INDIA, EMPIRE, AND]
WAR CULTL

C000180844

Based on ten years of research, Santanu Das's *India, Empire, and First World War Culture: Writings, Images, and Songs* recovers the sensuous experience of combatants, non-combatants and civilians from undivided India in the 1914–1918 conflict and their socio-cultural, visual and literary worlds. Around 1.5 million Indians were recruited of whom over a million served abroad. Das draws on a variety of fresh, unusual sources – objects, images, rumours, street-pamphlets, letters, diaries, sound-recordings, folksongs, testimonies, poetry, essays and fiction – to produce the first cultural and literary history, moving from recruitment tactics in villages through sepoy traces and feelings in battlefields, hospitals and POW camps to post-war reflections on Europe and empire. Combining archival excavation in different countries across several continents with investigative readings of Gandhi, Kipling, Iqbal, Naidu, Nazrul, Tagore and Anand, this imaginative study opens up the worlds of sepoys and labourers, men and women, nationalists, artists and intellectuals, trying to make sense of home and the world in times of war.

Educated in Kolkata and Cambridge, Santanu Das is Professor of English Literature at King's College London and joins All Souls College, Oxford, as Senior Research Fellow in English in 2019. He is the author of the award-winning monograph *Touch and Intimacy in First World War Literature* (2006) and the pictorial history *Indian Troops in Europe, 1914–1918* (2014), and the editor of *Race, Empire and First World War Writing* (2011) and the *Cambridge Companion to the Poetry of the First World War* (2013). He presented the series 'Soldiers of the Empire' for BBC Radio 4 and has contributed to various events commemorating the war, from radio and television programmes to exhibitions, performances and concerts.

INDIA, EMPIRE, AND FIRST WORLD WAR CULTURE

Writings, Images, and Songs

SANTANU DAS

King's College London

CAMBRIDGE
UNIVERSITY PRESS

CAMBRIDGE
UNIVERSITY PRESS

University Printing House, Cambridge CB2 8BS, United Kingdom

One Liberty Plaza, 20th Floor, New York, NY 10006, USA

477 Williamstown Road, Port Melbourne, VIC 3207, Australia

314–321, 3rd Floor, Plot 3, Splendor Forum, Jasola District Centre, New Delhi – 110025, India

79 Anson Road, #06-04/06, Singapore 079906

Cambridge University Press is part of the University of Cambridge.

It furthers the University's mission by disseminating knowledge in the pursuit of education, learning, and research at the highest international levels of excellence.

www.cambridge.org
Information on this title: www.cambridge.org/9781107081581
DOI: 10.1017/9781139963244

First published 2018

Printed in the United Kingdom by TJ International Ltd. Padstow Cornwall

A catalogue record for this publication is available from the British Library.

ISBN 978-1-107-08158-1 Hardback
ISBN 978-1-107-44159-0 Paperback

For Ma and Hugh, and in loving memory of Baba

'Literature fills in the gaps left by history'

(Novalis)

God knows whether the land of France is stained with sin or
whether the Day of Judgement has begun in France. For guns
and of rifles there is now a deluge, bodies upon bodies, and
blood flowing… Our guns have filled the German trenches with
dead and made them brim with blood. God grant us grace, for
grace is needed. Oh God, we repent! Oh God we repent!

(Amir Khan, 129th [Baluchis] from France to his
brother in Punjab, 18 March 1915)

The war pains me like hot sand in a cauldron
Every household now has widows.
' "Married men win battles"
Tell me, O *firangi* [foreigner],
Where is this written?'
Take the bachelors to war,
then victory will be yours.

(Punjabi First World War folksong, sung by
women, translated by Amarjit Chandan)

In India, when the upper classes ruled over the lower, they forged
their own chains. Europe is closely following Brahmin India,
when she looks upon Asia and Africa as her legitimate fields for
exploitation … She seems to have exhausted the oil that once
lighted her lamp. Now she is feeling a distrust against the oil
itself, as if it were not at all necessary for the light.

(Letter from Rabindranath Tagore to
C.F. Andrews, 11 July, 1915)

It is nearly two years ago, that my dear eldest son went out to
the War for the last time and the day he said goodbye to me –
we were looking together across the sun-glorified sea – looking
towards France with breaking hearts – when he, my poet son, said
these wonderful words of yours – 'jabar diney ei kathati boley
jeno jeo [sic] – ja dekhechi, ja peyechi tulona tar nei' – 'when
I leave, let these be my parting word, what my life received, is
unsurpassable' And when his pocket book came back to me –
I found these words written in his dear writing – with your name
beneath.

(Letter from Susan Owen, mother of Wilfred Owen,
to Rabindranath Tagore, 1920)

Contents

Colour plate section can be found between pages 232 and 233.

Plates

Illustrations

Maps

xv

Acknowledgements

This work has occupied me for over a decade. What began as a postdoctoral query grew into something I had never quite envisioned, as the whole field of colonial memory and the First World War shifted in the lead-up to the centennial commemoration. Research for the book has pushed me in new directions, taken me to parts of India and the world, introduced me to new languages and brought me in touch with people – from military officials and local community groups to writers and musicians – in ways that have been thrilling. Serendipity has been a constant force. After a long day in the National Archives in Delhi in 2005, a taxi took me to the airport. On being asked what had brought me to the city, I told the chatty man at the wheel about my research. His eyes lit up. His grandfather, he told me, had served in France in the 'European War' and, in his native place in Ambala, there is still an iron chest with his grandfather's papers and memorabilia!

The length of the book has only been matched by the kindness of a large number of people working in a variety of fields. I would like to thank the readers whom I now know to have read the typescript in an official capacity: Laura Marcus, Mrinalini Sinha, Vincent Sherry and Jay Winter. Given the interdisciplinary nature of the book, it was extremely helpful to have their wonderfully detailed engagement with the project as a whole and astute advice on particular areas. The support of my former supervisor Dame Gillian Beer has been invaluable: her capacity for immersion in the texture of the past and constant sense of pleasure in investigating its complexities remain a source of inspiration. The encouragement of the writer Amitav Ghosh and his remarkable blogposts on the war have been an abiding force: the book will hopefully answer his puzzled query, on reading my first book, about why I did not mention the Indian experience while writing on touch and intimacy in wartime.

A book of this scope would not have been possible without the generous institutional support I have had over the years. I am deeply grateful to the British Academy, the Leverhulme Trust and the Humanities in European

Research Area (HERA) for funding parts of the project at crucial stages; such support enabled me to work in various archives and commission translations of important material. I started thinking about the topic as a research fellow at St. John's, Cambridge in 2004; it continued to grow during my time at Queen Mary, University of London, and reached fruition at King's College London. I would like to thank my colleagues in all three institutions, and particularly at the English department at King's, where I wrote most of this book. In the summer of 2011, a visiting fellowship at the wonderful Zentrum Moderner Orient in Berlin through the kindness of Heike Liebau allowed me to work at the sound archives of the Humboldt University. In 2014, Gallimard invited me to do the visual sourcebook *1914–1918: Indian Troops in Europe* (2014) and facilitated access to various photographic archives in Paris, while BBC Radio 4 and the Arts and Humanities Research Council (AHRC) sponsored a field trip to India and Belgium to interview the descendants of war veterans for the programme 'Soldiers of Empire'. From 2013 to 2016, I directed a large pan-European HERA collaborative research project on 'Cultural Encounters in the Time of Global Conflict: Colonials, Neutrals and Belligerents in the First World War' which involved organising concerts, exhibitions, conferences and workshops, including one on 'Beyond Commemoration: South Asia and the First World War'. These various activities have possibly delayed but definitely enriched the book. I would like to thank the HERA team in London, particularly Natasha Awais-Dean, Suzanne Bardgett, Anna Maguire and Daniel Steinbach, who were often my first audiences and interlocutors.

While writing *India, Empire, and First World War Culture*, I always had the sense of being part of an engaged, supportive and diverse community of scholars: literary critics, First World War historians, scholars of South Asia, archivists and museum curators, and 'citizen-historians' working on centennial community projects. They invited me to speak at various venues, asked unexpected questions, provided references to peruse and opened up fresh lines of enquiry; without such stimulation and generosity, this project would have languished. It is difficult to name a few people when I feel indebted to so many, but I would like to express my gratitude to those friends and colleagues who read individual chapters and provided important feedback: Suzanne Bardgett, Jonathan Black, Rustom Bharucha, Arshdeep Singh Brar, Rana Chhina, Pragya Dhital, Diya Gupta, Kate McLoughlin, Abhishek Sarkar, Sumit and Tanika Sarkar, Gajendra Singh, Radhika Singha, Sejal Sutaria and K. C. Yadav. It is a particular pleasure to recall various conversations, over the years, with the individuals mentioned above, as well as with the following fellow-travellers in the field of First World War studies: Michèle Barrett, Shrabani Basu, Claire Buck, Amarjit Chandan, Debrae Rae Cohen, Virginia Crompton, Dominiek Dendooven, Alison Fell, Margaret R. Higonnet, John Horne, Andrew Tait

Jarboe, Vedica Kant, Jennifer Keene, Edward Madigan, Kaushik Roy, Anne Samson, Samiksha Sehrawat, Jasdeep Singh, Richard Smith, Sir Hew Strachan, Trudi Tate, Kim Wagner and, finally, David Omissi and Rozina Visram. Like anyone working on the Indian sepoys, I owe a particular debt to the work of the last two and they have always been open-handed with their knowledge and expertise. In London, George Morton-Jack has been a regular and exciting point of contact: it has been a real privilege to discuss with him the minutiae of the British Indian army as well as his important research into the military history of the sepoys as I tried to reconstruct their experiential and socio-cultural worlds. Radhika Singh has seen this book take shape and grow since the conference at ZMO, Berlin, in 2007: I have greatly benefitted from her formidable scholarship and constant encouragement. I would also like to mention the kindness and tireless efforts of Rana Chhina, retired Squadron Leader and current secretary of the United Services Institution of India, New Delhi, to gain recognition for the Indian soldiers in the First World War: he has been at the centre of various commemorative activities to all of which he brings his deep military knowledge and Buddha-like serenity.

One of the most rewarding and challenging aspects of this research has been the recovery of primary works in different languages and I am grateful to a veritable army of translators: Jan Braueburgher, Asad Ali Chaudhry, Pragya Dhital, Upasana Dutta, Diya Gupta, Adeel Khan, Luithui Khanthing, Arshdeep Singh Brar, Dilgeer Singh, Anna Stirr, Bhadra Vadgama and Jolita Zabarskaite. They did not just translate but often spent hours discussing the work with me, reading out passages or reciting verses (and being told off by the British Library staff!) so that I could get the sonority and nuances of the language. Abhishek Sarkar and Arshdeep Singh Brar were heroic in helping me navigate the weird and wonderful world of diacritics. Elizabeth Robertson provided valuable help at an early stage, while Christine Okoth was brilliant in the final processes of reference-checking. I owe a particular debt to Arshdeep and Diya: in the lead-up to the submission and during copy-editing of the typescript, I have bothered them with all sorts of queries and have only marvelled at their patience and goodwill.

It is a particular pleasure to thank the descendants of several war veterans who feature in this book for their generosity with time and material: Mahmood Awan, Sunanda Das, Mohan Kahlon, Indrani Haldar, the Sarbadhikari family and Raj Singh. It is a cause of great sorrow that four people involved with the book will not get to know the final outcome: the late Barleen Kaur, Arun Das, Romola Sarbadhikari and Jon Stallworthy. A remarkable young woman, Barleen translated some of the POW sound-recordings from Punjabi before her life was tragically cut short through illness. Based in Delhi, she wanted to come to London to study theatre. For several years, I had regularly visited and interviewed Romola Sarbadhikari, the daughter-in-law of Sisir Prasad Sarbadhikari who wrote *Abhi Le Baghdad* and Dr Arun Das whose father Captain Manindranath Das, MC, served as a doctor in Mesopotamia. And finally, Jon Stallworthy – teacher, friend and the doyen of First World War literary studies – who is sorely missed.

People at various archives and libraries whose resources have nourished this project have been unfailingly efficient and courteous. At some of these places, people have been helping me for over a decade: they include the British Library and the Imperial War Museum in London, the National Archives in Delhi and the National Library in Kolkata. I am particularly grateful to the following scholars and archivists for pointing me to important material or facilitating access to specific collections: Iqbal Hussein (National Archives, Kew), Jasdeep Singh (National Army Museum), Sukhdeep Jodha and Parmjit Singh (UK Punjab Heritage), Francesca Orsini (SOAS) in London and Kevin Bacon in Brighton; K. C. Yadav (Haryana Academy, Gurgaon), Subarno Chatterjee, Surja Shankar Ray, Rangan Datta and the late Jasodhara Bagchi in Kolkata; Uma Dasgupta in Shantiniketan; Bharti Gandhi at Meherjirana Library, Navsari and Dilgeer Singh at Punjab State Archives, Chandigarh; Dominiek Dendooven (In Flanders Fields Museum) in Ypres; Britta Lange, Heike Liebau, Larissa Schmid and Elisabeth Tietmeyer in Berlin; Elisabeth de Farcy in Paris and Peter Stanley in Canberra. A big thank you to friends and colleagues who invited me to speak at different conferences and workshops, and offered warm hospitality. More recently, Mira Kaushik at Akademi and Nima Poovaya-Smith at Alchemy took me far beyond my comfort-zone by asking me to collaborate on the dance-adaptation of the war story 'Us Ne Kahā Thā' and music project 'Sacred Sounds: Sikh Music Traditions and the First World War' respectively.

Warm thanks to friends with whom I have shared the book and much else over the years: Barnita Bagchi, Sudesna Banerjee, Subhadip Basu, Yajnaseni Bhattacharya, Elleke Boehmer, Amit and Rosinka Chaudhuri, Sukanta and Supriya Chaudhuri, Sarah Cole, Nandini Das, Mary Jacobus, John Kerrigan, Kate McLoughlin, Subha Mukherji, Jahan Ramazani, Sejal Sutaria and Ruth Vanita. In my department at King's, I would like to thank Jon Day, Richard Kirkland, Ruvani Ranasinha, Anna Snaith, Sejal Sutaria, Mark Turner, and particularly Jo McDonagh who managed to infuse daily life with a sense of style and fun. In a book about memory and feeling, it is important to get beyond names to remember some particular moments: the trip to the recruitment village of Bhondsi in Haryana with Professor Yadav, Philippa Goodrich and Radhika Singha; visiting the Indian sites around Ypres with fellow-enthusiasts, led (yet again) by Dominiek Dendooven; the visit with Rozina Visram to the exhibition

'Empire, Faith and War' organised by UK Punjab Heritage at SOAS; the trip to Dar Es Salaam with the BBC World Service group; and the First World War concert in the candle-lit chapel at King's College London, with Amanroop Kaur singing the Punjabi women's war-laments.

My commissioning editor Ray Ryan has been a tremendous force and has taken an exceptional degree of interest in the project from the start: I am deeply grateful for his enthusiasm and support for my work over the years as well as for telling me when to stop revising! The whole team at Cambridge University Press – Edgar Mendez, Sarah Lambert and Amy Watson – have been remarkably supportive and efficient. Céline Durassier at OOH Publishing has been a wonderfully sympathetic project manager while Steven Holt has been a heroic copyeditor, incorporating minute changes. Mike Leach kindly compiled the index.

Hugh Steven has been by my side far longer than it has taken me to do this book: his conviction in the book remained steadfast even when mine wavered. Many thanks for his constant support and for bearing with me as I cancelled yet one more engagement or vanished into the archives! One of my fondest memories is of our trip to France and Flanders, with his parents Neil and Marianne Stevens and his cousins Melanie and Nick, to visit the graves of his great grandfather Joseph Chitty and great-uncle McKenzie Stevens who came from New Zealand to serve in the First World War. As indeed I remember my trip with my mother Anuva Das to the Dupleix Museum in Chandernagore where I came upon the glasses of war veteran Jogen Sen. Her relief, I know, will be even greater than mine when this book finally sees the light of day. As always, she continues to put every interest of mine above her own; she remains remarkably independent even in the most difficult of times. The book is dedicated to her and to Hugh, and to the memory of my dear father Subhash Chandra Das whom I lost in December 2016.

Some of the material used in Chapters 1, 5 and 6 had previous outings, though in different form, in the following publications: 'Counter-Encounters in Mesopotamia, 1915–1918' in *Peripheral Visions: European Military Expeditions As Cultural Encounters in the Long 19th Century* (ed. Joseph Clarke and John Horne), 2018; 'Reframing Life/War "Writing" in *Textual Practice* (ed. Kate McLoughlin, Lara Feigel and Nancy Martin), Volume 29:7, 2015; 'Indian War Experience: Archive, Language and Feeling' in *Twentieth Century British History* (ed. Martin Francis), Volume 25:3, 2014; 'The Indian Sepoy in Europe, 1914–1918' in *The World During the World War* (ed. Anorthe Kremers and Helmut Bey), 2014; 'Writing Empire, Fighting War' in *India in Britain: South Asian Networks and Connections, 1858–1950* (ed. Susheila Nasta), 2013; 'Sensing the Sepoy' in *Comparative Critical Studies* (ed. Marina Warner), October 2012; 'Imperialism, Nationalism and the First World War in India' in *Finding Common Ground: New Directions in First World War Studies* (ed. Jennifer Keene and Michael Nieberg), 2011; 'Indians at Home, France and Mesopotamia, 1914–1918: Towards an Intimate History' in *Race, Empire and First World War Writing* (ed. Santanu Das), 2011; 'India, Empire and First World War Writing' in *The Indian Postcolonial: A Critical Reader* (ed. Elleke Boehmer and Rosinka Chaudhuri), 2010; 'Ardour and Anxiety: Politics and Literature in the Indian Homefront' in *The World in the World War: Experiences, Perceptions and Perspectives from Africa and Asia* (ed. Heike Liebau, Katrin Bromber, Katharina Lange, Dyala Hamzah and Ravi Ahuja), 2011; 'India and the First World War' in *A Part of History* (ed. Sir Michael Howard), 2008.

I am grateful to various individuals, libraries and institutions, mentioned in the following pages, for granting me permission to use material in the book. All efforts have been made to trace and contact the copyright holders of such material.

Note on the Text

After careful consideration, I have decided to use 'India' rather than 'South Asia' to refer to the subcontinent in 1914–1918 out of a sense of historical sympathy and fidelity to the people I write about and their structures of feeling. They knew and referred to their land as 'India'. The word, in this context, means undivided India under British rule which today comprises the nation-states of Bangladesh, India, Pakistan and Myanmar (formerly Burma, separated from British India in 1937). The British Indian Army also included a substantial number of Gurkha soldiers who belonged to the independent kingdom of Nepal as well as trans-frontier Pashtuns. In the 'Afterword', when I discuss the complexities of war memory, I use the term 'South Asia' to register the weight of postcolonial and post-partition history for us. Similarly, I refer to the cities as they were called then – Calcutta rather than Kolkata, Bombay rather than Mumbai – except when I refer to those places today.

Since the book is written in English, I have gone for the popular term 'sepoy', the official generic rank for an Indian infantry soldier, over the Persian word *sipāhī* from which it was originally derived. Within the book, this all-encompassing term signifies Indian troops of all ranks and from all branches of the army, including *sowars* or cavalrymen.

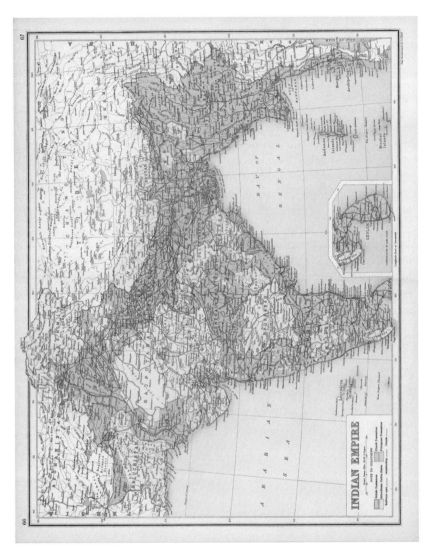

Map 0.1   Map of British India, 1914.

Figure 0.1   Artefacts, including a pair of 'blood-stained' glasses, of Jogendra ('Jon') Sen, Dupleix House and Museum, Chandernagore, India.

Introduction: 'Only Connect'
Fragments, Feeling and Form

It was on a chance visit one winter afternoon in 2005 to the quaint Dupleix House and Museum in Chandernagore – a former French colony by the Hoogly river and some 40 kilometres from Kolkata – that I first saw the pair of glasses (Figure 0.1). They lay in a cabinet ringed with dust in a darkened room. At the same time as noticing the glasses, my eyes took in the label 'blood-stained' next to them, though all I could detect was a smudge on the right lens. Delicate, fragile yet intact they lay, with their arms gently curving around the photograph of their master wearing them, as if locked forever in a protective embrace. The label identified the wearer as 'J. N. Sen, M.B., Private, West Yorkshire Regiment, who died in action on the night of 22–23 May in 1916, France. He was the first Bengalee, a citizen of Chandernagore, killed in 1914–1918 War'.[1] The glasses reminded me of the pocket-watch found on the body of the British war poet Edward Thomas, its hands perpetually fixed at 7.36 am as they recorded the time of Thomas's death; both had borne testimony to the final moments of their owners' lives. Next to the glasses was a collection of artefacts: a dog-tag (to identify the injured), a razor, a photograph of a young European woman, a 'Book of Friendship' possibly given by this lady (signed as 'Cis') and a small leather wallet. The fragility of the objects, combined with their stubborn persistence and the distance from the scene of action, made them seem uncanny. But more was to come. Several years after my discovery, I was speaking at the University of Leeds and, as I showed an image of Sen's artefacts, I was stopped

---

[1] J. N. Sen, Artefacts at the Dupleix Museum, Chandernagore, West Bengal. The story of the glasses led to a surge of interest in Sen and, in 2015, BBC Yorkshire commissioned a short *Inside Out* documentary on him. Some of his objects and photographs can be seen at www.bbc.co.uk/news/uk-england-leeds-31761904. An enthusiastic team at the University of Leeds did a community project on him in 2015 and there is now a webpage (www.leeds.ac.uk/news/article/3670/the_unlikeliest_of_pals_an_indian_soldier_alone_among_yorkshiremen).

3

mid-sentence by an excited English gentleman: 'Jon' Sen, he burst out, was a student at the university, and his name appeared at the university's war memorial. More research followed. Jogendra ('Jon') Sen, having just gained a degree in engineering from the University of Leeds, had volunteered in the opening months of the conflict in the Leeds Pals Battalion and was the only non-white member of the West Yorkshire regiment. He was a much-loved member. Arthur Dalby, a comrade, remembered him as 'the best educated in the battalion and he spoke about seven languages but he was never allowed to be even a lance-corporal because in those days they would never let a coloured fellow be over a white man'. Yet, after his death, the *Yorkshire Evening Post* published an obituary on 2 June 1916, with the heading 'Leeds "Pals" Lose an Indian Comrade'.[2]

It was two years later, in 2007, in a cabinet-filled room in the Humboldt Sound Archive in Berlin that I felt the same shiver as in Chandernagore. I was listening to a tremulous yet incantatory voice speaking largely in Punjabi (with a few Hindi words), interrupted by awkward silences and sharp intakes of breath:

Line	Transcription	Translation
1	Ek ādmi si … je makhan khāndā si Hindustān mein	There was a man who would have butter back in India
2	Do ser dūdh, pīndā sī	He would also have two sers of milk
3	Usne Angrejān kī naukrī kī	He served for the British
4	O ādmī Europe ki ladāī'ch āgayā	He joined the European War
5	Us ādmī nū Germany ne qaid kar leyā	He was captured by the Germans
6	Us nu India jānā chāhtā hai	He wants to go back to India
7	Je oh Hindustān jaūgā to usnu oh khānā milegā	If he goes back to India then he will get that same food
8	Oh ādmī nu tīn baras ho gaye hain	Three years have already passed
9	Khabar nahin kab sulah hovegā	There's no news as to when there will be peace
10	Je Hindustān mein oh ādmī jāyegā usko khānā oh milūgā	Only if he goes back to India will he get that food
11	Je do sāl oh ādmī etthe hor reh gayā tā oh ādmī mar jaūgā	If he stays here for two more years then he will die
12	Mahārāj kripā kare tā eh chheti sulah kar lein te assi chale jāiye	By God's grace, if they declare peace then we'll go back

[2] Interview with Arthur Dalby, 1988; *Yorkshire Evening Post*, 2 June 1916. Both can now be found at www.leeds.ac.uk/news/article/3670/the_unlikeliest_of_pals_an_indian_soldier_alone_among_yorkshiremen.

Figure 0.2   Voice-recording of a POW in progress at the POW
camp at Wünsdorf, Germany. Papers of Heinrich Lüders, Archiv der
Berlin-Brandenburgischen Akademie der Wissenschaften.

This is the story of Mall Singh, a Punjabi prisoner of war in the
'Halfmoon Camp' at Wünsdorf outside Berlin.[3] The recording was made
on 11 December 1916. He was made to stand in front of a phonograph
machine held before him by his German captors and instructed to speak
(Figure 0.2). Mall Singh's was among the 2,677 audio recordings made by
the Royal Prussian Phonographic Commission between 29 December 1915
and 19 December 1918, using the prisoners of war held in Germany.[4] A voice
calls out from the phonograph, strains itself in the act of recording: the

[3] Mall Singh, Voice-recording, Humboldt University Sound Archive, PK 619. Mall Singh speaks in a
mixed register, starting sentences in Punjabi and finishing them in Hindi and vice versa. Translation
by Arshdeep Singh Brar. Over the last ten years, this voice-recording has become known among
scholars in the field through the film *Halfmoon Files* by Phillip Scheffner and the efforts of a group
of German academics based at Berlin, particularly Heike Liebau and Britta Lange. I am grateful to
both of them for facilitating my work at the Humboldt archives. See Das, 'The Singing Subaltern',
Parallax, 17, 60 (2011), 4–18. Mall Singh's voice-recording can now be heard at www.tribuneindia
.com/news/spectrum/society/100-years-later-voices-from-wwi/591837.html
[4] See Heike Liebau, Ravi Ahuja and Franziska Roy (eds.), '*When the War Began, We Heard of Several
Kings': South Asian Prisoners in World War I Germany* (Delhi: Social Science Press, 2011).

trepidation, the timbre, the laboured enunciation, the slight breathless-
ness seem to bridge the gap between technological reproduction and lived
experience. As I listened to it, the body and emotion of the speaker seemed
palpable, filling in, flowing out, lending physicality to an encounter with
a disembodied voice from a hundred years ago. In some indefinable way,
Mall Singh was *present* in it. But why does he refer to himself as 'ādmī' in
the third person ('Ek ādmī si ... o ādmī Europe ... O ādmī nu teen baras')?
Unfamiliar with the genre of testimony but having grown up amidst the
robust oral culture of Punjab – recitations of *qissas* and folktales with their
third-person voices ('There was a King' or 'There was a parrot') – he falls
back upon familiar narrative form and intonation as he tells his life-story.
The voice rises and pauses and rises again until it reaches, and stresses, the
final words of each line ('khānā oh milūgā/ādmī mar jaūga/chale jāiye').
Desolate, homesick and hungry, he distils all the pain and longing into the
images of *makhan* (butter) and the two *sers* (a form of measurement) of
milk: home is remembered as taste.

Mall Singh served on the Western Front. However, for me, his story
resonates not with the homesick letters of his sepoy-brothers from France
and Flanders, but with something altogether more rare. It is a letter written
by a young girl called Kishan Devi from Punjab to her father Havildar
Sewa Singh, of the 23rd Sikh Pioneers, serving in Egypt (Figure 0.3):

> Dear Father, Ek Onkar Satguru Prasad ['There is One God by the grace of
> the True Guru'] This is Kishan Devi. I am writing in to inform that I am
> alright over here. We received your letter ... We came to know about you.
> We were really scared after receiving your letter. Mother says that you can
> write to us about what goes on in your heart. Father, I shall read all your
> letters. I do not fight with anyone. My heart is yours. You are everything
> to me, and I worry about you. I am like living dead without you ... Dear
> father please take leave and come to meet us. Please do come. We repeat
> again and again. My mother bows her head to you to pay respect. We do
> not have any more envelopes ... I am sending this letter on the 22nd day
> of Magh and the English date is 5th. Father, please write to us ... Father,
> please take leave and come and meet us. Please do come. Please do reply to
> our letter ... Reply to our letter soon.[5]

A child's scrawl in Gurmukhi script fills in all available space on the postcard; the words are joined together. In asking her 'bapuji' to pour out his
'heart' ('jo tere dil de vich hai'), Kishan Devi touches on, as we will see, a

[5] I would like thank its owner Avtar Singh Bahra, and Dominic Rai. Translated by Arshdeep Singh
Brar.

© Avtar S Bahra

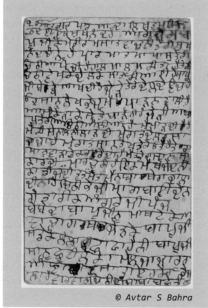

© Avtar S Bahra

Figure 0.3   Postcard of Kishan Devi to her father Havildar Sewa Singh, serving in Egypt, (a) front and (b) back. Private Collection of Avtar Singh Bahra, London.

central chord in the sepoy writing of the First World War: the tumultuous world of feeling. The distance between the war-front in Sinai and a village in Punjab suddenly narrows. If letters arriving from the front would usually be taken to the postal clerk to be read aloud to the non-literate family members, here Kishan Devi circumvents that by learning how to read and write. War serves as a catalyst for female literacy. But above all, we have here two people, caught in the maelstrom of war, each trying to reach out: the timbre of the voice finds its counterpart in the uneven scrawl of the hand. We do not know whether it reached the father. A daughter's heart-breaking appeal ('jāroor āyin' – 'please come'), like Mall Singh's desolate plea for butter, 'repeats again and again' in the chamber of First World War memories.

Quite early on during my research, in 2006, I had my first significant 'archival' find. While rummaging through the catalogue in the National Archives in Delhi, I glimpsed an entry saying 'Trench-note of Mir Mast'.[6] For anyone working on India and the First World War, Mir Mast is a remarkable if shadowy figure. On the rainy night of 2/3 March 1915, Jemadar Mir Mast, serving in the 58th Vaughan's Rifles (Bareilly Brigade) at Neuve Chapelle, deserted his camp and quietly crossed over to the German side with a group of fellow Pathans. He was an enterprising man. He became part of a Turko-German *jihad* mission and travelled via Constantinople to Kabul from where he fled to his homeland.[7] There, he trained fellow deserters and tried to foment an anti-colonial uprising; Anglo-Indian myth has it that the Kaiser decorated him with the Iron Cross. To make the story even more curious, his brother Mir Dast obtained a Victoria Cross for his performance in the Second Battle of Ypres in 1915. As I sat ruminating, a sealed envelope marked 'His Majesty's Office' was delivered to my desk and I was given permission to tear open the envelope. A thrill went through me. I thought I was about to touch the heart of the rebel sepoy: I expected words nothing short of 'jihad' and 'Hindustan' and 'dissent'. A hand-drawn trench map slipped out as my fingers pulled a small tatty notebook out of the envelope: did Mir Mast use it to navigate his way to the German trenches? What I found in his trench notebook was curiouser. Along with some casual jottings and numbers, it contained

---

[6] 'Jemadar Mir Mast's diary', National Archives of India, Delhi, Foreign and Political, War B (Secret), February 1916, 32–34.

[7] In the Political Archive of the Foreign Office in Berlin, a document mentions 'Mirmastshah Sipahi' among the Afridi deserters and includes 'Mirmast Sipahi' among the list of people who went to Constantinople (Politisches Archiv des Auswärtigen Amtes, Berlin, April, 1915, R 21082-1, 13, f. 6). For more details, see my entry on the Mir brothers at the *CEGC Sourcebook* (http://sourcebook .cegcproject.eu).

a long list of words, first in Urdu and then in English. The words range from the functional ('haversack', 'blanket', 'please') to the warmly human ('hungry', 'nephew', 'honeymoon') to a rather unusual list: 'turnip, carrot, parsnip, potatoes, prick, penus [*sic*], testacles [*sic*], harsole [*sic*], cunt, brests [*sic*], fuck, flour' (Figure 0.4)'. What had so distracted the Jemadar? The list was a good reality-check for the subaltern scholar and possibly an insight into what these young soldiers actually talked about in the trenches; or, maybe, it is a basic fact of language learning that we are always interested in concealed body-parts. Yet, amidst the carnage of the Western Front, it is also poignant testimony to a young man's appetite for life in its incorrigible plurality, the need for nourishment as well as for bodies to come together. Like Mall Singh's 'makhan', he had only the sound of words.

These moments have stayed with me and have shaped the book. Why do they matter so much? Jogen Sen's glasses, Mall Singh's voice, Kishan Devi's letter and Mir Mast's diary are not just fresh and tantalising sources but open up new ways of 'reading' – and writing – life, and particularly colonial lives, in times of war. At an immediate level, they confront us with the role of the sensuous, the material and the contingent: they force us to weave together a narrative of fugitive fragments, the flotsam, jetsam and lagan of life wrecked by war; they point to the importance of relicts as zones of contact between warm life and historical violence. They not only congeal time but also conceal processes of care: the fragility of the glasses, the wavering of the voice, the childish scrawl across the page, the crinkliness of the postcard are in many ways the hand-prints and face-prints of war in the act of writing its own violent life – its peculiar mode of communication – as it impacts human lives and reduces them to piecemeal narratives; they are the archives of touch and intimacy. Moreover, at a his-torical level, they acquire an altogether new level of importance as source-material the moment we step outside the Western world. If there has been a powerful material turn within cultural studies in recent years, some of its greatest yields have been in the field of colonial history; increasing use is made of ephemera, from calendar art to songs, in South Asian history, while Africanists have emphasised the importance of oral archives.[8] These materials present us with what the anthropologist Elizabeth Edwards has called 'raw histories'.[9] In a context where most of the colonial soldiers were

[8] See for example Christopher Pinney, *The Coming of Photography to India* (London: British Museum, 2001) and Tapati Guha Thakurta, *Monuments, Objects, Histories* (New York: Columbia University Press, 2004); among new work, see Priyasha Mukhopadhyay, 'On Not Reading the Soldier's Pocket-Book for Field Service', *Journal of Victorian Culture*, 22, 1 (2017), 40–56. Also see Joe Lunn, *Memoirs of a Maelstrom: A Senegalese Oral History of the First World War* (Portsmouth: Heinemann, 1999).
[9] Elizabeth Edwards, *Raw Histories: Photographs, Anthropology and Museums* (Oxford: Berg, 2001).

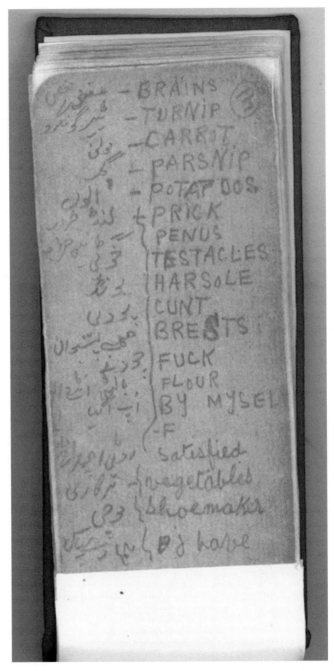

Figure 0.4   A page from the trench notebook of Jemadar Mir Mast, National Archives of India, Delhi. Foreign and Political War B (Secret), February 1916, 32–34.

non-literate and did not leave behind the abundance of diaries, journals, poems or memoirs that build up European war memory, it is necessary, I argue, to go beyond the solely textual to these other kinds of evidence – material, visual, oral – and establish a dialogue between them. Each has its ineluctable form to which we must attend; moreover, one fragment may change its meaning when considered alongside another. It is their cumulative power as well as their poignancy and serendipitous survival that help us recreate the texture of the past.

India, Empire, and First World War Culture: Writings, Images, and Songs examines the experiences of people from undivided India (comprising present-day India, Pakistan, Bangladesh and Myanmar (formerly Burma)) – both soldiers and civilians, men and women, sepoys, labourers, lascars, orderlies, doctors, politicians and intellectuals – in the First World War and the way such experiences were represented in a variety of forms: testimonial, political, visual, aural and literary.[10] It is a combination of extensive digging-and-delving and close investigative engagement with the material. Between August 1914 and December 1919, India recruited for purposes of war 877,068 combatants and 563,369 non-combatants, making a total of 1,440,437; in addition, there were an estimated 239,561 (Indian) men in the British Indian army at the outbreak of the war. Of them, 1,096,013 Indians, by conservative estimates, served overseas, including 621,224 combatants and 474,789 non-combatants, in places as diverse as France and Flanders, Mesopotamia, East Africa, Gallipoli, Egypt and Palestine, Salonika, Aden, Persia and Central Asia (see Table 0.1).[11] Between 50,000 and 70,000 of these men were killed.[12] 'The state of things is indescribable. There is conflagration all around, and you must imagine it to be like a dry forest in a high wind in the hot

[10] 'India' and 'Indian' at all points in this book refer respectively to the undivided India under British rule and its people, and not the present-day state of India. After agonising, long and hard, about whether to use 'South Asia' or 'India', I decided to go for the latter as the more historically sympathetic term for the pre-Partition history it excavates. The men discussed often refer to 'India' and saw themselves as 'Indian', though, in today's terms, they would be regarded as 'South Asians'. The British Indian army also included a substantial number of Gurkha soldiers, some resident in India and some from the independent kingdom of Nepal, as well as some trans-frontier Pashtuns.

[11] The above figures are from *Statistics of the Military Effort of the British Empire during the Great War, 1914–1920* (London: HM Stationery Office, 1920), 777 and reproduced in *India's Contribution to the Great War* (Calcutta: Superintendent Government Printing 1923), 79. These figures are still subject to revision and are therefore not set in stone.

[12] *India's Contribution* lists the figures of Indian casualties as 'Dead from all causes – 53,486; Wounded – 64,350; missing and POWs – 3762, as on 31 December 1919. Repatriated prisoners are not shown (176).

Table 0.1   Number sent on service overseas from India up to 31 December 1919

Theatre	Combatants				Non-combatant Indians	Totals		Grand total of all ranks (British and Indian)
	British officers	British other ranks	Indian officers and warrant officers	Indian other ranks		British	Indians	
France	2,395	18,353	1,923	87,412	49,273	20,748	138,608	
East Africa	928	4,681	848	33,835	13,021	5,609	47,704	
Mesopotamia	18,669	166,822	9,514	317,142	348,735	185,491	675,391	
Egypt	3,188	17,067	2,204	107,742	34,047	20,255	143,993	
Gallipoli	42	18	90	3,041	1,819	60	4,950	
Salonika	86	85	132	6,545	3,254	171	9,931	
Palestine	—	4	4	1	28	4	33	
Aden	952	7,267	480	19,936	5,786	8,219	26,205	
Persian Gulf	991	1,059	967	29,408	18,823	2,050	49,198	
	27,251	215,356	16,162	605,062	474,789	242,607	1,096,013	1,338,620
The above figures exclude 42,430 British of all ranks sent from India to England, all, or nearly all, of whom doubtless proceeded on to service from the United Kingdom.								42,430
								1,381,050

Statistics of the Military Effort of the British Empire During the Great War, 1914–1920 (London: His Majesty's Stationery Office, 1922), 777.

weather, with abundance of dry grass and straw. No one can extinguish it but God himself – man can do nothing. What more can I write?' observed Sohan Singh, a sowar in the 9th Hodson's Horse, on 10 July 1915, as he lay convalescing at the Kitchener Indian Hospital at Brighton.[13] The unprecedented violence of the First World War pushed men to the very edge of language. Yet, paradoxically, the war also produced an extraordinary outpouring of words, images and songs. And India was no exception.

In recent years, there has been a growing interest in the Indian sepoy in the First World War, particularly in his adventures on the Western Front.[14] In David Omissi's excellent collection of the censored letters, in a rush of publications commemorating the centenary of the war, in television documentaries and community projects, and in government-level commemorative events, the sepoy has become a far more visible figure than he was before 2014. If attention has focussed on the sepoy and his adventures abroad – from military histories to popular narrative accounts – this book engages with the power and poignancy of his story through a more diverse collection of material than hitherto available. At the same time, it also looks *beyond* his story abroad to embed the conflict in the larger socio-historical and cultural processes in India. From the heated debates of the time about what India's war participation might mean for its political future

---

[13] *Censor of Indian Mails 1914–1918* (henceforth *CIM*), India Office Record and Library (IOR), L/MIL/5/825/4, 571, British Library, London. The term 'Sowar' ['one who rides'] means 'cavalryman'.

[14] See David Omissi, *Indian Voices of the Great War: Soldiers' Letters, 1914–1918* (London: Macmillan, 1999) and *The Sepoy and the Raj, The Indian Army, 1860–1940* (London: Macmillan, 1994). Recent full-length books include Liebau *et al.* (eds.), *'When the War Began, We Heard of Several Kings'* (2011); Shrabani Basu, *For King and Another Country: Indian Soldiers on the Western Front, 1914–1918* (London: Bloomsbury, 2015); Simon Doherty and Tom Donovan, *The Indian Corps on the Western Front: A Handbook and Battlefield Guide* (Brighton: Tom Donovan Editions, 2014); George Morton Jack, *The Indian Army on the Western Front: Indian Expeditionary Force to France and Belgium in the First World War* (Cambridge, 2014); Gajendra Singh, *The Testimonies of the Indian Soldiers and the Two World Wars: Between the Self and the Sepoy* (London: Bloomsbury, 2014) and Peter Stanley, *Die in Battle, Do Not Despair: The Indians on Gallipoli, 1915* (London: Helion, 2015). In addition, there have been some visual histories: Vedica Kant, *'If I Die Here, Who Will Remember Me?': India and the First World War* (Delhi: Roli Books, 2014); Santanu Das, *L'Inde dans la Grande Guerre: Les cipayes sur le front de l'Ouest* [*1914–1918: Indian Troops in Europe*], trans. Didier Debord and Annie Perez (Paris: Gallimard, 2014) and Rana T. S. Chhina, *Les Hindous, The Indian Army on the Western Front, 1914–1918* (Delhi: USI, 2016). Rozina Visram wrote a pioneering article on the Indian sepoys in the 1980s and a number of historians, including Andrew Tait Jarboe, Kaushik Roy, Samiksha Sehrawat and Radhika Singha, have written important articles or book chapters, referenced below. Also see Gordon Corrigan, *Sepoys in the Trenches: The Indian Corps on the Western Front 1914–1918* (Staplehurst: Spellmount, 1999) and DeWitt C. Ellinwood and S. D. Pradhan (eds.), *India and World War I* (Delhi: Manohar, 1978). While this book was in production, the volume *India and World War I: A Centennial Assessment* (London: Routledge, 2018) edited by Roger D. Long and Ian Talbot came out. Also see the powerful and popular blogposts of Amitav Ghosh on the First World War: 'At Home and the World in Mesopotamia' (http://amitavghosh.com/blog/?cat=27).

to the recruitment speeches of Mahatma Gandhi, from photographs, testimonies and voice-recordings of the troops to women's folksongs in Punjab, from fictional representations by Indian and British writers to the imagining of a post-war world by intellectuals such as Mohammed Iqbal and Rabindranath Tagore, the country's involvement in the war, the book claims, produced a distinct and recognisable *culture*. *India, Empire, and First World War Culture* thus excavates the interwoven lives and cultural forms of several groups of people, including the Indians who served abroad, the people whom they encountered or who represented them, particularly in Europe, Britain and Mesopotamia, and, finally, men and women back in India. The impulses of the study are both recuperative and analytic. First, it seeks to examine the 'many-layered cake'[15] that the First World War was in India through a more *heterogeneous* collection of sources, and a more capacious lens that takes in both the sepoy and the civilian, the subaltern and the elite. Second, the book is actively interested in processes of *representation*. It places letters, diaries, memoirs, photographs, art objects, songs and above all literary writings at the centre of the investigation, delves into their formal complexities and shows how they allow a more intimate investigation of issues raised by more conventional historical sources. Indeed, what happens to cultural forms – from European photography and portraiture to Punjabi folksongs or Bengali and Urdu poetry to the Indian novel in English – when they are asked to bear testimony to Indian war experience? Together, these two moves – the use of an expanded and unconventional archive and the examination of the cultural and artistic forms themselves – enable a richer, more textured and affective understanding of the First World War in India.

The story of sepoys in foreign fields was the starting point of my research, taking me from the tiny recruitment village of Bhondsi in present-day Haryana through museums, barns and cemeteries in Western Europe and East Africa to archives in Australia and New Zealand. In 1914, India had the largest voluntary army in the world, though a question mark hangs over the word 'voluntary'. In spite of India's vast population, these men were recruited from a narrow geographical and ethnic pool, spread across Northern and Central India, the North West Frontier province and the kingdom of Nepal in accordance with the theory of 'martial races'. According to this construct, only certain ethnic and religious groups – such as the Pathans, Dogras, Jats, Garhwalis, Gurkhas and Sikhs,

---

[15] R. Danzig, 'The Multilayered Cake: A Case Study in the Reform of the Indian Empire', *Modern Asian Studies*, 3, 1 (1969), 57–74.

among others – were deemed fit to fight; incidentally, these were men from rural backgrounds who had traditionally been 'loyal' to the government, as opposed to the politicised Bengali who were branded 'effeminate'.[16] Various strands – from Victorian interest in physiognomy and Darwinism to indigenous notions of caste and political calculation – combined to form this elaborate pseudo-scientific theory. Forged in the aftermath of the Sepoy Uprising of 1857, it was enormously influential and shaped the formation of India's armed forces.[17]

During 1914–1918, India sent overseas seven expeditionary forces (see Table 0.1).[18] These included infantry, artillery and cavalry units as well as sappers, miners and signallers, Labour and Porter Corps, Supply and Transport Corps, the Indian Medical Service and Remount and Veterinary Services. Between 1914 and 1917, hundreds of thousands of Indians voyaged across the 'kālā pānī' or 'black waters' to the heart of whiteness and far beyond – from the tsetse-fly-infested bushes of East Africa to the rugged foothills of Gallipoli to the vast tracts of Mesopotamia. The camera captured this varied experience through its distinctive language, from the abject horizontality of dead Indian sepoys after the debacle of Tanga in 1914 (Figure 0.5) to the triumphant verticality documenting Indian sentinels escorting Turkish prisoners after the fall of Baghdad in 1918 (Figure 0.6). During 1914 and 1915, some 140,000 served on the Western front, where the sepoys saw action in the battles of Ypres, Festubert, Neuve Chapelle, Second Ypres and Loos. The infantry was withdrawn from Europe at the end of 1915, and thereafter Mesopotamia formed their main scene of action, where around 600,000 Indians were employed. The cavalry, however, stayed back in France until March 1918, seeing action on the Somme and at Cambrai. In 1918, they were sent to Palestine, where they took part in 'the last great cavalry campaign in history'.[19] Alongside them, in obscurity, several hundred thousand 'followers' toiled day and night. The government of India provided 50,000 non-combatants

[16] See Mrinalini Sinha, *Colonial Masculinity: The 'Manly Englishman' and the 'Effeminate Bengali'* (Manchester: Manchester University Press, 1995).

[17] There has been much work on the topic: for then-contemporary versions, see P. D. Bonarjee's *A Handbook of the Fighting Races of India* (Calcutta: Thacker, Spink & Co., 1899) and G. F. MacMunn, *The Martial Races of India* (London: Sampson Low, 1933); for recent analysis, see Heather Streets, *Martial Races: The Military, Race and Masculinity in British Imperial Culture, 1857–1914* (Manchester: Manchester University Press, 2004); for critique, see Gajendra Singh, *Testimonies*, 11–34.

[18] For a very helpful 'tabulated list' of military engagements, see *India's Contribution*, 4–57.

[19] Chhina, *Les Hindous*, vii.

Figure 0.5   Dead Indians after the Battle of Tanga, October 1914. Bundesarchiv
(Federal Archives), Berlin. Bild 146-1971-057-05/cc-BY-SA 3.0.

for the Western Front, and by the end of 1919, it had provided some
348,735 non-combatants for Mesopotamia.[20] Bearing the double
cross of race and rank, they comprised a 'dizzying variety', from depart-
mental followers, providing medical, ordnance and transport services, to
regimental followers such as the *bhistis* (cooks), *kahars* (water-carriers),
dhobies (washermen) and *chamaars* (tanners), the very terms bristling with
the violence of caste hierarchies.

These men have been doomed to wander in the no man's land between
the Eurocentric narratives of the 'Great War and modern memory' and
nationalist histories of India. But amnesia does not mean absence. During
my research travels during the past twelve years, I was repeatedly struck
by how memories persisted – privately, silently, stubbornly. When, in
2014, I visited Bhondsi, a heavily recruited Rajput village in what is today
Haryana, to interview the descendants of Punjabi veterans, a whole crowd
turned up in the panchayat-hall with a fund of stories and souvenirs
belonging to their grandfathers and great-uncles who had served in the
war: cigarette cases given as Christmas gifts in 1914 in the Western Front,
medals, coins, photographs, trinkets. Outside the panchayat-hall was the

[20] See Radhika Singha, 'Labour (India)' in the 1914–1918 Online Encyclopedia (https://encyclopedia.1914-
1918-online.net/article/labour_india). Singha has pioneered research in this field: see 'The Short Career
of the Indian Labour Corps in France, 1917–1919', *Journal of International Labour and Working Class
History*, No. 87 (2015), 27–62 and 'Finding Labour from India for the War in Iraq: The Jail Porter and
Labor Corps, 1916–1920', *Comparative Studies in Society and History*, 49, 2 (2007), 412–445.

Figure 0.6   Indian sepoys escorting Turkish POWs in Mesopotamia.
Courtesy of the Council of the National Army Museum, London.

Figure 0.7   Dance hat from Nagaland, north-east India, comprising a
German military helmet brought back from the Western Front by a Chang
Naga labourer and adorned with horns and hair. Pitt Rivers Museum, Oxford.

war memorial with names of the fallen from different wars, including sixteen from the First World War. As I left, I was even given a military salute
by a retired but rather fierce Subedar-Major who said 'Hum yodhaon ki
qaum hain, humein ladna hi aata hai' ('We are warriors; to fight is what
we know').[21] There was a certain clinging to the idea of 'martial races' and
discomfort in acknowledging the economic incentives of military service.
Later, just outside Ypres in Belgium, I visited a barn which had served as the
casualty-station for the wounded sepoys after the Battle of Neuve Chapelle
in 1915. I met the owner of the farm, Paul Jacobs, who told me how his
grandfather had housed the sepoys even though they could be pretty fierce,
for they used to chop off German ears and string them together into a
necklace round their necks![22] Paul Jacobs's fantasies would have run riot

[21] Interview at Bhondsi, Haryana in June, 2014 for BBC Radio 4 programme *The Soldiers of the
Empire: Fight in Fairyland*, October 2014 (www.bbc.co.uk/programmes/b04m9rxg).
[22] Interview with Paul Jacobs, Ypres, Belgium, September 2014, Ypres. Can be seen in the YouTube
video *From Bombay to the Western Front* (www.youtube.com/watch?v=6stybO5v7SY).

Figure 0.8   *Lota* or water-vessel with a name in Hindi inscribed.
Courtesy of Domique Faivre, Ypres.

if he had accompanied me to the Pitt Rivers Museum in Oxford. There I came across a most peculiar headdress (Figure 0.7) – a German helmet fitted with horns and human hair – found with Chang Nagas who served as labourers. In contrast, the soil of Ypres still keeps yielding up bodies of its Indian war dead. A couple of years ago, while digging a road, the body of a Gurkha sepoy was exhumed, not to speak of the regular crop of *kookris* (fish-shaped knives), shell-cases or *lotas* (water-vessels) with the name of the user inscribed (Figure 0.8).[23] In the Australian War Memorial and Museum in Canberra, I came across the diary of an Australian private where an Indian had written his name 'Pakkar Singh' in three languages (English, Urdu, Gurmukhi) (Figure 0.9). Such artefacts point to the world of inter-imperial encounters forged in the heat of battle yet taking place outside the empire; the simultaneity of Gurmukhi and Urdu scripts, on the other hand, opens up the plural linguistic world of undivided Punjab, and suggests how languages and religions cohabited.

[23] I am very grateful to Dominiek Dendooven from In Flanders Fields Museum, Ypres, who has taken me on numerous tours of the war cemeteries around Flanders, and to Domique Faivre, collector *par excellence*, for showing me his Indian trench artefacts.

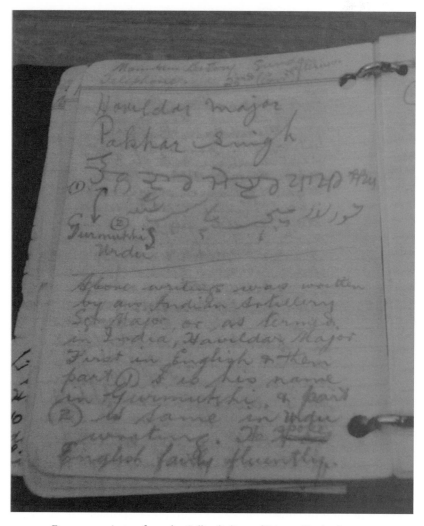

Figure 0.9   A page from the Gallipoli diary of Private Charles Stinson,
where an Indian had signed his name in English, Urdu and Gurmukhi.
Australian War Museum, Canberra, PR 84/066.

As my research evolved, I realised to my astonishment that three members
in my own extended family in Kolkata had served in the First World War –
two as doctors, and one as an interpreter. Captain Dr Manindranath Das
served in Mesopotamia and was awarded the Military Cross; his daughter-
in-law Mrs Sunanda Das took out from the family wardrobe his trench-coat,

Figure 0.10   Artefacts, including a tiffin-box and a German shell-case,
belonging to Captain Dr Manindranath Das in Mesopotamia, 1915.
Courtesy of Sunanda Das, Kolkata.

medals and other artefacts, including his tiffin-box and a German shell-case
he had found (Figure 0.10).[24] Similarly, Dr Prasanta Kumar Guha – a cousin
of my grandmother – served in France, and, in the course of interviews
with my cousins, his war diary in Bengali emerged.[25] But it was the third
family member, Hiren Basak – my maternal great-uncle who had served
as an interpreter in France – whom I had actually met and remembered
vividly. He lived next-door to my grandmother's and would come to her
house every morning and read the newspaper. War memories in India are
like the artefacts in the wardrobe – powerful but subterranean. In order to
salvage such memories and materials, it was essential to reach out to families and the community, the first step to coax private memories into the
more public domain of what Jay Winter and Emmanuel Sivan have called
'remembrance'.[26]

---

[24] I would like to express my thanks to Sunanda Das and her late husband Dr Arun Das whom
I interviewed in their house in Kolkata over a number of years, from 2012 to 2016.
[25] Interview with Indrani Haldar, July 2014, Kolkata.
[26] See Jay Winter and Emmanuel Sivan (eds.), *War and Remembrance in the Twentieth Century*
(Cambridge: Cambridge University Press, 1999), 6. In 1972, S. D. Pradhan and DeWitt Ellinwood

There is no one homogeneous 'Indian' war experience, any more than
there is a single 'British' or 'Ottoman' war experience. It is not sufficiently
appreciated just how varied the worlds of even the combatants were,
depending on rank, duty, theatre of battle or the period of service. On one
end of the spectrum, we have 'stars' such as Subedar Khudadad Khan who
became the first Indian to win the Victoria Cross for keeping his machine-
gun going at Hollebecke on 31 October 1914 even when grievously injured
and every comrade had been killed; or the nineteen-year-old Indra Lal
Roy ('Laddy' Roy), the Indian First World War flying ace, who brought
down ten German aeroplanes in fourteen days (so much for the 'non-martial' Bengali!) before plunging to his death in a dogfight on 22 July 1918.[27]
On the other hand, we have reports about some sepoys with self-inflicted
wounds on their left hand in their first week in the trenches (October 1914),
or going mad during the Siege of Kut (7 December 1915–29 April 1916). We
hear abject stories about the Indian Labour Corps – of working in blistering
heat or cutting with bruised hands through shingle while railway-laying in
Mesopotamia, or of a labourer trying to commit suicide by strangling himself with his *pugree* (turban) for having been forced to do a job not suitable
for his caste.[28] There were others too – princes, interpreters, assistant-sur-
geons, POWs, postal officers and doctors. How did these differences in
rank, caste, class, education and occupation play out in the way these men
were perceived and represented in photographs and memoirs, in the kind of
encounters they had, and in the creation of their own testimonies?

At the same time, the topic of the war and India cannot be reduced
to Indian experiences 'overseas'. Even though the country was dragged
into the war as part of the empire, there was widespread enthusiasm.
The princes, people and political parties, including the Indian National
Congress, all supported the war effort. 'I love the English Nation', wrote
Mahatma Gandhi to Charles Hardinge, Viceroy of India, as he threw
himself into the recruitment campaign.[29] India's war service, it was hoped,

conducted a series of interviews with Punjabi veterans of the First World War, funded by the
State University of New York; former Squadron Leader Rana Chhina also interviewed some of
the veterans in the 1980s. On behalf of the United Services Institution of India, Chhina has been
spearheading the centennial commemoration of the First World War in India and is currently
building up an important digital resource (http://usiofindia.org/Projects/View/?pid=72).
[27] See Rozina Visram, *Asians in Britain* (London: Pluto Press, 2002), 172, and Shrabani Basu, *For King
and Another Country*, 136–139.
[28] I am grateful to Radhika Singha for these details, which will appear in her forthcoming book *The
Coolies' Great War*. See Singha, 'Labour (India)' (https://encyclopedia.1914-1918-online.net/article/
labour_india).
[29] Mahatma Gandhi, 29 April, 1918, *The Collected Works of Mahatma Gandhi* (Ahmedabad:
Government of India, 1965), Volume XIV, 380.

would secure her 'the jewelled medal of Self-Government within the Empire'.[30] Chapter 1 investigates this oft-repeated assumption to argue for a more complex structure of feeling whereby imperial service was constructed as a point of national honour. Social and economic historians have drawn attention to India's substantial material contribution, from mineral, food grains and some 172,815 animals to the gift of 100 million pounds which was partly raised through war bonds.[31] But what has gone unnoticed is the remarkable process of ideological and cultural mobilisation or the experiential texture of lives on the home front. Meetings were held in all major cities, newspapers blazed with pictures, war journals in English such as *Indian Ink* (1914–1916) and *All About the War* (1915) were published, prayers were offered in mosques, temples and gurdwaras. Pandit Ram Prashad Sharma, one of India's foremost 'astronomers and astrologers' predicted 'confidently' that *Golak Jog* – the alignment of the five planets via the sun – will ensure 'His Imperial Majesty's decisive victory', while the Goddess Kali, the arch-deity of the Bengali anti-colonial revolutionaries, was said to have joined the Allied cause![32] Middle-class women too played their part, from knitting socks to taking part in 'Our Day' collections in the imperial centre (Figure 0.11). But no province registered the war as intensely as Punjab, which contributed more than half the total number of Indian combatants. How did the province feel and articulate the impact of war, from its poets and journalists to the non-literate village women?

A more expansive understanding of a First World War culture necessitates a corresponding redefinition of the 'archive', an expansion that is both horizontal and vertical. If investigations of the sepoys have largely been based on quotations from the censored letters, accepted as transcripts of experience, I examine their narrative strategies and textual complexities, and also draw on a fresh and wider range of sources: rumour, gossip, memoirs, photographs, sketches, sound-recordings, songs, poems and imaginative literature; it is through such dialogue that one can begin to understand the sepoy world. At the same time, the study recovers several

---

[30] Quoted in G. A. Natesan (ed.), *All about the War: India Review War Book* (Madras: G. A. Natesan, 1915), 267.

[31] See Sugata Bose and Ayesha Jalal, *Modern South Asia: History, Culture, Political Economy* (London: Routledge, 2011), 102–108; Radhika Singha, 'India's Silver Bullets: War Loans and War Propaganda, 1917–18', in Maartje Abbenhuis, Neill Atkinson, Kingsley Baird and Gail Romano (eds.), *The Myriad Legacies of 1917: A Year of War and Revolution* (London: Palgrave, 2018), 77–102

[32] Sharma, Pandit Ram Prashad, 'Astronomy and the War', *The Bengalee*, 28 February 1918.

Figure 0.11   Indian women collecting money for 'Our Day' Fund on
19 October 1916 in London. Getty Collection.

important textual testimonies, including the journal of an interpreter from
the Manipur Labour Corps, the account of a footloose Parsi lascar-turned-
Tommy, the memoir of a pretentious postal-officer in Egypt and an outstanding body of writing by a group of educated middle-class Bengali
POWs in Mesopotamia. Alongside such life-stories, the book draws on
a range of cultural productions in the home front – from recruitment
verses and lectures, including those by Gandhi, to street performances
and folksongs. I have often let sources argue amongst themselves to show
the contested nature of some of the histories. These various testimonies
are then supplemented by a corpus of self-consciously literary works by
writers, British and Indian, from Rudyard Kipling and Talbot Mundy
to Tagore, Sarojini Naidu, Chandradhar Sharma Guleri, Swarnakumari
Devi, Kazi Nazrul Islam and Mulk Raj Anand. The final chapter looks at
a range of more intellectual responses during but also beyond 1914–1918,
as it concludes with a chapter on Aurobindo Ghosh, Iqbal and Tagore,
ruminating on Europe, empire and a post-war 'future for mankind'. The

book thus attends to diverse voices, both subaltern and elite, the street performer and the Nobel Laureate, and reads the material, in conjunction and cumulatively, to argue for a powerful cultural and literary sphere during wartime. The recovery and translation of a substantial amount of vernacular material – from Urdu, Punjabi, Hindi, Bengali, Gujrati, and Nepalese (alongside a few Flemish, French and German sources) – have fundamentally shaped the scope of the book and the terms of its enquiry. These materials revealed for me the depth of the war's penetration, from the folk culture of Punjab to a variety of combatant and non-combatant experiences far beyond the reach of the censored letters; above all, they gave a certain 'palpable' quality to the research.

India, Empire, and First World War Culture is the first cultural and literary history of India and the First World War, though it necessarily engages with the social and the political. At a deeper level, it tries to capture what the cultural critic Raymond Williams has called 'structures of feeling', where 'different ways of thinking [are] vying to emerge at any one time in history'. Williams further notes

> We are concerned with meanings and values as they are actively lived and felt, and the relations between these and formal or systematic beliefs are in practice variable ... we are talking about characteristic elements of impulse, restraint and tone; specifically affective elements of consciousness and relationships: not feeling against thought, but thought as felt and feeling as thought: practical consciousness of a present kind, in a living and inter-relating continuity.[33]

As in my past work, what I have tried to capture most, by employing diverse means, is the *texture* of experience, thought and feeling. Instead of engaging explicitly with theories of affect or emotion, I have let my sources speak while being alert to the sensuous and affective dimension of their forms.[34] The sustained use of the 'literary' in the book, both as the practice of close reading and as source-material, is intimately related to such a purpose. If photographs, paintings or quotations from letters and literature are sometimes used by scholars as embellishment or a transparent envelope of experience, *India, Empire, and First World War Culture* instead prizes the act of *reading* and attention to *form*. Sources, whether an

---

[33] Raymond Williams, *Marxism and Literature* (Oxford: Oxford University Press, 1977), 132.
[34] The history of emotions has been a longstanding interest: see my *Touch and Intimacy in First World War Literature* (Cambridge: Cambridge University Press, 2006). For this study, I have found Barbara H. Rosenwein's *Emotional Communities in the Early Middle Ages* (Ithaca: Cornell University Press, 2007) and Rajat Ray: *The Felt Community: Commonality and Mentality before the Emergence of Indian Nationalism* (2003) particularly illuminating.

object, a photograph or a painting, are not just used as bedrocks to facilitate the flow of narrative but are dredged up, scrubbed and inspected in
all their grit and multidimensionality. Photographs, sketches, paintings,
poems, short stories and novels are here recruited not to serve as history by
proxy but to open up through their poetics a more complex psychological
and sensuous space. The enigma of form paradoxically can provide deeper
insights into the past and thus help to take us from the 'grey' of official
records to what Sigmund Freud calls the 'green of experience'.[35]

India, Empire, and First World War Culture is situated at the intersection of
three principal areas: First World War studies, South Asian history, and colonial and postcolonial literature. In the last several decades, the field of First
World War studies has been one of the most burgeoning fields of enquiry.
The work of cultural historians has reconceptualised our understanding
of war from 'combat' to one of 'conflict', one that encompasses civilians,
women and children as well as combatants.[36] In the last few years, our idea
of the war has been further transformed by the recovery and examination
of colonial and non-white experiences.[37] Four million non-white men,
including combatants and non-combatants, were recruited into European
and American armies during the First World War. If India contributed the
highest number from across the colonies and dominions, France recruited
some 500,000 colonial troops between 1914 and 1918, including 166,000 West
Africans, 140,000 Algerians, 47,000 Tunisians and 50,000 Indochinese. Over
two million Africans were involved in the conflict, as soldiers or labourers;
on the other hand, nearly 140,000 Chinese contract labourers were hired
by the British and French governments.[38] The Indian experience has to be

---

[35] Sigmund Freud, 'Neurosis and Psychosis' (1924), *The Standard Edition of the Collected Psychological Works*, under the general editorship of James Strachey (London: Random House, 2001), 149.
[36] This reconceptualisation has been spearheaded by a range of scholars, including Annette Becker, Claire Buck, Margaret Higonnet, John Horne, Antoine Prost and particularly Jay Winter. Winter's works, notably *Sites of Memory, Sites of Mourning: The Great War in European Cultural History* (Cambridge: Cambridge University Press, 1996) and *War beyond Words: Languages of Remembrance from the Great War to the Present* (Cambridge: Cambridge University Press, 2017), have a rich affective quality which has been as important to me as his scholarship.
[37] See Das (ed.), *Race, Empire and First World War Writing* (Cambridge: Cambridge University Press, 2011); Richard Fogarty and Andrew Tait Jarboe, *Empires in World War I: Shifting Frontiers and Imperial Dynamics in a Global Conflict* (London: I. B. Taurus, 2014); Robert Gerwarth and Erez Manela (eds.), *Empires at War 1911–1923* (Oxford: Oxford University Press, 2015). In addition, there has been much work on individual nations or ethnic groups. See the Introduction to *Race, Empire and First World War Writing* for a more elaborate historiography, 1–32. An unusual and illumin-ating literary intervention is Claire Buck, *Conceiving Strangeness in British First World War Writing* (London: Palgrave, 2014).
[38] See *Race, Empire and First World War Writing*, 4.

seen in the context of these diverse colonial troops, with their finely striated and insidious racial hierarchies. While French colonial troops served on the Western Front, Britain allowed only Indians, among its non-white troops, to fight in France and Flanders; within Europe, West Indians, Maoris, Egyptians and indigenous South Africans worked as pioneers or labourers.

It is a scandal that it has taken us a whole hundred years to recognise the extent of the non-white participation. Eurocentrism is, however, not the only cause. Most non-white colonial soldiers were non-literate, and, until recently, we did not have even a dozen full-length diaries and memoirs from the four million people. Moreover, unlike the (white) dominions, such as Australia, New Zealand and Canada, where the experience at Gallipoli or Vimy Ridge was proclaimed loudly and turned into the site of their emergence as nations, the colonies – after their transition into nation-states – distanced themselves from their imperial pasts. The First World War experience did not fit with the nationalist narratives of these former colonies and was thus largely airbrushed out of their official histories; it is only recently, sometimes in the light of the centennial commemoration, that many countries, including India, have started to *own* their war experience.[39] Still, we do not have the rich archives that one has in the Australian War Memorial in Canberra or the Canadian War Museum in Ottawa. One of the lasting legacies of the centennial commemoration will be not just the greater recognition of the colonial contribution but the recovery of fresh material. Our knowledge base has expanded substantially since I edited *Race, Empire and First World War Writing* in 2011. In an extraordinary outpouring of energy and enthusiasm, community groups have participated in the process as much as academics; digital sources and crowd-sourcing have led to the availability and sharing of material to an unprecedented degree. The commonest form this has taken has been a reclaiming of the 'voices', 'contribution' and 'hidden histories' of hitherto marginalised groups. Within academia too, there has been an exciting swell of interest in recovering the colonial and non-European aspects, signalled in the very title of works such as *The World in World Wars: Experiences, Perceptions and Perspectives from Africa and Asia* (2010). As the editors of this volume noted recently, in spite of the much-celebrated 'global turn' in First World War studies, there seems to be 'no consensus as to what global means'.[40] More

---

[39] In Britain, David Olusoga's popular BBC series and his book *The World's War* (2014) - a compendious and compelling narrative of how 'Europe's Great War became the World's War' - have powerfully drawn attention to the war's multiracial and multinational aspects at a national level.

[40] I am particularly grateful to Katrin Bromber, Katharina Lange and Heike Liebau for sharing with me their rich survey paper 'First World War Historiographies: Commemoration, New Research and

generally, work in this area falls into two broad categories. First, we have
the work of a number of military historians, who have looked at archives,
often located in Europe, but have significantly enriched our understanding
of non-European theatres of war.[41] Second, we have a number of social
historians who have reconstructed with great sensitivity and insight the
lives of non-white combatants and non-combatants, from French colonial forces to German askaris and British West Indian troops, by engaging
primarily with textual sources – including censored letters, occasional testimonies and official archival records. Both impulses have been present in
the ongoing work on Indian troops, a subject of burgeoning interest in
recent years: works have ranged from excellent military and social histories
of the Indian experience in France and Gallipoli to powerful attention
to the condition of the labourers in Mesopotamia largely through official
records, censored letters and interviews.[42]

  India, Empire, and First World War Culture marks a departure in two ways.
First, it tries to situate the war *within* the country through the experiences
of an array of people – politicians, journalists, artists, preachers, writers,
the ordinary men and women in the village – as well as in the life-stories
of those serving overseas. In this, the book is consonant with some of the
work happening on the Middle East, such as Leila Fawaz's rich social history *A Land of Aching Hearts: The Middle East in the Great War* (2014).[43]
Second, while the existing scholarship on extra-European aspects has been
either military or social or, more recently, economic, my focus is on *the cultural and the literary*, whereby I extend the frame to include photography,

Debates during the Centennial in/on Africa, the Middle East and South Asia' where they speak of
the 'two categories' I mention below.
[41] The classic example is Hew Strachan's work *The First World War: To Arms* (Oxford: Oxford
University Press, 2001); also see Omissi, *The Sepoy and the Raj* and George Morton-Jack, *The Indian
Army on the Western Front: India's Expeditionary Force to France and Belgium in the First World War*
(Cambridge: Cambridge University Press, 2014). In the context of Indian military history, the
various publications of Kaushik Roy, based on extensive research both in India and in Britain, have
played an important part.
[42] See, for colonial dimensions, Richard Smith, *Jamaican Volunteers in the First World War: Race,
Masculinity and the Development of National Consciousness* (Manchester: Manchester University
Press, 2004); Richard Fogarty, *Race and Empire in France: Colonial Subjects in the French Army,
1914-1918* (Baltimore: Johns Hopkins University Press, 2008); Michelle R. Moyd, *Violent
Intermediaries: African Soldiers, Conquest, and Everyday Colonialism in German East Africa*
(Athens: Ohio University Press 2014). For a list of the important works in recent years in the con-
text of India and First World War, please refer back to footnote 14. Needless to say, the war has
routinely appeared in classic works on Indian history, from Sumit Sarkar's *Modern India 1885–1947*
(Delhi: Macmillan India, 2002 [1983]) to Sugata Bose and Ayesha Jalal's *Modern South Asia* or, more
powerfully, in Sugata Bose's *A Hundred Horizons: The Indian Ocean in the Age of Global Empire*
(Cambridge: Harvard University Press, 2006).
[43] Also see Mustafa Aksakal, *The Ottoman Road to War in 1914: The Ottoman Empire and the First World
War* (Cambridge: Cambridge University Press, 2008).

painting, songs, life-writing and imaginative fiction. It is indeed curious that the 'cultural turn' that revolutionised our understanding of the war has not so far taken place for these colonial histories: there has so far been no equivalent to Jay Winter's seminal *Sites of Memory, Sites of Mourning* (1996) for the colonial non-white sphere. More time and digging are needed to produce a work of such comparative scope in the colonial context, but it also leads us to ask the following question: what shape should such history take? Indeed, to do cultural history in the extra-European context, it becomes even more vital *to de-Eurocentricise our tools as well as our sources.* We must rethink about what would constitute the archive in a situation where most of the participants were non-literate, the postcolonial states themselves ambivalent about their war participation, and both official archives and national memory woefully inadequate.[44] While not abandoning the traditional sources, it becomes crucial to visit, anthropologist-like, the 'sites' and seek out the families and communities, to raid archives of other countries whose war histories intersected with ours, to supplement official records with unconventional sources, and – equally importantly – *to know what questions to ask of our material.*

This book is focussed tightly on India, but many of the questions my material raises have relevance for the whole field of colonial war experience and representation. What did the former colonies hope to gain by dint of their war service? Why did the men enlist? How were the non-white soldiers viewed in the longer history of race and representation? The research of scholars in adjacent fields and often in the context of other racial groups has constantly helped me to clarify issues, provide fresh lines of enquiry and above all throw up eerie points of contiguity. If debates in the past have been locked into questions of whether the colonial soldiers were 'loyal' soldiers or ruthless mercenaries, whether they were merely cannon-fodder or had some agency, we are now increasingly moving towards a much more complex and nuanced vocabulary. While the use of multiple, shifting frameworks to understand the mixed motives of the African *askaris* helps to illuminate the world of their Indian cousins, the exploration of British fantasies and anxieties underpinning representations of West Indian troops is revealing for interpreting the iconography around the sepoys.[45] Moreover, literary accounts from

[44] An unusual and beautiful example is Raghu Karnad, *Farthest Field: An Indian Story of the Second World War* (London: William Collins, 2015); Yasmin Khan's *The Raj At War: A People's History of India's Second World War* (London: Penguin, 2015) is also a bold intervention in this direction.
[45] See Moyd, *Violent Intermediaries*; for race and representation, see Smith, *Jamaican Volunteers in the First World War*.

the period often show a highly sophisticated understanding of motive, agency and ambivalence.

In *Postcolonial Melancholia* (2005), Paul Gilroy has noted how the 'narcissism of minor differences' should be balanced by what he calls, inverting Freud, 'the invaluable solidarity of the slightly different'.[46] In spite of the great differences in the war participation of various non-white colonies, I have been struck by commonalities in thought and structures of feeling. A basic aspiration expressed in a 1915 article in the Jamaican journal *Grenada Federalist* – 'We will be fighting to prove to Great Britain that we are not so vastly inferior to the white' – resounds across a range of Indian newspaper articles and verses and finds its inimitable expression, with regional inflection, in a Bengali war limerick: 'Who calls me now a coward base,/ And brands my race a coward race?/I'll brook no more such scoffing word:/ My King himself has washed the shame/That fouled so long my stainless name.'[47] The strange paradox of imperial war service as a tool to salvage racial honour that I examine in Chapter 1 occurs, with local variations, across a range of non-white participation, from former colonies such as the West Indies to particular ethnic groups such as the Maoris and aboriginal Australians. The similarities are even more pronounced if we move to the area of recruitment, from the mobilisation of oral culture to the blurring of lines between 'voluntary' and 'involuntary' recruitment to the centrality of the economic incentive. Recruitment in Punjab (Chapter 2), even in the coercive stages of 1918, was perhaps not as brutal as that unleashed in parts of Africa, but consider the following accounts, the first from Malawi and the second from Punjab:

> The government told the chief that there was war; the chief informed his people. He asked us young people to help the government fight the Germans. I lost confidence in the chief; he was a betrayer. He would make us die in the war.[48]

> The Tehsildar's method was to have a list of all men in a village prepared by the Patwari. When he had got the list, it was the Tehsildar's practice ... to ask a family of 3 or 4 brothers to provide one of two recruits for the army.[49]

[46] Paul Gilroy, *Postcolonial Melancholia* (New York: Columbia University Press, 2005), 79.
[47] Quoted in M. B. L. Bhargava, *India's Services in the War* (Allahabad: M. B. L. Bhargava, 1919), 218.
[48] Interview with Sam Kamaga, 4 August 1973, as quoted in Melville Page (ed.), *The Chiwaya War: Malawians and the First World War* (Boulder: Westview Press, 2000), 215.
[49] Testimony of Muhammed Khan, *Congress Report on the Punjab Disorders*, March–June 1920, Vol. 20 (http://gandhiserve.org/cwmg/VOL020.PDF). Also see V. N. Datta (ed.), *New Light on the Punjab Disturbances in 1919* (Simla: Indian Institute of Advanced Study, 1975).

In both, the village hierarchy is mobilised; both, interestingly, are oral sources. And, in fact, resistance to such pressures from the most vulnerable groups takes similar forms – the folksongs of lament sung by Punjabi women excavated here resonate most powerfully not with the chiselled verse of elite Indian women, but with their similarly distraught African sisters: 'Helter-skelter! Helter-skelter! Germany has completely finished off our young men.'[50] This book is thus part of a larger project of how we remember the wider colonial world of the First World War. I am increasingly convinced that one needs to go beyond the textual towards oral histories and visual clues the moment we step outside Europe.

In recent years, the field of colonial and postcolonial studies has been energised by concepts such as 'cultural encounter', 'affective communities' and 'cosmopolitan thought-zones' which have opened up the imperial past in fresh ways. Scholars such as Elleke Boehmer, Antoinette Burton, Leela Gandhi and Kris Manjapra, among others, have alerted us to more complex 'webs' and 'networks' of exchange, as well as to the presence of 'lateral contact zones' outside the imperial axis.[51] If, in the past, the 'sepoys of the Raj' were problematic figures for the country's nationalist historiography or even for the subaltern project, the 'new military' historians are exploring their complex relations to the colonial state and society.[52] Colonial soldiers, I argue, were some of the most important and unacknowledged nodes for such transnational contact; in the context of India, they participated, through the long nineteenth century, in campaigns in Cyprus, Egypt, Abyssinia, South Africa and most recently China. If the First World War is usually understood as a military conflict between European empires, I have argued elsewhere that it can equally be reconceptualised as a turning point in the history of cultural encounter and entanglement.[53] If

[50] African soldiers' song, quoted in Melvin Page (ed.), *Africa and the First World War* (Basingstoke: Macmillan, 1987), 15.
[51] Antoinette Burton, *At the Heart of the Empire: Indians and the Colonial Encounter in Late Victorian Britain* (Berkeley: University of California Press, 1998); Leela Gandhi, *Affective Communities* (Durham, NC: Duke University Press, 2006); Mrinalini Sinha, *Spectres of Mother India* (Durham and London: Duke University Press, 2006); Elleke Boehmer, *Indian Arrivals 1870–1915: Networks of British Empire* (Oxford: Oxford University Press, 2015); Sugata Bose, *A Hundred Horizons*; Sugata Bose and Kris Manjapra (eds.), *Cosmopolitan Thought-Zones: South Asia and the Global Circulation of Ideas* (London: Palgrave, 2010).
[52] Kaushik Roy (ed.), *War and Society in Colonial India, 1807–1945* (Delhi: Oxford University Press, 2006).
[53] See my Introduction to the online sourcebook on 'Cultural Exchange in the Time of Global Conflict' (http://sourcebook.cegcproject.eu/introduction); also see the important doctoral dissertation of Anna Mary Maguire, *Cultural Encounters during the First World War: The Experience of Troops from New Zealand, South Africa and the West Indies*, King's College London (2017), https://kclpure.kcl.ac.uk/portal/files/66980846/2017_Maguire_Anna_1239996_ethesis.pdf.

Figure 0.12   An Indian soldier exchanging coins with a man of the Greek
Labour Corps at Salonika. © Imperial War Museum (Q 13716).

the names in different First World War cemeteries bear testimony to the
macabre cosmopolitanism of the battlefields, a parallel world of contact
and exchange was opening up for the sepoys: in the billets, hospitals, POW
camps, railway stations, estaminets and markets. In Gallipoli, they shared
chapathis with the Australians; in France, they formed intense bonds with
their French 'mothers'; in Salonika, they exchanged coins with Greek
labourers (Figure 0.12); and in Mesopotamia, a North Indian sweeper
Jumman adopted a recently orphaned Armenian boy he had found crying
near a well and named him Babulal. Having witnessed the Armenian
genocide, Sisir Prasad Sarbadhikari – a member of the Bengal Ambulance
Corps and an educated middle-class prisoner – observed of his Armenian
friends that 'Their lives have become ours'; similarly, a wounded Turkish
soldier told him that 'This war that we are fighting – what is our stake in
this? ... We became enemies overnight because one or two people [the
British and the German kings] deemed it so.'[54] In academic studies on

[54] Sisir Prasad Sarbadhikari, *Abhi Le Baghdad* (Kolkata: privately printed, 1957), 158.

Figure 0.13   Indian sepoys billeted with a family in France.
Courtesy of Eric Deroo, Paris.

transnational exchanges, the 'politics of anti-Westernism' is often limited to exchanges among the intellectual elite, but texts such as Sarbadhikari's extraordinary Mesopotamia POW memoir *Abhi Le Baghdad* or some of the censored sepoy letters point to a parallel version of 'anti-colonial cosmopolitanism' from below.[55] Such points of contact may have contributed to the burgeoning nationalist consciousness.

Some of the most moving cross-cultural encounters are recorded by young sepoys describing their intense bonds with their French 'mothers' (Figure 0.13). Consider the following letter:

> The house in which I was billeted was the house of a well-to-do man, but the only occupant was the lady of the house, and she was advanced in years. Her three sons had gone to the war. One had been killed, another had been wounded and was in hospital, and the third was at the time in the trenches … Indeed, during the whole three months she ministered to me to such an extent that I cannot adequately describe her [kindness]. Of her own free will

---

[55] See Santanu Das, 'Entangled Emotions: Race, Encounters and Anti-colonial Cosmopolitanism', in Santanu Das and Kate McLoughlin (eds.), *First World War: Literature, Culture, Modernity* (London: British Academy and Oxford University Press, 2018), 241–261.

she washed my clothes, arranged my bed, polished my boots for three months
... When we had to leave that village this old lady wept on my shoulder.[56]

Such translated and censored extracts, I argue in Chapter 5, are complex
palimpsests where, underneath various accretions, one can hear echoes of
the sepoy heart. Yet the above extract, as I shall show, was hijacked by none
other than Rudyard Kipling, adding another layer to the intertwined histories. *India, Empire, and First World War Culture* views the world at war from
both European and Indian perspectives. Starting with visual and testimonial
accounts, it then asks how such encounters, in Europe and Mesopotamia, are
in turn represented by both British and Indian writers. If ideas of 'military
orientalism', 'exoticism', 'otherness' and 'alterity' often provide us with too
easy a vocabulary, the book contends that the processes of perception and
representation on both sides were far more complex, informed by diverse histories, fantasies and anxieties. One of the findings of my research is that Kipling
was given access to the censored sepoy letters for propaganda purposes. Yet,
the resultant work, *The Eyes of Asia* (1915), I argue, resists a reductive reading as
just imperial propaganda: racial prejudice co-exists with a more intimate history of emotions, including vulnerability, maternity and yearning. Through
a series of readings of photographs, letters and literary texts by European
soldiers and artists (Chapters 3 and 4), as well as letters, testimonies and literary texts by Indians (particularly Chapters 5–9), I show how race was often
only one factor, though an important one, which intersected with class, rank,
theatre of battle and the specificity of the context. Representational practices,
as noted above, are key to some of my analyses of structures of experience and
feeling, from sepoy letters and songs to Kipling's *The Eyes of Asia* and Mulk
Raj Anand's war novel *Across the Black Waters* (1940).

As should be evident by now, the book does not aim to present a compendious survey of war culture: such an enterprise requires several volumes
and a team of scholars. Instead, I have focussed on particular 'sites' of experiential and cultural representation. The archives, in particular, are asymmetrical and have guided my focus; in the light of the uneven documentation
of Indian service overseas, I have decided to focus on the Western Front,
and on Mesopotamia, which has so far received little attention.[57] Given
the heterogeneity of sources, the chapters are interdisciplinary in scope.
This heterogeneity and interdisciplinary nature are something I wish to

---

[56] Letter of Sher Bahadur Khan, Secunderabad Cavalry Brigade, France, 9 January 1916, *CIM*,
L/MIL/5/828/1, 112r as well as in IOR, L/MIL/5/826/1, 115.
[57] For example, there is very little, by way of Indian testimonial sources, on the experience in Egypt,
Palestine, East Africa or Gallipoli. For a different approach, see Peter Stanley's important socio-
military study *Die in Battle, Do Not Despair* which documents the Indian war experience at Gallipoli
through largely Western sources in the absence of Indian testimonies. Such an approach is however
not suitable for the more intimate 'history from below' I wish to recover.

emphasise as necessary to understanding the many-stranded and multidirectional nature of the history. In her inspired study *Body Parts: Essays in Life-Writing* (2010), the literary critic Hermione Lee notes that

> Readers of biography are greedy readers, with an insatiable appetite for detail and story. There are all kinds of ways of satisfying these appetites. Coming at a likeness will always involve a messy, often contradictory, mixture of approaches. It's that all-encompassing quality which gives biography some of its appeal – and makes it so resistant to theorising. History, politics, sociology, gossip, fiction, literary criticism, psychoanalysis, documentary, journalism, ethics and philosophy are all scrambled inside the genre. But the target of all these approaches is a living person in a body, not a smoothed-over figure … What makes biography so curious and endlessly absorbing is that through all the documents and the letters, the context and the witness, the conflicting opinions and the evidence of the work, we keep catching sight of a real body, a physical life.[58]

India, Empire, and First World War Culture is a work of cultural and literary history rather than biography, but it is driven by, and hopes to whet, the same kind of appetite. In the course of this study, I have not just, magpie-like, picked on various source-materials but actively feasted on what Lee calls a 'messy, even contradictory, mixture of approaches', guided by the nature and genre of source-material: gossip shares the same pedestal as governmental decrees; political and social histories rub shoulders with visual culture and art history; the grand narratives of military history are brought into dialogue with the granularity of anthropological research; literary studies have been leavened with insights from the history of emotions. The heterodox methodology of 'life-writing' is one with which *India, Empire, and First World War Culture* shares its critical affinity, but by the very dint of its subject – a largely non-literate sepoy community – it goes beyond 'writing' to engage with visual, material and aural cultures. There is a difference between writing 'lives' and writing an individual 'life', but I firmly believe that our understandings of history are deepened by efforts to imagine how such histories are experienced by different individuals in specific places, rather than a series of bloodless discursive spaces. The aim, as with Lee, is not a smoothed-over historical narrative but to glimpse a 'real body' – of people, experiences, ideas – in the very act of being articulated, framed and contested. Underlying the variety and mixture of approaches mentioned above are two main critical tools employed throughout the monograph: archival recovery, supplemented by other

---

[58] Hermione Lee, *Body Parts: Essays on Life-Writing* (London: Pimlico, 2010), 3.

historical and literary material; and the practice of close reading – whether of word, or song, or image. It is only by making such words and images and objects speak and breathe and connect with each other, while respecting their specific contexts and forms, that we feel the warmth of human life across these fugitive fragments which, like the sepoy bodies they mourn, lie strewn across the globe.

PART I

The Restless Home Front

CHAPTER I

The Imperial–Nationalist Self
Anti-discrimination, Aspiration and Anxiety

On 29 July 1914, Dr Ramji Lal, a civil servant in Rohtak district in Punjab wrote in his diary: 'Read the *Panjabee*. There is fear of war between Austria and Serbia. If other powers will join the combatants, the result will be horrible. May God help them to avert the war.'[1] The very next day, fellow Lahore-based newspaper *Zamindar* predicted that

> War will not be confined to Austria and Serbia but will be a universal war in which all the great empires of Europe will be involved; for having partitioned Asia and Africa, they have no hunting grounds left, and will now descend into the arena and hunt each other. The result of it all will be that the giant which has so far been ruining Asia will now be engaged in ruining himself; the materials of war which have so far been used to destroy Orientals will now be employed in the destruction of Europeans.[2]

Eerie as it is acute, the prophecy shows the depth of engagement, if with a touch of anti-colonial *Schadenfreude*, with the war in one of the most heavily recruited colonial home fronts: Punjab. In the pre-war years, the province evolved, as is well known, as 'the sword-arm of the Raj'; during the war years, it was, like large parts of undivided India, a discursive battlefield.

As Britain declared war on 4 August 1914, Lord Hardinge, the Viceroy of India, declared that India too was at war, without even consulting the Indian leaders. But news of the war's outbreak was accompanied by widespread proclamations of 'loyalty', even though some, like Dr Lal, privately expressed fear and trembling. 'On the question of loyalty to the British Government all people are united', declared the *Tribune* on behalf of the

---

[1] Unpublished diary of Dr Ramji Lal, written in English. Haryana Academy, Gurgaon, New Delhi.
[2] *Zamindar*, 30 July 1914, India Office Records, British Library, London (henceforth IOR), Punjabi Newspaper Reports (PNR), L/R/5/195, 914. All references to the Punjabi newspapers here are to the IOR collection in the British Library. An important selection of some of these newspapers can be found in Andrew Tait Jarboe (ed.), *War News in India: The Punjabi Press during World War I* (London: I. B. Tauris, 2016).

'educated classes', while the Calcutta-based *Amrita Bazaar Patrika* reported 'spontaneous expressions of loyalty ... throughout the length and breadth of the Indian Empire'.[3] The native princes named the hospital ship they had contributed *Loyalty*.[4] Parties closed ranks, politicians and the public concurred: 'loyalty ... had swept the country', 'loyal toasts were drunk', 'our duty as Muslims now is to remain loyal', 'the duty of Mahomedans of India [is] to adhere firmly to their old and tried loyalty to the British Government', 'key to the whole situation is Loyalty'.[5] Even the 'extremist' nationalist leader Bal Gangadhar Tilak issued a pledge of 'loyalty' as early as 4 October 1914 in the *Mahratta*, adding that 'Indian hearts will be thrilled to know that Indian troops have landed in France.'[6] In April 1918, after attending the Imperial War Conference in Delhi, Mahatma Gandhi wrote to the Viceroy 'I love the English Nation, and I wish to evoke in every Indian the loyalty of the Englishman.'[7]

What was the mottled texture of the banner of such 'loyalty'? Of course, with a battery of anti-sedition laws imposed by the government, the Indian press was cribbed and confined, but still the word seems to protest a bit too loudly.[8] Does such enthusiastic support show the success of the colonial state in 'purchasing loyalties' from different groups by offering post-war 'rewards', or was it a shrewd continuation of what Sanjay Seth has called the 'discursive strategy of moderate nationalism' for greater political autonomy?[9] While recognising the importance of both, this chapter

---

[3] *Tribune*, 26 August 1914, IOR, PNR, L/R/195, 822, British Library, *Amrita Bazaar Patrika*, 7 August 1914 and 2 October 1914, National Library Kolkata. The word recurs in British media, too, as in various articles in *The Times*: 'The Loyalty of India: Speeches at the National Congress' (31 December 1914), 'Rajput Fighting Forces – Indian Loyalty' (8 January 1915) and 'Loyal India' (14 January 1915).

[4] See, for example, *Speeches of Indian Princes on the World War* (n.p., 1919).

[5] G. A. Natesan (ed.), *All about the War: The India Review War Book* (Madras: G. A. Natesan, 1915), 267, 270, 269. For contemporary records, see *Statistics of the Military Effort of the British Empire during the Great War, 1914–1920* (London 1920), 777; *India's Contribution to the Great War* (Calcutta: Superintendent Government Printing, 1923).

[6] *Mahratta*, 4 October 1914, quoted in Bal Ram Nanda, *Three Statesmen: Gokhale, Gandhi and Nehru* (Delhi: Oxford University Press, 2004), 447.

[7] Mahatma K. Gandhi, Letter to Viceroy, 29 April 1918, *The Collected Works of Mahatma Gandhi* (Ahmedabad: Government of India, 1965), Vol. XIV, 380 (hereafter *CWMG*).

[8] In the government archives, one comes across a high level of anxiety, at times bordering on panic, about the 'loyalty' of the Muslim populations in India; this is also evident in the renewed communiques issued, stating that the 'sacred places of Islam' in the Middle East would not be attacked. A revealing report in August 1915 states that there is 'the strong notion' among 'the semi-literate class' in Bengal that 'Germany is a great friend of Turkey'. See 'Vigilance over the Muhammedan Press', 25 August 1915, Intelligence Bureau (IB), Confidential 312/14/(1–2), West Bengal State Archives, Kolkata.

[9] See Aravind Ganachari, 'First World War: Purchasing Indian Loyalties. Imperial Policy of Recruitment and "Rewards"', *Economic and Political Weekly*, 19 February 2005, 779–788; Sanjay

argues that India's phenomenal rhetoric of loyalty both intersected with and went beyond mere political expediency and instrumentality towards a more complex 'structure of feeling'. Through close engagement with diverse sources – from proclamations by the native princes and newspaper articles in the Punjabi press to recruitment speeches by Bal Gangadhar Tilak and Mahatma Gandhi to a Bengali recruitment play – this chapter examines the process by which India's contribution to the imperial war effort came to be constructed as a point of national honour. In a world marked by a European imperial ideology, the idea of war service in France and Flanders was seized upon by the educated middle classes as an opportunity to combat racist discrimination and inequality across the empire. Such an agenda in turn played itself out in national, regional, ethnic and institutional contexts through the axes of political aspiration and racial anxiety, among a range of other factors. Aspirations ranged widely, from trying to use India's war service to retool the country's political position within the empire to raising issues of imperial citizenship to calling for an end to the racist double standards in the treatment of Indians at home and abroad. Anxiety, an equally powerful current, eddied and pulled in a slightly different direction. If gender is the principal modality 'in which race is lived',[10] service on the blood-brown fields of France and Flanders was seen as the arena in which a fretful colonial masculinity could finally 'prove' itself on the international stage. Other impulses and ideas, as we will see, crested and winked in the wake.

In South Asian historiography, there has been a distinct shift over the last few decades from a nationalist perspective to an interrogation of nationalism itself and its transnational dimensions.[11] Moreover, revisionist scholarship has questioned the automatic conflation of anti-colonialism with territorial nationalism and has drawn our attention to a wider range

Seth, 'Rewriting Histories of Nationalism: The Politics of "Moderate Nationalism" in India, 1870–1905', in Sekhar Bandyopadhyay (ed.), *Nationalist Movement in India: A Reader* (Delhi: Oxford University Press, 2009), 35.

[10] Paul Gilroy, *The Black Atlantic: Modernity and Double Consciousness* (London: Verso, 1993), 85.

[11] For broad-ranging studies, see Sumit Sarkar, *Modern India 1885–1947* (Delhi: Macmillan India, 2002 [1983]) and Sugata Bose and Ayesha Jalal, *Modern South Asia*. For important studies of early cultural nationalism, see Partha Chatterjee, *The Nation and Its Fragments: Colonial and Postcolonial Histories* (Princeton: Princeton University Press, 1994) and Tanika Sarkar, *Hindu Wife, Hindu Nation: Community, Religion and Cultural Nationalism* (Bloomington: Indiana University Press, 2001). For the transnational and revolutionary aspects, see Arun Coomer Bose, *Indian Revolutionaries Abroad, 1905–1922: In the Background of International Developments* (Patna: Bharati Bhawan, 1971) and Maia Ramnath, *Haj to Utopia: How the Ghadar Movement Charted Global Radicalism and Attempted to Overthrow the British Empire* (Berkeley: University of California University Press, 2011).

of anti-colonial imaginaries.[12] In this respect, the years of the First World War – largely consigned even today to the waiting-room of history within South Asian studies – can provide us with an uncommon vantage point before the post-war moment inaugurates a more definite vision of nation-state politics. The First World War caught the Indian psyche at a critical juncture in the country's history between an imperial identity which was increasingly being tested and a burgeoning nationalist consciousness which did not yet define itself in terms of a territorial nation-state. With one singing its death-aria and the other waiting to find a clear voice, it was a moment in parenthesis. In terms of Indian high politics, it was the moment between Gopal Krishna Gokhale's death, Tilak's departure and Gandhi's arrival. Even for the more 'extremist' political faction, particularly the Home Rule Leaguers led by Tilak, the demand was not yet for *purna swaraj* or full independence but for greater self-representation and 'Dominion' status within the empire.[13] Except for a handful of radical revolutionaries, such as the Bengal nationalists or the Ghadrites, Indian nationalism at this stage did not yet flow into the clear stream of the nation-state but swelled and strained against the still-solid banks of empire loyalism.

What such a situation generated was a structure of feeling marked by what I had elsewhere called the 'imperial–nationalist' dyad, which enabled the imperial war service to be constructed the way it was.[14] In a mirror image from the top-end perspective of wartime imperial polity, in a way that is highly germane here, Mrinalini Sinha has discerned a similar 'imperial nationalising conjuncture'; she reads the famous declaration of Edwin Montagu in 1917, promising gradual development of free institutions in India with a view to ultimate self-government, as a 'nationalising' strain within the political structure of the Indian empire.[15] The aim of this

[12] For a perceptive commentary on recent trends in South Asian studies, see Mrinalini Sinha, 'Premonitions of the Past', *The Journal of Asian Studies*, 74, 4 (2015), 821–841. Sugata Bose has also drawn attention to the 'variety of individuals, linguistic groups and religious communities seeking to contribute to imagining it [the nation] into being'; there were 'territorial as well as universalist aspects', though it is only the former, he regrets, that get theorised: Sugata Bose, 'The Spirit and Form of an Ethical Polity', in Peter Heehs (ed.), *Situating Sri Aurobindo: A Reader* (New Delhi: Oxford University Press, 2013), 113.

[13] H. F. Owen, 'Towards Nation-wide Agitation and Organisation: The Home Rule Leagues, 1915–1918', in D. A. Lowe (ed.), *Soundings in Modern South Asian History* (Berkeley: University of California, 1968), 159–195.

[14] Santanu Das, 'Imperialism, Nationalism and the First World War', in Jennifer Keene and Michael Nieberg (eds.), *Finding Common Ground: New Directions in First World War Studies* (Leiden: Brill, 2010), 75.

[15] Sinha, 'Premonitions of the Past'. One of the few historians to investigate this complex 'conjuncture' at this point, Sinha further adds that 'Gandhi's postwar mobilization of a national–popular collective … [was] also a critical political intervention precisely to change the terms of the emerging imperialist nationalizing of the Indian empire' (828).

chapter is to interrogate this moment, without the retrospective shadow of Amritsar or the overdetermined trajectory of the nation-state.

Moreover, the idea of 'India' at the time embraced Indians domiciled abroad.[16] On 24 March 1875, Lord Salisbury, the Secretary of State for India, had decreed that 'Indian settlers ... will be in all respects free men, with privileges no whit inferior to those of any other class of Her Majesty's subjects resident in the colonies.' In reality, however, they were, in Hugh Tinker's classic phrase, 'separate and unequal'.[17] Racist opposition escalated during the late nineteenth century, with New Zealand, Australia and Canada all adopting an aggressive 'white colony' policy; and, as is well known, it was the institutionalised inequality of another white colony – South Africa – that led Gandhi to launch his *satyagraha* movement, which powerfully brought the overseas Indians to the attention of the Indian government. The beginning of the war coincided with the biggest internal upheaval regarding the treatment of Indians overseas. In 1914, the *Komagata Maru*, a Japanese ship hired by a Sikh businessman, had sailed from Hong Kong, picked up some 340 Sikhs, 24 Muslims and 12 Hindus, all British subjects, and arrived in Vancouver on 23 May 1914, in defiance of the Canadian government's exclusion laws.[18] The authorities did not allow the ship to dock, alleging that it harboured members of the revolutionary Ghadar party. The ship headed back to India and, by the time it reached Budge Budge near Calcutta on 27 September, the war had broken out and some of the passengers were marked as political agitators. On 29 September, the British police tried to arrest Baba Gurdit Singh and some twenty others and, following an altercation, opened fire, resulting in the deaths of nineteen people. Racist discrimination abroad, it was felt, was matched by the colonial brutality at home.

Given the context, India's phenomenal war enthusiasm may seem extraordinary today. Yet, it was precisely on the double cross of race and colonialism that the recruitment rhetoric was nailed – indeed, imperial war service was conceptualised as a badge of national honour. My enquiry will be two-fold. First, I will be examining how India's war service opened up a space between empire loyalism and burgeoning nationalism across a

[16] See Itty Abraham, *How India Became Territorial: Foreign Policy, Diaspora, Geopolitics* (Stanford: Stanford University Press, 2014).

[17] Hugh Tinker, *Separate and Unequal: India and the Indians in the British Commonwealth 1920–1950* (London: Hurst, 1976), 22.

[18] See Hugh J. M. Johnston, *The Voyage of the Komagata Maru: The Sikh Challenge to Canada's Colour Bar* (Delhi: Oxford University Press, 1979). Also see the resource-rich website 'Komagata Maru: Continuing the Journey' (http://komagatamarujourney.ca) developed by Simon Fraser University.

range of subject groups. Second, I intend to investigate the underworld of grievances, slights, insecurities and resentments that the war brought to the fore, issues which were intimately bound up with but not reducible to the political.[19] In order to examine the imperial–nationalist dyad, both in its political imagining and in its affective undertow, I explore four sites of its articulation: the speeches of native princes who occupied a strange position and had an angular but vital relationship to the debates; reports in the public sphere, with reference to Punjabi newspapers; the high politics of Indian nationalism, with reference to the war writings of Tilak and Gandhi; and, finally, a Bengali recruitment play which provides a regional twist on the debate. The elephant in the room is obviously the sepoy; he will be my subject in the next chapter. However, it is important to acknowledge here that it is not known how much he was touched or moved by these debates.

The Native Princes: Tradition, 'Legitimate Aspirations' or Bargain?

In August 1914, when King-Emperor George V sent a message to the 'Princes and People of My Indian Empire', the pledges of support from the native princes were extravagant.[20] With varying alliances, treaties and partnerships with the British Raj, the native princes ruled about one-third of India, from Jammu and Kashmir and parts of Punjab (particularly Patiala and Kapurthala) in the north to a massive block of Rajput- and Maratha-ruled states, to Hyderabad and Mysore in the south; there were also smaller kingdoms scattered throughout the country. In 1909, the *Imperial Gazetteer of India* had listed a total of 693 native states including the Shan states of Burma and Nepal.[21] The policy of indirect British rule left these rulers with considerable influence and autonomy over their Indian subjects while subordinating their sovereignty and authority to imperial British suzerainty. David Cannadine's thesis of 'imperialism as ornamentalism', of 'hierarchy made visible, immanent and actual', fits this group with their palaces, elephants and gun salutes even if it irons out the 'wrinkled texture' of their treatment by the British

---

[19] For early works that consider the role of emotions, see Rajat Kanta Ray, *The Felt Community: Commonality and Mentality before the Emergence of Indian Nationalism* (New Delhi: Oxford University Press, 2003) and Tapan Raychaudhuri, *Europe Reconsidered: Perceptions of the West in Nineteenth-Century Bengal* (Oxford: Oxford University Press, 2005).

[20] Quoted in G. F. MacMunn, *India and the War* (London: Hodder and Stoughton, 1915), 40–41.

[21] See Barbara N. Ramusack, *The Indian Princes and Their States* (Cambridge: Cambridge University Press, 2004), 2; also see Tony McClenaghan and Richard Head, *Maharajas' Paltans: History of the Indian State Forces, 1888–1948* (Delhi: Manohar, 2013).

Raj.[22] However, in recent years, a number of scholars have reassessed the role of the native princes and convincingly argued that, rather than being mere 'puppets', they exercised considerable autonomy in several spheres and often contested British authority and successfully ushered in modern reforms in their states.[23] It is in this delicate position, between the psychology of a severely diminished sovereignty and yet enough authority over their subjects and agency to manoeuvre their complex role within the Raj, that some of the extravagant war enthusiasm of the princes can be located, rather than it being mere imperial subservience.

'Your excellency is aware that the whole resources of my state are at the disposal of the British governement': the pledge of the Nizam of Hyderabad, the foremost ruling chief of India, summed up the enthusiasm of the group as a whole.[24] The Imperial Service Troops of all the twenty-seven states in India were placed at the disposal of the Viceroy while the seventy-year-old Sir Pertab Singh, the Regent of Jodhpur and a favourite of the late Queen Victoria, vowed to go and sit at the doorstep of the Viceroy until he was allowed to go and fight! The princes started competing with each other with offers of men, money and material. On 9 September 1914, when the names of the princes selected by the Viceroy to serve in Europe – the chiefs of Bikanir, Patiala, Coochbehar, Jodhpur, Rutlam and Kishengarh, among others – were announced, it caused a sensation in the House of Commons.[25] Meanwhile, vast sums of money flowed from the 700-odd native princes according to their wealth and prestige, from contributions of over 50 lakhs of rupees from the likes of the Nizam of Hyderabad and Maharajah of Mysore to 5 lakhs of rupees from Maharajah Gaekwar of Baroda for the purchase of aeroplanes for the Royal Flying Corps.[26] There were also interest-free

---

[22] David Cannadine, *Ornamentalism: How the British Saw Their Empire* (Oxford: Oxford University Press, 2002), 122.

[23] See, for example, Janaki Nair, *Mysore Modern: Rethinking the Region under Princely Rule* (Minneapolis: University of Minnesota Press, 2011), where she draws on a range of visual, social and legal texts to reconceptualise the history of Mysore in the late nineteenth and early twentieth centuries as one of the inaugural sites of Indian modernity, despite 'the well-known limits to its economic and political sovereignty' (25).

[24] Quoted in Bhargava, *Indian Services in the War*, 38.

[25] See *India's Contribution to the Great War* (Calcutta: Superintendent Government Printing, 1923), particularly the chapter on 'The Imperial Service Troops', 190–202; M. B. L. Bhargava, *India's Services in the War* provides a helpful list of services of the native states and individual princes, 226–333, alongside detailed chapters on 'Indian Mussalmans', 'Press', 'Educated and Political Classes', 'Womanhood' and so forth; among recent accounts, see Budeshwar Pati, *India and the First World War* (Delhi: Atlantic Publishers, 1996) for an effective summary with some valuable details, including contemporary newspaper accounts, 7–29.

[26] Foreign and Political, Internal B, April 1915, no. 319, National Archives of India, New Delhi (henceforth NAI); Political (Confidential), 1915, Proceeding 505, West Bengal State Archives, Kolkata (henceforth WBSA).

loans, in addition to offers of troops, labourers, hospital ships, ambulances, motorcars, flotillas, horses, materials, food and clothes. Some of the gifts were specific. The Begum of Bhopal sent 500 copies of the Qur'an and 1,487 copies of religious tracts for the Muslim soldiers, while the Maharajah of Patiala sent *romals* (covers for the Adi Granth or Sikh holy scriptures) and *chanani* to the Sikh prisoners in Germany.[27] The munificence of the princes was duplicated by smaller landowners and chieftains: the Thakur of Bagli thus contributed 4,000 rupees for the Indian troops in East Africa, Mesopotamia and Egypt to be spent on 'socks, shirts, mufflers, waistcoats, cardigan jackets, tobacco, cigarettes and chocolates'.[28] In Jhansi, some *zamindars* reinstated the ancient Indian custom of *jangmat*, whereby the householder every morning set aside in an earthen vessel a few grains which were then sold and the proceeds handed over to war funds.[29]

The financial contributions of the native princes were substantial, but of equal value to the colonial state was the sphere of their influence. As early as 1876, Lord Lytton had observed that, 'Politically speaking, the Indian peasantry is an inert mass. If it ever moves at all it will move in obedience, not to its British benefactors, but to its native chiefs and princes.'[30] Consider the following two speeches, the first given by the Hindu queen Taradevi in Calcutta on 25 December 1914, and the second delivered by the (Muslim) *Begum* of Bhopal at the Delhi War Conference in April 1918:

> Gentlemen, though I am a lady of such an advanced age yet I am Kshatriya and when my Kshatriya blood rises up in my veins and when I think I am the widow to the eldest son of one who was a most tried friend of the British Government, I jump on my feet at the aspiration of going to the field of war to fight Britain's battle. It is not I alone, I should say, but there are thousands and thousands of Indian ladies who are more anxious than myself, but there is no such emergency, neither will there be one for the ladies to go to the front when there are brave men who would suffice for fighting the enemies.[31]

> Is it not a matter for regret then that Turkey should ... join hands with the enemies of our British Government? All gentlemen like you have read, I suppose, in the papers, how the British Government is now, as ever, having Mohamedan interests at heart ... India will leave nothing undone to justify the confidence, the love, the sympathy with which the King-Emperor has always honoured us. The need of the Empire is undoubtedly India's

[27] Punjab Civil Secretariat, Chandigarh, Political Part B, February 1917, 6427/74, 139–143.
[28] NAI, Foreign and Political, Internal B, April 1915, nos. 972–977.
[29] NAI, Home (Political Deposit), December 1914, no. 29.
[30] Lytton to Lord Salisbury, 11 May 1876, quoted in Ramusack, *The Indian Princes*, 164.
[31] Quoted in M. B. L. Bhargava, *India's Services in the War*, 205.

opportunity … Now that the war has entered upon a more intense phase we assure you that it will never be said that in this supreme crisis India, when weighed in the balance, was found wanting.[32]

Speeches such as the above fly in the face of any attempts to equate colonial femininity with pacifism, or, indeed, with anti-colonialism. Made by two powerful women rulers of the time, they try to galvanise a version of heroic colonial masculinity by appeals to issues of caste and religion. If the first speech joins Hindu caste hierarchies – Kshatriya is the martial caste – to colonial patriarchy in the service of the empire, the second points to a specific issue: how to retain the loyalty of India's Muslim population when they are being made to fight their co-religionists in Mesopotamia after the entry of the Ottoman Empire into the war? As early as 14 November 1914, in Constantinople, the Sheikh-ul-Islam declared a holy war against the Western nations, including Britain and its Allies, and promised the fire of hell. As Hew Strachan observes, 'This was a call to revolution which had, it seemed, the potential to set all Asia and much of Africa ablaze.'[33] Echoing the Begum's exhortations, we have similar appeals from the Nizam of Hyderabad, the Nawab of Palanpur and the Aga Khan, telling their subjects that 'it is the bounden duty of the Mohammedans of India to adhere firmly to their old and tried loyalty to the British Government'.[34]

Why did the native princes support the war efforts so ardently? There was of course the question of status: few of these status-obsessed if beleaguered princes, whom Lord Curzon described as a set of 'undisciplined schoolboys', could resist the seductions of imperial titles and honours and gun salutes.[35] But the impulses went deeper; memory blended with motive; family tradition was combined with hard-nosed political strategy. At the Princes' Conference in 1915, the Nizam of Hyderabad invoked family tradition: 'In 1887, my revered father offered to Her Imperial Majesty, Queen Victoria, the sum of Rs 60 lakhs when danger merely threatened the borders of the Indian empire. I should be untrue alike to the promptings of my own heart and to the traditions of my house if I offered less to

---

[32] *Ibid.*, 278–280. A very similar speech under the title 'H.H. The Begum of Bhopal' can be found in Natesan, *All about the War*, 270.

[33] Hew Strachan, *The First World War* (New York: Viking, 2003), 99–100.

[34] 'Indian Mussalmans and the War', in Natesan, *All about the War*, 269. For a detailed account, see Yuvaraj Deva Prasad, *The Indian Muslims and World War I* (New Delhi: Janaki Prakashan, 1985); 'Expressions of Loyalty from Mohammedan Bodies in India', NAI, Foreign and Political, Internal B, April 1915, nos. 259–305.

[35] Curzon to Hamilton, 29 August 1900, in Adrian Sever, *Documents and Speeches on the Indian Princely States* (Delhi: B. R. Publishing Corporation, 1985), Vol. 1, 343. Nor was Curzon himself any less obsessed with titles and honours.

His Imperial Majesty, King George V, in this just and momentous war.'[36] Some, such as Sir Pertab Singh of Jodhpur and Maharajah Ganga Singh of Bikanir, had served in the imperial wars in China; for others, such as Maharajah Holkar of Indore, a European war was, like polo or Riviera tennis, a 'sport'.

Sugata Bose and Ayesha Jalal have noted how 'the colonial state juxtaposed to its own conception of monolithic, unitary sovereignty at the centre a shallow, if not fake, version of sovereignty reposed in the persons of "traditional" rulers', which involved a 'very dramatic change in ideas of sovereignty and legitimacy'.[37] It has also been argued that it led to a crisis in ideas of imperial masculinity as *shikar* (hunt) took the place of warfare.[38] At the same time, as more recent scholarship has suggested, many of these native princes, rather than just wearing a 'hollow crown' in relation to the paramount power, aspired to renegotiate their relationship with the Raj as well as to 'strengthen the bonds with their subjects through modalities of remembered sovereignty'.[39] In such a fluid context, the prospect of service on the battlefields of France and Flanders could be said to present the ideal opportunity to restage and materialise fantasies of sovereignty and martial glory on a global stage; 'nationalism', in this context, obviously worked on a regional and cultural axis, as the recognition and validation of the contribution of a particular princely state. On the other hand, such princely pride was matched by political calculations and designs at the national level. At the war conference in January 1917, the Prince of Alwar dismissed any 'mere selfish hope that the fruits of our efforts may be sweet' but insisted, in the same breath, that 'when such constitutional changes take place, it is not possible to think that the destinies of our one-third India are likely to be ignored'.[40] At the Princes' Conference in October 1916, the Prince of Baroda had similarly stated that 'we should have a regularly assigned and definite place in the constitution of the Empire'.[41]

Such aspiration in a fast-evolving imperial structure was fulfilled through the appointment of Maharajah Ganga Singh of Bikanir as the country's representative in the Imperial War Cabinet in 1917. It also showed the clout these princes enjoyed. At a lavish banquet on the eve of his departure

[36] Quoted in Bhargava, *India's Services in the War*, 38–39.
[37] Bose and Jalal, *Modern South Asia*, 83.
[38] See, for example, Satadru Sen, 'Chameleon Games: Ranjitsinhji's Politics of Gender and Race', *Journal of Colonialism and Colonial History*, 2, 3 (2001), 23–24. See also Ramusack, *The Indian Princes*, 132–169.
[39] Nair, *Mysore Modern*, 63.
[40] *Speeches of Indian Princes on the World War*, 2.
[41] *Ibid.*, 25.

to London for the Imperial War Conference to celebrate India's 'proper
place in the Empire', he made the following observation:

> And I know I am voicing the feelings and sentiments of your Highnesses
> when I further state that we of the Indian States – who yield to no one
> in the whole of the British Empire in steadfast loyalty and deep devotion
> to the Person and Throne of our King-Emperor – happily it is quite con-
> sistent to be at one and the same time – in the best and truest sense of the
> terms – staunch loyalists and Imperialists as well as true patriots of our
> Mother Country, deeply sympathising with all the legitimate aspirations
> of our brother Indians in British India, just as much as, we feel sure, our
> brethren in British India sympathise with the legitimate aspirations of the
> Princes and peoples of the Indian States and our desire to see maintained
> un-impaired our dignity, privileges and high position.[42]

If the decision to invite India to the Imperial War Cabinet was an
example of the 'imperial–nationalising conjunction' at the level of
imperial polity, Ganga Singh's self-fashioning as 'staunch loyalist' cum
'imperialist' cum 'patriot' is its affective counterpoint in a rebooting of
imperial identity in wartime. At the same time, he tries to connect the
'legitimate aspirations' of the subjects of British India with those of the
princes and people of the native states. The repetition of 'legitimate' is not
coincidental: imperial war service 'legitimises' India's 'aspirations', but, in
the course of the speech, such aspirations get largely reduced to those of
the native princes. Chosen above Tilak to represent India at the Versailles
Peace Conference, Ganga Singh – with his bejewelled red turban and
flamboyant moustache – spent most of his time arguing for the privileges
of the princely states and only occasionally made the argument for self-
government. 'India has earned herself a clown', the Chinese nationalist
Mao Zedong would bitterly note, whereby 'the demands of the Indian
people have not been granted'.[43]

'Invidious Distinction': 'Educated Classes', Discrimination and Self-respect

In an article titled 'The war and the educated classes', Sir P. S. Sivaswami,
Vice Chancellor of Madras University, expressed surprise at the 'loyalty and
devotion' shown by the 'educated classes who were such frequent and severe

---

[42] Speech delivered in January 1917. *Ibid.*, 48.
[43] Quoted in Erez Manela, *The Wilsonian Moment and the International Origins of Anticolonial Nationalism* (Oxford: Oxford University Press, 2009), 217.

critics of the administration'.[44] Within the Indian National Congress, both
the moderates (who dominated it in 1914) and the extremists extended
their support. But war enthusiasm went far beyond the 'microscopic
minority' represented by the Congress and infected the middle classes at
large – though, as we will see, underneath the enthusiastic proclamations
there sometimes seethed a world of tension and discontent. Fundraising
was organised and meetings were held in cities such as Calcutta, Bombay,
Lahore and Allahabad. Pamphlets were produced pledging support, one
typical title being 'Why India Is Heart and Soul with Britain in This
War'.[45] A 'ladies-only' play was performed in Calcutta to raise money,
while a war journal, *Indian Ink*, was launched.[46] Prayers for British victory
were offered in temples, mosques and gurdwaras, from the Jama Masjid in
Delhi to the scared ghats in Benares.[47] The goddess Kali, it was claimed in
Calcutta, had declared her support for George V, while special *pujas* were
offered 'for the victory of British arms' during the spring festival of Holi.[48]
From intellectuals such as Rabindranath Tagore, Muhammed Iqbal and
Kazi Nazrul to the editors of various vernacular newspapers to the future
revolutionary leader Subhas Chandra Bose, everyone seemed to endorse
the Allied cause in 1914. Pandit Ram Prashad Sharma, one of India's foremost 'astronomers and astrologers', predicted 'confidently' that *Golak Jog* –
the alignment of the five planets via the sun – would ensure 'His Imperial
Majesty's decisive victory'.[49]

How should one explain such widespread support? While the nation-
wide press, including the substantial vernacular media, was abuzz with war
news, there was one province where the discussions took place with a particular intensity: Punjab. From the late nineteenth century, the province
had a burgeoning urban print industry: by 1901, 186 vernacular newspapers
and periodicals were being published, in a variety of languages, particularly
Urdu, mainly in Lahore and Amritsar, but also in Multan, Sialkot, Jhelum
and Rawalpindi.[50] Lahore was home to an influential coterie of writers,
journalists and activists; as early as 1881–1882, it had some thirty-two

---

[44] Natesan, *All about the War*, v–vi.
[45] Bhupendranath Basu, *Why India Is Heart and Soul with Britain in This War* (London: Macmillan, 1914).
[46] *Bengalee*, 3 February 1915. Copies of the newspaper from 1914 to 1918 can be found in the West
Bengal State Archives (WBSA), Kolkata.
[47] Associated Press of India, Bangalore, 31 October 1914; NAI, Home (Political Deposit), December
1914, no. 29, 9.
[48] *Bengalee*, 28 February 1915.
[49] Sharma, Pandit Ram Prashad, 'Astronomy and the War', *Bengalee*, 28 February 1918, WBSA.
[50] See N. G. Barrier and Paul Wallace, *The Punjabi Press, 1880–1905* (East Lansing: Michigan State
University, 1970), 159.

'licensed vernacular presses'.[51] The newspapers were obviously subject to intense governmental scrutiny, but many were feisty organs and give insights into some of the dissident undercurrents.[52] While today it is often asked why India supported the war efforts, these newspapers show how very different the stakes were in 1914: debates revolved not around whether the country *should* join in the war effort but whether it would be *allowed* to do so. For a colour ban was in force which forbade the non-white subjects of the British Empire to fight against the 'white races'; in the Boer War, the Indians were involved only as non-combatants.[53] 'Will British statesmanship rise to the height of the occasion and permit India to do her duty to the Empire?', asked the *Panjabee* on 8 August 1914.[54] While there were occasional references in the papers to 'freedom' and suggestions that 'India will not be forgotten', it was the end of racial discrimination rather than a clear-cut agenda for political sovereignty that emerged as the immediate goal: 'It is a step towards the eventual obliteration of existing racial prejudice, so essential to India's self-fulfilment as a nation and an integral part of the Empire.'[55] Nation and empire had not yet defined themselves as antithetical terms. The other pressing issue was the Arms Act which forbade Indians to carry firearms. Reporting that '408 persons were killed by wild animals', the *Bengalee* queried 'Would an Englishman like to face a tiger with no better weapon than a stick?'[56]

One adjective comes up repeatedly in the translated extracts: 'invidious'. Consider the following: 'when the present war broke out and Indians showed their loyalty to the Empire in its hour of need, it was hoped that the old *invidious* distinctions between Indians and Europeans would be abolished'; 'the *invidious* distinction was sufficiently galling already; it will become twice as galling after their [the Indian soldiers'] return from Europe'; 'though Indians are inferior to none in loyalty, courage and

---

[51] *Punjab Government Gazetteer of the Lahore District, 1883–4* (Lahore: Sang-e-Meel Publications, 1989), www.asafas.kyoto-u.ac.jp/kias/pdf/kb6/14sunaga.pdf; *Paisa Akhbar*, the largest selling newspaper, had a weekly circulation of only 13,500. This lively and robust public sphere was more the product of a college-educated middle class than an English-educated elite, though there was obviously some overlap. See Sanjay Joshi, *Fractured Modernity: Making of a Middle Class in Colonial North India* (Delhi: Oxford University Press, 2001), 16–43.

[52] These extracts exist because, like the sepoy letters, they were collected and translated by the colonial state for purposes of monitoring, with anything vaguely dissident or contrary being clamped down upon as 'seditious' under the Press Act of 1915. See Jarboe, *War News in India*, 10–11.

[53] See Morton-Jack, *The Indian Army on the Western Front*, 134–139.

[54] *Panjabee*, 8 August 1914, IOR, PNR, L/R/5/195, 782, British Library.

[55] *Khalsa Akhbar*, 1 October 1915, IOR, PNR L/R/5/196, 588, British Library; *Desh*, 12 September 1915, IOR, PNR, L/R/5/196, 535, British Library; *Panjabee*, 5 September 1914, IOL, PNR, L/R/5/195, 853, British Library.

[56] *Bengalee*, 6 October 1914, WBSA.

initiative … they are not treated with equality… Is it too much to hope that these *invidious* distinctions should now go the way of all indefensible things?'[57] It is a familiar adjective that points, beyond war and India, to contemporary debates around imperial citizenship and the rights of non-white immigrants.[58] In *Racism and Empire: White Settlers and Coloured Immigrants in the British Self-governing Colonies, 1830–1910*, Robert A. Huttenback cites an interesting letter, written on 13 November 1901 by Lord Chamberlain to Sir John Forrest, the former Premier of Western Australia and Minister for Defence in the Commonwealth Government:

> I think the Australians are right in taking steps to prevent the country from being over-run by the coloured races but I also feel, as you do, that the matter is full of difficulty, and that we, as imperialists, must take care not to make *invidious distinctions* between the different races who live under the British flag.[59]

Empire here paradoxically gets in the way of the otherwise full-hearted endorsement of Australian racism. However, for the colonial subject, even such a tokenistic semblance of equality was a valuable passport and the first step towards self-respect. Just the previous year, the Bengali weekly *Sanjivani* had noted that

> Every part of the British Empire will send troops to Australia to celebrate the federation of the Australia Republics on the 1st of January. India too will send Gurkha, Pathan and Sikh soldiers to take part in the ceremony. Cannot Lord Curzon take the opportunity to have that obnoxious Australian law repealed which prohibits the Indians, who do not know English, from entering that colony? … Australian colonists are allowed to come freely to this country. Why then should not the Australians give the same privilege to Indians?[60]

The ornamentalism of this imperial pageantry with its display of the Indian 'martial races' is seized upon by the vernacular press to ask for actual change in the inter-imperial relations. The Indian sepoy becomes the cue for demanding the rights for his immigrant, if less glamorous, cousins.

Demand for political rights went hand in hand with an internal sense of lack. 'Psychological damage', Ashis Nandy has argued, was one of the most

---

[57] *Jhang Sial*, 7 July 1915, IOR, L/R/5/196, 396, British Library; *Tribune*, 25 July 1915, IOR, PNR, L/R/5/196, 427, British Library; *Panjabee*, 17 May 1917, IOR, PNR, L/R/5/199, 392, British Library. My italics.

[58] See Tinker, *Separate and Unequal*; see also Robert A. Huttenback, *Racism and Empire: White Settlers and Coloured Immigrants in the British Self-governing Colonies, 1830–1910* (Ithaca: Cornell University Press, 1976).

[59] Chamberlain Papers, JC/14/1/1/17, quoted in Huttenback, *Racism and Empire*, 282. My italics.

[60] *Sanjivani*, 15 November 1900, IOR, RNN, quoted in Huttenback, *Racism and Empire*, 282.

insidious features of British colonialism in India.[61] Constantly made to feel small in myriad ways before the 'superior' powers of the West, Indian battlefield experience in Europe was viewed by the educated middle classes, much like the princes as discussed before, as a way of salvaging racial and national pride: '[Indian] active service and the bravery and self-restraint … [now would] remove the wrong impression which obsessed the minds of certain people that Indian soldiers are not equal to European soldiers.'[62] Such sentiments were by no means limited to India. Thus, the *Grenada Federalist* in 1915 expressed the following view: 'As Coloured people we will be fighting for something more, something inestimable to ourselves. We will be fighting to prove to Great Britain that we are not so vastly inferior to the white.'[63]

The two imperatives – the demand for the end of public discrimination and the need for private self-validation – often went hand in hand. Consider the following extracts from the *Panjabee* and the *Zamindar*, respectively, both published in the opening months of the conflict:

The question is one not so much of sending the Indian volunteers, as soon as they are recruited, to the front, as of enabling the Indian community to feel that they too can have their rightful share in the defence of the Empire … The distinction that has hitherto been made in this respect between Indians and other classes of the King's subjects is galling to the self-respect of the Indian and is a great hindrance in the way of his thinking 'imperially' … The distinction must be removed if Indian loyalty is to be placed on an active and satisfactory footing … To them the question is, above everything else, one of national self-respect.[64]

The war has its advantages and disadvantages. Its disadvantages consist in the terrible loss of life and the consequent suffering which inevitably ensues. Its advantages will be seen in the benefits which it will bring to India. We are convinced that self-government will be granted to this country – even if it be compensation for the services of Indians during the war. Our sepoys who have gone to the front will see Europe with their own eyes. They will see European institutions and will see that there is no difference – except in colour – between Indians and Europeans. Their ideas will broaden and this

---

[61] Ashis Nandy, *The Intimate Enemy: Loss and Recovery of the Self under Colonialism* (Delhi: Oxford University Press, 1983). See also Frantz Fanon, *The Wretched of the Earth* (London: Penguin, 1991 [1961]).
[62] *Desh*, 4 December 1915, IOR, PNR, L/R/5/196, 728, British Library.
[63] *The Federalist*, 27 October 1915, quoted in Glenford Howe, *Race, War and Nationalism: A Social History of West Indians in the First World War* (Kingston: James Currey, 2002), 17.
[64] *Panjabee*, 15 August 1914, IOR, PNR, L/R/5/195, 808, British Library; *Panjabee*, 20 August 1914, IOR, PNR, L/R/5/195, 809, British Library.

will naturally have some effect on their fellow countrymen. We hail with joy the approaching day of our liberty and we feel that it is not far distant.[65]

Both illuminate the complex reasoning behind the push towards recruitment. The first letter in many ways echoes the same concerns as Chamberlain's but 'from below': British racial discrimination is shown to get in the way of the realisation of a full imperial identity and colonial loyalty, which co-exists with a sense of 'national self-respect' and furnishes the ground for loyalty. The 'galling' distinction refers to the policy within the British army of withholding the King's Commission from the Indian officers. As early as September 1914, the *Tribune* had questioned it: 'France has its Arab Generals and Russia has many Asiatic Generals, but Liberal England restricts its best native officers to posts subordinate to that of sergeant-major.'[66] Amar Singh, one of the few Indians to hold a King's Commission, writes bitterly in his diary about the racist hierarchy in the army.[67] Yielding to continued pressure, nine Indian officers, including Amar Singh, were granted the 'regular' King's Commission in 1917. One of the direct legacies of India's war involvement was the 'Indianisation of the military', a move that the *Panjabee* heralded with 'genuine enthusiasm' as the 'first step' towards the 'eradication' of the 'barriers of inequality'.[68] The second extract makes two conjoined predictions, both of which would bear fruit: the journey towards self-government, as borne out by Edwin Montagu's August declaration of 1917, and the politicisation of the war veterans through travel and exposure to foreign cultures.[69] In fact, as we will find in the next section,

---

[65] *Zamindar*, 16 October 1914, IOR, PNR, L/R/5/195, 945–6, British Library. According to the Criminal Intelligence Department, the *Panjabee*, with a circulation of 1,000, was classified as 'Hindu, advanced nationalist', while the *Zamindar* was considered nothing less than 'seditious', being shut down repeatedly. Quoted in Jarboe's helpful 'Introduction' to *War News in India*, 11–12. Also see N. Gerald Barrier and Paul Wallace, *The Punjab Press, 1880–1905* (East Lansing: Michigan State University Press, 1970) and Graham Shaw and Mary Lloyd (eds.), *Publications Proscribed by the Government of India* (London: The British Library, 1985).

[66] *Tribune*, 3 September 1914, IOR, PNR, L/R/5/195, 838, British Library.

[67] Amar Singh, 'Some Notes, 6 April 1915', *Diaries of Major General Amar Singh*, Nehru Memorial Museum and Library, New Delhi, Microfilm R3541, Index 10. See the section on Amar Singh in Chapter 7, 293–295.

[68] *Panjabee*, 25 February 1917, IOR, PNR, L/R/5/199, 187, British Library. See S. L. Menezes, *Fidelity and Honour: The Indian Army from the Seventeenth to the Twenty-First Century* (Oxford: Oxford University Press, 1999), 306–339; Philip Mason, *A Matter of Honour: An Account of the Indian Army, Its Officers & Men* (London: Jonathan Cape, 1974), 444–466.

[69] Interview with Lance Naik Khela Singh conducted by DeWitt Ellinwood and S. D. Pradhan, quoted in Pradhan, 'The Sikh Soldier in the First World War', in DeWitt Ellinwood and S. D. Pradhan (eds.), *India and World War I* (Delhi: Manohar, 1978), 224.

the above points would find their fullest exposition in the writings of Bal Gangadhar Tilak and Gandhi.

At the same time, the vernacular newspapers kept a close watch on international developments, from women's suffrage movements to the Easter Rising of 1916 to the Bolshevik revolution of 1917. Indeed, the Russian Revolution sent shockwaves through the Indian subcontinent. Kazi Nazrul Islam, the only sepoy-poet of India, recalled receiving the news of the revolution in his training camp in Nowshera, while the Lahore newspaper *Desh* reported how 'one of the greatest empires in the world, which was the chosen home of despotic rule, has thrown off the rotten chains and secured the exalted blessing of Swarajya'.[70] The application of the word *swarajya* shows the clear lines of political identification. Tilak in turn noted that 'all over the world self-government is on the anvil and India alone cannot be expected to sit still'.[71] Similarly, when Lloyd George, in a speech on 12 April 1917, commended America's entry into the war – which he called a 'struggle for freedom' – the English-language *Tribune* immediately seized upon it:

> People of India welcome this great speech of the British Premier [Lloyd George, on the value of democracy] … The next question is that after the war this principle of freedom should be extended beyond Europe to Asia and Africa … Will these pioneers, after the war, say that freedom and democracy is good for themselves and not good for Asiatics and Africans – and give some excuse, such as their backwardness, poverty, want of education and organization, to back their refusal? Will they say that sugar tastes sweet in European mouths but will cause dyspepsia to Asiatics?[72]

If 1917 was a momentous year, with the Russian Revolution and the entry of the United States into the war, within India this was the year of Secretary of State Edwin Montague's famous declaration of 'the progressive realisation of responsible government' as the British aim for India. Montague left key conditions vague and tilted towards the 'raj's friends, not its critics', causing widespread frustration, even among the moderates.[73] But still it was a hard-won concession. While, at the beginning of the war, the stress had rested on the first term of the 'imperial–nationalist' conjunction, by the end of the war the focus had shifted steadily towards the

[70] Pranatosh Chattopadhyay, *Kazi Nazrul* (Kolkata: A. Mukherji & Co., 1977); *Desh*, 24 March 1917, IOR, PNR, L/R/5/199, 263, British Library.
[71] Babu Aurobindo Ghose (ed.), *Bal Gangadhar Tilak: His Writings and Speeches* (Madras: Ganesh & Co., 1919), 296.
[72] *Tribune*, 17 April 1917, IOR, PNR, L/R/5/199, 315, British Library.
[73] See Bose and Jalal, *Modern South Asia*, 105.

second. If the 'Wilsonian moment' of 1918–1919 provided a crucial impetus to the Indian nationalists, as Erez Manela has argued,[74] the Punjabi press shows how such claims were deep in the making in the public sphere long before 1918.

'I Might Rain Men on You': Gandhi's Recruitment Speeches

But how was the recruitment campaign addressed at the high end of the Indian political spectrum? Nowhere was the interconnectedness between war service, the push for anti-discrimination and political autonomy, and the imperial–national dynamic more densely evident than in the wartime writings of the two main political leaders and fellow barristers: Bal Gangadhar Tilak and Mahatma Gandhi. The extremist nationalist leader, recently released from jail in November 1914, was very much the popular nationalist hero at the time, while Gandhi, just returned from South Africa, was quietly establishing himself on the Indian political scene. The different attitudes and rhetoric of the two men around war recruitment show the diverse strains within Indian high politics at the time. Moreover, while Tilak's stance remains the most powerful example of the instrumental use of Indian war service, Gandhi's writings invite diverse frames of interpretation as war service gets linked to his vision of *swaraj* (self-rule) on the one hand, and the concept of *ahimsa* (non-violence) on the other.

Let us start with the Indian National Congress (INC) in 1914. It was a divided and diminished body, after the pyrrhic victory of the 'moderates' and the expulsion of the 'extremists' in the Surat Congress of 1907.[75] The war paradoxically offered the party a platform to come together: the decision to mobilise Indian soldiers was endorsed by both camps. The most high-profile and respected member in the 'moderate' camp was Gopal Krishna Gokhale, the mentor of Gandhi and the person through whom the latter had drawn international attention to the plight of Indians in South Africa. As soon as the war was declared, Gokhale pledged unconditional support and requested that the King's Commission be thrown open to Indians. As Sanjay Seth has observed, such 'loyalism' can be viewed as part of the 'discursive strategy of moderate nationalism' to 'furnish the very ground from which criticism became possible'.[76] The 'extremist'

---

[74] Manela, *The Wilsonian Moment*, 77–98.
[75] See Nanda, *Three Statesmen*, 435–470, for an excellent record of these years.
[76] Seth, 'Rewriting Histories of Nationalism', 35.

Tilak would strike a different note.[77] At a speech in Nasik in 1917, he noted that

> The Indian soldiers have saved the lives of the British soldiers on the French battlefield and have shown bravery. Those who once considered us as slaves have begun now to call us brothers. God has brought about all these changes. We must push our demands while the notion of this brotherhood is existing in the minds of the English. We must inform that we, 30 crores of the Indian people, are ready to lay down our lives for the Empire.[78]

Tilak would thus support India's involvement but, unlike Gokhale, would insist on *conditional* recruitment in self-respecting terms – commissions for Indian officers, equal pay for the soldiers and wholly Indian regiments commanded by Indians.[79] The only nationalist leader to take such a stance, he would argue his case in a series of articles in his two influential newspapers, *Kesari* and *Mahratta*.[80] Seizing upon a comment made by Lloyd George that India 'can do vastly more and will do so if her war heart is touched', Tilak would present a political bargain as an emotional prerequisite for successful war mobilisation:

> Surely Rs 11 or Rs 16 is not what is calculated to *touch* the hearts of the people … The people see their adored leaders interned and externed without rhyme or reason … The army laws and rules make most revolting discriminations between Europeans and Indians. Surely these are not ways of *touching* the hearts of the people. Surely these things must tell, and tell prejudicially in the work of recruitment. The greater the information and intelligence a class is based with, the greater must be its unwillingness to supply recruits to the Army under present conditions … The appeals [for fresh recruits] have not produced the desired result. Why not? What makes people deaf to the appeals of even their most trusted leaders?[81]

The strategist *par excellence* here turns the 'invidious distinctions' made by the colonial state into the very reason for the lack of recruitment. The demand for conditional recruitment, or what the British condemned as 'left-handed co-operation' is presented through the logic of the 'heart'; a nationalist agenda is moulded into a loyalist language of touching and feeling between the empire and her subjects. Out-Lloyding Lloyd George,

---

[77] Speech at the Nasik Conference, 1917, in Ghose, *Tilak: His Writings and Speeches*, 241. See also Richard Cashman, *The Myth of Lokmanya: Tilak and Mass Politics in Maharashtra* (Berkeley: University of California Press, 1975).

[78] Ghose, *Tilak: His Writings and Speeches*, 244.

[79] See Ganachari, 'Purchasing Loyalty', 785.

[80] *Kesari*, 5 March 1918, 9 March 1918, IOR, Bombay Newspaper Report (BNR), L/R/174, 8, British Library.

[81] *Mahratta*, 9 March 1918, IOR, BNR, L/R/5/174. Emphasis in original.

he would reiterate his point at a popular meeting in November 1917 at Godhra: 'What was wanted was that India's heart should be *touched*.'[82]

During the war years, Tilak would take on an increasingly prominent role. In 1916, in co-operation with the Irish Theosophist Annie Besant, he would start the Indian Home Rule League, which marked a new direction in Indian nationalist politics.[83] The Home Rule League agitated for *swarajya* or India's self-rule as a 'Dominion' within the empire. During its initial years, the movement was successful, with a membership of about 60,000 in 1917–1918 across India, particularly in Gujarat, United Province, Bihar and parts of South India.[84] Refuting British allegations that he discouraged recruitment, he claimed that it was a 'disgrace to our traditional devotion to duty' that out of 25 crores of people, only 6,000 had come forward.[85] If there were an end to discrimination, if '*Swarajya* under empire is given', the resultant 'pride' and 'devotion' would make thousands of young men come forward of their own accord: 'Allow us to fight for the Empire.' The imperial–national dynamic is here posited as the necessary psychological ground for recruitment, reminding one of some of the Punjabi newspapers. Moving from such analysis to direct bargaining, he would say the following: 'If Government want, they may give *Swarajya* and have 25,000 or even 25 lakhs of men.'[86] And to his fellow countrymen at a recruitment rally in Poona in 1917, he said 'If you want Home Rule be prepared to defend your home. Had it not been for my age I would have been the first to volunteer.'[87] Tilak also believed that military training would make the men fitter for self-rule, a point to be developed by Gandhi.

Enter Gandhi. In many ways, Gandhi's approach to the war can be interpreted as the classic middle path, but it would be useful to revisit first his thoughts in 1914. As he received news of the outbreak of war in Madeira on 4 August 1915, on board the *S.S. Kinfauns Castle*, he wondered 'What is my duty?'[88] Stranded in London, he would raise a volunteer field

---

[82] Ghose, *Tilak: His Writings and Speeches*, 295. My italics.

[83] Tilak set up his Indian Home Rule League in April 1916 and Annie Besant her own All India Home Rule League in September, with the two working in co-operation. See Owen, 'Towards Nationwide Agitation and Organisation'.

[84] See Shekhar Bandyopadhyay, *From Plassey to Partition: A History of Modern India* (Hyderabad: Orient Blackswan, 2009), 291.

[85] *Kesari*, 12 February 1918, IOR, PNR, L/R/5/174, British Library.

[86] *Kesari*, 12 March 1918, IOR, PNR, L/R/5/174, British Library.

[87] Ghose, *Tilak: His Writings and Speeches*, 365.

[88] For details about Gandhi's time in London, see James D. Hunt, *Gandhi in London* (Delhi: Promilla, 1978), 174. For a pioneering article on Gandhi's ambiguous attitude to war, see Peter Brock, 'Gandhi's Non-violence and His War Service', *Gandhi Marg* (New Delhi), 23 February 1981, 601–616. Two books that

ambulance corps to work with the Red Cross to help Indian troops fighting in Europe. It would be comprised of 'Indian residents of Great Britain and Ireland'.[89] He was acutely aware that 'as satyagrahis, we cannot even help by nursing the wounded for such help also amounted to supporting a war', since 'one who would not help a slaughter-house should not help in cleaning the butcher's house either'. He explained his war involvement to his uneasy followers thus: 'London owes the food it gets in war time to the protection of the Navy. Thus to take this food was also a wrong thing … It seemed to me a base thing, therefore, to accept food tainted by war without working for it.'[90] The explanation shows a combination of subtlety and strenuousness that would characterise many of his war-related arguments. In a chapter titled 'A Spiritual Dilemma' in his *Autobiography*, he would note that 'All of us recognized the immorality of war.'[91] It is important to remember, though, that this was the *third* time that Gandhi was volunteering for imperial war service.[92] The question that will arise, time and again, is how to read Gandhi's wartime writings. Do we treat them as exercises in strenuous argumentation, lurching between the twin poles of political instrumentality and moral philosophy, or should we consider them as examples of what David Hardiman has called 'the Gandhian dialogic'[93] – fraught 'communions' both with the self and others? It was one thing to raise an ambulance corps in 1914, and quite another matter to send young men to the battlefields in 1918. To understand his decision to join the recruitment campaign requires the opening of multiple, if intersecting, frames of reference.

were particularly stimulating were Erik Erikson, *Gandhi's Truth: On the Origins of Militant Nonviolence* (New York: W. W. Norton, 1969) and Faisal Devji, *The Impossible Indian: Gandhi and the Temptation of Violence* (Harvard: Harvard University Press, 2012). I owe a particular gratitude to the author of the latter work, who kindly shared with me a copy of his essay 'Gandhi's Great War' ahead of its publication.

[89] See Hunt, *Gandhi in London*, 181. In 1914, Gandhi successfully raised the corps; and, by December, the number of volunteers had grown to 150, including 60 serving at the hospital at Netley, 58 at Brighton and 20 at Brockenhurst. But the corps was disbanded in 1915, following a protracted squabble with the authorities and refusal to let Gandhi visit Netley, out of fear that 'I might make mischief'.

[90] Letter to Maganlal Gandhi, September 18, 1913, *CWMG*, XII, 531. He writes an almost identical letter on 15 November to Pragji Desai: *CWMG*, XII, 554.

[91] M. K. Gandhi, *An Autobiography or The Story of My Experiments with Truth* (London: Penguin, 1982), 39.

[92] Peter Brock, 'Gandhi's Non-violence and His War Service', 371.

[93] David Hardiman, *Gandhi in His Time and Ours* (London: Hurst, 2003), 6. Among the vast amount of scholarship on Gandhi, see Judith Brown, *Gandhi: Prisoner of Hope* (New Haven: Yale University Press, 1989); for a more loyalist and somewhat 'sinister' Gandhi, see Ashwin Desai and Goolam Vahed, *The South African Gandhi: Stretcher-Bearer of Empire* (Stanford: Stanford University Press, 2015), which addresses, in convincing detail, his imperial war experiences.

Gandhi returned to India in January 1915. After watching the political scenario for one year, he launched his first *satyagraha* campaigns in India – in Champaran in 1917 and in Ahmedabad and Kheda in early 1918 – working with the peasants and workers against extortive rents and taxes. But in April 1918, he attended – with 'fear and trembling' – the war conference in Delhi and supported the new governmental resolution to raise half a million Indian troops.[94] On 29 April 1918, he wrote to the Viceroy promising 'ungrudging and unequivocal support to the Empire, of which we aspire, in the near future, to be partners in the same sense as the Dominions overseas'.[95] His approach was effectively an act of triangulation between the 'unconditional' support of his moderate mentor Gokhale and the push towards Dominion status that had the stamp of Tilak. He told Maffey that 'if I became your recruiting agent-in-chief, I might rain men on you'[96] and reached out to both Tilak and Annie Besant, urging them to turn 'every Home Rule Leaguer' into 'an active recruiting depot'.[97] Over the summer of 1918, he threw himself into the recruitment campaign: he travelled across Gujarat and Bihar, where he delivered speeches, held rallies and issued leaflets; he stopped only in August when, wholly exhausted, he fell seriously ill. Such zeal has baffled scholars. Peter Brock asks 'How was he ever to succeed in combining recruitment of his fellow countrymen for the most destructive war … with the continued devotion to the doctrine of non-violence?'[98] Was this a case of 'an irrational outbreak of filial devotion' or a 'flexible adjustment of his idealism to the demands of his nationalism'?[99] Or, as some recent scholarship has suggested, was it the reverse? In other words, was the recruitment campaign not in spite of but precisely *because* of his investment in non-violence beyond the realm of instrumental politics? Like an intricate piece of Gothic fan-vaulting, his various pronouncements both ramify and interconnect, revealing in the process startling ideas, from issues of gender and caste to his concepts of *abhay* (fearlessness), *aapbhog* (self-sacrifice) and *ahimsa* (non-violence).

Let us start with an actual recruitment speech, delivered on 26 June 1918 at Ras and subsequently published in *The Bombay Chronicle*:

---

[94] Letter to J. L. Maffey, 27 April 1918, *CWMG*, XIV, 374.
[95] Letter to Viceroy, 29 April 1918, *Ibid.*, 377–380.
[96] Letter to J. L. Maffey, 30 April 1918, *Ibid.*, 382 (also in NAI, Home (War) Deposit, October 1918, no. 26).
[97] *CWMG*, XVI, 116.
[98] Brock, 'Gandhi's Non-violence', 379, 374.
[99] Erikson, *Gandhi's Truth*, 369; Paul F. Power, *Gandhi on World Affairs* (London: George Allen and Unwin, 1960), 35.

Voluntary recruiting is a key to Swaraj and will give us honour and manhood. The honour of women is bound up with it. Today we are unable to protect our women and children even against wild animals. The best way of acquiring the capacity of self-protection is joining the army. Some will ask, 'Why get killed in France?' But there is a meaning in being thus killed. When we send our dear ones to the battle-field, the courage and the strength which they will acquire will transform all the villages. The training we can get today we may never get again ...

Taking the population of a village at one thousand we should have twenty recruits from each village or two per hundred. What are two in a hundred? How many men do cholera and such other diseases take away every year? These men die unmourned except by their relatives. On the other hand, soldiers' death on the battle-field makes them immortal, if the scriptures are right, and becomes a source of joy and pride to those left behind. From the death of Kshatriyas will be born the guardians of the nation and no Government can withhold arms from such men ... For years we have been deprived of our fighting capacity. How are we to acquire the use of arms for which our ancestors practised penances and took severe pledges? ...

Sisters, you should encourage your husbands and brothers and sons and not worry them with your objections. If you want them to be true men, send them to the army with your blessings. Don't be anxious about what may happen to them on the battle-field. Your piety will watch over them there. And if they fall, console yourselves with the thought that they have fallen in the discharge of their duty and that they will be yours in your next generation.[100]

The future 'Mahatma' here sounds more like the finger-pointing Lord Kitchener of recruiting posters rather than a votary of the anti-war Wilfred Owen. He made similar speeches over the summer of 1918 in Nadiad, Karamsad, Ras, Kheda, Kathlal and Jambusar. What is remarkable is the variety of discourses at play, from invocation of the Arms Act to the 'martial' *Kshatriya* and address to the village women to rural mortality rates. Few people refashioned their masculinity as spectacularly as Gandhi, parading his vulnerable body before the world, but here he harps on 'manhood', 'true men', 'brave men', 'manly' and 'warriors' as he invokes the Kshatriya warrior ethos. Pointing out the ubiquity of the warrior image in Gandhi's work, Ajay Skaria notes that it was from the time of his recruitment speeches to the villagers, many of whom were Kshatriyas, that Gandhi started describing the *satyagrahi* as the 'true warrior' and even claimed a 'Kshatriya [warrior caste] genealogy' for *ahimsa*.[101] In 1920, he

[100] Speech at Ras, 26 June 1918, *CWMG*, XIV, 453–454.
[101] Ajay Skaria, *Unconditional Equality: Gandhi's Religion of Resistance* (Minneapolis: University of Minnesota Press, 2016), 94.

even claimed to be 'one of the greatest Kshatriyas of India'.[102] While these contexts may help to make sense of the warrior image in Gandhi, they cannot surely be used to condone or justify in any way his recourse to gender and caste politics or the lure of battlefield 'honour' and 'immortality'. Indeed, one may even be tempted to say that the prophet of peace is here preaching 'the old Lie: Dulce et Decorum est' and that too for the empire at a time when heroic masculinity was being debunked in the trenches. If, at the outbreak of the war, he had written about 'weeping sisters, wives and mothers',[103] here they are supposed to find 'joy' and 'consolation' in the war service of their men: their 'piety' would be the men's safeguard, presumably, against industrial artillery. Even more startling was his support for the quota system: on 22 June 1918, in a speech at Nadiad, he noted that, 'If every village gave at least twenty men, Kheda district would be able to raise an army of 12,000 men … this number will then work out at 1.7 per cent, a rate which is lower than the death rate.'[104] Even a biographer as empathetic as Erik Erikson has called this logic 'appalling', while Tanika Sarkar has observed with admirable succinctness that 'Gandhi knew – and none better – how to speak to the peasant. But he did not always speak for the peasant.'[105] Having exhausted all his rhetorical armoury, he finally falls back on the central reality: 'It is my view that, in the final analysis, soldiering is more paying than other professions.'[106]

A slightly different perspective emerges as we move from Gandhi speaking *to* peasants to him speaking *about* the peasants at the Gujarat Political Conference in 1918:

> When the peasantry of India understands what swaraj is, the demand will become irresistible … We often refer to the fact that many sepoys of Hindustan have lost their lives on the battlefields of France and Mesopotamia. The educated classes cannot claim the credit for this. They were not sent out by us, nor did they join up through patriotism. They know nothing of swaraj. At the end of the War they will not ask for it. They have gone to demonstrate that they are faithful to the salt they eat. In asking for swaraj, I feel that it is not possible for us to bring into account their services.[107]

Gandhi was possibly the only nationalist leader to point out so clearly the gap between the educated discourse around war service as a push for

---

[102] *Ibid.*
[103] *CWMG*, XII, 523.
[104] 'Appeal for Enlistment', Leaflet No. 1, Nadiad, 22 June 1918, *CWMG*, XIV, 443.
[105] Erikson, *Gandhi's Truth*, 371; Sarkar, 'Gandhi and Social Relations', in Judith M. Brown and Anthony Parel (eds.), *The Cambridge Companion to Gandhi* (Cambridge: Cambridge University Press, 2011), 175.
[106] Appeal for Enlistment, Leaflet No. 2, 22 July 1918, *CWMG*, XIV, 495.
[107] 'Speech at Gujarat Political Conference – I', 3 November 1917, *CWMG*, XIV, 55.

greater political autonomy and the motives of the actual sepoys. His critical intervention in the debate was his call to the middle-class nationalists to own – 'claim the credit' for – the Indian war contribution and effectively *nationalise* the imperial recruitment campaign by linking it to the Home Rule movement. He thus wrote to Mahadev Desai that, in any case, 'they ... are going to raise their 5 lakhs of men. Why not then anticipate them and offer them an army of our own selection?' and, then again, in a lengthy letter to Srinivasa Sastri on 18 July 1918:

> The gateway to our freedom is situated on the French soil ... If we could but crowd the battle-fields of France with an indomitable army of Home Rulers fighting for victory for the cause of the Allies, it will be also a fight for our own cause. We would then have made out an unanswerable case for granting Home Rule, not in any distant time or near future but immediately.[108]

He further added that 'by enlisting in the war, we will be patriotic': 'sacrifice for the empire, for the sake of Swaraj ... [and] helping the Government means nothing but helping ourselves'.[109] Such statements as the above blur the divisions between 'loyalist' and 'nationalist' motives, taking us to the recesses of the imperial–nationalist space. There was another equally important reason. As he noted in a recruitment leaflet on 22 July 1918, 'by enlisting in the army, we shall learn the use of weapons'; military training for him was 'essential', for 'we shall be unfit for Swaraj for generations to come if we do not regain the power of self-defence'.[110] Military experience would also politicise the peasantry but, beyond such politicisation and self-defence, there was an even more important fallout for Gandhi: this was self-discipline, and its roots lay in his personal battle-field experience.

In a speech delivered in Calcutta in 1902, just after returning from his medical stint in the Boer War, Gandhi had said: 'As a Hindu, I do not believe in war, but if anything can even partially reconcile me to it, it was the rich experience we gained at the front.' He recalled how freely the 'lovable' Tommy had shared his water and rations with the Indian bearers; in the topsy-turvy world of the front, the khaki uniform or the Red Cross badge was a 'sufficient passport' to racial equality and fraternity:

[108] Letter to V. S. Srinivasa Sastri, 18 July 1918, *Ibid.*, 489.
[109] *Ibid.*, 443, 484. He also noted that 'India would be nowhere without Englishmen', Speech at Karamsad, 14 July 1918, *CWMG*, XIV, 484.
[110] Recruitment Leaflet, 22 July 1918, *CWMG*, XIV, 495; Letter to Hanumantrao, 17 July 1918, *Ibid.*, 485. He further noted that 'the first essential for swarajya is, thus, the power of self-protection'.

There was perfect order, perfect stillness. Tommy was then altogether lovable. He mixed with us … freely. He often shared with us his luxuries whenever there were any to be had … There was, shall I say, a spirit of brotherhood, irrespective of colour or creed … It was certainly not the thirst for blood that took thousands of men to the battlefield … they went to the battlefield because it was their duty. And how many proud, rude, savage spirits had it not broken into gentle creatures of God![111]

The war-zone is constructed as a democratic space; the extremity of the situation and the bonds of male camaraderie suspend codes of civilian society, including racial discrimination. And more. Gandhi's experiences in the two imperial wars made him come to the paradoxical conclusion that it was the military – an institution trained to maim and kill – that fostered some of the qualities he held most precious for 'character building', the prerequisite to 'nation-building': self-discipline, self-sacrifice, bravery, courage, resilience, order, control, fellowship. The ancient Gujarati proverb in which Gandhi believed – *tapne ante raj, ne rajne ante tap* (discipline is power, power is discipline) or the concept of *atmashakti* so central to the Swadeshi movement in Bengal seemed to have found its perverse realisation in the imperial British army. 'I think if anything from the West deserves copying, it is drill.'[112] During his political experiments in Champaran and Kheda, Gandhi had repeatedly been frustrated by the eruptions of violence and the lack of discipline. And yet, as he had famously said in *Hind Swaraj* (1909), 'It is Swaraj when we learn to rule ourselves.'[113] And, for the philosopher of *ahimsa*, the concepts of 'freedom', 'sovereignty' and 'unconditional equality' led to the battlefield.

In recent years, the 'Father of the nation' has been reinvented as 'the ancestor of the Global Indian', and there has been a shift from Gandhi the arch-negotiator to Gandhi the political philosopher. In *The Impossible Indian: Gandhi and the Temptation of Violence* (2012), Faisal Devji has powerfully argued that 'it was the battlefield that provided him with a site

<hr/>

[111] Speech at Public Meeting in Calcutta, 27 January 1902, *CWMG*, III, 264–265.
[112] 'Speech at Second Gujarat Educational Conference', 20 October 1917, *CWMG*, XIV, 30. Hardiman (*Gandhi in His Time*, 27) observes that discipline has a dual character – empowering and repressive – and that, while Foucault emphasised the latter quality, Gandhi stressed the former.
[113] Anthony J. Parel (ed.), *Hind Swaraj and Other Writings* (Cambridge: Cambridge University Press, 1997), 73. 'Neither freedom nor sovereignty', Faisal Devji reminds us, 'could be obtained by means of a deal, but must be possessed unconditionally.' Faisal Devji, 'Gandhi's Great War', in Roger D. Long and Ian Talbot (eds.), *India and World War I: A Centennial Assessment* (London: Routledge, 2018), 196. I am grateful to Devji for kindly sending me a copy of this article ahead of its publication.

to think about such violence, specifically the battlefield of the *Bhagavad-Gita*.[114] More recently, Ajay Skaria, in *Unconditional Equality: Gandhi's Religion of Resistance* (2016), has drawn attention to the image of the 'satayagrahi as warrior' in Gandhian thought and suggests that the image helped Gandhi to conceptualise the idea of self-sacrifice (*aapbhog*) in two ways. First, to quote Skaria, in 'sublative' terms where 'the warrior masters his fear of his own death'; second, as marked by 'an economy of the gift, by an immeasurable equality and inequality'.[115] But let us first consider Gandhi's own reflections.

During the *satyagraha* campaign in Champaran and Kheda, Gandhi wrote of his 'terrible discovery' that the peasants had adopted *satyagraha* not as an exercise in superior morality but as a 'weapon of the weak'.[116] For him, it was a betrayal of the basic principles of *satyagraha* (non-violent resistance; in Sanskrit, 'satya' – truth, 'agraha' – insistence). A month later, on 17 July 1918, he wrote to Hanumant Rao on the same subject:

> It is my practice of ahimsa and failure to get our people even to understand the first principles of ahimsa that have led me to the discovery that all killing is not himsa, that, sometimes, practice of ahimsa may even necessitate killing and that we as a nation have lost the true power of killing. It is clear that he who has lost the power to kill cannot practise non-killing. Ahimsa is a renunciation of the highest type. A weak and an effeminate nation cannot perform this grand act of renunciation, even a mouse cannot be properly said to renounce the power of killing a cat ... The noblest warrior is he who stands fearless in the face of immense odds. He then feels not the power to kill, but he is supremely triumphant in the knowledge that he has the willingness to die when by taking to his heels he might have easily saved his life.[117]

This was one of the clearest expositions of the *satyagrahi* as warrior, with the twin gifts of sovereignty and self-sacrifice: in 'dying without killing' lies the ultimate triumph of *ahimsa*.[118] Yet, Gandhi's radical understanding of

[114] Devji, *The Impossible Indian*, 96, 116. More recently, he notes how extreme situations like the war could harbour for Gandhi 'incalculable possibilities': 'Non-violence was one such incalculable, as was the bravery that characterised both it, and certain kinds of violence' ('Gandhi's Great War', 202).

[115] Skaria, *Unconditional Equality*, 96. He further notes that 'The warrior's life is immeasurable ... because he receives life from and through an equality with his own death, which is always immeasurable to him.' (103). Such reading, while complex, may risk what the philosopher F. H. Bradley called 'the bloodless ballet of categories', especially within the context of war recruitment.

[116] *CWMG*, XIV, 462.

[117] Letter to Hanumantrao, 17 July 1918, *CWMG*, XIV, 485.

[118] Skaria notes that the phrase appears only in the English version and that, for a thinker as tenacious as Gandhi, 'dying without killing, and by extension satyagraha or ahimsa, is an impossible possible'. *Unconditional Equality*, 134.

'renunciation' is based on some of the most conventionally gendered language ('effeminate nation'). In a letter to his friend C. F. Andrews, he continued as follows: 'I find great difficulties in recruiting but do you know that not one man has yet objected because he would not kill. They object because they fear to die.'[119] These men, he concluded, were too 'weak' to 'walk to the gallows, or stand a shower of bullets'; the war experience would, by implication, inculcate the ethos of the true *satyagrahi*.[120] To his admirer Esther Faering, who had also queried his zeal for recruitment, he made a careful distinction:

> What am I to advise a man to do who wants to kill but is unable owing to his being maimed? Before I can make him feel the virtue of not killing, I must restore to him the arms he has lost ... A nation that is unfit to fight cannot from experience prove the virtue of not fighting. I do not infer from this that India must fight. But I do say that India must know how to fight.[121]

Ahimsa was not the absence but the active *renunciation* of violence which must therefore be predicated on actual knowledge of it. What we have, in the context of war, is a radical reinterpretation of both *ahimsa* and *satyagraha*.

It is important to recognise the complexity and subtlety of Gandhi's formulation. At the same time, the question that goes strangely unasked is whether the intricacies of political and moral philosophy, however subtle, can provide justification for war recruitment on ethical grounds. While the battlefield as a moral site and the image of the ancient warrior as *satyagrahi* help Gandhi to reconceptualise the idea of *ahimsa*, the landscape shifts seismically as we descend from the philosophical ether to the muddy reality of the trenches. What happens when the metaphor of the warrior gets grotesquely literalised? First, notwithstanding the problematic gender politics, it is important to note that the 'warrior' image in the recruitment speeches and letters functions largely as a philosophical–literary *idea* fighting a bloodless combat against a bloodless enemy; absent is the body in pain, the wounds in the body, the pain in the wound. In her classic study *The Body in Pain* (1985), Elaine Scarry has argued that the '*concrete objects of consciousness*' – moral convictions, reciprocity, habits – all fade into 'weightlessness' in the face of extreme pain.[122] Second, if the *Gita*, Nietzsche and Derrida provide one framework, as in Skaria, the killing

---

[119] Letter to C. F. Andrews, 29 July 1918, *CWGC*, XIV, 510.
[120] Letter to C. F. Andrews, 6 July 1918, *CWMG*, XIV, 475. He further notes, 'They were too weak to undertake the methods of violence' (475).
[121] Letter to Esther Faering, 30 June 1918, *Ibid.*, 462–463.
[122] Elaine Scarry, *The Body in Pain: The Making and Unmaking of the World* (Oxford: Oxford University Press, 1985), 31–32.

fields of France and the Middle East in 1914–1918 open up a different one. In the mass industrialised warfare where the enemy was invisible and daily reality consisted of being cooped up and shelled passively, the classical image of the 'warrior' was rendered obsolescent, if not obscene. Soldiers came back from war not with the psychic rearrangement Gandhi desired but with shellshock. In a letter to Andrews, Gandhi had written the following: 'There is not a single recruiting speech in which I have yet said, "Let us go to kill the Germans." My refrain is, "Let us go and die for the sake of India and the Empire." '[123] While the refrain is one of the most effective and instrumental uses of the imperial–nationalist idea for war recruitment, the shearing off of the killing from the dying is something that poets such as Owen would demolish in their verse by recasting the sacrificial victim as the murderer: 'I am the enemy you killed, my friend.'[124] The contexts and pressures are admittedly different, but the recruitment speeches almost show Gandhi, as noted above, preaching called 'the old Lie'. It was as if, even before these Indian peasants had reached the battlefields of empire, they had become the fodder in the experimental laboratory of Gandhi for a 'greater cause' – be it moral philosophy, empire or nation. The fact that Gandhi was rather unsuccessful in recruiting does not mitigate against such claims.

As always, Gandhi himself would have been acutely aware. A letter to a member of his *ashram* shows a far more ambivalent attitude: he conceded that fighting in war, though a 'powerful' way of acquiring 'heroism', was also 'an evil one': 'We can cultivate manliness in a blameless way.'[125] In his classic psychobiography, Erik Erikson has argued that the terrible illness that afflicted Gandhi in 1918 was actually a nervous breakdown brought about by this terrible conflict.[126] The recruitment campaign, it must be admitted, was a significant but short phase in his career. Ironically, while doing the Congress report after the Amritsar massacre, it was Gandhi who would launch a full-scale investigation about the strong-arm tactics around recruitment and denounce the sepoy in 1921 as a 'hired assassin' of the Raj.[127]

---

[123] Letter to C. F. Andrews, 6 July 1918, *CWMG*, XIV, 477. Gandhi's idealism in this letter gets out of hand when he says that Indian sepoys, trained by him, may 'fill the trenches and with hearts of love lay down their guns and challenge the Germans to shoot them – their fellow men – I say that even the German heart will melt'.

[124] Wilfred Owen, 'Dulce et Decorum Est', in *The Poems of Wilfred Owen*, ed. Jon Stallworthy (London: Chatto & Windus, 1990), 126.

[125] 'Letter to Nanubhai', 24 September 1918, *CWMG*, XV, 52.

[126] Erikson, *Gandhi's Truth*, 378.

[127] Quoted in Sugata Bose, *His Majesty's Opponent: Subhas Chandra Bose and India's Struggle against Empire* (Cambridge: Harvard University Press, 2011), 51.

Bāṅgāli Palṭan [*The Bengali Platoon*]: Regionalism, Realism and Literary Form

We have so far been considering the 'imperial–nationalist' dynamic and its undertones in a variety of sites, from the context of princely India through that of Punjabi newspapers to the war writings of Tilak and Gandhi. In this concluding section, I would like to briefly explore a regional variation of the recruitment rhetoric through a new form – literature, more specifically a play written for recruitment purposes. Two questions will guide my investigation. First, how is the recruitment rhetoric shaped by and in turn played out against the socio-political and cultural specificities of a particular region? Second, how does literature open up an affective space that at once embodies and interrogates the 'imperial–nationalist' dynamic, particularly in relationship with the socio-economic conditions of the region?

In July 1916, a certain Dr S. K. Mullick of Calcutta wrote to the Chief Secretary of the Government of Bengal with a unique offer to raise and equip a regiment of citizen soldiers of 1,000 men.[128] The organising committee would bear the expenses for recruitment, uniform and pay. Each recruit would be paid a separation allowance of 18 rupees per month. Initially, it was supposed to comprise 100 men recruited from different provinces, but ultimately it was confined to Bengal. In a war speech delivered at the Young Men's Union in Calcutta, on 22 May 1917, the local *zamindar*, Kumar M. C. Sinha, credited Mullick as 'the first who saw [the] Bengalee soldier coming'.[129] The offer was accepted and, on 7 August 1916, a Double Company of Bengalis for the Regular Army was sanctioned. Though the number required for the Double Company was 228, nearly 400 names were registered within a fortnight and thus the Bengali 49th Regiment was formed.[130] These recruits, unlike the semi-literate peasant-warriors from the Punjab, were well-educated Bengali youths belonging to the *bhadralok* class. In an overcrowded meeting in the Star Theatre in September 1916, people came to see off the first batch of Bengali soldiers amidst tremendous excitement. Even the anti-colonial revolutionary C. R. Das could not contain his thrill: 'This is the first time in the history of British rule in India that the Government has decided to admit Bengalis into the army.'[131] The widespread war enthusiasm, recorded by the poet-soldier Kazi Nazrul

---

[128] WBSA, Political File 1W-53 (1–5), B, April 1916, Proceedings 697–701.

[129] 'The War through Indian Eyes' (1917) in *Writings and Speeches by Kumar Manindra Chandra Sinha* (Calcutta: unknown publisher, n.d.), 24.

[130] *Ibid.*, 25.

[131] 'Motilal   Ghose', www.archive.org/stream/motilalgosho35420mbp/motilalgosho35420mbp_ djvu.txt. The 49th Bengali Regiment would go on to have a rather inglorious record. It reached

Islam in *Bāndhan-Hārā*, was remarkable, given that the province had so recently been rocked by the Swadeshi movement and had long been the site of anti-colonial revolutionary activities.[132]

Before the year was out, the recruitment campaign was made into a play —*Bāṅgāli Palṭan* [*Bengali Platoon* in English, though the 49th Bengalis were a regiment].[133] It was written in September 1916 by the novelist Satish Chandra Chattopadhyay and was premiered to full houses at the Presidency Theatre. This two-act play, written in close consultation with Mullick and first read out in a private gathering at his house, mixes fact and fiction. Its dramatis personae include Dr Mullick, Kumar Sinha and contemporary political figures, along with fictional representations of village youths and their feisty mothers. The play is set in a small village in Bengal and traces the fortunes of the educated middle-class Nirmal and the buffoonish Keblā (meaning 'silly') from their desultory, seemingly insignificant village life to their glorious enlistment as soldiers of the First World War. If Bernard Shaw's famous pronouncement 'No conflict, no drama' remains one of the central tenets of the genre, the conflict in the play is not so much representational as it is ideological. With its propagandist imperial agenda on the one hand and its mode of social realism on the other, the play bears testimony to a discursive tension between its overarching ideology of 'loyalty' and the economic reality of enlistment; it is also acutely diagnostic of the regional inflection of the 'imperial–nationalist' dynamic and its affective undertow.

Bāṅgāli Palṭan is marked as much by the absence of any pan-Indian nationalist consciousness as it is by the lack of awareness of the one million Indian soldiers serving abroad. 'Bengali mother', 'Bengali son' and the 'Bengali race' are the recurrent phrases in a play obsessively and exclusively rooted in the 'prestige' of Bengal. Consider the speech by Dr Mullick in the play:

MULLICK: The Bengali race should be particularly grateful to the English government for the warm generosity it has shown in imparting military training to

---

Mesopotamia in September 1917, but never saw combat and struggled with the desert conditions and disease. A commanding officer divided the regiment into 'Measles Squad', 'The Whooping Cough Squad' and 'Scarlet Fever Squad'. More seriously, there was infighting and a junior member opened fire on three senior colleagues while they were asleep, and the regiment was disbanded soon after the war.

[132] The authoritative book on the subject remains Sumit Sarkar, *The Swadeshi Movement in Bengal 1903–1908* (Ranikhet: Permanent Black, 2011 [1973]).

[133] Satish Chandra Chattopadhyay, *Bāṅgāli Palṭan* (Calcutta: Madhuri Workshop, 1916). All translated passages from this play are mine. Page references are given in the text.

the Bengalis. At this hour of peril of our King, we should no longer just sit back. It is one's duty to help in whatever way one could. One more word – it is my belief that it is a red-letter day in the national life of Bengal – because Bengali soldiers are leaving for the battlefield today. Arise Bengal! Go forward, Bengalis! Carve out bravely the path of name and fame! Remember the slurs of yester-years! People have often looked down on us as a cowardly, weak and effeminate race! Let the Bengali soldiers demonstrate to the world the inner strength of the Bengalis. (23)

Mrinalini Sinha has shown how, in late-nineteenth-century British discourses, Englishmen were cast as the highest ideal of masculinity, characterised by their chivalry, love of sport and work ethic, and defined in opposition to the Bengalis who were regarded as effeminate, bookish and overly serious.[134] In the play, Keblā's mother says 'Do you mean to say that the Bengali boys will fight? Well, if they go to battle, who will become the clerks for the English?' (16), a point that is taken up by the character Pānckaḍi: 'Our honoured government [is] … now welcoming Bengali youths to train as soldiers. This is indeed a singular opportunity for us' (27). The 'effeminate' Bengalis were defined in contrast not only to fox-hunting Englishmen but also to the 'warrior-gentlemen' of the Raj – the turban-wearing Sikh or the kookri-wielding Gurkha – and were barred from joining the army. Hence, the wartime enlistment was a 'singular opportunity', a point not lost upon the narrator in a piece of doggerel penned by 'A Bengalee': 'Who calls me now a coward base,/And brands my race a coward race?/I'll brook no more such scoffing word:/My King himself has washed the shame/That fouled so long my stainless name.'[135]

In recent years, research on wartime Bengal has revealed how, under a veneer of wartime support, even enthusiasm, there seethed an underworld of racial tensions, anti-colonial plots and traces of social radicalism.[136] While such events are completely glossed over in the world of the play, its realist mode cannot ignore the socio-economic conditions that prevailed during the war years. Wartime Calcutta registered a sharp hike in the prices of essential commodities, including rice, wheat, salt, cooking-oil and cloth; by 1918, prices had risen by 78% but wages had remained static since 1914; moreover, unemployment soared.[137] The loyalist–nationalist agenda in

---

[134] Sinha, *Colonial Masculinity: 'The Manly Englishman' and the Effeminate Bengali*.
[135] Quoted in Bhargava, *India's Services in the War*, 218.
[136] Suchetana Chattopadhyay, 'War, Migration and Alienation in Colonial Calcutta', *History Workshop Journal*, 64, 1 (2007), 212–239.
[137] Kenneth McPherson, *Muslim Microcosm: Calcutta, 1918–1935* (Ann Arbor: University of Michigan, 1974); also see Chattopadhyay, 'War, Migration and Alienation', 230. Also see Upendra Narayan Chakravorty, *Indian Nationalism and the First World War 1914–18* (Kolkata: Progressive Publishers,

the play rubs against the economic imperatives of recruitment, as in this conversation between three potential recruits:

KHAGEN: The way our lives are going, it seems we've no option left ... The monster of poverty seems to be engulfing the whole of our country. Malaria and famine are now our constant companions. On top of that, the daily grind of poverty. I cannot see a single family that hasn't felt its sharp pinch.

BIMAL: Not only that. We become penniless trying to fund our education and then we cannot find any work. Can there be anything worse that can happen to us? ...

...

SUREN: That is why I'm saying, our condition is so miserable – without a job, our right hand doesn't seem to work – instead of thinking of anything else, we should join the Bengal Platoon. Without it, there seems to be a lot of hardship ahead of us.

KHAGEN: Far better to die in battle than to live a life of shame like a dog or a cat. (7–8)

As Keblā prepares to flee to Calcutta to enlist, he thinks of the salary of 11 rupees and the further 50 rupees he will get at the time of leaving. The play trades in double irony: first, mass unemployment – which had propelled many Bengali youths into revolutionary nationalist activities – is here seen to fuel imperial war recruitment; second, the 'loyalist' agenda of the play is undercut by a realism that exposes the economic underpinnings of the whole enterprise. The village wives now voice their protest:

KEBLĀ'S MOTHER (CRYING): What horrors have befallen me! I see that the crocodile has invaded my house first. Is it to undo me that the red-faces [*lalmukho* - contemporary Bengali racist slang for the English] came to the village?

KEBLĀ: Look, don't call these eminent people such awful names.

KEBLĀ'S MOTHER: Why shouldn't I? I will, a hundred times over. First the burntfaces invade our country, and now they are trying to raid my larder! (36)

Any serious critique of empire or war is diffused through humour, but it nonetheless casts its shadow over the play: the 'uneducated' village women function as voices of dissent.[138] In the final act of the play, Nirmal, Keblā and other village youths, all in military uniform, march towards a ship amidst strains of joyous singing – 'Sing the glories of the English! Sing the praise of the emperor! ... Sing the glories of the Bengalis' – as

---

1997) for a detailed exploration of the effects of the war on Indian industries, price rises and workers' movements.

[138] For a more detailed exploration of the responses of Indian women to the conflict, see Santanu Das, 'India, Women and the First World War', in Alison S. Fell and Ingrid Sharp (eds.), *The Women's Movement in Wartime: International Perspectives, 1914–1919* (London: Palgrave, 2007), 18–37.

empire loyalism, Bengali nationalism and war service here are a trinity become one.

The 1914–1918 war therefore catches the Indian psyche at a fragile spot between a continuing or rather residual loyalty to the empire and a welter of ambitions, anxieties and agendas which varied according to the interest group – from princes trying to secure their future in a post-war imperial world to the middle classes pushing for the end of racial discrimination and nationalist leaders bargaining for greater political autonomy. War service, for each, becomes a fraught game-plan which at once illuminates, puts pressure on and in turn leads to the manipulation of the imperial self. A close examination of the various speeches and writings – from those of the princes to the debates in the vernacular newspapers to the lectures of Tilak and Gandhi – suggests a certain richness and plurality of discourses that go far beyond the straightforward nationalist agenda of the subsequent years; what the play foregrounds is the seamless fluidity between opposed political identities as well as the underpinning of economic incentives even on the part of middle-class Bengalis. The vibrancy of such discourses gives lie to the idea of an apathetic or passive colonial home front; instead, some of the most immediate and urgent issues, particularly the bid for racial equality and national self-respect, are hammered on the anvil of battlefield service. But 1919 would be a huge watershed: the passing of the Rowlatt Act and the subsequent Amritsar massacre would irremediably change the very meaning of war service in the national psyche, and gradually airbrush it out of the nation's history.

Figure 2.1 'Farewell' by Pran Nath Mago. Fine Arts Museum, Punjabi University, Patiala and estate of the artist. Courtesy of Chadrika Mago, Chandrahas Mathur and Punam Mathur. (See the plate section for a colour version of this figure.)

CHAPTER 2

Sonorous Fields
Recruitment, Resistance and Recitative in Punjab

As a family we all feel very proud of my grandfather. I keep telling my
children. Everyone should remember his name for the sacrifices he
made. (Interview with Raj Singh, grandson of Pat Ram, a recruiter,
Delhi, India, 2014).

I feel sad. I think sorrow is the appropriate word to use. The way
he [my great grandfather] was used as cannon fodder. These
sickle-handlers who had never seen a gun, in a sense put into all
this warfare. (Interview with Mahmood Awan, great-grandson of
Havildar Ghulam Mohammed, a soldier, Dublin, Ireland, 2014).[1]

> May you never be enlisted,
> You who have left me crying.
> 'Married men win battles'
> Tell me, O *firangi* [foreigner], where is this written?'
> 'Take the bachelors to war,
> O *firangi*, then victory will be yours.'[2]

Let us start with a scene of farewell (Figure 2.1). A son touches the feet of
his mother as we see soldiers embark on the train to the front. The elderly
father looks on as the mother wipes away her tears with her *chunni* (scarf).
Emotion is suggested through gesture and colour rather than through the
art of close-up. White, the colour of mourning, visually unites the grieving
parents and spills over through the world of fabric to a similar scene on the
right-hand corner with two distraught women, suggesting a wider female
community of mourning, before the white is carried over to the waiting

---

[1] The interviews were carried out by me as part of the Radio 4 programme 'Soldiers of Empire: Recruitment
and Resistance' in October 2014. See www.bbc.co.uk/mediacentre/proginfo/2014/41/soldiers-of-the-
empire.

[2] The above folksong, recently recovered, has been translated by Amarjit Chandan and UK Punjab
Heritage. It was performed by Amanroop Kaur at the concert 'Terrible Beauty: Literature and Music
from the First World War' we organised at King's College London on 11 November 2014. A YouTube
recording of the concert can be found at www.youtube.com/watch?v=yVyyrm-Feno.

train – the cause of the sorrow, the harbinger of death. The painting, by
the Punjabi artist Pran Nath Mago, is titled 'Farewell' and was painted in
1945.[3] The emollient contours and the flowing clothes of the civilian figures contrast with the Western military uniform and rigid gestures of the
soldiers, while the three distant figures on a bridge amidst the billowing
smoke of the train take the painting to a different place, different time –
the world of no-return. The immediate trigger of the painting was the
Second World War, but it was based on Mago's childhood memories of
soldiers taking leave at the Gujar Khan railway-platform for the front
during the 1914–1918 war. The painting fuses the two wars as both depleted
Punjab of its young men.

The painting lifts the veil on what still remains one of the weakest links
in First World War history: the colonial home front. Of the over one
million Indians who served abroad, some 480,000 came from Punjab.[4]
The massive recruitment figures from a single province were the fruition
of a process that had begun in the nineteenth century – the 'militarisation of Punjab' and the 'Punjabisation of the Indian army'.[5] Scholars have
noted how Punjab's frontier location with relation to Afghanistan and the
display of Punjabi loyalty during the Sepoy Uprising of 1857 influenced
the shift of the Indian army's recruitment centre to this province.[6] Political
expediency was soon welded to Victorian racial ideology. As early as 1879,
the Eden Commission Report noted that 'the Punjab is the home of the
most martial races of India and is the nursery of our best soldiers'.[7] Lord
Frederick Roberts – the Commander-in-Chief in India from 1885 to 1893 –
was an enthusiastic proponent of the theory of the 'martial races' and
reshaped the class components of the Indian army, in particular replacing
men from the 'unmartial' south with the 'martial' races of the north. The
army was further reorganised by Lord Herbert Kitchener, who became
the Commander-in-Chief in India in 1902. The province soon evolved
into the recruiting ground for soldiers and policemen for the empire. In

[3] Pran Nath Mago became an important figure in the Punjabi art scene around the time of the
Second World War, with paintings such as 'Farewell', 'Catching Fish', 'Rumour' and 'Mourners'. His
paintings often represent the effects of war or the Partition on the villages of Punjab. See Pran Nath
Mago, *Contemporary Art in India* (Delhi: National Book Trust, 1985).
[4] *The Punjab and the War* (1922) compiled by M. S. Leigh (Lahore: Sang-e-Meel Publications and
Superintendent Government Printing, Punjab, 1997 [1922]), 40.
[5] See Rajit Mazumder, *The Indian Army and the Making of Punjab* (Ranikhet: Permanent Black,
2003), 7–45.
[6] See Ian Talbot, *Punjab and the Raj, 1849–1947* (Delhi: Manohar, 1988).
[7] 'Eden Commission Report on Organisation and Expenditure of the Army in India', IOR, L/MIL/
17/5/1687. Also see G. F. MacMunn, *The Armies of India* (London: Adam & Charles Black, 1911). For
critical works, see Streets, *Martial Races* and Singh, *The Testimonies of Indian Soldiers*, 10–34.

August 1914, Punjab (including the British districts and princely states) had 100,000 men in its armies, including 87,000 combatants and 13,000 non-combatants; by the end of the war, Punjab had contributed one-third of all the Indian recruits and over 40% of the total number of Indian combatants mobilised.[8] However, the conventional idea of Punjab as the 'exceptional' colonial state – prosperous, loyal and unified – has increasingly come under pressure.[9] As Mark Condos has recently argued, the 'garrison state' was also the 'insecurity state' *par excellence*, bristling with anxiety, almost bordering on panic, about its 'warlike' inhabitants.[10]

This chapter focusses on the cultural and literary lives of the war in Punjab. Research on wartime Punjab has largely been military, political and socio-economic in nature, from analysis of the logistics of recruitment to the relationship between the army and the state.[11] Most of this work is based on governmental archives. This chapter, in contrast, is interested in the testimonial and the cultural, and how they may help in the recovery of a more immediate and sensuous sphere of experience. I read official documents alongside war posters, reports of rumour, songs, vernacular journals, newspaper reports, interviews, treatises, poems and lectures, which in turn open up a far more contested space, politically, socially and psychologically. The lines of investigation here are two-fold. If debates continue about whether the sepoys were voluntary loyalists or seasoned mercenaries, I suggest the need for a more psychologically and culturally nuanced framework. For that, I first revisit the familiar recruitment story, through unconventional archives, in the first two sections to factor in the grittiness of the social and the economic, before moving to the cultural. Second, the chapter seeks to excavate a wider war culture in Punjab, recovering a substantial number of hitherto unknown texts, and argues for a more palpable, complex and ambivalent relationship to the war. In a context when the press was gagged and political dissent could not

---

[8] See M. S. Leigh, *The Punjab and the War*, 40–41.

[9] See Mridula Mukherjee, *Colonizing Agriculture: The Myth of Punjab Exceptionalism* (Delhi: Sage, 2001).

[10] See Mark Condos, *The Insecurity State: Punjab and the Making of Colonial Power in British India* (Cambridge: Cambridge University Press, 2017), 10.

[11] See Tan Tai Yong, *The Garrison State: The Military, Government and Society in Colonial Punjab, 1849–1947* (New Delhi: Sage, 2005); also see Talbot, *Punjab and the Raj*; Imran Ali, *The Punjab under Imperialism, 1885–1947* (Princeton: Princeton University Press, 1988); Mazumder, *The Indian Army*; Kaushik Roy, 'Introduction' to *War and Society in Colonial India, 1807–1945* (Delhi: Oxford University Press, 2006), 1–52 and Tahir Mahmood, 'Collaboration and British Military Recruitment: Fresh Perspective from Colonial Punjab, 1914–1918', *Modern Asian Studies*, 50, 5 (2015), 1474–1500. I am grateful to K. C. Yadav of Haryana Academy for kindly sharing his unpublished paper on 'Donning the Khaki: Recruitment in Punjab during World War I' with me and reading my chapter.

be voiced openly, cultural forms such as verse, song and rumour became the modes of enquiry and protest. There is a related methodological point. To mine such war culture necessitates engaging with the oral, the aural and the performative. I have used the phrase 'recitative' (from Italian *recitativo*) in order to suggest this robust culture where the oral interacted with the textual in complex ways: narrative pleasure resided in reciting, quoting, narrating, singing or the practice of 'sung enunciation' with regular shifts between the different registers.[12] The Punjabi home front, I argue, was intensely literary even though it was largely non-literate – sometimes seething, sometimes somnolent but always sonorous.

Given the fraught history of the province because of the subsequent Partition, it is important to bear a few things in mind. In spite of the winds of nineteenth-century revivalism, the field of literary production in undivided Punjab was polyglossal: songs, poems and propaganda were articulated or written in Urdu, Punjabi (written both in Gurmukhi and in Nastaliq), Haryanvi (written in Devanagari) and Hindi. Moreover, identity was often plural, as was the language; caste identity intersected with and cross-cut across religious differences in complex ways. Cultural practices did not neatly map on to religious or ethnic affiliations; most people would have been familiar with both Urdu and Punjabi. Whether people wrote in Devanagari or Nastaliq script did not depend on religion only, and the sanitisation of language according to religious more had not happened. It is telling that *Jat Gazette*, one of my sources, was meant for the Hindu communities in eastern Punjab but was written in the Nastaliq script. Similarly, what would later become the state of Haryana in 1966 was still very much part of undivided Punjab, with districts such as Hissar and Rohtak being important recruitment centres.

The pre-war years, particularly 1905–1913, saw a burgeoning of new kinds of anti-colonial movements. Punjab too felt the restlessness. In 1907, there was widespread rural upheaval in the province in response to casualties from plague and malaria, rural landlessness and the 'Colonisation Bill', with the movement giving the Punjabis a revolutionary 'rhetoric and symbology'.[13] Moreover, Pan-Islamism had been a distinct presence since the Balkan wars,

---

[12] See Farina Mir, *The Social Space of Language: Vernacular Culture in British Colonial Punjab* (Berkeley: University of California Press, 2010); also see Susan S. Wadley, 'Why Does Ram Swarup Sing? Song and Speech in the North Indian Epic Ḍholā', in Arjun Appadurai, Frank J. Korom and Margaret A. Mills (eds.), *Gender, Genre, and Power in South Asian Expressive Tradition* (Philadelphia: University of Pennsylvania Press, 1991), 201–223.

[13] See Gajendra Singh, 'Revolutionary Networks', in 1914–1918 Online Encyclopedia (https://encyclopedia.1914-1918-online.net/article/revolutionary_networks_india); also see Mark Condos, *The Insecurity State*, 199.

and provided the context for the eruption of the 'Silk Letter' conspiracy in 1916.[14] The more immediate threat, however, was the Ghadar movement. Meaning 'rebellion' or 'mutiny', the 'Ghadar' was an anti-colonial revolutionary movement. It was started in 1913 by a group of Indian migrants, including a substantial number of Punjabi Sikhs in the United States and Canada, with Lala Har Dayal as their future leader.[15] It espoused the complete overthrow of the British empire. With the declaration of the war, the newspaper *Ghadar di Gūnj* issued its clarion-call: 'Let us unite and strike. This is our opportunity.'[16] Har Dayal now encouraged the Ghadar members to return to India to subvert the loyalty of its soldiers and turn them into revolutionaries. The movement created widespread panic, and the notorious Defence of India Act of 1915 was partly a response.[17] In reality, the impact of the Ghadarites was limited: their plans were largely foiled, and the movement was 'officially' declared to have been crushed.[18] But it would indeed be reductive to view wartime Punjab through the extremes of 'loyalty' and 'rebellion'. If military and social historians in recent years have shown us a more nuanced understanding of dissent, it is the oral culture of the time – verse, lectures and folksongs – that conveys its various shades and shows a deeply ambivalent, if not sharply critical, attitude to the war. But first, let us consider the much-debated world of war recruitment.

Mixed Motives: Livelihood, Tradition and Incentives

In 1914, India had one of the largest voluntary armies in the world. Of the 27,522 new recruits enlisted in India between August and 31st December 1914, 13,400 were from Punjab alone.[19] The total number of men to have served from Punjab, including the British districts and the Indian states,

---

[14] See, for example, Burak Akçapar, *People's Mission to the Ottoman Empire: M. A. Ansari and the Indian Medical Mission, 1912–1913* (Delhi: Oxford University Press, 2014).

[15] See Harish K. Puri, *Ghadar Movement: Ideology, Organisation and Strategy* (Amritsar: Guru Nanak Dev University Press, 1993); Maia Ramnath, *Haj to Utopia*; Mark Condos, *The Insecurity State*, 198–201; Seema Sohi, *Echoes of Mutiny: Race, Surveillance, and Indian Anticolonialism in North America* (New York: Oxford University Press, 2014).

[16] 'The Determined Purpose of Revolution', *Ghadar di Gūnj* (San Francisco: Hindustani Ghadar Press, 1916). The translation comes from the collection of 'hostile oriental propaganda' in the British Library, Mss Eur E288, 7.

[17] Michael O'Dwyer, *India As I Knew It, 1885–1925* (London: Constable, 1925), 189.

[18] Mark Condos, *The Insecurity State*, 212.

[19] 'Numbers Recruited by Province from 1 August to 31 December 1914', App IX in *Recruiting in India*, BL, IOR L/MIL/17/5/2152. This is the official authoritative document of recruitment in India with detailed lists and appendices of men recruited according to region, religion, time-period, theatre of war etc.

by the end of the war was 480,000, including 410,000 combatants and 70,000 non-combatants. Of the 282,170 combatants recruited from Punjab from 1915 until 1918, some 156,300 were Muslims, some 63,900 were Hindus and 61,970 were Sikhs, though the last religious group – the Sikhs – comprised only 12% of the population.[20] These men were mostly 'peasant-warriors' belonging to tribes designated as the 'martial races' as mentioned in the Introduction. Why did they enlist for a foreign war? The question has provoked much debate. The men, it was officially claimed, fought for their *izzat*; in his introduction to the letters of the Indian soldiers, David Omissi has observed that 'Indian soldiers fought, above all, to gain or preserve *izzat* – their honour, standing, reputation or prestige', a notion he goes on to develop in greater complexity elsewhere.[21] On the other hand, Kaushik Roy, among others, has labelled them 'quasi-mercenaries', pointing to the dense network of 'tangible goods and intangible incentives'.[22] Part of the problem lies in the very definitions; can there be more of a common ground, particularly if we up-end the telescope and move from the colonial archives to popular culture?

At the outset, it must be admitted that even within Punjab it is not possible to impose a common motive for enlistment of the 480,000 men from this province, who ranged from members of the vast land-owning families of Western Punjab to the struggling peasant-proprietors of Gujrat,

---

[20] M.S. Leigh, *The Punjab and the War*, 44–45. It is difficult to state the precise numbers mobilised from undivided Punjab. Some of the most detailed data and statistical tables are to be found in the aforementioned 'Recruiting in India: Before and During the War of 1914–1918' (L/MIL/17/5/2152) which gives the total recruitment from Punjab 'since the beginning of the war up to November 30th, 1918' as 446,976, including 349,688 combatants and 97,288 non-combatants. M. S. Leigh compiled a mass of statistics pertaining specifically to the province in *The Punjab and the War* (1922), in the section titled 'Manpower', 34–62. The figure of 480,000, quoted in the text, is from Leigh; he arrives at this by including 370,000 combatants and 70,000 non-combatants from Punjab serving in the army at the end of 1918, plus 30,000 casualties suffered during the war, and allowing another 10,000 for wastage for retirement, discharges or invaliding (40). The most detailed study of the recruitment process in Punjab through official sources in recent years is Tan Tai Yong's excellent book *The Garrison State* (2005); also see Omissi, *The Sepoy and the Raj*, 1–152.
[21] David Omissi, *Indian Voices*, 12. Omissi develops a nuanced notion of *izzat* in his exploration of the 'fighting spirit' in *The Sepoy and the Raj*, 77–84
[22] Kaushik Roy, 'Logistics and the Construction of Loyalty: The Welfare Mechanism in the Indian Army 1859–1913', in Partha Sarathi Gupta and Anirudh Deshpande (eds.), *British Raj and Its Indian Armed Forces, 1857–1939* (Delhi: Oxford University Press, 2002), 98–124; and *Sepoys against the Rising Sun: The Indian Army in Far East and South East Asia* (Leiden: Brill, 2015), 397. Philip Mason has referred to the relationship as a 'combination of loyalty and expectation', see Philip Mason, *A Matter of Honour*, 406.

Rawalpindi and Jhelum to the impoverished Dogras of Kangra. Motives varied widely, from military service being a source of livelihood to family tradition and rank within the army to how crops had done that season. Enlistment was often intimately related to the history of a particular village, tribe and caste. Moreover, men from families with several generations of soldiers would have had a different relationship to the army from that of the combatants from 'non-martial' races recruited for the first time in 1917 when the recruiting base was substantially broadened. For each group, economic incentive was a central aspect, but one must take into account too nuances related to the more specific socio-cultural story of the region that intersected with issues such as family and community traditions, livelihood, faith and masculinity, among other factors.

In the absence of testimonies, let us begin with what was promised on the recruitment posters. A common poster, depicting some scenes from the 'early life of a recruit', promises 'Good Food, Good Pay, Good Treatment and a Healthy Life'.[23] Another shows a sepoy in full military uniform, rifle in hand (Figure 2.2). A closer look reveals that there is no actual figure under the dress; instead, in the place of the face, there is a big question mark, next to which is a question in Urdu: 'Who will take this money [Rupaiye], rifle [Bandooq] and uniform [Wardi]?' Below the inscription is a cupped pair of hands with a pile of coins, with the answer 'He, who immediately enlists in the army'.[24]

One can read the Urdu poster along with a popular wartime recruitment song, which circulated both in Punjabi ('Bharti ho ja ve') and in Haryanvi ('Bharti ho lyo re'):

> Get enlisted, the recruits who stand out there,
> Here you get broken slippers, there you'll get full boots, get enlisted,
> Here you get torn rags, there you'll get suits, get enlisted,
> Here you get dry bread, there you'll get biscuits, get enlisted,
> Here you'll have to struggle, there you'll get salutes, get enlisted.[25]

---

[23] See 'Some Scenes in the Early Life of a Recruit', www.iwm.org.uk/collections/item/ object/31096. The average pay of the sepoy or infantryman was Rs 11 and he received *batta* or special allowance for foreign or field service; a sowar or cavalryman was paid Rs 14, and an additional Rs 20 for the horse, totalling Rs 34.

[24] IWM, Art. IWM PST 12574, 'Who Will Take This Uniform, Money and Rifle?' (www.iwm.org.uk/ collections/item/object/31123).

[25] *Jat Gazette*, November 1914. Translated by Arshdeep Singh Brar. It was possibly composed by Bhai Chhaila Patialewala, a famous singer in early-twentieth-century Punjab, in Punjabi and then adapted by Deepchand into Haryanvi. Many of these songs are marked by a strong Urdu–Persianate lexicon, showing a highly syncretic culture.

Figure 2.2　'Who Will Wear This Uniform?', War Recruitment Poster, Imperial War Museum, 2Art.IWM PST 12574.

In the Haryanvi version in *Jat Gazette*, 'suits', 'boots' and 'salutes' (mentioned in English) are contrasted with an alternative rhyme of 'toote littar' (broken slippers), 'phatt chitthde' (torn rags) and 'sukhe tittar' (dry bread). Absent in both poster and song is any explicit appeal to imperial 'loyalty'. In spite of the official rhetoric around 'honour' or 'izzat', did the recruiting authorities know the hard truth, leading them to focus solely on incentives? The song tunnels deep into the history of military service in Punjab and translates economic logistics into the fabric of everyday life, felt on the skin and in the gut, and within the heart. Military expenditure was the largest item in the colonial budget; 10% of the entire governmental budget went to Punjabi soldiers in 1912–1913.[26] Once in the army, young recruits, used to rough village *khaddar*, would wear uniforms of machine-made finer cotton and enjoy a better diet, including a wider selection of vegetables. The key word, however, is 'salute', indicating how such service was perceived in the community. If the idea of an organic *izzat*-fuelled sepoy is now being increasingly dismissed as the product of colonial myth-making, the idea of the sepoy as a hardened mercenary, on the other hand, speaks to a post-nationalist moment rather than to the complex psychosocial world of the sepoy in 1914. The craved-for 'salute', while intimately related to, and dependent on, land and money, could not wholly be reduced to them; a Victoria or Military Cross, or even a far lesser medal, had a certain aura and prestige in the community that went beyond the colour of money.[27]

While military historians have increasingly noted the role of 'society and politics' in shaping the army, such observations also need to be nuanced to a more intimate history of feelings.[28] The colonial patronage, high visibility and consequent prestige accorded to the Punjabi soldier from 1880 to 1920 created their own particular affective structures. Two issues, in particular, should be noted. First, as discussed in Chapter 1, in 1914 – when Indian nationalism had not fully defined itself and the prestige of the empire was

[26] See Mazumder, *The Indian Army*, 1, 22–23. Mazumder provides the statements of financial returns and in-depth discussion of military expenditure on Punjabis, 5–6, 19–30.
[27] In this regard, I was highly struck by Shrabani Basu's recovery of the fascinating story of Satoori Devi, the widow of Gabar Singh Negi, who would pin her dead husband's Victoria Cross on her sari, and accept the salutes of the people on the streets, or later at the Memorial, on behalf of her husband. See Shrabani Basu, *For King and Another Country*, 192. The soldier was accorded a certain respect, particularly in the rural communities, and the British built upon this with their notion of *izzat*, as motivation for the Sirkar. However much we deconstruct the idea of *izzat*, I realised during my field trips in Punjab in 2014 that it continues to hold remarkable emotional power, particularly in the villages.
[28] According to Amitav Ghosh, the one thing that has remained 'constant' in such history is 'the sepoy's ambivalent relationship to his job', Foreword to Kant, *'If I die here'*, 9.

unmatched – employment in the British Indian army was a source of considerable pride and prestige; at the same time, there was ambivalence too, conscious or unconscious (as both Anand and Ghosh point out) about serving in the colonial army, but held in check by a range of factors, tangible and intangible. Second, as the economic historian Imran Ali has observed, military service was much more than just a 'career': 'such "professionalism" had not clarified itself in the consciousness of the Punjabis. Instead, military service was regarded as a vehicle for establishing one's status, as an individual but more importantly as part of a social group'.[29] The 'welfare mechanism' of the colonial state towards its sepoys went far beyond economic incentive into a dense network of socio-cultural relations.[30] They help one to understand the curious logic of another poster which states 'This soldier is defending India. He is protecting his home and family. The best way to help your family is to join the army.'[31] Enlistment in a colonial army is here constructed as service for 'India' and the 'defence' of the country slips into 'protection' of the family. While it is important not to confuse the state-commissioned posters and songs as 'subaltern' documents, they nonetheless take us one step closer to the sepoy.

Economic incentive was central, but it needs to be considered in conjunction with a variety of factors. Military service in Punjab was indissolubly associated with its agricultural economy.[32] For many in the arid tracts of Shahpur, Jhelum and Attock, the army was the main source of livelihood; for small-scale peasant proprietors, it supplemented agricultural income.[33] In *The Punjab Peasant in Prosperity and Debt* (1925), Malcolm Darling noted that 'the bulk of cultivators of the Punjab are born in debt, live in debt and die in debt'.[34] A survey done at the time revealed that 83% of the land-proprietors were in debt.[35] A land survey done in 1926 showed that 23% of the cultivators had 1 acre or less, 33% had 1–5 acres, 20% had 5–10 acres and 24% had over 10 acres.[36] It is revealing that the most heavily

---

[29] Imran Ali, *The Punjab under Imperialism*, 110–111.

[30] Kaushik Roy, 'The Construction of Loyalty'.

[31] The above-mentioned poster can be viewed at 'This Soldier Is Defending India', www.iwm.org.uk/collections/item/object/31129.

[32] This is indeed a standard observation among historians of Punjab: see in particular Talbot, *Punjab and the Raj* and Imran Ali, *The Punjab under Imperialism*.

[33] See Richard Fox, *Lions of the Punjab: Culture in the Making* (Berkeley: University of California Press, 1985), 44. Indeed, army service was one of the standard avenues of employment for the Punjabi cultivator, along with wage labour abroad that saw many work as policemen and watchmen in Hong Kong and Burma or as agricultural labourers in North America.

[34] Malcolm Lyall Darling, *The Punjab Peasant in Prosperity and Debt* (Oxford: Oxford University Press, 1925), 246.

[35] Darling, *The Punjab Peasant*, 4. For details about military income, see Mazumder, *The Indian Army*, 7–45.

[36] *The Agricultural Journal of India*, March 1926, 109.

recruited part of India was Rawalpindi, where the average landholding was less than 5 acres, while some of the most 'disappointing' rates of recruitment happened in the more prosperous canal colonies.[37] On the other hand, in the arid tracts of northern Gurdaspur and the Kangra districts where numerous recruits for the Dogra companies were raised, enormous amounts of cash flowed in during the war years, providing a lifeline to the entire tribe; in Gurgaon, between 1915 and 1917, remittances and pensions for military service exceeded the land revenue by Rs 75,000.[38] The army, for Darling, 'has not only saved these people from penury but has even made them prosperous'.[39] Often, there was a direct connection between the recruitment rate and the debt levels of the village: a post-war survey found that the life of the villagers in Rawalpindi, though hard, was relatively debt-free, whereas Muzaffargarh, which consisted of similar-sized land-holdings but without the military presence, was debt-ridden. The novelist Mulk Raj Anand put his finger unerringly on the pulse of war recruitment in his war novel *Across the Black Waters* (1940):

> As the second, third or fourth sons of a peasant family overburdened with debt, they had to go and earn a little ready cash to pay off the interest on the mortgage of the few acres of land, the only thing which stood between the family and its fate … Besides, the soldier pledged to fight the battles of the King-Emperor, brought the necessary prestige to keep the policeman at bay and bail out brothers, fathers or uncles, who were arrested for non-payment of rent or debt.[40]

If the governmental archives provide us with the figures and statistics, Anand – having himself been brought up in a similar family in Punjab – shows how a dense network of economic incentives and social privileges could flower at once into a pledge of loyalty.

As several scholars have noted, power and wealth in Punjab were concentrated in the hands of a few rich landholding families.[41] They were galvanised for the recruitment campaign through an elaborate system of 'rewards', including 'titles, robes and swords of honour, guns, revolvers, complimentary *sanads* (parchment rolls), cash rewards, grants of

[37] Darling, *The Punjab Peasant*, 127; Leigh, *The Punjab and the War*, 47.
[38] Talbot, *Punjab and the Raj*, 46; Home Military, B, July 1919, No. 266, Punjab State Archive, Chandigarh, 10. Also see Mazumder, *The Indian Army*, 25–27.
[39] Malcolm Lyall Darling, *Wisdom and Waste in the Punjab Village* (London: Oxford University Press, 1934), 51. Also see Mustapha Kamal Pasha, *Colonial Political Economy: Recruitment and Underdevelopment in the Punjab* (Karachi: Oxford University Press, 1998), 107–111.
[40] Mulk Raj Anand, *Across the Black Waters* (Delhi: Orient Longman, 1940).
[41] Talbot, *Punjab and the Raj*, 13–18; Imran Ali, *The Punjab under Imperialism*, 16, 98.

Government land'.[42] Moreover, there was also a strong 'chit culture' among
the military and the collaborating elite alike, enumerating the number of
recruits they had raised, in anticipation of material reward or social recognition.[43] During the war, 75,000 acres of land were made available in the
freshly constructed Lower Bari Doab Colony in order to encourage recruitment, in addition to 103,000 acres already reserved for war veterans.[44] The
land-owning families who had helped were generously rewarded. At the
end of the war, some 420,000 acres of Colony land were given to around
6,000 officers.[45] Such statistical data can be read directly alongside some of
the letters sent to the soldiers in France. A father wrote, to his son serving
at the front, 'Tell me how many times you have been in the trenches',
adding 'Remember that all who distinguish themselves in this war will certainly obtain a grant of land from the Government. I have myself read it in
the *Lyallpur Gazette* and it is also commonly spoken of'.[46]

While it is essential to uncover these deep economic underpinnings and
challenge the construction of loyalty as organic to sepoy identity, it would
be going too far to reduce the sepoy to a mercenary. According to the OED,
a 'mercenary', as commonly defined, is 'a professional soldier serving in
a foreign army'; or, as an adjective, 'mercenary' denotes 'making money
at the expense of ethics'. As mentioned earlier, in 1914, the sepoy did not
ordinarily see his service as 'unethical': as examined in Chapter 1, nationalism had not yet defined itself strongly, and the indifference or even hostility of most farmers to the Ghadar movement was revealing. A certain
ambivalence, and potential for dissent, pulsed underneath, but would not
yet erupt. Moreover, a remarkable feature of the British Indian army was
that, even in 1914, it was largely viewed as a 'native' army – in fact, so dis-
proportionately high was the representation of the peasantry that it put
checks on the coercive power of the state. In the absence of any underpinning nationalist or religious fervour, the British Indian army evolved
its own affective structures – from the notion of *nām*, *namak* and *nishān*
[name or reputation, loyalty to the salt one has partaken, flag or insignia] to
the *mā-bāp* [parental] relationships between the officer and the sepoy to the
ethos of 'honour and shame' – which cannot be wholly dismissed, just as

[42] O'Dwyer, *India As I Knew It*, 224.
[43] Tahir Mahmood, 'Punjab and the First World War: Expectations and the Enticement of the
"Oriental Mind"', http://pu.edu.pk/images/journal/history/PDF-FILES/2%20TM_v5iNo2_2014
.pdf.
[44] See Imran Ali, *The Punjab under Imperialism*, 115.
[45] See Rana and Adil Chhina, 'Commemoration, The Cult of the Fallen', https://encyclopedia.1914-
1918-online.net/article/commemoration_cult_of_the_fallen_india.
[46] Letter from __ (name withheld), Sikh, from Chachrauli, Punjab to __, 3rd Skinner's Horse, France,
19 December, 1915, *CIM*, IOR, L/MIL/5/828, 111, British Library.

they cannot be wholly accepted at face value. Similarly, a singularly thorny issue is the much-discussed notion of *izzat*. Even if 'martial valour', as Ravi Ahuja has persuasively argued, was no longer the only (or necessarily most important) route to *izzat*, a diffused sense of the idea still clung to military service and betrayal still had enormous power to bring 'shame' to the family and village.[47] Military medals and decorations, as noted before, still enjoyed their aura. What I am trying to suggest is a more nuanced frame of reference, where incentive, *izzat* and varying degrees of ambivalence about their position in the colonial army were finely blended. Economic necessity or incentive, family and community traditions, an internalised ethos of 'martial races' and the cult of heroic masculinity were all combined, hinting at a complex structure of feeling that went beyond the reductive categories of organic loyalty or mercenary impulse, and point to an emotional world where, as we will see in Chapter 5, loyalty to one's regiment and comrades could co-exist with reservations against the colonial state. It is important to remember that, apart from occasional and isolated cases (as in Mesopotamia and Singapore), the army held together; at the same time, the very need to use force in 1917 and 1918 – whether it be because of over-recruitment from one community or broadening of the recruitment base – suggests a certain loosening of its emotional appeal, especially in times of war.

Coercion, Resistance and Reprisal: 1917–1918

It is not known when the first aggrieved letter from the front reached Punjab. As early as May 1915, letters such as the following began to arrive: 'For God's sake, don't come, don't come, don't come to this war in Europe … tell my brother Muhammud Yakub Khan for God's sake not to enlist.'[48] And traditional enticements gradually began to lose their allure.[49] As Tan Tai Yong has examined in *The Garrison State: The Military, Government and Society in Colonial Punjab, 1849–1947*, the civil and military branches came together in the war years with progressive turns of the colonial screw, with the 'class recruiting system' being replaced by the 'territorial system'.[50] The whole recruitment campaign can be divided into three rough phases: from 1914 to 1916, it was largely 'voluntary', even if propelled

---

[47] For perceptive, if differing, takes on 'izzat', see Omissi, *The Sepoy and the Raj*, 77–84, and Ravi Ahuja, 'The Corrosiveness of Comparison', in Heike Liebau, Katrin Bromber, Dyala Hamza, Katharina Lange and Ravi Ahuja (eds.), *The World in World Wars: Experiences, Perceptions and Perspectives from Africa and Asia* (Leiden: Brill, 2010), 136.

[48] Letter from Havildar Abdul Rahman from France to Naik Rajwali Khan in Baluchistan, 20 May, 1915, *CIM*, IOR L/MIL/5/825/3, 394, British Library.

[49] Report of the Chief Censor, Boulogne 29 May 1915 in Censor Vol. 1, Part III, IOR L/MIL/5/825, 394.

[50] Tan Tai Yong, *The Garrison State*, 101.

by economic incentives; in 1917, we see the beginning of the use of force, though in combination with more traditional incentives and methods; and from April to November 1918, it was largely coercion. July 1917 marked a turning point. With a fresh directive to 'double the previous flow of recruits', the province was called upon to provide a monthly total of 14,290 fighting men.[51] Recruiting became one of the main duties of the village revenue officials, who worked through 'local men of loyalty and influence'; it was also the date from when coercion became legitimised.[52] The districts of the province at the time were divided into units called 'tehsils', which were further sub-divided into 'zails'. The entire socio-administrative hierarchy – from the head of a tehsil or 'tehsildar', often an Indian civil servant, to his subordinate or the 'zaildar', usually a major landholder in the zail, to the safed posh who assisted the zaildar to the village headman or the lambardar working under him – would now be exploited.[53] Recruiting durbars were held and local depots were set up.[54] Soon a 'quota-system' was introduced, first for districts and later for villages, whereby the zaildars, sufed poshes and lambardars were required to raise a certain number of men, through their influence or by means of force.[55]

If the district war histories furnish us with names and numbers, the freshly unearthed volumes of the vernacular propaganda journal *Jat Gazette* recreate the texture of such events. Consider the following extracts, which can be read alongside the rare photograph of a Dogra recruitment meeting (Figure 2.3):

> A recruitment drive was held on the 20th of December [1917], in Jhajjar at the Jahanara Bagh. Major Pye [Recruitment Officer] and other officers, Zaildars, Lambardars, Zamindars, Safedposh were present. Various people appealed for recruitment. After that, Pandit Harswarup Shastri provided accounts of the Kshatriya *dharma* by citing classical texts and historical events and emphasized upon recruitment. Rai Sahab Pandit Prabhudayal drew the attention of the Brahmins towards recruitment and appealed to them to provide the maximum number of men. The event, to a large extent, was successful and many enlisted in the army.[56]

---

[51] V. N. Datta (ed.), *New Light on the Punjab Disturbances in 1919* (Simla: Indian Institute of Advanced Study, 1975), 488, 484.

[52] Army Department (Secret), Note No. 417 of 1917, NAI.

[53] See Tan Tai Yong *The Garrison State*, 118; also see Omissi, *The Sepoy and the Raj*, 1–46.

[54] V. N. Datta (ed.), *New Light on the Punjab Disturbances in 1919*, 484. Also see Leigh, *The Punjab and the War*, 42.

[55] In Ludhiana, four zaildars and two sufed poshes were sacked for failing to recruit the required numbers, *War History of Ludhiana District*, 17, IOR: POS 5540.

[56] *Jat Gazette*, 25 December 1917 and 26 February 1918.

Figure 2.3 Recruiting meeting taking place at the foothills of the Himalayas.
Published in *The Sphere*, 12 October 1917.

Such entries show the art of colonial recruitment brought to its insidious pitch of perfection. The entire administrative hierarchy is mobilised, local scholars, singers and folklorists are hired, caste hierarchies tapped into; often, entries in the gazette were used to encourage inter-tribal and inter-district rivalry. The *Jat Gazette*, throughout 1917 and 1918, abounds with references to such meetings held in schools, parks and community halls; such reports were meant to further enhance the recruitment drive.

From July 1917 onwards, such practices were supplemented by a whole range of coercive measures, which have largely been written out of the colonial archives. If M. S. Leigh's *The Punjab and the War* (1922) provides hints of 'non-official exertions', an alternative history from below emerges from the Congress Report on the Punjab Disturbances in 1919, believed to have been written by none other than Gandhi.[57] During the official enquiry into the Punjab disturbances in 1920, Andrew Thompson, the Chief Secretary to the Punjab Government admitted to a series of coercive measures, from the cutting off of the supply of water for irrigation to

[57] Much important material is collected in *New Light on the Punjab Disturbances* (488) which includes the 'Minutes of Evidence' & 'Note on Recruiting Methods' as appendices. See https://archive.org/stream/reportofthe commi032063mbp/reportofthecommi032063mbp_djvu.txt for the Congress Report.

levying excessive penalties on *zails* which failed to meet the recruitment quota, to the use of 'sitting *dharnas*' by recruiters until the quota had been met.[58] A direct fallout of the quota system was the practice of 'buying and selling recruits' whereby landlords, unwilling to give up their sons, would pay 'suitable men' to enlist, while urban notables 'openly purchased recruits from agencies'.[59] The rate of desertion from recruiting-centres shot up in 1917, to about 26,702, of whom 17,338 were arrested; in places such as Muzaffargarh, Multan and Gujranwala, desertion was as high as 25% of the enlistment.[60] By March 1918, 'the official and non-official exertions' had reached such a 'breaking-point' that the Lieutenant-Governor Michael O'Dwyer intervened and asked for the suspension of recruitment for ten weeks from 1 April 1918.[61] But the situation in Mesopotamia dictated otherwise, and, for the colonial officials, it involved the balancing of 'the risk of the German menace against the risk of internal disturbances'.[62] Forced into changing his mind, O'Dwyer promised to raise 200,000 men over the coming year. The governmental report hailed the results as 'astonishingly good'; Mahmood Awan, whose grandfather was recruited, described it as a reign of terror.[63]

Between April and October 1918, O'Dwyer was able to raise 77,728 men.[64] Tan Tai Yong has noted that, in these six months, recruits were raised 'through a mixture of coercion, pressure and inducements propagated by the rural elites'; O'Dwyer was also helped by the fact that men were trying to flee from a province freshly ravaged by the 'outcome of plague, malaria and influenza'.[65] In 1920, Thompson noted that, in 1918, in places such as Gujranwala, one man in every fourteen of military age was enlisted, going up to one man in three in some places.[66] The picture gets more sinister if we up-end the telescope, and move from the colonial archives to oral testimonies:

> The *tehsildar* came to our village [in Gujranwala] in the month of *Baisakh*. At night, it was proclaimed by beat of drum that all should present themselves in the morning at the village hall. As it was harvest time and also

---

[58] 'Minutes of Evidence, Punjab Government' in *New Light on the Punjab Disturbances*, 95, 192, 188.
[59] 'Minutes of Evidence', 192; also see Leigh, *The Punjab and the War*, 43.
[60] 'Minutes of Evidence', 190.
[61] Fortnightly Report, Punjab, 31 March 1918, Punjab State Archives, Chandigarh.
[62] 'Minutes of Proceedings of the Sub-Committee of Provincial Recruiting', Home (Political), 'B', 1920, February, No. 373, NAI.
[63] Home (Political Deposit), March 1918, No. 39, NAI; Awan, interviewed by author in 2014.
[64] Fortnightly Report for the Punjab, April to September 1918, Punjab State Archives, Chandigarh.
[65] Tan Tai Yong, *The Garrison State*, 138.
[66] 'Minutes of Evidence', 187.

as the people were afraid of being forcibly taken as recruits, only a small number of people attended in the morning. The tehlisdar therefore fined some 60 or 70 persons. The total amount of the fine was Rs. 1,600 ... The other people were abused and beaten and told to bring more recruits.[67]

I heard a complaint that he [the recruiter] made men to stand naked in the presence of their womenfolk ... Ghulam Muhammad of Hazara Miani told me that some women had been ill treated at Kaura Kot and also in some Pathan village, perhaps Gurna. He told me that some women had been taken to ... induce their relations either to return or to enlist. I also heard that the companions of the *tehsildar* had grazed the crops of the absconders and looted their houses ... The villagers' grievance was only about recruiting. They did not want to be recruited.[68]

The first extract is from Sardar Khan, part-proprietor of Ratali in the Gujranwala district; the second is a court testimony by Ahmad Hussain Khan, a revenue assistant, in relation to the murder of the 'overzealous' recruiter Nadir Hussain Shah, who was hacked to death by the angry villagers. Both accounts appear in the appendices of the Congress Report on the Punjab disturbances.[69] During the summer of 1918, the district officers and lambardars, themselves threatened with losses of jobs and titles if they failed to recruit, resorted to a spree of brutal measures: lists were compiled of families which had more than one son; recruits began to be bought and sold for large amounts of money; farmers who did not offer their sons were denied remission from income tax.[70] The number of men charged with offences or 'chalaned' went up by 300% in 1918 and charges were dropped when they enlisted; in Attock and Mianwali, men fled to the North West Frontier province to avoid being recruited; the water-supply to parts of Multan was cut off.[71]

Such brutality fuelled reprisal and resistance: a dangerous restlessness was setting in across the land in 1918. Vulnerable, desperate, angry, the villagers hit back. As early as April 1917, a retired subedar-major was threatened with death by a desperate mother if he did not give up her son whom he had induced to enlist, while in Hoshiarpur, mothers

---

[67] Extract from Sardar Khan, part-proprietor of Ratali in the Gujranwala district, deposed before Mr Labh Singh, M.A., Bar-at-Law, who was specially deputed to collect evidence. *The Congress Punjab Inquiry, 1919–1920*, to be found online at 'Report of the Commissioners', https://archive.org/stream/reportofthecommi032063mbp/reportofthecommi032063mbp_djvu.txt.

[68] Extract from Khan Ahmad Hussain Khan, quoted in Congress Report, 20–21.

[69] It is now widely accepted that the report was written by Gandhi: 'The task of drafting the report of this Committee was also entrusted to me.' Gandhi, *An Autobiography*, Part V, Ch. XXXV. Much of the recruitment process is detailed in Chapter II.

[70] These cases are detailed in Chapter II of the Congress Report.

[71] 'Minutes of Evidence', 190–192.

threatened recruiting officers with self-immolation if their only sons were not released.[72] An actual death occurred in January 1918 in Hissar when a villager assaulted a recruiter with a stick.[73] The next month, in Multan, a recruiting party, including the Deputy Commissioner, was waylaid into a house with the promise of recruits and then assaulted.[74] An extreme example was the murder of the above-mentioned Nadir Hussain Shah, the *tehsildar* of Bhera in Shahpur and a brutal recruiter, who was hacked to pieces on 27 July 1918 by the village lambardar; similarly, a subedar who had received several decorations and five squares of land for his recruiting effort was killed with 'every brutality and indignity'.[75] 'Severe friction' took place between the villagers and recruitment officials in Muzaffargarh, while in Shahpur, a mob resisted the arrest of seven villagers, who did not want to enlist, upon which the police opened fire.[76] A full-scale altercation erupted in June 1918 in the village of Jangae Sikanderbad in Multan when a 120-strong armed recruiting party, sent to get two recruits, was assaulted by the villagers, and an armed police force had to be installed.[77] One of the best-organised protests happened at Lakk in Shahpur, where around 1,000 men belonging to 'Janglis' or pastoral tribes inhabiting several villages got together to oppose enlistment.[78] When the police arrived, a mob surrounded the police. The landed classes, particularly the Tiwana Maliks, provided contingents of mounted men and crushed the resistance. Yet, resentments would continue to simmer for another year and find their vent in what the Congress Report called the 'unexpected exhibition of mob fury' in 1919.[79]

The Printed Voice of an Oral World: From Rumours to Recruitment and Civilian Verse

If the recruitment drive created such an upheaval in the socio-political life of the province, what were its effects on the cultural and the literary

---

[72] NAI, Home (Political Deposit), April 1917, No. 60.

[73] NAI, Home (Political Deposit), January 1918, No. 59.

[74] NAI, Home (Political Deposit), March 1918, No. 41.

[75] NAI, Home (Political Deposit), September 1918, Proc. No. 40, p. 19. A court-case into the murder was launched in which Khan, mentioned above, gave testimony; Home (Political Deposit), September 1918, Proc. No. 20, p. 16 – the murder, however, was not officially linked to recruitment.

[76] Congress Report, 19.

[77] Home (Political Deposit), (July?) 1918, Proc. No. 31, 19.

[78] The whole case is detailed in *War Services of Shahpur District*, Punjab Civil Secretariat, IOR POS 5545, 10.

[79] *New Light on Punjab Disturbances*, 16.

sphere? In the field of war studies, it is only in recent years that cultural and literary historians have turned their attention to the civilian home front – even in the context of Europe where there is an abundance of documents.[80] Such an enterprise becomes far more difficult in the context of early-twentieth-century Punjab with a literacy rate of only 6.4% among men and 0.3% among women.[81] The rates would have been significantly lower in the villages from where the soldiers were recruited. But being non-literate, as I have suggested earlier, does not mean being non-literary: like Prospero's island in *The Tempest*, this land of five rivers seemed to have been 'full of noises/Sounds and sweet airs that give delight and hurt not'.[82]

Early-twentieth-century Punjab was marked by a divide between its urban intelligentsia and rural peasantry, spread across the Muslim-dominated West and the Hindu-heavy east. As mentioned in Chapter 1, there was a flourishing print culture in the urban centres, particularly centred around Lahore. The Lahore-based *Paisa Akhbar*, the largest-selling newspaper, had a weekly sale of 13,500. However, as N. G. Barrier has astutely pointed out, the effective readership would have been higher as the newspapers would often be read out to the illiterate villagers.[83] These newspapers, however, had a very limited presence in the rural areas, where the heartbeat of society lay in its robust oral culture. The oral interacted in complex ways with the textual, particularly with the burgeoning early-twentieth-century world of print, but the spoken word dominated. It was a society that might have been illiterate but was robustly literary, abuzz with oral tales and performances: the soundscapes would have ranged from sacred sounds such as the daily *adhan* (*azan* in Urdu – call to prayer) and the reading of Guru Granth Sahib to the singing of *bhajan* and roadside performances.[84] Above all, there would be the constant flow of speech conducted in a variety of sites: the water-well, the panchayat hall, at the

---

[80] See John Horne (ed.), *State, Society and Mobilization in Europe during the First World War* (Cambridge: Cambridge University Press, 1997).

[81] *Census of India, 1901*, Vol. 1 (Calcutta: Government Printing of India, 1903), 178.

[82] William Shakespeare, *The Tempest* (Arden Shakespeare), ed. Alden T. Vaughan and Virginia Mason Vaughan (London: Bloomsbury, 2011), 254.

[83] N. G. Barrier and Paul Wallace, *The Punjabi Press, 1880–1905* (East Lansing: Michigan State University, 1970), 159; also see N. G. Barrier's seminal work *Banned: Controversial Literature and Political Control in British India, 1907–1947* (Delhi/Columbia: Manohar/University of Missouri Press, 1974); Talbot, *Punjab and the Raj*, 79. Also see Nazar Singh, 'Newspapers, Politics, and Literature in Nineteenth Century Delhi and Punjab', *Punjab Past and Present*, 24, 2 (1990), 401.

[84] See Farina Mir, *The Social Space of Language*, 91–122. In their introduction to *Another Harmony: New Essays on the Folklore of India* (Berkeley: University of California Press, 1986), Stuart Blackburn and A. K. Ramanujan note how many texts were 'probably composed orally, written down by disciples and then disseminated orally again' (4).

barber, the local grocer, the sweet-maker, in the public fairs, the cattle-market and private quarters.[85] Between 1914 and 1918, Punjab hummed continuously with stories of the war. While this world has vanished, what we do have are printed traces of this soundscape which help us to access, however partially, this sonorous world.[86]

Rumours have a hallowed place in the history of warfare, and war-time Punjab was no exception.[87] They seemed to have spread like wild-fire as soon as news of the war came through. 'How can false rumours about the war be suppressed?'[88] ran the headline of one of the issues of the Lahore-based *Dipak* in September 1914, while the Amritsar-based *Vakil* published a list of 'fantastic rumours' afloat in October.[89] 'It is difficult to stop rumours', noted *Siraj-ul-Akhbar* on 7 December 1914, while, that very week, the colonial government included a long list of 'rumours that are still in circulation'.[90] Recoverable today only from the world of print, the relation between the two was intimate: in rural Punjab, the printed word would be read out by the handful of people able to read, such as the village elder or postmaster, but then would course through the community as speech, often assuming a fresh life as it sallied forth. Combining information, misinformation, exaggeration, distortion and hearsay, rumours are deeply revealing of local anxieties, excitabilities, susceptibilities and pressure points; in times of war, they assume particular intensities of meaning and serve as lightning-rods into half-articulate fears and fantasies.[91] Given how bewildering the 'fog of war' must have been to the people of Punjab, rumours in the opening months spread like wildfire.

[85] See for example the anthropologist Haroon Khalid's article 'A World without Written Words: The Remnants of Pakistan's Oral Tradition', www.dawn.com/news/1316665; Anshu Malhotra and Farina Mir (eds.), *Punjab Reconsidered: History, Culture and Practice* (Delhi: Oxford University Press, 2012).
[86] One of the classic studies on 'soundscapes', from a more recent period and in an Islamic context, is Charles Hirschkind, *The Ethical Soundscape: Cassette Sermons and Islamic Counterpublics* (New York: Columbia University Press, 2006).
[87] In the context of India, see Indivar Kamtekar, 'The Shiver of 1942', *Studies in History*, 18, 1 (2002), 81–102; also see Sarkar, *Modern India*, 153–154; Kim Wagner, *Of Rumours and Rebels: A New History of the Indian Uprising of 1857* (London: Peter Lang, 2016). Interestingly, hardly any attention has been paid to wartime rumours in India in 1914–1918, except a brief mention by Heike Liebau, 'Kaiser Ki Jay: Perceptions of World War I and the Socio-religious Movement among the Oraons in Chota Nagpur, 1914–1916', in *The World in World Wars*, 252.
[88] *Dipak* (Lahore), 15 September 1914, Punjab Newspaper Reports (PNR), IOR/L/R/5/195, 866, British Library.
[89] *Vakil* (Amritsar), 3 October 1914, PNR, IOR/L/R/5/195, 947, British Library.
[90] NAI, Home (Political Deposit), December 1914, No. 29, 1.
[91] See Pamela Stewart and Andrew Strathern, *Witchcraft, Sorcery, Rumours and Gossip* (Cambridge: Cambridge University Press, 2004), 1–28.

The appearance of the light cruiser *SMS Emden* in the Indian Ocean captured the imagination of a nation. *Emden*, it was claimed, was a Turkish cruiser called *Muhammedan*.[92] And soon, one cruiser multiplied into several cruisers in the imagination until it was a veritable 'fleet' with a 'large contingent' about to attack various Indian ports, particularly Karachi.[93] And if war knocked on the sea front, could the home front be far behind? In November 1914, a village fair at the temple of Mohan Lal Ganj Tahsil in neighbouring Lucknow was reportedly disrupted by German soldiers and the villagers fled with their women folk, 'leaving behind them their children, and their ornaments'; car-loads and train-loads of wounded European soldiers, apparently seen in Howrah Station in Calcutta, further fanned fears.[94] German spies were reported in Lahore, German planes began to be spotted in Multan, some 62,000 German soldiers were said to have landed in Chittagong.[95] And, to add to the woes, the Emir of Afghanistan was said to have sent 400,000 soldiers to attack Peshawar.[96] Paranoia about a home invasion was closely followed by anxiety about the fate of men in the trenches: some rumours claimed that the Germans had cut off the heads of the Gurkha and Sikh soldiers and sent them to the English as punishment for mobilising non-white troops, while a parallel rumour spread that the German soldiers had refused to fight the Indians, claiming that they were friends![97] What is remarkable is the way these rumours pick on international events and discourses and provide their own gloss: the contradictory rumours of German troops in relation to the Indian sepoys actually pick up on and respond to the discursive tension in the German propaganda machine between its racist propaganda against Britain's use of colonial troops on the one hand and its attempt to befriend Indian Muslims and foment global *jihad* on the other. Similarly revealing is the timing of the rumour and the nature of transformation: oral reports that German soldiers had been carrying 'syringes … filled half with air and half with oil' which threw 'a current of fire' beset the villages in August

---

[92] *Vakil* (Amritsar), 3 October 1914, PNR, IOR/L/R/5/195, 943, British Library.
[93] Home (Political Deposit), December 1914, No. 29.
[94] *Dipak* (Lahore), 12 November 1914, PNR, IOR/L/R/5/195, 1011, British Library; also mentioned in the report of Home Department Political December 1914 Proc. No. 29, NAI.
[95] *Zamindar*, 13 October 1914, PNR, IOR/L/R/5/195, 931, British Library, *Dipak*, 22 September 1914, PNR, IOR/L/R/5/195, 885, British Library and *Hindu* (Lahore), 25 September 1914, PNR, IOR/L/R/5/195, 885, British Library; also mentioned in report of the Home Department, December 1914, NAI.
[96] *Hindu* (Lahore), 6 November 1914, PNR, IOR/L/R/5/195, 1011, British Library.
[97] *Paisa Akhbar*, 20 September 1914, PNR, IOR/L/R/5/195, 881, British Library; *Jhang Sial*, 22 September 1914, PNR, IOR/L/R/5/195, 881, British Library.

1915, a reference to the gas attack at Second Ypres on 22 April 1915 or more probably the novel use of the *Flammenwerfer* or flamethrower by the Germans, while zeppelins reached the streets of Calcutta in the guise of 'flying submarines'.[98]

For the *Zamindar*, 'the ignorance and illiteracy of the general public' afforded a 'fertile soil' for such 'dissemination', but what the rumours actually testify to is the rich inner life – the fears and fantasies – of these 'ignorant and illiterate' people, and that interiority is by no means the preserve of the bourgeoisie.[99] If the colonial state commandeered the people into allegiances of loyalty, rumours provided the much-needed space for the articulation of internal conflicts, contradictions and contestations suppressed in the official sphere. Consider, for example, the following report published in the newspaper *Akhbar-i-Am* on 7 June 1916:

> One of these rumours is that the Kaiser has captured Lord Kitchener with ten thousand troops ... A report which has gained currency among these simple-minded persons is that the Kaiser himself went to Mecca and waited at the sacred shrine for three days and three nights to know the will of God, when a voice came from above saying: 'Rise, O Messenger of God and Protector of Islam; take the Divine sword in thy hand and slay thy enemies!' ... Another mischievous rumour similarly spread by the Germans ascribes to the English the intention of digging up the grave of the Prophet Muhammed and carrying his remains to the British Museum, an intention which the English are determined to carry out at all costs ... A thousand curses on those ... who invent such rumours; ten thousand on those who spread them, and a hundred thousand on those fools who believe them![100]

Here, Lord Kitchener is being confused with General Townshend – with the latter's surrender on 25 April 1916, with indeed 10,000 Indian men – but it gets connected with the whole conflict about Muslim participation in the war. The above story of the Kaiser going to Mecca and receiving the oracle has to be read alongside an earlier rumour, reported and dismissed in the same newspaper on 3 May 1915, that the Kaiser had embraced Islam.[101] The entry of the Ottoman empire in October 1914 and the declaration of a global *jihad* through the German–Turkish propaganda machine created widespread consternation among the Indian Muslims who were threatened by Sheikh-un-Islam, on behalf of the Caliphate,

[98] *Shahid*, 11 August 1915, PNR, IOR/L/R/5/196, 471, British Library; *Siraj-ul-Akhbar*, 12 March 1917, PNR, IOR/L/R/5/199, 236, British Library.
[99] *Zamindar* (Lahore), 30 October 1914, PNR, IOR/L/R/5/195, 991, British Library.
[100] *Akhbar-i-Am* (Lahore), 7 June 1916, PNR, IOR/L/R/5/197, 488, British Library.
[101] *Akhbar-i-Am* (Lahore), 3 May 1915, PNR, IOR/L/R/5/196, 240, British Library.

with the 'fire of hell'.[102] Despite repeated assurances by the Muslim princes and religious leaders, such as the Agha Khan, many Muslim soldiers felt deeply conflicted, and it is on this fraught territory that the above rumours trade. Yet the narrative jouissance of such reports was considerable, evident in the rather extravagant bestowal of curses by the writer. Indeed, the above extract is an example of the state-sponsored burgeoning print media trying in vain to control and contain a sphere which during the war years remained largely outside the reach of the colonial authorities.

In her fascinating study *The Social Space of Language: Vernacular Culture in British Colonial Punjab* (2010), Farina Mir recovers the polyglot oral and aural world of what she calls the 'literary formation' of colonial Punjab whereby multifarious individuals shared the practices of 'producing, circulating, performing and consuming Punjabi literary texts'.[103] Key to this sphere was the age-old tradition of oral performances, from the daily recitation of religious texts and the singing of devotional songs to the narration of *qissas* such as *Heer Rānjhā* in village fairs to the performances of street-poets and *mirasis* (professional singers-cum-storytellers). A number of features underpinned this culture. First, though Urdu was declared the official language and became the principal bearer of the public sphere, Punjabi retained a stronghold as the everyday colloquial language for the ordinary people. Second, though some sectarian tensions were beginning to be felt in the wake of religious revivalism, particularly the militancy of the Arya Samaj, many of the sites of the Punjabi literary formation in the villages continued to attract plural audiences, cutting across both caste and religious divides.[104] Third, the oral and the textual did not just co-exist but evolved through constant interaction: many of the stories existed in both textual and oral versions, as with the classic *qissa Heer-Rānjhā*, and the literary culture was based around the act of public recitation and listening – the artful turn of phrase, battle of the poets, or love play among characters. Between 1884 and 1901, when Richard Temple decided to collect folktales – the basis of his three-volume *Legends of the Punjab* – he hired 'bards' to *perform* these texts, for they were stored in oral memory rather than in script; in *Romantic Tales from the Panjab* (1903) Charles Swynnerton recounts a wedding group, 'standing or squatting under a pipal tree listening to the black-bearded minstrel' narrating the story of Heer and Rānjha.[105]

[102] Quoted in Hew Strachan, *The First World War*, 100.
[103] Mir, *The Social Space of Language*, 6.
[104] *Ibid.*, 17.
[105] The continuity of this tradition of oral narratives and street performance in the 'foreign fields' of the First World War can be seen in some of the photographs in the Imperial War Museum, as of the

25

It is this popular sphere of folk and religious performances that the
colonial state tried to infiltrate. M. S. Leigh in *The Punjab and the War*
(1922) notes the 'very effective use of the local bards in working up enthusiasm'.[106] Again, the *Jat Gazette* provides tantalising insights into the cultural and literary dimensions of war mobilisation in East Punjab: leading
bards and singers were hired, recruiting songs and verses commissioned
and special performances organised during village fairs and public
meetings. A genre that was mobilised was the *Swāng*. Literally meaning
disguise or impersonation, it was a sort of open-air folk theatre involving
a group of ten to twelve people which incorporated elements of song,
enunciation, dialogue, pantomime, verse, dance and acting, and with
the orchestra seated in the middle.[107] During the war years, one of its
foremost proponents was Deepchand – partly the founder of the genre –
whose services were hired in Karnal, Hissar and Rohtak.[108] Deepchand
would often add a special session of recruiting songs at the end of the
Swāng; 'I inspire people to enlist by singing in their own language',
he once said.[109] The very titles – 'Duty', 'The Spirit of Bravery', 'The
Flag-Bearers of George V', 'The Bravery of the Jats' or 'A Jat Soldier' –
announce the dominant themes and the exhortations: 'Brave warriors
of Hindustan', 'Have courage and be a man!', 'Devour the enemy' or
'Punch the Germans'.[110] Such 'songs' were often laced with war news
('We forced Hindenburg's forces to flee/Ludendorff was handed a strong
defeat') and tied to issues of regional, clan or tribal prestige rather than
the imagination of a nation – 'The popularity of the Jats goes far and
wide/In Baghdad, in France, Basra and Egypt.' Indeed, these songs

---

outdoor performance of the Indian Porter Corps at Kut-al-Amara (see Q 24576, IWM archives).
Even more tellingly, there is a wonderful photograph of a scene from a bazaar in Kut-al-Amara,
with an Arab boy relating the story of the siege on the anniversary of the recapture of the town,
showing the importance of oral narratives to capture the non-European dimensions of the war (Q
24577, IWM archives).

[106] Leigh, *The Punjab and the War*, 42.

[107] Deepchand was different from the later Dip Chand of Sonepat, the 'Kalidas of Haryana'. See
Durga Das Mukhopadhyay, *Folk Arts and Social Communications* (Delhi: Ministry of Information
and Broadcasting, 1994), Chapter XIII; also see Anjum Katyal, *Habib Tanvir: Towards an Inclusive
Theatre* (New Delhi: Sage, 2012). For a brief introduction, see 'Theatre in Haryana', www
.indianetzone.com/37/theatre_haryana.htm.

[108] *Jat Gazette*, 15 January 1918, 6.

[109] There was controversy over Deepchand's *swāngs* after some people noted that his 'passionate songs'
might inspire 'impure thoughts'. This idea was perhaps because of the influence of Arya Samaj. See
Jat Gazette, 15 January 1918, 6.

[110] These are some of the texts sung which were extracted in *Jat Gazette* on 1, 8 and 22 January, 27
August, and 17 and 24 September 1918.

might have been part of the recruitment meeting in Gurgaon that the *Jat Gazette* records on 8 August 1918:

> Nearly 1500 people turned up at the recruitment drive at Bahadurgarh …
> A couple of songs were sung. The commissioner saw the recruits. There was
> about a hundred. A man presented both his sons … Most of the recruits were
> healthy. Four of them were quite tough and their chests were measured.[111]

At a recruitment meeting in Jhajjar, a Sanskrit scholar provided 'accounts of Kshatriya *dharma* by citing classical texts and historical events and emphasised recruitment'; buoyed by their success rates, the people of Gohana brought their sons on camels and playing 'the drum with immense joy', while, in another village, an English band accompanied some forty-seven fresh recruits, playing the *algojhā*, the flute and the *veenā*.[112]

While this rich sonic world has been lost, what we do have is a powerful corpus of printed war texts in Punjabi and Urdu published across northern India, particularly in Punjab. Over a decade, I have managed to recover several works, indicative of a much larger field of literary production arising out of the war. These range from recruitment verses such as *Bharti: On Recruiting* (1915) and *Na'ra-i-Jung* (1918) to historical treatises and pamphlets to *Qissas* and *Fasānahs*, even, including *Fasānah-i-Jung Yurap* (*A Story of the European War*) (1914), *Jarmani ke asli Halat* (*The Real Condition of Germany*) (1915), *Bahār-i-Jarman* (*The Spring of the Germans*) (1915), *Haqiqat-i-Jung* (*The Truth of the War*) (1915), *Jarman Nāmah* (*Book of the Germans*) (1915), *Bahār-i-Inglish* (*The Spring of the English*) (1916), *Bahri Jung* (an account of the naval battle of Jutland on 31 May 1916) (1917) and finally *Vaddā Jung Europe* (which I shall discuss in Chapter 8). Very little is known about their sites of circulation, but there are clues, both internal and external, that these works were meant to be read out and performed, in whole or in part, in public venues, ranging from meetings and festivals to schools and colleges. Here, I shall briefly focus on two recruitment pieces – *Bharti* (*On Recruiting*) (1915) by Tara Singh and *Nā'ra-i-Jung* (*The Call of War*) (1918) by Master Sant Singh, both published in Punjabi in Lahore, and then a selection of short Urdu poems titled *Bahār-i-Jarman* (1915), collected and published in Moradabad in United Provinces.

In a climate where Punjabi literature had very little colonial patronage (as opposed to the Urdu literary scene), the propaganda machine would have given it a definite boost. *Bharti*, written in Nastaliq script, is an odd

---

[111] *Jat Gazette*, 8 August 1918.
[112] *Jat Gazette*, 25 December 1917, 26 February and 24 September 1918.

collection of short pieces, including verses, morals, aphorisms, requests (*Dar khwast*), stories (*kahani*) and fables, each trying to justify and encourage recruitment. These short pieces habitually blend a certain Sufi mysticism about life's transience with appeals to heroic ideals of loyalty and gallantry ('Brave souls, consider this world a dream; do not be afraid to be recruited, dear friend'), which are often in tension with the stress on the economic imperatives. Consider the following verses, which mix the 'noble cause' with the lure of 'pakorās',

> 'Hold/hug tightly'
> Put your name down for recruitment
> Put your life up for a noble cause
> Be remembered by the world as a (true) Man
> Notice ['Ishtehar']: Woman, wealth and enemy flee; the one
>   who gets recruited eats *pakorās* [fried dough balls] with joy.[113]

to the uneasy coalition of morals and incentives,

> 'Sound of the clock'
> The contented people do not knowingly do wrong in the British Raj
> All those who wish the King well have a joyous time
> Death comes to the ignorant who worry for their lives, they are the ones
>   who keep their wealth buried
> Estate, authority and wealth all come from the government, Tara Singh,
>   [to] those who get recruited.
> Moral: Enlist, Celebrate the King's peace, be rewarded in both the worlds.
>   Perform your duty. Do not be a traitor ('*namak harām*').

to almost irritated hectoring tone as the 'benefits' are laid out:

> 'For the benefit of all'
> What objection do you have against recruitment? Food is from the
>   government,
> uniform is from the government, expenditure is from the government,
> protection is from the King. Be alert in the Service of the state. Sincerely.
> Note: Do not let this opportunity go away …

What each of the above pieces tries to navigate is a complex space between a strenuous ideological appeal – whether to the transience of life or heroic masculinity or the benefits of British rule – and financial incitement. The resulting tension makes for formal dissonances. In the first of the three pieces quoted above, the solemnity of the exhortation is undermined – abruptly, humorously – through the metonymy of the

---

[113] Tara Singh, *Bharti* [*On Recruiting*] (Lahore, 1915). Translated by Arshdeep Singh Brar.

'pakorās' or fried dough-balls popular across India. A tribute at once to local wit, verbal felicity and the love of food, it takes us back to the war posters promising 'good life' and the song 'Bharti ho lyo re'. The second quotation shows the complex ethos behind enlistment we have been discussing, joining immediate material rewards with a larger hinterland of 'intangible' benefits ('estate, authority and wealth') and then folding both into a rhetoric of 'duty', to be rewarded in both worlds. The key word is 'namak haram' ('disloyal' or 'betrayer'), grafting the protection extended by the colonial state to the ancient norm of loyalty; indeed, ingratitude is the implication behind the irritated query of the final piece and its advice: 'Rozgari de vich hoshiyari' ('Be smart in the choice of profession'). Partly ethos, partly incentive and partly moral pressure, the verses put their finger on the varied pulse of the recruitment psychology.

A different note is sounded in *Na'ra-i-Jung*, composed in 1918, by Master Sant Singh of the Punjab Temperance Federation, Amritsar, which had links with the Recruitment Committee. *Nāra* literally translates as 'call' or 'burst out with a gushing noise'; meaning variously 'vociferation', 'clamour', 'noise' and 'shout', the word sums up the tonal variety of this quite extraordinary collection of lyrics, written in Punjabi and Urdu.[114] It would have been part of the final push in 1918 for more troops for Mesopotamia, as is evident in the following lines: 'Suddenly emerges a cry again/Send out more help/Friends, with one more push/Fight, sons of Punjab.' Opening with 'Raag of Recruitment', with a multi-faith invocation, the poem goes on to knit together the regional, national and imperial identity in a trinity become one: 'Fight, sons of Punjab … You are brave sons of Bharat Mata … All increase the glory of King George' (3–5). As in the recruitment play *Bāṅgāli Palṭan* discussed in the previous chapter, the imperial and the nationalist claims on the sepoy are secondary to the regional identity: he is first and foremost the son of *Punjab*. Compared with *Bharti,* the tone is more hectic, even hectoring, particularly as it erupts into the roisterous song 'German Harega' ('Germany will lose'):

> The German was arrogant,
> he was whimsical,
> he vanishes into thin air (like camphor)
> along with his allies.
> Germany will lose.

---

[114] The poems are all in the 'Nastaliq' script. However, the introduction, prefatory 'Dua' (Prayer) and the last verse 'Dilawaran-e-Hind se Khitab' are in Urdu, but 'German Harega' and 'Jangi Geet' are in Punjabi.

Forced him to retreat from Paris,
Evicted from Basra,
Far away from Baghdad,
Forcing him into submission

Germany will lose

Forced him out of Jerusalem,
Destroyed them in Gaza,
Life slipped out of them
Leaving behind some possessions.
…

Germany will lose,

Hindus and Muslims,
Accompanied by Sikhs,
Send out help to the government
Salvage their 'dharam'[115]

Humour, invective, braggadocio and recruiting zeal are combined, as the
very title of this song 'German Harega' ('Germany will lose') becomes
an index of the increasing sense of desperation. The strenuous anti-
German rant is undermined by the humorous rhymes 'ghuroor' (arro-
gant), 'fitoor' (whimsical) and 'kāfoor' (vanish): what comes across is a
certain linguistic jouissance and a global imagining of the war through
the pathways of the sepoy. The final appeal to 'dharam' – defined as 'duty'
or 'religious ethics' – would be developed in the section 'Jangi Geet'
('War Song'):

One day everyone will die, then why are you are afraid of death
Wage a righteous war, may your life be worthwhile
There are many benefits to this [British] rule, highly prized and no sorrows
There is no hunger, everyone celebrates
Hospitals, railways, lakes, look at the wonders of this Raj
There is mirth, there are villages and cities, there is no end.
Hindus, Muslims, Christians … all reap benefits
Tighten your belts and fight.[116]

The very proliferation of motives – from the claims of righteous war
(referred to as 'Dharam Yudh') to the financial 'benefits' to the celebration of the wonders (referred to as 'Lehran', literally meaning 'waves') of
the British Raj – points to the absence of a strong ideological force for

---

[115] 'German Harega', *Na'ra-i-Jung*, 4–5. Translated by Arshdeep Singh Brar.
[116] 'Jangi Geet', *Na'ra-i-Jung*, 6–8.

enlistment. The First World War, unlike the Sikh wars, was anything but 'Dharam Yudh'; earlier, the poem had announced bluntly 'Earn greater respect/May poor turn rich.'

If both *Bharti* and *Na'ra-i-Jung* were part of the recruitment effort, even though composed by locals, was there any literature beyond state-sponsored propaganda? Such a speculation may seem idle in view of the paucity of sources, but the hitherto unknown *Bahār-i-Jarman* (*The Spring of the Germans*) (1915), an extraordinary anthology of short poems in Urdu edited by one Fazl-i-Hussain, hints at nothing less than a lively poetic subculture or even counterculture to mainstream literary propaganda. The title as well as the occasional anti-German rant might have been a tactical necessity to evade censorship. A collection of short subversive verses, it is a tribute to local talent and ingenuity and shows how a global conflict was appropriated, domesticated and critiqued through the twin modes of satire and comedy. Printed on cheap paper and written in colloquial Urdu, it begins with a strange, extended allegory of 'A Cricket's Funeral': 'today, when I entered the bathroom for ablution before prayers, I saw black ants dragging his [the cricket's] dead body over the wall'. No explanation of the cricket's identity is given, as the preface is followed by humorous couplets:

> Germany has fallen for the beauty of France
> Germany has fallen for the beauty of France, just as dew falls
>   on the dead grass.
> Germany runs to France like a hungry donkey runs for grass.
> Why should they not then put Belgium on a stick, life in Europe
>   is passing only on dry grass.[117]

If the refrain 'Germany has ... France' is a stock device of the oral tradition of *shayaris*, the three-fold repetition of 'ghās' (grass) or the image of Germany as 'bhukhā gadhā' (hungry donkey) hints at a more demotic kind of verse: it is debatable, though, whether it actually was such, or merely meant to parade as 'street literature'. One of the most brilliant poems in the whole collection is 'Khelne lag gaye Mamoon Mumaani Holi':

> Uncle (*mamoon*) started to Play Holi with Aunty (*mumaani*)
> Holi brought youth in old age, the merchant is playing Holi
>   with another merchant
> Why should the nephew not be shocked, Uncle starting to
>   play Holi with aunty.

---

[117] Muhammed Fazl-i-Hussain (ed.), *Bahār-i-German* [*The Spring of the Germans*] (Moradabad, 1915), 5. Translated by Asad Ali Chaudhry.

> The War in Europe has caused so much devastation, times are not
>   peaceful, nor is Holi sweet.
> Rivers of blood are flowing in Europe, in what new colours has
>   arrived the old Holi.[118]

Comedy, critique and quotidian detail are combined as the Hindu
festival of colours (Holi) is imagined as a family sport. The keyword is
'seth' ('Seth se khelne … hai sethani holi'), which means merchant with
an undertone of ill-gained wealth: the casting of the war as 'holi' between
merchants now reframes the war as a frivolous game between capitalist
nations, with hints of illegitimate colonial plunder. Such a tone is kept up
in the ironic description of the war as 'ghazab ki gadbad', literally translating as 'marvellous mess', before the grotesque transformation of the
sacred festival into 'rivers of blood' ('khoon nadiye ki'). The juxtaposition
of Holi and 'jung-e-Europe' is shocking; the key word, stitching the two,
is 'rang', meaning at once colour, style or form. In retrospect, the war
itself is constructed as a blood sport between two capitalists, showing a
far cannier and ambivalent attitude. Other poems in the collection range
across a variety of topics, from exaggerated reports of Allied offensives,
with claims such as 'Two hundred thousand [Germans] killed at midnight'
to the effects of war on everyday life in Punjab. While classic historical
accounts, such as Bose and Jalal's *Modern South Asia* (2011) tell us about
wartime inflation in India, particularly the rising prices of food grains and
kerosene, we have its sensuous evocation here through imagery and sound:

> Germany has been going on with its 'chaaein chaaein' for four
>   days, crows are teasing lions with their 'kaaein kaaein'
> We are facing inflation in market where trading is slow, such wind
>   is blowing from the West with 'saaein saeein'
> …
> First there was grain that became short in supply, now ink has become
>   expensive.[119]

Onomatopoeia and rhyme here function as both ironic and mnemonic
devices, hinting at a whole culture of recitation, quotation, repetition and
circulation: if recruitment verses exult honour and bravery, the critique of
the war is here embodied through the very poetic form, its images, sounds
and rhythms.

---

[118] *Bahār-i-Jarman*, 6.
[119] *Bahār-i-Jarman*, 10.

Unfortunately, we know very little about the origins of the anthology or these anonymous poets, but it is nonetheless an ode to local ingenuity and wit, serving as a lightning-rod into how the war was perceived and represented in popular culture and its subversive verse forms, beyond the active reach of state propaganda. The volume ends with a poem titled 'Sulahkije bas ladai ho chuki'[120] ('Reconcile, Enough, an End to Fighting Already'): what was perhaps paraded as anti-German propaganda ends up condemning the war itself, something we will see time and again. It is possible that direct critique of the Allied war efforts or of the empire, being prohibited through the Press Act, is being voiced through this seemingly 'low-quality', street-level, scurrilous publication. Though published in Moradabad, it would have resonated deeply with similar productions in Punjab, where again cultural forms such as poetry were being similarly drawn upon to articulate dissent. Consider the following poem published in the newspaper *Dodharakhanda* in Amritsar, in September 1916:

> War is nowadays waged in Europe,
> The storm of Death has spread below the sky
> Hundreds of thousands of young men have fallen prey to the
>   arrow of Death
> As if life was a borrowed thing to be returned afterwards ...
> Every youth is riddled with wounds
> It is thus that tomb is being raised on tomb
> Those soldiers who used to vaunt their prowess
> Are receiving Dum Dum bullets on their breasts
> The brave soldiers are very glad,
> For true pleasure lies in dying.
> This is, however, not war;
> It is merely the bridge over which the righteous will pass into paradise.
> To say nothing of men, angels too are afraid.
> Even Jesus Christ, who is in the fourth Heaven, is afraid,
> Lest an aeroplane should appear there.[121]

As with *Bahār-i-Jarman*, the poem is ambivalent, fractured and dissonant, veering between the officially sanctioned idea of the war as sacrifice ('brave soldiers', 'true pleasure') and the image of youths 'riddled with wounds', until it tries to get out of the ideological deadlock through the humorous image of a rather terrified Christ. But the point about the basic contradiction between religious dictates against killing and modern industrial warfare is not to be missed, and will be taken up by other writers and orators.

[120] *Bahār-i-Jarman*, 6.
[121] 'A Picture of the Battlefield', *Dodharakhanda* (Amritsar), September Edition 1916 edition, PNR, IOR/L/R/5/195, British Library.

Ambivalence and Dissent: From War Pamphlets
to Women's Folksongs

In wartime Punjab, the most powerful form of literary dissent against the imperial war effort was to be found in the pages of *Ghadar dī Gūnj*, the collected poetry and literature of the movement which first appeared in 1914. 'Oh men in arms why are you supporting my oppressors', queries Mother India in a poem called 'The Cry of the Motherland to Her Soldiers', published in 1914, adding 'Do you not know that the merciless are my enemies.'[122] However, as noted earlier, the Ghadar did not capture the popular mood. Moreover, its protest was against empire rather than against warfare; in fact, it was a parallel call to arms. What I would instead like to draw attention to in this final section is resistance to the war itself in the literature of the time, ranging from ambivalence to dissent to active denunciation, on humanistic and religious grounds rather than political ideology. I would briefly focus on two kinds of literature from the opposite ends of the social spectrum: a couple of scholarly Urdu pamphlets and lectures, namely *Fasānah-i-Jung-i-Yurap* (*The Saga of the War in Europe*), published in Lahore in 1914, and *Haqīqat-i-Jung* (*The Truth of War*), published in Delhi in 1915, and a collection of folksongs, largely in Punjabi, which survived in oral memory and was written down during the Second World War.

The *Fasānah* was co-authored by Piyare Mohan Dattatreya, a brilliant student of philosophy and economics at the Government College of Lahore, and Bishan Sahai Azad, a well-known Urdu journalist and future author of a celebrated book on the Amritsar massacre.[123] Comprising some 149 pages and a dozen illustrations with inlaid captions, the *Fasānah* was written, as the preface notes, to 'save' people from 'false rumours' and aims 'to explain how Germans forced other kingdoms to get militarily involved'. It was probably a commissioned piece of propaganda but, instead of being an anti-German diatribe, it ends up being a critique of European civilisation itself. Starting with a list of wars to have ravaged Europe from the eighteenth century onwards, it goes on to discuss various 'social ills' afflicting the continent, such as escalation in the number of divorces in France, which apparently had shot up from 10,818 in 1908 to 13,058 in 1911! In a historical treatise meant to elucidate the Allied cause, any belligerent

---

[122] *Ghadar dī Gūnj*, BL, IOR, Mss Eur E288, 16.
[123] For details on the authors, see 'Dr. Ram Mohan Dattatreya', www.ikashmir.net/tributes/rmdatatreya.html.

agenda or defence is undercut not by anti-colonial dissent but by exposure of the horrors of the war itself. It describes the battlefield repeatedly as a place of slaughter ('maqtal') rather than a site of honour or sacrifice. The most remarkable passage in the text is the opening section, titled 'Day of Judgement-like Scenes in the World of the Living'. Any analogy for this, the authors note, must surely be the present war. They then go on to develop the idea with imagery so extraordinary that it deserves to be quoted at length:

> Red clouds overcast the land of Europe and send down a rain of arrows and spears creating torrents of blood. Hundreds and thousands of innocent people are being killed and their souls in unison are begging the creator of all the worlds for mercy and justice. Thousands of young women are becoming widows through no fault of theirs. Their remaining lives will be spent crying and mourning.
>
> Hundreds and thousands of children have been orphaned … Dozens of cities have been affected and hundreds of families affected. Thousands of human beings drift aimlessly from city to city and country to country … The theatre of war reminds us of the doomsday scenario. Hundreds of thousands of soldiers move towards each other carrying deadly weapons to kill each other. Deadly sound from guns and cannons booms all around. Everything is engulfed in smoke. Cries of the injured soldiers can melt even rocks. But the bloodthirsty warriors are not moved by these sights. And if we peep through the smoke shield created by cannons and guns, what we see is even more frightening. Injured horses are running around scared. Rivers of blood are flowing on the land. Soldiers who were hale and hearty only hours ago are lying crushed on the ground beyond recognition. Dead are lying in heaps. Trenches and bunkers which were there to protect the living are now full of those who either have their arm torn away or are without a leg …
>
> All around are mounds of bloody unshrouded bodies. Occasionally we see a uniformed soldier, who himself is perhaps minutes away from the claws of death, going through the pockets of his dead colleagues. Can there be a more dreadful scene? Can there be a more frightening place? War is a calamity greater than any other calamity.[124]

The visceral power of the above passage is almost unmatched in literature produced in India in 1914–1918: a generic mythic imagination about warfare, crowded with 'arrows and spears', evolves into a graphic vision of trench warfare one would expect in the writings of Wilfred Owen or Henri

---

[124] Bishan Sahai Azad and Piyare Mohan Dattatreya, *Fasānah-i-Jung-i-Yurap* (Lahore: C. L. Alam and Company, 1914), 2–4. I am grateful to Asad Ali Chaudhry and Pragya Dhital for translating the text and for discussing it with me in illuminating detail.

Barbusse. What makes it remarkable is that it would be produced by two civilian Indian writers as early as 1914.

It is likely that both authors were Hindu, and that Azad was an adopted pen-name, tagged after 'Bishan Sahai'. It is indeed a tribute to the syncretic culture of the time that not only was the text written in Urdu but also the apocalyptic imagery recalls the tradition of *Marsiya, Nūhah* and *Soz* – elegiac laments sung for the martyrs of Karbala.[125] The immediacy of the address, the list of rhetorical questions and the cumulative intensity of calamitous details are all redolent of the aforesaid elegiac forms and traditions of religious sermons; they are here employed to redress the problems of distance, scale and communication for the general public: how can the war, so remote and yet so immense, be brought home? Moreover, for many Muslim subjects, the First World War would have been a continuation of the Balkan Wars, marked by European expansionism; the entry of the Ottoman Empire into the war, and the Ottoman–German propaganda of a global *jihad*, added to the consternation.[126] Written to expose the 'greediness of Kaiser Wilhelm', it shows a deeply conflicted attitude to Europe itself, reminiscent of the critiques of Tagore and Iqbal we will discuss in the final chapter. But what distinguishes the above is its combination of narrative drama and visceral imagery. Starting with the apocalyptic imagery of the clouds, it moves from the general cost of war – widows, orphans, damaged cities – to the immediacy of cannon booms and cries of injured soldiers until we are asked to 'peep through the smoke shield' and view modern industrial war in all its gory detail. As in trench poetry, protest is voiced through a structure of bodily damage. The key imagery is that of blood ('khoon' or 'lahu'), from the opening reference to 'khooni bādal' ('blood-laden clouds') and 'khoon ki nadiyā' ('torrents of blood') through the bloodthirsty ('khoon ke pyāse') warriors to the description of 'rivers of blood' ('lahu kā dariyā') and 'bloody unshrouded bodies' ('khoon aludā bekafan'), the 'kafan' poignantly evoking the shroud used to cover the dead. One is reminded of the Bengali doctor Kalyan Mukherji, who, serving injured soldiers in Mesopotamia, had exclaimed 'Rivers of blood, red in colour – everywhere – I was covered in blood. Why is there so much blood?', while the British trench soldier-poet Ivor Gurney, serving on the Western Front, wrote memorably about 'that

[125] During Ashura, the tenth day of Muharram, this is expressed through both verbal/aural and physical 'mātam' (mourning), the latter ranging from the beating of the chest as elegies are heard/recited to cutting oneself.
[126] See Hew Strachan, *The First World War*, particularly his chapter on 'Jihad' (97–128).

red wet/Thing I must somehow forget'.[127] If Mahatma Gandhi had used statistics of cholera deaths in villages as an argument for enlistment ('How many men does cholera ... take away every year?'), *Fasānah* provides its fierce rebuttal: 'Has anyone ever heard of cholera bringing down beautiful palaces?' Through intimate physical details – from 'pushtie aur bunker' ('ditches and bunkers') to descriptions of soldiers crushed to the ground ('zamin par kuchle para hey') to mutilated body parts – it builds up its critique of the war as 'wehshiānā' (barbaric). Such knowledge, the treatise argues, should teach Europe not to give 'cannons and torpedoes' any more 'qadar' (respect) than is 'wajib' (needed). In a text written to distinguish the 'good war' from the 'bad war' and justify killing when needed for self-defence, what comes across most powerfully is the religious injunction 'Qatl Na Kar' ('Do not kill').[128]

Such conflict is even more pronounced in *Haqiqat-i-Jung*. Its author Joel Waiz Lall was a teacher at a Christian boarding school, where he was involved in evangelical, literary and pastoral work; in 1914, he wrote *A History of Persian Literature*.[129] In *Haqiqat*, Waiz set out to give a potted history of the war. The introduction makes clear that the book was based on a series of wartime lectures given in various places. Being much more of a socio-historical study than *Fasānah*, it provides precise information about the geographical area and population of the belligerent states, gives logistical details of the war in terms of army numbers, weaponry and finance, and is accompanied by a remarkable Urdu map of the world at war. Yet, as in *Fasānah*, there is a central tension between its overall agenda to justify this 'good' war against 'German barbarism' and an anti-war protest which ends up being a critique of Europe itself. Consider the following passage:

> Who would have thought that such a cry will be raised from the same Europe which was a guide to the other nations? Who would have thought that at the beginning of July last year such an earthquake will take place on this continent, which was the source of light for the entire world, that this earthquake's blows will destroy lakhs of homes and darkness will spread all around? Who knew that in the bright age of sophistication there will be bloodletting on a scale beyond imagination and very difficult to put in words?
>
> The whole world considered Europe to be the source of wisdom and knowledge and skill, but before our eyes this house was burnt down in its own

---

[127] Letter from Nasiriyah, 26 July 1915, *Kalyān-Pradīp*, 292–293; Ivor Gurney, 'To His Love', in Tim Kendall (ed.), *Poetry of the First World War* (Oxford: Oxford University Press, 2013), 122.

[128] *Fasānah*, 5–15.

[129] *115th Annual Report of the Baptist Missionary Society* (London: Baptist Missionary Society, 1907), 7.

fire … In this horrific war, in one year, the number of the injured and the
dead has risen to one crore. In these times, the advances of science have
been turned into tools for killing … In the olden times people fought with
arrows and spears and swords. At the most, a million people were engaged.
But in this war, which has caused havoc in Europe, 20 million people are
fighting with all types of weaponry …

There is sadness in every house. It is absolute chaos all over … Lakhs of
young people have crossed over to the 'land of peace' … lakhs of women
face the prospect of widowhood and their innocent and orphan children
face nothing but trouble and pain.[130]

Like the *Fasānah*, the *Haqiqat* adopts the oral medium and rhetorical
devices of the Islamic religio-political sermon through its series of
questions, the use of anaphora, or the catalogue of calamities. But, instead
of dwelling on battlefield horrors, it focusses on how the war had changed
the idea of Europe in the eyes of the world.

The rhetorical questions build up the image of Europe as a source of
'Ataleeq aur rahnuma' ('learning and guidance'), 'nūr aur Tahzeeb' ('light
and civilisation') and 'hikmat kā markaz' ('source of wisdom'), only to
suggest shock and surprise at the outbreak of such a barbaric war in its heart-
land. Waiz Lall here echoes a sentiment widely shared among (anti-)colo-
nial and particularly Muslim intellectuals: if a so-called superior morality
and governance had been used in the ideological justification of European
colonialism, the war had irreversibly changed it. In Punjab, as we shall
see, the sentiment had found its greatest exponent in Muhammed Iqbal,
who had predicted even before the war that 'your civilisation will commit
suicide/With its own sword', now chiming in with the image of the house
'burnt down in its own fire'.[131] The visceral language of *Fasānah* is here
replaced by a sort of hysterical realism: 'in Europe twenty million people are
fighting … cannons with a range of sixteen miles are in operation … the
daily cost of war is more than Rs 500 million'. Such linguistic jouissance
was very much part of the oratorical style of Muslim preaching; here, it is
peculiarly affective, evoking the emotional 'truth' of the war.

The *Fasānah* and the *Haqiqat* are remnants of what would have been
a much larger literary culture of the war, the counterpoint to the heated
political discourses we discussed in Chapter 1. With their explicit aim
to combat 'false propaganda' and justify the 'good' war against German

[130] Joel Waiz Lall, *Haqiqat-i Jung* [*The Truth of the War*], trans. Asad Ali Chaudhry and Pragya Dhital
(Delhi: J. & Sons Barqi Press, 1915), 5–7.
[131] Quoted in Ayesha Jalal, *Self and Sovereignty: Individual and Community in South Asian Islam since
1850* (New York: Routledge, 2000), 170.

militarism, they were both probably commissioned pieces; yet what they end up revealing is a far more fraught and conflicted relationship to the war, as a supposed critique of German militarism ends up being a critique of Europe itself. Both draw upon the oral style of the Friday prayers to impress the immensity of the war on the masses as well as to suggest the inherent unholiness of the enterprise; the religious injunction against killing gets filtered through what Ceymil Aydin calls the 'politics of anti-Westernism'. It is debatable whether the sermons were implicitly influenced by the revolutionary sentiments of the Ghadar (which was not limited to the Sikhs) or the burgeoning Pan-Islamism during the war years. Indeed, for many Muslim subjects, the First World War would have been the latest episode in the history of European aggression; the two works follow the path of a longer tradition of Pan-Islamic dissent against colonialism, going back to Jamal al-Din al-Afghani. While both of these texts were the products of elite culture, their style and imagery, as discussed, were calculated to move the masses, and would have crossed not just the urban–rural but also the civilian–soldier divide.

If the anti-war sentiments in the above extracts were couched in a general genre of the 'history of the war', there would, however, be one group in Punjab who would unequivocally denounce the war: the village womenfolk. While elite women, from Sarojini Naidu and Sarala Devi to the 'modern girls' depicted in the *Bāṅgāli Palṭan* to aristocrats such as Sophia Duleep Singh, took an active part in the recruitment campaign, the actual victims of the war – the mothers, wives or daughters of the Punjabi soldiers – had a very different take on the conflict. Yet seldom, if ever, do they surface in the archives, except through such rare examples such as the Kishan Devi postcard, or a letter from an irate woman to her husband: 'Why do you not return? Your mother has gone out of her mind and does not sleep at home so I am alone all night. The winter and dark nights are ahead and how can I, a lone woman, stay by myself?'[132] 'Subaltern as female', writes Gayatri Spivak, 'is more deeply in the shadow.'[133] What *have* serendipitously survived are folksongs improvised and sung during the war years by these women. Coaxing, cajoling, anxious, passionate, rueful, angry, desperate, mournful, bitter and desolate in turns, these folksongs provide us with a veritable archive of female emotions, pointing to a

[132] Letter to Lance Dafadar Nasab Ali Khan from his wife, 3 November 1916, *CIM*, IOR, L/ MIL/5/826/9, 1446, British Library.
[133] Gayatri Spivak, 'Can the Subaltern Speak?', in Cary Nelson and Lawrence Grossberg (eds.), *Marxism and the Interpretation of Culture* (London: Macmillan, 1988), 257.

buried subaltern tradition of female protest. The distinguished Punjabi
poet Amarjit Chandan, who has recovered and translated many of these
songs, has called them 'the voice-overs of historical events'.[134] Most of these
songs exist in both Urdu and Punjabi versions.[135]

The emotional acuity and realism of these songs are remarkable, from
their angry initial protests against enlistment,

> May you never be enlisted
> You who leaves me behind at my parents' house
> Before we have even lived together

to desperate pleading with their husbands to be allowed to accompany
them 'take me with you to Basra then/So I will work through the night
for you/Spinning cotton on the wheel' to the moment of farewell with
which we started this chapter, as the heaviness of the eye and the heart is
set against the speed of the locomotive:

> Go slowly, O train, go slowly
> My husband is going to Basra
>
> He wears a tussar shirt,
> Go slowly, O train, go slowly, you carry
> A passenger bound for Basra.

One can read the couple of letters that have survived – 'My heart feels
that it could not sustain separation from you for a single moment'[136] – with
the sense of desolation that runs through these songs:

> Son of my father-in-law has registered for the *laam*
> He has left without even talking to me
> I don't even know where to post my letters.
>
> The roadside is lined with Jandi trees
> (All else having been ruined)

[134] See Amarjit Chandan's blogpost (www.sikhfoundation.org/sikh-punjabi-language-studies/punjabi-poetry-on-war-amarjit-chandan) and 'World War I and Its Impact on Punjabis', where many of the songs are quoted and translated (http://apnaorg.com/articles/amarjit/wwi). Also see Mahmood Awan, 'The Feminine Metaphor' (http://tns.thenews.com.pk/poetry-the-feminine-metaphor/#.V6cNoegrKUl). *TNS: News on Sunday*, January 25 2015 and 'Not Their War', *TNS*, December 7 2014 (http://tns.thenews.com.pk/world-war-1-not-punjabis-war/#.V6cPTOgrKUl). Over the last several years, I have been in conversation with Chandan and Awan.

[135] Jasdeep Singh and his wife Amanroop have now set some of these lyrics to Punjabi classical tunes from the time to bring out their emotional range and rawness.

[136] Letter to Dafadar Prayag Singh from his wife, written in Hindi, December 1915, quoted in Omissi, *Indian Voices of the Great War*, 129, 276.

> O wicked Germany, stop!
> Every household now has a widow.[137]

The word 'laam' may be a variation of the French phrase 'l'arme', a linguistic vestige from the days of the Sikh empire when former army officers drilled Punjabi soldiers using French words of command, showing how language and folk traditions remember a longer history of war and military contact. The song itself is an example of how, in the recesses of literary form, an older war was overlaid by the current conflict, only to be updated further during the Second World War: 'They have picked up our youth, this is how British Raj recruits/Many of our boys in Sudan and Burma/yearn for their motherland.'[138] These songs are 'recitative' in the sense that they were usually 'recited' rather than 'sung', bearing the rhythms and patterns of everyday speech. At the same time, the anti-German diatribe might be indicative of the work of colonial propaganda, with this most intimate of genres giving the lie to myths of authenticity. 'Testimony', observes Spivak, 'is the genre of the subaltern giving witness to oppression … editorial control varies in degree but is never absent.'[139] At the same time, they try to bargain with the British as they try to protect their husbands – 'Married men win battles/Tell me, O *firangi*/Where is this written?'

Perhaps the most poignant testimonies to have emerged from the war, they soon erupt in a fury of denunciation, delving into a much longer history of war and suffering and death in this troubled region:

> War destroys towns and ports, it destroys huts
> I shed tears, come and speak to me
> All birds, all smiles have vanished
> And the boats sunk
> Graves devour our flesh and blood.[140]

---

[137] The originals are extracted in S. S. Bedi (ed), *Punjab da lok sahit* (Navyug, 1968). The above translations are all by Amarjit Chandan, and they appeared, alongside the originals, in the exhibition 'The Sikhs and the First World War' put on by UK Punjab Heritage, SOAS, 2014. Some of them can be found in 'The World War and Its Impact' and *The Singing of the Scythe*, 2014, No. 3 (www.mptmagazine.com/poem/punjabi-folksongs-703).

[138] Quoted and translated in Mahmood Awan, 'The Feminine Metaphor'. I am grateful to Amarjit Chandan for his suggestion that 'laam' is a variation of 'l'arme'; however, Rana Chhina offers a different interpretation, noting that 'laam' refers to 'lamba', or 'long': the long war.

[139] Gayatri Spivak, 'Three Women's Texts and Circumfession', in Alfred Hornung and Ernstpeter Ruhe (ed.), *Postcolonialism & Autobiography: Michelle Cliff, David Dabydeen, Opel Palmer Adisa* (Amsterdam: Rodopi, 1998), 7.

[140] Chandan, 'World War I and Its Impact'. According to Chandan, 'The women hate war and the warmongers, whether the British or the Germans … There is nowhere any hint of martyrdom in these songs. They knew their men were mercenaries and not fighters in the Sikh or Rajput or *jihadi* tradition.'

The references to the destruction of 'sheher' (cities), 'bandargāh' (ports) and 'jhuggiyān' (huts) repeat what we already heard in *Fasānah-i-Jung-i-Yurap* and *Haqiqat-i-Jung* but in a key far more searing and personal; what they testify to is a world of broken relationships ('tut gaiyān yāriyān'). and the harsh facts underlying recruitment – 'children of poor people perishing in Basra' ('bachde ghareebān de/Basre wich moye ne'). When placed next to such simple, honest, brutal poetry, the chiselled aestheticised English verse of the upper-class nationalist woman-poet Sarojini Naidu extolling the 'sacrifice' of Indian sepoys sounds obscene:

> Scattered like shells on Egyptian sands
> They lie with pale brows and brave, broken hands.
> …
> And you honour the deeds of the deathless ones,
> Remember the blood of thy martyred sons![141]

The juxtaposition shows how support for the war was fundamentally split not on the axis of gender – lots of Indian women, such as Sarala Devi, Sophie Duleep Singh and Mrs P. Roy, rallied to the cause of war and empire – but often along the axis of class. The cousins of these Punjabi women were not their upper-class, privilege-encrusted sisters but the wives and mothers and daughters of other colonial recruits across the world, pointing to a transnational poetics of female protest from below. A line from a First World War Punjabi folksong, 'Stop butchering now, our sons are already dead', finds its echo in the songs of East African village women: 'Helter-skelter! Helter-skelter!/What have you done, Sir?/Germany has completely finished off our young men.'[142]

In one of the most celebrated and moving poems in Punjabi, 'To Waris Shah', written in the aftermath of the Partition (1947), the poet Amrita Pritam would directly address her literary ancestor:

> Once wept a daughter of the Punjab [Heer], your pen unleashed
> a million cries
> Today millions of them weep and to you, Waris Shah, they say:
> O sympathiser of sufferers! Rise and look at your Punjab![143]

[141] Sarojini Naidu, 'The Gift of India', in *The Broken Wing: Songs of Love, Death and Destiny 1915–1916* (London: William Heinemann, 1917), 5–6.
[142] Song quoted by Awan in 'Not Their War'; *Communication for New Loyalties: African Soldiers Song*, quoted in Page, *Africa and the First World War*, 15.
[143] Amrita Pritam, 'To Waris Shah', in *Alone in the Multitude*, ed. and trans. Suresh Kohli (New Delhi: Indian Literary Review, 1979), 11.

The lines could be equally applied to the effects of the First World War in the history of this blighted province. If war historians in recent years have started to look at the province beyond just the stories of the soldiers sent to various battles, what the variety of forms that I have examined lays bare is a rich, complex and multi-stranded culture that the 1914–1918 war catalysed in the province – as wars here had done before, and will do again, as with Pran Nath Mago's painting with which I began. If the Punjab government fell upon oral modes of transmission for its war efforts, texts such as *Fasānah-i-Jung-i-Yurap*, *Haqiqat-i-Jung* and the folksongs show how literary and cultural forms did not just testify to a far greater ambivalence than is usually acknowledged, but also came to function as protest when other modes of articulation were suppressed. And it is only by keeping our ear close to the ground, listening to its chants, cries and half-articulate whispers, that a fuller view of Punjab can emerge; we will return to the theme with *Vaddā Jung Europe* in Chapter 8.

PART II

Race and Representation

Figure 3.1 'Indian attending to his ablution' © Paris – Musée de l'Armée, Dist. RMN-Grand Palais/image Musée de l'Armée.

CHAPTER 3

Five Shades of 'Brown'
The Sepoy Body in Western Visual Culture

It is a photograph which has not made up its mind whether to belong to ethnology, war or art. Two sepoys, interrupted in the middle of their shower, stand like a pair of polished statues by a railway-track in France facing the camera: static, upright, semi-naked (Figure 3.1). Three uniformed European men – possibly railway officials – look on, one standing on the right and the other two squeezed in the recessive space between the two sepoys; the uniformed duo, like a visual rhyme, mirror in miniature the two sepoys in the foreground. There is a further layer of onlookers, though barely visible – the sepoys sitting at the carriage-entrance at the right, and those squatting on the ground across the tracks on the far left – in this drama of spectatorship. We also see the back view of a turbaned stooping figure who is lifting a bucket. The functional accoutrements of the shower, such as the bucket and brass water vessel or *lota* (placed in front of the sepoy on the left), are appropriated as markers of authenticity in an aesthetic project, while the nakedness of the statuesque sepoy-bodies – the smooth torso, the wet glistening skin, the soft down near the navel – contrast with the hats, uniform and brass buttons of the European officers. The photograph, labelled 'Indian attending to his ablution', was part of a series of 'photographic types' by the French photographer Jean Segaud, which includes images of uniformed Gurkhas and turbaned sepoys 'performing' their cultural habits. Segaud took the pictures in September 1914 as the first contingent of Indian troops arrived in France and made their long, circuitous journey from Marseilles to the Western Front.[1] Racialised, embellished and 'exotic', Segaud's photograph of the sepoys is the fine point where an ethno-photographic project such as *The People of India* (1868–1875) by John William Kaye and John Forbes Watson meets the aestheticism and voyeurism of Edgar Degas's toilette series (1886–1890).

---

[1] See Das, *Indian Troops in Europe*, 45–77; also see Morton-Jack, *The Indian Army on the Western Front*, 134–153.

What is remarkable about Segaud's image is the copiousness of the detail and the camera's power to render capaciousness as the profusion of bodies and objects not only define space and perspective but introduce chance. 'No matter how artful the photographer, no matter how carefully posed his subject', notes Walter Benjamin, 'the beholder feels an irresistible urge to search a picture for the tiny spark of contingency, of the here and now, with which reality has (so to speak) seared the subject.'[2] Indeed, the barely visible body-parts that unintentionally intrude into the frame – the turbaned heads of the onlookers squatting at the carriage-entrance, the white-clad back of the stooping figure or the left arm and leg of the third similarly undressed sepoy (largely hidden behind the left-hand figure) washing himself – are all 'tiny sparks' that animate the photograph and assert sepoy-life and movement. The pile-up of clothes and shoes and the running water are the material deposits of the 'here and now', the trace of contingency. The aura of the photograph partly lies in the quality of light as it illuminates the wet, smooth, brown skin, especially around the torso and the hands, with the sheen spilling onto the flooded surfaces of the railway tracks. The short turban on the head of the tall, young man, his soft growth of beard (partly in shadow) and the *kara* (bracelet) on his left arm identify him as a 'Sikh'. But this is not the conventional 'martial' Sikh: instead he looks somewhat uncomfortable – brows knitted, arms stiffened, toe curled – as the European camera, Actaeon-like, gazes at his body. Indeed, the tableau of the 'Sikh bathing' becomes an 'item' in memoirs, photographs and sketches. A strikingly similar photograph, treading a fine line between war and ethnology, can be found in one of the war albums of General Reginald Savory (Figure 3.2) who served with the Indian troops in Egypt and Gallipoli.[3] The close-up shows a young Sikh with his hair loose and tumbling down, while the second image bears an uncanny resemblance to the one by Segaud above – though the figures seem somewhat more relaxed in Savory.

Visual theory and cultural history can be uneasy bedfellows. If scholars working on photography stress its formal dimensions, reminding us of the 'poetics of flash', social and cultural historians, it is often alleged, 'flatten' photographs into narrative embellishments or naive ideological gestures, or worse, to a direct flash of reality.[4] The relationship is particularly

[2] Walter Benjamin, 'A Little History of Photography', in *Selected Writings, Volume 1 Part 2, 1931–1934*, trans. Rodney Livingstone and others, ed. Michael W. Jennings (Cambridge: Belknap Press, 1999), 510.

[3] Photograph Album of General Reginald Savory, NAM, 1976-05-51 (86).

[4] For works on photography, some of the classic texts remain Roland Barthes, *Camera Lucida: Reflections on Photography* (New York: Hill and Wang/Farrar, Straus and Giroud, 1981) and Rosalind Krauss,

Figure 3.2   Sikhs at toilette. Album of General Reginald Savory, 1976-05-51 (86). Courtesy of the Council of the National Army Museum.

complex in the field of colonial photography because of the 'doubled history', as Christopher Pinney has noted, of the disciplines of anthropology and photography.[5] If the subjects of such photographs have traditionally been viewed as the muted objects of the colonial gaze, recent research has stressed a more reciprocal, though admittedly asymmetrical, relationship. Thus, the recent reconceptualisation of photographs as 'raw histories' by anthropologists such as Elizabeth Edwards helps us to go beyond a straight-forward vocabulary of power and domination in favour of a more complex Barthesian 'semiosis'.[6] In the bathing photographs above, the racialisation of the sepoy-body co-exists with a process of individuation which marks the genre's difference from nineteenth-century ethnographic photographs. If the war had turned Europe into an ethnological theatre, these men start

The Optical Unconscious (Cambridge: MIT Press, 1994); also see Ulrich Baer, 'Photography and Hysteria: Towards a Poetics of the Flash', *The Yale Journal of Criticism*, 7, 1 (1994), 41–77.

[5] Christopher Pinney, *Photography and Anthropology* (London: Reaktion, 2012), 17–29; also see Christopher Pinney, *The Coming of Photography to India* (London: The British Library, 2008) and Zahid R. Chaudhary, *Afterimage of Empire: Photography in Nineteenth-Century India* (Minneapolis: University of Minnesota Press, 2012).

[6] Elizabeth Edwards, *Raw Histories: Photographs, Anthropology and Museums* (Oxford: Berg, 2001), 10. Also see her *The Camera as Historian: Amateur Photographers and Historical Imagination, 1885–1918* (Durham: Duke University Press, 2012).

impinging on the European visual unconscious as individuals rather than as types. Moreover, the 'native' in the modern European setting, as I shall examine below, causes a certain shift in the relation between subject and landscape. *Mis-en-scène* and 'raw history', staged tableau and quotidian detail, stasis and movement, ethnology and individuation are all combined.

The anonymous sepoy stands at the intersection not only of railway tracks but of different ways of looking at the sepoy-body: nineteenth-century ethnography and anthropology, the theory of the 'martial races' as well as the history of colonial warfare are all rolled into a generalised 'military orientalism'.[7] The images discussed above are among the several thousand photographs of Indian sepoys and non-combatants in the different theatres, from France and Mesopotamia to Gallipoli and Egypt (photographs of the East African campaign are rare).[8] Who took them? In *First World War Photographers* (1989), Jane Carmichael notes three main categories of photographers – official, press or commercial and private or amateur. The official and the press photographers mainly used one or a combination of the following four kinds of cameras: hand-held folding plate, single-lens reflex, panoramic and field cameras.[9] The Indian Expeditionary Force (IEF) did not have a strictly 'official' photographer but several distinguished commercial photographers and agencies – Horace Grant in Marseilles and Orléans, Jean Segaud, Roger Viollet and H. D. Girdwood on the Western Front, and Ariel Varges in Macedonia and Mesopotamia – took a keen interest in them. Some were exploited for propaganda and commercial purposes and published in newspapers, magazines and journals. In addition, there are hundreds of 'private' photographs from army officers, amateurs and enthusiasts. If the Crimean War was the first war to be photographed extensively, the First World War was marked by what Jay Winter has called the 'Kodak' revolution.[10] The availability of these slim pocket-sized cameras at comparatively cheap prices allowed the ordinary European soldier and civilian to photograph the war on an unprecedented scale. A small number of Indian officers and non-combatants (particularly doctors) owned cameras, but it was rare; the

---

[7] Patrick Porter, *Military Orientalism: Eastern War through Western Eyes* (London: Hurst and Company, 2009).

[8] One of the very few military historians to use visual material as cultural artefact is Peter Stanley's inventive *Die in Battle, Do Not Despair*, but Stanley's focus is on what the pictures tell us rather than their form.

[9] Jane Carmichael, *First World War Photographers* (London and New York: Routledge, 1989), 1, 4.

[10] Jay Winter, *War beyond Words: Languages of Remembrance from the Great War to the Present* (Cambridge: Cambridge University Press, 2017), 36.

vast majority of sepoy photographs we have in the First World War was
taken by Europeans.[11]

This chapter examines some of these art forms, mainly photographs,
as 'visual manuscripts' and seeks to both excavate and analyse the formation of a complex and multi-striated visual culture around the sepoy. The
Indian sepoy, I argue, causes a certain *tremor in the European field of perception and representation* and opens up a surfeit of meaning that could
not be contained within the existing vocabularies of race, war and empire,
while being shaped by them. Moreover, in the absence of first-person testimonies, these images – photographs as well as sketches and paintings –
remain some of the most eloquent descriptions of sepoy activities abroad;
occasionally, they open their worlds up in more oblique ways, suggesting
moments, emotions and impulses around which there is otherwise only
silence. If photographs are too often used as embellishments in First World
War histories, I wish here to investigate both their contextual and formal
properties, and tease out their multiple intensities of meaning. Three
related points need to be made. First, how can we use these photographs as
source-material in a recuperative project while acknowledging, at the same
time, the problem of the colonial 'frame' and power-hierarchies? Second,
in visual discourses around colonial war experience, there is often a certain
essentialism at work as even the most thoughtful scholars often flatten
substantial differences of class, rank, context or the eye behind the camera
into a generalised representation of the 'black body in white imagination'.[12]
If race and war remain important categories for our analysis, I wish to
pay attention to how they intersect with and are at times overtaken by
a host of formal and circumstantial features, ranging from what Pinney
calls 'techno-materiality'[13] to issues of rank and status (combatant versus
non-combatant), the nature of the encounter and the context, the subject at hand and the landscape, and finally the aim and experience of
the photographer. In this chapter, I examine the representation of the

---

[11] There would have been some exceptions, such as the Rajput aristocrat Amar Singh, the Bengali journalist Ashutosh Roy and Captain Dr M. N. Das, among others, whom we will discuss in later chapters.
[12] Christian Koller has recovered important material on German perceptions of colonial troops but without much engagement with the specificities of the context or complexities of representation (see Christian Koller, 'German Perception of Enemy Colonial Troops' in Franziska Roy, Heike Liebau and Ravi Ahuja (eds.), *'When the War Began, We Heard of Several Kings': South Asian Prisoners in World War I Germany* (Delhi: Social Science Press, 2011), 130–148). A more sophisticated engagement is to be found in Richard Smith's study *Jamaican Volunteers in the First World War*, 100–121, where the above phrase appears.
[13] Pinney, *The Coming of Photography to India*, 9.

sepoys across five sites – Marseilles, the Western Front, Mesopotamia, the Brighton Pavilion Hospital and, finally, the POW camp at Wünsdorf – to reveal, as it were, *at least* five shades of meaning or 'brownness'. Third, the photographs did not exist by themselves but alongside, and in dialogue with, a substantial 'art archive': sketches, drawings, cartoons, watercolours and oils by artists, amateurs and officials. Examining photography within these diverse artistic processes makes possible a fuller understanding of the thickness of the visual culture.

How was the Indian sepoy viewed in the pre-War years? In terms of photography, he brings together two fields which have curiously remained separate: colonial photography and the cultural history of warfare.[14] Indeed, one of the questions this chapter asks is 'When does a war photograph become a colonial photograph?' In *Picturing Empire: Photography and the Visualization of the British Empire* (1997), James Ryan has shown how imperial–military photography was an established genre by the end of the nineteenth century. The most important photographic project in colonial India was the massive, eight-volume *The People of India* begun in 1858 by John William Kaye and J. Forbes Watson.[15] In the immediate aftermath of the Sepoy Uprising (1857), photography here did not just serve as 'imperial surveillance' but also marked out a 'stage in the transformation of ethnological curiosity into a structured framework – a sort of grid to be found in museums and exhibitions' – through which colonial subjects could be classed, raced and understood.[16]

The field where photography would prove itself particularly persuasive was in the theory of 'martial races'.[17] Soon after the Sepoy Uprising of 1857, men such as General Lord Frederick Roberts started to manipulate Victorian media, particularly *The Times*, to propagate their theories about the martial prowess of particular groups, especially the Sikhs and the Gurkhas.[18] Handbooks, photographs and sketches of

---

[14] See Santanu Das, Daniel Steinbach and Larissa Schmid (eds.), *Colonial Photography in the Era of the First World War* (London: Bloomsbury, 2019).

[15] Also see R. McKenzie, '"The Laboratory of Mankind: John McCosh and the Beginnings of Photography in British India', *History of Photography*, XI (1987), 109–118.

[16] James Ryan, *Picturing Empire: Photography and the Visualization of the British Empire* (Chicago: Chicago University Press, 1997), 158 and Thomas R. Metcalf, *Ideologies of the Raj* (Cambridge: Cambridge University Press, 1998), 119. Also see Pinney, 'Classification and Fantasy in the Photographic Construction of Caste and Tribe', *Visual Anthropology*, 3 (1990), 259–288.

[17] See Introduction, 14–15.

[18] See Heather Streets, *Martial Races*, 134. Frederic Sleigh Roberts's *Forty-One Years in India: From Subaltern to Commander-in-Chief* (London: Macmillan, 1897) went through twenty-seven editions in one year. For the popularity of the theory, see P. D. Bonarjee, *The Fighting Races of India* (1899).

the various 'fighting races' of India – the 'Gurkha', the 'Pathan', the 'Sikh', the 'Punjabi Mussalman', the 'Dogra Rajput' – began to flood the market.[19] Indian soldiers appeared on cigarette cards which were avidly collected by schoolboys, the most popular being that of the Bengal Lancer. Moreover, the Second Anglo-Afghan War (1878–1880) was perhaps the most photographed war at the time, and narratives and images of gallant Indians fighting on horseback in narrow mountainous passes fired the imperial imagination.[20] Moreover, tall and fine-limbed sepoys, with their flamboyant moustaches and regimental regalia, were an integral part of the ornamentalism of the grand *durbars*, from the proclamation of Queen Victoria as the Empress of India in 1877 to the coronation of King George V in 1911. Victorian fiction endorsed and further encouraged such notions. Rudyard Kipling's focus was on the British soldier in India, but the sepoy was never out of sight. Imperialism, orientalism, derring-do, martial race theory and heroic masculinity all blended to manufacture the image of the Indian sepoy in a range of publications, from manuals and journals to paintings, postcards and cartoons, to advertisements for boot-polish.[21] Of the various ethnic groups, images of two 'types' dominated the press: the Gurkha with his kukri and the Sikh with his whiskers and turban. Even before the sepoys had landed in France in September 1914, *Punch* published their pictures, on foot and horseback, with the caption 'India for the King'.[22] In the years leading up to the First World War, the sepoy was a recognisable type; by 1915, he had become a species.

The 'Arrival' Images: Orientalism, Self-orientalism and Beyond

The most visible of the colonial troops in the British press in 1914 were the 140,000 Indian soldiers on the Western Front. On the morning of 26 September 1914, amidst autumnal skies and a gentle breeze, the ships carrying the first of the Indian troops from the Lahore Division nudged their way into the harbour at Marseilles. The excitement exceeded all

[19] For a perceptive analysis of the theory, see Singh, *Testimonies of Indian Soldiers*, 11–34.
[20] Such paintings include *10th Bengal Lancers Negotiating the Jugdulluk Pass Supervised by a British officer, December 1879* (www.gettyimages.co.uk/detail/news-photo/second-anglo-afghan-war-10th-bengal-lancers-negotiating-the-news-photo/463901241) and *Storming the Heights at Peiwar Kotal, Afghanistan, during the Second Anglo-Afghan War, 1878* by Harry Payne (www.lookandlearn.com/blog/9556/harry-payne-artist).
[21] See John M. MacKenzie (ed.), *Imperialism and Popular Culture* (Manchester: Manchester University Press, 1989).
[22] *Punch*, 9 September 1914.

expectations. Herbert Alexander, who accompanied the Indian Mule Corps to France, remembered it thus: 'Even at that early hour the streets were alive with people. From docks to camp [we] passed through streets lined with the good folk of Marseilles, who clapped their hands, cheering vociferously and shouting ... At some places we had almost to force our way through the cheering crowds.'[23] 'It was a delirious scene' noted Massia Bibikoff, a Russian artist, who stayed back to sketch the princes. 'People who were drinking in the cafes of the Canebière, men, women, officers, stood up on their chairs and shouted, "Vive Angleterre! Vivent les Hindous! Vivent les Allies.'[24] No army was so hotly pursued by the imperial paparazzi or subjected to such a variety of visual documentation as the Indian sepoys and sowars in France: they appeared in photographs, postcards, posters, water-colours, oils and cartoons. If the panoramic depiction of the Indian tents dotting the outskirts of Marseilles fell back on traditions of nineteenth-century military photography,[25] the representation of the actual men was different. Such photographs drew on two distinct but overlapping traditions: the representation of sepoys as sentinels of the Raj, exotic, martial and statuesque, going back to nineteenth-century imperial spectacles such as durbar photography and court painting; and an anthropological curiosity in their everyday habits, generating a parallel stream of 'manners and customs' images reminiscent of *The People of India.*

'There was not one less than some five feet eleven in height, slender, beautifully proportioned', rhapsodised Massia Bibikoff.[26] The wide-eyed wonder was translated by the camera into the expansiveness of the panorama which sought to capture both the 'exotic' visitors and the local audience to establish 'a setting, a situation, a social context'.[27] One of the most iconic early pictures, taken by the British photographer Horace Grant and appearing in the *Daily Mirror* on 2 October 1914, shows Indian lancers 'in swinging gait', marching along the cobbled streets of Orléans, followed by mule-carts; jubilant French men and women throng on either side, several layers deep (Figure 3.3). Hats, heads and hands clapping frame our view of the 'procession'. This is very much in the tradition of 'high-altitude'

---

[23] Herbert Alexander, *On Two Fronts, Being the Adventures of an Indian Mule Corps in France and Gallipoli* (New York: Dutton, 1917), 27–29. Alexander's nephew Norman Wimbush would do some wonderful sketches of sepoys in Gallipoli.

[24] Massia Bibikoff, *Our Indians in Marseilles*, trans. L. Huxley (London: Smith, Elder, & Co., 1915), 1.

[25] For a discussion of photography during the Abyssinia campaign, see James Ryan, *Picturing Empire*, 78–83.

[26] Bibikoff, *Our Indians in Marseilles*, 17.

[27] Pinney, *Photography and Anthropology*, 55.

Figure 3.3 Indian soldiers marching at Orléans. *Daily Mirror*, 2 October 1914.

imperial spectacles.[28] At the same time, there is a reversal of the colonial visual trope. Instead of the lone European against the 'swarming crowd' of natives, the sepoys are here surrounded by hundreds of French people. Second, in an example of how war influences the cultural history of photography, there is the inauguration of a new tradition already seen in the opening photograph of this chapter: the Indians are not viewed against some native bush or purling brook, but framed against Western iconic landmarks, such as the cathedral at Orléans, the statue of Jean d'Arc or the Gare du Nord. This iconography of 'ornamentalism'[29] reaches a climactic point in a series of photographs taken by the acclaimed French agency Roger Viollet showing the Indian troops marching on the Champs-Élysées on 14 July 1916 for the Bastille Day Parade (Figure 3.4). Here, the local French people no longer just watch and clap, as in the 'arrival' pictures, but join the sepoys, who, after two years in France, look more relaxed. The contrast with the opening bathing photograph cannot be greater; the sepoys here confidently grin at the camera, enjoying the attention of the crowd. Some of the Parisians too pose for the camera, wanting to be part of the moment: an imperial tableau is turned into an image of cultural encounter. The photograph of a French woman giving flowers to a Jat officer was reproduced in the French newspaper *J'ai vu* (Figure 3.5) and made into a popular postcard, while a silk postcard depicted the Sikh sepoy as a 'heart-killer'.

From October 1914, photographs of the Indian arrival started appearing in a range of newspapers, journals and magazines, from *L'Illustration* and *Le Petit Journal* in France to *The Times*, *The Illustrated London News* and weekly tabloid *The Bystander* in Great Britain.[30] They were depicted through the tropes of loyalty and gallantry, partly out of imperial conviction, and partly to counter the German depiction of Allied colonial troops as cannibals.[31] 'To uphold the Izzat of the British Raj against an aggressive and relentless enemy' announced *The Bystander* (Figure 3.6) on 7 October 1914; it combined crowded 'arrival' scenes, discussed above, with insets of two figures, described as martial 'types', marching through the streets

---

[28] *Ibid.*

[29] David Cannadine uses the phrase in *Ornamentalism*, where, in a different context, he has described the troops as 'veritable walking Christmas trees of stars and collars, medals and sashes', 95.

[30] See *L'Image de la Guerre* (1914–1915) with its caption 'Les Hindous Marseilles'; a watercolour-postcard showing some turbaned Indians leading some horses is labelled 'La Grande Guerre – Les Hindous'.

[31] See Christian Koller, 'Representing Otherness: African, Indian and European Soldiers' Letters and Memoirs', in Santanu Das (ed.), *Race, Empire and First World War Writing* (Cambridge: Cambridge University Press, 2011), 127–142.

Figure 3.4   Indian soldiers surrounded by the local people in Paris after the Bastille Day
Parade in July 1916. Courtesy of BDIC, Paris (fonds Valois).

of Marseilles to their resting-ground – a series of white camps depicted
'from above' (reminiscent of nineteenth-century military photography, as
in pictures of the 'Balooch Regiment' in camp in the Abyssinia campaign
of 1868 in which Indian troops were used).[32] *The Sphere*, on the other hand,
carried a double-spread, using some of the same images, on 10 October
1914, describing the Indians as 'noble and majestic specimens of mankind'.[33] *The Times* ran a series of illustrated articles, with captions such as
'Our Indian Soldiers' (2 September), 'For the Indian Soldiers: Gifts from
the King and Queen' (23 October) and 'Indian Comrades of the British'
(23 December), which were in turn reproduced in a variety of newspapers
in India.

At the same time, a parallel 'manners and customs' set of representations
started to flood the market. Small-scale, domestic and at close-focus, they

---

[32]   The image can be viewed at 'The Baloch Regiment in Camp', https://en.wikipedia.org/wiki/British_
Expedition_to_Abyssinia#/media/File:The_Abyssinian_Expedition,_1868_Q69868.jpg.
[33]   *The Bystander*, 7 October 1914; *The Sphere*, 10 October 1914, 28–29.

Figure 3.5   A French woman giving flowers to an Indian (Jat) soldier.
Published in *J'ai vu*.

capture the sepoys in small groups or by themselves at the camp at Parc
Borély and later at Orléans in October 1914: resting, smoking, lounging,
cooking, playing cards, having a shave, bathing, chatting, unpacking
or practising with their new Mark III rifles, often facing away from the
camera. Most of these photographs are anonymous, and the taking of such
photographs continued well into the next year, showing the *dhobis* (washermen) hanging clothes and the barbers at work (Figure 3.7). As early
as October 1914, many of these photographs started appearing both in
British and in French newspapers; some of the popular ones were turned
into a series of postcards titled 'Guerre 1914 – Au Camp de l'"Indian
Army"– Marseilles'.[34] Taken for propaganda purposes or out of simple
curiosity, these photographs give us insights into a selection of 'everyday'

---

[34] *Image de la Guerre* ('The Indians in France', 8 October 1914, which shows them cooking). See Das,
Indian Troops in Europe, 50 for the image of one such postcard.

"To uphold the Izzat of the British Raj against an aggressive and relentless enemy"

—H.M. THE KING-EMPEROR

THE LANDING OF THE INDIAN CONTINGENT IN FRANCE
A novel spectacle much to the taste of the Marseillais

INDIAN SOLDIERS (OF WHICH THE TWO SEPARATE FIGURES ARE TYPES) MARCHING THROUGH THE STREETS OF MARSEILLES TO THEIR CAMPING GROUND

A GENERAL VIEW OF THE TROOPS "GOING INTO RESIDENCE" AT THEIR CAMP ON THE RACECOURSE
Although the Indian troops arrived at Marseilles on September 26, the message announcing the event was "delayed in transmission," presumably by the Censor, and London did not know of it till the morning of October 2. They had a great reception, and seemed greatly pleased thereby

Figure 3.6   'To uphold the Izzat of the Raj against an aggressive and relentless enemy'.
The Bystander, 7 October 1914.

Figure 3.7   An Indian barber at work. © Imperial War Museum (Q 004071).

life in the Indian camp in all its sensuousness. These photographs at once continue with and significantly depart from the tradition of *The People of India*: at one level, they are 'types', but they are also individualised, depicted in the daily quotidian round of camp activities. What is often of great interest in these photographs is not the racialised physiognomy *per se*, but rather the brown body as enmeshed in cultural habits in foreign fields: a form of *ethno-cultural phenomenology witnessed within the heart of whiteness*.

Consider the following accounts, one from the irrepressible Massia Bibikoff at Marseilles and the second from the British private George Taylor, commenting on the two most 'popular' areas of action:

> What a group! It deserves a master's pencil. The most fertile imagination could not conceive such a picture. One is bare to the waist with a sort of white skirt draped round him ... yonder is a Sikh, engaged in taking down his long hair, like a woman, and then rolling it up again in a little chignon on the top of his head. They are all squatting or lying down in the strangest

and most diversified attitudes. They are so slender, so thin, so supple that they can literally bend in two. Their knees almost touch their chin.[35]

We got amongst the Indians, the other day, they were making cakes, confectionary style. They are generally sit [*sic*] on their heels when they are working, a position which they can keep for any length of time. In this fashion they were baking. By their sides on iron plates, was their 'dough'. It looked to me like putty which had been soaked in oil. Opposite them were fires which burned on the ground. After taking a handful of dough he commenced to slap it until he had made it into the shape of a cake, which was as well rounded as if it had been done with a rolling pin. After this performance he again took the cake, put it on the plate, thence onto the fire … After a few minutes, it was baked and ready for eating.[36]

What fascinates Taylor and Bibikoff is not just the cultural but the phenomenological novelty – the perch, stretch, posture or bend of the sepoy-body in cooking or doing up the hair, in the ways it inhabits space. The sepoys had brought to Europe – along with their lances, kukris and *lotas* – different forms of bodily gestures. Particular ways of sitting, perching, squatting, holding, eating, grooming or shaving impinged on the local people of France and Flanders as surely if silently as the news of the battle of Neuve Chapelle. Consider the photograph 'An Indian barber at work' (Figure 3.7) where the camera is fascinated by the ease, intimacy and posture of the bodies during an everyday ritual. Colonialism and orientalism are categories too grand and overused to help one understand the granularity of such everyday perceptual shifts that the sepoys occasioned.

Bibikoff's *Our Indians in Marseilles* (1915) is a singularly charming diary, if slightly feverish in its orientalism. Her impressions of the Indians, both in prose and in pencil sketches, provide a wonderful parallel to the hundreds of photographs coming out of Marseilles capturing the daily activities of the sepoys. However, the most powerful sketches came from Paul Sarrut, who made some seventy pencil and ink sketches of British and Indian troops, the majority being of the latter. Very little is known about Sarrut except that he was a young French liaison officer and had access to the Indian camps; a sketch, signed 'Béthune – 16/12/1914' – offers a rare clue to when and where he operated.[37] (Figure 3.8(a)) These wonderfully intricate and deeply felt sketches, the opposite of 'martial images' or 'ethnological types', capture Indian combatants and followers in the 'most diversified attitudes': loading or unloading a cart, making a fire to cook or watching the kettle boil while sitting on their haunches (Figure 3.8(b)). His

[35] Bibikoff, *Our Indians in Marseilles*, 26.
[36] Papers of Private G. (George) Taylor, IWM, 02/55/1.
[37] Paul Sarrut, *British and Indian Troops in Northern France – 70 Sketches 1914–1915* (Arras: H. Delepine, 1915).

sketches take us to spaces not accessible to the camera or not recorded in the letters: inside a billet; or a medical station with two wounded sepoys waiting for the ambulance; or a moment of unspoken intimacy between two sepoys lying side by side, redolent of the delicate homoeroticism evoked by Owen and Remarque (Figure 3.8(c)).

Alongside Sarrut's works, there is a number of paintings, sketches and portraits of Indian soldiers by British artists, of which the most beautiful and luminous is perhaps Eric Kennington's 'The Indian Doctor' (Figure 3.9). Kennington was an official war artist and made a number of sketches of Indian sepoys. 'The Indian Doctor' was done in France in late 1917 when he was attached to the Jodhpur Imperial Service Lancers, 4th Cavalry Division (Indian). It was possibly done in a couple of hours in the Regimental Transport Lines – about three or four miles behind the front line in the Cambrai sector.[38] We do not know the identity of the young man, except his name ('Daler Singh'?) scribbled on the left-hand corner but not clearly legible; he was perhaps a doctor from the Medical Service, seconded to the Jodhpur Lancers. It is one of Kennington's finest works: done in charcoal with touches of pastel, the drawing glows. There is a certain softness and delicacy – in the half-wistful, half-dreamy look in the deep-set sensitive eyes, the play of light and shade on the contours of the face, and the soft growth of facial hair – that give it an extraordinary poignancy. Of all the sepoy images, this is the image I have come back to, time and again, while writing the book; the expressiveness and sensitivity of the face remind me of Lalu, the protagonist of Mulk Raj Anand's *Across the Black Waters*, whom I shall discuss in Chapter 8.

Scholars of South Asian history are often reluctant to draw on these sketches, which were framed by the European gaze. But works such as Sarrut's pen and ink drawing or Kennington's charcoal speak to the need for going beyond such rigid notions and all-encompassing theories of orientalism. One needs to carefully distinguish between different forms of art; Sarrut's work, for example, is radically different from the beautiful but highly orientalised pastel portraits of Indian troops by the Swiss artist Eugène Burnand.[39] Instead, his sketches are like

---

[38] I am grateful to Jonathan Black for his help with this image. He is one of the few art historians to powerfully draw attention to colonial war experience in his chapter 'Our Brown Brethren': Identity and Difference in images of non-white soldiers' in Michael Walsh and Andrekos Varnava ed. *The Great War and British Empire* (London: Routledge, 2017), 129–150.

[39] These 104 pastel portraits were drawn over a number of years in Paris, Marseilles and Montpellier, and form his celebrated *Les Alliés dans la Guerre des Nations* (The Allies in the War of Nations) (www.eugene-burnand.com). In addition to Sarrut's sketches, there is a substantial archive of pastels, paintings and sketches done of the Indians, from Gerald Spencer Pryse's *Indian and Motorbuses near Poperinge* (1914) to Philip Laszlo's enigmatic double portrait of Risaldar Jagat Singh and Man Singh. Much of this art is now slowly coming to light.

(a)

(b)

(c)

Figure 3.8   (a), (b) and (c) Pen and ink drawings by Paul Sarrut, from *British and Indian Troops in Northern France – 70 Sketches 1914–1915.*

Figure 3.9   Eric Kennington, 'Indian Doctor from the Jodhpur Imperial Service'.
Courtesy of the Estate of Kennington.

camp-notes – hurried, delicate, intimate – as he manages to capture the 'raw history' of sepoy-life behind the lines. They remain stubborn proof of how European art does not always or exclusively have to do with power relations, and that even subaltern lives can occasionally move under an European artist's touch.

Bodies in Combat: Cartoons, Posters and the Photographic World of H. D. Girdwood

Much of the substantial visual archive on the Indian sepoys on the Western Front comes from the camera of a single individual – the Canadian-born photographer Hilton Dewitt Girdwood. At once a relentless self-promoter and a genuine enthusiast for the Indian Corps, he invented the bogus title 'Geographer and Historical Photographer to the Government of India' for himself and thus remains the first self-ordained 'official cameraman' of the IEF 'A'.[40] Having spent most of his pre-war years as a commercial photographer in Europe, South Africa and India, this thirty-six-year-old man sensed opportunity and sailed with the first units of the IEF 'A' from India. After much wrangling and bitterness with the War Office, he was finally granted permission to visit the front and photograph the Indian Corps.[41] Though imperial propaganda was his stated aim, part of the reason might have been financial gain and self-advancement – though he claimed to have lost a lot of money in the process. However, through sheer tenacity and dogged determination, he built up what is possibly the most extensive visual archive of the sepoys in any theatre of the war.

Girdwood's photographs provide insights into how the Indian sepoys on the Western Front were perceived and 'framed'; occasionally, such photographs intervened in such discourses and further excited the

---

[40] For a detailed account on Girdwood, see Nicholas Hiley 'Hilton DeWitt Girdwood and the origins of British official filming', *Historical Journal of Film, Radio and Television*, 13, 2 (1993), 129–148.

[41] See Girdwood's letter to Seton, July 1915, Papers of H. D. Girdwood, India Office Records L/ P & J/6/1440, British Library. The wartime papers of Girdwood, including his fraught correspondence with the War Office, advertisements for his war film and details of post-war lecture tours, are archived in the India Office Room, British Library (L/P & J/6/1440 and L/P&J/ 6/1454, File 3569) and make fascinating reading. Also see the collection of 631 photographs, under the title 'Indian Army in Europe during the First World War by H D Girdwood', British Library Photo 24; some of these images can be viewed online at the British Library website.

then-contemporary fantasies around the sepoy-body. Girdwood carried both ordinary and stereoscopic cameras, allegedly spending some £1,000 on the equipment, and even covering his camera in 'protective brass'. During his tour, he was not allowed near the front line but, in the first four days, he managed to take photographs at around seventy locations and film at half of them, shooting a number of behind-the-lines scenes: the wounded being tended, camp-life, sepoys digging communication trenches or interacting with the locals. While these images today open up the whole world of cultural encounters behind the front line, Girdwood at the time was sorely disappointed: 'every effort was made by me to obtain permission to photograph howitzers, bursting shells, German prisoners and aeroplanes, but these four things were absolutely denied to me at every stage'.[42] Of all the war photographers, Girdwood exemplifies most powerfully the desire for what the literary critic James Campbell has called 'combat gnosticism'. Through an examination of trench poetry, Campbell argues how First World War literature constructs the idea of the body in combat as the sole source of meaning and authenticity at war so that only 'the experience of fighting provides a connection to Reality, an unmediated Truth'.[43] Similarly, Girdwood desperately tried to capture the sepoy-body in combat, and even tried to generate a sense of the photographer too being at risk. He named his company 'Realistic Travels' and described himself, in the film advertisements, as 'the man who actually faced death to take the film'.[44] Of the several hundred pictures that form Girdwood's collection, the most striking are a sequence of stereoscopic images of sepoys in the 'front line': members of the Scottish Black Watch Regiment and the 41st Dogras keeping guard in a trench, two British officers and some sepoys in an officer's shelter, or sepoys digging and reinforcing trenches. In keeping with the simulacrum function of the stereoscope – as opposed to the panorama or diorama – the images manipulate distance and perspective to emphasise immediacy and depth and 'immerse' the viewer. Consider his image of an infantry unit from the 58th Rifles undergoing training against gas attacks in Fauquissart (Figure 3.10).

<hr/>

[42] Letter of 28 October to Seton, British Library, IOR, L/P + J/6/1440. Also see Hiley, 'Girdwood', 134.
[43] Campbell analyses how trench poetry reduces a complex culture of conflict to combat-action alone, leaving out the war experience of civilians, women and non-combatants. See James Campbell, 'Combat Gnosticism: The Ideology of First World War Poetry Criticism', *New Literary History*, 30 (1999), 207.
[44] 'As we near the firing line the sound of the guns becomes terrible. Shells are continually screeching over our heads, hundreds of them from field guns, and every now and again the air would be rent like the tearing of heavy cloth', 'With Sir James Willcocks in Our Frontline Trenches', L/P & J/6/1454, File 3569, 375.

Figure 3.10 Indian Infantry from 58th Rifles training for gas attack.
© The British Library Board (Girdwood Collection, Photo 24/300).

Here, the art of the close-up creates a drama between the horizontal and vertical axes of the image – between the immediate and elongated foreground, marked by the diagonal row of rifle-barrels and bare hands clasping them, on the one hand, and the longitudinal view of the trench zigzagging its way into the distance on the other. The British smoke-hoods with their celluloid window – an early version of the gas mask – complete the air of eeriness. The reality was different. When the Indians came under gas attack for the first time in the Second Battle of Ypres in April 1915, they were largely defenceless, their only protection being their turbans, on which they were advised to urinate before then pressing them against their mouths and noses in an effort to curb the effects. By passing off a training session as an actual gas attack, Girdwood's photograph veils and dissembles.

The whole relationship between photography, propaganda and 'truth-telling' reaches its climax over Girdwood's attempts to pass off his photographs and six minutes of film footage taken in July 1915 of a Gurkha battalion rehearsing a 'practice attack' in a wood near Merville as actual

Figure 3.11   Combat Action – 'With impetuous charge, our brave hill-men of India
charge'. © The British Library Board (Girdwood Collection).

'combat shots' taken in the front-line trenches (Figure 3.11).[45] In his film
With the Empire's Fighters, now lost but widely shown at the time, the
scenes were edited into a single sequence with the following caption:

> How our Brave Troops carry a German position – Gurkhas charging a
> German trench – First line clearing out the trench and storming the second
> line – Our second line consolidates a trench captured by the stormers –
> Carrying off the wounded – Well done (136).

One of the surviving stereocards shows 'our' much-vaunted Gurkha troops
in action while a second group advances through the woods, with a plume
of smoke billowing in the background.

The possessive pronoun is kept up in the caption which reads: 'With
an impetuous charge, our brave hill-men of India charge the first line of
German trenches and pass on to capture the second line' (Figure 3.11).[46] The
War Office was not impressed. In the India Office Record of the Great War,

[45] See Hiley, 'Hilton DeWitt Girdwood', 135.
[46] L/P & J/6/1454 File 3569, IOR, BL, 374.

one finds a version of the above photograph, on which the a war official had written 'a deliberate "fake", it is a photograph of practice manoeuvres'; another photograph, 'Cutting the Wire – Where Our Gallant Heroes Fell' is similarly annotated: 'disturbing image of corpses – but is this faked?'[47] Girdwood was expressly forbidden to describe it as 'a real scene of action'.[48] Yet, in an example of the hypocrisy of the War Office itself, the faked shots were banned in the UK but allowed to be shown in India.

Girdwood's fakery was, however, an index of the obsessive contemporary interest in the sepoy-body and has to be understood in the context of a wider visual culture. If the 'arrival' images flooded the newspapers in early October, the focus soon shifted to their 'brave deeds'. The Indians held around one-third of the British line in the opening months of the war and would take part in the battles of Neuve Chapelle (March), Aubers Ridge and Festubert (May) and Loos (September–October). Stories of Khudadad Khan, with his gallantry and the Victoria Cross, filled newspaper columns. Indian sepoys would occasionally be spotted, in villages, in towns and even in Paris. Popular war imagination ran riot. In the absence of front-line images, the old 'arrival' photographs, alongside cartoons, sketches and drawings imagining the sepoy-body in action, were published in the newspapers and journals, from *The Daily Mail* to *The Sphere* and *The Bystander*. More than photographs, these drawings and their captions give clues concerning imperial imaginings around the sepoy-body. Consider the two images (Figure 3.12) from *The War Illustrated*, the first appearing on 7 November 1914 and entitled 'The Terror by Night: Our Gurkhas at Work', while the second, appearing only two weeks later, was captioned 'Sikhs and Gurkhas Cut Up the Germans in Lille'. In both, the kukri – the fish-shaped blade famously associated with the Gurkhas – is the source of drama. In the first, we have the Gurkha with the kukri creeping up on an unaware German soldier and the caption reads

> The fighting qualities of the Gurkhas, the little hillmen from Northern India … are well-known. In addition to a rifle, the Gurkha carries a keen knife with a broad fish-shaped blade. This knife he can throw for some distance with deadly accuracy. With cat-like noiselessness the Gurkha, knife in hand or in teeth, can glide through the grass until he is close to the isolated outpost and then comes the fatal throw.[49]

[47] See *India Office Official Record of the Great War*, British Library Photograph 21/48. Also see Pinney, *The Coming of Photography to India*, 80.

[48] *Ibid.*

[49] Also see *The Illustrated London News*, 7 November 1914, for a very similar representation, with the caption noting 'The Indians in the field: a gallant and successful charge at a certain place'.

Figure 3.12   'The Terror by Night: Our Gurkhas at Work', *The War Illustrated*,
7 November 1914; and 'Sikhs and Gurkhas Cut Up the Germans at Lille',
The War Illustrated, 21 November 1914.

What we have here, though, is heroism-tipping-into-primitivism: if the
phallic kukri is the point of titillated curiosity, the 'cat-like noiseless'
suggests a subhuman non-white body – furtive, stealthy, agile – now
pressed into the service of the empire. A more lurid account appeared
in the same month on the pages of *The Bystander*, which carried a full-
length cartoon of a British Tommy in conversation with an elegant society
hostess; the caption reads as follows:

> A Story from the Front:
>   TOMMY: 'One of them Ghurkas cut off a German's 'ead so clean 'e never
> felt it. 'Ye've missed me', ses the German. 'Oh! 'ave I' ses the Ghurkha – 'jest
> you try an' shake it?'[50]

And, as the German apparently tried to nod his head, it just rolled off
his shoulders! If the kukri-wielding Gurkha became a recognisable trope,
the image of the Sikh with the dagger, in hand or between his teeth, soon
became the subject of postcards.[51] The French *Petit Journal* (Figure 3.13)

---

[50] *The Bystander*, 4 November 1915, 161.
[51] A sketch captioned 'A Black Look' published in *The Bystander* (25 November 1914) shows two Indian
   soldiers – one with a rifle, the other with a dagger – hiding behind a wall, ready to ambush – in
   classic North West Frontier-style fashion – while an unsuspecting German officer rides into view.

Figure 3.13   'Nos amis d'Orient – Soldats indiens au combat'. Contemporary
Postcard, Bibliothèque Nationale de France, Paris.

depicted a Sikh soldier in fierce, flying motion, bearing down on the
thigh of a rifle-carrying but helpless German with the weight of his knees,
as he prepares to plunge the dagger into the German's breast! The most
remarkable variation on the theme, however, were two fan-shaped tab-
leaux in Japanese style by the French–Italian graphic artist Alberto Fabio
Lorenzi. The first one showed a group of Sikhs, rifles in hand and daggers
in mouth, advancing through tall trunks of trees, possibly alluding to Hill
60 (Figure 3.14). The second one dramatised the Battle of Neuve Chapelle
(10–13 March 1915), transforming what was horrendous reality – cannon,
machine-guns, artillery – into a highly aestheticised and miniaturised
version of hand-combat, in exquisite format.

The Gurkhas and the Sikhs were well-recognised 'martial types' in the
British imperial imagination.[52] But what the above images bring out is a discursive tension in the construction of such types, between the sepoy as a loyal
colonial subject and as a primitive brute. The non-white soldier mobilised
racial fantasy: the roots, as we have seen, go back to nineteenth-century

---

[52] See Lionel Caplan, *Warrior Gentlemen: Gurkhas in the Western Imagination* (New York and
Oxford: Berghahn Books, 1995); Fox, *Lions of the Punjab*.

Sikhs chargeant dans un bois de sapins raviné par l'artillerie anglaise

Cote 60. — SUD-OUEST D'YPRES

Mai 1915.

Figure 3.14   Alberto Fabio Lorenzi, 'Sikhs charging in a fir-wood furrowed
by English artillery: southwest of Ypres, May 1915'. Imperfectly circular
shape with indentation, diameter about 29 cm. Courtesy of BDIC
Collection Nanterre: EST FL 1049. (See the plate section for a colour
version of this figure.)

racial science, but how does the war affect these impulses? A popular story about the non-white soldier – applied to Indians, the *spahis* and Moroccans – was that they chopped off the ears of German soldiers and made them into a necklace round their necks. Thus, Emil Spaet, a former German civilian internee in Britain, reported that he was told by an English lieutenant that 'Indians always came back from battle with the cut-off ears and heads of German soldiers.'[53] In 2014, during an interview at his family farm outside Ypres, Paul Jacobs narrated the same story to me, saying that he had heard it from his grandfather whose farm was turned into a casualty-station after the battle of Neuve Chapelle. Sigmund Freud, in 'Thoughts for the Times on War and Death' (1915), observed that 'War strips us of the later accretions of civilisation and lays bare the primal man in each of us' and that 'We ourselves are, like the primaeval man, a gang of murderers.'[54] As European soldiers descended to the level of the 'primaeval man', was the inner paranoid acknowledgement of barbarity projected onto the racial other? The image of the Indian sepoy did not exist by itself but in relation to the British Tommy as the latter regressed into a troglodyte figure. At the same time, there might also have been an element of wish fulfilment: the fantasy of heroic hand-to-hand combat, rare in the stalemate of the trenches but vividly imagined in cultural forms (such as in Wilfred Owen's 'Strange Meeting': 'as you jabbed and killed/I parried'), gets projected too onto the sepoy.[55] The Indian sepoy becomes the site where beleaguered white mascu-linity inscribes its own anxieties and fantasies.

Girdwood's photographs both mobilise and update such fantasies. In his photographs – unlike in sketches, cartoons or even the propaganda film *With the Indians in France* (1916) – the Indian sepoys are no longer kukri-wielding pre-industrial warriors of the East but modern infan-trymen, adequately prepared by the Raj, even if this was far from the truth. In visual terms, his photographs can be said to be the rebranding of the Indian sepoys as twentieth-century fighters: they are shown to don gas masks and handle rifles, while remaining ineluctably exotic as Girdwood shows primitivism meeting modern technology. The film *With the Empire's Fighters* was premiered on 11 September 1916, and Girdwood went on an

[53] Quoted in Heather Jones, 'Imperial Captivities: Colonial Prisoners of War in Germany and the Ottoman Empire, 1914–18', in Santanu Das (ed.), *Race, Empire and First World War Writing* (Cambridge: Cambridge University Press, 2011), 181.
[54] Sigmund Freud, 'Thoughts for the Times on War and Death' (1915), in *The Standard Edition of the Complete Psychological Works*, trans. James Strachey (London: Hogarth Press, 1953–1974), Vol. XIV, 297, 299.
[55] 'Strange Meeting', *The Poems of Wilfred Owen*, ed. Jon Stallworthy (London: Chatto & Windus, 1990), 126.

extended 'lecture-tour'; he claimed to have given 866 lectures in Great Britain, reaching a million people, including 250,000 children. The film is lost, but what we do have are some of the responses it elicited.

The schoolchildren were invited to write down their reflections after watching the film. Thus, thirteen-year-old Isaac Silverman from Liverpool Hebrew Higher Grade School wrote about the most 'wonderful' and 'splendid' Gurkhas who had 'come all these thousands of miles ... to help this Great Empire' while eleven-year-old Constance Fletcher from St Paul's Girl's school wrote at greater length:

> The Gurkha Regiment, the Sikhs and Jats have distinguished themselves by their true skill, courage and bravery in the great French battles. We cannot realize the soldiers' lives of hardship and suffering ... We saw the Indian soldiers going into action, how fearless and brave they are. We saw the valuable gifts given by the native Princes of India for use in France ...
>
> The Indian soldiers interested us by the way they cooked their food and we were amused by their strange customs and manners. It is wonderful how the soldiers have endured the severe weather in France, from the tropical climate of India and some were being sent back there.[56]

The level of engagement, with its combination of sympathy, curiosity and a certain imperial consciousness, is quite astonishing; a common point of reference for both children is the kukri. Silverman wrote how the Gurkhas with 'their terrible keen-bladed kukris have instilled in the foe a dread and awe of silent death', while Fletcher noted the 'terrible Gurkha knives which have filled the Germans with terror and awe'. Meanwhile, Girdwood went on an extensive lecture-tour, first to Canada and then across India in 1920, including Bombay, Calcutta, Allahabad, Lucknow and Peshawar.[57]

While the images of the 'valiant' Sikhs and Gurkhas were being assiduously promoted, both in photography and in print, there was, however, one substantial group which was airbrushed from popular representation: the huge number of Indian non-combatants, particularly the labourers. While they mostly toiled in Mesopotamia, a contingent of 50,000 served in France, where they played an essential role.[58] While cooks and *dhobis* were woven into images of exoticism of the 'culture and manners' kind, the porters and labourers working in France are nowhere to be seen in popular drawings, magazines or newspaper articles. But, deep in the archives, one finds them too. In the BDIC archives in Paris, one comes across a hitherto

[56] 'Papers of Girdwood', L/P & J/6/1454 File 3569, 289.
[57] 'Papers of Girdwood', L/P & J/6/1454 File 3569,115, 116, IOL, BL.
[58] See Radhika Singha, 'The Short Career of the Indian Labour Corps in France', 27–62.

unknown set of images of a group of Indian labourers, without proper gloves or boots, toiling at a construction-site for a British aerodrome at Azelot in north-eastern France in February 1918: digging drainage trenches, felling trees and chopping wood. An English officer recorded that it was 'bitterly cold' and the Azelot communal cemetery – close to where the aerodrome was sited – contains the graves of four Indians, all of whom died between February and April 1918.[59] We will examine the experiences of some of these men in Chapter 7, but they appear far more frequently in images from the Levant and the Middle East, where they were engaged in a greater range of activities. The sheer variety of their supporting roles as well as the nature of battle or occupation in these far-flung theatres meant that these non-combatant bodies were not just more visible, but constructed differently by imperial eyes.

Images from the Levant and the Middle East: Ariel Varges and James McBey

In *First World War Photographers* (1989), Jane Carmichael notes a strange paradox about photography and the 'outer theatres' of war. On the one hand, from the logistics of supply as well as publication of the photographs, the distances created 'insurmountable problems'. On the other hand, there could be far greater opportunities for wartime photographers in these far-flung theatres, removed from the largely static Western Front and less fettered by official prohibitions.[60] The terrain of some of these theatres – the flood-prone flat plains of Mesopotamia or the vast tracts involved in the Sinai and Palestine campaign – provided more space for the individualistic and the adventurous, perhaps best exemplified in the documentary *With Allenby in Palestine* which created and celebrated the myth of 'Lawrence of Arabia'. In the context of the Indian troops, the most sustained engagement comes from the lens of the highly talented American photographer and cinematographer Ariel Varges. Varges was attached to the British army from July 1916 as their official photographer in Salonika, and then, in November 1916, he moved to Mesopotamia.[61]

---

[59] See Das, *Indian Troops in Europe*, 105.

[60] Jane Carmichael, *First World War Photographers*, especially her chapter 'Unorthodox Achievement: The Outer Theatres of War', 76–97.

[61] Varges initially worked for Hearst's International News Pictorial, and by July 1916 he was reportedly the 'official photographer of the British forces' at Salonika. But Hearst's organisation was renounced on account of its apparent pro-German bias in October 1916. Varges, in order to continue working with the British forces, was supposed to have become a captain in the British army, but it seems that,

Varges's aesthetic and unfailingly humane vision went far beyond his official role. His time in Macedonia coincided with those of some 10,000
Indians, including 6,543 combatants and 3,254 non-combatants, who were
stationed at the Macedonian front and engaged in light duties.[62]

Among the various war photographers, Varges was singularly alive to
the possibilities of the photograph as a *visual form* rather than just a historical record. The distinctiveness of his vision is evident in a remarkable sequence of shots of an Indian sports meet in May 1916. Girdwood's
self-aggrandising imperial heroics are replaced in Varges's photographs by
the constant drama of the lens, as in his photograph of sepoys seemingly rushing towards the camera during a race or the balletic poise of
synchronised bodies during a gymnastic display.[63] However, the most
striking series is that of muleteers wrestling on their mules (Figure 3.15).
Here the camera seems to exult in the interplay of light, shadow, speed
and collision of bodies: the focus is on the smooth, naked shoulders
and the back of the muleteer, lurching horizontally between the two
animals, as he is grabbed by the neck and dragged off his mule by his
opponent. If the grinning, turbaned figure on the right sums up the mood
of joviality, the Barthesian *punctum* is perhaps in the all-seeing eye of
the mule on the left, directly accosting the viewer and providing a wry
comment on the whole scene! Varges's photograph also shows the emerging art of motion photography as his cinematographer's eye relishes
the drama between bodies, animal and human, as the camera moves out
of its imperialist high-altitude omniscience to exult in its own formal
strategies. The camera's orientalist lingering caress of brown flesh, reminiscent of Jean Seguet, is complemented by a sense of excitement and
drama. The image shows how the seemingly innocuous and the aesthetic
could become enmeshed in racial politics; indeed, the line between the
depictions of heroism and horse-play on the one hand and implications
of subhuman bodily presence on the other, as we saw in relation to the
Gurkha troops, could be very fine. In a strange twist, this photograph
ends up in the German ethnological work *Der Völkerzirkus unserer Feinde*

from November 1916, he was attached to the War Office Cinematograph Committee (WOCC). He
travelled to Mesopotamia, where he remained until the end of the war, continuing to supply the
WOCC with films such as *With the British in Baghdad* and *Our Troops in Mesopotamia* in August
1918. Also see 'Ariel L. Varges', http://bufvc.ac.uk/newsonscreen/search/index.php/person/952.
[62] See *Military Statistics*, 777. For details of the British mobilisation in Salonika, see Alan Wakefield and
Simon Moody, *Under the Devil's Eye: Britain's Forgotten Army at Salonika 1915–1918* (Stroud: Sutton
Publishing, 2004).
[63] See, for example images Q 32063 and Q 32064 in the Imperial War Museum, London.

Figure 3.15   Indian cavalrymen wrestling on mules. Photograph by Ariel Varges.
© Imperial War Museum (Q 3205).

[*The Circus of Peoples of Our Enemies*] published in 1916, with the derisive label 'Gymkhana: World-battle on Mules'.

If the sports images show Varges's fondness for the dramatic, his scenes of daily life on the Macedonian front are no less remarkable. Here he captures the non-combatant engaged in everyday tasks: laying bricks; tying firewood into a bundle using both hands and feet; straightening an overturned mule cart; or repairing the mules' harnesses in their tents. Some of his most interesting images are of encounters – an Indian sepoy and a Greek labourer exchanging coins across a ditch (see Figure 0.12 in the Introduction) or a Serbian colonel showing an Indian officer how to use a camera. In *Photography in Hindostan or Reminiscences of a Travelling Photographer* (1877), John Blees wrote about the influence of classical portraiture on photography and pointed out the 'Rembrandt-effect' in photographs of upper-class Indians. Varges's muse, I would argue, would have been Johannes Vermeer and, more immediately, Courbet. As with the intimate paintings of Vermeer and Courbet, Varges's photographs often depict solitary figures deeply absorbed in the moment

(a)

(b)

Figure 3.16   (a) The carpenter of an Indian transport camp smokes a
home-made pipe, constructed from a pickle jar, a tin funnel and two hollow canes.
© Imperial War Museum (Q 32321). (b) An Indian cook grinding pepper in a Turkish
shell case. The shell was fired into their camp when they were stationed in Egypt.
Salonika, March 1917. © Imperial War Museum (Q 32818). Both photographs are by
Ariel Varges and part of the Ministry of Information First World War Official Collection.

or in a particular act; what comes across in the images is almost a process
of self-dialogue. Thus, he focusses not on the busier scenes of army life,
but on quiet, unguarded moments of everyday activities: he shows us a carpenter, all by himself (or at least in the photograph), smoking an improvised
hookah, or a cook, grinding pepper into a Turkish shell-case (now working
as a mortar) that was fired into the camp (Figure 3.16). Intimate and deeply
humane, such photographs also show us the ingenuity, intelligence and
creativity of these nameless camp followers, as an object of destruction is
domesticated and put to good use. In many ways, Varges's images are a hymn

to these camp followers: their daily little acts, their resourcefulness and art of bricolage, their rare moments of pleasure.

One of the most poignant of his images is, however, of a solitary sepoy paying homage at a makeshift memorial. We do not know the exact location. Against an expansive sky and a desolate landscape – we see nothing but barren land and a rough-hewn brick wall – stands a sepoy, slightly bowed, with his right hand on his knee and the left extended to touch a tall pole-like object. As with many war images, it is only when we read the caption that we grasp its meaning: 'An Indian Sepoy pays a visit to the grave of two British airmen who were brought down in the desert by the enemy, who erected the propeller of their machine as a memorial to them' (Figure 3.17). Nothing could be more distant from the world of Girdwood with its celebration of Gurkha antics: this is the sepoy as the mourner – alone, elegiac, thoughtful – even though the cartridge-belt strapped around him is a reminder of his killing role. Why did the enemy plant the propeller where the plane came down – was it intended as a symbol of triumph or a gesture towards memorialisation, or both? Were the mourner and the killer mingled in this act of memorialisation by the enemy, in 'one body and one heart'? The memorial neither celebrates nor sentimentalises but stands enigmatic amidst the desert; the focus instead is on the bowed figure paying homage. Framed against the cosmic expanse of open skies and featureless land, the rifle-carrying cartridge-laden sepoy in silent repose for his dead comrades in a foreign land could be any soldier, in any battle. Particularly poignant is his need to touch the propeller, at once trophy and memorial and debris and relict – bearing traces of the dead comrades, of the tumult in the skies and, more recently, of 'enemy' hands – in what must surely be one of the strangest moments of touch and intimacy in the material culture of the First World War.

In January 1917, Varges moved to Mesopotamia. He arrived in the aftermath of the siege of Kut when the command had passed to Charles Monro and Stanley Maude, and the Indian troops were preparing for their advance to Baghdad. Priya Sathia has argued that, in 1916–1918, Mesopotamia offered the British army not only 'release from the killing fields of France into fabled locales' but rather the mission of 'developing Iraq'; she further argues how, for the colonial administrators, Mesopotamia becomes the key site for the 'redemption of empire and technology'.[64] The main agents in such technological rejuvenation of Mesopotamia were the

---

[64] Priya Sathia, 'Developing Iraq: Britain, India and The Redemption of Empire and Technology in the First World War', *Past and Present*, Vol. 197, Issue 1, 1 November 2007, 211–255.

Figure 3.17   An Indian soldier visits the grave of two British airmen brought down in the desert by the enemy, who erected the propeller of their machine as a memorial to them. Photograph by Ariel Varges © Imperial War Museum (Q 24255).

Figure 3.18   Indian camp followers crossing the Diala, who seem to be more particular in removing their shoes than the soldiers following them. Photograph by Ariel Varges. © Imperial War Museum (Q 24498).

British Indian army – its labourers, sappers, miners, engineers, signallers. Varges's Mesopotamia photographs, taken for propaganda purposes for the Ministry of Information, accordingly show how the British Indian army was bringing 'modernity' to Mesopotamia: engineers drawing and chlorinating water at an advanced post, building bridges and creating roads. At the same time, as always with Varges, there is humanity and humour: the flooding of the Diala, in Varges's vision, becomes a moment of rich human drama as he photographs a group of camp followers crossing the river, with their shoes in their hands and lanterns to guide them (Figure 3.18). It is a motley crowd of people. While the young man in the foreground strides ahead with casual ease, with two pairs of shoes – carrying one along with the lantern while holding another pair in his left hand – the slightly older bearded man on his left is intensely focussed on the act, as he pulls up his trousers so as not to get them wet while carrying a lantern, a stick and a small bundle. Like the cook with the mortar and pestle, it is a moment of intense absorption in the act. At the same time, there is a distinct sense of community and warmth among the people, and even a shared sense of amusement: in the background, one can see a young boy laughing, possibly at the camera and as a comment on the scene.

A small but powerful body of etchings and watercolours by the British artist James McBey provides another visual record of the sepoys in the Middle East. McBey, a self-taught artist and etcher who had succeeded greatly against the odds, was barred from military service because of poor eyesight. After a short stint in the Army Printing and Stationary Service in Rouen, in January 1917, McBey was appointed as the official artist of the Egyptian Expeditionary Force. In that capacity, throughout 1917 and 1918, he accompanied the Allied forces in Palestine and Syria, from Damascus to Gaza, and a number of his watercolours are devoted to the Indian troops stationed in Mesopotamia, Egypt and Palestine. Like Paul Sarrut, he is interested in capturing them in their daily round of activities – sitting in a group, guarding the mosque of Omar or fetching water at the wells at Samarra. Instead of the intimacy of Sarrut, his sepoys are usually distant figures and reduced to silhouettes, smudges or huddled masses in a vast elemental drama of the sands and the sky, as in 'A Listening Post in the Desert: Indian Lancers', 'Near Aceldema' or 'Indian Prisoners Escaped from the Turks'. However, there is a powerful series of full or half-length portraits of 'Punjabis' in Arsuf, including a tantalising double portrait of two Punjabi men huddled close together for warmth, with the camp-fire eerily lighting up their faces (Figure 3.19). The single most startling quality about the painting is its use of chiaroscuro, investing the figures with a sense of the spectral. Out of the surrounding darkness emerge these two figures, every feature shrouded (including the head of one) except their faces, mouth slightly ajar and eyes eerily intense, almost mirroring each other. The mantle of light at once caresses, covers and joins the two figures as they come together for warmth: warmth from the fire as well as the mutual warmth of their bodies, set against the coldness of the night, of death. The painting shows a different configuration of body space and intimacy among sepoys from what we see among Tommies, even though, as I've argued elsewhere, civilian tactile codes of Victorian England collapsed in the trenches. The date (4 November 1918) and the two sets of signatures – of the artist, in English, and presumably of one of the sitters in Devnagari script (on the right) – suggest that the painting was based on a real-life moment. The censored sepoy letters, as we shall discuss in Chapter 5, are peculiarly silent on the theme of

Figure 3.19   James McBey, *A Double-Portrait of Punjabis at a Campfire.*
© Imperial War Museum (Art 1595). (See the plate section for a colour
version of this figure.)

male intimacy in the war; consequently, it is through such paintings and photographs, along with memoirs and imaginative literature, that a history of touch and intimacy among sepoys must begin to be recovered.[65]

Medical Care As Propaganda: The Brighton Pavilion Hospital

If photographs of Indian sepoys in action on the Western Front appeared regularly in the British press, a very different – and more popular – set of images was being manufactured within Great Britain itself: the wounded sepoys being cared for by the empire and nursed back to health in various hospitals along the south coast of England. 'Tenderly lifting a serious case – stretcher bearers at work' had read one of Girdwood's stereo-views; 'Tender care of Our Wounded' was the label of a sequence in his film *With the Empire's Fighters*.[66] 'Tenderness' indeed set the tone for these hospital photographs as British imperialism sought to blazon to the world its supposedly philanthropic and paternal face.[67]

By 31st December 1914, the Indian Corps had suffered 9,579 casualties, including both British and Indian soldiers, with 1,397 killed, 5,860 wounded and 2,322 missing: nearly one out of four of the sepoys who landed in Marseilles in early October had suffered some sort of injury.[68] By the end of 1915, the number had leapt to 28,800.[69] Initially, the wounded Indians were nursed in improvised hospitals in France, but, by the end of 1914, Lord Kitchener had appointed Sir Walter Lawrence as Commissioner for the Indian Sick and Wounded, and tried 'to get the Indians quickly into warm and dry buildings'.[70] In reply to a plea from Lawrence that 'nothing is too good for Indians who have fought for us in Flanders', Lord Hardinge, the Viceroy of India, wrote back: 'You are right in saying that nothing can be too good for them after they have fought for us … In my opinion this kindness shown to our soldiers in England is of priceless value, all retold in length and possibly with exaggeration in the villages and, for it is only tends to increase our prestige in this country.'[71] Paternalism, pragmatism

---

[65] All three watercolours are in the IWM and can be viewed online at the IWM 'Art and Popular Design' website under 'James McBey'.

[66] Programme for *With the Empire's Fighters*, IOR, L/P&J/6/1454 File 3569, 254.

[67] There is a substantial archive of private images in the Imperial War Museum, among other places, consisting of photographs taken by doctors, orderlies and military or ambulance staff.

[68] Lt Col. J. W. B. Merewether and Sir Frederick Smith, *The Indian Corps in France* (London: John Murray, 1918), 199.

[69] Willcocks, *With the Indians in France*, 324.

[70] Report by Lawrence, TNA WO 32/5110.

[71] Papers of Sir Walter Lawrence, MSS Eur F143/73, British Library.

and desire for further prestige were finely blended as medical care became the bedrock of imperial propaganda. The wounded Indians were sent to a cluster of hospitals along the south coast of England: the famous Dome and Pavilion Hospital, the Kitchener Indian Hospital and York Place Hospital in Brighton, Lady Hardinge and Forest Park at Brockenhurst as well as hospitals in Netley, Bournemouth and Milford-on-Sea.[72] Of these, the most celebrated was the Brighton Pavilion Hospital. The Royal Pavilion, originally a modest neo-classical structure but transformed by John Nash between 1815 and 1823 into a grand palace, was Orientalism run wild. The exterior was Indian, the interiors an extravagant *chinoiserie*, with Chinese vases, lamps, paintings and wallpaper. As has been documented widely, it was hastily converted into a hospital for the Indian wounded: elaborate arrangements were made to cater to cultural and religious sensitivities; it had nine kitchens with caste cooks for each, three water-taps for Sikhs, Hindus and Muslims in each ward and signs in Urdu, Gurmukhi and Hindi.[73] The hospital has been the subject of intense scrutiny, from extensive academic research to being the centrepiece in the British centennial commemoration of the Indian contribution, from inspiring exhibitions and light-and-sound programmes to fiction, paintings and cartoons.[74] Much of the interest now has been driven by its extraordinary visual archive. Of all the Indian hospitals, the interiors and inmates of the Brighton Pavilion were the most photographed, sketched, painted and filmed; regularly used today – as illustrations in academic articles to book covers to conference posters – these photographs are seldom analysed, as if they were the transparent envelope of sepoy life in Brighton.

On 14 December 1914 – a cold and wet Monday – two trains steamed into the Brighton station, carrying its first shipment of the Indian wounded. 'No trains that have entered Brighton have ever been so eagerly awaited', noted *The Brighton Herald* as it announced 'Arrival of Indian Wounded' in a bold, big font.[75] Throughout 1915, the local press was rapturous with descriptions of these 'magnificent men', 'brown warriors' and

---

[72] Rozina Visram, *Asians in Britain*, 260.

[73] See Jessica Rutherford, *The Royal Pavilion: The Palace of George IV* (Brighton: Brighton Borough Council, 1994).

[74] For an illuminating account of encounters between Indians and the local people in Brighton, see Suzanne Bardgett, 'Indians in Britain during the First World War', *History Today*, 65, 3 (March 2015), also see Andrew Tait Jarboe, ' "Healing the Empire": Indian Hospitals in Britain and France during the First World War', *Twentieth Century British History*, 26, 3 (2015), 347–369; also Samiksha Sehrawat, *Colonial Medical Care in North India: Gender, State and Society, c. 1840–1920* (Delhi: Oxford University Press, 2013), 187–248. For two evocative accounts of the arrangements made for the Indian troops and their responses, see Visram, *Asians in Britain*, 180–192, and Shrabani Basu, *For King and Another Country*, Chapter 7 ('Badobast Sahib'), 95–108.

[75] *The Brighton Herald*, Saturday, 19 December 1914, 1.

'Eastern warriors', 'stalwart Indian warriors' and 'our guests from beyond the seas'.[76] Some of the classic images were reproduced in a booklet *Indian Military Hospital: Royal Pavilion Brighton 1914–1915*. It was produced by the government in 1915 with the text in three languages, and a copy was given to every convalescent sepoy at the Pavilion. Included within the booklet was a set of thirty-five lavish photographs, some thirty-three of them taken by the celebrated local photographer Arthur Henry Fry. These images, showing the sepoys ensconced in the Dome itself or in the gardens, and with captions such as 'Sunshine in the Grounds' and 'India in the Lawns', emphasise space and freedom as images of British upper-class leisure and idyll were transposed onto the Indian subaltern. These are deeply ironic, for it was freedom of movement that was at issue in these hospitals and created widespread resentment, including a murder attempt.[77]

The centre-piece of Fry's visual cavalcade was a set of three photographs of the interior of the Pavilion. Inaugurating the volume and spread across two pages, the famous first image is a soft-focus panoramic sweep of the Dome taken from a recessive angle below the balcony in the north so that our gaze is filtered through the inner arcade: we are invited to a grand circular space, with rows of beds but the figures indistinct so that our eyes travel and rest on the three ornamented arches. The blur of turbaned figures and white-clad doctors is completely dwarfed by the expanded background, with the whiteness of the linen matching the chandeliers and the star-like bursts of light on the ceiling. This was photography as imperial spectacle, reminiscent of the panoramas taken during the Delhi Durbar. The most iconic image was, however, the more vertical celebration of the Dome (Figure 3.20): the foreground, populated by beds with the Indian wounded, is shortened to just over one-third of the frame and the expanded background takes in the three-tiered Regency architecture. What we get is a combination of the tradition of church painting, high-altitude photography and what David Cannadine calls the ornamentalism of the Raj, as our gaze is pulled upwards towards the ceiling, with the chandelier right in the centre and framed by bright bursts of light. The wide-angle view captures the sense of wonder and awe the sepoys must have felt about their surroundings; 'if there be paradise on earth, it is this, it is this', wrote one

---

[76] *The Brighton Herald*, Saturday, 19 December 1914, 1; *Brighton Graphic*, 12 December 1914; *Brighton Graphic*, 16 January 1915, *Brighton Season, 1914–1915*.
[77] Visram, *Asians in Britain*, 80.

Figure 3.20   The Dome of the Brighton Pavilion from the Platform on the South, as taken by Arthur Fry and published in the booklet *Indian Military Hospital: Royal Pavilion Brighton 1914–1915* (1915).

sepoy, quoting a couplet from the wall of Diwan-i-Khas in Delhi.[78] This was contemporary propaganda at its most powerful: not just to dazzle the peasant-soldiers with imperial regalia but use them as images of philanthropy and beam them across the empire. The photograph immediately inspired two paintings: C. H. Burleigh's *The Dome As an Indian Hospital* (1915) (Figure 3.21) and Douglas Fox Pitt's *An Interior View of the Brighton Pavilion* (1919) (Figure 3.22). In contrast to Fry's panoramic angle, Burleigh's painting is more contained: the visual drama between the diagonal rows of beds, with black bed-frames and white linen, and the sweeping curve of the majestic Oriental arcade serves more as a spectacular background to the triumvirate of figures having a chat in the foreground, vivid in their blue uniform and orange turbans, a visual counterpoint to the imposing chandelier. In contrast, Fox Pitt was more of a true inheritor of Fry. In his vertical rendering of the same scene, the sepoys are flattened into blobs of blue against the white linen, licked into the white and blue

---

[78] Letter written 16 January 1915, *CIM*, IOR, L/MIL/5/525/1.

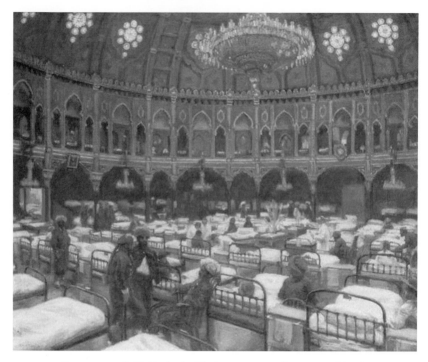

Figure 3.21   C. H. Burleigh, *The Dome As an Indian Hospital* (1915).
Courtesy of the Royal Pavilion & Museums, Brighton & Hove.
(See the plate section for a colour version of this figure.)

of the dramatically expanded background of the Regency architecture. In both Fry and Fox Pitt, what is highlighted is the imperial spectacle rather than any engagement with the sepoy.

The sepoy letters from the Brighton Pavilion, however, tell a different story. Thus, the much-publicised photograph of King George V pinning the Victoria Cross on Jemadar Mir Dast, included in the above-mentioned booklet, acquires a sober meaning when read alongside his letter: 'It [the gas] gives me great pain and will go on doing so … The Victoria Cross is a very fine thing, but this gas gives me no rest. It has done for me.'[79] Indeed, the horrors of war leak into the most sanitised of photographs, such as that of 'A Pathan, a Garhwali and Two Young Gurkhas, Bal and Pim Bahadur' (Figure 3.23), taken not by Fry but by Girdwood. The wheelchairs with

[79] Letter of Mir Dast, 55th Coke Rifles, attached to 57th Rifles, 12 July 1915, from Brighton Pavilion Hospital to Subedar Khan, North West Frontier Province, *CIM*, L/MIL/825/4, 563, British Library.

Figure 3.22   Douglas Fox Pitt, *An Interior View of the Brighton Pavilion* (1919).
Courtesy of the Royal Pavilion & Museums, Brighton & Hove.
(See the plate section for a colour version of this figure.)

the severely injured young men are positioned to fit the horizontal frame. Immaculately dressed, they face the camera and are shown to be enjoying a smoke: the photograph is meant to be an advertisement for the post-war care and reconstruction. Yet, the young faces, together with the empty sleeves and blankets hiding gaps where limbs were supposed to be, create

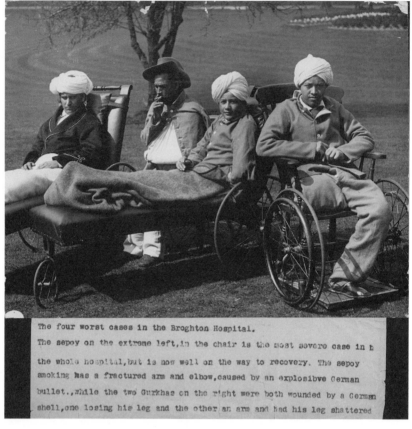

The four worst cases in the Broghton Hospital.

The sepoy on the extreme left,in the chair is the most severe case in h

the whole hospital,but is now well on the way to recovery. The sepoy

smoking has a fractured arm and elbow,caused by an explosibve German

bullet.,while the two Gurkhas on the right were both wounded by a German

shell,one losing his leg and the other an arm and had his leg shattered

Figure 3.23   The four worst cases in the Brighton Hospital – a Pathan,
a Garhwali and two young Gurkhas, Bal and Pim Bahadur. The latter two are
brothers and were wounded by the same shell. © Imperial War Museum.

an immense sense of futility, reminiscent of Wilfred Owen's lines 'He sat
in a wheeled chair, waiting for dark/And shivered in his ghastly suit of
grey/Legless, sewn short at elbow.'[80] We realise the full extent of the tragedy as we further read in the booklet *Indian Military Hospital*: 'The latter
two are brothers and were wounded by the same shell.'

Apart from trying to draw a veil over the horrors of war, the photographs
also conceal some of the murkier aspects of the hospital. First, the British
officials, anxious that the presence of Indian troops might imperil 'white

---

[80] 'Disabled', *The Poems of Wilfred Owen*, 152.

prestige' through liaisons with the local women, instituted a draconian policy of segregation. High fences were erected around the Pavilion grounds, wires ran around the hospital at Barton-at-Sea and police guards were stationed outside the Kitchener Indian Hospital. From this hospital, a wounded sepoy wrote 'Our people are very angry. They [the English] do not allow us out to the bazaars ... The English have now become very bad. They have become dogs', while an Indian storekeeper stationed in Barton similarly complained 'True, we are well-fed, and are given plenty of clothing; but the essential thing – freedom – is denied.'[81] The closely supervised and elaborately stage-managed nature of Fry's images is revealed through a photograph not included in the booklet: it shows a room with Indian patients in their beds while, unknown to the photographer, a mirror at the back of the room reflects two army officers standing at the other end of the room supervising the 'photo-shoot'.[82] Second, the decision of the colonial government to send the sepoys, once they had recovered, back to the trenches caused widespread discontent. For the wounded sepoy, a stay in the hospital was the first step in his return to India: it had to do not just with his intense homesickness and horror at the war, but with his understanding of the 'moral contract' on the part of the 'Sarkar': he had fought gallantly and he had been wounded and that signified to him the end of the job. Instead, what he saw around him alarmed and outraged him. 'The wounded go back to the trenches. Some men come here who have been wounded twice over', wrote Gulab Singh from a war hospital on 3 April 1915; 'only the lame with one leg and broken bones are sent home', added another.[83] In the Brighton Pavilion, a petition was submitted by Mir Dast, while, at the hospital in Milford-at-Sea, a remarkable letter, addressed 'to the King', was written in Urdu but in the Roman alphabet:

> Your majesty's order was that a man who had been wounded once should be allowed to return to India or that if he had recovered should not be made to serve again ... the heart of India is broken because they inflict suffering on the sick ... The Indians have given their lives for 11 rupees [the Indian soldier's pay]. Any man who comes here wounded is returned three or four

[81] Letter of Sepoy Pirzada, 40th Pathans, Kitchener India Hospital, 3 June 1915, *CIM*, L/MIL/828/2, 404(v); Letter of Mithan Lal, Storekeeper, Indian Convalescent Home, New Milton, England, 2 December 1915, *CIM*, IOR, L/MIL/5/828/1, 93, British Library.
[82] I am grateful to Kevin Bacon of the Brighton Pavilion Museum for this insight. Some of the images can be found at 'WW1 and the Royal Pavilion', https://brightonmuseums.org.uk/royalpavilion/history/wwi-and-the-royal-pavilion.
[83] Gulab Singh, 57th Rifles, England, to Bhur Singh, 25th Cavalry Bannu, 3 April 1915, *CIM*, IOR, L/MIL/5/825/2, 211, British Library; Sikh Sepoy, 59th Rifles, England, to his brother in India, 5 April 1915, *CIM*, IOR, L/MIL/825/2, 219, British Library.

times to the trenches. Only that man goes to India who has lost an arm or
leg or an eye.[84]

Yet, what greets us in the photographic archives is the smiling faces of
sepoys, strolling by the beach, or about to go on a motor-ride.

Ethnology, Photography and Art in Wünsdorf: Hermann Struck and Otto Stiehl

If the sepoy-body became the site of imperial propaganda both in France
and in Great Britain, how was it viewed in Germany? In fact, it was across
no man's land in the POW camps in Germany – particularly the twin
campsites in Zossen (Weinberglager) and Wünsdorf (Halbmondlager or
Halfmoon Camp) – that the sepoy-body underwent some of its most
extraordinary investigations and representations, being subjected at once
to racist propaganda and ethnological study.

At the end of 1914, the twin camps of Zossen and Wünsdorf were built
to house a large number of colonial POWs of African, Tatar, Georgian and
South Asian origin. Within Wünsdorf, a separate camp – the *Inderlager* (the
Indian camp) – was created, where around 1,000 Indian troops, captured
on the Western Front, along with some 860 Indian civilian POWs, were
detained.[85] The Wünsdorf camp was singular in two respects. First, it was
something of a propaganda camp where the Indians were subjected to
sustained anti-British propaganda co-ordinated by the *Nachrichtenstelle für
den Orient* (NfO; Intelligence Bureau for the East). A mosque was built,
religious ceremonies were encouraged, and a special newspaper, *El Jihad*,
was produced in different languages; the Indian version, published in Urdu
and Hindi, was renamed *Hindostan*.[86] Second, the Wünsdorf camp was
the site of serious academic research by a team of distinguished German
academics, which included Heinrich Lüders, the professor of the Oriental
seminar of Berlin University, Felix von Luschan, an expert on ethnology,
and Luschan's doctoral student Egon von Eickstedt.

In *Anthropology at War: World War I and the Science of Race in Germany*
(2010), Andrew Evans has argued how anthropology in early-twentieth-
century Germany spanned several overlapping fields of study, including

[84] Anonymous letter addressed 'To the King', 24 May 1915, Milford-at-Sea, *CIM*, IOR, L/MIL/5/825/3, 403, British Library.
[85] See Roy, Liebau and Ahuja (eds.), '*When the War Began, We Heard of Several Kings*' for a won-derfully detailed account; also see Heike Liebau, 'Prisoners of War (India)' in the *1914–18 Online Encyclopedia* (https://encyclopedia.1914-1918-online.net/article/prisoners_of_war_india).
[86] Indian nationalists from the Indian Independence Committee (IIC) in Berlin were invited to give lectures to the POWs and infuse them with anti-British and *jihadist* sentiments.

ethnology and physical anthropology. Photography held a privileged position: race became partly a 'visual phenomenon' as photographs (usually
in the format of 'mug shots') were central both to 'seeing' racial difference
and to constructing various physical 'types'.[87] During the First World War,
'the camps functioned', as Britta Lange has astutely noted, as 'a substitute
for the ethnographic field and became a sort of colonial laboratory'.[88]
Throughout the war years, a group of anthropologists, ethnologists and
linguists, headed by Carl Stumpf and Wilhelm Doegen and working
under the aegis of the Royal Prussian Phonographic Commission, paid
regular visits to various POW camps across Germany and Austria,
including the campsite at Wünsdorf (Figure 3.24). The bodies of these
colonial troops were measured and photographs were taken; their voices
were recorded and their speech patterns were analysed, and their cultural
habits were intensively observed. Photographs reveal a variety of attitudes
and moods in the interaction between the sepoys and the academics, from
a group of Gurkhas excitedly speaking to a team of linguists to a rather
disturbing image of a naked Nepalese soldier being measured by Egon
von Eickstedt.[89]

Photographs of Indian POWs from the Wünsdorf camp feature in a
number of contemporary ethnological studies, ranging from Professor Dr
Backhaus's *Die Kriegsgefangenen in Deutschland* (1915) and Leo Frobenius's
Der Völkerzirkus unsere Feinde (1916) to the linguist Wilhelm Doegen's
Unter fremden Völkern (1925). The images vary according to the nature of
the publication, but in each the individuals photographed usually stand
in for 'types'. While the anthropologists were careful not to establish a
direct relationship between moral nature and physiognomy, the images of
Indian POWs and the accompanying commentary, when viewed together,
show how the photographs of POWs nonetheless 'played on prejudices

---

[87] Andrew Evans, 'Capturing Race: Anthropology and Photography in German and Austrian
Prisoner-of-War Camps during World War I', in Eleanor M. Hight and Gary D. Sampson (eds.),
Colonialist Photography: Imag(in)ing Race and Place (London: Routledge, 2002), 229. This chapter is
reproduced in his monograph *Anthropology at War: World War I and the Science of Race in Germany*
(Chicago: University of Chicago Press, 2010), 155–188. Also see Reinhard Johler, Christian Marchetti
and Monique Scheer (eds.), *Doing Anthropology in Wartime and War Zones: World War I and the
Cultural Sciences in Europe* (Bielefeld: transcript Verlag, 2010) and H. Glenn Penny and Matti Bunzl
(eds.), *Worldly Provincialism: German Anthropology in the Age of Empire* (Ann Arbor: University of
Michigan Press, 2003).

[88] Britta Lange, 'South Asian Soldiers and German Academics', in *'When the War Began, We Heard of
Several Kings'*, 155. Also see Lange, 'Archive, Collection, Museum: On the History of the Archiving
of Voices at the Sound Archive of the Humboldt University', *Journal of Sonic Studies Issue 13 Online*
(http://sonicstudies.org/post/156170371867/journal-of-sonic-studies-issue-13-online).

[89] Evans, 'Capturing Race', 238.

Figure 3.24   The Prisoner of War Camp at Wünsdorf.
Photograph Album of Otto Stiehl. Courtesy of Staatliche Museen
zu Berlin – Museum Europäischer Kulturen.

and depicted a racially strange and menacing enemy'.[90] Thus, in an article by the popular anthropologist A. Korbitz, the heads of the Nepalese troops were said to exhibit a 'massiveness and brutality', characteristic of the 'yellow race people', and in keeping with their skill with kukris, used in 'cutting off the heads of those they overrun'.[91] The insidious relationship is even more evident if we turn from photography to art. In Wünsdorf, the renowned Jewish portraitist Hermann Struck was commissioned to do a series of lithographs of the POWs which were published as part of the volume *Prisoners of War* (*Kriegsgefangene*) by the famous Austrian explorer and anthropologist Felix von Luschan in 1917; they include a number of portraits of Indian sepoys (Figure 3.25), with several bearing the names of the subjects. In the introduction, Luschan acknowledged these vivid

[90] Evans, 'Capturing Race', 245.
[91] A. Korbitz's, 'Types from the German POW Camps', quoted in Evans, *Anthropology at War*, 173.

Figure 3.25 Sketches by Hermann Struck, published in Felix von Luschan, *Kriegsgefangene* (*Prisoners of War*) (1917).

charcoal drawings as 'works of art first' but insisted on their 'scientific meaning [*wissenschaftliche Bedeutung*]'.[92] The research of Andrew Evans into the correspondence of Struck, Luschan and Eickstedt has shown how, in his words, 'in the case of POW images – both the photographs and drawings – the artistic and the scientific collided and merged'. In a letter to Luschan, Struck wrote 'your remarks in relation to the Negro-type were thoroughly correct, and I immediately did his hair. He now has received the very pretty, frizzy Negro hair'. Racial theories, rather than artistic fidelity, thus seemed to have guided Struck in the painting. And the lithographs, in turn, fed into further consolidation of racial types. After the war, Egon von Eickstedt wrote to Luschan to ask permission to have some of Struck's portraits appear alongside his photographs, and noted that 'I photographed about 15 Sikhs. I presume that I captured the average type and it appears to deviate only slightly from Struck's drawings.'[93] Struck's

[92] Felix von Luschan, *Kriegsgefangene* (Berlin: Dietrich Reimer, 1917), 2.
[93] See Evans, 'Capturing Race', 235, where the whole correspondence is detailed. Evans further notes that, when Eickstedt's article was published in 1921, 'Struck's drawings appeared alongside photographs to illustrate the various racial elements present in the Sikh population' (235).

charcoal drawings – themselves actively manipulated to accord with racial thinking – seemed to have become the yardstick against which ethnological photographs of the Sikh 'heads' were judged. The Indian POWs here, like their fellow non-white POW-brethren, become chattels in the complex transaction between ethnology, photography and art in wartime Germany.

It is in this context that I would now like to turn to the photographs of someone who was neither an ethnologist nor an anthropologist but an amateur photographer, and who left possibly the most extensive visual documentation of life in Wünsdorf: the camp commander, Otto Stiehl. A complex individual, Stiehl was a professor at the Technische Universität Berlin and a member of the Prussian Academy of Architecture.[94] He volunteered for war service in 1914; he initially worked as a first lieutenant at the headquarters of Weinberg Camp and then, from June 1917, was second in command of headquarters and in charge of the Halfmoon Camp where the Indians were interned. He took a number of photographs, and in the 1980s, a whole collection of glass-slides and negatives was discovered by the archivist Margot Kayleyss. In 1994, Stiehl's granddaughter donated two photograph albums which Stiehl had kept as a personal souvenir of his time at the Halfmoon Camp.[95] These two substantial albums, now housed at the Ethnological Section of the Museum of European Culture in Berlin, are extraordinary records: they contain photographs (mostly by Stiehl), notes, letters, newspaper-cuttings, memos, sketches and watercolours (including the three by the Indian inmate Gangaram, whom we will address in Chapter 5), and give insights into the daily texture of camp-life.[96] Stiehl gave occasional lectures on POWs during the war years and, in 1921, he published the study *Unsere Feinde: 96 Charakterköpfe aus deutschen Kriegsgefangenenlagern* (*Our Enemies: 96 Faces with Striking Features from German POW Camps*), with a long introduction and using many of his photographs. It is instructive to compare the two unpublished albums,

[94] Margot Kayleyss, 'Indian POWs in World War I Photographs as Source Material', in Franziska Roy, Heike Liebau and Ravi Ahuja (eds.), *'When the War Began, We Heard of Several Kings': South Asian Prisoners in World War I Germany* (Delhi: Social Science Press, 2011), 217. Here Kayleyss recounts how she came across the glass-slides in a wooden box, and how they were divided into four categories – 'Camp Premises', 'Camp Occupancy', 'Camp Life' and 'Art Activities' (216). Also see Kayleyss, *Muslime in Brandenburg – Kriegsgefangene im 1. Weltkrieg: Ansichten und Absichten* (Berlin: Staatliche Museen zu Berlin, 2000).
[95] Margot Kayleyss, 'Indian POWs in World War I Photographs as Source Material', in *'When the War Began, We Heard of Several Kings'*, 216.
[96] I am very grateful to the chief archivist Professor Elisabeth Tietmeyer for making these two extraordinary diaries available to me on my trips to Berlin over the last five years.

bulging with notes and photographs, with the published book and its carefully tailored selection of photographs he chose to reproduce.

In the 'Introduction' to *Unsere Feinde*, Stiehl aligns his work with the genre of ethnological writing, noting 'the rare possibility to collect examples of the most different peoples'. The language, however, veers between a wartime racist vocabulary of describing the colonial armies as 'savages and half-savages' and a closely observed and nuanced commentary on their 'good aspects', which fascinate him. He writes about the 'curious mellowness' of the features of the Gurkhas, the 'magnificent Afghans' and the 'proud' Sikhs with an 'outstanding sense for their outer appearance', and goes beyond the limits of standard ethnological writing:

> The worst situation was for the Thakurs, who were forbidden to eat bread prepared by strangers. They refused to eat while on the move, as well as in the camp. Finally the administration found a solution. They delivered flour and the prisoners were allowed to bake flat bread using the heating stove. After a while they started eating raw rice and baked potatoes … Asked about their relationship to the world war, they said that they were brought to Calcutta with no explanation of where they were going, and then shipped to France. Until the battle in which they were captured, they had not known against whom and for what they were fighting.[97]

He then goes on to single out 'the only Indian who understood and spoke a little English', and mentions that it was 'exhilarating to see how much he knew about his importance and how often he used to assert himself'. This was possibly Ganga Ram, whom we will discuss in Chapter 5. The same tension between racial stereotyping and sharp individuation marks his choice of photographs. Of these 96 character-sketches in *Unsere Feinde*, about twelve are of Indian POWs: Stiehl provides portraits, which allow glimpses of their clothes as well as their general bearing and demeanour. Though photography in the camp obviously operated within the stark asymmetries of power and racial hierarchies and was framed by the racist discourse of ethnology, it is important to note that Stiehl at least makes a point of mentioning that 'no POW was photographed against his will'. Moreover, the three-quarter-length portrait format that Stiehl adopts (as also in Doegen's *Unter fremden Völkern*) is more individualised and less degrading

---

[97] Otto Stiehl, *Unsere Feinde: 96 Charakterköpfe aus deutschen Kriegsgefangenenlagern* [*Our Enemies: 96 Faces with Striking Features from German POW Camps*] (Berlin, 1916), 4–11. He ends on a high nationalist and militarist note, denouncing the 'colourful flocks' as 'crude and morally inferior' and declaring that Germany's sons would be able to defeat this 'Sturmflut' ('storm tide'). I am grateful to Jan Braueburgher for translating the Introduction for me.

Figure 3.26   'Inder, Zhafur, Sauliah Singh, Mhow', published in Otto Stiehl,
Unsere Feinde: 96 Charakterköpfe aus deutschen Kriegsgefangenenlagern (*Our Enemies: 96
Faces with Striking Features from German POW Camps*) (1921).

than the mugshots of unnamed subjects often to be found in the pages of
Leo Frobenius's *Der Völkerzirkus unserer Feinde* (1916).[98] Compared with the
selection of figures in Frobenius, the men in Stiehl's photographs emerge
more as individuals than as types; this is evident in their engagement with the
camera as well as from the captions, which do include their names. Thus, we
have the profile of a remarkably young Nepalese man, described as 'Gurkha,
Kallu Gurung, Parbat, Nepal' with his headdress and uniform, while in
another we have a man, 'Inder, Zhafur, Sauliah Singh, Mhow', staring into
the distance with somewhat glazed, wistful eyes (Figure 3.26).[99] Personal

---

[98] Frobenius put together a collection of photographs from various sources, including some by Varges
      and Girdwood. They are supplemented by men photographed in the POW camps, such as the
      mugshot of a young Senegalese man with the caption 'Mandingo [tribe] rifleman from Senegal',
      or a group of Indian sepoys drawing on their hookas as 'Hubble-bubble in Indialager'. See Leo
      Frobenius's *Der Völkerzirkus unserer Feinde* (Berlin: Eckart-Derlag, 1916).
[99] Otto Stiehl, *Unsere Feinde*, 52, 55.

acquaintance and the time available for these studies perhaps account for the sense of ease that some of the photographs radiate, which cannot be reduced solely to their propagandist or ethnological function; instead, they suggest that some degree of familiarity and even trust were established between subject and photographer.

Since he was an amateur photographer, it is likely that Stiehl's interests were more visual than ethnological, and that he fell back on the ethnological discourse of the day to frame and market the material in *Unsere Feinde*. The photographic interest is particularly evident if we move from *Unsere Feinde* to the original photograph albums. The photographs here are far more intimate, lively and engaged than the ones chosen for publication. Stiehl captures the regular rhythm of 'camp-life', such as the soldiers playing cards, holding a ram, fetching a bucket, pouring grain together or staring into the distance. Some of them might have been used for propaganda but what emerges strongly is his innate curiosity about the lives of these men: what the photographs capture above all is the ambivalence of his position, at once an academic and a military officer. One particularly remarkable photograph taken in February 1917 shows a group of Indian POWs dressed up for a performance during what Stiehl referred to as the 'Indian Spring Festival'. It shows the men, including some whose portraits appear in the book, with painted faces, false beards, elaborate head-dresses and improvised weapons, parading as gods and ready to act out a scene from a mythological play (Figure 3.27); one POW is cross-dressed as a goddess, complete with nose-ring. An image such as this acts like a lightning-rod into sepoy-life in the POW camps. Equally interesting is the role of the photographer: rather than mug shots or profiles, what Otto Stiehl is interested in capturing is the cultural life of the Indians – without always trying to collapse otherness into alterity. Being the camp-commander, his photographs are obviously embedded within structures of power and shaped by the orientalist and racist worldview of the time, but, while these must be recognised, they are not the sole frameworks through which to see the photographs: quiet individual moments, group activities during festivals, or men just sitting together or lounging around seemed to have attracted his attention more than spectacles of military drill in the camp. Such images show a deep absorption in and sustained engagement with the daily lives of these men which were undoubtedly shaped by his position as the camp commander as well as contemporary racial science but seem to go beyond these categories into a more complex structure of feeling, which we will investigate

Figure 3.27   'Indian Spring Festival'. Photograph Album of Otto Stiehl.
Courtesy of Staatliche Museen zu Berlin – Museum Europäischer Kulturen.

in the next chapter with reference to British literary representations of
the sepoys.

Thus, from the arrival of the sepoys in France or Mesopotamia,
through their convalescence in the hospitals at Brighton to their internment in the POW camps in Germany, the Indian sepoy-body was the
site of multiple intensities of meaning and was subjected to a variety of
visual representations that went far beyond simple 'military orientalism'.
Orientalism often formed the starting-point and provided a common
vocabulary but, as I hope to have shown, such preconceptions were
challenged and altered during the actual encounters. Such photographs,
paintings, sketches and watercolours habitually defy the thesis of the
naive 'othering' of the sepoy, which was initially adopted by some of the
photographers and artists, and is all too easily accepted and recycled by
many scholars today. If the 'Senegalese' or the 'Indian' or the 'West Indian'
soldiers are increasingly becoming objects of academic enquiry, and often
on a fascinating comparative axis, what we learn from the representation

of one broad racial group from one part of the world – placed in a variety of contexts and spaces – is how racial or ethnic identity was not the only or necessarily always the most important factor in these representations; place, context, rank and motives were just as important, and intersected with the minutiae of race in endless combinations.

CHAPTER 4

Imperial Antibiotic
The Indian Sepoy in British War Writing

This man in his own country prayed we know not to what Powers.
We pray Them to reward him for his bravery in ours.
(Rudyard Kipling, 'Hindu Sepoy in France')

Lieutenant-Colonel Venour, an officer in the 58th Rifles, had just success-fully retaken a trench on the Western Front when he was suddenly thrown flat on his back in the mud by Havildar Lashkarai, an Afridi Pathan. Venour had momentarily stood up to survey the trenches when Lashkarai had jumped on him and brought him down: 'Venour's comments, in the most virulent Pashto, of which he was a past master, left Lashkarai unmoved and ready to repeat the performance'.[1] We realise, retrospectively, that Lashkarai had just saved Venour's life. The Havildar had spotted a German sniper taking aim at his officer and acted with lightning quickness. The inexperienced lieutenant-colonel, however, decided to look over the top again but, this time, the Havildar was a second too late: the sniper's bullet went through Venour's head and he fell back into Lashkarai's helpless arms. The incident marks the first appearance of a sepoy in the memoir of Lieutenant A. G. Lind, 58th Rifles Frontier Force, who had travelled from Karachi with the Indians and served alongside them on the Western Front.

The above vignette is representative of the way the British officers of the Indian army often represent their men – experienced, loyal, canny. Such intimate and precise accounts defy the generalised discourse of 'otherness', a combination of 'racism and exoticism', which some scholars often attribute *en masse* to European perceptions of Indian and African soldiers.[2] The testimonies by the British officers similarly differ sharply from the pictures

---

[1] A. G. Lind, *A Record of the 58th Rifles F.F. in the Great War 1914–1919* (Waziristan: Commercial Steam Press, 1933), 9.
[2] See Koller, 'Representing Otherness: African, Indian and European Soldiers' Letters and Memoirs', in Das (ed.), *Race, Empire and First World War Writing*, 127–142; Andrew Evans, 'Representing Race', 226–256.

174

and reports about the Indian troops that flooded the British press in late 1914 and early 1915, ranging from weekly updates in *The Times* to full-page illustrations, sketches and cartoons in *The Illustrated London News*, *The Bystander* or *The Sphere*.[3] The media accounts often adopt an 'exotic' line, either in their open celebration of these 'gallant Oriental warriors' or racist humour at their 'primitive' traits, as in 'A Black Outlook' where two Sikh sepoys lurk behind a house, with their lances drawn, ready to jump on an unsuspecting German cavalryman.[4] In contrast, the representations of the sepoy-figure in the diaries, memoirs and letters of the British officers open up a far more complex and nuanced space where regimental histories and personal and cultural familiarity from pre-war times in India and the intensity of shared battle experience at the front are brought into strenuous negotiation with the overarching ideology of empire and hierarchies of race and rank. Lind notes how the Indians on the Western Front were thrown into action 'at a moment's notice' in trenches 'little better than open ditches': 'The rank and file, with a pathetic faith in the superiority of the British "bandobost" above all other armies, could not understand why they could not have the same [i.e. weaponry as sophisticated as that with which the British troops were equipped].'[5] Similarly, his fellow officer J. W. Barnett, serving with the 34th Sikh Pioneers, writes: 'Don't think it is fair that men should have to dig in open in daylight 200 yards from Germans – it is murder really'; a few pages later, we encounter the most awful moment in the diary when, during intense shelling, a Gurkha sepoy gets 'jammed under beams in burning house': 'Had to shoot him in head as could not be got out. Horrible. Curse thus war – it is murder.'[6] Pity, sympathy, even outrage on behalf of the men punctuate these officers' diaries, but they are seldom evolved into any sustained critique of the war or empire. As Michael Lieven notes in a different context, 'The question of whether cruelty is part of the pathology of European imperialism or merely a failing of its villains, who can be expelled from their caste leaving a virtuous liberal imperialism to spread the benefits of civilisation, is left hanging.'[7] Indeed, the

---

[3] See *The Times*: 'Our Indian Soldiers', 2 September 1914, 9; 'Indian Loyalty', 16 September 1914, 7; 'Soldiers of India', 3 October 1914, 7; 'Hospital for Indian Troops', 9 October 1914, 5. Also see 'Our Brave Indian Troops', *The Illustrated News*, 7 November 1914 and 'With the Indian Troops at the Front' (9 January 1915) and 'With the Indian Troops in France' (6 February 1915), both in *The Sphere*.
[4] 'A Black Outlook', *The Bystander*, 25 November 1914.
[5] Lind, *A Record of the 58th Rifles*, 9.
[6] Lt. Col. J. W. Barnett, 'Diaries', IWM 90/37/1, 8, 17.
[7] Michael Lieven, 'Contested Empire: Bertram Mitford and the Imperial Adventure Story', *Paradigm*, No. 25 (1998), unpaginated, available at http://faculty.education.illinois.edu/westbury/paradigm/lieven2.html.

contradictions at the heart of a putative 'liberal imperialism' were pushed to an extreme on the battlefields of the First World War to which the private diaries of these officers bear complex testimony.

As I argued in the previous chapter, the meanings around the sepoy depended not just on racial otherness and colonial ideology, but on a host of other factors too, ranging from the theatre of war to his status (combatant/non-combatant) to specific contexts; a resplendent sepoy and a downtrodden *bhisti* (water-carrier) engendered very different set of representations, just as the wounded sepoys encountered in Brighton were perceived very differently by the British from those held as fellow prisoners in a POW camp in Mesopotamia. Similarly, the representations of Indian combatants and non-combatants by the British officers lurch between certain broad stereotypes and the minutiae of differences, depending on the specific circumstances and levels of knowledge and exposure. Consider the following accounts, all appearing in private unpublished accounts of the British officers:

> Jiger the Indian ward boy with the Turkish prisoners in the ward is a real joy. He is very fat, with a huge smile on his face and very black. He is very serious when he is gesticulating wildly, with Johnny Turk, trying to find out what he wants, but soon his face lights up and he darts off laughing to himself with a cup of water, or a box of matches or whatever the Turk wants. He treats it all as a huge joke, but he would rather be with the 'sahibs' [aboard the *H.S. Takada*, carrying Turkish POWs to India].[8]

> My orderly Bhir Singh, a dear fat old smiling Sikh has particularly requested me to send to England for a watch for him ... as he is a Sikh he has probably saved as much as a Punjabi Mussalman would have got into debt ... It is rather amusing one of my guns is manned by Sikhs and the other by Punjabi Mussalmans. When one starts a sort of 'are we down-hearted' shout, the other gun tried to outshout it – so each day as we march off, each gun tries to outshout the other with its 'jai ke wange' – shout of victory – much to the amusement of the British troop of the column.[9]

> Eventually a little Gurkha, one of a handful who had got mixed up with our gallant band of defenders, volunteered to be water drawer ... He loaded himself with about a dozen empty bottles and returned unscratched ... I shall never quite understand how he escaped, unless it was owing to his dusky skin and undoubted skill in scout craft. One of his dodges was to prop up his hat to draw the enemy rifle fire while he was drawing

---

[8] E. G. Wade, 'A Sideshow on the Tigris', Diary, 17 March 1916, IWM 90/17/1.
[9] Letter of Lt. Col. Arthur MacGregor, written on 20 November 1916 from a paddle steamer on the Tigris, IWM 05/38/1 and 05/38/2.

the water. At the first opportunity I commended him for a distinction which his bravery so justly merited [at Ali Garbi, during the Mesopotamia campaign].[10]

These accounts are very different from the heroic representation of the sepoy figure in France and Flanders that we saw in the photographs and postcards. The infantilisation in each of these accounts shows how discourses of racial difference intersected with those of class; at the same time, each is alive with a certain precision of impression that is shaped by yet goes beyond the generalised discourses of 'orientalism'. The racist condescension co-exists with a certain affection and warmth, pointing to a complex emotional response that goes beyond easy categories; the colonial hierarchies are maintained but adjusted. The fabric of prose captures these mixed feelings. Phrases such as 'very fat', 'very black', 'a dear old fat smiling Sikh' and 'a little Gurkha' with 'his dusky skin' are all bristling with various shades of racist humour based on infantilisation; yet, interwoven with it is Wade's 'real joy' in and warmth for Jiger's *joi de vivre* ('gesticulating wildly', 'huge smile', 'face lights up', 'darts off laughing'), MacGregor's intricate (if clichéd) distinction between Sikhs and Punjabi Mussalmans or Byrom's admiration for the 'bravery' of the Gurkha sepoy. Class often is a strong underlining factor: MacGregor, who served with the Indians in Mesopotamia, mentions Sikh, Muslim and Hindu sepoys fondly, but the tone changes abruptly as he talks about the 'low caste swine – *nai, moochi*, and *kahar* caste only and intended for ammo [ammunition] column work only': 'I feel like getting into a strong antiseptic bath after every parade with them.'[11] Race and class are often inextricably linked in fanning prejudice, but here it is more the latter that fuels the pitch of racist hysteria as the British officer, the so-called agent of sweetness and light, ends up internalising Indian caste prejudices.[12]

The focus of this chapter is on the literary writing of the time, particularly fiction, both by British officers and civilians, and how it engages with the subject of India and the war. Their importance is two-fold: they provide insights into the wartime discourses around the sepoy, but also move

---

[10] Captain J. A. Byrom, 'Memoir', written 1919–1920, IWM 99/84/1, 26.

[11] Letter of Lt Col. Arthur MacGregor, written on 20 November 1916, IWM 05/38/1 and 05/38/2.

[12] Nicholas Dirks has argued that caste 'is, in fact, the precipitate of a history that selected caste as the single and systematic category to name, and thereby contain, the Indian social order', Nicholas Dirks, *Castes of Mind: Colonialism and the Making of Modern India* (Princeton: Princeton University Press, 2001), 13.

beyond the war years into a longer history of race and representation. Does literary writing mobilise the standard Oriental tropes, as in the visual iconography and popular media, or do fiction, memoirs and stories put pressure on such ideologies and delve deeper into the affective dimensions and mixed feelings of these moments and processes? Does literature, more than photography, provide a diagnosis of the fears and fantasies around the Indian participation in the conflict?

It is difficult to pinpoint the first published literary piece on the First World War sepoy. An early example was *Indian Ink: Splashes from Various Pens* (1914–1915), a Calcutta-based propaganda journal founded to raise money for the Imperial Reserve Fund and relieve 'the distress caused by war'. There, we have a variety of material, from Shirley Hodginson's 'India to England' – possibly the first example of colonial ventriloquism for purposes of war propaganda and Indo-British 'brotherhood' ('Proud Rajputs, gallant Gurkhas …/Thy soldiers are we, England') – to R. C. Lehmann's more restrained 'Epitaph' for an 'English Soldier and an Indian Soldier buried together in France'.[13] As we would see, both these impulses – the hijacking of the 'native' voice for propaganda as well as memorialisation of the sepoy – would soon appear first in the hands of Rudyard Kipling. Meanwhile the Indians start impinging on classic European war memoirs: Siegfried Sassoon in his diary notes how the Indian cavalry made occasional 'spots of poppy-colour' among the 'browns and duns and greys'; Robert Graves, in *Goodbye to All That* (1929), refers to 'Mohammedan Indians'; while the German soldier-writer Ernst Jünger would devote one whole chapter in his memoir *Storm of Steel* to the Indian sepoys.[14] At the same time, certain accounts move beyond the sepoy-figure to articulate some of the broader anxieties framing the Indian participation in the conflict, particularly in the light of Turkey's declaration of *jihad*, the burgeoning nationalist movement within India and German attempts to win over the Muslim population in India. Frederick Britten Austin's 'The Magic of Muhammed Din' trades exactly on such fears: a German spy tries to infiltrate an Indian village and stir up a revolution, only to be exposed by an Indian fakir-cum-enchanter named Muhammed Din.[15] Similarly, we have an Indian spy in Somerset Maugham's First World War story 'Giulia

---

[13] Both poems are extracted from *Indian Ink: Splashes from Various Pens* (Calcutta: Thacker, Spink and Co., 1915), 12.

[14] Siegfried Sassoon, *Memoirs of an Infantry Officer* (London: Faber & Faber, 1965 [1930]), 96; Robert Graves, in *Goodbye to All That* (London: Jonathan Cape, 1929), 233; Ernst Jünger, *Storm of Steel*, trans. Michael Hofmann (London: Allen Lane, 2003 [1920]) 141–155.

[15] 'The Magic of Muhammed Din', *The Strand Magazine*, August 1917, 54, 320, 99–107.

Lazari' (1928). A later but sustained exploration is John Masters' full-length novel *The Ravi Lancers* (1972) about Indian war experience on the Western Front, shot through with the story of inter-racial romance and friction.

In recent years, a number of historians have drawn attention to how the British empire, from the Sepoy Uprising of 1857 onwards, was a highly 'insecure' empire, plagued by constant fears of the various faces of dissent, from small-scale riots to full-fledged mutinies.[16] The task of controlling a vast far-flung empire through a 'native' army created a constant state of anxiety; the theory of the martial races, it has been argued, lurched between scenarios of 'colonial fantasy' and 'colonial nightmare', with one regularly slipping into the other.[17] If a previous generation of scholars looked at the British Indian army as 'sentinels of the Raj', scholars now have started examining how it became a site of 'chronic malaise and insecurity for the British imperial establishment'.[18] Such fears intensified acutely during the First World War. First, there was the extensive German–Ottoman propaganda of a global *jihad*, trading on a general Pan-Islamic sympathy, with active points of contact with transnational networks of Indian revolutionary nationalists, which was meant to stir up anti-colonial rebellion within India.[19] To this was added the activities of the Ghadar party. The actual impact of the Ghadar revolutionaries, as mentioned in Chapter 2, was limited, but the panic they caused through their networks, which stretched from the United States and Canada to Japan, Singapore and Paris, was quite unprecedented. For Michael O'Dwyer, the Lieutenant General of Punjab, the Ghadar was 'by far the most serious attempt to subvert British rule in India' and the notorious Defence of India Act of 1915 was partly a response.[20] This wider context, as well as the figure of the sepoy in the battlefield, becomes crucial to understanding the literary representation of the sepoys. While the photographs in the previous chapter depict

---

[16] See Mark Condos, *The Insecurity State*. Condos focusses on Punjab, as we have already seen, but refers to other provinces as well; moreover, he gives a pre-history of 'colonial insecurity' in early British India, going back to 1757, and extends his analysis to the pre-First World War period. The forthcoming work of Gajendra Singh titled *Spectres of Violence* and focussing on the Ghadar movement is also a step in this direction.

[17] Gajendra Singh, *Testimonies of Indian Soldiers*, 11–34.

[18] Condos, *The Insecurity State*, 182.

[19] For transnational and anti-colonial networks during the war years, Arun Coomer Bose's *Indian Revolutionaries Abroad, 1905–1922* still remains an exemplary study. Also see Kris Manjapra, *Age of Entanglement: German and Indian Intellectuals across Empire* (Cambridge: Harvard University Press, 2014); for links between Germans and Indian nationalists, see Heike Liebau, 'Prisoners of War (India)' in *1914–18 Online Encyclopedia* (https://encyclopedia.1914-1918-online.net/article/prisoners_of_war_india).

[20] Michael O'Dwyer, *India As I Knew It*, 189.

the sepoys and the colonial frames around them, British literature of the period, on the other hand, gives us insights not just into such frameworks but also into the various fantasies, anxieties and paranoia surrounding the very involvement of India in the war.

Here, I discuss three works written during the war which show sustained engagement with the sepoy-figure as well with some of these wider currents: *Hira Singh: When India Came to Fight in Flanders* (1918), an Orientalist pot-boiler by Talbot Mundy; *The Eyes of Asia*, a propaganda text by Rudyard Kipling based on a cache of real-life letters; and, finally, the war diary and subsequent novella 'The Experiences of Ram Singh' by the officer-writer 'Roly' Grimshaw who fought alongside the Indian troops. Underpinning each of them is the logic of what I have termed 'imperial antibiotic'. Literature, I shall argue, provides the space for the articulation of the fear of the imperial body being possibly 'infected', as well as for the inoculation against such fear through the injection of a strong dose of narrative 'antibiotic'.

Double Trouble: Panic, Assurance and the Genre of Imperial Adventure

In July 1915, the *New York Times* carried a report on one of the most curious episodes of the First World War:

> One hundred Indian troops of the British Army have arrived in Kabul, Afganistan, after a four months' march from Constantinople. The men were captured in Flanders by the Germans and were sent to Turkey in the hope that, being Mohammedans, they might join the Turks. But they remained loyal to Great Britain and finally escaped, heading for Afghanistan. They now intend to join their regimental depot in India, it is reported.[21]

The one hundred troops possibly refer to the 'Afghan Mission' – a collective mission of German, Indian and Ottoman military and diplomatic personnel to Kabul with the aim of winning the neutral Emir of Afghanistan over to the side of the Central Powers, and fomenting anti-colonial rebellion in India. It was part of the dense German–Ottoman–Indian anti-colonial revolutionary network during the war years.[22] There

[21] Extracted in the Preface to Talbot Mundy, *Hira Singh: When India Came to Fight in Flanders* (1918), available as an Etext of Project Gutenberg (www.gutenberg.org/files/4400/4400-h/4400-h.htm). All further references to the work are to Talbot Mundy, *Hira Singh's Tale* (London: Cassell & Co., 1918).
[22] See Arun Coomer Bose's *Indian Revolutionaries Abroad*.

were several such missions in 1915 and 1916. The most high-profile of them was the Niedermayer–Hentig expedition of 1915 comprising the German army officers Oskar von Niedermayer and Werner Otto von Hentig, the exiled Indian prince Mahendra Pratap, the Muslim scholar and nationalist Maulavi Barkatullah, and a handful of Indian prisoners and defectors. The group made one of the most gruelling and thrilling journeys ever across Central Asia amidst extreme climactic conditions; von Hentig's party travelled with twelve pack horses, twenty-four mules and a camel caravan.[23] The Indian nationalists, including Mahendra Pratap, finally reached Kabul, but the prevaricating Emir ultimately decided not to support the mission. In addition to these two expeditions, the German Foreign Office also sent to Turkey a substantial number of Muslim POWs, particularly Tatars and North Africans, in the hope they would join their Muslim brethren; one delegation included forty-four South Asians, but they seemed to have vanished after reaching Turkey. The expeditions were thus failures, but their links with Indian revolutionary nationalist networks in Berlin, including the India Independence Committee, and the spectre of a global *jihad* created widespread panic in the British Raj: the expeditions became the stuff of legend, apocrypha and rumour.

The article published in the *New York Times*, as well as the swirling panic around the Ghadar movement, directly inspired what is possibly the earliest full-fledged novel about the Indian involvement in the war: Talbot Mundy's *Hira Singh: When India Came to Fight in Flanders*, first serialised in *Adventure Magazine* in 1917 and then published in 1918. The catalyst – the brief report – is extracted in full in the preface. Aged thirty-four, Talbot Mundy had by the time of the First World War established his reputation with novels such as *The King of the Khyber Rifles* (1916) and *The Winds of the World* (1917), with their blend of adventure, Orientalism and pseudo-mysticism. Earlier, at sixteen, he had run away from home and had lived in India, Africa and the Far East, eking out a living as a confidence trickster.[24] The story of this extraordinary journey of a group of conspirators and

[23] See Rajah Mahendra Pratap, *My Life Story 1886–1979*, ed. Vir Singh (Delhi: Originals, 2004). Niedermayer himself wrote a couple of books on the expedition: *Meine Rückkehr aus Afghanistan* [*My Return from Afghanistan*] (Munich: Wolf, 1918) (under the pseudonym Hadschi Mirza Hussein) and *Unter der Glutsonne Irans: Kriegserlebnisse der deutschen Expedition nach Persien und Afghanistan* [*Under the Scorching Sun of Iran: War Experiences of the German Expedition to Persia and Afghanistan*] (Dachau: Einhornverlag, 1925). A succinct summary can be found in 'The German Mission to Afghanistan 1915–16 (The Niedermayer–Hentig Expedition)', http://s400910952.websitehome .co.uk/germancolonialuniforms/afghan%20mission.htm.

[24] See Brian Taves, *Talbot Mundy, Philosopher of Adventure: A Critical Biography* (London: McFarland Books, 2006).

defectors from Berlin across the vast tracts of Central Asia to Afghanistan
must have had a special appeal to him. Yet what he does with the story is
diagnostic not just of his personal investment in the tale but also of British
perceptions, fantasies and anxieties around the Indian war participation at
large. At the same time, it also shows how the war as the 'great game' could
be rewritten in a post-Somme world and its implications for the genre of
imperial adventure stories.

The small report gave Mundy a singular vantage-point. The world's first
industrial war is recast as an imperial adventure-cum-quest narrative, full
of intrigue and subterfuge, transnational escapades and homosocial camaraderie and shot through with romance. The mixed group of German,
Turkish and Indian travellers is replaced by an all-Sikh cavalry squadron
of a princely state, drawing at once on warm memories of Sikh loyalty
during the Sepoy Uprising and the contemporary anxiety about Ghadarite
impulses. Thus, the German–Ottoman–Indian links get imaginatively
fused with the Ghadar threat for the novel to play on the full range of
imperial anxiety and fears, if only to seek finally to negate it. The novel
tracks the journey of this cavalry unit – on foot, horseback, mule, caravan,
boat, ship – from India through the Suez to the Western Front, and then
back from the German POW camps, through Persia and Afghanistan to
India. After a brief, perfunctory 'tale within a tale' structure, the novel
unfolds as a first-person narrative by Hira Singh, a lance dafadar, recounting
his 'tale' of the cavalry leader and hero Prince Ranjoor Singh. The prince
is a figure of impossible charisma and dark intentions: fluent in German
and with a fondness for speaking in riddles, he is an agent provocateur.
He is given to vanishing acts, only to reappear at crucial moments and
command his squadron, but this behaviour leads to widespread fear and
suspicion. Playing Horatio to a hyper-active Hamlet, Hira Singh is the
loyal and trusting aide, in thrall to and in love with his hero of dark corners.
The narrative moves from France through Germany and Central Asia to
Kabul: Ranjoor Singh leads his men on the Western Front but is forced to
surrender; taken a POW, he pretends to co-operate and signs a declaration
to join the Germans (much to the horror and dismay of his men) in a bid
to escape via Turkey to India. Once in Central Asia, he strikes a series of
deals, negotiates with the warring Kurds and Turks, and, after a glorious
cavalry charge amidst hail and lightning, manages to obtain Kurdish help
and reach Afghanistan, and finally makes his way back to India with the
133 Indians under his command, as well as a German prisoner, a Syrian linguist and a Greek doctor. If the mud and blood of the trenches mark the
end of the epoch of the Victorian adventure, *Hira Singh* is one of its last

gasps: Mundy shows that, for the genre of the imperial adventure story to survive and incorporate the war, it has to move away from the trenches of Europe onto another theatre, another kind of story, as he crafts his Indian counterpoint to Lawrence of Arabia. But the colonial hierarchies intrude, anxieties abound.

Hira Singh constantly lurches between the twin poles of realism and fantasy, just as its men swerve between trusting and doubting their leader. The first-person narrative enables Mundy to create a sense of immediacy and 'authenticity', while it hijacks and orientalises the Indian voice. Mundy, through Hira Singh, drenches the prince and the story in a vocabulary of romance: Ranjoor Singh looms out of a 'violet mist'; he makes his men ride 'like a storm in the night' (27); the squadron ploughs into the German defence as 'wind cut into a forest in the hills' (27). In this world, the 'battle' is a 'dream' (9). But what would have been a mere Oriental war romance is ballasted by Mundy's intricate loading of every narrative rift with historical ore. Grafted onto this otherwise bizarre romance is a whole wealth of contemporary historical details – from 'Sikh, Muhammadan, Dogra, Gurkha, Jat, Punjabi, Rajput, Guzerati, Pathan, Mahratta' journeying together across 'kalo pani' and French women throwing flowers at the sepoys to alleged instances of self-wounding ('Has the sahib ever heard of "left-hand casualties"?' (35)) or German propaganda pamphlets being dropped on Indian trenches. The cumulative intensity of these details jars against the improbability of the central romance plot.

In his classic work *Dreams of Adventure, Deeds of Empire* (1979), Martin Green has noted that adventure tales were 'the energizing myth of English imperialism': 'They were, collectively, the story England told itself as it went to sleep at night; and, in the form of its dreams, they charged England's will with the energy to go out into the world and explore, conquer and rule.'[25] If such myths underpinned Victorian stories of imperial adventure by writers such as Rider Haggard and Rudyard Kipling, *Hira Singh* at once inherits and interrogates this tradition in the context of imperial panic in times of a global war. At the outset of the war, the Caliph in Constantinople had declared an Islamic holy war against the Allies; the transnational revolutionary links between the German and Turkish officers and the Indian nationalists, exemplified in the 'Afghan mission', posed a new threat; the Ghadar movement, as we have noted, caused widespread consternation. In times of war, the dreams could suddenly morph into nightmare. Mundy both registers the change and provides reassurance: the novel is at once *an*

---

[25] Martin Green, *Dreams of Adventure, Deeds of Empire* (Routledge: London, 1979), 3.

acute diagnosis of and inoculation against the fears and anxieties about Indian 'loyalty' in the war. What he does is to evolve the panoply of anxieties into a narrative strategy of double-dealings and derring-do. An opening master-stroke is to change the group of bedraggled Muslim sepoys into a dashing Sikh cavalry squadron, thus interweaving the German–Islamic threat with the Ghadar strand. The Sikhs had become almost a cliché of colonial loyalty ever since their role in helping to crush the Sepoy Uprising of 1857; forming only 2% of the population, they formed 20% of the Indian army during the First World War.[26] Yet, as discussed in Chapter 2, there was always also a certain degree of fear about this 'warlike' community, which would produce during the war years the most extensive transnational revolutionary network in the form of the Ghadar. Seeking to take advantage of the war, the Ghadrites tried to infiltrate the ranks among the 23rd cavalry at Lahore, the 26th Punjabis at Ferozepur and the 5th Light Infantry in Singapore.[27] Their success was limited, but we have already noted the widespread panic they created. *Hira Singh* trades exactly on these fears. In the novel, the British visitor asks Hira Singh – 'You have talked with Sikhs in California?', referring to the Ghadrites – to which our protagonist replies 'Then you have heard lies, Sahib', and he continues thus: 'A bad Sikh and a bad Englishman alike resemble rock torn loose … I am told that in America men believe what hired Sikhs write for the German papers.' It is against this background that the novel has to be understood, as Mundy transfers British panic around the Indian participation in the war into doubting within the Indian camp itself against Ranjoor Singh. As he finally vindicates himself and his men regain their trust, it becomes an exercise in imperial reassurance.

The novel's construction of the Sikh sepoy hovers around a single word – 'true'. 'I am a true Sikh', claims Hira Singh; and, of Ranjoor Singh, he notes 'I knew him to be a true man'. Rumours circulate: 'I asked whether it was true that the Kaiser had turned Muhammadan' (11). Ranjoor Singh warns his men to 'Remember the oath of a Sikh! Remember that he who is true in his heart to his oath has Truth to fight for him!', to which Hira Singh replies 'I am a true man' (63). Chapter III opens with an Eastern proverb: 'Shall he who knows not false from true judge treason' (65). When his disbelieving men accost Ranjoor Singh with 'What is our destination?',

---

[26] S. D. Pradhan, 'The Sikh Soldier in the First World War', in DeWitt C. Ellinwood and S. D. Pradhan (eds.), *India and World War I* (Delhi: Manohar, 1978), 217.

[27] See Condos, 'Imperial Insecurity and the Ghadar Movement', in *The Insecurity State*, 198. Also see Maia Ramnath, *From Haj to Utopia*.

he replies enigmatically 'If ye be true men why are ye troubled about destination? Can the truth lead you into error? Do I seem afraid?' (86). As the men are captured by the Germans, Ranjoor Singh notes that 'We shall discover before long which are false and which are true' (94). 'There is work to be done that calls for true ones', says Hira Singh, to which the men reply 'Such men be we' (113). A few pages earlier, we have been given insights into what this 'truth' was:

> Above all and before all we were all true men, loyal to our friends, the British, and foes of every living German or Austrian or Turk so long as the war should last. The Germans had bragged to us about the Turks being in the war on their side, and we had thought deeply on the subject of their choice of friends. Like and like mingle, sahib. As for us, my grandfather fought for the British in '57, and my father died at Kandahar under Bobs Bahadur. (66)

And then, a few pages later, 'Nay', said I, 'I am a true man. No man can make me fight against the British' (69). Allegiance to the British Raj becomes the index of the 'true' Sikh as the tropes of masculinity, faith and imperial loyalty are combined. And more: Mundy projects this idea onto Hira Sigh so that war propaganda speaks with a Punjabi accent; ancestral support for the British during the Sepoy Uprising is drawn upon to seal the nature of this 'truth' exactly at a time when this essentialist link between Sikh masculinity and political allegiance was being powerfully contested in the wake of the Ghadar movement and its parallel pantheon of Sikh revolutionary heroes such as Baba Gurmukh Singh. Mundy's obsessive reiteration of the word 'true' is a desperate attempt to shore up this colonial construction of organic Sikh loyalty to the British Crown: it becomes an index of the mounting panic around Indian loyalty while at the same time delivering a narrative antibiotic against the feared infection of the anti-colonial upsurge. In fact, *Hira Singh* can be regarded as a double dose in narrative inoculation, against the Ghadrites in California as well as the German–Indian nexus in the Halfmoon Camp in Berlin. We witness Ranjoor Singh sign the following petition:

> We, being weary of British misrule, British hypocrisy, and British arrogance, thereby renounced allegiance to Great Britain, its king and government, and begged earnestly to be permitted to fight on the side of the Central Empires in the cause of freedom. (82)

The nationalist sentiment is articulated, only to be, as we will see, countered and dismissed. As Ranjoor Singh signs his name 'with a great flourish', his men feel 'he had let them through the gates of treason' (82–83). Like the men, the readers go through the motions of consternation, but they are supposed to know better as Ranjoor Singh plays double-bluff, honourably acquits himself and his men, and takes Tuggenheim prisoner.

Though circumscribed by the imperial ideology, Mundy does something radical in *Hira Singh*, both formally and ideologically. First, the colour of the hero of imperial fiction changes, even though he is a colonial agent – the equivalent of having an Indian James Bond in terms of the genre. Second, and more importantly, Mundy gives agency to an Indian officer, Ranjoor Singh. If, according to the racist construction of the day, Indians were supposed to be gallant warriors but ineffective leaders – men who could fight but not think – Ranjoor Singh is the strategist and leader *par excellence*: in the German camp and in Turkey, he negotiates adroitly with the Germans, the Turks, the Kurds and the Afghans. It is only through the world of the Indian cavalry against the Turks on the plains of Stamboul, far away from the trenches of northern France, that the 'Charge of the Light Brigade' could have its last stand in an age of industrialised warfare: 'The hail was in our backs. No man ever lived who could have charged forward into it and not one of the Turkish sentries made pretence at anything but running for his life' (254).

Propaganda or Projection?: Kipling's *The Eyes of Asia*

If Mundy evolves British fears and suspicions around Indian participation into an Orientalist fantasy of double-dealing and assurance through his fictional prince, the master-teller and champion of empire – Rudyard Kipling – set himself an altogether more difficult task: to write a commissioned piece of imperial war propaganda. *The Eyes of Asia* (1918) was the result of two years' endeavours.[28] A series of four letters where Kipling imagines himself to be a sepoy writing home from France or England, it is at once one of the most acute and insidious representations of the sepoy. The first literary text to give the ordinary sepoy a voice and capture some of his sense of wonder and bewilderment, it is also a grotesque travesty of such experience, reducing many of its complexities and ambivalences to colonial mimicry.

---

[28] Remarkably, this work has received very little attention. I have previously written on this work in 'Writing Empire, Fighting War', in Susheila Nasta (ed.), *India in Britain: South Asian Networks and Connections, 1858–1950* (London: Palgrave, 2013), 28–45. All references are to *The Eyes of Asia* (New York; Doubleday, Page & Co., 1918). A new edition, by Charles Allen, came out in late 2017.

The origin of this work is as compromised as it is tantalising. On 19 June 1916, Major Sidney Goldman of the Intelligence Department engineered a meeting between Brigadier-General Cockerill and Kipling on 'how best to give intelligence to neutrals at home'. On 26 June, Kipling 'starts work on some Indian letters from men who have been at the front', which were secretly forwarded to him by Sir Dunlop Smith. These were the censored letters of the Indian troops which we investigate in the next chapter. Finding the letters 'a complete revelation', he asked for more. On 6 October 1916, he thanked Smith for another batch of letters. He wanted, he intuited, to 'get together a whole collection of letters giving points of view from all parts of the Empire, of quite humble folk'.[29] The result was *The Eyes of Asia*. It was published in the American *Saturday Evening Post* in six parts over the months of May and June, and appeared in book form in the United States in 1918. In November 1918, Kipling forwarded to Smith a copy of the book, assuring him that there was nothing in the letters that would land Smith in trouble with India House and yet concluding 'It's to the censored letters I owe it.' Here indeed, in a small packet, was the essence of the India Kipling adored and idealised: the land of 'manly', 'humble', 'loyal' and usually semi-literate men from Northern India and the North West Frontier province, now fighting at the empire's hour of need – a far cry from the revolutionary Ghadars or Bengali nationalists.

In a context in which these letters have survived, Kipling's 'recreations' with their points of fidelity, departure or exaggeration provide singular insights into how they were being understood and utilised for propaganda purposes by the greatest British writer of the time. Was there conflict or contiguity between his roles as an artist, a jingo-imperialist and a war propagandist? The work comprises four short pieces. Three of these – 'A Retired Gentleman', 'The Fumes of the Heart' and 'A Trooper of Horse' – take the form of 'letters' where Kipling imagines himself to be a wounded Rajput, a Sikh and a Muslim sepoy, respectively, writing from English hospitals or France; 'The Private Account', on the other hand, recreates the scene of reading of one such letter by the family of the sepoy in a village in the North West Frontier Province. In each of them, the sepoy is a predictably semi-educated and infantile figure overwhelmed by the supposed superiority, generosity and fairness of the Raj. But what makes the construction both tantalising and disturbing is the combination of the 'real'

---

[29] The papers are to be found in the Kipling Archive, University of Sussex Library, The Keep, Sx MS 54/3/1, Ad. 1. Also see the succinct 'Introduction' on the Kipling Society website, www.kiplingsociety.co.uk/rg_asia_intro.htm.

and the 'propagandist'. Kipling mentioned to Smith that what struck him
was how, on coming to Europe, the soldiers had 'discovered the nakedness
of their own land'.[30] Kipling's Sikh soldier, in 'Fumes of the Heart' writes
from the Brighton Pavilion hospital as follows:

> The rain in Franceville is always sure and abundant and in excess. They grow
> all that we grow such as peas, onions, garlic, spinach, beans, cabbages and
> wheat. They do not grow small grains or millet, and their only spice is mus-
> tard. They do not drink water, but the juice of apples which they squeeze
> into barrels for that purpose. A full bottle is sold for two pice. They do not
> drink milk but there is abundance of it. It is all cows' milk, of which they
> make butter in a churn which is turned by a dog.

At first reading, it comes across as predictable in its parody of
'Occidentalism from below'.[31] But a comparison with some of the censored
sepoy letters shows how closely such a passage resonates with the actual
voices of the sepoys as they encounter France for the first time:

> The country is very fine, well-watered and fertile. The fields are very large,
> all gardens full of fruit trees. Every man's land yields him thousands of
> *maunds* of wheat … The fruits are pears, apricots, grapes and fruits of many
> kinds. Even the dogs refuse them at this season. Several regiments could eat
> from one tree. The people are very well-mannered and well to do. The value
> of each house may be set down as several *lakhs* and *crores* of rupees. Each
> house is a sample of paradise.[32]

Kipling the writer is perceptive to the 'fine excess' in such descriptions, but
the propagandist draws a veil as these initial raptures modulate into cries of
despair in their real-life letters: 'God knows whether the land of France is
stained with sin or whether the Day of Judgement has begun in France.'[33]
What we have in Kipling is the selective appropriation of the sepoy voice
for purposes of propaganda and recruitment. 'We Mussalmans should
have at least two troops out of four', writes the fictional Dafadar Abdul
Rahman to his mother, while his real-life cousin Havildar Abdul Rahman
warns his relatives 'For God's sake don't come, don't come, don't come to

---

[30] Sussex Kipling Archive, *Ibid*.
[31] The phrase has been used by Claude Markovits to describe some of the sepoy letters, Claude
Markovits, 'Indian Soldiers' Experiences in France during World War I', in Heike Liebau,
Katrin Bromber, Dyala Hamza, Katharina Lange and Ravi Ahuja (eds.), *The World in World
Wars: Experiences, Perceptions and Perspectives from Africa and Asia* (Leiden: Brill, 2010), 40.
[32] Saif Ali Khan, 40th Pathans or 129th Baluchis, 17 August 1915, France to Kasim Din, Persia, *CIM*,
IOR, L/MIL/5/825/5, 715, British Library.
[33] Amir Khan, 129th [Baluchis] from France to his brother in Punjab, 18 March 1915, *CIM*, L/MIL/5/
825/2, 141–142.

this war in Europe.'[34] In 'A Retired Gentleman', the convalescing Rajput's observation that 'it is the nature of the English to consider all created beings equal' (14), in accordance with the principles of British liberalism, is richly ironic in the context of the contemporary racist hierarchies of the British Indian army that ruled that the senior-most Indian officers would nonetheless be lower in rank than the junior-most British officer.

The Eyes of Asia is an unsettling work in the way it lurches between moments of acute, unerring understanding of the sepoy heart and a constant undertone of racist condescension that layers and distorts that understanding. The letters written by Kipling's sepoys are full of intimate details that chime closely with their real-life counterparts, from wonder at 'air machines' in the battlefield and admiration for the women in France ('It is the women who do all the work') to the need for education ('We must cause our children to be educated') to their astonishment at the Brighton Pavilion hospital ('a dome of gold and colours and glittering glass work') (37, 28). But such wonder or astonishment is habitually translated into words, phrases, pronunciations and spellings that go beyond either 'orientalism' or 'realism' into something rather tawdry for so gifted a writer: in the letters, the soldiers express their astonishment at 'Seyn Paul' (St Paul), they are obsessed with 'Ul or Baharun' (Earl and Baron), they refer to 'Baraich' (Bridge) and one of the princesses of Rajputana who had been educated at 'Ghatun' (Girton) (12–14): infantilisation and mockery become the mode of humour. Even at the time, such formulations would have come across as mawkish, let alone their offensiveness to our modern-day ears. Scenarios such as 'This Sahib says he will be my letter-writer at home ... Two annas! I give you one ... You've forgotten, we Sikhs always bargain' (25) come across as tired at best and racist at worst. Kipling's delicate understanding of human vulnerability, as in *Kim*, or linguistic inventiveness in evoking British soldiers, loafers or administrators in India, seems to be strangely missing or misplaced when it comes to evoking the sepoys.

What comes across in Kipling's text is a group of men who are naive, semi-educated and wholly beholden to the empire, with little of the poignancy, poetry and emotional intelligence that mark the actual censored letters. The mother in 'The Private Account', while listening to her son's letter being read out, interjects – 'He writes like a poet, my son' – but Kipling fails to provide any of the natural poetry of the letters. Similarly,

---

[34] *The Eyes of Asia*, 86; Havildar Abdul Rahman, 59th Rifles, in France to Naik Rajwali Khan in Baluchistan, 20 May 1915 (originally in Urdu), 20 May 1915, *CIM*, IOR, L/MIL/5/825/3, 394, British Library.

much of the mischief that often animates the letters – for example, the elaborate codes devised to avoid the censors or risqué references to French women – are strikingly absent. It is debatable whether Kipling's creativity was hemmed in through the requirements of propaganda or whether he failed to connect with the Indian soldiers in spite of the sympathy he showed in his fine couplet on a 'Hindu Sepoy in France' in 'Epithets of War'.[35] One wonders whether admission of such distance and difference from the sepoy, as in the couplet, rather than the identification and empathy that the ventriloquism of *The Eyes of Asia* demanded, was revealing of the affective structures of empire. Occasionally, he lifts sentences directly from the originals: 'This is not war. It is the ending of the world. This is not such a war as was related in the Mahabharata about our forefathers' becomes, in 'Fumes of the Heart', 'This war is not a war. It is a world-destroying battle.'[36] Or consider the following two extracts, each describing the lady of the house where an Indian sepoy had billeted, the first from an actual sepoy letter, the second written by Kipling's imaginary soldier in 'The Fumes of the Heart':

> Of her own free-will she washed my clothes, arranged my bed [and] polished my boots ... Every morning she used to prepare and give me a tray with bread, butter, milk and coffee ... When we had to leave that village the old lady wept on my shoulder. Strange that I had never seen her weeping for her dead son and yet she should weep for me! Moreover, at [our] parting she pressed on me a five franc note to meet my expenses en route.[37]

> Of her own free-will she washed my clothes, arranged my bed, and polished my boots daily for three months ... Each morning she prepared me a tray with bread, butter, milk and coffee. When we had to leave that village the old lady wept on my shoulder. It is strange that I had never seen her weep for her dead son, but she wept for me. Moreover at parting she would have had me take a fi-farang [five franc] note for the expenses.[38]

The exactness of reproduction is astonishing; in today's vocabulary, it would constitute a case of plagiarism, but actually one could read it to unearth a more intimate history of emotions.

For, while Kipling's construction of the sepoy is disappointingly reductive, his evocation of the mother–son relations is elaborate and

[35] 'Hindu Sepoy in France', 'Epitaphs of the War', in *The Collected Poems of Rudyard Kipling*, ed. R. T. Jones (Ware: Wordsworth, 2001), 399.
[36] Letters from a wounded Punjabi Rajput (England), 29 January, 1915, *CIM*, IOR L/MIL/5/825/1, 54, British Library; *The Eyes of Asia*, 42.
[37] Letter from Sher Bahadur Khan, 9 January 1916, France, *CIM*, IOR, L/MIL/5/826/1, 115, India Office Library, British Library.
[38] 'The Fumes of the Heart', *The Eyes of Asia* (New York: Doubleday, Page & Company, 1918), 36.

compelling: the trope of the 'French mother', a recurring theme in the letters, seems to have deeply engaged him. The third story centres around a son reading out to his parents a letter from his older soldier-brother in France, and the final story swells to a crescendo of longing of the sepoy for his mother in India:

> Mother, think of me always as though I were sitting near by, just as I imagine you always beside me ... I shall come in the dead of the night and knock at your door ... Oh, my mother, my mother, I am your son, your son; and as I have said at the beginning I will return to your arms from out of this country, when God shall permit.[39]

This extended dialogue with the mother, so vividly imagined, gains special resonance in the context of Kipling's own life. As is well documented, Kipling spent eight idyllic years in Bombay where he apparently spoke, wrote and even 'dreamed' in Hindustani. Yet, like many children from the colonial administrative class, he was separated from his mother and sent off to England, an experience that haunted him throughout his life – he would write later of his sense of being abandoned by his parents. In his old age, does this imaginative identification with the Indian soldier make Kipling revisit his childhood and create a fantasy of maternal warmth still located in India? As Edward Said observes in his beautifully nuanced introduction to *Kim*, 'Kipling not only wrote about India, he was *of* it.' 'The imperial experience, while often regarded as exclusively political', Said notes, 'was also an experience that entered into the cultural and aesthetic life as well.'[40] Through its tender descriptions of the mother–son dyad, *The Eyes of Asia* shows how the imperial experience entered the most intimate sphere of the emotional life as well. Another sub-current also pulses beneath this sense: more recently, in September 1915, his eighteen-year-old son John (Jack) Kipling, a Lieutenant in the 2nd Battalion Irish Guards, had disappeared in the battle of Loos. The imagined Indian soldier writes 'Mother, once I was reported "missing, killed or believed taken prisoner"', exactly the message that Kipling and his wife received. The painful story of their subsequent life-long search to find their son and Kipling's intense involvement in the work of imperial war commemoration is well known. In these contexts, *The Eyes of Asia* is deeply revealing of the complex emotional history of the writer himself: the grief of the father and the desolation of the child arising from the dislocations of war

---

[39] 'A Trooper of the Horse', 77, 78, 101.
[40] 'Introduction' to Edward Said (ed.), *Kim* (London: Penguin, 1987), 12.

and colonialism. This is not to excuse the imperialistic elements in the text or his patronising, if affectionate, attitude towards the sepoy, but rather to suggest, as Said notes with reference to *Kim*, that 'there is more than one history in it to be remembered'.[41]

The Experiences of Ram Singh: Touch, Intimacy and Ideology

One of the most remarkable and intimate accounts of the Indian war experience on the Western Front would appear from a British officer a decade after the war – the trench diary of Captain Roly Grimshaw – which would then form the basis of his novella *The Experiences of Ram Singh, Dafadar of Horse: An Echo of 1914*. The diary is an almost daily record from the outbreak of the war to 2 June 1915 (when he got wounded), while the novella, somewhat like Kipling's text, is a fictionalised account of the opening months of the conflict imagined through the perspective of an Indian dafadar (or cavalry sergeant) Ram Singh. It was first serialised in 1930 in the *Assam Journal* in India. The date of publication is significant. On the one hand, it is part of the publishing boom of trench memoirs in the late 1920s, where it takes its place alongside Edmund Blunden's *Undertones of War* (1928), Siegfried Sassoon's *The Memoirs of a Fox-Hunting Man* (1928) and Robert Graves's *Goodbye to All That* (1929), all of which mention, though in passing, the presence of Indian troops; at the same time, its publication in India rather than in Britain places it, as we will explore, in a very different context. The differences between the diary and the novella are illuminating in understanding the fluctuating representations of the Indian sepoy and the complex impulses at work.

Roly Grimshaw had completed two years of service in India as the instructor at the School of Cavalry and Equitation at Saugor when the war broke out. An officer with the 34th Poona Horse, he re-joined his regiment in Egypt en route to France and arrived at Marseilles at 4pm on 14 October. 'I never thought I should be in Calais with a squadron of the Poona Horse', he wrote on 31 October.[42] On arrival, the 34th Poona Horse was immediately dismounted, and the sepoys were made to dig trenches. In November, along with a British cavalry unit (7th Dragoon Guards), the

---

[41] 'Introduction' to *Kim*, 12.
[42] Captain 'Roly' Grimshaw, 'Diary of an Indian Cavalry Officer', in Captain 'Roly' Grimshaw, *Indian Cavalry Officer, 1914–1915*, ed. Col. J. Wakefield and Lt Col. J. M. Weippart (Tunbridge Wells: Costello, 1986), 28.

34th Poona Horse was sent to relieve the infantry and take part in the Battle of Festubert (15–25 May 1915); and in December, when the Indian Corps was seriously depleted and demoralised, it was used in a fierce but unsuccessful counter-attack. The 34th Poona Horse thus became one of the first Indian units to see action and register the full intensity of trench warfare in the opening months of the conflict. Grimshaw was severely wounded, and was brought back under fire by an Indian sepoy and a British officer; he was invalided out of the line and sent to England, where he spent much of his time visiting and cheering up the wounded in different war hospitals. Meanwhile, the Poona Horse went on to win battle honours at the Somme in 1916 and Cambrai in 1917.

On arrival at the Western Front, on 3 September, Grimshaw wrote in his diary that, 'if anything, my whole nature recoils with horror from the prospects of killing with my own hands some inoffensive German … I jot them down because I wish to record my exact feelings and mentality and not merely to conform to what is expected of one' (19–20). It is this scrupulous effort towards honesty and precision that marks – in the absence of a trench diary by an Indian combatant – what is so far possibly the most intimate record of the Indian war experience in the opening months on the Western Front. He describes the sea-voyage and arrival of the Poona Horse in Marseilles, the men being made to 'dig like hell' and 'frozen stiff', the plight of the horses with oversized frost-shoes and the battles of Neuve Chapelle, Festubert and Givenchy as experienced by both the British officers and the sepoys – the bombing-raids, rescue-missions, walking on the dead, and the loss of comrades. Grimshaw's diary is like the classic English trench account turned upside down as it bears traumatic testimony to the everyday trench deprivations of the Indian army: of Ashraf Khan horribly mutilated by a shell; of Fateh Hyder Shah carefully feeling bodies in no man's land; or of Abdul Gafoor pulling Grimshaw to safety. On 20 December 1914, as the sepoys stumbled their way to the hospital, wounded and dazed after the battle of Givenchy, Grimshaw wrote

> The state of the wounded beggars all description. Little Gurkhas slopping through the freezing mud barefooted; Tommies with no caps and plastered in blood and mud from head to foot; Sikhs with their hair all down and looking more wild and weird than I have ever seen them; Pathans more dirty and untidy than usual; all limping or reeling along like drunken men, some helping an almost foundered comrade … I asked myself, is that what civilisation means? … I stopped some of the Gurkhas and asked them why they walked in bare feet. Those that replied said, 'Sahib, our feet hurt us terribly, but in boots they hurt us worse.' (54)

More like the opening stanza of Wilfred Owen's 'Dulce et Decorum Est' rather than Girdwood's manufactured images of heroic Sikhs and Gurkhas, this is the Indian sepoy's traumatic entry from orientalism and myth into the war's blood-dimmed history. Grimshaw's adulation of the men – 'What my feelings were about our poor men I can find no words to express. Their almost dumb suffering was infinitely worse than if they had complained openly' (44) – was a common sentiment in the British officers' diaries and resonates with fellow officer Andrew Kerr's observations about the Jammu and Kashmir Rifles in East Africa: 'I can never say enough about the men.'[43] It is frustrating for us today that Grimshaw's 'deep concern for, and love of, his men', like that of countless fellow officers, is never evolved into any powerful critique of the campaign or war or empire, and the hierarchies of race and rank within the army remained intact, but that should not blind us to pockets of intimacy that sometimes developed between the British officers and the Indian sepoys.

In *Touch and Intimacy in First World War Literature* (2006), I argued that the trench experience and writing were marked by moments of bodily contact and tactile tenderness that went beyond the strict categories of gender and sexuality.[44] Grimshaw's diary is haunted by similar memories across the line of colour: he recalled standing amidst the muddy slush of the trench on what felt like a 'sand-bag', only to shine his torch downwards and realise, to his horror, that he was standing on the corpse of a young Pathan; a bit later, on the same day, when Ashraf Khan, 'one of the nicest looking fellows I have seen', was badly injured and dies, Grimshaw had the corpse 'carefully put on one side' to avoid it being trodden upon until it could be buried, and later 'moved him myself and was astounded at his extraordinary lightness' (39). A couple of months later, in December, when a *sowar* slipped into the mud, Grimshaw 'hauled' him out and 'took the poor chap, almost pulseless, to a ruined house a few feet away, stripped him, and four of us massaged him' (55). If, in Clare Buck's perceptive reading, these scenes are designed to contribute 'to the image of Grimshaw as an officer whose genuine concern for his men is indexed through physical touch',[45] such charged moments – particularly recorded in a private

---

[43] See Andrew Kerr, *I Can Never Say Enough about the Men: A History of the Jammu and Kashmir Rifles throughout Their World War One East African Campaign* (Gloucestershire: PMC Management Consultants, 2010).
[44] Santanu Das, *Touch and Intimacy in First World War Literature*, 109–136.
[45] Buck, *Conceiving Strangeness*, 26. According to Buck, 'Grimshaw thus finds in the conventions of war writing a way to enable a militarily authorized trans-cultural bonding' (26). For her, Grimshaw's response to the inadvertent bodily contact with the dead Pathan is informed by 'disgust' (27), which is supplanted by 'horror' in the imagined reconstruction of the scene when Ram Singh has to stand on the shoulders of the dead Pathan (31).

diary with no immediate intention of publication – equally testify, I would argue, to an alternative history of emotions between the British officer and the Indian sepoy, often forged at an individual level and yet circumscribed by the colonial ideology of the day. It is an intimacy which is fraught and asymmetrical, perilously forged amidst the heat of battle and yet informed by hierarchies of race and rank and for which we are still trying to find a nuanced vocabulary.

Roly Grimshaw is a classic example of a substantial number of British Indian officers who, in the warmth of their affection and care for these men, would have considered themselves non-racist and liberal and protested against many of the discriminatory policies – and yet they were an integral part of the colonial establishment, its ideology and hierarchies. Grimshaw recalled a huge row with a racist R.A.M.C. officer who was trying to throw Indian officers out of a first-class carriage and he noted bitterly how 'typical of the attitude towards Indians' it was and yet, faced with tough choices on the battlefield, he towed the official line that 'a British officer is worth more than a wounded sepoy' (43). Race and rank, as is often the case, are difficult to disentangle. In the diary, he speaks about 'the carefully suppressed repulsion that many weak-minded Englishmen cultivate with regard to all who are not "white"' (47). In many ways, this is the classic blind-spot of early-twentieth-century liberalism, which was made to accommodate, quite comfortably, the project of empire: cases of racism, discrimination or subjugation, so abhorrent otherwise to the liberal ideology, were blamed on a 'few weak-minded' individuals rather than being questioned as something intrinsic to the very ideology of empire. That deeper critique was starting to be voiced during the First World War by intellectuals such as Tagore, Iqbal and Aurobindo Ghosh, as we will examine in the final chapter of the book.

The novella *The Experiences of Ram Singh* (1930), on the other hand, is a palimpsest, mixing first-hand testimony, report, fiction, hearsay, ventriloquism, dream, wish-fulfilment and propaganda, with one running into the other. It follows the fortunes of Ram Singh – a dafadar or sergeant – from his mobilisation and the rigours of the sea journey through his arrival in Marseilles with his cavalry unit, his baptism by fire and his share of horrors to him being injured and hospitalised in the Brighton Pavilion. Ram Singh is Grimshaw's Indian alter ego in what essentially is 'a literary act of going native'.[46] The narrative follows, to a large degree, Grimshaw's own trajectory, from mobilisation to injury, but is layered with the thick description

[46] Buck, *Conceiving Strangeness*, 29.

of an Indian sepoy just arrived in Europe. Grimshaw's use of Hindi words –
'Mar gaya' (has died), 'dushman' (enemy), 'behosh' (unconscious) – is precise and unerring. Traumatic memories leach from diary to fiction. The
memory of standing on the much-trodden and submerged 'young Pathan',
recorded on 23 November 1914 – 'I decided to say nothing and tried to
blot the hideous picture from my brain' (38) – resurfaces in the novella
as Ram Singh notes: 'I wonder if that will be my end … He tried to blot
the scene from his mind but could not.' (138). If trauma is the common
ground between the diary and the novella, so is the hushed intimacy of the
successful rescue mission. Consider the following accounts, the first from
the diary and the second from the novella:

> When it was dark, I got Fateh Hyder Shah to organise the little rescue party
> under my direction … Firstly a man [Fateh Hyder Shah] crept out and
> made a round of the bodies lying grouped together some 150 yards off. He
> had to feel each carefully to see if any life existed. After about 20 minutes,
> I heard the long faint whistle (by mouth), followed by a single short note.
> This was the signal, prearranged, that told me that only one survivor existed
> amidst that group. I therefore sent out four men to bring him in. (*Diary*, 44)

> [Ram Singh] examined the first man and, finding the hands and face quite
> cold, opened the *kurta* in order to put his own hand on the man's chest. The
> body was stone cold … Satisfied that only one man was alive, Ram Singh
> gave the prearranged whistle … In a few minutes he could just discern four
> figures crawling towards him. They soon arrived. (*The Experiences of Ram
> Singh*, 146)

The act of 'feeling' the sepoy-body, carried out by Fateh Hyder, is re-
imagined and re-enacted through the consciousness of Ram Singh. While
such an act is an exercise in 'combat gnosticism' as a marker of authenticity,[47] it is also a phantasmatic moment of touch and intimacy with the
sepoy-body the British officer was denied in real life.

Such subliminal impulses are examined in a remarkable chapter titled
'Ram Singh's Dream'. War nightmares were the commonest symptoms of
shellshock, prompting Sigmund Freud to move *beyond* the pleasure principle. But Ram Singh must be one of the handful of war fiction's heroes
who still can experience dream as wish-fulfilment. As the train leaves for
the front, Ram Singh dozes off and we are given a vivid and elaborate
dream-sequence. He dreams that he guides his men to food and shelter,
proudly noting 'Had he not fully demonstrated himself a leader of men?
What would these miserable creatures have done without him?' (111).

[47] Campbell, 'Combat Gnosticism'.

This is particularly poignant given the contemporary construction of the sepoy as congenitally incapable of leadership: '[The Indians] are of course splendid fighters, but are very lost without their officers.'[48] What we have in the scene is Grimshaw's fantasised reconstruction of the sepoy psyche. Yet, his grasp of the complexities of the sepoy heart is acute, reminding one of similarly delicate moments in Mulk Raj Anand's novel *Across the Black Waters*. Ram Singh's careful recovery and handing over of the dead English officer's 'identity disc, wrist watch and gold ring' to the doctor – 'Please take them from me, otherwise I may be accused of theft' (168) – is touchingly perceptive of the trepidations of the sepoy. In the dream-world, the sepoys' night of rest is broken by the arrival of a badly wounded British trooper. The Indian sepoys take turns to nurse him, but he dies: 'With tender care the body was carried out then, wrapped in the trooper's greatcoat, laid to rest.' Is this Grimshaw's passionate defence of his men and fierce rebuttal of the wartime stereotype of the 'savage Oriental' robbing and defiling the dead? Yet, in spite of this sensitivity, there is a touch of imperial/Oriental fantasy. The next morning, Ram Singh does not just abort a sudden ambush but kills a German trooper, driving his blade 'deep into the man's [German's] vitals' (115). At one level, we are back to the world of newspaper cartoons about Sikh and Gurkha gallantry-tipping-into-brutality; on the other hand, following the logic of the scene, is it the imperial unconscious shoving 'deep' into the 'vitals' of Ram Singh's consciousness the British officer's fantasies of the loyal sepoy avenging the death of his British officer?

What makes *The Experiences of Ram Singh* such a complex text is the uneasy combination of the genuine affection of an army officer towards his men and the adherence to the myth of an 'imperial bond of brotherhood' that draws a veil over institutional racism and double-standards or the ideology of empire itself. Thus, during the battle of Neuve Chapelle, when Ram Singh complains against the decision of retaining the 'corpse-like' sepoys further in the trenches without relief, 'Smith Sahib' places his arm across his N.C.O.'s shoulders and replies 'What you say Ram Singh is true ... but as there are no men we must support the trials together.' (149). Protest is voiced and glossed over; blame for the 'terrible ordeal' is shifted from any critique of Indians being used as 'cannon-fodder' to the peculiar predicament of war; sympathy is generated both for Ram Singh and for Smith Sahib, the two selves of Grimshaw; the imperial ideology remains intact. While the 'Diary' is studded with intimate moments actually shared

---

[48] Lt R. L. Benson to Hardinge, November 1914, Hardinge Papers, 102/1/10066, Cambridge University Library.

between the British officer and the sepoys, the 'great bond of sympathy' between the two in the novella veers between imperial romance and government propaganda. Compare one of the most poignant moments – the death of Ashraf Khan – in the *Diary* with its rewriting in the novella, where the latter becomes the young Beji Singh:

> The killed was Ashraf Khan, one of the nicest looking fellows I have seen. Both his legs were blown off below the knee, and one arm, and half his face. I saw he was a hopeless case and did up the others, two of whom were quite bad. Poor Ashraf Khan, an only son, and his mother a widow. He lived for 40 minutes. I did what I could for him but, as he was unconscious, it was not much use (39).

> Lying in the bottom of the trench was Beji Singh with one leg severed at the knee, the other almost cut away at the fork. The mangled boy was quite conscious ... Smith Sahib bent close over the lad in order to administer a tabloid of morphia. Beji Singh, whose arms were uninjured, brushing aside the proffered drug, seized his Squadron Commander by both hands. Momentarily, he held him in a vice-like grip uttering the words 'Sahib, Sahib', then letting go, subsided lifeless. Smith Sahib turned to Ram Singh with the words '*Guzar gea*'. Both of them gently lifting the battered remnants, laid the body in the niche where had rested the Hun and the other Indian. Tears stood in Ram Singh's eyes: what would he say to Beji's mother, she a widow and Beji an only son?

> Covered with blood from the death grip of a young soldier for whom he entertained more than a passing regard, Smith Sahib felt strangely unnerved at the incident. (150)

What does Grimshaw gain by changing the real-life account of being a witness, and largely unable to help, to the fictional death-embrace with Beji Singh in the novella? First, the Muslim sepoy, with his potentially divided allegiance in view of Turkey's war involvement, is changed to a loyal Sikh. Second, the fictional representation is almost a reassuring literalisation of the so-called 'ma–baap' (mother–father) system which structured the British Indian army. However, it was in the trenches of the Western Front that this construction was being sorely tried, as in the following letter: 'We are like goats tied to a butcher's stake.'[49] At a time when some of the sepoys, thrown into the battle, were beginning to recast the colonisers as 'butchers', Grimshaw not only portrays Owen Sahib as the all-caring *pater* but hijacks the sepoy voice itself to wring out a desperately wishful endorsement of the 'ma–baap' ethos ('Sahib, Sahib') at the moment of

---

[49] Letter from Abdul Rahim Khan, 7 February 1917, to Mir Hassan Khan, Hyderabad, *CIM*, IOR, L/MIL/5/827/1, 143, British Library.

death. But rather than just an act of 'going native' or overdetermined by the Saidean framework of power and knowledge, such moments, I would argue, are complex emotional flashpoints and hint at a deeper history of feeling – intensities and intimacies heightened by racial difference in an all-male environment – that the British officers felt for their men but could not articulate. Such feelings, delicately fringing the text through phrases such as 'a young soldier for whom he entertained more than a passing regard' or 'one of the nicest looking fellows I have seen' in the diary, could perhaps only be perversely consummated in the death-grip. There might also have been a personal dimension. When Grimshaw was wounded, he was carried to safety by an Indian sepoy. Is 'Sahib, Sahib', with its combination of trust and forgiveness, a textual rewriting of a desired moment that never happened in real-life, a fictional salve for the British officer's own seared conscience when, instead of protecting his men like a 'baap' (father), he had in fact led them, like a 'butcher', to their death?

The extraordinary rewriting and ventriloquism could also be understood in a wider formal and political context. In terms of the genre, one may note that the tearful embrace between comrades at the moment of dying – a standard trope of trench narratives, from Kat and Paul's in Eric Maria Remarque's *All Quiet on the Western Front* to Raleigh and Stanhope's in Sherriff's *Journey's End*, both published a year earlier, in 1929, is re-imagined here across the divide of race and nationality. In many ways, it is reminiscent of the death-embrace between the black Peter and the white Meriwether (whose family had formerly owned Peter's grandfather as a slave) on the battlefields of France in the African-American writer Jessie Fauset's war novel *There Is Confusion* (1924). But, as I have been trying to demonstrate, the political contexts of Grimshaw's novella were very different from those of either its European or its American cousins. *The Experiences of Ram Singh* was serialised in India in 1930 – the year when the nationalist movement in India reached a new point of intensity and focus, with Gandhi's Dandi March, the launch of the Civil Disobedience movement and the declaration of Purna Swaraj or full self-rule by the Indian National Congress.[50] At such a fraught moment, the resurrection of the shared war experience and ventriloquism of the Indian sepoy-voice, culminating in his dying acknowledgement of the homosocial bond on the battlefields of France, could be read as a desperately wishful rewriting of a previous moment in the history of empire, the swan-song of Indo-British amity itself.

[50] Sarkar, *Modern India*, 254–348; Bose and Jalal, *Modern South Asia*, 120.

What each of these texts seeks to do, in different ways, is to reimagine the war from the perspective of the Indian soldier, from the aristocratic Hira Singh to the sepoy in the Brighton pavilion to Ashraf Khan at the moment of death, for the purposes of empire. The imagination in each of these texts uneasily lurches between imperial fantasies and paranoia: emotional ambivalence spurs formal complexity. In spite of the adherence to or open celebration of empire, each of these men occasionally shows a remarkable understanding of the sepoy psyche. What each suggests is a complex structure of feeling: it was not just an imperial relationship, or racist hierarchy, nor homosocial bond in the trenches. A touch of all three, it gave rise to a certain assumption of intimacy, felt or imagined, for which fiction provided the playing field. Power, propaganda, racism, infantilisation, warmth, affection, difference and perhaps a diffused eroticism were all fused and confused, resulting from but spilling beyond the work of the empire.

PART III

The Sepoy Heart

Figure 5.1 'An Indian, unable to write, is putting his thumb impression on the pay-book'. © Imperial War Museum (Q 12500).

Figure 5.2 'A wounded soldier dictating a letter to a fellow soldier or a scribe on the grounds of the Brighton Pavilion hospital'. © Imperial War Museum (Q 053887).

CHAPTER 5

'Life-Writing' from Below
Letters, Poems, Prayers and Songs of Sepoys
in Europe, 1914–1918

It is the close-up of three anonymous hands – differentiated by colour, gesture and uniform but severed from the faces or the rest of the body – that is startling (Figure 5.1).[1] A 'white' hand – confident and bureaucratic – grasps and guides the thumb of the 'coloured' hand, protruding from the left-hand side of the picture, to get a thumb-impression. We see part of the officer's uniformed torso and both his hands – but little of the non-white person. The camera, it seems, knew; consciously or unconsciously, it replicated the drama of marginalisation as well as the anonymity of the act. The caption says 'An Indian, unable to write, is putting his thumb impression on the pay-book.' Insurgent under the touch are not just body parts but the weight of colonial history. The gesture captures across the line of colour not just the recruitment process but the story of colonialism itself, with its systemic inequalities and asymmetries. This brisk, bureaucratic touch is answered by another more lingering, tactile moment captured on the grounds of the Brighton Pavilion.[2] Here, a similarly non-literate sepoy dictates a letter to a fellow sepoy or a scribe (Figure 5.2). The violent traces of war are evident on his wheelchair-bound body. What was probably meant to be a staged tableau of imperial medical care evolves into something far more poignant as the sepoy leans across to touch the scribe or his fellow sepoy. It is a gesture of gratitude, trust and intimacy: thank you for writing, the hand says, as the body fills in the gap left by language. It is this intimate body and the inner world of the sepoy in Europe – in the Western Front, in hospitals in England, and in the POW camp of Wünsdorf in Germany – that this chapter examines.

The First World War marked the high-water mark in British life-writing. As Wilfred Owen wrote, 'Above all I am not concerned with Poetry. My subject is War, and the pity of War.'[3] If Owen's was the most spectacular

---

[1] IWM Photograph Archives, Q 12500.
[2] IWM Photograph Archives, Q 053887.
[3] Owen, in *The Poems of Wilfred Owen*, 192.

refashioning of poetry as testimony in wartime, his fellow comrades were not far behind. If the mouth could not articulate what the eyes had seen or ears heard, the hand wrote. Letters, memoirs, diaries, biographies, auto-biographies, fiction and poetry poured out to the extent that much of war writing became a form of life-writing, from trench poetry to Robert Graves's *Goodbye to All That* (1929) to VAD nurse Vera Brittain's *Testament of Youth* (1933). But what about the colonial life-writing in the time of war? In recent years, there has been growing interest in recovering colonial and non-European life-stories, though these works often focus on the highly literate, if not the cultural elite, within these communities. In *Postcolonial Life-Writing: Culture, Politics and Self-Representation* (2009), Bart Moore-Gilbert traces the 'detailed poetics of a subgenre' through the writings by figures as diverse as Mahatma Gandhi, Wole Soyinka and Edward Said; his focus is on the decentred but on the scripted and the literary. But can there be 'life-writing' from below? What will our sources be then and does such a project put pressure on the very textual bias of the definition which omits the life-stories of the majority of the world's people in the early twentieth century?

While the emphasis in Part II was on European representations of the sepoy, our focus here is on the sepoys' various experiences in Europe, as expressed by themselves. Like their European and Dominion comrades, these men 'lived, felt dawn, saw sunset glow/Loved and were loved', but we have very few full-length records.[4] In recent years, several testimonies have surfaced, particularly a handful of remarkable diaries and memoirs by non-combatants that we will investigate in the next two chapters. Our main sources of information remain the translated and censored letters by the sepoys.[5] While the letters are often quoted and extracted without much textual or formal analysis, here I seek to read them more closely – their materiality, their narrative and psychological structures, their liter-ariness – for a more formally and emotionally nuanced understanding of

---

[4] John McCrae, 'In Flanders Fields', in George Walter (ed.), *The Penguin Book of First World War Poetry* (London: Penguin, 2004), 155.

[5] See Omissi's excellent selection *Indian Voices of the First World War*; also see 'Europe through Indian Eyes: Indian Soldiers Encounter England and France, 1914–1918', *The English Historical Review*, 122, 496 (2007), 371–396. A number of scholars have written powerfully on the letters: see, among others, Visram, 'Indians in the First World War', in *Asians in Britain*, 254–299; Susan VanKoski, 'Letters Home 1915–16: Punjabi Soldiers Reflect on War and Life in Europe and Their Meanings for Home and Self', *International Journal of Punjab Studies*, 2, 1 (1995), 43–63; Claude Markovits, 'Indian Soldiers' Experiences in France during World War I'; Singh, *The Testimonies of Indian Soldiers*; and Basu, *For King and Another Country*.

this extraordinary archive. Second, I consider them alongside the poems they often contain as well as the sound-recordings of songs, stories and prayers from the POW camp at Wünsdorf. They help to illuminate not just what these men did but the underworld of their consciousness. If the biographer, in Richard Holmes's classic formulation, is a ferry-man, like Charon, between the living and the dead, how do we 'track the footsteps'[6] of people who could not read or write? What I wish to recover here is not the life-trajectory of any particular sepoy or the collective biography of the Indian war experience, but rather certain 'moments of intimacy, revelation, or particular inwardness'[7] that enable us to understand the inner world of the sepoy.

Before we begin our investigation, it may be worthwhile to provide a brief outline of the sepoys' engagements in Europe.[8] In late September and early October, the first Indian units started to arrive at Marseilles, totalling around 24,000 men. They comprised two infantry divisions, renamed Lahore and Meerut, and a cavalry brigade. They formed the Indian Expeditionary Force 'A' (IEF A), and were put under the command of Lt-General Sir James Willcocks, arriving at a time when 'Ypres was trembling in the balance and each man was worth his weight in gold'.[9] It was a first in many senses. For the first time in history, the British empire was 'allowing' its non-white troops to fight against Europeans on European soil, a 'privilege' extended to Indians but not to West Indians or indigenous South Africans. Between August 1914 and December 1919, 138,608 Indians, including 1,923 officers, 87,412 other ranks and 49,273 non-combatants served in Europe.[10] Wonder had piled upon wonder as they were transported via railways to Bombay or Lahore, then put on huge ships, row upon row ploughing the seas, while submarines kept watch; and then to arrive in 'Marsels' and to be cheered by white men in coats and even kissed by white women in hats. Harnam Singh Bath records in his diary that some women, seeing Sikhs for the first time, even offered to shave off their beards, thinking they had been in the ship too long, while Singh thought that they were so 'fair-skinned' because they had 'prayed

---

[6] Richard Holmes, *Footsteps: Adventures of a Romantic Biographer* (London: Flamingo, 1995), 27.
[7] Hermione Lee, *Body Parts: Essays on Life-Writing* (London: Random House, 2010), 3.
[8] See Merewether and Smith, *The Indian Corps in France*; there is a range of recent books, including Corrigan, *Sepoys in the Trenches*; Morton-Jack, *The Indian Army on the Western Front*; Basu, *For King and Another Country*; for illustrated accounts, see Chhina, *Les Hindous*; Das, *Indian Troops in Europe, 1914–1918*; Kant, *If I Should Die*.
[9] Willcocks' letter to Hardinge, 2 September 1915, Hardinge Papers, Cambridge University Library.
[10] *Statistics of the Military Effort*, 777.

and meditated too much' in their previous lives![11] Europe and civilisation and modernity melted in a dream so sweet that, if these sepoys woke, they wished Caliban-like to dream again. 'We have seen things that our eyes never dreamt of seeing', wrote Sepoy Suleiman Khan from France.[12] What Claude Markovits has called 'occidentalism from below' is written as a state of sensuous rapture: Paris is compared to a 'Fairyland', every house is 'a sample of Paradise', and 'the bazaars are most magnificent'.[13] From 17 October, 1914, the sepoys would be moved to the trenches; in the course of the next one year, they would take part in the battles of First and Second Ypres, Neuve Chapelle, Festubert and Loos. If the trauma of the Western front defied, as Walter Benjamin noted, the limits of 'communicable experience' even for trained European soldiers, one could imagine the plight of these men who had just arrived in their summer cotton tunics. 'This is not a war; this is the end of the world': lack of measure yielded to apocalyptic imagining.[14]

Letters As Literature: Materiality, Form and Emotion

'Oh happy paper, how I envy your lot. We shall be here but you will go and see [India]': thus addresses a sepoy in Pashto a letter written otherwise in Urdu, pointing to a certain epistolary self-consciousness.[15] It has been said that the First World War produced, among other things, 'a sudden and irrepressible bulimia of letter-writing'.[16] Whether it was bulimic outpouring or conscious testimony, the Indians were not far behind. 'Why only one', wrote back an Indian medical officer from a hospital ship, 'You ought to write to me every week or at least every fortnight.'[17] Between March and April 1915, Indian soldiers from France were writing around 10,000 letters a week. The Indian sepoy, however, was no stranger to letters, even though he could not read. For centuries, he had been

---

[11] Harnam Singh, Personal Diary, by kind permission of UK Punjab Heritage who, along with Rana Chhina, are translating it for publication.
[12] Suleiman Khan, France, October 1916, Censored Indian Mail of the First World War (*CIM*), India Office Records (IOR), L/MIL/5/826/8, 1272, British Library.
[13] Sirdar Ali Khan, Sialkot Cavalry Brigade, 6 August 1916, *CIM*, IOR, L/MIL/826/1, 1023, British Library.
[14] 'A wounded Punjabi Rajput', 29 January 1915, *CIM*, IOR, L/MIL/5/825/1, 54, British Library.
[15] An Afridi Pathan to his brother [55th Rifles India], 27 June 1915, *CIM*, IOR, L/MIL/5/825/4, 516, British Library.
[16] Quoted by Martyn Lyons, *The Writing Culture of Ordinary People in Europe, c. 1860–1920* (Cambridge: Cambridge University Press, 2012), 77.
[17] A Sub-Assistant Surgeon (Hindu) to a friend (Peshawar District, NWFP), late January or early February 1915, *CIM*, IOR, L/MIL/5/825/1, 49, British Library.

travelling as an imperial sentinel – in Somalia, China, Malta, Egypt; as early as the 1840s, each sepoy was entitled to send one letter home free of postage and get one back; there was great resentment when this privilege was withdrawn in the 1850s.[18] But the scale of letter-composition in the First World War was completely different; above all, the processes of colonial censorship now ensured that substantial chunks from these letters survived for posterity.[19]

The original letters are now lost. What we have are extracts from them, as selected from the originals and translated by the colonial censors. We usually read the extracts in the censors' cold print, but a couple of the original letters have recently surfaced, and highlight their materiality (Figure 5.3)

War letters are never just read; as missives from the war-zones, they serve as both physical trace and report. In semi-literate communities, they assumed an exaggerated 'aura' as both material and content – viewed, circulated and preserved, they served as much as visual and tactile objects as they did as decipherable texts.[20] As the note from Kishan Devi cited in the Introduction suggests, the letters would often be taken to the village school-master or the postal officer to be read aloud. If letter-writing was a collaborative act, letter-reading was a communal one. These processes of composition and reception raise questions about the very nature of the letters: were they private or public? How did the knowledge of colonial censorship affect composition? What narrative traditions did they draw upon?[21] These extracts were used by the colonial censors to assess the 'morale' of the troops; often a selection would be forwarded to the Chief Censor, E. B. Howell. Can an archive, thus created to police the thought-processes of the sepoys, be opened up to provide a history of emotions from below?

By early 1915, the men had realised that their letters were being read, and they drew on ingenious codes to avoid censorship. Perhaps the best-known

---

[18] I am grateful to Radhika Singha for alerting me to this point.
[19] This extensive collection is housed in the British Library and mainly comprises extracts from letters written by soldiers from the Western Front, and England, with occasional extracts from letters to these men from their relatives in India or comrades in other fronts.
[20] Priyasha Mukhopadhyay makes a similar point in the context of colonial documents in 'Of Greasy Notebooks and Dirty Newspapers: Reading the Illegible in *The Village in the Jungle*', *The Journal of Commonwealth Literature*, 50, 1 (2015), 59–73. For an example of how anthropological insights can open up the process of reading (or not reading), see Veena Das, 'The Signature of the State: The Paradox of Illegibility', in Veena Das and Deborah Poole (eds.), *Anthropology in the Margins of the State* (Santa Fe: SAR Press, 2004), 225–252.
[21] Primers for letter-writing were being made available as part of colonial education at the time, though we do not know whether the sepoys or scribes were familiar with them.

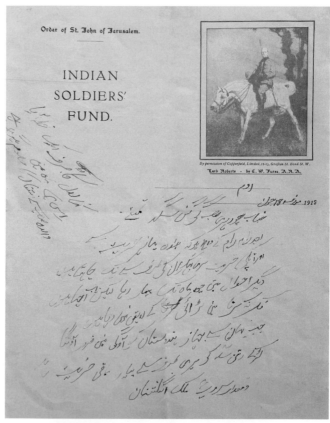

Figure 5.3   A letter in Urdu and envelope stamped 'Brighton, 9pm 18 Ju 15' from Saroop Singh to his cousin in Punjab. Courtesy of Haryana Academy of History and Culture, India.

example is a letter written shortly after the battle of Neuve Chapelle in April 1915: 'The black pepper which has come from India has all been finished, so now the red pepper is being used. But the red pepper is little used and the black more.'[22] The 'black pepper' refers to Indians while the 'red pepper' refers to the English; the letter is advice against further enlistment. The threat of censorship incited at least one sepoy to poetry:

> Oh bulbul, hide your voice in your throat.
> Kings have very sensitive temperaments,
> And cannot endure words.[23]

The Indian song-bird 'Bulbul', a stock image for longing in *ghazals*, strays into a poem about the war.[24] The heavily mediated nature of these letters, as well as the knowledge that they were being read, somewhat undermine their testimonial value but, as Omissi notes, 'The crucial issue is, surely, less what we cannot learn from these letters, than what we can learn from them.'[25] Given their multiple sites of production – speech to hand, hand to print, vernacular to English, whole to part – these letters are best read, I argue, not as transparent envelopes of sepoy experience but as palimpsests where, underneath various accretions by different agencies, one can still hear the heart-beat of the sepoy.

If the letters are usually used to illuminate the sepoys' social world,[26] they are also some of the earliest testimonies to a subaltern history of feeling. One can imagine the range of emotions – thrill, wonder, excitement, fear, terror, horror, homesickness, grief, envy, religious doubts – that the sepoy must have gone through, as he encountered new lands, people, cultures as well as separation, loneliness and industrial warfare. What forms did they take? Extracted, quoted and summarised, these letters are usually squeezed for their last drop of information but seldom read, in the sense that their narrative structures, the web of associations and assumptions, or the sociocultural codes and nuances of the 'felt' community within which they have their meaning are rarely investigated. To read the letters properly, we need

---

[22] Mausa Ram from Kitchener's Indian Hospital to Naik Dabi Shahai, 2 April 1915, *CIM*, IOR, L/MIL/5/825/2, 208, British Library.
[23] Hussein Shah, from Kitchener's Indian Hospital, 5 December 1916, *CIM*, IOR, L/MIL/5/826/9, 1493, British Library.
[24] *Ghazals* are verse narratives, often centring around themes of love, loss and beauty. Originating in pre-Islamic Arabic poetry, they were very popular in India in the eighteenth and nineteenth centuries and were marked by complex metrical traditions. See, for example, K. C. Kanda, *Urdu Ghazals: An Anthology: From 16th to 20th Century* (New Delhi: Sterling, 1995).
[25] Omissi, *Indian Voices of the Great War*, 9.
[26] See Omissi, 'Europe through Indian Eyes'; Visram, *Asians in Britain*, 169–401.

to evolve careful strategies that address not only what they say but how they say it, to whom they address it, and what they do not say. Consider the following letter written on 18 March 1915 by Amir Khan to his brother in Punjab:

> The enemy is weakening. In the fighting of the 10th March, up to the 12th, according to my estimate, 5,525 Germans were taken prisoners of war, and 25 guns and machine guns … Our new army is collected in great numbers. Wherever he shows strength, our guns at once knock him flat. Please God, I speak with certainty, our King – God bless him – is going to win and will win soon …

> [On a separate scrap of paper] God knows whether the land of France is stained with sin or whether the Day of Judgement has begun in France. For guns and of rifles, there is a deluge, bodies upon bodies, and blood flowing. God preserve us, what has come to pass! From dawn to dark and from dark to dawn it goes on like the hail that fell at Swarra [?] camp. But especially our guns have filled the German trenches with dead and made them brim with blood. God grant us grace, for grace is needed. Oh God, we repent! Oh God, we repent![27]

The letter refers to the offensive at Neuve Chapelle (10–13 March 1915) in which the Indians formed half the total fighting force and more than 12,500 men were killed or wounded. Referring to the same offensive, another sepoy writes that 'when we reached their trenches we used the bayonet and the kukri and blood was shed so freely that we could not recognise each other's faces.'[28] Such descriptions of hand-to-hand combat and slaughter are absent in Amir Khan's account; instead, we have the textual drama of two bits of paper. Is it an attempt to avoid the censors, or is it testimony to an internal conflict between the (official) endorsement of victory and inner anguish, an imperial super-ego and a traumatised id? *Izzat*, as discussed in Chapter 2, is a remarkably complex polysemous term.[29] The letter provides a counterpoint to the loud proclamations of 'loyalty' and 'valour' in many of the letters and pushes the thesis of the 'embattled self' that Leonard Smith has argued for the French troops to their non-white counterparts.[30] Letters such as the above enable us to move beyond the simple categories of sepoys as gallant warriors or hapless victims – or the equally reductive

[27] Amir Khan, 129th [Baluchis], from France to his brother in Punjab, 18 March 1915, *CIM*, IOR, L/MIL/5/825/2, 141–142, British Library.
[28] Rifleman Amar Singh Rawat (Garhwal Rifles) to a friend (India), Kitchener's Indian Hospital, 26 March 1915, *CIM*, IOR, L/MIL/5/825/2, 184–185, British Library.
[29] Ahuja, 'The Corrosiveness of Comparison', in *The World in World Wars*, 131–166.
[30] Leonard V. Smith, *The Embattled Self: French Soldiers' Testimony of the Great War* (Ithaca: Cornell University Press, 2007).

binaries of 'loyalists' and 'mutineers' – and show them, like their European counterparts, as individuals – complex, tormented and sometimes highly ambivalent.[31] If official victory was ideologically the province of a state-sponsored notion of *izzat* or honour, the moral core, a competing province of *izzat*, is here violated by a visceral sense of guilt, and the need to atone: 'Oh God we repent, oh God we repent.' The phrase refers to the Arabic word 'Tawba', meaning to 'retreat', 'return' or 'repent', a recurring word in the Qur'an and central to Islamic thought, which foregrounds the idea of atonement as a way of rectifying one's life.

Neither the transcript of trench experience nor just scribal embellishment, these letters are some of the earliest encounters between textual form and South Asian subaltern history. Given the problems of literacy and censorship, it is astonishing how *much* the sepoys managed to pack into their missives, from detailed accounts of their first impressions of Europe to vignettes about the war to observations on issues such as gender, education and class. On first reading, these letters seem to be chiefly functional, with a threefold aim: to provide information, offer advice and issue requests. And yet, if we read more intensely, breaking through these reports – encoded in narratives, embedded in metaphors – there is the tumultuous inner world. The letters are haunted by images of the heart: 'My heart wishes to unburden itself'; 'My heart was day and night fixed on home'; 'My heart is sadly failing'; 'My heart is not at ease, for I can see no way of saving my life.' The word 'heart' comes straight out of Punjabi and Urdu poetry. However, it is here not just a reiteration of the conventional trope but embedded in a matrix of affect and associations through which the sepoy made meaning of himself, the war and the world.

Perhaps because of the censors or the need to communicate, or of internal pressures of masculinity, feelings are often not voiced directly. Instead, they lead to a thickening of language as emotions such as horror, resignation or homesickness erupt through images, metaphors and similes:

> The condition of affairs in the war is like leaves falling off a tree, and no empty space remains on the ground. So it is here: the earth is full of dead men and not a vacant spot is left … the bullets flew about more thickly than drops of rain [Amar Singh Rawat (Garhwal Rifles), from Kitchener's Indian Hospital, to Dayaram Jhapaliyal in Garhwal, 1 April 1915].[32]

---

[31] Michelle Moyd in her chapter on ' "We Don't Want to Die for Nothing": Askari at War in German East Africa, 1914–1918', in Santanu Das (ed.), *Race, Empire and First World War Writing* (Cambridge: Cambridge University Press, 2011), 90–107 makes a similar point about *askaris*.
[32] Amar Singh Rawat (Garhwal Rifles) from Kitchener's Indian Hospital to Dayaram Jhapaliyal in Garhwal, 1 April 1915, *CIM*, IOR, L/MIL/5/825/2, 245, British Library.

> For God's sake don't come, don't come, don't come to this war in Europe
> ... Cannons, machine guns, rifles and bombs are going day and night, just
> like the rains in the month of Sawan. Those who have escaped so far are like
> the few grains left uncooked in a pot [Havildar Abdul Rahman (Punjabi
> Muslim), from France, to Naik Rajwali Khan in Baluchistan, 20 May 1915].[33]

> There is conflagration all round, and you must imagine it to be a dry forest
> in a high wind in the hot weather, with the abundance of dry grass and
> straw [Sowar Sohan Singh, from Kitchener Indian Hospital, Brighton, 10
> July, 1915 to Jodh Singh, Bitaspur, Punjab].[34]

> As tired bullocks and bull buffaloes lie down in the month of Bhadon so
> lies the weary world. Our hearts are breaking, for a year has passed while we
> have stood to arms without a rest ... Germany fights the world with ghastly
> might, harder to crush than well-soaked grain in the mill. For even wetted
> grain can be ground in time ... We have bound ourselves under the flag
> and we must give our bodies [Santa Singh, from hospital in Brighton, to his
> uncle in India, 18 August 1915].[35]

These are some of the most sensuous examples of writing in the whole
pantheon of First World War letters: sensuous in the double sense of a
record of sense impressions and the employment of the language of the
senses. The image of themselves as 'leaves falling off a tree' or a 'few grains
left uncooked in a pot' or 'tired bullocks' and of the war as a 'conflagration'
in a 'dry forest in a high wind' match up to the pastoral similes of British
war-poets such as Edmund Blunden and Edward Thomas. But, for these
men, these images are not literary embellishments or even communicative
gestures: they are *repositories of feeling*. They show how deeply their perceptual and narrative processes were still rooted in the agrarian worlds they
had left behind as the world's first manifestation of industrial warfare, with
its employment of gas and artillery, is articulated through pastoral images.[36]
Sometimes, the images cross over to the world of myth and religion.
A wounded Hindu sepoy writes that 'This is not war. It is the ending of the
world. This is just such a war as was related in the *Mahābhārata* about our
forefathers', while a Muslim sepoy adds 'But it is not [ordinary] fighting,

---

33 Havildar Abdul Rahman (Punjabi Muslim) from France to Naik Rajwali Khan in Baluchistan, 20
   May 1915, *CIM*, IOR, L/MIL/5/825/3, 394, British Library.
34 Sowar Sohan Singh, Kitchener's Indian Hospital Brighton, to Jodh Singh, Bitaspur, Punjab, 10 July
   1915, *CIM*, IOR, L/MIL/5/825/4, 571, British Library.
35 Santa Singh, hospital in Brighton, to his uncle in India, 18 August 1915, *CIM*, IOR, L/MIL/5/825/5,
   758, British Library.
36 Of course, we do not know the balance between sepoy and scribal input, but that does not affect
   my argument. Both would have come from, and communicated the experience to, the same
   community.

it is Karbala.'[37] The *Mahābhārata* is a legendary epic of the Kurukṣhetra War between the Kaurava and the Pāṇḍava princes, while Karbala was the place of a battle in October 680 where Husayn ibn Ali was defeated and killed, and the anniversary of the battle is an annual holy day of mourning among Shi'ite Muslims.[38] Whether occurring at the level of experience or representation, these letters, freighted with images, similes and allusions, can be read as *Indian literature of the trenches*: these men may have been non-literate, but being non-literate does not mean being non-literary.

The letters are often treated as linguistic bubbles on the dark sea of South Asian plebeian history, but they are rooted in local regional and cultural traditions. Claude Markovits has suggested an antecedent for the letters in I'tisam al-Daula's *Wonders of Vilayet* (1827) through the person of the literate scribe.[39] While this is an interesting suggestion, it is highly doubtful whether the sepoy or scribe would have access to such elite texts. Instead, in view of our discussion on the literary formation of Punjab, from where more than half the troops came, I would instead suggest that the censored letters bear testimony to a remarkable transition from a vibrant and robust oral culture to a textual culture of letter-writing. In her book, Farina Mir notes how, between 1884 and 1901, when the British army officer Richard Temple decided to collect folktales – the basis of his three-volume *Legends of the Punjab* – he hired 'bards' to perform these texts, showing the deep connections between oral memory and narrative traditions.[40] Similarly, between 1914 and 1918, a whole generation of men who had grown up listening to *qissas*, myths, prayers and recitations were forced to write or dictate letters which unsurprisingly draw on these oral traditions. 'I have learnt to read and write myself', writes a sepoy.[41] Of course, particular phrases or letters have to be placed within specific linguistic, cultural and religious frames and traditions, but we need to start thinking of these letters as belonging to and in turn creating particular 'emotional communities'.[42]

---

[37] A wounded Punjabi Rajput,' 29 January 1915, *CIM*, IOR, L/MIL/5/825/1, 54, British Library; Allah Ditta from France to his father in Punjab, 23 April 1915, *CIM*, IOR, L/MIL/5/825/3, 293, British Library.

[38] Omissi, *Indian Voices of the Great War*, 56.

[39] See Claude Markovits, 'Indian Soldiers' Experiences in France', 42.

[40] Farina Mir, *The Social Space of Language: Vernacular Culture in British Colonial Punjab* (Berkeley: University of California Press, 2010), 17.

[41] Letter from Alam Khan, attached to 4th Cavalry, Base Depot, Marseilles, 1 October 1915, *CIM*, IOR, MSS EUR F143/ 86–88 (microfilm), 60, British Library.

[42] See Barbara H. Rosenwein, *Emotional Communities in the Early Middle Ages* (Ithaca: Cornell University Press, 2007); Rajat Kanta Ray, *The Felt Community: Commonality and Mentality before the Emergence of Indian Nationalism* (New Delhi: Oxford University Press, 2003).

There is often a tendency in the letters to erupt into verse, which resonates with our findings about the fluidity between genres in Punjabi literary culture. It is an impulse that at once disturbs and intrigues the Chief Censor, E. B. Howell, a highly talented linguist. He calls it a sign of 'bad morale', but painstakingly translates or comments on them.[43] Some of the Punjabi poems appearing in the letters chime with the recruitment verses and songs considered in Chapter 2. Compare the poem appearing in a letter sent from Amritsar on 15 March 1916 – 'Like heroes of Bharat, trample the foe down/Make streams of blood flow, soldiers of India!'[44] – with recruitment verses such as 'The Raag of Recruitment' from *Nara-i-Jung* (1914) which we considered earlier: 'Roar like lions in the battlefield/ … Go to the battlefield and stir up a storm, let rivers of blood flow.'[45] The literary value of these verses is highly uneven, but their place in the emotional lives of the sepoys was central. Letters sometimes evolve into verse without a break or mediating pause, as in the following:

> From ＿＿＿, Brahmin, Lady Hardinge Hospital, Brockenhurst, to Pandit ＿ ＿＿, Garhwal (Hindi, 30 November 1915):
>
> My brother, I have written a few verses and couplets. They will show you what has happened and what is happening. I will tell you in ordinary language about the heroes and glorious deeds done here:

When the Lord of Raghu's race heard he said, 'Who can blot out the
　　writing of fate?'
When Hanuman places his foot on a mountain
It falls to pieces
The army of the Rakshashas melts away
Before the arrow of the Lord Rama just as the darkness of night disappears
On the rising of the sun …
How shall I tell you about the things that happened here? No tongue can
　　describe them.
When the aeroplane mounts into the sky
The bullets fall around like rain in July.
When the shells burst, the heroes cry, 'Glory to the Lord Ragunath'
By one shell many fell and are wounded,
And many are missing
Everyone cheers the German heroes and calls out, 'Bravo!'
They show an extraordinary spectacle.
The German heroes are very strong, and

---

[43] See Markovits, 'Indian Soldiers' Experiences in France', 39. Markovits suggests that Howell's selection might have a literary bias (38–39).
[44] From Amritsar to France, 15 March 1916, *CIM*, IOR, L/MIL/5/828/2, 337r., British Library.
[45] 'The Raag of Recruitment' from *Nara-i-Jung* (Amritsar, 1914). Translated by Asad Ali Chaudhry.

Those who fight with them are overthrown!
Brave, Mothers' sons! For every one that falls may a thousand spring up![46]

'Poetry' here functions as a way of giving structure to a world of perceptual and metaphysical disorientation. As in the shell-shocked poems of the British trench poets, formal devices – rhythm, rhyme, imagery – try to hold together a world disintegrating to 'pieces'. But the imperial–heroic mode registers the strain and is pushed to breaking-point as the men try to make meaning of the conflict. While the epics *Ramayana* and the *Mahabharata* provide a model for comprehending the horrors of the Western Front, the mention of aeroplanes, shell and bullets (one wonders whether the words appeared in English in the original) shows how Punjabi poetic form bears the weight of historical trauma. In English literature, we similarly have the romantic lyric trying to accommodate the blood-dimmed reality of the trenches – mud, gas, mines and barbed wire. If Wilfred Owen had refashioned poetry as testimony, as missives from the trenches – 'My subject is War and the pity of war. The poetry is in the pity' – the unlettered sepoy shows a similar impulse to record, to testify and to communicate.[47] There is a tension between the grandiose mythic framework ('Glory to Lord Ragunath') and appeal to martyrdom on the one hand, and the stark realism of 'many fell and are wounded … many are missing'. What is curious above is the reference to German prowess: is this a coded message, within an elaborate literary framework, about the severity of the conflict? However, some of the most moving poems are the short impromptu ones, as in the following lyric addressed to the postman:

> My letters, postman, guard with care
> Remember that my heart is there
> My life is crushed with griefs and pains
> Yet cruel Fate says, 'Death remains'.

Witty, simple and heartbreaking, such missives make us question where letter-writing ends and verse-making begins.

Articulate Flesh: Pain, Vulnerability and 'Malingering'

From 23 October to the end of First Ypres in early November 1914, the Indian Corps held around twelve miles or one-third of the entire British

---

[46] From __ (name withheld), Brahmin, Lady Hardinge Hospital, Brockenhurst to Pandit __ (name withheld), Garhwal, 30 November 1915, The censor noted that 'The first sklok (verse) is from the Ramayana of Tulsi Das, and probably the skloks 2, 3 and 4 are from the same source.' *CIM*, IOR, L/MIL/5/825/8, 1389, British Library.
[47] Wilfred Owen, *The War Poems*, ed. Jon Stallworthy (London: Chatto & Windus, 1994), 98.

line. The British trenches were shallow and open, little more than ditches, and German rifle-fire and shrapnel tore into the sepoys. Between 22 October and 3 November, some 1,848 sepoys, comprising a startling 57%, were admitted to hospitals, of which some 1,049 had wounds to their left hand.[48] The hand-wound rates dropped after Willcocks had five sepoys shot for cowardice that winter; they again went up after the battle of Neuve Chapelle in March 1915.[49] There was widespread suspicion of the wounds being self-inflicted, even though Colonel Bruce Seton conducted an investigation of 1,000 'wounds' and dismissed such allegations as false.[50] The topic of self-wounding has been a severely contested area among military historians. While Jeffrey Greenhut analysed the statistics and turned it into a thesis of sepoy under-performance through the lack of training, both Gordon Corrigan and George Morton-Jack have noted that many of these wounds were probably the result of unintentional exposure to shellfire in the first few months of the conflict.[51] At the same time, some were indeed self-inflicted, and Morton-Jack estimates them at 'several hundred'; such wounding, however, was not confined to the Indian camp, but also happened among British, French and German troops in 1914.[52] While high occurrences of hand-wounds at two specific periods cannot be used to make any sweeping claims about sepoy morale or performance on the Western Front, they were nonetheless distinct pressure-points: how were such moments articulated and what insights do they provide into the sepoy-body, emotion and agency?

The battle of Neuve Chapelle (10–13 March 1915) sent shockwaves through the Indian army. On 26 March, a wounded Aamir Singh Rawat wrote that 'We have been constantly fighting for six months, but we have not even seen the sun; day and night the rain has fallen; and the country is so cold that I cannot describe it.'[53] The sepoys from northern India

---

[48] Jeffery Greenhut, 'The Imperial Reserve: The Indian Corps on the Western Front, 1914–1915', *Journal of Imperial and Commonwealth History*, 12 (1983), 57.

[49] The National Archives, London, WO 154/14, 'Return Showing Court-Martial Convictions in Indian Corps from October 1914 to February 1915'.

[50] Bruce Seaton, 'Analysis of 1000 Injuries', BL, IOR, L/MIL/17/5/2402.

[51] Corrigan, *Sepoys in the Trenches*, 182; Morton-Jack, *The Indian Army*, 171–175. However, Gajendra Singh, in *The Testimonies of Indian Soldiers*, notes that 'there was a far higher incidence of this type of wounding among Indian sipahis' (90).

[52] Morton-Jack, *The Indian Army*, 172. He mentions self-wounding among European troops in 1914 and notes that self-infliction of wounds was not 'endemic among the Indians of the Indian Corps': 'It occurred as a discernible problem in October 1914, and among a minority in spring 1915, but not otherwise.' (175).

[53] Aamir Singh Rawat (Garhwal Rifles), Kitchener's Indian Hospital, 26 March 1915, *CIM*, IOR, L/MIL/5/825/, 184, British Library.

might have been used to low temperatures, but not to the darkness or wetness of Flanders. From around this time, a number of letters start to drop tantalising hints. 'Eat the fat but preserve the bone carefully', advised Colour Havildar Mir Haidar Jan on 20 March 1915 from his hospital bed in England to his comrade Shah Nawaz Khan serving in France.[54] As late as September 1915, similar letters continued, such as the following one from Uttam Singh of 57th Wilde's Rifles: 'the grey beards call the winning wrestle "bacha" [save or escape]. If you are wrestling with your friends, wrestle carefully and save your legs and arms'.[55] Said Khan was being more cautious when he wrote that 'my foot does not trouble me any more now ... So act, that honour may be preserved and life too may not be destroyed.'[56] Not every ploy was successful, but there was persistence. 'The Doctor will not pass me as unfit, but I hope ... [that] the Commanding Officer will declare me unfit, because of the wound to the foot.'[57] Inzar Gul nearly faced prison for his hand-wound, until a friend testified and managed to save him.[58] It is not possible to know exactly what had actually happened, but the sepoys' sense of relief at the prospect of being slightly wounded was widespread and openly expressed: 'I have been wounded by a bullet in the hand. A little bit of bone was broken above but I am glad because my life is safe'; or 'I was wounded in the index finger of the right hand ... Do not be at all anxious about me but give thanks on my behalf.'[59] Given that many sepoys knew that their letters were being read, such candour is remarkable. Consider the following letter from Naik Main Ram, recovering from his wounds in Kitchener's Indian Hospital, to sepoy Dani Ram, serving in Muscat:

> You should know that you should not on any account come out to the war ... You are an old soldier and are intelligent. If a man wishes to remain [away] he can do so in any case – there are many subterfuges for a man, and you should endeavour in every manner to protect your life ... my brother,

[54] Colour Havildar Mir Haidar Jan to Shah Nawaz Khan, 20 March 1915, *CIM*, IOR, L/MIL/5/825/2, 140, British Library.

[55] Uttam Sing of 57th Wilde's Rifles France, 1 September 1915, *CIM*, IOR, L/MIL/5/825/5, 850, British Library.

[56] Sepoy Said Khan, Pathan, to Jemadar Amir Khan of the 59th serving in France, from hospital in England, section directed at the writer's brother Nadir Khan, not dated, *CIM*, IOR, L/MIL/5/825/2, 140, British Library.

[57] Letter from Lance Naik Palak Khan, 129th Baluchis, Indian General Hospital, Brighton, *CIM*, IOR, MSS EUR D681/18, 374 Eur, British Library.

[58] Afridi Pathan, 58th Vaughan's Rifle, from hospital, England, February 1915, *CIM*, L/MIL/5/821/1, British Library. For a discussion of some of these cases, see Singh, *Testimonies*, 90–92.

[59] From a Garhwali wounded and in England to his guru in India, 17 February 1915, *CIM*, IOR, L/MIL/5/825/90, British Library; Name not given, Kitchener Indian Hospital Brighton, 26 July 1915, *CIM*, IOR, L/MIL/5/828/3, 415r., British Library.

you will see that it is necessary for a man to save his life by all means …
There are a hundred things you can say – [that you are] weak, [or have] a
pain in the chest, or asthma – there are fifty excuses. And here [at the front]
they slash with their knives until there is nothing of you left.[60]

The reference to 'old soldier' suggests that such impulses were not restricted
to fresh recruits; the advice to 'protect your life' is presented as a need, almost
a duty to oneself, rather than a matter of shame or guilt. There is a similar
canniness, with advice for caution, from Khan Mohammed of 40th Pathans,
himself recovering in a hospital in England, as he wrote to his friend Sher
Jhang: 'Your complaint, that of having had the trench fall on you – is a
very good one. But do not straighten your back. Wherever you go, do not
straighten your back.'[61] Thus, again and again, we have such insinuations
and innuendoes that provide insights into an underworld, marked by fear
and resourcefulness, bristling under the proclamations of loyalty.

By the middle of 1916, references to such wounds cease; instead, as
Gajendra Singh has acutely noted, we come across references to more
subtle forms of self-harm. From early 1917, one finds regular requests in
letters being sent to India for substances that would 'produce sores on the
legs or on the neck or on the chest'.[62] The substance most commonly used
was the seed of the *bhailawa* plant, a nut used by *dhobis* or washermen to
mark clothes; according to the censor's gloss, they 'cause the body to swell
and pimples to appear'.[63] On 17 July 1915, sepoy Diwana wrote to his friend
Ramdatta serving in Marseilles 'you should mash them up, and then smear
on the body … fumigate yourself also with it'; a week later, another wrote
'Fumigate yourself with the bhilawan [sic], grind it to powder and smear
it over your loins.'[64] For Mansingh Rawat, it was the passport to India: 'If
only I could get that medicine [*bhailawa*] … then perhaps I should get
back to India.'[65] Indeed, the censor's report in October 1915 notes that
'bhilawa [sic] continues to be in strong demand'.[66] However, the most

[60] Naik Main Ram, Kitchener's Indian Hospital, to Dani Ram, Muscat, 9 June 1915, *CIM*, IOR, L/
MIL/5/825/4, 476, British Library.
[61] Khan Mohammed of 40th Pathans from a hospital in England to Sher Jhang, 26 July 1915, *CIM*,
IOR, L/MIL/5/825/4, 616, British Library.
[62] Abdul Karim, France, to Risaldar Shahzad Khan, Saharanpur, U.P., India, 19 December 1915, *CIM*,
L/MIL/5/825/6, British Library. See Singh, *Testimonies*, 90–92.
[63] Censor's Note, 25 July 1915, *CIM*, IOR, L/MIL/5/828/3/416v., British Library. 'Bhailawa' is variously
referred to as 'bhilawan' and 'bhilawa', and occasionally as 'teliya'.
[64] Sepoy Diwana, Kitchener Indian Hospital, to Sepoy Ramdatta, Marseilles, 17 July 1915, *CIM*, IOR,
L/MIL/5/828/3, 413v., British Library; Name not given, Kitchener Indian Hospital, 25 July 1915,
CIM, IOR, L/MIL/5/828/3/416v., British Library.
[65] Letter from Man Singh Rawat, Indian Military Depot, New Milford, 22 September, 1915, *CIM*,
IOR, MSS EUR F143/ 86–88 (microfilm), 34.
[66] E.B. Howell, Censor's Report, 11 October, 1915, *CIM*, IOR, MSS EUR F143/ 86–88 (microfilm), 52.

extraordinary letter comes from Mohammed Gaki Khan, who wrote the
following on 6 June 1915 to Sowar Mohammed Rafi Khan:

> I went and saw Khalka Pershad today and asked him about the matter. He
> said that he had no experience of his own but that he knew so much, that
> the smoke of the bhalwa [sic] plant is used for this purpose. The plant is
> ground down and then thrown on the burning coals … That part which
> the smoke touches by the grace of God becomes inflamed. Its effect lasts
> three days … There is another method which will succeed in deceiving the
> doctors – that is, to pretend to suffer from sciatica … Also I learnt from
> other people that if you want to make your eyes sore, you should do as
> follows: grind the seed of the *rand* plant and apply it to the eyes as one
> does *surma*. Then lie down with closed eyes. The eyes will at once become
> reddened. But you must apply the stuff two or three times a day. By grace
> of God no harm will be done to the eyes. Another prescription of the eyes
> is as follows: apply the wax from your ears with a blunt-pointed needle to
> your eyes. The eyes become reddened. A method for bringing about fever is
> as follows: mix some safrida [white lead] in curds and drink it. Fever will set
> in at once … The first and most important thing is to try and have yourself
> sent to Hospital as soon as possible. Do not think of pension or anything
> else … Lalla Hajjan also told me a method of causing injury to the foot.
> First, make a cut in your foot with a knife and then put a piece of copper
> in the wound.[67]

The precision about the plant's effects on body-parts, the range of options
presented and the exactness of description, all marked by an extraordinary
calmness of tone, suggest a subterranean fund of accumulated knowledge embedded in the community. There is little shame, or dilemma or
dithering; instead, the invocations to God present the action, as in the
above letter from Dani Ram, as legitimate, sanctioned, 'necessary'.

Before we examine the above letter, it is important to have some caveats.
The above 'malingering' letters constitute only a handful, erupting at particular periods, among a vast collection of correspondence which otherwise professes loyalty, gallantry, *izzat* and *dharma* (it is another question
whether they were genuine or aimed at the colonial censors). Second, the
recovery of such letters is politically sensitive. During the centennial years,
when Indian military organisations and community groups are trying
their best to gain recognition for the Indian troops on the axis of heroism
and sacrifice, such letters do not just cause embarrassment but may even
undermine the recuperative process at the public level. Above all, there
is the risk of a few letters being blown out of proportion to pathologise

[67] Mohammed Gaki Khan to Sowar Mohammed Rafi Khan, 6 June 1915, *CIM*, IOR, L/MIL/5/825/4,
538, British Library.

the Indian troops and further marginalise their contribution; they may also play into the hands of white nationalists. Such risks make even the most post-national academic feel acutely awkward. In historical terms, it is important to note that there was no mutiny or mass-desertion on the Western Front in 1914–1918; instead, the British Indian army won 9,200 gallantry awards, including eleven Victoria Crosses (now shared between India six, Pakistan three and Nepal two). The letters thus cannot be woven into a thesis of any large-scale political dissent; at the same time, they cannot be brushed under the carpet. The calm tone, the depth of bodily knowledge, the recurrence of such letters and the networks within community militate against the idea of 'malingering' as an isolated aberration. Instead, they point to the potential for dissent as well as structures of control in the military.[68] While dissent is to be found in all armies, it is possible, though debatable, that instances such as the above were specifically linked to the reality of the Indian army being a colonial army; more data and comparative analysis are needed for any firm conclusion. However, it cannot be denied that the sense of serving so far from home, the hostile climate, the intensity of the battle and, above all, the idea of fighting for a country not theirs would all have been contributory factors.

Self-inflicted wounds are often calculated and limited assaults on the body to prevent greater damage. While such 'malingering' letters, in the colonial context, are conventionally interpreted through the lens of loyalty and dissent, what is surprisingly not mentioned is the body, its vulnerability, its capacity for endurance. In *The Body in Pain* (1990), Elaine Scarry argues that, in the act of war, the soldier's 'fundamental relation between body and belief takes many degrees and radiates out over thousands of small acts': from putting on the uniform every morning and taking up the gun to more specific acts of defence and killing.[69] The above letters put pressure on this 'fundamental' relation between body and belief; it pits the virtues of *izzat*, *dharma*, regimental loyalty or the fear of shame, all underpinned by heroic masculinity, against the materiality of that too, too solid flesh. If shellshock was, among other things, the unconscious language of masculine protest,[70] some of the Indian sepoys made their bodies *speak*: they took up their guns, polished their boots, and guarded the

[68] See, for example, Rajit Mazumder, *The Indian Army and the Making of Punjab*, where he argues convincingly about the 'restraint of imperial power' within the army (93–138).
[69] Elaine Scarry, *The Body in Pain: The Making and Unmaking of the World* (New York: Oxford University Press, 1985), 153.
[70] In *The Female Malady: Women, Madness and English Culture* (New York: Virago, 1987), Elaine Showalter makes the controversial and highly contested claim that 'men were silenced and immobilized and forced, like women, to express their conflicts through the body' (171).

trenches; when pushed to the limit, a number of them asked for *bhailawa*, made their bodies erupt into boils and warts, and claimed that their backs had been crushed under the trenches. Paradoxically, these acts asserted, in however circumscribed or extreme a manner, their agency. These acts can be taken as a variation of what James Scott, in a different context, has called 'hidden transcripts' – acts of resistance taking place off-stage.[71] In addition to battlefield trauma, there would have been other factors, such as the sense of contractual obligation being exceeded, or of insufficient belief in the cause, or lack of incentive, and homesickness.[72] Colonial and racial difference should not be fetishised but, equally, cannot be ignored. What deterred the majority of the men, sepoys and Tommies alike, from such 'malingering' was not just harsh disciplinary measures, let alone notions of 'izzat', nor loyalty to Pax Britannica, but a deep sense of loyalty and love for their comrades.

Intimacies: Camaraderie, Eros and Romance

The French soldier Pierre La Mazière, who later worked as a nurse, recounts a curious encounter with a wounded black soldier in 1915:

> I took the poor Black to my arms to help him. I leaned over him on the table. His head rested on my chest. He continued to scream. Huge tears rolled down his cheeks. I felt sorry for him, I cradled him. At one point, I told him he was a handsome guy.
>
> Then, with his lovely smile, he stretched out his arms and kissed me.[73]

Pain, sympathy, vulnerability and a diffused sensuousness are combined; Captain Roly Grimshaw's *Experiences of Ram Singh*, as we examined in the last chapter, almost verges on such a moment between Beji Singh and 'Smith Sahib'. Were similar moments of inter-racial contact articulated by the sepoys? Both British and Indian accounts mention examples of Indian sepoys risking their lives to save their British officers. The most celebrated account is that of Subedar Manta Singh during the battle of Neuve Chapelle on 12 March 1915. On finding the wounded Lieutenant (later Captain) George Henderson on the battlefield, he placed his officer

---

[71] James C. Scott, *Domination and the Arts of Resistance: Hidden Transcripts* (New Haven: Yale University Press, 1992).
[72] Michelle Moyd, discussing the world of African *askaris*, speaks of a similarly complex world of checks and balances in *Violent Intermediaries: African Soldiers, Conquest and Everyday Colonialism in German East Africa* (2014).
[73] Pierre La Mazière, *L'H.C.F.: L'hôpital chirurgical flottant* (Paris: Albin Michel, 19919), 11, quoted in Smith, *The Embattled Self*, 84.

in a wheelbarrow he had found in no man's land and pushed him to safety; in the process, he himself got shot and later succumbed to his injuries.[74] There were other such examples: Havildar Mula Singh and Sepoy Rur Singh ventured out under fire to rescue Captain Turnbull; Havildar Dewa Singh went out with Lieutenant Drysdale under fire to drag Brunskill to safety; and when 'Bickford Sahib was wounded', Rayab Khan 'picked him up and carried him in'.[75] Today, these moments are celebrated as examples of Indo-British 'camaraderie' in the First World War. True, these are immensely moving stories, and testify to the warmth of the relations as well as gallantry; yet what saddens me is that, in my twelve years of research, I have not come across a single example of an English soldier, officer or private, risking his life for an Indian sepoy.

This is not to deny that there were moments of warmth and generosity between the officers and the sepoys such as the above, but to recognise that the underlying structures of power and hierarchies of race continued largely intact even in the trenches. In the sepoy letters, the British officers usually seem more of an absence; when occasionally mentioned, they are kindly, but remote, figures of paternal authority. A rare exception is the following letter from a Jemadar of 9th Hodson's Horse in France to a lady addressed as 'Dearer than Life':

> My life! What can you know of the vicissitudes of my existence here. Perhaps I wrote the card on horseback during a wild charge! Or perhaps I wrote it under a shower of bursting shells! Or perhaps I wrote it at the last gasp of life! My unjust Beloved, you reproach me when you should praise …
>
> Listen, I will tell you of an incident which occurred to me, the day before yesterday. I was on the battlefield accompanied by a sowar, and came upon a wounded British soldier. 'Well friend', I said to him, 'how are things going with you?' 'Quite all right', he replied. 'I am proud I was of service in the fight, but I was thirsty.' I gave him water to drink, and asked if he wanted anything else. 'I regret nothing', he said, 'except that I shall not meet my sweetheart.' … 'My friend', I said, weeping with pity, 'my own condition is the same as yours.' I told the sowar to remove him to a safer place, as shells were falling near. He lifted him and was carrying him

---

[74] Manta Singh died of his wounds in the Kitchener Indian hospital a few days later in March 1915. Henderson survived the war and ensured that Manta Singh's son, Assa Singh Johal, was taken care of. Assa Singh Johal developed a friendship with Robert Henderson, the son of Captain Henderson, and the two of them actually served together in the Second World War. Their sons are friends too and are serving in the army, carrying the tale of friendship into the third generation. (See 'Brighton Warrior: Manta Singh', www.sikhmuseum.com/brighton/warriors/manta/index.html.)

[75] *47th Sikhs: War Records of the Great War, 1914–1918* (Chippenham, 1992 [1921]), 88; Sepoy Raja Khan of the 59th, wounded in England, to Havaldar Diwan Ali Khan, 21 March 1915, *CIM*, IOR L/MIL/5/825/2, 144, British Library.

away, but he had not gone a hundred paces when the soldier cried out 'my beloved' and expired.[76]

Identification here occurs across the line of colour: distinctions of race, hierarchy and power are temporarily brushed aside as one lover encounters and comforts another under the shadow of death. Yet, given the stylisation and the playful imagination with which the letter begins, we cannot be sure whether the encounter actually happened or not. Whatever the case may be, we have here a narrative of heterosexual romance encased within a framework, fantasised or real, of inter-racial homosocial camaraderie at a moment of extremity.

But what about camaraderie among the sepoys themselves? Some of the most important shifts in their thinking happened in their relationship to each other. While the arrangements in the Brighton Pavilion highlighted the caste and religious divisions among the sepoys through the nine kitchens and three water taps, it was exactly at this time that these lines began to break down in France under the pressure of new circumstances and exposure to European norms. Tara Singh, a Sikh sowar (cavalry man), wrote from France that, 'When I returned from Marseilles to the firing line, we had to change trains en route, and we wandered about Paris for eight hours. On that day, we all ate at the same table. Our company was composed of five sepoys (of whom three were Sikhs and two Muslims), two sweepers and three cooks; but we all ate together at the same table. Moreover, we have often eaten food and drunk tea prepared by Muslims.'[77] The censored letters are curiously silent on the main subject of European war-writing: camaraderie. Mutilation and mortality, loneliness and boredom, and the strain of constant bombardment led to a new level of intimacy and intensity in the trenches under which the tactile norms of civilian society collapsed. Men were often haunted by the *touch* of a comrade's body: C. H. Cox, an English private, remembered how his comrade 'laid back in my arms and his last words were for his mother as he died in my arms'.[78] Such warm individual relations are rarely mentioned in the sepoy letters, but that does not mean they did not happen. Indian same-sex intimacy and touch have a very different structure and history, and bodily contact between men – linking arms, holding someone by the shoulder, or constant, casual horseplay – was part of the daily tactile continuum, unlike in England, in a post-Wilde era, when it was coming under strain.[79]

[76] Jemadar Hasan Singh, 19 September 1916, *CIM*, IOR, L/MIL/826/7, 1168, British Library.
[77] Tara Singh, 6th Cavalry, France, 17 July 1916, *CIM*, IOR, L/MIL/5/826/6, 927, British Library.
[78] C. H. Cox, 'A Few Experiences of the First World War', IWM, 88/11/1.
[79] See Das, *Touch and Intimacy in First World War Literature*, 109–136.

Even the most cursory look at photographs of sepoys shows them almost always in small groups: smoking, chatting, playing cards, or working jointly. The unit diaries often point to such moments of individual intensities and generosities. After the second battle of Ypres, a distraught Mala Singh ventured into no man's land to carry back a wounded comrade. On one occasion, a Naik was found performing the duty of a sentry who was a young and terrified boy; three older sepoys went looking for a rifle which a young sepoy had left behind by mistake so that he would not get into trouble. After Lance Naik Buta Singh from the 47th Sikhs had been killed, with his body left near the German lines, a patrol from his Company (No. 2) went out and recovered his body.[80] These stories do not appear in the letters: perhaps the sepoys did not have an adequate language to communicate such intimacies; perhaps such bonding was such an integral part of the Indian homosocial culture that it did not attract special comment; being professional soldiers, rather than conscripts, the sepoys were used to such bodily contact; above all, the censors might have objected and the sepoys, writing home, did not want to alarm their families. Interestingly, such moments are occasionally mentioned in Mesopotamia diaries and reminiscences by the educated middle-class medical staff; perhaps it was as much a question of form and expression as of memory. Above all, it is in the art and literature of the time – from Paul Sarrut's delicate sketches to Chandradhar Sharma Guleri's 'Usne Kahā Thā' to Mulk Raj Anand's *Across the Black Waters* – that we have the fullest record of this rich world of friendship and generosity which sustained the men.

However, a few letters show a degree of intensity that goes beyond the world of war camaraderie and trespasses into the world of romance. These are rare, but they do show that some of the Indians, as with men (including soldiers) from any other country, were not immune to the charms of members of their own sex. Consider the following letter, sent by Dilbar in Lahore on 21 May 1916 to Abdul Hakim Khan, 19 Lancers, in France:

> Go, my letter, and tell him that when you were leaving me I was weeping and overwhelmed with grief. Tell him that when the rain of his presence falls on me again the dust of separation will be swept away … In the expectation of a single letter from you he is, as it were, prostrated by sickness. If you did not know it before know it now that he remembers you day and night in his affliction.[81]

---

[80] *47th Sikhs*, 88, 96, 108, 112.
[81] Dilbar (Pathan), Veterinary College, Lahore, Punjab, to Abdul Hakim Khan, 19 Lancers, France, 21 May 1916, *CIM*, IOR, L/MIL/826/5, 762. I am grateful to Gajendra Singh for the reference.

This is the language of romance: in its self-conscious stylisation and excess, it resonates with much of the Urdu and Pashto love poetry, often exchanged between men, that scholars such as Ruth Vanita and Saleem Kidwai have so laboriously recovered.[82] A letter such as the above is very different from the inarticulate or dictated sepoy letters we were discussing earlier; some of the sepoy letters (as from the inveterate letter-writer and assistant-surgeon Godbole) are remarkably sophisticated. These letters cannot be confined to the parenthesis of wartime, but open up larger histories of male intimacy and longing. Consider the following two poems included in the letters:

> Since the day you went to the field, Oh heart of my heart,
> From that day I know no ease …
> My soul languishes for communion with you
> And my body is like water.[83]

> Oh letter mine make no delay
> Take, on the wings of love, your way,
> Gain strength in blessed India's air,
> And quickly reach my dear one there.
> Give him the message you have brought
> To keep him in his loving thought
> Alive I'll meet him here again
> And dying, on his astral plane.[84]

In *Lads: Love Poetry of the Trenches* (1989), Martin Taylor highlights the homoerotic aspects of trench poetry and convincingly argues how English war poetry has the distinction of being the most moving 'love poetry' of the twentieth century. The above poems show that such verse was by no means confined to the writings of European authors. There is, however, a vital difference: while the poems Taylor recovers are addressed to comrades, the two poems quoted above are addressed by the soldiers to men they had been separated from. Unfortunately, we do not have the originals: it is debatable whether poetry here provides the 'legitimate' form to express love that 'dares not speak its name' or whether it is just an over-heated poetic vocabulary. Yet, the romantic pulse cannot be missed as it dances and leaps even around the translated extract.

[82] Ruth Vanita and Saleem Kidwai (ed.), *Same-Sex Love in India: Readings from Literature and History* (London: Palgrave, 2000).
[83] Kot Dafadan Kutubuddin Khan (Pathan), 3rd Corps Remount, Lahore, to Gulab Khan, 11 Lancers attacked the 19 Lancers, France, 7 March, 1917, *CIM*, IOR, L/MIL/5/827/2, 263, British Library.
[84] Firoz Khan (PM), Secunderabad Cavalry Brigade, France, to Palwan Khan, Jhelum, Punjab, 3 July 1916, *CIM*, IOR, L/MIL/826/6, 866, British Library.

Far more common, and better-known, is the world of inter-racial heterosexual liaisons and romance that was opening up beyond the battlefield: these
ranged from fleeting glances and awkward greetings in market-squares and
across shop-counters to more sustained relationships.[85] Though there were
strict official policies to limit contact between non-white troops and white
women, fuelled by racist fears of 'miscegenation', there are clear examples
of sexual contact between French women and non-white men in wartime
France.[86] 'The apples have come into excellent flavours [...] They are ripe.
We wander in the orchards all day', teasingly wrote a sepoy; or 'There are
crowds of "machines" here also, and the sight of them delights us, but we are
ashamed to touch them lest we lose caste.'[87] While historians have tried to
assess the extent of such relationships, what is almost equally intriguing is the
form of articulation of such relationships in the letters themselves, with their
conjoined politics of gender, race and (as in the last letter) caste. Misogyny
was common to the world of the trenches across race or rank. However, the
mystification of 'whiteness', combined with colonial power-structures and
indigenous categories (such as caste here), added a particular fetishistic logic.
Compare the following letters, the first written by a Tunisian worker and the
second by an Indian sepoy:

> In this land called France there are no longer any men at all, there are only
> women who are very numerous. They tell us that when we have finished our
> work in France and are about to return home, they will give each of us three
> women that we will be allowed to bring to Tunisia.

and

> If you want any French women there are plenty here, and they are very
> good-looking. If you really want any I can send one to you in a parcel.[88]

The pleasure here lies not so much in the act but in the narrative jouissance and homosocial boast; the woman is not just to be enjoyed but
'parcelled' back. The novelist Mulk Anand in *Across the Black Waters*, as we
will examine in Chapter 9, delves into this complex world. While some

---

[85] Markovits, 'Indian Soldiers' Experiences in France'.
[86] Tyler Stovall, 'Love, Labour and Race: Colonial Men and White Women in France during the Great War', in Tyler Stovall and Georges Van Den Abbeele (eds.), *French Civilisation and Its Discontents* (Lanham: Lexington, 2003), 307.
[87] Fom Sowar __ (name withheld), Field Post Office 12 France to Kot Havildar __ (name withheld), Kurram Militia, India, 25 Oct, 1915, CIM, IOR/L/MIL/5/828/3. 448v, British Library. A Sikh sepoy to Gurun Ditta Mal (Depot, 47th Sikhs), 12 May 1915, L/MIL/5/825/3, 353, British Library. A number of historians, including Rozina Visram, Claude Markovits and Gajendra Singh, have written about these inter-racial romantic liaisons.
[88] Quoted in Tyler Stovall, 'Love, Labour and Race: Colonial Men and White Women in France during the Great War' 307; Letter from Umed Sing Bist (Dogra) to Sali Seok (Lohana, Kangra District Punjab), November 1915, CIM, IOR, L/ MIL/5/825/7, British Library.

of the letters were sexual fantasies, actual liaisons took place too. When the Indian cavalry moved in 1915 to a new neighbourhood, some letters of a 'violently amatory nature' addressed to them from the French women they had left behind were intercepted.[89] At least one of these 'violently' amorous relationships ended in a pregnancy and eventual marriage that created quite a furore among the sepoy community. Indeed, a romantic liaison happened in my own family. Dr Prasanta Kumar Guha, a great-uncle of mine, went to France as a doctor and even got engaged to a French girl. However, being a nationalist, he decided to return to India, putting country before love, but the two continued to correspond in French. When he later got married in Calcutta, the French lady sent bangles as a wedding-gift for his Bengali bride![90]

POW Sound Recordings: Longing, Faith and Hope

Of all the Indian testimonies, the most haunting are the voice-recordings made in the German POW camp at Wünsdorf which we mentioned in the context of visual representation in Chapter 3.[91] In addition to the elaborate propaganda mechanism and ethnological study, there was an active scholarly interest in the camp's inmates by linguists and ethnomusicologists. In fact, Mall Singh's soulful lament, with which we began the book, was one of the several hundred South Asian recordings in this extraordinary 2,677-strong collection, produced by the Royal Prussian Phonographic Commission, and masterminded by the philologist Wilhelm Doegen, between 29 December 1915 and 19 December 1918.[92] The Commission comprised thirty academics who toured thirty-one prison camps in Germany and made the recordings in approximately 250 languages and dialects. The photograph Figure 0.2, which we briefly touched on in the Introduction, while discussing the case by Mall Singh, shows us about

[89] Censor's Notes, 21 August 1915, *CIM*, IOR, L/MIL/5/825/4, 703, British Library.
[90] Interview with Indrani Haldar, July 2014, Kolkata.
[91] A number of these recordings, particularly from Nepalese, Urdu, Punjabi and Bengali, have been recovered and translated here for the first time. I am grateful to Heike Liebau for facilitating a month's fellowship at the Zentrum Moderner Orient, Berlin, which allowed me to work on these audio-recordings, and to Britta Lange for her hospitality during this period.
[92] See *'When the War Began, We Heard of Several Kings'* and, in particular, the wonderful accompanying disc, which contains some of the songs, paintings and photographs. Also see in that volume the important essay by Britta Lange, 'South Asian Soldiers and German Academics', 149–186 which discusses some of the recordings, including the detailed story of Mohammed Hossin which I translated for the piece. Since the translation is extracted there in full, I do not mention it here. Also see Heike Liebau, 'Prisoners of War (India)', in *1914–18 Online Encyclopedia* (https://encyclopedia.1914-1918-online.net/article/prisoners_of_war_india).

the way in which these audio-recordings were made: the person being recorded is flanked by German officials; an officer places his hand on the sepoy's shoulders to steady him while his other hand holds a sheet of paper from which the sepoy is made to read out.

In her celebrated essay on subaltern speech, Gayatri Chakravorty Spivak tells us the remarkable story of Bhubaneswari Bhaduri, with its combination of nationalism, suicide and the tragic failure of communication, and makes her famous claim that 'The subaltern cannot speak.'[93] Part of the power and controversy of this essay lies in our question: has not Bhubaneswari Bhaduri spoken eloquently through her dead, menstruating body? Rajeswari Sunder Rajan has perceptively observed that

> [Bhubaneswari] serves as the figural example of the subaltern who cannot – but in fact, does speak. 'Cannot' in this context signifies not speech's absence but its failure ... In other words and more generally, the locution 'Can the Subaltern speak' is an invitation to rethink the relation between the figural and the literal.[94]

The plangent materiality of the POW recordings pushes this differential relation between the literal and the figural to a crisis-point: here at long last, or so it seems, is the subaltern voice, in all its grainy materiality. It is highly debatable whether the sepoys could be called 'subaltern', directly involved as they were in safeguarding the empire and given their access to power and authority which they sometimes did not hesitate to exercise. Yet, in the context of them being shipped to Europe and their powerlessness as prisoners of war in Germany, they can temporarily be referred to as 'subalterns'. Moreover, following Spivak's logic, these men were muted in the very act of speaking: they recorded some pre-arranged text into the funnel of the phonograph-machine, except a very few, such as Mall Singh, who decided to tell his life-story. Was it a desperate attempt to reach out to the wider world for help? Even as they spoke, it has taken almost a century for these voices to be heard. Spivak's troubling question – 'With what voice-consciousness can the subaltern speak?' – becomes freshly resonant in the context of these extraordinary recordings.[95]

Of the over 2,677 sound-recordings in the archive, around 300 recordings are of South Asian prisoners. The languages of these recordings include

---

[93] Gayatri Chakravorty Spivak, 'Can the Subaltern Speak?' (1988), in Rosalind C. Morris (ed.), *Can the Subaltern Speak? Reflections on the History of an Idea* (New York: Columbia University Press 2010), 104.

[94] Rajeswari Sunder Rajan, 'Death and the Subaltern', in Morris (ed.), *Can the Subaltern Speak?*, 122.

[95] Spivak, 'Can the Subaltern Speak?', in Morris (ed.), *Can the Subaltern Speak?*, 255.

Hindi, Urdu, Punjabi, Bengali, Garhwali, Pashto, Khasi and Nepalese. They range from minimal machine-like utterances, like the 1′ 9″ recording of Karamar Ali reading out the letters of the Bengali alphabet, to the 3′ 20″ recording of Mohammed Hossain telling the astonishing story of his capture and of life in the POW camp.[96] It seems both from the recordings and from the archival material that many of these texts, particularly those in Nepalese, were first written down and then read out.[97] In terms of genre too, these recordings vary: the majority of the men read out a well-known tale or legend, or sing devotional or religious song, and only a very few, like Mall Singh – exceptionally, tantalisingly – decide to tell their life-stories. But the demarcations are often porous. Thus, Chota Baghua, a farmer and trained at the Amritsar regimental school in Kohat, starts with a parable of the 'King and his four daughters', then sings a *shabad* and proceeds abruptly to say that 'The German King is very intelligent. He fights with all the kings.'[98] Parable, music and contemporary commentary are all rolled into one. These are some of the earliest voice-recordings by South Asians, and they are invaluable at once to ethnomusicologists, linguists, cultural historians and literary scholars.

One of the problems we have here, akin to that in the letters, is that we have very little, except the recordings themselves and the 'Personal-Bogen' forms which give us basic information about the age, place of birth and pre-war profession of the subjects.[99] To uncover a subaltern history of emotions from so aggressive an ethnological and propagandist archive – especially when the recordings themselves are so stubbornly recalcitrant and were extracted under duress – is to stretch the practice of reading the colonial archive against the grain to its limit. While the work of scholars such as Heike Liebau and Britta Lange has greatly expanded our understanding of the complex network of interactions among German officials, academics and prisoners at Wünsdorf, what interests me here is the testimonial and affective dimensions of the recordings. Any reading

---

[96] Karamar Ali, Lautarchiv, Humboldt University, PK 1159; Mohammed Hossin, 'Story from the Gull', Lautarchiv, Humboldt University, PK1151. My translation of the story can be found in Lange, 'South Asian Soldiers', 180–182.

[97] Papers of Heinrich Lüders, Berlin-Brandenburgische Akademie der Wissenschaften. The papers in the folders '5Bd 1' and '5Bd 2' deal with the extensive documentation and hair-splitting philological analysis of Nepalese texts, possibly by the linguist Heinrich Lüders himself.

[98] Chotta Bagua, Song and Prayer, Lautarchiv, Humboldt University, Berlin, PK0610.

[99] Owing to the remarkable investigative efforts of Heike Liebau, we now have been able to piece together the various traces of the thirty-five-year-old Gurkha sepoy Gangaram Gurung who did a recording of the 'Prodigal Son' in English and three religious paintings; we also have his photograph. See Liebau, 'Encounters of a Gurkha in Europe (1914–1918): Gangaram Gurung', forthcoming.

has to be necessarily tentative and incomplete. But why was a particular story chosen over another by the narrator? The choice partly depended on what the sepoys remembered; some of the stories have no direct relevance to their contemporary plight.[100] But sometimes, hovering underneath or around the fringes of the stories, are parallels and parables that echo the sepoys' own predicament. Thus, the story of 'a parrot who died shivering with cold' gathers extra meaning when we realise that it was recorded in December 1916 in the Wünsdorf camp which had a mortality rate of 16.8% among Indians.[101] On the other hand, the story of rifleman Ranbir Sahi of a journey in the dark, and his sudden encounter with a house and dwellers who lavish fruits and water, hospitality and kindness on him, hovers somewhere between hope and wish-fulfilment.[102] These stories cannot be read as neat allegories or clear parables of the situation, but rather must be taken as hints and suggestions to suggest certain structures of feeling.

Very occasionally, there are striking parallels, as in this story of the 'Swan and Heron':

> Swan and Heron became friends. Swan lived in his own homeland but Heron was staying in Swan's homeland away from his own homeland. Heron used to feel nostalgic about his own homeland. Swan asked him the reason for his unhappiness. The Swan asked the Heron: 'why are you unhappy and why don't you eat anything'? Heron replied that he has received news about his homeland and is therefore nostalgic. Swan thought that perhaps the Heron's home is far better than Swan's homeland and therefore he is missing it. The Swan concludes by saying that one's nation (vatan) is very dear to one, it may not be very good, but even then, one is desirous to return to one's own land.[103]

The resonance with the sepoy's own condition cannot be missed: longing, homesickness and nostalgia get translated into a tale of separation. Similarly, in another recording, we have a reference to the folktale of Sassui Punnhun from North India:

> Santa Singh became as dry as a bamboo; he looks love-struck and
> heart-broken.
> Without his Sassi, he is wholly heart-broken.[104]

---

[100] Stories such as 'The King with Seven Sons', narrated by Malla Singh and 'The Rajah of Aligarh' told by Jeet Singh show a narrative world populated by kings and queens, marriage, loss and recovery.

[101] See Gerhard Höpp, *Muslime in der Mark: Als Kriegsgefangene und Internierte in Wünsdorf und Zossen, 1914–1924* (Berlin: Verlag das Arabische Buch, 1997), 50.

[102] Lautarchiv, Humboldt University, PK244.

[103] Lautarchiv, PK828. Translation by Barleen Shahi.

[104] Lautarchiv, 05970102. Translated by Harleen Singh. Sassui Punnhun is a love story from Sindhi folklore about a wife who is separated from her husband.

Here, Santa Singh, the homesick POW, is compared to the languishing lover Punnhun, separated from his beloved Sassi who here can be said to stand in for his homeland.[105] While most of the recordings are narratives or songs from northern India, there are a few Bengali recordings, including a wonderful 'tappa', possibly by a Bengali lascar: 'Let me go, let me go, I feel like a bird/Why keep me captive, preying on the weak.'[106] Perhaps the most haunting among these was one recorded in Khas by Bhawan Singh, from Darjeeling, on 8 December 1916:

> When a person dies,
> He constantly roams about
> And thus becomes a ghost.
> It is the soul that roams about.
> The roaming is like the air.
> So a ghost is like air
> He can go everywhere.[107]

According to Heinrich Lüders, the German scholar and linguist who closely studied the Indian prisoners, Bhawan Singh was one of the 'most intelligent' prisoners, a man who spoke Khas, Hindustani, English and even a bit of German. Lüders was hence surprised that '*he* of all people' would believe in ghosts. Singh claimed to have seen 'the ghosts of his dead comrades as they strolled up and down the training ground in moonlight'.[108] Was this merely 'Oriental' superstition, or a case of aggravated war trauma? The English soldier-poet Siegfried Sassoon, for example, had visions of dead bodies littering Piccadilly Circus on a visit to London. Or was Bhawan's story at once one of acute alienation and of fantasies of freedom so that the figure of the free-roaming ghost becomes the twin bearer of paranoia and wish-fulfilment?

In April 1915, J. B. Jackson, a representative of the American embassy in Berlin, visited the camp at Wünsdorf and reported on the '400 Indian soldiers and four officers in the camp'; he was particularly struck by a part of the barracks 'kept clean for prayer'.[109] Indeed, religion played a

---

[105] Recording of Santa Singh, Humboldt Lautarchiv, 05970102.

[106] Humboldt Lautarchiv, PK1612; my translation. 'Tappa' was an enormously popular genre in India in the late nineteenth and early twentieth century, particularly in Bengal, where it was patronised by the *zamindars* or landlords. Love and loss were popular themes, set to semi-classical tunes.

[107] Bhawan Singh from Almora, Lautarchiv, PK 591. The translation used is from Britta Lange's article, who uses the theme to highlight the idea of 'haunting' and 'ghostliness' in 'South Asian Soldiers and German Academics'.

[108] *Ibid.*

[109] Leonhard Adam, 'A Marriage Ceremony of the Pun-Clan (Magar) at Rigah (Nepal)', *Man: A Monthly Record of Anthropological Science*, 34, 23 (1934), 17–21. I am grateful to Heike Liebau and Ravi Ahuja for this reference.

central role in the daily lives of the inmates; photographs have surfaced of the barrack-walls lined with images of deities (Figure 5.4) and we have already seen photographs of the Dusserah festival being performed. In fact, the only artworks by an Indian soldier that have survived are three watercolours depicting Indian deities by Gangaram Gurung, one of which is shown in Figure 5.5.[110]

Above all, the sound-recordings are replete with religious (particularly Sikh) hymns and music, including *shabad, kirtan, gurbani* and *bhajan*.[111] They all point to the rich oral tradition of northern India and its connections to everyday religious practices. More than in the letters, it is through these grainy recordings – men singing together *shabads* or the *gurbani* – that one seems to come palpably close, a hundred years on, to the actual presence of these men as well as to the underworld of their feelings, welling up and spilling over through the power of devotional song:

> Hey Gobind, Hey Gopal Hey Dayal Lal
> Pran Nath Anath Sakhe Deen Dard Nivar
> Hey Samarat Agan Puram Mohe Mya Dhaa
> Andh Koop Maha Bhayan Nanak Par Utaar.[112]

> O Lord of the Universe, O Lord of the World, O Dear Merciful Beloved
> You are the Master of the breath of life, the Companion of the lost, and
>   the forsaken, the destroyer of the pains of the poor,
> O All-powerful, Inaccessible, perfect Lord, please shower me with
>   Your Mercy
> Please carry Nanak across the terrible deep dark pit of the world to the
>   other side.[113]

With only their faith and the sacred sonorous sounds they had carried with them from Punjab, these men bared their souls as their voices united in fragile hope. The above *shabad*, with its plea for mercy amidst the 'terrible deep dark pit', is deeply moving, especially if one listens to it; there is a plaintive rendition of another *shabad* by Namdev, whose poetry dealt with the marginalised sections of the society, particularly the underprivileged castes.[114]

---

[110] A Gurkha sepoy from the Punjab, he was one of the few camp inmates who had some English and did a recording of the 'Parable of the Prodigal Son' in English.

[111] *Shabad* is the term used by Sikhs to refer to a hymn or section of the Holy Text that appears in their several Holy Books, particularly the Guru Granth, each of whose parts can be set to music. Gurbhani literally means 'bani' or 'words' of the Guru, while bhajans are usually songs with a religious or spiritual idea, often set to ragas, and occur across Hinduism, Jainism and Vaishnavism.

[112] Lautarchiv, PK 05970100.

[113] I am grateful to Harleen Singh for the translation.

[114] Lautarchiv, PK 05970101.

Figure 2.1 *Farewell* by Pran Nath Mago. Fine Arts Museum, Punjabi University, Patiala and estate of the artist. Courtesy of Chadrika Mago, Chandrahas Mathur and Punam Mathur.

Figure 3.14   Alberto-Fabio Lorenzi, *Sikhs charging in a fir-wood furrowed by English artillery: southwest of Ypres, May 1915*. Imperfectly circular shape with indentation, diameter about 29 cm. Courtesy of BDIC Collection Nanterre: EST FL 1049.

Figure 3.19   James McBey, *A Double-Portrait of Punjabis at a Campfire*. © Imperial War Museum (Art 1595).

Figure 3.21   C. H. Burleigh, *The Dome As an Indian Hospital* (1915).
Courtesy of the Royal Pavilion & Museums, Brighton & Hove.

Figure 3.22   Douglas Fox Pitt, *An Interior View of the Brighton Pavilion* (1919).
Courtesy of the Royal Pavilion & Museums, Brighton & Hove.

Figure 5.5 A religious painting depicting the goddess 'Saraswati' by Gangaram Gurung. Photograph Album of Otto Stiehl. Courtesy of Staatliche Museen zu Berlin – Museum Europäischer Kulturen.

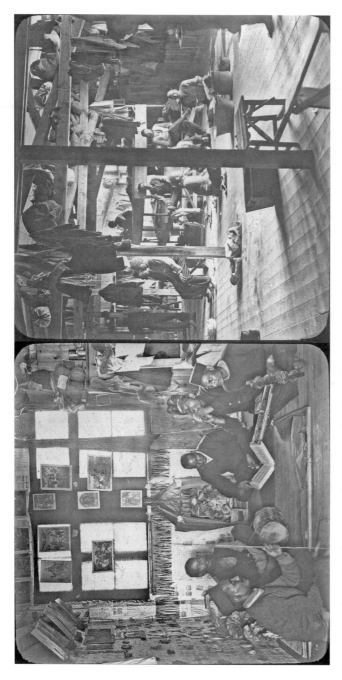

Figure 5.4   The insides of an unnamed POW camp housing Indian troops. BayHStA, Abt. IV, BS-D (Bildersammlung Diapositive), Nr. 9275.

Figure 5.5   A religious painting depicting the goddess 'Saraswati' by Gangaram
Gurung. Photograph Album of Otto Stiehl. Courtesy of Staatliche Museen zu
Berlin – Museum Europäischer Kulturen. (See the plate section for a colour
version of this figure.)

According to Lüders, the majority of the Indian prisoners did not have
'the confidence to tell a story, but preferred to sing a song ... Old verses
are constantly altered, extended and copied until something utterly new

emerges.[115] Indeed, one such song was recorded on 6 June 1916. All that is known about it is that it was sung by 'Jasbahadur Rai', a twenty-three-year-old Gurkha sepoy from Sikkim/Darjeeling, and that it was a 'Gurkha song, own words'. Jasbahadur must have died shortly afterwards, for his grave can be found outside the Zossen camp. The song is recorded in two instalments. Here is the first one:[116]

Line	Nepali transcription	English translation
1	Sisai kholā badhi jyān āyo bagāyo bulbule	With the rising of the Sisai river, I came, carried in its bubbling flow
2	Germany deshmā āipugyau hamī Angrezko hukumle	We arrived in the country, Germany, at the orders of the British
3	Hai suna suna, sun lāune charī, Angrezko hukumle	Listen, oh listen, gold-wearing birdie, at the orders of the British
4	Nepālī jyānko tīn dhāre pānī mul pāni tururu	Nepalis have three water taps, water flowing from the source
5	Nepālī jyānko marne na bāchne man pani durūrū	Nepali people, neither dying nor surviving, the heart also sobbing
6	Na uḍī jānu na basī āunu, man rūnchha durūrū	Neither can we fly away, nor can we arrive while staying put, the heart cries, sobbing
7	Hai suna suna, sun lāune didī, man rūnchha durūrū	Listen, oh listen, gold-wearing sister, the heart cries, sobbing
8	Pāniko bulbul, yo manko chulbul, bujhāũchhau katin din	The bubbling of water, the restlessness of this heart, how many days will it take to console yourself?
9	Hai suna suna, sun lāune kānchhī, bujhāũchhau katin din	Listen, oh listen, gold-wearing little one, how many days will it take to console yourself?
10	Dui paisa bathe tabalmar sigret salkāula mārchisle	If I save two cents, I'll light a Tabalmar cigarette with matches
11	Hindustān pāri, ke rāmro pahāḍ, ghāsaiko khaliyo	Across Hindustan, what beautiful hills, storage places for fodder
12	Baseko pirtī, chutāunam bhayo, man bādha baliyo	The love we've had, we now have to break apart, bind your heart and be strong
13	Hai suna suna, sun lāune charī, man bādha baliyo	Listen, oh listen, gold-wearing birdie, bind your heart and be strong

[115] Heinrich Lüders, 'Die Gurkhas', in Wilhelm Doegen (ed.), *Unter fremden Völkern. Eine neue Völkerkunde* (Berlin: Stollberg, 1925), 135.
[116] Jasbahadur Rai, Sikkim/Darjeeling, 'Gurkha song, own words', recorded on 6 June 1916 at 4 pm, Lautarchiv PK 307. Transcription and translation from Nepali by Anna Stirr with Ram Kumar Singh. Through a happy coincidence, Anna was then working on *Jhyaure*, a genre to which Jasbahadur's song belongs. See her important article, 'Sounding and Writing a Nepali Public Sphere: The Music and Language of Jhyaure', *Asian Music*, 46, 1 (2015), 3–38. More recently, Alaka Chudal has also started a project on these Nepalese POW sound-recordings.

Then it continues in another file:

Line	Nepali transcription	English translation
14	Europai jyānko ke rāmro tarī gā̃seko tillī pāt	The Europeans have such beautiful fields, shining leaves sewn together
15	gwāpeko hunchha Tihara kisim dunaiko Dillī pāt	They're joined together as if for Tihar, a bowl made of leaves from Delhi
16	he suna, sun laune didī, dunaiko Dillī pāt	Listen, oh listen, gold-wearing sister, a bowl made of leaves from Delhi
17	Europai jyānko baganai rāmro, torīko phul phulchha man	The Europeans have such beautiful gardens, mustard flowers bloom – when flowers bloom, so does the heart
18	chaudhai sālko laḍāiko suru dunyaiko bhukta man	When the war of the year 14 began, the world's hearts suffered greatly
19	garmiko mausam – garmiko mausam, garmi jyān bhayo, pankhaile humkaideu	Hot summer weather – Hot summer, my body is hot, cool it off with a fan
20	Europeko deshmā basnu man chhaina, India pathāīdeu	I don't want to stay in a European country, please send me to India
21	Gorkhālī khānchha khasiko shikhār khā̃daina rājai hā̃s	A Gorkhali eats goat meat, he doesn't eat swans
22	Na bachdā gati, na mardā mati, Belgiumko mahārāj	Surviving brings no progress, dying brings no knowledge, king of Belgium
23	Jānu jyān jānu, jādā nai mero,dhou bhane kati dhou	Bodies must go, and when mine goes, if you wash it, how much can it be washed?
24	Parālko āgo, jiu bhayo dāgo,rou bhane kati rou	Fire of straw, my body has become like a string, if I cry, how much can I cry?
25	Pharānse jyānko kyā ramro tarī, ṭhulo chha suntalā	The French have such beautiful fields, and there are large orange trees
26	Pharāns ni miche ma herdā kheri, jiu baḍhchha tīn tolā	I pushed through France too, and when I look back at it, my body gains 36 grams [out of fright]
27	Usai ra mero sāno jyān sāno ma kholdai kholdina	That and my body is small, so small, I don't open up
28	Germanko deshmā bātai jyān bujhdaina ma lājaile boldina	In the country of the Germans, I don't understand their talk, and out of embarrassment, I don't speak
29	Ki bhannu ṭhulo bhagavān bhannu dāju ke lāī?	Tell me, brother, what can we call powerful – God?
30	Madeshe jyānko hariyo pipal ghā̃s kātū yellāī	Our green pipal tree of the plains might as well be cut down for fodder.

In the whole pantheon of First World War culture, this must count as one of the most haunting testimonies. Like Mall Singh's, the song is interrupted by awkward pauses and sharp intakes of breath. Yet there is a passionate intensity to the singing, a compulsive need to tell: the voice rises and falls, high-pitched, desolate, undeterred. Traumatised by his experience and perhaps haunted by the knowledge of his approaching death, Jasbahadur turns an ethnographical experiment into one of the most powerful examples of life-narrative.

In both metre and melody, Jasbahadur draws on a genre of Nepali song called 'jhyaure'.[117] The 'jhyaure' was essentially a love song, often a feminine lament. If there is a relationship between the feminisation of 'jhyaure' songs and their theme of marginalisation, both political and economic, Jasbahadur spectacularly expands the scope of this folk genre to address his wartime imprisonment and emasculation. Repeated throughout the song is the word 'Jyān', a word meaning life as well as its material manifestation; he also mentions 'jiu', meaning body in the more conventional sense. Both suggest his desperate efforts to cling on to life even as he sings his own elegy. The refrain 'Hai suna' ('Listen, oh listen', lines 3, 7, 9, 13), Ancient Mariner-like, draws the listener into the song through an intricate sonic structure, combining alliteration (suna/sun/laune) with a pattern of repetition with variation centring around the addressee or companion – a young woman, referred variously as 'didi' (elder sister), 'kanchi' (little girl), 'chari' ('birdie', or girl in folksongs). Water ('pani') courses through the song, first entering as torrents of the river ('Sisai', either the name of a river or 'susāī' meaning 'whistling', a term commonly used to describe the sound of flowing streams), only to later emerge as bodily tears ('cries, sobbing') before becoming water for his own funerary rituals ('how much can it be washed'). Memory, metaphor and mourning are knitted together through onomatopoeia and rhyme ('paniko bulbul, ei monko chulbul') as sound becomes the sense. Cigarettes and matchsticks get mixed with mountains and flowers, Belgium and Germany are brought together, the year of the war's eruption is remembered through sense perception. Tellingly, in the whole song, it is only once, in line 28, that Jasbahadur breaks the poetic metre – a line where he talks about his difficulty in speaking in a foreign language. The closing reference to the 'pipal tree', worshipped as a symbol of divinity, is particularly poignant: the cutting down of the tree suggests the ebbing away of faith. Jasbahadur is the First World War poet par excellence, for he records history not as grand narrative or even cultural memory but as 'a structure of feeling'. Blurring the boundaries between song, reportage, lament, *j'accuse*, prison-narrative and compulsive testimony, it is also

---

[117] See Anna Stirr, 'Sounding and Writing a Nepali Public Sphere', 3–38. Anna Stirr has also substantially enriched my understanding of the song through detailed annotation. The song, she tells me, is also related to the subgenre of songs called 'Gurkha dukha' ('The Sorrows of the Gurkhas').

the birth of life-writing as the form of Nepali folksong – the *jhyaure* – is called upon to bear lyric testimony to historical trauma.

One of the most tantalising and frustrating aspects about Jasbahadur's song – as with most of the testimonies discussed in this chapter, including the censored letters – is the fact that, unlike their European counterparts, we know so very little about them or their authors. While their historical value cannot equally be overemphasised, their literary, formal and affective qualities cannot be overlooked: Amir Khan's letter, the short poems, the prayers and parables, Mall Singh's voice and Jasbahadur's broken melody are sensuous evocations of the past, resistant to flattened narratives or neat theorisations; instead, they take us to the very contact-zone where testimony is born. At the same time, they also show how the very idea of 'life-*writing*' needs to be loosened and rethought if we are to recover the lives of the majority of the world's people. Messy, fragmentary, fugitive and wholly compelling, these testimonies give us no compendious history or definitive account of 'sepoy life in Europe', but, perhaps more probingly and definitely more movingly, *recreate* moments, moods, emotions, situations, crises, contingencies, summoning up a real body, a palpable life – as we turn the pages of the censors' extracts or listen to the recordings, each alone.

CHAPTER 6

'Their Lives Have Become Ours'
Occupation, Captivity and Lateral Contact in Mesopotamia, 1914–1918

Framed by the sun stands a small Arab girl, unadorned and alone, in a slightly frayed *thwab* and sporting a *tarboosh* (Figure 6.1).[1] Remarkably composed, even slightly quizzical, for someone so young, she stands her ground, with the right foot thrust forward, hands firmly clasped together and the face slightly askance.[2] The *punctum*, one may say, lies in the unsmiling eyes and mouth as they hold the camera's gaze at an angle. The effect is rare. Curiosity, suspicion, trepidation, war-weariness: it is difficult to read the expression but child-like delight or ease is not one of them. It is the knowing look of someone much older than her years. The photograph would have been striking even in the collection of Ariel Varges, but what makes it remarkable is that I came across it in the 'war album' of Captain Dr Manindranath Das, mentioned in the Introduction, who served as a doctor in Mesopotamia in 1916–1918. We know very little about his war experiences, except that he was a distinguished doctor, and that he pretended to be dead and stayed behind to treat wounded soldiers when others had retreated after an attack. He risked his own life to bandage their wounds, for which he was given the Military Cross.[3] Family lore has it that he would have got the Victoria Cross, had he been white. But we know hardly anything beyond these details. The story is typical of how little is known of the experiences of the participants of the Mesopotamia campaign, even when the subjects were educated, articulate and decorated.

For the Indians, Mesopotamia was the main ground of battle: the largest number of Indians – some 588,717, including 7,812 officers, 287,753 other ranks and 293,152 non-combatants (often forming porter and labour corps) – served there between 1914 and 1918.[4] The campaign, which was

---

[1] A *thwab* is an ankle-length Arab garment, akin to a robe, while a *tarboosh* is a close-fitting, flat-topped brimless hat.
[2] Photograph album of Captain Dr Manindranath Das, owned by Mrs Sunanda Das, Kolkata.
[3] Interview with Mrs Sunanda Das, daughter-in-law of Manindranath Das, December 2014.
[4] *India's Contribution to the Great War*, 97.

Figure 6.1   An Arab girl wearing a *thwab* and a *tarboosh*, photographed somewhere in Mesopotamia by Captain Dr Manindranath Das. Courtesy of Sunanda Das.

managed by the Government of India rather than the War Office in London, was a classic example of the colonial government's Macbeth-like 'vaulting ambition which o'erleaps itself/And falls on the other'. What began as a limited defensive operation in 1914 to protect the oilfields of Abadan and pre-empt any serious *jihadi* threat evolved in 1915 into a full-fledged offensive to capture Baghdad, and resulted in what is often considered the British Army's greatest humiliation in the First World War. In a campaign marked by dust, disease and death, the biggest debacle was the five-month-long siege in the city of Kut-al-Amara (7 December 1915–29 April 1916), and two years of abject degradation for the non-officer prisoners of war, both British and Indian, who would be dragged across Iraq, Greater Syria and Turkey. At the time of surrender, the number of Indians captured was around 10,440, including 204 officers, 6,988 rank and file and 3,248 camp followers.[5] While we have British POW first-person accounts, there have

---

[5] The figures are quoted in Major E. W. C. Sandes, *In Kut and Captivity: With the Sixth Indian Division* (London: John Murray, 1919), 261. These figures are close to the figures cited in *Statistics of*

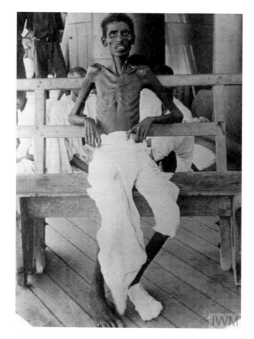

Figure 6.2   An Indian POW, in an advanced stage of starvation, recently freed
after the Siege of Kut in Mesopotamia, 1916 during an exchange of prisoners.
© Imperial War Museum (Q 79446).

been no corresponding Indian accounts. Instead, the much publicised
photograph of a sepoy in an advanced state of starvation fills that silence
with horror (Figure 6.2). Part of the aim of this chapter is to break this
deafening silence around the Indian experience in Mesopotamia through
the investigation of freshly unearthed material.

In her powerful study *A Land of Aching Hearts: The Middle East in the
Great War* (2014), Leila Fawaz notes that 'World War I was not only a global
event, but also a personal story that varied across the broad Middle East.'[6]
If experiences in the Middle East, like the campaign itself, long remained
marginalised, the stories of the British POWs as well as of the local men
and women from Iraq, Lebanon and Turkey are being increasingly heard

the Military Effort of the British Empire, 330. The Table of Prisoners in *Statistics* mentions a separate
category for 'Indian Native Kut' but gives only the combined figure for 'Indian Native' (captured
elsewhere during the Mesopotamia campaign) and 'Indian Native Kut' at 200 Indian officers and
10,486 'other ranks' (330).
[6] Leila Fawaz, *A Land of Aching Hearts: The Middle East in the Great War* (Harvard: Harvard University
Press, 2014), 2. See her chapter 'South Asians in the War', *A Land of Aching Hearts*, 205–232.

and examined.[7] While there has been some work on the military logistics of the Indian army in Mesopotamia, the actual experiences of the men have remained unknown. In recent years, the novelist Amitav Ghosh has powerfully drawn attention to this area through his remarkable blogposts.[8] What I wish to recover and examine here are the 'personal stories' of the men from the Indian subcontinent as well as how such stories intersected with those of their allies and enemies across the broad Middle East over the four years. While discussing 'cosmopolitan thought-zones', the political historian Kris Manjapra makes the following observation:

> To frame the global circulation of ideas within the lone axis of centre versus periphery is to view the world through the colonial state's eyes and through its archive. As theorists of interregional and transnational studies have pointed out, the practice of taking sideways glances towards 'lateral networks' that transgressed the colonial duality is the best way to disrupt the hemispheric myth that the globe was congenitally divided into an East and West, and that ideas were exchanged across that fault line alone.[9]

The South Asian war experience in the Middle East provides a singular vantage-point for examining such 'lateral' encounters: what we have in this extraordinarily cosmopolitan theatre is a multi-ethnic, multi-lingual and multi-religious army from British India interacting with people from a vaster but similarly multi-ethnic, multi-lingual and multi-religious empire at a time when the strains of the war effort had started triggering the genocide of the Ottoman Armenians. The plural identities of the Indians – as invaders, victims, fellow colonial-subjects and often co-religionists (for the Muslim sepoys) – interacted with an internally divided local population, often defying any neat political, racial or religious grid. What drives the present chapter, among other issues, are the testimonial, affective and intimate dimensions of these encounters between Indians, both sepoys and educated medics, and a range of Ottoman subjects in several contexts: occupation, combat, siege and captivity.

The military campaign remained the backbone for cultural encounters.[10] On 6 November 1914, the Sixth Indian (Poona) Division crossed over

---

[7] Fawaz's study is partly responsible for the excavation of the daily experiences of the local men and women, soldiers and civilians, particularly from what is today Lebanon. For an Ottoman perspective, see Mustafa Aksakal, *The Ottoman Road to War in 1914: The Ottoman Empire and the First World War* (Cambridge: Cambridge University Press, 2008); also see Eugene Rogan, *The Fall of the Ottomans: The Great War in the Middle East, 1914–1920* (London: Allen Lane, 2015).

[8] Amitav Ghosh, 'At Home and the World in Mesopotamia', blogpost, archived on his website www.amitavghosh.com. Kaushik Roy, 'The Army in India in Mesopotamia from 1916–1918: Tactics, Technology and Logistics', in Ian Beckett (ed.), *1917: Beyond the Western Front* (Leiden: Brill, 2009), 131–158.

[9] Kris Manjapra and Sugata Bose (eds.), *Cosmopolitan Thought-Zones*, 2.

[10] There has been a number of important works on the Mesopotamia campaign, of which A. J. Barker, *The Neglected War: Mesopotamia 1914–1918* (London: Faber, 1967) remains one of the best. Also see Kaushik Roy, 'From Defeat to Victory: Logistics of the Campaign in Mesopotamia, 1914–1918', *First*

the bar of the Shatt al-Arab into Turkish waters, captured the Ottoman fort at Fao and headed towards Basra; by the end of the month, it had captured the city. Having tasted easy success, the ambitious cavalry-officer General Nixon, Commander of the IEF 'D', craved for more. 'Having swallowed Basra and retained it in the face of Ottoman counter-attack', as Leila Fawaz notes wryly, 'fanciful aspirations of sacking the minarets of Baghdad, glittering some five hundred miles upstream, appeared as enticing as a Mesopotamian mirage.'[11] The responsibility fell on General Charles Townshend, the commander of the Sixth Division. In May 1915, Townshend continued his offensive up the Tigris towards Amara aboard *HMS Espiegle* and then *HMS Comet*; his men, known as Townshend's 'Regatta', got onto small local boats called *bellums* to chase through weeds and marshes a retreating Ottoman army. By September 1915, the British flag flew over Basra, Amara, Qurna, Nasiriyah and Kut. Townshend continued his unstoppable advance towards Baghdad but, on 22 November, the whole show came to an abrupt halt: his exhausted and malnourished army faced a numerically superior, well-camouflaged and entrenched Turkish army at Ctesiphon. In the ensuing battle, the Indian casualties were enormous, estimated at 4,300. Townshend now retreated to Kut, expecting reinforcements and hoping to regroup over the winter; instead, he would be faced with one of the longest sieges in British history.[12] There were several significant but unsuccessful attempts to relieve the town, first by Lieutenant-General Aylmer in March and then by Captain Gorringe twice in April.[13] Townshend finally surrendered on 29 April 1916. While the captured officers received preferential treatment, the privates, both British and Indians, suffered 'two years of horror'.[14] After the fall of Kut, the campaign was rethought and the control passed from India

---

World War Studies, 1, 1 (2010), 35–55; Roy, 'The Army in India in Mesopotamia'; Charles Townshend, *When God Made Hell: The British Invasion of Mesopotamia and the Creation of Iraq 1914–1921* (London: Faber, 2010); Paul K. Davis, *Ends and Means: The British Mesopotamian Campaign and Commission* (Madison: Associated University Presses, 1994); and Ross Anderson, 'Logistics of the IEF D in Mesopotamia, 1914–1918', in Kaushik Roy (ed.), *The Indian Army in the Two World Wars* (Leiden: Brill, 2011), 105–144. Also see Mark Harrison, *The Medical War: British Military Medicine in the First World War* (Oxford: Oxford University Press, 2014), 204–227 and Priya Satia, *Spies in Arabia: The Great War and the Cultural Foundations of Britain's Covert Empire in the Middle East* (Oxford: Oxford University Press), 2008.

[11] Fawaz, *A Land of Aching Hearts*, 63.

[12] For a detailed history of the siege using British sources, see Nikolas Gardner, *The Siege of Kut-al-Amara: At War in Mesopotamia, 1915–1916* (Bloomington: Indiana University Press, 2014) and Patrick Crowley, *Kut 1916: Courage and Failure in Iraq* (Stroud: The History Press, 2009).

[13] 'Despatch by Lieutenant-General Sir G. F. Gorringe', British Library, IOR, L/MIL/17/15/109.

[14] Patrick Crowley, *Kut 1916: Courage and Failure in Iraq*, 181.

to Britain. Under General Maude, the British forces advanced carefully up both sides of the Tigris, occupied Kut in December, and finally entered Baghdad on 11 March. Throughout the campaign, religion was often a flash-point. As early as 14 November 1914, the Sheikh-un-Islam, on behalf of the Caliphate, had declared a *jihad* or holy war against the British and French empires and promised the Muslims who supported them 'the fire of hell'.[15] Even though the colonial government repeatedly reassured the Muslim sepoys that the 'holy places of Islam' would be protected, there was consternation; for example, the 15th Lancers refused to open fire on their Turkish co-religionists in Basra in 1915 with the whole regiment 'taking an oath not to fight against Muslims'.[16]

What were the 'undertones' of such an arduous campaign and what are our sources? British memoirs provide tantalising glimpses, from accounts of men 'going mad in the heat' and 'dancing in no man's land' to Major Carter's famous account of a hospital ship bringing Indians covered in their own faeces after the battle of Ctesiphon.[17] Indian testimonies on the Mesopotamia campaign are very rare, as we have nothing similar to the archive of censored Indian mail from France. While it is possible to recover the activities of the relief forces from the substantial visual archives and the unit diaries, the most 'silent' of the fronts in the campaign is the world of siege and captivity: there have so far been no POW diaries or letters or memoirs from the Indians. This chapter recovers and examines this shadowy world through freshly unearthed and unusual material – the writings (in Bengali) of a group of educated and largely middle-class Bengali men who served as medical personnel – doctors, orderlies, stretcher-bearers and clerks. Their value is two-fold. First, if Indian testimonies have largely been sepoy-centric, here we have the voices of non-combatants. Coming out of a more educated milieu as well as being acutely conscious of the histor-ical importance of the experience, several of these men wrote memoirs.[18]

---

[15] Hew Strachan, *The First World War* (New York: Viking, 2003), 100. See his chapter on 'Global Jihad', 95–124.
[16] Letter of Ashraf Ali Khan to Signalling Instructor Dafadar Fateh Mahomed Khan, 6th Cavalry, France, 24 March 1916, *CIM*, IOR, L/MIL//826/4, 582, British Library.
[17] *A Land of Aching Hearts*, 65; A. J. Barker, *The Neglected War*, 137.
[18] These include Prafulla Chandra Sen, 'Bengal Ambulance Corer Katha' ['The Story of the Bengal Ambulance Corps'], serialised in *Mānasī O Marmavāṇī* (the instalments I have been able to locate include December 1922, Vol. 5, Part 2, 459–466, January 1924, Vol. 6, Part 2, 536–542 and June 1925, Vol. 5 Part 1, 495–500); Ashutosh Roy, 'Yuddhavandīr Ātmakathā' ['The Autobiography of a Prisoner of War'], *Bhāratvarṣa* (in January 1920, Vol. 2, Part 2, 194–197 and March, 1920, Vol. 2, Part 4, 511–514); Krishna Behari Ray, 'The Story of a Bengali Prisoner of the Turks in Kut', as narrated by Shitanath Bhatta, Supply and Transport Department, 6th Division, *Mānasī O Marmavāṇī* (September 1919), 121–125. All translations are mine unless stated otherwise.

Second, we have here for the first time glimpses into life under captivity. Starting with the initial impressions of the occupied land and its people through these memoirs as well as the few extant sepoy letters, I shall then examine Indian experiences and encounters in the context of combat, siege and captivity largely through the lens of two extraordinary testimonies – a set of letters by Dr Kalyan Kumar Mukherji and a 209-page-long memoir *Abhi Le Baghdad* by Sisir Prasad Sarbadhikari. I shall read them alongside the writings of their friends and colleagues as well as those of British prisoners in Mesopotamia.[19]

Between the Primitive and the Familiar: Basra, *Bazaars* and *Boodhus*

Orientalism, mythic history and muddy reality jostled together in British soldiers' first impressions of Mesopotamia: space was perceived as deep time. If an 'Arabian Nights' quality hung over the desert air in the north, the British soldiers knew that the country 'spanned the whole land of Holy Writ, from Jerusalem to Babylon and from Babylon to Shush'.[20] The British traveller D. G. Hogarth anticipated the responses of the Tommies by some ten years when he noted, in 1904, that travelling in Mesopotamia was 'to pass through the shadow of what has been': the cradle of civilisation was now a forsaken land.[21] Depopulation, disrepair and dereliction had set in over the centuries and Mesopotamia, as the soldiers found it in 1914, was alternately a desert and a swamp. Every spring, water would stream down the Taurus and Zagros mountains and flood the low-lying land, with its innumerable creeks, canals and ditches, and the sand would morph into mud.[22] If the mud on the Western front was the product of industrial

[19] During the Balkan Wars of 1912–1913, three medical teams were despatched from India to treat wounded Ottoman soldiers. There were regular letters back home by the team organised by Mohammad Ali Jauhar and directed by Mukhtar Ahmad Ansari. These letters were published in the weekly *Comrade* journal, but the Bengali writers do not seem to mention it. For this mission and its remarkable collection of letters, see Burak Akçapar, *People's Mission to the Ottoman Empire: M. A. Ansari and the Indian Medical Mission, 1912–1913* (Delhi: Oxford University Press, 2014). Harald Fischer-Tiné kindly sent me a copy of his article 'Keep Them Pure, Fit, and Brotherly! The Indian Y.M.C.A.'s Army Work Schemes during the Great War (1914–1920)', which opens up a fresh dimension to the war experience; see his forthcoming piece '"Unparalleled Opportunities": The Indian YMCA's Army Work Schemes for Imperial Troops during the Great War (1914–1920)', *Journal of Imperial and Commonwealth History*.
[20] Edmund Candler, *The Long Road to Baghdad* (London: Routledge, 2016 [1919]), Vol. II, 198.
[21] D. G. Hogarth, 'The Eastern Mind', *Monthly Review*, 15, 43 (1904), 122. Also see Nadia Atia's excellent article '"A Relic of Its Own Past": Mesopotamia in the British Imagination, 1900–14', *Memory Studies*, 3, 3 (2010), 232–241.
[22] See *The Land of Aching Hearts*, 61–62. Also see Charles Townshend, *When God Made Hell*, 3–10.

artillery, the British soldiers saw the mudflats in Mesopotamia as the natural habitat for the so-called 'primitive people' of 'Turkish Arabia': 'It is a mud plain so flat that a single heron, reposing on one leg beside some rare trickle of water in a ditch, looks as tall as a wireless aerial. From this plain rise villages of mud and cities of mud. The rivers flow with liquid mud. The air is composed of mud refined into a gas. The people are mud-coloured.'[23] Did the Indians too see the land and its people through a similar lens – myth-fringed but mud-splattered?

Orientals are often most prone to Orientalism. On reaching Basra, Dr Kalyan Mukherji wrote to his mother: 'Ahre Ram, is this the Basra of Khalif Haroun al-Rashid? Chi! Chi! There is not even the faintest sign of roses; instead what we have here is a 10–12-hand-long, 5–6-hand-wide and 20–21-hand-deep ditch. Into it flows the water of the Tigris, knee-deep or waist-deep. Each of these ditches is home to at least two hundred thousand frogs – small, big and medium-sized. Most of them are bull-frogs. What a terrible din they make.'[24] The language of the land which housed the Tower of Babel seemed to have degenerated into a cacophony of frogs but the spry Orientalist humour is free of any racialising discourse. Mukherji was stationed just outside Basra; the account of his fellow Bengali Ashutosh Roy of the actual city was different:

> The town reminds me of our own towns. The shops are well-decorated. The bazaar is covered ... At the entrance of the canal that leads from Shat-el-Arab to Basra is another bazaar, called 'Ashar'. The well-to-do live around here and the bazaar is not small. The canals and the rivers are full of boats called 'Mahellas' – they are like the ones we have back at home ('chip naukār mato') but smaller. They are good for fast travel. Most well-to-do people have their own mahellas. At every lane here, you will find 'Kāwākhānā' or Coffee-shops; they can be compared to the street-side tea-shops in our country. The big difference is that in our country, only in the morning and in the evening, people crowd around these places to have tea; but here are crowds of coffee-drinkers at all times of the day.[25]

Neither the fantasy-town of Haroun al-Rashid nor the site of dereliction as in British accounts, Basra emerges here as bustling, stratified, *familiar*. While we have photographs of 'Ashar' bazaar from the British travel-writer

---

[23] Robert Byron, 'Road to Oxiana', quoted in Townshend, *When God Made Hell*, 7–8.
[24] Letter dated 13 April 1915, quoted in Mokkhada Devi, *Kalyān-Pradīp: The Life of Captain Kalyan Kumar Mukhopadhyay I.M.S.* (Calcutta: Satish Chandra Mukhopadhyay and Rashik Law Press, 1928), 250. My translation.
[25] Ashutosh Roy, 'The Autobiography of a Prisoner of War', *Bharatbharsha*, March 1920, Vol. 2, Part 2, 195.

Gertrude Bell, Roy records its daily rhythm: Arabs and Armenians having bread with meat for lunch and drinking coffee or performances by Bedouin street-dancers. The streetscape of Al-Qurna reminds him of his own native Varanasi; he also records the Ottoman army in retreat and a Turkish cruiser on fire. A seasoned traveller who had previously written an account of his travels in China, Roy mixes travelogue, ethnology and military expedition in his account, which was serialised in a Bengali journal and illustrated with photographs.

The accounts of Kalyan Mukherji and Ashutosh Roy are exceptional. The authors were educated, middle-class and culturally confident, and there is a close engagement with the land, its people and its history which is absent from the few sepoy-letters we have from Mesopotamia. But their gaze, like that of the British travellers, is often ethnological: the Arabs are described as sturdy and bold but 'lazy', while the Armenians are depicted as intelligent, good-looking, well-dressed ('their food, manners, and dress are far superior to the Turks'), but somewhat cowardly and untrustworthy.[26] As Roy enters Al-Qurna, 'the Garden of Eden', a rogue Armenian interpreter points to 'the tree of knowledge'; a sceptical Ray notes, with wry humour, 'Whatever the truth, all I can say is that the mosquitoes of this place are beyond description – a suitable place indeed for our ancient father and mother.'[27] However, the real objects of his fascination as well as of racist opprobrium are the Bedouins or 'Boodhus': 'They are uncivilized. They eke out a living through looting and plunder. They also try to earn a livelihood by raising sheep, goat, bulls, camels, horses and donkeys. They have no fixed address – they pitch big blankets like tents and live at one place for two to three months … The Boodhus are very fierce. They do not hesitate to kill people even without proper reason.'[28] Such comments are echoed in other accounts; the diary of the 47th Sikhs refers to them as a 'treacherous and thieving race, whose habit it is to appear to side with the stronger party … Boodhus, flies and dust are the plaguers of the country', while there are references in both British and Indian memoirs to their alleged habits of looting and massacring people.[29] But Roy is fascinated: he lingers on, and photographs their gestures, clothes and ornaments, not just reminiscent of British travellers in Mesopotamia, but bearing traces of Kaye and Watson's ethnological project *Peoples of India*. Ethnology did not act

---

[26] Roy, 'The Autobiography of a Prisoner of War', *Bhāratvarṣa*, March 1920, Vol. 7, Part 2, Issue 4, 513.
[27] *Ibid.*, 513.
[28] *Ibid.*, 513.
[29] *47th Sikhs*, 121; Barker, *Neglected War*, 242.

solely on an East–West axis, nor was it just a racial science. Class, as much as race, underpinned these ethnological forays; if the British colonials had photographed 'primitive' Indians, Roy in turn draws on an ethnological vocabulary to understand the Bedouins.

Such engagements with the locals, ethnological or otherwise, are absent in the handful of letters from sepoys in Mesopotamia that have survived by dint of being written to their friends serving in France. Though these letters are from soldiers involved in the relief efforts of 1916–1917, they are revealing of the general sepoy attitude towards Mesopotamia, particularly in the light of our discussion in the last chapter:

> The country in which we are encamped is an extremely bad place. There are continual storms and the cold is very great, and in the wet season it is intensely hot ... If I had only gone to France, I could have been with you and seen men of all kinds. We have all got to die someday, but at any rate we would have had a good time there.[30]

> You know very well that I am not in India. I am with Force 'D'. You must know very well where Force 'D' is. Since coming here I have met many men who were formerly in France. From them we have heard all about France. In truth, you must be very comfortable there, since the 'public' there is so civilised, and money too is plentiful. The particular part of the world where I am is a strange place. The seasons here are quite different from what you experience anywhere else. We have already experience of the cold and wet. Now the heat is threatening us from afar. It rains very heavily and the entire surface of the land becomes a quagmire ... Except for the barren, naked plain, there is nothing to see.[31]

Experienced or imagined, France is the yard-stick and the obscure object of desire: the difference between France and Mesopotamia, according to another sepoy, is that 'between heaven and earth'.[32] If the sepoy letters describing France are often rhapsodic, leading Markovits to call them 'Occidentalism from below',[33] the descriptions here are unremittingly negative. Mesopotamia confronted the sepoys with an underdeveloped version of their own country: 'uninhabited', 'desolate' and 'barren' are recurrent words used to describe the landscape.

---

[30] Sowar Jivan Mal, 28th Cavalry, to Lance Dafadar Ganda Singh, 28th Cavalry, France, 17 November 1915, British Library, IOR, MSS Eur E420/10.
[31] From _, Field Ambulance, Force 'D', Mesopotamia, to _, Dafadar, 21 May, 1916, BL, IOR, L/MIL/828, Part 2, 345.
[32] From sub-assistant surgeon, Force 'D', Mesopotamia to _ Dafadar, France, 21 May, 1916, BL, IOR, L/MIL/828, Part 2, 344 (v).
[33] Markovits, 'Indian Soldiers' Experiences in France', 40.

Figure 6.3 Indian army engaged in chlorinating water at an advanced post in
Mesopotamia, 1917. © Imperial War Museum (Q 24489).

Priya Sathia has argued that, after the horrors of industrial combat on
the Western Front, British war officials made the mission of 'developing
Iraq' into a key site for the 'redemption of empire and technology', a point
we briefly touched upon in Chapter 3.[34] As early as 1916, Edmund Candler
had noted that a military infrastructure – the construction of roads, bridges,
dams – was cast as a way of 'bringing new life to Mesopotamia' at a time
when 'the war had let loose destruction in Europe'.[35] The main agents in
such technological rejuvenation of Mesopotamia were the British Indian
army – its labourers, sappers, miners, engineers, signallers – as photographs
portrayed them engaged in a wide variety of roles: building bridges and
dams, chlorinating water at an advanced post (Figure 6.3), laying telephone
cables, working at a slipway near the Shatt al-Arab waterway or fixing signalling posts, or driving a tractor to haul a howitzer across the Diala. While

---

[34] Priya Satia, 'Developing Iraq: Britain, India and the Redemption of Empire and Technology', *Past
and Present*, No. 197 (2007), 211–255.
[35] Edmund Candler, *The Long Road to Baghdad* (London: Cassell, 1919), 183.

such activities were woven into an imperial narrative of Britannia bringing progress and development to Mesopotamia through the work of another colonised race, i.e. the Indians, the actual labourers who were doing the hard work were less impressed. Being the orderlies of both war and empire, they had neither the imperial guilt nor the humanistic angst of men such as Candler and expressed their opinions bluntly. The harsh climate, the rickety infrastructure and the meagre provisions fuelled discontent: 'They do not give us postcards to write. In France there was no lack of anything. It has remained for us to encounter the greatest of difficulties in this place. There is no sign of milk or sugar, and for drink, we have nothing but the water of the Djlah.'[36] While it is possible to partly reconstruct the later years of the campaign through an interweaving of the army unit diaries, occasional letters and photographs, we know very little about the Indian experience during the early years, particularly during the siege or under captivity. It is in this context that we now turn to Kalyan Mukherji's letters and Sarbadhikari's memoir.

Kalyān-Pradīp: Politics, Protest and Mourning

Kalyān-Pradīp is as unique a document in the history of South Asian literature as it is in the literary history of the First World War. A 429-page-long memoir, it was written by an eighty-year-old widow, Mokkhada Devi, as a tribute to her thirty-four-year-old grandson Kalyan Mukherji who died as a POW in Mesopotamia.[37] *Kalyān-Pradīp* – literally meaning *Kalyan-Lamp* – was written to keep alive the 'flame' of his memory. Mukherjee was born into an upper-middle-class family in Calcutta, and trained as a doctor in Calcutta, London and Liverpool before joining the prestigious Indian Medical Services (I.M.S.). In the memoir, Devi closely follows the arc of Kalyan's life, from his time in Calcutta and England to the outbreak of the war and his service in Mesopotamia until his death on 18 March 1917; framing the life-story is a vivid re-imagining of the Mesopotamia campaign with a degree of familiarity with operational details which is astonishing for an eighty-year-old woman in Calcutta. Amidst her account, set like jewels, are Mukherji's own letters from various battle zones, and under siege and in captivity, to his mother. Blurring the boundaries between Bengali home front and Middle Eastern

---

[36] From __ (name withheld) Force D, Mesopotamia to __ (name withheld) France, 7 February, 1916, BL, IOR, L/MIL/5/828/2, 335(v).

[37] Mokkhada Devi, *Kalyān-Pradīp*. 'Kalyān' in Bengali means 'well-being' or 'goodness' while 'Pradīp' means 'lamp'. All translations are mine.

war front, *Kalyāṇ-Pradīp* is as much a first-hand testimony to the campaign in Mesopotamia as it is to how the war was being understood, remembered and re-imagined in colonial Calcutta.[38]

Mukherji's wartime missives are exceptional in at least two respects. First, for once, they are complete and original rather than censored and translated fragments that we have in the case of sepoys from the Western Front. Second, Mukherji's are the only letters from an Indian that cover two full years of the war on any front, from the time of his arrival in Basra in April 1915 until his death on 18 March 1917. Equally remarkable are the sophistication of his sensibility and its evolution as, Owen-like, he bears testimony to front-line horrors and turns them into the vale of soul-making. Attached to the Ambulance Corps of the 6th Division, he bore first-hand witness to the battle of Amarah in June 1915 and then the battle of Nasiriyah on 25 July, where he managed a dressing station behind an orchard-wall 300 yards behind the trenches. Missives from the front, his letters – like those of his British colleagues in the Western front – are acute sensory palimpsests, resonant with the 'shai-shai' of rifle-fire, the 'boom-boom' of artillery or the description of the shrapnel spreading like 'a shower of hail-stones against the sky, as if an invisible hand from the sky is throwing a handful of pebbles' (314). These letters can be compared, across the imperial divide, with the letters of fellow non-combatant and officer Spink who arrived in Basra at a similar time, witnessed the same battles, experienced the siege and captivity and wrote at length to his parents. Thus, after the battle of Nasiriyah (25 July), Spink wrote to his father about the 'big show' and stated that 'we whacked them once again',[39] but, for Mukherji, it became a turning point towards disenchantment:

> At five in the morning, we left the camp with bandages, medicines, iodine, milk and brandy in order to take care of the wounded. From 5 pm our cannons started.
>
> Boom! Boom! roared around twenty or twenty-five cannons at once. After fifteen or twenty minutes, our soldiers began to advance from behind us firing above our heads like hail-stones … After two or three hours, unable to bear the bombardment any more, the enemy started to retreat … Around 3 pm, a group of prisoners and some of the wounded enemy soldiers began

---

[38] Mokkhada Devi's extraordinary talents and achievements co-exist with a certain social and religious conservatism which is deeply revealing about sections of the Bengali bourgeoisie of the time.

[39] Letter of Spink, 10 August 1915, from Amara to his sister, 'Papers of Spink', British Library, IOR Mss Eur 188/1.

to arrive. From 6.30 in the morning till 1 pm, I did not have time even to breathe. Rivers of blood, red in colour – everywhere – I was covered in blood. Whom to nurse first? Like Dhruva in 'Immersion', I wondered, 'Why is there so much blood?' Why such bloodshed? What more can I describe? I shall never forget such a scene in my life.[40]

His documentation fast devolved into acute soul-searching and critique: 'What I have seen – it is impossible to describe. Today the English flag has been flown here.'[41] The juxtaposition is telling: the 'English' flag, though secured through Indian sepoys, brings no sense of pride. Throughout his letters, the campaign, like the victory above, is referred to as 'English', never as 'ours'.

Kalyan's letters provide vivid snapshots of the offensive, from Nasiriyah in July and Kut in September, when he spent three days in the trenches and was commended by Nixon for 'collecting the wounded from a shell-swept area' (423). Their documentary value, singular as it is, is outweighed for the reader by the tumultuous world of feeling that the letters record following Townshend's advance from Nasiriyah to Kut-al-Amara. His growing sense of disenchantment was perhaps a direct response to the change in the nature of the campaign from a defensive expedition to one of aggressive offensive action, spurred by the ambition of Townshend and Nixon: 'I understand that we won't advance any more. But then I have heard that so many times.' Later, from Aziziyah, sixty miles upriver from Kut: 'We have advanced a lot – why more? It is us, having tasted victory, who are snatching away everything from the enemies; the enemies have not yet done anything.'[42]

On reaching Aziziyah on 3 October after the victory at Kut, an anxious Townshend asked for an order 'in writing over Sir J. N.'s signature' about the viability of a further advance and received an immediate order to 'open the way to Baghdad'.[43] In sharp contrast, Mukherji was rent apart by conflict. In quick succession, he wrote to his mother, first from Kut on 4 October:

> I have had my fill of warfare. I have no more desire to see the wounded and the dead.
>
> Rows and rows of injured men are being sent by ships, belonging to us or the Turks, to Amara. Many of them will be going to Bengal Ambulance.

---

[40] Letter from Nasiriyah, 26 July 1915, *Kalyāṇ-Pradīp*, 292–293.
[41] *Kalyāṇ-Pradīp*, 293.
[42] Letters of 13 October 1915 and 28 October 1915 in *Kalyan-Pradeep*, 330, 336.
[43] Holdich to Moberly, 16 October 1922, The National Archives, CAB, 45/91; *Mesopotamia Commission Report* (London: HMSO, 1917), 27, The National Archives, WO 106/911.

Some have lost a hand, some a leg – everyone is asking for water. And still men continue speak about the glory of war and try to prove its advantages. In the name of patriotism and nationalism, they go on to cut each other's throats. There is nothing as narrow-minded as nationalism in this world … If the word 'patriotism' (or 'nationalism') did not exist in the European dictionary, there would have been far less bloodshed.

In our country too, in the name of patriotism, many leaders are teaching small schoolchildren how to kill. Murder, the greatest sin, becomes morally acceptable when committed in the name of patriotism. If a person, by guile or force, takes away another's property, it is burglary or dacoity – again a sin. But when a nation snatches away another's land – then it is celebrated as empire. Well, there's little point in discussing all this now – just hope that the war ends soon.[44]

and then again on 20 October:

Great Britain is the teacher. The patriotism the English have taught us, the patriotism that all civilised nations celebrate – that same patriotism is at the root of this bloodshed. All this patriotism – it means snatching away another's land. In this way, patriotism leads to empire-building. To show the love of one's country or race by killing thousands and thousands of people and grabbing someone else's land, well, that's what the English have taught us.

The youths of our country, seeing this, have started to practise this brutal form of nationalism. Therefore, the random killing of people, throwing bombs at a blameless Viceroy – all these horrific things, they have started. Shame on patriotism. As long as this parochialism does not end, bloodshed in the name of patriotism will not cease. Whether a man throws a bomb from the roof-top or fifty men start firing a cannon – the cause of this bloodshed, this madness is the same.[45]

The level of intellectual maturity and anti-war fervour are reminiscent of the letters of war poets such as Owen and Sassoon. His letters are very different, however: they are not just condemnations of violence or narrow patriotism, as in the trench-letters of Owen and Sassoon, but complex reflections on the relationship between war, empire and nation. Mukherji's radicalism is two-fold. As a colonial subject, he exposes the intimate relationship between war and imperialism. However, his anti-colonial critique, even as he acknowledges the deep educational influence of England upon the Indian bourgeoisie, cannot be equated with Indian nationalism. Through acute reasoning, he associates imperial aggression

[44] Letter of 4 October 1915, 317–318.
[45] Letter dated 20 October 1915 in *Kalyāṇ-Pradīp*, 333–334. My translation from Bengali. Also see Amitav Ghosh's blogpost, 'I spit in the face of patriotism'. 'At Home and the World', archived at www.amitavghosh.com.

with its obverse – nationalist terrorism. For Mukherji, imperialism, revolutionary nationalism and the European war were all implicated in the same
vicious cycle of violence, reminding one of the similarly anti-colonial and
anti-nationalist stance of Rabindranath Tagore who was writing his novel
Ghaire Baire (*The Home and the World*) – a critique at once of imperialism
and nationalism – the very same year.

Mukherji sustained a slight injury in the battle of Ctesiphon on 25
November but, brushing aside a generous offer to take leave, he accompanied 400 injured soldiers on a steamer to Kut-al-Amara. At Kut he
became part of the besieged 6th Division and, after the surrender on 29
April, he was taken captive. He bore traumatised testimony to the siege,
which we will discuss later in relation to Sarbadhikari. Being an officer, he
was treated relatively well after the surrender and was allowed to write home
at least once a month. His are so far the *only letters* we have from among
the 10,000 Indians besieged at Kut. In *The Secret Battle: Emotional Survival
in the Great War* (2010), Michael Roper has discussed how soldiers wrote
obsessively to their mothers; elsewhere, I have written about the importance of the mother's kiss in the trenches.[46] Mukherji's letters, written under
captivity, are similarly beset by his longing for and anxiety about his ageing
mother: 'Please don't catch your death by worrying about me … I want
to see you when I come back.'[47] With almost Sophoclean irony, this was
the time when Mukherji, in Ras al-'Ain, received a letter about the sudden
death of his daughter and his mother's grave illness. He immediately wrote
back to his mother:

> Ma, please take care of yourself, please get well. I want to see you so very
> much – I shall come home soon! Please don't leave the world before I get
> back. I know my eldest daughter has died, but it is not the end of the world.
> You too lost your eldest daughter. When I come back home, I will have
> lots of children – so please don't worry about that! I am desperate to hear
> your news, to read letters in your hand … When I read your voice, I feel
> very happy. Please don't worry about me. I'm very well here but I'm always
> thinking and worrying about you.[48]

Kipling's fictional letter about the Indian soldier pining for his mother
finds its eerie echo not in sepoy letters but in that of a middle-class Bengali
doctor. Kalyan's mother died in November, but he did not receive the news
until 3 March 1917. Meanwhile, an epidemic had broken out in the camp,

[46] See Michael Roper, *The Secret Battle: Emotional Survival in the Great War* (Manchester: Manchester
University Press, 2010); Das, *Touch and Intimacy in First World War Literature*, 109–136.
[47] Letter dated 1 May 1916, *Kalyāṇ-Pradīp*, 408.
[48] Undated letter, *Kalyāṇ-Pradīp*, 411–412.

and he wrote in February 1917 that, 'if people are not removed from here, no one will survive' (416). This was to be his last letter.

His final days are pieced together by his grandmother from his friend and fellow captive Dr Puri, who remembered how Mukherji, on learning the news of his mother's death, 'lost all enthusiasm for life and his instinct for survival': he could not eat or sleep, and started muttering 'Oh dear, my goodness'. He soon came down with fever and became delirious on 12 March: 'In his delirium, he would speak constantly in Bengali. The other doctors and I could not understand Bengali but we could clearly make out the words "Mother! Mother! Oh dear mother! What happened my mother!"' After six days of delirium, he died on 18 March.'[49] The grand-mother was sent back Kalyan's belongings: his horse's saddle, his reins, watch, shoes, clothes and bags. To read the last few pages of *Kalyāṇ-Pradīp* is to listen to a threnody of loss and mourning: Kalyan's mother mourning the death of her grand-daughter; Kalyan mourning the death of his mother and daughter; Dr Puri mourning the death of his friend ('Kalyan laid me on his breast and saved my life, but I could not save him')[50] and, above all, an eighty-year-old woman – the author – mourning the death of three generations: Kalyan's mother, Kalyan and Kalyan's young daughter. In *Kalyāṇ-Pradīp*, Mesopotamian history evolves into mourning diary without a break or mediating pause.

Abhi Le Baghdad: Battlefield Trauma, Hunger at Kut and the March

Sisir Prasad Sarbadhikari's *Abhi Le Baghdad* (1957) begins where Mukherji's letters end. While Mukherji's letters become sparse after the debacle at Ctesiphon, Sarbadhikari's 209-page-long memoir evokes in harrowing detail the battle itself, the resultant siege and life under captivity. Mukherji and Sarbadhikari were fellow Bengalis in Calcutta (Sarbadhikari in fact refers to Mukherji) but, as an elite medical officer and an Indian orderly, their experiences were markedly different. As are the tone and genre. Mukherji's letters are missives from the front, blending vivid snapshots with acute reflections; Sarbadhikari's book is a memoir *sui generis*, reading in turns like battlefield notes, nursing memoir, POW diary and travel narrative. It is possibly the most powerful and sustained piece of Indian life-writing to have emerged so far from the war.

---

[49] Letter from Dr Puri, in *Kalyāṇ-Pradīp*, 416–417.
[50] Letter from Dr Puri, 25 May 1917, in *Kalyāṇ-Pradīp*, 416.

Abhi Le Baghdad is alone of its kind: there seems to be no precedent for it in the annals of Indian literature. Paradoxically, Sarbadhikari's literary cousins would be Remarque and Blunden from across the racial divide. Written with the same combination of immediacy, literariness and anti-war fervour, *Abhi Le Baghdad* is *All Quiet on the Western Front* turned upside down – from a non-combatant, non-white and non-Western Front perspective. The title is revealing: it does not flaunt its historical authenticity, such as E. O. Mouseley's *Secrets of a Kuttie: An Authentic Story of Kut* (1921), nor is it an exercise in self-aggrandisement, such as postal officer Kunal Sen's *Through War, Rebellion & Riot 1914–1921*. Instead, it is taken from the bitter aside of an anonymous Muslim soldier during the retreat to Kut: 'Ya Allah, abhi le Baghdad' ('Oh Allah, so much for taking Baghdad'). The whole memoir, similarly, is a view 'from below' or, as his fellow captive the British NCO P. W. Long named his memoir, *Other Ranks of Kut* (1925). It is written in Bengali, but, as in many such books by the educated Bengali middle-classes, it shows intimate familiarity with English literature and frequently refers to it, from the Scottish song 'Auld Lang Syne' to Oliver Goldsmith's 'The Deserted Village'.

Sarbadhikari had just completed a degree in law when the war was declared. He volunteered as a private in the newly formed 'Bengal Ambulance Corps' (BAC) for Mesopotamia primarily because of, in his own words (in English), a 'spirit of adventure'.[51] The Corps comprised four British commissioned officers, three Viceroy's Commissioned Officers (VCOs), sixty-four Non-commisioned Officers (NCOs) and privates (including Sisir) and forty-one camp followers, including cooks, water-carriers and cleaners. They reached Amara on 15 July and set up the Bengal Stationary Hospital in Amara where they were stationed for the first two and half months.[52] In September, some thirty-six of them, including Sarbadhikari, were chosen to be sent to the firing line as part of the 12th Field Ambulance of the 16th Brigade. The story centres around this group of idealistic Bengali youths as they encounter the battle of Ctesiphon (November 1915), the resultant siege of Kut (December 1915–29 April 1916) and captivity for the next two years. As a medical orderly who knew English and picked up Turkish, Sarbadhikari was made to work in

---

[51] Sisir Prasad Sarbadhikari, *Abhi Le Baghdad*, Preface (Kolkata: privately printed, 1957). Page references will be given in the text. I am very grateful to Dutta for translating the text for me: I have drawn on her translation of *Abhi Le Baghdad*, unless stated otherwise.

[52] The Bengal Ambulance Corps was masterminded by Dr S. P. Sarbadhikari and it did important medical work in Mesopotamia. See 'The Bengal Ambulance Corps', Confidential File 312/16, West Bengal State Archives, Kolkata for detailed information.

hospitals in Ras al-'Ain and Aleppo, and then in the German camp at
Nisibin. The memoir is closely based on his wartime diary, which has its
own tale of trauma and survival to tell:

> It would be a mistake to believe that the diary I have maintained till now
> or what follows is the original version. After surrendering at Kut, I had
> torn up the pages of the diary and stuffed the pieces in my boots; I had
> written a new version at Baghdad from the remnants. This copy, too, was
> spoilt when we walked across the Tigris – although the writing was not
> rubbed off entirely since I had used copying pencil. I kept notes about the
> Samarra–Ras-el-Ain march and onwards in that copy itself, after I dried it.
> I had to bury the copy for a few days at Ras-el-Ain but not much harm had
> been done as a result. I copied the whole thing again in the Khastakhana at
> Aleppo. (156–157)

The diary travelled with him to Calcutta and was converted into a memoir
with the help of his late daughter-in-law Romola Sarbadhikari, a remarkable woman, with whom I had a series of interviews, from 2007 to 2010.
Since my discovery of this privately printed text in 2006, it has become
better-known, thanks largely to the brilliant blogposts of Amitav Ghosh,
who has called its survival 'insistently miraculous' and notes its 'extraordinary immediacy': 'at times, the book has the quality of a diary'.[53]

Such diary-like immediacy is evident in Sarbadhikari's description
of the battle of Ctesiphon (22 November 1916) where he accompanied
the army as part of the Field Ambulance. It was his first proper taste of
combat: 'As we kept advancing, bullets were whizzing above our heads
and cannon balls exploding noisily behind us.' (35). His colleague Prafulla
Chandra Sen distinguishes, in his reminiscence, between the different
sounds on the battlefield: the 'miao' sound of the .303 British bullets, the
'bumblebee-like buzzing' ('bhramarer guñjan') of the bullets fired by the
Arab soldiers and the 'hiss' of shells.[54] Sarbadhikari instead focussed on the
aftermath of the attack as the next day dawned:

> Ctesiphon – the second of the two days.
> It is beyond my power to describe what I witnessed as the 23rd dawned.
> The corpses of men and animals were strewn everywhere. Sometimes the
> bodies lay tangled up; sometimes wounded men lay trapped and groaning
> beneath the carcasses of animals. The highest death toll was in the front of
> the trenches where there were barbed wire fences. In places there were men

[53] Amitav Ghosh, unpublished paper, 'Shared Sorrows: Indians and Armenians in the prison camps of
Ras al-'Ain, 6. Also see Ghosh, 'At Home and the World in Mesopotamia'.
[54] Prafulla Chandra Sen, 'The Story of Bengal Ambulance Corps', *Mānasī O Marmavāṇī* (March
1925), 175.

stuck in the barbed wire and hanging; some (fortunately) dead and some still living. There might be a severed head stuck in the wire here, perhaps a leg there. A person was hanging spread-eagled from the wire – his innards were spilling from his body. There were spots within the trenches where four or five men were lying dead in heaps; Turks, Hindustanis, British, Gurkhas – all alike and indistinguishable in death.

'In a death embrace

Grasping each other by the neck

Lay the twain' ... [Original in English]

We saw a Sikh sitting and grinning by himself in one place – his teeth bright in the middle of his black beard. I wondered what the matter was with him – how could he be laughing at a time like this? I went close to him and realised that he had long since been dead. Perhaps he had grimaced in his death-throes.

It fell to me and Phani Ghose to note down the names and numbers of the wounded. And what a task it was! (42–43)

'If I live a hundred years, I shall never forget that night bivouac', Charles Townshend would write in his memoir.[55] Sarbadhikari not only had to count the wounded but also had to disentangle the living from the dead and arrange the wounded 'with their own haversacks under their heads and a blanket to cover them' (40); Prafulla Sen, working alongside him, remembered the eerie silence: 'Some have had their whole rib-cage shattered, some had lost their jaws but there was hardly any sound.' But the most difficult part for the two Bengali boys was having to show empty bottles to British Tommies who were crying for 'a drop of water for heaven's sake' or having to leave the seriously injured to be collected later: 'This terrible chill on top of the injuries – many died of the cold itself.'[56]

How does Sarbadhikari remember and represent the scene? In *The Great Push* (1917), Patrick MacGill, an Irish stretcher-bearer on the Western Front, notes that 'The stretcher-bearer sees all the horror of war written in blood and tears on the shell-riven battlefield. The wounded man – thank heaven! – has only his pain to endure.' On the other hand, the French novelist Henri Barbusse in *Le Feu* (1916) concludes his harrowing description of the battlefield with the image of a German and French soldier in death-embrace.[57] Sarbadhikari combines the visual testimony of MacGill with the anti-war critique of Barbusse: his account moves from the optical

[55] Townshend, *My Campaign in Mesopotamia*, 176.
[56] Sen, 'Bengal Ambulance Corps', 179.
[57] Patrick MacGill, *The Great Push* (London: Herbert Jenkins, 1917), 96; Henri Barbusse, *Under Fire* (London: Dent, 1965 [1916]), 323–324.

rectitude of 'severed head' and 'innards' through the macabre multiculturalism of the battlefields to focus on the single Sikh soldier who blurs
the boundaries between life and death, laughter and grimace. Combining
testimony, reportage and exposure of the horrors of war, such visceral
description is the Indian counterpoint to Robert Graves's 'dead Boche',
'Dribbling black blood from nose and beard'.[58] If theories of trauma dwell
on gaps in consciousness, the First World War accounts circle round visceral memories. Sarbadhikari's memoir is no exception: he describes how
he woke up to find himself lying next to a corpse; in Basra, he witnessed a
shell explode within the makeshift tented hospital in a garden, 'taking off'
half the face of a sepoy lying in the hospital tent. There was nothing left
of his face – blood was gushing from a gaping hole where his mouth, nose
and eyes had been' (66). Like Owen drenched in the blood of his 'poor
little servant George', Sarbadhikari could easily have said 'My senses are
charred.'[59]

Yet, such extremity also produces rare moments of intimacy.
Sarbadhikari mentions how his colleague Bhupen Banerjee took off his
'British warmer' and gave it to a British casualty; Sen, in his account
of the night, remembered a young English captain, who had lost part
of his leg, gazing forlornly on the cross that hung from his neck: 'As we
[members of the BAC] gave him some water and saluted him before
lifting him on to the stretcher, he gave us a wan smile which, even
after eight years, I remember clearly.'[60] In one of his letters, Dr Kalyan
Mukherji mentions a very similar episode. On his way from Ali Gharbi
to Sannaiyat, he encountered a severely wounded British soldier; as he
poured some water into his mouth, the latter tried to kiss Mukherji's
feet and tears rolled down his cheeks, and, as Kalyan took him in his
arms, he died.[61] Records of such intimate moments, particularly across the
colour-line, are very rare in Indian accounts and here form the real-life
counterpart to Grimshaw's fantasised death-embrace between the English
officer and the dying Beji Singh; however rare they were, Mukherji's
account shows that moments of touch and intimacy were by no means
restricted to the Western front or between European comrades alone.
Neither Sen nor Sarbadhikari mentions nursing the enemy, though that

---

[58] Robert Graves, 'A Dead Boche', in *The Collected Poems of Robert Graves* (London: Penguin Classics, 2003), 27.

[59] Wilfred Owen to Siegfried Sassoon, letter dated 4 November 1918, in *Wilfred Owen: Collected Letters*, ed. Harold Owen and John Bell (Oxford: Oxford University Press, 1967), 581.

[60] Sen, 'The Story of Bengal Ambulance Corps', 177.

[61] *Kalyāṇ-Pradīp*, 303.

Figure 6.4   A Royal Army Medical Corps officer and some Indian staff tending to
wounded Turks at an advanced dressing station after the action at Tikrit,
November 1917. © Imperial War Museum (Q 24440).

does not mean that they did not do so. A number of images have recently
surfaced which show officers from the Royal Army Medical Corps, along
with Indian medical orderlies and stretcher-bearers, tending to wounded
Turkish soldiers at an advanced dressing station in Tikrit in November
1917. One shows the Turks laid out in rows on stretchers, with the sun
beating down, and Indian and British medical personnel at work; another
shows a Turk sprawled on the ground, with two Indian medical orderlies
poring over him (Figure 6.4). Though they were taken within the context of professional duty, these photographs, like the nursing memoirs by
British women, suggest spaces of contingent contact between men across
the political lines.
     Much ink has been spilt over Charles Townshend's decision to retreat
from Kut after the Battle of Ctesiphon.[62] For over 140 days, the Sixth

---

[62] See Charles Townshend, *My Campaign in Mesopotamia* (London: Thornton Butterworth Ltd, 1920);
      Gardner, *The Siege of Kut-al-Amara*, 68–71; Ron Wilcox, *Battles on the Tigris: The Mesopotamian
      Campaign of the First World War* (Barnsley: Pen & Sword, 2006), 80–82.

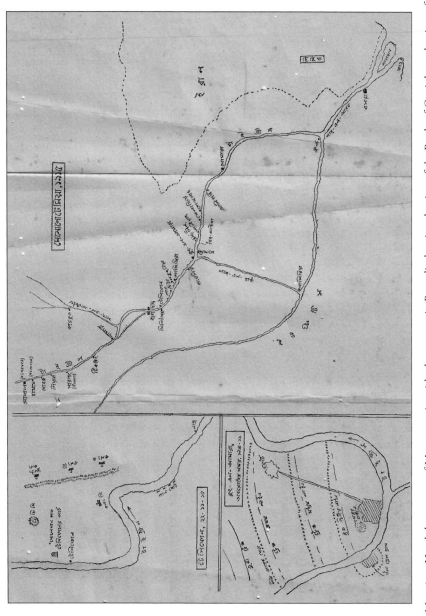

Map 6.1 Hand-drawn map of Mesopotamia, with place names in Bengali, showing the sites of the Battle of Ctesiphon, the siege of Kut, and finally the route of the brutal desert march Sarbadhikari would be forced to undertake in 1916. Included in *Abhi Le Baghdad*.

Division was besieged in Kut. He laid the blame on the 'dejected, spir-
itless and pessimistic' sepoys: 'How easy the defence of Kut would have
been had my division been an *all British one* instead of a composite one.'[63]
Since he was an educated medical orderly, Sarbadhikari's experiences were
perhaps not typical, but his is so far the fullest account of life inside the
town. He initially worked in a makeshift tented hospital set up in a date-
orchard, on the outskirts of the city, which was regularly bombed. Several
patients and BAC workers were killed or injured; Sarbadhikari was then
transferred to the British General Hospital, but movement across the city
was difficult, with regular bombings and air-raids which killed the native
Arabs as well. Through gradual details, he builds up a picture of life in
Kut: the regular round of injuries, British planes dropping a few paltry
bags of wheat flour, the daily fluctuations of hope around Aylmer's Relief
Force, the big but unsuccessful push to capture Kut on 24 December, the
diminishing stock of food and medicine, and the 'perennial hankering for
something sweet' (85).

'Hunger', Townshend wrote to his Turkish counterpart, 'forces me to
surrender.'[64] Much of the discussion around Kut had revolved around
the question of horsemeat. Faced with dwindling supplies, Townshend
prescribed horsemeat for the men, only to be faced with rebellion en
masse by the sepoys (except for the Gurkhas). The entry in Sarbadhikari's
diary for 28 January reads as follows: 'Horseflesh started being served today
onwards. Most of the Indian sepoys, Hindu and Muslim, did not eat it. We
had it. The meat was very tough.' (72). April was the cruellest month. In
mid-April, after the 13th Division's failed attack on Sannaiyat, an increasingly anxious Townshend cut down the rations from 10 to 5 ounces of
attah (whole wheat flour), with the sepoys getting only 'the sweepings, full
of husk and dirt and mouldy'.[65] Starved and hungry, 5,000 sepoys on 11 April
finally accepted horsemeat, though the remaining half still refused; on 12
April, a desperate Townshend threatened to demote non-meat eaters, both
officers and NCOs, from their ranks and, by 14 April, most of them were
taking horsemeat. But it was too late. According to Colonel Patrick Hehir,
the chief medical officer in Kut, 'on an average fifteen men were dying
daily: of these, five a day were dying of chronic starvation and ten with
chronic starvation with diarrhoea, bronchitis or some other simple malady

[63] A. J. Barker, *Townshend of Kut: A Biography of Major-General Sir Charles Townshend, K.C.B., D.S.O.*
(London: Cassell, 1967), 197.
[64] Quoted in *Abhi le Baghdad*, 73.
[65] Private Papers (Diary) of Major A. J. Anderson, IWM 9724.

supervening'.[66] Hehir, in his account, did not distinguish between British and Indian troops; in *The Siege of Kut-al-Amara* (2014), Nikolas Gardner mentions a study that apparently indicates that 'the number of Indians who died from disease and starvation inside Kut exceeded the number of British personnel by ten times'.[67] Sarbadhikari's evocation of the final month is remarkable, from his detailed account of how the BAC members burnt dung cakes and horse-bones to cook horsemeat and their efforts to ward off scurvy by picking leaves, grass and weeds, to descriptions of how the 'healthy frames' of the sepoys gradually became 'skeletal' (85). Desertions increased too, for which he blamed hunger, rather than religion. He mentions a young boy from the 19th regiment who tried to desert but was caught and executed: 'The firing party was formed from his own company – perhaps there were men from his village, perhaps even from his kin' (83). The members of the BAC pulled through the crisis, though 'their constant companion' was hunger:

> Even in the midst of these troubles the eighteen of us spent our days merry-making. There would be songs every evening. Our billet was like a small club. Sanyal Moshai from Supply and Transport, Ashu babu and Raj Bahadur-babu used to drop by whenever they had time. A havildar from 4th Rajputs attached to our No. 2 Field Ambulance was a daily visitor. A driver from the Artillery, Malaband, used to come often. He was very religious and was later driven insane and committed suicide. A few others were also driven to suicide at Kut. All of them had gone insane. (87)

Part of the achievement of *Abhi Le Baghdad* is the way it manages to be an ode to the spirit of human resilience and warmth and contact without sanitising any of the horrors. Friendship, fellow-feeling and the indomitable spirit of *adda* [chatter] co-exist with horror and insanity, but the balance gradually begins to tip. Kalyan Mukherji wrote in mid-April that 'For the last fifteen days, people are starving to death. What is the use of medicine when there is no food? … How can I cure them when there is nothing to eat?'[68] On 28 April, Sarbadhikari wrote 'Not a single grain of ration today'; the next day, Townshend surrendered.[69]

If hunger was the predominant memory of the siege, the moment of horror in *Abhi Le Baghdad* was the forced march of the privates to Ras al-'Ain via Bagdad and Mosul, under a blazing sun and on minimal rations and water. Many collapsed while marching and were left to die, and British

[66] Gardner, *The Siege of Kut-al-Amara*, 156.
[67] *Ibid.* It is not known how accurate or precise this study was.
[68] *Kalyān-Pradīp*, 400.
[69] *Abhi Le Baghdad*, 92.

accounts stress the gratuitous cruelty by both Arab and Turkish guards.[70]
Heather Jones has pointed to the 'dominant scandal' around class: while
the British and Indian officers were relatively well-treated and transported
on steamers, the privates – both Indian and British – were forced on a
500-mile-long march.[71] In *Other Ranks of Kut*, P. W. Long, a private, has a
whole chapter on 'Horrors of the March', which were for him 'the tortures
of the damned': 'Daylight came but still no water … I put one foot before
the other like an automaton. My lips were hard and dry and my tongue
was like a piece of leather.'[72] Long could complete the march only because
he was given some boots by a kindly Havildar of the Mahratta regiment.
Being a member of the BAC, Sarbadhikari was transported in a steamer
from Kut to Baghdad, and from there was sent by train to Samarra, some
sixty miles away.[73] From Samarra, he was made to march to Mosul via
Tikrit and Sargat, and again from Mosul via Nisibin to Ras-al-Ain, where
he arrived on 25 August: in total they had marched for 500 miles over
forty-six days. (Figure 6.5) The march is the most traumatic episode in the
whole memoir and is evoked with a sort of hallucinatory intensity:

> This march under the torment of the guards, with starved, parched,
> exhausted bodies, crossing mile after mile of mountainous land or barren
> desert on foot, was horrifying – a nightmare never to be forgotten. I shall
> remember it forever.
>
> See that White swaying over there? Catch hold of him now before he falls
> to the ground.
>
> What is the matter with him? A sunstroke?
>
> Whatever it might be, take him along with you somehow, he must not be
> left here.
>
> You have not had anything to eat for four days? Cannot take another step?
>
> There is no use saying that, you must march. The guards will not wait for
> you, nothing will sway their stony hearts.
>
> You sold off your boots in Baghdad because you were starved. Your feet are
> bleeding, sore after walking barefoot over sand and stones and thorns, you
> are walking with strips of cloth tied around your feet …
>
> Your chest is parched, your tongue is hanging out, you cannot speak from
> the thirst after walking since morning till noon. You keep seeing 'buttermilk

---

[70] See Patrick Crowley, *Kut 1916: Courage and Failure in Iraq*, 181.
[71] Heather Jones, 'Imperial Captivities', 185.
[72] P. W. Long, *Other Ranks of Kut* (Uckfield: The Naval and Military Press, n.d.), 66.
[73] Some of his friends in the BAC were, however, repatriated, as is evident from the list at the end of
      Abhi Le Baghdad, i–v.

sherbat' written on red cotton floating in front of your eyes, you cannot will it away however much you try.

That means that it is not too long before you go insane – even so, walk on you must. You cannot lie here. Surely you know what the consequences are of lying here alone? Dying bit by bit in the hands of the Bedouins.

There goes the scream of the guards 'Haidi, iyalla!' ['Get up, get moving!']

Those yells of 'Haidi, iyalla!' by which the guards drove us on are never to be forgotten. You would wake up with a start – are they not screaming 'Haidi, haidi? No? Well, let us fall back asleep, then. (134–135)

Reminiscence, flashback, testimony and *j'accuse* are fused and confused as he refers to the march in the Bengali original as '*bhayāvaha*' ('horrifying'), '*duḥsvapna*' ('nighmar(ish)') and '*vibhīṣikā*' ('terror'). The only other Indian record of a similar march appears in the reminiscence of fellow Bengali Shitanath Bhatta, of the Supply and Transport department of the 6th Division, who referred to the ordeal as 'indescribable'.[74]

Sarbadhikari's account, in contrast, is strikingly vivid. Memory here is both the cutting-instrument and an open wound: he does not just remember but seems to relive the moment as he reverts to the present tense – the eternal now – of the trauma victim who, as Sigmund Freud noted with reference to the soldiers on the Western Front in *Beyond the Pleasure Principle* (1920), is 'doomed to a compulsion to repeat past experience as present'.[75] The string of rhetorical questions, often combining Bengali and English ('*Ki hoyeche or? Sunstroke?*') in the original, the sudden intrusion of second-person pronouns (Sarbadhikari uses the semi-formal 'tomake' and 'tomar'), the regular addresses ('*take dharo*' - 'please hold him', '*calte pārcho nā*' - 'you can't walk anymore', '*tomāke coltei hobe*' - 'you have to walk'), the claim on the body – feet, tongue, chest – cancel the gap between the past and the present and draw in the reader. 'All that long day', notes Long, 'the air resounded with "Yellah, haidi, goom, yellah, yellah'.[76] Bhatta too remembers such shouts, accompanied by beatings with whips, rifle-butts and shoes.[77] If Sarbadhikari and Bhatta dwell on the horrors, Long records an extraordinary act of friendship: 'a sepoy, who had been helped for several miles, finally collapsed and could

[74] Krishna Behari Ray, 'The Story of a Bengali Prisoner of the Turks in Kut', as narrated by Shitanath Bhatta, Supply and Transport Department, 6th Division, *Mānasī O Marmavāṇī* (September 1919), 123.
[75] Sigmund Freud, 'Beyond the Pleasure Principle' in *Standard Edition of the Works of Sigmund Freud*, trans. James Strachey (London: Hogarth Press, 1920–1922), Vol. XVIII, 27.
[76] Long, *Other Ranks*, 74.
[77] Roy, 'Bengali Prisoner', 123.

not rise again, not even when the Onbashi tried kicking him to his feet. He was a Hindu and a naik of his regiment pleaded to stay with him. But the request was denied and the man left to die.'[78] Bhatta attributes such cruelty specifically to the Turkish race, who, he claimed, have hearts 'harder than stones'.[79] Such essentialist categories or racist discourse are wholly absent in Sarbadhikari's account.

Cosmopolis in Extremis? Vulnerability, Empathy and Encounters

According to Major E. W. C. Sandes, 'our Indian rank and file suffered severely it is true, but not to the extent of the British'.[80] This has led some historians, including Nikolas Gardner and Patrick Crowley in their other-wise excellent works, to conclude that 'British personnel suffered even more acutely'.[81] It is true that, in captivity, 1,767 of the 2,949 British POWs died or remained untraced, compared with 3,032 dead or untraced among the 10,686 Indian captives.[82] But, in the absence of any detailed breakdown of a timeline for the casualties, Indian or British, it is impossible to say that the Indians suffered any less on the *march* itself.[83] Preferential treatment by the Turks towards the Indian Muslims started only at Ras al-'Ain, where the Muslim troops were separated and sent to various camps in Turkey, while the Hindus and Sikhs were subjected to back-breaking labour at the Ras al-'Ain railhead. British narratives of Ottoman captivity are crowded with the sight, sound and even festering touch of their Indian subjects–allies–fellow POWs. Long recalled how men working at the railhead resembled 'animated skeletons hung about with filthy rags'; Captain Mouseley remembered how at night one heard 'the high Indian wail': 'Margaya Sahib, Margaya' ['Dying, Sahib, I'm dying']; Charles Barber, a doctor attached to the 6th Division, noted how, for these malnourished and overworked men, 'large wounds would sometimes begin by showing promise of healing for a few days, but would then stop and progress no further; would bleed when touched'.[84]

As a medical orderly with English and some Turkish, Sarbadhikari was more fortunate. He worked for a couple of months in a makeshift

[78] Long, *Other Ranks of Kut*, 62.
[79] Roy, 'Bengali Prisoner', as narrated by Bhatta, 123.
[80] E. W. C. Sandes, *In Kut and Captivity*, 451.
[81] Gardner, *The Siege of Kut-al-Amara*, 165.
[82] *Statistics of the Military Effort of the British Empire*, 330.
[83] See also Heather Jones, 'Imperial Captivities', 187.
[84] Long, *Other Ranks*, 112; Mouseley, quoted in Wilcox, *Battles on the Tigris*, 137; Charles Barber, *Besieged in Kut and After* (London, 1918), 191.

hospital in a Bedouin tent at Ras al-'Ain, then for more than a year at the Central Hospital in Aleppo and finally in the German camp at Nisibin. The narrative centre of the memoir is the story of a group of about twenty boys from the BAC who were taken prisoner at Kut. Sarbadhikari's evocation of the sense of mounting anxiety and desperation is superb as he describes the group getting separated during the march and scattered across different camps in Mesopotamia, Turkey or Greater Syria. On his way to Ras al-'Ain, Sarbadhikari was stunned to see scribbled on a wall of the POW camp in Mosul, in familiar handwriting, the name of his friend 'Saachin Bose', who had been reported 'missing'; he also learnt that two of his friends, Amulya Chatterji and Sushil Laha, had died during the march; in Ras al-'Ain, he was reunited with the sixteen-year-old Bhola. As Sarbadikhari got transferred to the Aleppo General Hospital, a feverish Bhola, who was being looked after by Sarbadhikari, clung to him, and sobbed hysterically 'Dādābhāi [Elder brother], I will never survive if you leave me' (143). If men formed intense bonds on the Western Front, Sarbadhikari shows a similar intimacy flowering among members of the BAC among the barren sands and open skies of Mesopotamia.

Life in Kut was precarious, but in Ras al-'Ain and Aleppo, the BAC boys actually started to die, including Priyo Roy, Mathew Jacob, Sailen Bose and their beloved commanding officer Amarendra Champati; Sarbadhikari also mentions the death of Kalyan Mukherji. Like the British and French nurses working on the Western front, Sarbadhikari – surrounded by the dead and dying – had trouble comprehending at night whether 'I was alive or dead' (148).[85] The lines between sanity and insanity, reality and nightmare began to blur: Probodh went clinically mad; Priyo seemed to see his grandmother near the hospital door just before his death in Ras al-'Ain; Jagdish, delirious from typhoid-fever, dreamt that his leg was being burnt as kindling, a grotesque impingement on the dream-world of the practice of burning the leg-bones of horses for fire (167). Sarbadhikari dreamt that he was in the firing-line and shooting at a Turk, but the bullet ricocheted off and struck his friend Dhiren Bose in Calcutta as Owen's 'Strange Meeting' gets realised in the unconscious of a Bengali non-combatant.

On 20 November 1916, Sisir was sent on a mail train to the Aleppo General Hospital or Markaz Khastakhana with fifty seriously injured patients. In contrast to the daily degradation and gratuitous cruelty of

---

[85] For experiences of the British nurses, see Santanu Das, ' "The Impotence of Sympathy": Service and Suffering in the Nurses' Memoirs', in *Touch and Intimacy*, 175–203.

Ras al-'Ain, the Aleppo Khastakhana, overseen by the Germans, is depicted as a more civilised space:

> Aleppo is not like the cities we have seen so far, such as Baghdad and Mosul. The houses are nice to look at; the roads are not bad. We hear it looks like towns in Europe. The people on the streets look cultured; their clothes are nice; European costume predominates. There are people of many communities – Turks, Syrian Christians, Rums (i.e. Greeks) and Jews.
>
> I was at Aleppo's Markaz Khastakhana (hospital). We were, on the whole, friendly with the Turkish soldiers …
>
> There were one or two Indians here, and a Romanian named Alda Sava. The Armenian doctor Shagir Effendi is a great man, he cares very much for his patients. There were two *khadamas* in the *kaus*: one was an Armenian woman called Maroom, the other a Syrian Christian man called Musha. The two of them looked after us very well. Their responsibilities were to make the bed, sweep the wards etc. …
>
> There was another man at the Markaz khastakhana with whom we were quite friendly. He was an Armenian and his name was George. His home was in Diyar Bakr, his children had all been killed – he was the only one to escape with his life to Aleppo. George was given the task of cleaning the toilets. He cooked, slept – all at one spot. On cold days we used to go to him and we would chat while warming our hands over his *angithi* (coal-fire brazier). We had only a single stove in our ward and we received very little fire for kindling. (144–159)

If Kut was the realm of daily hunger and Ras al-'Ain a place of trauma, the hospital in Aleppo in contrast was, to borrow the title of Fawaz's masterly study, 'the land of aching hearts': at once a microcosm of the general displacement in the Middle East caused by the war and a place of temporary refuge for the displaced, the wounded and the derelict.

The core of the memoir in this final part is the web of encounters and relationships that developed through the way Sarbadhikari's multiple, often contradictory, identities – as POW, as a British colonial subject, as fellow Asian, as educated and middle-class, as both friend and enemy – intersected with the multi-racial and multi-ethnic fabric of an empire in the process of modernisation, with its own hierarchies, alliances and tensions.[86] The patients in the hospital were largely Turkish as well as a few Indian, British and Russian POWs and some German and Austrian soldiers; the staff comprised Armenian doctors and *muhajirs*, Turkish and Arab orderlies, Kurds, Syrian Christians, Jews, Rumis. The racialising discourse that we

---

[86] For the processes of modernisation in the Ottoman empire just before the war, see Fawaz, *A Land of Aching Hearts*.

find in English POW memoirs around the 'barbaric Turk' or 'cruel Oriental' is absent in *Abhi Le Baghdad*, though the author does not shy away from mentioning the regular dose of brutalities: he distinguishes between the Turkish guards, who beat him up, and the wounded Turkish soldiers, who are described as 'pathetic'; he mentions how the hospital barber spat on his face when he went for a shave and yet, when he was ill, the Turkish orderly physically lifted him and carried him to the toilet. Hierarchies were further reversed when one day he gave the Turkish orderly ten piastres and the latter broke down in tears. It is this tessellated attention to the mixed yarn of human interaction, rather than any reductive racial discourse, which makes *Abhi Le Baghdad* such an exceptional piece of literature. We meet, for example, a wounded thirty-year-old Turkish soldier who, having lost his wife, would take his five-year-old daughter to battle with him, and would leave her with an acquaintance when he had to go to the front line; when Sisir would ask him about her future if he got killed, he would reply 'Allah Biliyor' ('Allah knows') (155). We meet too an elderly Turkish soldier who had come to the ward to collect cigarette-butts, only to discover that the man on the next bed was his own son with whom he had lost contact for three years!

In the hospital, Sarbadhikari was assigned to the ward of wounded Turkish soldiers; conversations started:

> None of the Turkish soldiers were literate, but most of them had great fellow-feeling. They used to say, 'You are not at war with us now, so we are all *kardes* [brothers].' 'Kardes' was an oft-used word ...
>
> We spoke of our lands, our joys and sorrows ... One thing that they always used to say was, 'This war that we are fighting – what is our stake in this? Why are we slashing each others' throats? You stay in Hindustan, we in Turkey, we do not know each other, share no enmity, and yet we became enemies overnight because one or two people deemed it so.' Is this on the mind of every soldier of every nation?
>
> Another thing that was notable about them was their hatred for the Germans. All of them used to despise the Germans – they used to say that Germany was responsible for getting them into this war. The particular cause of dissatisfaction was that the Germans would receive the best of all of Turkey's produce. Eggs, for example, would be sent first to the German hospitals, and after their requirements were met, what remained (if anything did) would go to the Turks. It was the same with everything else. We used to think that the situation was the same in our country, but our consolation was that we were actually under British domination, but Germany and Turkey were allies![87]

[87] *Abhi Le Baghdad*, 158.

What brings captive and captor together as 'kardes' here is the shared yoke of European subjugation and a sense of being caught up in a war that is not theirs. In contrast to the conscious 'politics of anti-Westernism' that Ceymil Aydin has uncovered among Asian intellectuals during the war years or even the 'anti-colonial cosmopolitanism' that Kris Manjapra detects among the South Asian elites, this is an international brotherhood of the dispossessed and the displaced premised on the vulnerability of being.[88] What gives Sarbadhikari's memoir its singularity is its poignant undertow of raw experience: he captures with eerie precision the fabric of a transnational community formed not because of any conscious political ideology but out of human vulnerability at a time of conflict.

Such Indo-Turkish 'brotherhood' was in sharp contrast to Sarbadhikari's cordial but somewhat distant relationship with his British fellow staff and superiors. His colleague Prafulla Chandra Sen recalled the friendship between members of the BAC and the English orderlies: they used to exchange English novels and teach each other English and Bengali songs.[89] Similarly, in Aleppo, Sarbadhikari records pockets of intimacy between the Indian captives and their colonisers-turned-fellow captives, as when he cooked a very spicy curry for Corporal Shaw, setting his haemorrhoids aflame. Yet the institutional hierarchies remained intact:

> The discrimination that is always practised between the whites and the coloured is highly insulting. The white soldier gets paid twice as much as the Indian sepoy. The uniform of the two is different – that of the whites is better ... In fact, whatever little provision could be made is made for the Tommy. Even the ration is different – the Tommies take tea with sugar, we are given only molasses.[90]

He similarly records that, in the steamer voyage to Baghdad after the surrender at Kut, the British troops were provided with sleeping places in the lower deck while 600 sepoys were crammed into the exposed upper deck. Accounts of such everyday casual racism and colonial hierarchies are inadvertently corroborated by Major Sandes in *In Kut and Captivity* (1919): 'our first business was naturally to get separate accommodation for the Indian officers': 'we explained also that Indian officers ... were always of inferior ranks to British officers'.[91]

---

[88] Cemil Aydin, *The Politics of Anti-Westernism in Asia: Visions of World Order in Pan-Islamic and Pan-Asian Thought* (New York: Columbia University Press, 2007); Kris Manjapra, *Cosmopolitan Thought-Zones*, 2.
[89] Sen, 'The Story of Bengal Ambulance Corps', *Mānasī O Marmavāṇī*, January 1924, 537.
[90] *Abhi Le Baghdad*, 188.
[91] Major F. W. C. Sandes, *In Kut and Captivity*, 285, 287.

If *Abhi Le Baghdad* plunges us into the minutiae of everyday life in the hospital, it is also acutely aware of the larger currents outside: it is one of the few South Asian works that bears witness to the Armenian genocide. Sarbadhikari notes that, 'From what we hear these terrible mass killings were not perpetrated by the Turkish soldiers; they were done by Chechens and Kurds.' (176–177). Sarbadhikari uses the word '*hatyākāṇḍa*' (literally 'killing-event'). At Ras al-'Ain, one of the epicentres of the genocide, he provides an eye-witness account from his friend Sachin: 'A group of Armenians were made to stand up, with their hands tied, and their throats were slit one by one' (177). On the way from Ras al-'Ain to Aleppo, Sarbadhikari met two boys of around ten who told him in broken Arabic that their parents had been killed by the Turks; as he went past a well, he saw a cloud of flies: 'It is not at all advisable to drink from these wells; there are Armenian corpses rotting in most of them.' (129–30). As he went past empty villages, he remembered Oliver Goldsmith's famous 1770 poem 'The Deserted Village', where Goldsmith speaks about rural depopulation in wake of the Irish Famine: 'Along thy glades, a solitary guest/Amidst the bowers, the tyrant's hand is seen.' (129). Yet, only a few hundred kilometres away from Ras al-'Ain, the hospital in Aleppo, presumably under German protection, was a relatively safe zone: the chief doctor was Armenian and there was a significant Armenian presence. The most meaningful encounters in the text are those between Sarbadhikari and his Armenian fellow workers: Sarbadhikari used to idolise the chief doctor, while the Armenian *muhajir* looked after him like a 'mother' and asked about 'the smallest details of my home and family' (171). Similarly, Sarbadhikari records how a Punjabi sweeper rescued an Armenian boy, named him Babulal, and brought him up; it is possibly the same child whom Major E. A. Walker referred to when he mentioned 'a small Armenian boy about ten or so' being brought up in the Indian sepoy camp at Ras al-'Ain.[92] At one point, Sarbadhikari observes that 'Their lives have become ours'.

Could the above milieu at the Aleppo *Khastakhana* (hospital) be called 'cosmopolitanism from below'? In *Writing Culture: The Poetics and Politics of Ethnography* (1986), the anthropologist Paul Rabinow observes that the term should be extended to transnational experiences that are particular rather than universal, to experiences that are not privileged, even coerced. He defines the term as 'an ethos of macro-interdependencies, with an

---

[92] IWM, 76/115/1, Diary of E. A. Walker, 17 July 1916. I am grateful to Heather Jones for bringing to my notice this diary which corroborates Sarbadhikari's claim in *Abhi Le Baghdad*. See Jones, 'Imperial Captivities', 187–188.

acute consciousness (often forced upon people) of the inescapabilities and particularities of places, characters, historical trajectories, and fates'.[93] In Sarbadhikari's account of the hospital, Indians, Turks, Armenians, Syrian Christians, British and Russians co-habit and share life-stories, heat and food; George the Armenian receives temporary refuge and Armenian doctors tend to Turkish patients. However, these men and women come together not because of their commitment to some ethical or socio-political ideal in times of war but through the 'unbearable vulnerability'[94] produced by historical and geopolitical entanglements. The most moving relation-ship in the text is the one between Sarbadhikari and the fifteen-year-old Armenian orderly Elias; as the situation worsens, Elias prepares to flee one night and Sarbadhikari gives him his most precious possession – the only warm coat he has (178). Thinking beyond yourself and giving your only warm coat to an orphan from a foreign country may be the first powerful gesture, more than any ratiocinative or intellectual exercise, towards a true cosmopolitan ethic, described as 'feeling and thinking beyond the nation'.[95]

Abhi Le Baghdad is the fullest and the most detailed among the small but immensely powerful body of testimonies on Mesopotamia by the group of Bengali non-combatants. Together, they lift the veil from over this 'bastard war'.[96] An ode to non-combatant experiences, these memoirs show that the 'Indian voices' of the war can by no means be reduced to combat experience alone. Educated, nuanced and cosmopolitan, these non-combatants point to the remarkable lateral spaces, opened up by the war and empire and yet operating beyond the usual imperial axis. Indeed, these accounts help us to reconceptualise our definition of colonial war experience from one of battlefield 'combat' to that of conflict that includes experiences in hospitals and POW camps: what they bear witness to is not the trauma of the trenches, but a different form of experience, one that accommodates hunger and torture and forced marches as well as the kindness of strangers. What they emphasise is not the heat of battle but the precarious everydayness of war. This chapter is in many ways just a first glance, as it were, into an extraordinary range of human experiences and encounters in a part of the world which today, a hundred years on, is

---

[93] Paul Rabinow, 'Representations Are Social Facts', in James Clifford and George E. Marcus (eds.), *Writing Culture: The Poetics and Politics of Ethnography* (Berkeley: University of California Press, 1986), 258.

[94] Judith Butler, *Precarious Lives: The Power of Mourning and Violence* (London: Verso, 2006), xi.

[95] Pheng Cheah and Bruce Robbins (eds.), *Cosmopolitics: Thinking and Feeling Beyond the Nation* (Minneapolis: University of Minnesota Press, 1998), 1–19.

[96] The phrase refers to the 1967 title of A. J. Barker's classic book *The Neglected War*.

witnessing the same scenes of hunger and desperation. In 1919, the Arab-American poet Mikha'il Na'ima wrote poignantly of the Middle East after the war:

> My brother, who are we?
> There are neither home nor people
> Nor neighbours for us anymore.
> When we sleep, and when we rise,
> our garment is shame and ignominy.
> The world has swept us away,
> as it swept away our dead.
> Just bring the shovel and follow me;
> let us dig another trench
> to shelter our living [...][97]

A hundred years later, the same images return. Let us hope for small mercies, that Elias meets another Sarbadhikari and finds shelter.

---

[97] Mikha'il Na'ima, 'Ankhi', originally in Arabic. A slightly different translated version can be found at www.poemhunter.com/poem/my-brother-83.

CHAPTER 7

Transnational Lives
Peripheral Visions of the War

In the tale 'The Imam and the Indian', Amitav Ghosh makes the following observation:

> The men of the village had all the busy restlessness of airline passengers in a transit lounge. Many of them had worked and travelled in the sheikdoms of the Persian Gulf, others had been in Libya and Jordan and Syria, some had been to the Yemen as soldiers ... And none of this was new: their grandparents and ancestors and relatives had travelled and migrated too, in much the same way as mine had, in the Indian subcontinent – because of wars, or for money and jobs, or perhaps simply because they got tired of living always in one place ... The wanderlust of its founders had been ploughed into the soil of the village: it seemed to me sometimes that every man in it was a traveller.[1]

Ghosh's surmise about that 'quiet corner of the Nile Delta' holds true of large parts of his native land as well. If countless Indians, like their Egyptian brethren, had been on the move – as traders, migrants, convicts, indentured labourers, sepoys and lascars – throughout the eighteenth and nineteenth centuries, few events in world history churned up the soil in the quiet corners of India as much as the First World War. The war not only flung its dwellers far and wide; it also turned a handful of them, as we saw in the last chapter, into writers. However, given that more than one million Indians served overseas, the number of first-hand testimonial accounts remains depressingly low. It has taken almost a century for the first substantial and perhaps the most extraordinary of these memoirs – *Abhi Le Baghdad* – to surface in the public domain; I still remember my sense of thrill and near-disbelief when, after tracking down the family, I first saw a copy of the book in the hands of Romola Sarbadhikari, the daughter-in-law of Sisir, in Calcutta; it had been within the family all these

---

[1] Amitav Ghosh, 'The Imam and the Indian', in *The Imam and the Indian: Prose Pieces* (New Delhi: Ravi Dayal Publisher, 2006), 5.

years. Before then, the only other extensive first-person testimony by an Indian I had known was the unpublished war diaries of the Rajput aristocrat Amar Singh, who was more of a sheltered witness rather than an active participant and whose account gives a very particular view of the conflict. In the last few years, several more first-person accounts have emerged.[2] This chapter pursues the argument of the last two chapters. First, it continues the project of recovery, examining a number of hitherto largely unknown texts; second, it examines the textual and generic aspects of these more self-conscious accounts and their relationship to questions of life-writing and narrative strategy.

Here I shall focus on four such testimonies, all of which are rather exceptional, by dint of their rarity as a genre and in terms of their scope and subject-matter. Of these, two are hitherto wholly unknown (translated here for the first time) and are perspectives 'from below' – a chronicle of the experiences of the Manipur Labour Corps in France by an interpreter who was among the first literate members of the Tangkhul community in Manipur, and the memoir of a young Parsi runaway who joined the Middlesex Regiment and served as a 'Tommy' in France, Egypt and Palestine. The other two accounts are in English, stylised and self-consciously elite: the war diaries of the Rajput prince Thakur Amar Singh, modelled after the diary of Samuel Pepys, and the memoir of Kunal Sen, an Anglicised and upper-middle-class Bengali *babu* who worked as a postal officer on four fronts. Together, the four accounts traverse a remarkable range, from being the first example of life-writing in the Tangkhul community to the only hitherto known travelogue-cum-trench-account by an Indian 'Tommy' to the laboriously crafted accounts by a Rajput aristocrat and a Bengali *babu*. Much of the interest in all of the four accounts lies in the fact that none of these men was a 'sepoy' (Karkaria was in the British army) and they all have a certain angular relationship to the war, generating a kind of 'peripheral vision'. If there is often a tendency to reduce *all* Indian participants of the First World War to the figure of the non-literate

---

[2] In addition to the ones discussed in the chapter, I would particularly like to mention Subedar M. B. Sinha, *Soinik Bangali: 1914 Shaler Mahajuddhe France, Mesopotamia O Kurdistan-e Bāngāli Polṭon* [*Sainik Bengali: The Bengali Palton in France, Mesopotamia and Kurdistan in the 1914–1918 War*] (Calcutta: M. B. Sinha, 1939) in Bengali and *Major General A. A. Rudra: His Service in Three Armies and Two World Wars*, ed. Major General D. K. Palit (New Delhi: Reliance Publishing House, 2000); I came across these compelling memoirs only when this book was going to press and hence have not been able to include them. The most substantial unpublished testimony to have recently surfaced is the diary of Harnam Singh Bath, which is being translated by Rana Chhina, under the auspices of UK Punjab Heritage.

sepoy, these accounts show the heterogeneous nature of the Indian war experience. There is often a 'double consciousness' at work in these texts: on the one hand, there is an acute awareness on the part of these men of their being imperial subjects in a European war, bolstered by signs and traces of the power of the British empire; on the other hand, the war also paradoxically takes them beyond the India–Britain axis, from Baku to Gallipoli, opening up alternative spaces and contexts for encounters and experiences.

'I Lacked Writing Skills': First-Time Chronicler

Putanleng Shinglai, a young man of the Tangkhul tribe in the then princely state of Manipur, was just two months into his marriage when R. S. Ruichumhao, the first Christian convert of the State, recruited him for the Indian Labour Corps in 1916. Putanleng was sent to France in 1917 as a labourer; the next year, he was dead. His grave can be found at the St Sever Cemetery Extension in Rouen, France. The family decided to marry off Putanleng's young widow to his brother rather than send her back to her parents. Meanwhile, the King of Manipur was given a CBE and then a KCSI for his 'services'.[3]

If the 140,000 Indians on the Western Front are the best documented among all non-white participants in the conflict, little is known about the 50,000 non-combatants who served alongside them, including the 28,000-strong Indian Labour Corps that was sent over to France in 1917 and served there for one year.[4] Described by Lord Ampthill, the adviser to the Corps and their general spokesperson, as 'tribal groups' – 'hill-men' or 'primitive people who had never been beyond their villages'[5] – they have remained, like Spivak's female subaltern, 'even more deeply in shadow',[6] by dint of both their social class and their non-combatant status. Radhika

---

[3] See Yumnam Rajeshwor Singh, '87 Brave Manipuries of the First World War', http://kanglaonline .com/2015/11/87-brave-manipuries-of-the-first-world-war.

[4] While the figure of 49,278 appearing for 'Non-Combatants' for France in *Statistics of Military Effort*, 777 was initially thought to refer to the Indian Labour Corps influx of 1917, it now seems likely that the number includes some 22,000 non-combatants (mostly camp followers) who accompanied the Indian infantry and cavalry divisions in France between 1914 and 1918, and a further 28,000 labourers of the ILC sent in 1917. See *Fourth Supplement to London Gazette*, 25 July 1919, 9541, in conjunction with *India's Contribution*, 96. I am grateful to George Morton-Jack for investigating and sharing these figures with me and Radhika Singha.

[5] 'Correspondence on the Indian Labour Corps in France', IOR, L/MIL/5/738, British Library.

[6] Gayatri Chakravorty Spivak, 'Can the Subaltern Speak?', in Morris (ed.), *Can the Subaltern Speak? Reflections on the History of an Idea*, 40.

Singha, who has done more than anyone else to recover the experiences of the Indian Labour Corps, notes that 'there are very few sources that allow us to assess how the labourers communicated their own understanding of this historical moment'; the subaltern experience, she notes, becomes visible at the points at which it had to be 'probed and managed by those raising and supervising the ILC'.[7] These men were recruited from some of the most isolated and depressed parts of the country – Assam, the Assam–Burma frontier, the Naga hills, the mountainous tracts of the Manipur princely state and the Lushai hills – with very low levels of literacy; only a handful of letters from these 50,000 men survive.[8] It is in this context that the freshly unearthed memoir *Apuk Apaga Rairei Khare. France Khava, 1917–1918* (*The First Great War Worldwide. To France, 1917–1918*), written in Tangkhul dialect by Kanrei Shaiza – a Tangkhul who accompanied the 66th Manipur Labour Corps Company to France as an assistant interpreter – accretes extraordinary significance.[9] How did he understand and write about the experience, especially when compared with colonial propaganda such as *Indian Labourers in France* (1919) by Captain Kashi Nath,[10] who supervised the 23rd Labour Corps in France, or the voluminous correspondence of Lord Ampthill, for whom these men, 'from the hills and jungles, who have barely emerged from barbarism',[11] were perhaps not fit even for the task of the labourer?

Apuk Apaga Rairei Khare is the first known example of life-writing among the Tangkhuls; it would have been the journey of the men to France that provided the rationale. Born in 1896, Kanrei Shaiza would have been among the bare handful of first-generation literates among the Tangkhuls. He was part of the second batch of students in the Ukhrul Mission School

---

[7] See Radhika Singha's seminal article 'The Short Career of the Indian Labour Corps in France', *ILWCH*, 87, 2015, 27–62. We eagerly await her monograph *The Coolies' Great War*.

[8] 'The bulk of the Labour Corps letters received are in languages which we cannot read and the few in Hindi and Urdu contain nothing of the slightest interest.' Censor's Report, 7 April 1917 and 14 November 1917, IOR/L/MIL/5/828, quoted in Radhika Singha, 'The Short Career of the Indian Labour Corps in France'.

[9] Kanrei Shaiza, *Apuk Apaga Rairei Khare. France Khava, 1917–1918* [*The First Great War Worldwide. To France, 1917–18*] (Imphal, publisher not known, 1974). I am very grateful to Luithui Khanthing for translating the text and discussing the contexts, and to Subarno Chatterji for facilitating the process. According to Khanthing, this book was among the first works of 'Tangkhul literature', published in the 1960s and 1970s. The book is in two parts, the first describing his trip to France with the Manipur Labour Corps, and the second dealing with his state-sponsored visit to Delhi on the occasion of the Republic Day in 1974. After the war, Kanrei became a school-teacher and a member of the 'village authority'.

[10] Described by Lt-Gen. Sir H. V. Cox as 'an extremely able and energetic Indian officer who belongs to our Provincial Civil Service', 'Diary of Tour in France, 27 February to March 1918', 25.

[11] 'Correspondence on the ILC', IOR, L/MIL/5/738, 113, British Library.

founded by the English missionary Reverend William Pettigrew who came to Manipur in 1891. Kanrei accompanied the 66th Manipur Labour Corps to France in 1917, but it was only in 1974 that he wrote his record in Tangkhul dialect and titled it *Apuk Apaga Rairei Khare. France Khava, 1917–1918*. In the preface he notes that

> It was my desire for a very long time to write about the experiences which we came across during the War, but since I lacked writing skills it took a while to write this book. However, despite this, I have tried to write to the best of my ability. It is my sincere and humble appeal to my people that this account be enthusiastically read. (Preface)

The fragile sense of authorship comes across in the text through the awkward, if endearing, tension between self-inscription and self-erasure. In a narrative where the 'I' is firmly subsumed into a communal 'we', Kanrei always refers to himself by name – possibly following the local oral tradition, or in an attempt to assert his identity as an 'important' member of the Corps, or in an effort to maintain an objective historical tone or possibly a touch of all three. Part of the difficulty of writing the account might have been his divided loyalties as a tribal member, native informant, interpreter and school-teacher. Even if these complex roles and his education necessarily set him apart from the men whose experience he records, his account is the nearest we can have to the subaltern experience before it dissolves into silences and ventriloquism in the colonial archives.

Compared with the confident and racy tone of Kashi Nath's *Indian Labourers in France*, Kanrei's account is taciturn, factual, report-like: information takes precedence over evocation and chronicling over storytelling as the personal is flattened into the collective. Yet, it is a 'we' that, as we will see, is fractured and contested, climaxing in a moment of high drama. Kanrei follows a strictly chronological account, starting with processes of recruitment and sea-journey through the experiences in France to eventual return and triumphant welcome by the King in Imphal. One of the most striking features of the text is its multi-vocality: Kanrei repeatedly punctuates his text with the 'voices' of others, recorded in the first person. *Apuk Apaga Rairei Khare* is possibly the only testimony unearthed so far that gives insights into the processes of recruitment among the labour battalions from the native perspective. In response to the Viceroy's request for labourers in January 1917, Maharajah Churachand Singh of Manipur State immediately offered to contribute the Manipur Labour Corps and in turn resurrected the repressive *thoukai* (a feudal system under which the 'hao' or the commoner was to supply free labour to the King) to recruit men from the hills.[12] Kanrei's first-person account takes us through the various stages of the process, from the stubborn resistance of the men ('Even if the government punishes us, we will not go. It is better to die at home than die in a war or in a distant place') to the manoeuvres of the political agent ('Punitive action is out of question as this will result in bloodshed') to the summoning of Reverend William Pettigrew 'so that he can convince the Tangkhuls' and his big recruitment speech:

> It is not for the purpose of fighting that you Tangkhuls are being asked to go to France. You are not soldiers and you don't know the trade of soldiers, who are fighting this war with rifles and artillery. When you go, you will not be deployed on the war fronts … You will be provided meals and above all, every labourer will be paid 22 rupees each month … More importantly the Government has decided that all those who enrol for service will be exempted for their lifetime from paying khazana, thoukai and begari. Also you will be accompanied by the Baro Sahib [Political agent] and other 'sahib' officers. You will be treated like children by these officers. You Tangkhuls should not disobey the Government. To look after you and act as interpreters for you, I have arranged for my Christian leaders and teachers to accompany you. (7–9)

Reproduced in the first person, the speech is indicative of the hold the Christian missionaries had over the people and the role they played in recruitment. Assurance of personal safety, promise of material benefits, exemption from corvee (still in force in parts of the Kumaon Himalayas and along the Assam–Burma border), religious instruction and pastoral care: various enticements are dangled, as Pettigrew treads the fine line between persuasion and coercion; Pettigrew's otherwise detailed offer does not mention contract hours or days of rest which would be debated 'above their head', while his promises of personal safety would later be queried even by Ampthill.[13] The 'Christian leaders and teachers' referred to above

---

[12] 'Thoukai', which can be broken into 'thou' ('responsibility') and 'khai' ('division') approximates to the forced compulsory labour which every Naga village was obliged to perform for a given period of time in a year in lieu of revenue exactions other than house-tax. However, the term does not appear in official wartime documents so as to portray the services of the Manipur Labour Corps as 'voluntary'. I am grateful to Luithui Khanthing for the information above. For the shifting meanings of 'hao', see Saroj Nalini Arambam Parrat, *The Court Chronicles of the Kings of Manipur* (London: Routledge, 2005), 32. In 1917, the recruitment for the ILC was done so aggressively that it sparked uprisings in the Kuki-Chin tracts on the Assam–Burma border and in Mayurbhanj, Orissa. See Radhika Singha, 'The Recruiter's Eye on "the Primitive": To France – and Back – in the Indian Labour Corps, 1917–18', in James E. Kitchen, Alisa Miller and Laura Rowe (eds.), *Other Combatants, Other Fronts: Competing Histories of the First World War* (Cambridge: Cambridge Scholars Press, 2011), 199–224.

[13] See Radhika Singha, 'The Short Career of the Indian Labour Corps in France', 38. Singha refers to another memoir, similarly written by an interpreter called Sainghinga Sailo, who went to France as a

would have included Kanrei, who is completely silent on the ethics of such recruitment. Inadvertently or not, his account of the decision of the Tangkhuls to enlist indicates the coercive measures at work: 'thereafter the government began requisitioning men i.e. *thoukai* for coolies from each village as to the size of the household', and households who could not provide labourers of their own 'hired' men at a rate of 30 rupees (9–10). The practice seems very similar to the coercive measures for sepoy enlistment in the Punjab discussed in Chapter 2. Kanrei's quiet, multi-vocal narrative – incorporating the voices of resistance, strategy, conversion or coercion – evokes minutiae of the recruitment process, as the boundaries of life-writing and war-writing collapse. In April 1917, a group of 2,000 recruits for the Manipur Labour Corps assembled in Imphal. They underwent a short, intensive period of training, lasting around three weeks, which involved rigorous physical exercise and imparted some basic knowledge of warfare.[14]

One of the most vivid memories in the text is of the journey to France. The sea-journey is a common motif in war memoirs, but the experience often depended on class and rank. If the aristocrat Amar Singh recalled the exhilarating sight of ship upon ship, packed with Indian sepoys and guarded by submarines, voyaging across *kalapani*, Kanrei's account is traumatic: the journey of the 66th Manipur is marked by sea-sickness, dizziness and the outbreak of cholera as he reports how 'the vomit and excrement of our coolies' had to be cleaned by water-hoses and that 'the dead bodies were wrapped and stitched in a fabric and heaved into the sea regularly' (17–18). To this very day, the sea-voyage of 1917 haunts Tangkhul cultural memory, with the belief being that not only the dead but the feeble and vulnerable too were thrown into the water.[15] Even amidst such conditions, the able-bodied are made to work during their various stopovers in Aden, Cairo and Alexandria. Surprisingly there is no sense of outrage or complaints from Kanrei. In his flat tone, he goes on to report that the men were quarantined in Taranto for a month in July 1917, and after a

---

clerk with the Lushai Labour Corps, which was recently recovered by Joy Pachuau, and it would be fascinating to compare the two accounts. Sainghinga's memoir is informed, Joy Pachuau notes, 'by the educated Mizo's drive for *changkanna*, or self-improvement through knowledge of the modern world, a characteristic of travel accounts published in *Mizo leh Vai* ', as quoted in Singha, 'The Short Career of the Indian Labour Corps in France', 29. The list of enticements is also reminiscent of the ILC recruitment poster published in the propaganda newspaper for the sepoys *Jangi Akhbar*, No. 18, 1918.
[14] See Yumnam Rajeshwor Singh, '87 Brave Manipuris of the First World War', http://kanglaonline.com/2015/11/87-brave-manipuries-of-the-first-world-war.
[15] I am indebted for this information to the translator Luithui Khanthing.

medical examination – which involved the Italian doctors 'inserting certain instruments in our anus' – they were declared germ-free and allowed to proceed to France. They reached Marseilles in August and, after initially being employed in gathering 'rifles, ammunition, bayonets, shells, grenades, boots, gum boots' and in constructing trenches, they were sent to Blargies (23–25).

Official war diaries and correspondence, a few censored letters and the photographs of the ILC provide some insights into the experiences of these men in France: reading them alongside Kanrei's account enables a proximate understanding of the experiences of these men and the gaps and silences in each account. Of the official documents, the most illuminating is the correspondence of Ampthill, where a certain Victorian humanitarianism, colonial paternalism, contemporary racism, ethnology and imperial cover-up are mixed. In his tour of three labour units working on a British aerodrome construction-site near Nancy, he notes confidently that 'I am satisfied that anything possible is being done' and yet goes on to note 'barns and haylofts … big, dark, draughty places with imperfect roofs and somewhat rickety floor'; in a later tour of the labour units, including the 66th Manipurs, undertaken in March 1918, he comments on the 'new huts' which are 'distinctly better', even though 'the ground inside them is very cold and damp'. The accommodation for the ILC was markedly inferior to that offered to the sepoys, resulting in high rates of 'bronchial pneumonia': according to Ampthill's bizarre logic, this was due to the men's 'chronic disposition to malarial fever' and he asks for 'quinine, castor-oil and cough-mixture'.[16] Photographs speak out voluminously when the documents are silent. A deeply moving image shows the meagre food and clothing they were given, as we see two men from the Manipur Labour Corps having lunch, surrounded by wheel-barrows, at a place near Arras in October 1917 (Figure 7.1).[17] The winter months were even harder. Kanrei notes that 'the extreme cold of this place cannot be described' and again, a few pages later, 'the extremity of the cold cannot be described' and that 'at night the water stored in bottles would freeze'. On 6 January 1918, Ampthill observed that the men were bearing up with the cold – it was the same day that the Senior Medical Officer recorded the deaths of three

---

[16] 'Correspondence on the ILC', IOR, L/MIL/5/738, 113, British Library. As Singha bitterly notes, this was a classic colonial construct designed to shift the blame to 'malarial germs' rather than the poor health-care arranged by the colonial administration.
[17] See Santanu Das, *1914–1918: Indian Troops in Europe* (Ahmedabad: Mapin Publishing, 2015), 106–107.

Figure 7.1   Indian labourers from Manipur having lunch near Arras, 20 October 1917.
Copyright Imperial War Museum (Q 6124).

men of the 66th Manipur company from bronchial pneumonia.[18] Kanrei
mentions that one of his tasks was to accompany the dead, 'wrapped properly in a fabric', to the burial ground, where an officer would carry out the
burial service (33): one wonders whether this was the Blargies Communal
Cemetery extension, near where the 66th Manipurs were stationed and
where there are forty-four Indian graves.[19]

    In contrast to the Indian labour battalions working in Nancy, the 66th
Manipurs were put up in proper billets amidst a large labour camp that
housed 'different corps of Agamhao, Khasia, Tesiwali, Chinese as well as

[18] Singha, 'The Short Career of the Indian Labour Corps in France', 40.
[19] Follow the CWGC link to the cemetery: 'Blargies Communal Cemetery Extension', www.cwgc
      .org/find-a-cemetery/cemetery/26900/BLARGIES%20COMMUNAL%20CEMETERY%20
      EXTENSION.

those of the blacks, English and other Europeans' (27). This was rather unusual, for the colonial authorities usually insisted on a strict segregation of different national and ethnic groups. Kanrei does not mention any kind of interaction with workers from other countries. Instead, he gives a rather detailed account of their work:

> Our work was not restricted to earthwork alone. We would load and unload timber from the train. In that vast area timber was piled in vast quantities. It was transported to the war front, while from other locations, it was brought and deposited here. In this manner we spent the month of December 1917 and the months from January to May of 1918 working the same routine. Many would work at night. Their job was to use machines to saw wood … Meanwhile the Interpreters and the Headmen would supervise the entire working area by taking their usual rounds. At times when the loading–unloading could not be completed in time, leaders would join and render assistance. Work would commence at 7 AM in the morning and by 11 AM we would return to camp. 11 AM to 2 PM was our lunch time, and at 2 PM we would recommence our work till 5 PM in the evening and return. Everyday work begins at 7 AM without fail. (27–28)

The above account is at once illuminating and frustrating: we get a first-person account of the back-breaking labour but without any testimonial affect. The Indian labourers were considered reliable if not terribly hardy: Egyptians would carry 'two sacks, each weighing around 80 lbs, as they run up and down, laughing and singing' while 'the poor Indian, with all his willingness can only manage one sack and that with many sighs and groans'.[20] Such sighs and groans, or visceral accounts of 'hands bleeding' or 'sticking to frozen metal'[21] recovered paradoxically from governmental documents do not appear in Kanrei's first-person but curiously disembodied testimony. Was Kanrei himself involved in the loading–unloading, or did he work as one of the supervisors? Was there a sense of tribal shame or personal guilt, or was the deafening silence about the injustices and ignominies an act of cover-up by a colonial intermediary? Or was it a question of genre: was it that Kanrei, in writing the first history of the Tangkhuls, wanted to chronicle and highlight the positive dimensions of their 'contribution' to the momentous event?[22]

---

[20] India Office Library, British Library, L/MIL/5/738, 50.

[21] See Singha, 'The Short Career of the Indian Labour Corps in France', 58, 53.

[22] This is the case with some of the memoirs by members of the Chinese Labour Corps and the continuing reluctance by even some of the most eminent Chinese scholars and community leaders working on the subject in recent years to discuss fully the painful, unattractive and occasionally violent details of the time of the Chinese Labour Corps in France; instead, they are evolved into

But, even leaving aside such painful details, one of the most curious qualities about 'The First Great War Worldwide' is the absence of the personal, the affective, the intimate: how did the men feel when they first saw the trenches, or when their ungloved hands first delved into the marshlands, or when a shell whizzed overhead? Such sights and sounds and emotions are resolutely held in check in the narrative. In many ways, Kanrei is the chronicler *par excellence*, for what the narrative does is to chronicle their lives: what work they did, what they ate, what time they started and finished work, what games they played. However, the record of a single incident of high drama reveals the rich and complex inner world of these men, the web of obligations, expectations, honour and shame, trust, kinship and religion that marks the group. The issue at hand was the question of renewal of contracts. In a letter dated 10 December 1917, Ampthill noted that the present time is 'the worst possible moment for asking the men whether they will re-engage' after the expiry of their one-year contract: 'They are feeling the cold, they are very home-sick and they do not know what the winter has in store for them' and that 'money is no inducement'.[23] For once, Kanrei's account reveals the seething underworld of emotions that lies behind such single sentences in the official archives as his multi-vocal narrative rises majestically to the occasion. Kanrei begins with his characteristic third-person narrative style:

> When S. Kanrei, A. Porom Singh and R. Ruichumhao tried to reason with the men [to extend their contracts], they considered the three of them unwilling to make their representation … They did not pay heed even when we said that we cannot go against the 'sarkar' and that we should always obey our commanding officer. They were so aroused by the leaders from other communities that they flatly refused to hear our arguments. These other leaders secretly filled the coolies' ears by saying, 'the three of them are Christians and therefore are not afraid to die. So when they appeal to you to stay, you don't listen to them' (35–36).

We have here the voice of the colonial intermediary trying to thwart subaltern resistance; at the same time, it also shows how his Christianity, which had so far been an advantage to Kanrei, could equally go against him. But the events took a dramatic turn when the three interpreters, including Kanrei, were summoned by the colonial authorities and accused of instigating the

a celebratory narrative of self-improvement on the Western Front. The subject has often been the topic of lively debate between myself and Xu Guoqi: see for example Xu Guoqi's important book *Strangers on the Western Front: Chinese Workers in the Great War* (Cambridge: Harvard University Press, 2011).

[23] IOL, BL, L/MIL/5/738, 99.

rebellion; they were separated from the rest of the men as well as from each other as punishment. We have here in a nutshell the classic predicament of the colonial intermediary, caught between competing claims of tribal affiliation and colonial patronage. Smarting at the ignominy, Kanrei delivered a passionate address to the men, which is worth quoting in its entirety:

> The three of us have been disgraced because of you … In the olden days when the thoukai service was accompanied by the meiteis and mayangs, the coolies were beaten and their money was taken away, and because of this reason thoukai was detested. Think about it, we did not allow others to bully you, nor did we take away your money. We looked after you with much care and compassion, yet you do not listen to our counsel and now for this the three of us have been shamed (37).

Kanrei here reveals himself to be an experienced negotiator and skilled speaker. Smarting, anger, wounded pride, loyalty, betrayal, affection, power: various emotions and histories jostle as Kanrei – at once tribal member and colonial intermediary – argues with his men, trying to coax and bully them not in terms of imperial loyalty, but by invoking personal obligation and local histories. And the men change their minds! Possibly as a reward, Kanrei is selected for a trip to London, and to Buckingham Palace; but the men feel increasingly anxious about being on their own without Kanrei, with the result that Kanrei, in a fine display of tribal loyalty, cancels the visit and accompanies the men home. Nor was this just an isolated display of responsibility or affection. Throughout the narrative, Kanrei shows sustained concern for the men, and every Sunday would take them out on educational tours, for 'I wanted our jovial, anxious, young men to experience and learn the characteristics, manners, traits and conducts of other nations, other peoples' (34).

Taciturn yet passionate, *Apuk Apaga Rairei Khare. France Khava, 1917–1918* remains a singularly valuable account by a member of the community for a whole submerged population group in First World War history. Interestingly, the same combination of emotional reticence and a taboo on intimacy is found in a chronicle by a Chinese interpreter about his labour battalion that has just been unearthed, *Ou Zhan Gong Zuo Hui Yi Lu* (*Memories of My Work in the European War*).[24] There too, we have the same

---

[24] Gu XinQing, *Ou Zhan Gong Zuo Hui Yi Lu* [*Memories of My Work in the European War*] (Hong Kong: Commercial Press, 1937). The discovery was made by Katie Ng, who recovered this valuable document while doing research for an undergraduate dissertation on the Chinese Labour Corps at King's College London. See Katie Ng 'Identity in Perspectives of Chinese Labourers in WW1' (2017).

diligent tabulation of tasks accomplished and hours worked for, without any emotional outlet or any reference to the effects of such labour on the body.

While we – the twentieth-century readers – crave for confessional testimony, a record not of what the men did, but of the marks and scars on the subaltern body, such ignominies – which were often their daily lot – might have had little appeal or even might have been an active cause of shame for the actual sufferers or the local historian chronicling his community for the first time; also, there might not have been any precedence for such 'bodily testimony' in the oral tradition he was drawing upon. In the whole text, there are only two occasions when the world of feeling interrupts the nonchalant tone. The first is the memory of the football matches, when the text suddenly glows with pleasure and pride, as much on behalf of his unit as of his own sporting self:

> Our team would play and defeat teams from other Manipur Companies as well as three or four other Company teams of Agam Hao. At every game we would score 2–3 goals. These made our officers so euphoric that Lt. Brown would sanction one hundred francs, of which Agam Singh, the Jemadar, would give fifty francs to us. With this amount the players would hold a 'tea party' each time. All our players were students of the Ukhrul Mission School. S. Kanrei, A. Porom Singh and R. Ruichumhao, these three were very good football players with stamina, and skills. However, amongst the three, S. Kanrei was the most skilful player ... Because of his skill and good spirit, everyone watching the game, including his officers, was very pleased with him and showered him with praise.

Passages such as the above are rare and thrilling, a testimony to moments of joy which these players and their audience would narrate with such ardour after their return to Manipur that the sport would become part of the cultural memory of the war in the region and would be celebrated with a football match in their honour in 2017! The second example, on the other hand, looks inward and is laced with delicate sadness: homesickness was perhaps as far as he could allow himself to go in the direction of the intimate. The following account is the most direct eruption of the world of feeling into the most taciturn of texts:

> When we heard the sweet gratifying voice of the cuckoo calling out 'cuckoo' 'cuckoo' from the branches of trees in springtime, our thoughts turned to our homes, thinking of the echoes of the cuckoo calling out this time at home. We were filled with an inexpressible desire to return home.

We would think only of our homes, because this place during the warmer climate is inarticulately beautiful. We were stationed at Blargies during the time. (35)

Birdsong was by no means the preserve of British trench-poetry alone.

'I Become a Tommy': Wanderlust, Combat and the Memoir of a Lascar-Soldier

Of the life-stories of various people in this chapter, perhaps the most colourful and entertaining is that of Nariman Karkaria – one of the handful of Indians to be serving, like Indra Lal Ray and Jogen Sen, in a British Regiment. A young Parsi man from Navsari in Gujrat and possessed by wanderlust, he roamed the world, as we will see, in the pre-war years before enlisting in the British army: he served on multiple fronts – in France, Egypt, Palestine and Salonika – and took part in the battle of the Somme in July 1916 and in a sideshow of the battle of Beersheba in October 1917; he was also a compulsive storyteller. His 380-page memoir – written in Parsi Gujrati, first serialised in the Parsi newspaper *Gulabi* and then published as a book in 1922 – is referred to in the preface as *Rangbhumini Rakhad*, which translates as 'Roaming a Performance Stage' or 'Travels of Interesting Places'.[25] The title is revealing. Despite its being dedicated to 'my very close friend Lieutenant Colonel H. E. Lavie who too fought bravely on the battlefield of the last war' and a record primarily of the author's experiences as a soldier, it is nonetheless pitched as a travelogue: it shows how Karkaria conceptualised his war memoir as a travel narrative when the latter was an established genre while war testimony had still to be born; moreover, war and travel seemed to have been inextricably linked in his mind. A world war becomes for Karkaria a passport for world travel to such an extent that at one point, stationed in Jordan, he has to remind himself and his readers 'Don't think I can take you to Mecca or Medina. How can I afford to enjoy roaming around the world when I am actually enrolled to fight on a battlefield? So let me take

[25] Nariman Karkaria, *Rangbhumini Rakhshad* (Bombay: Manek Printing Press, 1922). I am very grateful to Vadra Bhadgama for translating the text with such great enthusiasm and care. Page references are mentioned in the text. I am grateful to Murali Ranganathan for first alerting me to the text, and to Bharti Gandhi at the First Dastoor Meherjirana Library, Navsari, for her help in accessing this rare text. For the contribution of Parsis more generally to the war, see Marzban Jamshedji Giara, *The Contribution of the Parsi Community during the First World War (1914–1918)* (Navsari: Sorabji Burjorji Garda College Trust, 2016).

you back to my platoon' (269). The statement is revealing of the traveller at heart who has temporarily become a 'Tommy'; it is also indicative of the colloquial ease and intimacy which characterises this most carefree and footloose of war narratives.

'My active brain kept questioning me: "Why don't you do something different and get to know the whole world?"' (4), asks Karkaria at the beginning of his memoir. It is indeed this longing that generates and subsequently underpins the whole narrative. On the 'dark, dangerous' night of 10 August 1910, 'as if seized by satanic power', the sixteen-year-old leaves home without a word to anyone, purchases a third-class one-way ticket to Bombay, and jumps on the Capri-bound ship for China. This marked the beginning of an extraordinary twelve-year peregrination, at once facilitated and disrupted by the war. A spirit of adventure alternates with a sense of vulnerability as, between 1910 and 1914, we see this young Parsi lad, 'holding bedding under his arm' – with hardly any money but gifted with a razor-sharp wit and exceptional charm – travel through Hong Kong, Peking, Petrograd, Finland and Sweden. *Rangbhumini Rakhad* at once is and is not a lascar narrative: Karkaria eked out a precarious living as a lascar, but his level of education, cultural awareness and Parsi contacts that add so much colour and character to the narrative would have marked him out from the average semi-literate lascar. It was at sea, during his second trip to China in February 1915, that the war finally hit him: 'It was a dangerous war – war in the air, war on the land, war on the sea. War, war, and war' (48). Having 'no idea what it meant to volunteer in the war', he initially decided to stay out of it. But communal pressure mounted, the lure of heroic masculinity proved irresistible, a dim sense of his Iranian ancestry dawned on him, and he decided to enlist: 'Yes, I will go to war and fight on battlefields and pull out the intestines of a couple of Germans!!' (49). The reality of the war, however, did not sink in as he travelled through Harbin and Petrograd and Karungi until, some fifty pages later in the text, we are told that he had arrived in London and immediately headed towards Whitehall. He was initially rejected, and was asked to register through the India Office; however, he argued and finally enlisted as private 'No. 3213' in the 24th [Reserve] Battalion of the Middlesex Regiment. His Parsi heritage and light complexion would no doubt have helped him. After six months of gruelling training, first at Northampton and then at Aldershot, his battalion was mobilised, and he finally went to France in November 1915.

It was in early 1916 that Karkaria had his first taste of combat. Movement of thousands of soldiers and vehicles, darkness lit up by flashes from bursting shells, and the constant thud of bombs greeted him as his battalion moved towards the front line at Fricourt: the descriptions are vivid and powerful, 'amazement and fear' abound. 'How much destruction can be caused by guns', he wonders as his company settles down in 'Liverpool Trench' and views the debris of war – 'broken rifles, bayonets, axes, spades, tattered German uniforms and overcoats' (141). In the course of the next few weeks, they dig trenches, repair damaged wire and encounter poison gas, and soon Karkaria finds himself in the Battle of the Somme, though it is not certain whether he was involved in the offensive on that fateful first day or subsequently. Injured, he is moved to Hospital No. 5 at Rouen and is finally sent to Southampton. After a period of recovery – and compulsory tourism, savouring London's theatres and parks and 'yellow fog' (178) – his regiment was transferred, via *HMS Saxon*, to Egypt. There the regiment was stationed outside the city of El Qantara, and was later caught up in a sideshow of the battle of Beersheba in October 1917 in the Sinai–Palestine campaign, incurring heavy casualties. Karkaria survived unscathed, and subsequently travelled through Palestine and Jordan, until his battalion was ordered to go to the Salonika Camp early in 1918. Here, he served for a few months as an 'unqualified doctor' and witnessed the Allied victory, and made his way, through Constantinople and Tiflis and Baku, back to England, where he finally embarked on *HMS Zeppelin*, to make his way back to India. It is an extraordinary story, and though Karkaria admits to have added some 'salt and pepper' to invigorate parts of his narrative, the main places and points of action mentioned can largely be corroborated.

One of the most far-flung and colourful accounts of the First World War, the central parts of *Rangbhumi Rakhad* read like a classic trench narrative – we have the night-march, the body 'stiff and cold' in the dug-out, reconnaissance, trench-raid, attack and counter-attack, snipers, teargas-shells and shrapnel, barbed wire and rats. The value of such an account increases exponentially when we realise that it is possibly the only trench narrative we have so far from an Indian, even though he served in a British unit; to have it serialised in a Gujrati paper and get it published as early as 1922 – when there is nothing of that sort in Indian writing and before classic accounts such as Sassoon's *Diary of an Infantry Officer* and Blunden's *Undertones of War* appeared in the late 1920s and early 1930s – is remarkable. Indeed, in its careful list of factual details and trench realism, its kinship is not with the sepoy letters but with the accounts of the European soldier-writers. Consider the following account about Karkaria's experience at Fricourt:

> One could only see miserably destroyed tattered trunks as a reminder of once very productive woods … All over we could see broken rifles, bayonets, axes, spades, tattered German uniforms and overcoats. Like others, I too picked up a crisp blue overcoat belonging to a German Officer as bedding. This has been a place where many infantry battles had taken place, so we came across broken limbs lying here and there. (141)

Similar accounts, listing the stubborn obduracy of objects when their owners and users have perished, punctuate British and French war writings, from Arthur Graeme West's posthumous *Diary of a Dead English Officer* (1915) to Henri Barbusse's *Under Fire* (1916). But, unlike the authors of most accounts of the Western Front, Karkaria is keenly aware that the world war is not limited to Europe: 'Those who have been on the battlefields in France believed that the war was only fought there and nowhere else. But now with my various experiences on various battlefields, I can see how incorrect that notion was. I will now describe how the brave soldiers who fought in Egypt and Mesopotamia overcame the hardship caused by nature' (186). And more: he goes on to describe how 'totally different' the war was in Egypt, where 'our eyes were swollen, red and sore. Only God knows how much sand we inhaled with every breath'; how, in the open plains of the Balkans, his tent was blown up in the middle of the night and he found himself almost burning to death; or the fear of submarines in the Caspian Sea; or the jubilant welcome extended to the British troops in Jerusalem. It is through such vivid detail that Karkaria cumulatively builds up his war narrative. It is equally striking that, in the course of a 380-page narrative, he does not mention a single person, let alone a friend, by name: camaraderie, the great theme of First World War trench experience, is strangely absent in the narrative. While training in Northampton, he had noted that 'I knew nobody there with whom I could have a laugh' (105).

Apart from its trench realism, the generic affiliation of *Rangbhumi* is with that of the travelogue. In the tradition of nineteenth-century Indian travel writing, such as Yusuf Khan Kambalposh's *Tarikh-i-Yusufi* (*The Travels of Yusuf Khan*, 1847) or Behramji Malabari's *The Indian Eye in English Life or Rambles of a Pilgrim Reformer* (1893),[26] Karkaria relegates autobiographical details to incidental asides rather than forming any continuum with them. Instead, time and again, he tries to cast his experiences

---

[26] See Javed Majeed, *Autobiography, Travel and Postnational Identities* (London: Palgrave, 2007), 51.

of travel as an almost empirical narrative, illustrated with photographs as touchstones of authenticity, and thus privileging an 'objective' account of sights seen and places encountered over a more intimate history of emotion and the senses. 'Let me show you China', 'If you ever wish to travel to Russia', 'Come on, join me in my trip' are regular narrative tics; accounts of fighting alternate with, and are often wholly outweighed by, his experiences as a tourist, as he takes us to the Mosque of Omar in Jerusalem or Hagia Sophia in Istanbul or the 'outstanding magic city of Tiflis with its multi-ethnic population'. The description of each of these visits is accompanied by a Wikipedia-like download of information rather than the warmth of personal encounter or thick description: this is perhaps in tandem with the aim to 'inform' and 'educate' the readers of the then-contemporary Indian travelogue, from which personal details are expunged. The exception, unsurprisingly, is the description of the imperial metropolis. As cultural and literary historians such as Antoinette Burton and Elleke Boehmer have documented, London was not just a city for the subjects of the empire, but an overwritten space where myth and reality, expectations and desire, hearsay and actual experience touched and blended.[27] Karkaria is no exception: 'What extraordinary pleasure it would be to be in London and my heart was engulfed in the anticipation of the pleasure. I must have irritated the Guard by asking him 50 times when we would reach London – I even washed my face 15 times' (95). Yet the London that greeted him was not the metropolis ablaze with 'the Imperial brilliance of the electric light in perfected power and majesty', as in Syed Ahmad Khan's description of his visit in 1869, as recalled in *Musafiran-i-London*[28] or the object of *ajaibat* (wonder), as in countless Urdu travelogues, but blacked out in fear of zeppelin raids:

> Getting out of the station, I had a shock. The whole place was engulfed in darkness. Was this the famous lively London? All my expectations were ruined. Such darkness. It made the roads of London look scary; they frightened me ... But what was the reason for this darkness? War, it was nothing but the devastating war. People were more scared to walk in the lit-up city and preferred this darkness as there was a constant fear of this enchanting city being bombarded ... This cursed war had turned such magnificent hotels and YMCAs into military offices. And with them were

---

[27] Antoinette Burton, *At the Heart of Empire: Indians and the Colonial Encounter in Late-Victorian Britain* (Berkeley: University of California Press, 1998); Elleke Boehmer *Indian Arrivals, 1870–1915: Networks of British Empire* (Oxford: Oxford University Press, 2015).

[28] See Majeed, *Autobiography*, 78, 297.

gone the waiters who earned wages as high as those of governors. Instead of
washing dishes in hotels, they were cleaning rifles on battlefields. (97–100)

Karkaria's account, possibly the only such account by an Indian during
the First World War, is not just the deflation of a cherished colonial fantasy: his thoughts about the waiters are necessarily a view of the imperial
metropolis from below, a subaltern perspective rather than that of the
privileged tourist, an extension of what he would have done, had not the
war disrupted his life.

Reading Karkaria's account of war and travel, one question that repeatedly comes to mind – and over which he draws a veil of silence – is about
his feelings as an Indian subject: what was it to be the only Indian soldier
in an English regiment? How did it feel to experience wartime London
or the Mosque of Hagia Sophia as an Indian? A sophisticated and light-
skinned Parsi, it seems that he had easily adjusted to his company, but was
there never any racist discrimination or feeling of alienation? Conversely,
in Egypt or the Balkans, was there any special rapport with the locals
as a colonised subject? We come across a blank for such questions. It is
not known whether Karkaria concerned himself with such questions, or
whether a certain embarrassed silence was at work or whether it was a generic consideration. Any reference to India or reflection about his role in
an imperial war is absent. Indeed, there seems to be a strange relationship
to his Indian identity: when he takes part in the Battle of the Somme, he
proudly titles the section 'How Indian soldiers fought on the Somme'; yet
later, when some Indian soldiers embark on a ship in which he is travelling,
his identification is more with British troops, as he notes patronisingly
that 'training the Indians was hard work'. Rather than a strong national
imaginary, there seems to have been more of a Parsi Gujrati identity and
sensibility at work, often at a socio-cultural and linguistic level, in the text.
He chose the Parsi Gujrati dialect (his mother-tongue) for his memoir,
and uses culturally familiar similes: after his first meal at the barracks
at Northampton, his face 'looked like *dhaal* [lentil soup] ruined while
cooking' (106); mistreated in China, he feels like a 'rotten egg curry' (22);
encountering the first (tear) gas attack on the Western Front, he writes that
'air as hot as red chillies spread across the trenches' (156). The one recurring reference and site of attachment in the text is to his home town; in
a narrative otherwise marked by a dead-pan voice, there is a spontaneous
outburst of feeling when he is asked 'where I came from in India': 'Before
I could give him the answer, I got so emotional thinking of my dear home
town of Navsari, that I began to cry' (288). The sole reference to India, or,

indeed, any admission of homesickness, appears only towards the end of the travelogue as he makes the final return voyage: 'To enter the threshold of your beloved mother country after years of being away is a feeling that has to be experienced, not described.' (380).

Honour and Slur: The War Diaries of Thakur Amar Singh

If there could be a perspective almost diametrically opposite to those of Kanrei or Karkaria, that is provided by the exhaustive and at times exhausting but consistently fascinating diaries of Thakur Amar Singh.[29] A Rajput aristocrat trained at the Imperial Cadet Corps and one of the first Indians to hold a King's Commission, the thirty-six-year-old Amar Singh was appointed the Aide-de-Camp to General Brunker, commanding the 9th Sirhind Brigade, which was part of the Lahore Division. He served intermittently in France from December 1914 to December 1915 and was near the war-zone during the Indian exploits in Festubert, Givenchy and Neuve Chapelle, though he did not take part in the actual fighting. In January 1916, he joined his brigade in Mesopotamia. Coming to his diaries after the memoirs of Kanrei and Karkaria is like entering a different planet, though all three were in France, and shows the sheer heterogeneity of the Indian war experience. However, Amar Singh's position was anomalous, being one of enormous privilege but of little power. His duties were restricted to the back of the front: he looked after the transport, visited the sepoys in the trenches, went riding and did the occasional translation; most importantly, he kept a daily diary in English, writing down everything he witnessed in exhaustive detail. The war years are part of his diaries, which stretch almost daily from 3 September 1898 to the day of his death on 1 November 1942, running to eighty-nine volumes.

The war diaries are an extraordinary combination of description, observation, emotion, opinion and analysis. Records of key events such as the battles of Givenchy (18–22 December 1914) and Neuve Chapelle (10–13 March 1915) are supplemented by more analytical accounts written shortly afterwards. If Merewether and Smith provide the official account of the

---

[29] Diaries of Amar Singh, January–December 1914 (Microfilm R3540 Index 9) and January–December 1916 and January–24 August 1917 (Microfilm R3541 Index 10), Nehru Memorial Museum and Library, Teen Murti House, New Delhi. The original diaries are housed in the Kanota fort, Rajasthan; all references in the text are to the microfilm version of the diaries in the Nehru museum, abbreviated as 'Diaries'. The pages in the diary are not numbered. See the majestic edition of the diaries (1898 to 1905) produced by Susanne Rudolph and Lloyd Rudolph (eds.), *Reversing the Gaze: Amar Singh's Diary: A Colonial Subject's Narrative of Imperial India* (Delhi: Oxford University Press, 2000) and the illuminating biography by DeWitt C. Ellinwood, *Between Two Worlds: A Rajput Officer in the Indian Army, 1905–1921* (Lanham: Hamilton, 2005).

Battle of Neuve Chapelle,[30] Amar Singh gives us a more personal account, from sensuous descriptions of bombardments to German guns 'mowing our men down' to a poignant account of a 'cold, hungry, thirsty, wounded' German in no man's land calling out to his comrades.[31] His meditation on the 'terrible' nature of war reminds one of European officer-writers but, unlike them, his 'structures of feeling' are created not so much by war trauma as by the complex conjunction of class, racial and colonial politics in wartime.

'Slur' is a recurrent word and emotion in the diaries; a constant oscillation between class privilege and racial discrimination forms their emotional core. Experiences of 'slight' range from the refusal of the English soldiers to salute him (though he was one of the King's Commissioned Officers) to being teased for not eating beef to being 'very rudely' asked to leave the room when important military details are discussed. The personal and the racial are interlinked. When Amar Singh had suggested sending an all-Indian force to Egypt, General Brunker had turned on him 'fiercely': 'you can't fight with native troops only'. Singh criticises General Brunker's decision to mix British and Indian troops, for 'the Indians must have felt it as a slur on them':[32]

> The great trouble under which we have laboured is that whenever we fail in the slightest degree anywhere people raise a hue and cry whereas, if the British troops fail under the same circumstances, no one mentions it. The Indian troops had done very well all along but when we had the reverse at Givenchy and Festubert there was a hue and cry ... Plainly the thing is that if there is a success it is due to the British element but if there is a reverse then it is all put down to the Indian troops. I do not know what is expected of the Indians.[33]

Amar Singh may have been occasionally too enthusiastic or defensive about the Indian performance, but what comes across powerfully is his frustration and resentment at the racist ideology of the British army. According to General Willcocks, the Indian officer 'can *never* replace ... the natural instincts of the white man'.[34] The uneven performance of the

[30] See Merewether and Smith, *The Indian Corps in France*, 218–219.
[31] Singh, Diaries, 'A few notes about the severe fighting at Neuve Chapelle', Thursday 8 April 1915, Boulogne.
[32] Singh, Diaries, 'Some notes about the severe handling we had at the fighting at Festuibert [*sic*] & Givenchy', Wednesday 31 March 1915.
[33] Singh, Diaries, 'Some notes', Tuesday 6 April 1915, Boulogne.
[34] Willcocks to Hardinge, 30 December 1914, Hardinge 102/1/1153a, quoted in Greenhut, 'Imperial Reserve', 72.

Indian Corps is understood in terms not of inadequate military training but of the Indians' 'natural inferiority'.

The diaries capture the emotional pulse of Indian army life and its hierarchies as Singh moves between the worlds of the British military elite and a semi-literate sepoy community. Singh is generally very sympathetic towards the sepoys. After the first day of the battle of Neuve Chapelle, he describes how wounded Sikh soldiers 'empty their magazines and throw all the ammunition in the ditch'; when he assures two Gurkha officers that they would be back in India in 'three or four months' time', they answer 'Jabtak kaun zinda rahega' ('As long as someone is alive').[35] Informed about desertion by a group of Pathans, he notes that 'perhaps they had enough of fighting'; when told about the low levels of recruitment in India, he writes 'He [the Indian] is perfectly safe at home and well protected ... He cannot see why he should hazard his life.'[36] Singh's understanding of the unnecessary nature of the conflict for the Indians and the waste of lives is acute, but, ironically, it is *his* 'education' in the imperial ideology as well as in Rajput aristocratic and masculine codes that prevents his sympathy from developing into a critique of the empire or into anti-war protest. As with the educated classes in Chapter 1, imperial war service becomes a way of salvaging national prestige: 'The lives of a few thousand is nothing compared to the honour of a nation.'[37]

On 19 December 1915, Amar Singh boarded the ship *Erinpura*, along with British and Indian soldiers, on his way to Mesopotamia. The journey is described as 'very happy and pleasant' but there is always a crippling sense of marginalisation: 'I hear that in Egypt Tommies have to salute Egyptian officers. Why not in India? ... There are very few Tommies indeed who take any notice of me ... though they know me and I am always with the General in my own brigade.'[38] The ship had a good library, and Amar Singh immersed himself in what seems to have been his primary activity during the war years: *reading*. He read omnivorously – from Byron and Dickens to the Urdu translation of Shakespeare's *Cymbeline* and the *Rubáiyát of Omar Khayyám*, to the novels of the Bengali nationalist Bankim Chandra Chattopadhyay. Paul Fussell's powerful thesis of the First World War as a singularly 'literary war' in *The Great War and Modern Memory* (1975) seems to have been realised more powerfully with Amar Singh than

[35] Singh, Diaries, 'A few notes about the severe fighting at Neuve Chapelle', Thursday 8 April 1915; 'Some notes', Tuesday 6 April 1915, Boulogne.
[36] *Ibid.*
[37] Singh, Diaries, 'Some notes', Tuesday 6 April 1915.
[38] Singh, Diaries, 'The Voyage', 27 January 1916.

with any other colonial non-white participant. Once in Mesopotamia, he again found himself in a limbo, though, in early June 1916, he was sent to Basra and Amarah to look after supplies and met some of the Indian POWs exchanged with the Turks after Kut:

> [The men] were simply a bag of bones and there was hardly any flesh on them ... I shall never forget the case of Virbhan Rajpoot who was from Shekhawati in Jaipur. He had a broken arm and he was literally nothing but skin and bones. His eyes were bulging out and as I talked to him sympathetically the poor fellow actually cried ... They were most pleased to see me and felt awfully grateful. Several of them took me for some Maharajah.[39]

The above passage is characteristic of the diary, both in terms of Singh's primary duty during the war, whether in France, the Middle East or Bombay – meeting, encouraging or consoling Indian soldiers – and in terms of the tone in which it is recorded. It is a voice that is gentle, compassionate, engaged, but it is essentially a view of the war from the above and the afar: 'most pleased', 'awfully grateful' or being mistaken for a 'Maharajah' only go to show the distance from these 'simple men', a distance that is peculiarly alienating.

In his biography *Between Two Worlds: A Rajput Officer in the Indian Army, 1905–1921* (2005), DeWitt Ellinwood has noted that 'It was evident that the army command did not know what exactly to do with him at the time', a problem peculiar to Amar Singh being an aristocrat, a graduate of the Imperial Cadet Corps and one of the handful of King's Commissioned Officers.[40] 'It was a change to have something to do', Amar Singh notes at one point in the diary; in May 1916, as Indian POWs were made to undertake the horrendous march across the desert, he plans 'for a couple of tennis courts at my garden' (14 May 1916). His diaries show how war experience was fundamentally split across class lines, sometimes even more than by race. The constant disquiet and sense of slight that haunt the diary cannot be located solely in the colonial racial ideology (though there are instances of racist discrimination, as when he is taunted for not taking beef, or his salute is not returned): Amar Singh's more specific problem is one of *not belonging*, of a sense of liminality, of constantly being made to feel redundant. He is soon transferred to India and spends the last two years of the war in Bombay, as A.D.C., again reading, or going to the theatre, or talking to arriving or departing troops. As the record of a member of a

[39] Singh, 'Notes about the Sick and Wounded That the Turks Gave Us after the Surrender of Kut-el-Amarah', 20 May 1916, 'Diaries'.
[40] Ellinwood, *Between Two Worlds*, 443.

privilege-encrusted minority, his diaries – though voluminous, accessible and historically invaluable – give a very particular view of the war, without much of the intimacy or power of Sarbadhikari, the pathos of Kanrei or the excitement of Karkaria. After reading Pepys's *Diary*, Singh notes that 'The only good I have got out of this book up to the present is a way as how to write a diary'; the statement can partly be applied to the experience, or rather peripheral visions, of the war of this lonely and deeply observant Rajput aristocrat, in France, Mesopotamia and Bombay.

The Call of 'Duty': The Bengali Babu as Postal Officer on Four Fronts

Honour is something that was at the top of the mind for our final memoirist – Kunal Sen – though, with him, it often comes down to his own personal advancement. *Through War, Rebellion & Riot 1914–1921: Being a Narrative of My Career in Egypt, the Dardanelles, the Balkans, Mesopotamia and in Iraq, under 'Shot and Shell', and Its Finale under the 'lathi' of Bombay Rioters*: the very fullness of the title of Kunal Sen's war memoir signals its difference, in sensibility, tone and experience, from any of the other memoirs discussed above. Opening with a photograph of himself, proud in his military uniform with two stripes and looking sideways at a distance, the memoir bristles with the sense of 'self' – its sense of entitlement, its authority, its stylisation – even more than in Amar Singh's diaries and so conspicuously absent in Karkaria. In contrast to Kanrei's traumatic sea-journey and Karkaria's passages in the third-class in ships, Kunal Sen's is a world where a first-class compartment is 'wangled' for him by his commanding officer-turned-friend, beer and sandwiches are called up to his cabin on the ship and he travels to the front because he 'burned to do my bit'.[41]

Born and brought up in 'Lily Cottage' in Calcutta, Kunal Sen epitomises, almost to a parodic level, Macaulay's dream-generation of Indians 'brown in colour but English in tastes, habits and preferences'. As a Postal Superintendent at the Postal Office in Shillong, Sen cannot resist the opportunity of going to the 'European War' or indeed penning a 'fine' paragraph about the process:

> I remember that week! After a rapid process of relinquishing charge, I left Shillong. Hurried preparations in Calcutta, adieu and firm grips at Howrah

---

[41] Kunal C. Sen, *Through War, Rebellion & Riot 1914–1921: Being a Narrative of My Career in Egypt, the Dardanelles, the Balkans, Mesopotamia and in Iraq, under 'Shot and Shell', and Its Finale under the 'lathi' of Bombay Rioters* (Calcutta: Art Press, n.d., according to Worldcat, between 1921 and 1939), 3.

to relations and 'pals', the best of them my brother 'Kabby' and my cousin 'Viccy', and I was *en route* to Bombay keen as mustard and with a heart filled with joy that this golden opportunity had come my way. Tears and fears, regrets and misgivings, I had absolutely none. It was the beginning of my *experimentum crucis*: all I heard, all I thought and all I felt was 'duty'! (2)

Both the sentiment and the vocabulary veer towards parody through excess and affectation; he is an almost extreme example of the highly Anglicised section within the Bengali middle-class bourgeoisie. The Bengali professional classes, largely the product of the colonial system and crucial to its administration but with a deeply ambivalent relationship to it, would also be at the forefront of the anti-colonial nationalist movement; as noted earlier, in the pre-War years, Bengal was rocked by the Swadeshi movement (1903–1908). Yet, certain sections of the Bengali bourgeoisie remained stubbornly 'anglicised', if not sycophantic of the Raj.[42] Important examples from this class would have included Indra Lal 'Laddie' Roy, the flying ace in the First World War, who famously 'forgot' his mother tongue after being sent to England. Yet Sen has a remarkable story to tell and he tells it with remarkable gusto: it is a deeply engaged and engaging, if sometimes irritating voice, informed by an observant eye and ear. As a postal officer, he is posted successively in Egypt, Gallipoli, the Balkans and Mesopotamia, along with the Indian Expeditionary Force. In each of these places, he is in charge of a number of Field Postal Offices: in Cape Helles, he opens an F.P.O. to serve the Indian Transport Corps, and introduces the system of money-orders for the Indian troops; in Monastir, he is involved in the opening and managing of a Field and a Base Postal Office (65); and in Mesopotamia he plays a central role in the setting up of the 'Iraq Posts' for the local populace as well as for the soldiers (108). He takes us deep into the logistics of the postal organisation to the 'most important' act of 'censoring uncensored letters from the front': 'The loves and tears, and hopes and fears, disclosed by the hundreds of letters I censored, must ever remain a sacred secret' (54).

Throughout his three years of service, Sen worked as a Postal Officer, yet what the memoir strains repeatedly to claim is combatant status: references to 'baptism of fire' (26), the 'theatre of war' and the prospect of 'mutilated death' are longingly dwelt upon, an elaboration of the 'shot and shell' in the memoir's title. This is a classic tendency within British war writing. British war memoirs by non-combatants, particularly stretcher-bearers,

---

[42] An extreme example would be the family of Aurobindo Ghosh: his Anglophile father had shipped him off to England so that the son would have nothing to do with India.

ambulance workers and nurses, often highlight moments of bodily risk and danger in anxious response to the dominant cultural discourse of 'combat gnosticism' as mentioned in Chapter 4 – an overriding belief that the 'real' war experience lay only in front-line combat experience.[43] Sen, at several points in the narrative, gives elaborate descriptions of being exposed to shelling in Achibaba; there is also a certain degree of self-dramatisation. As he comes under shelling in Cape Helles, he writes, with typical self-indulgence and congratulation, of how he found his 'grim, fearless and determined inner self': 'I trudged on, viewing without emotion a shattered corpse here and a disembowelled carcass there, listening without a tremor to the explosion of shells all around me and overhead' (28). One wonders whether such heroic self-fashioning was partly the result of being brought up on the stories of imperial adventure, combined with the anxiety of being a Bengali – a race constructed as 'effeminate', particularly in relation to the 'manly Englishman'.[44] His real moment of reckoning came, how-ever, on 10 June 1916 in Mesopotamia, when he and a fellow officer were caught in a vicious cross-fire on the banks of the Tigris, an episode narrated in a tone of 'derring-do' coming straight out of Kipling or Haggard. At the same time, there is a sort of grudging respect towards the Turks: Sen recounts a particular incident on Cape Helles when, in the face of heavy enfilade, the Turks stopped firing, seeing six casualties on stretchers being carried to a hospital ship. He observes that 'the bloodthirsty and ferocious Turk laying all Armenia waste showed he could be a sport!' (41). Later, in 1918, he reports that Mosul is 'teeming with refugees', mostly Armenians, fleeing from the Turks, but he does not show the concern or empathy one finds in Sarbadhikari.

Yet, Sen's account remains a valuable document, for it is a rare account of the Indian war experience in theatres such as Egypt, Gallipoli or the Balkans; it is also a curious antiquarian document with its unabashed orientalism and elitism, a record as much of a particular Bengali Anglophile mindset as of the people and places he records. Some of its most telling moments are not tales of danger but descriptions of places he visits – Port Twefik, Salonika,

[43] James Campbell, 'The Ideology of First World War Poetry', 203–215. Marginalised ethnic groups often registered the anxiety acutely; thus West Indian and Maori units, for example, were deeply distressed at being classed as 'non-combatant' on the Western Front, and felt it to be a slur both on their masculinity and on their race, especially when many of them had come under fire. See Richard Smith, *Jamaican Volunteers in the First World War*.

[44] See Mrinalini Sinha, *Colonial Masculinity: The 'Manly Englishman' and the 'Effeminate Bengali' in the Late Nineteenth Century* (Manchester: Manchester University Press, 1995).

Baghdad, Mosul – as potted histories of these places alternate with his personal impressions: the city of Suez is described as the haunt of 'Bohemian dissipation', where 'sirens wheedled the sale of cider under the pseudonym of "fizz"' (4); in Salonika, 'cobbled and filthy roads transmitted an uncouth welcome' (64); as he sails up the Tigris towards Baghdad, he encountered a 'half-naked, web-footed marsh Arab, who would emerge and walk along the bank with his wives, his children, his dog, his pony, pig and poultry' (95), even though, on reaching the city, he notes 'I went ashore, and was pleasantly surprised. There was culture and refinement among the people, and cleanliness in the houses.' (97). However, instead of any empathy for, or identification with, the local people through a shared history of colonial subjugation and destitution, there is a defensive sense of distance coupled with racism and an almost imperial superiority even though, growing up in colonial Calcutta, Sen would have witnessed at first hand 'filthy roads' or 'half-naked' poverty-stricken people. In comparison, the accounts of many of the British upper-class nurses are more interested in, or engage more deeply with, the lives of local people.

Such detached observation is, however, interrupted by two people for whom Sen displays a lot of affection, if not unmixed with a sort of colonial paternalism – the Arab pilot Abdullah who navigates his boat and his batman 'Chemba' who accompanies him on all four fronts. We first hear of Chemba running an 'illicit traffic' in his mail bag amidst the fire and flies of Gallipoli, selling 'Three Castles' for the price of 'Benson and Hedges' and sardine for the price of caviar, until Sen intervenes and 'it meant the end of an income for a hill wedding somewhere' (40). But his most flamboyant appearance happens in Salonika, where he tries to marry the daughter of a wealthy Jewish gentleman, pretending to be a much-decorated Gurkha officer. One of the most poignant stories, however, is his memory of 'a gigantic Australian coming down a neighbouring gully, arm in arm with a tiny Gurkha, whom he called "Bill", swapping jam with chapatti, singing "La Boheme" to him with a lovely tenor, and silently appreciating the response of a hill song about the purchase of a pair of velvet shoes in "Darjeeling kobazaroma"' (37). One may juxtapose such reminiscences with material artefacts such as the diary of Private Stinson, pointing to a world of encounters facilitated by imperial networks and yet taking place outside the empire (see Figure 0.9 in the Introduction).

Strikingly different from each other, and from the dominant sepoy narratives, all four accounts give the lie to any homogeneous definition of the Indian war experience. The accounts by Kanrei and Amar Singh seem to lie at the opposite ends not just of Indian or even non-white war experience, but of the very spectrum of First World War writing more generally. It is true that each of these accounts was, by the very dint of their respective genres, exceptional, but they remain testimonies to the capaciousness of the war. Travel, as much as war, seemed to have been constitutive of the self in each. Consequently, these writings occupy a strange space between life-writing, travel-writing and war-writing: one never knows where one ends and the other begins. Each puts pressure on the very label 'war diary' or 'war memoir', and indeed on our conceptualisation of colonial war experience. If the First World War is still often viewed as the military clash of empires, these accounts lead us not just to extend it from front-line combat to a wider definition of conflict but also to view it as a turning-point in the very history of cultural encounters – an idea to be spectacularly developed by Mulk Raj Anand in his war novel *Across the Black Waters* (1940).

PART IV

Literary and Intellectual Cultures

CHAPTER 8

Literary Imaginings
From Tagore and Naidu to Guleri, Nazrul and Nand Singh

'Literature fills in the gaps left by history' (Novalis)

I was introduced to the literature of the First World War as part of my English degree at Presidency College, Calcutta. Founded in 1817 to disseminate the fruits of Western learning, it haughtily regarded itself as the 'Oxford of the East' and claimed to have the oldest English department in the world. Every Thursday afternoon, during our second year, the grand colonial edifice with its high ceilings and sweeping balconies resounded with the notes of First World War verse. During my time at Presidency College, in the mid 1990s, First World War literature meant British trench poetry and spoke with an 'English' accent. I devoutly thumbed through my father's copy of Jon Silkin's *Penguin Book of First World War Poetry*; 'I am the enemy you killed, my friend', I still remember our professor saying, his voice choking with pity.[1] Our teenage hearts bled. Our distance had not dulled our sympathy for those doomed British youths; and the statues of the two English Tommies, who stood on either side of the cenotaph-like First World War Memorial in Calcutta, blended in my mind with the figures of Wilfred Owen and Siegfried Sassoon, whose poetry I could recite by heart. Literature, during my time at Presidency, started with *Beowulf* and ended with Virginia Woolf. And Indian literature of the First World War: did such a thing exist?

In the POW camp in Wünsdorf, on 9 December 1916, Sib Singh, a Sikh from Amritsar, noted that, 'When the war is over/Many *qissas* will be printed.'[2] Amar Singh even contemplated bringing 'charans' (hereditary poet-historians) from Jodhpur State; 'poetry', he noted, 'is the best form in which records ought to be kept' and, with the Indian troops fighting in Europe for the first time, 'we are missing the chance of immortalising our

---

[1] Wilfred Owen, 'Strange Meeting', *The War Poems*, 36.
[2] Sib Singh, 'Story' in Punjabi, recorded at the POW camp in Wünsdorf on 9 December 1916 at 5.15pm, Humboldt Sound Archives, PK 610.

305

deeds however poor they may be'.[3] In Parts I and III, I explored a variety of literary forms, from Punjabi recruitment verses and women's songs to letters and sound-recordings in the POW camps to the memoirs of combatants and non-combatants. Many of these forms draw upon the vernacular oral culture and put pressure on conventional definitions of 'war literature'; at the same time, one might ask, is there a more self-conscious body of war literature with a capital 'L' in the conventional sense from undivided India? Where is the Indian Wilfred Owen, the Pakistani Siegfried Sassoon, or the Bangladeshi Robert Graves? Such a question is, however, based on the reduction of the scope of war literature to a narrow and peculiarly English trajectory of war memory, as enshrined in Paul Fussell's otherwise brilliant work *The Great War and Modern Memory* (1975) and increasingly under attack as an exercise in 'combat gnosticism'.[4] In recent years, there has been a powerful expansion in the canon of British war literature to include civilian and women's war writing; as the Irish poet Michael Longley has suggested, 'if the cosmos of a poem is the Great War, then that's it. And it doesn't matter if it's a woman writing, or Edward Thomas writing in England.'[5] War memory and literature are necessarily even more diffused, oblique and angular in the colonial literary sphere, where it at once negotiates with indigenous traditions and accommodates other histories, local concerns.

The present chapter recovers and analyses war literature, in English and vernacular languages (Hindi, Bengali and Punjabi), produced in the Indian subcontinent during and immediately after the war. Rather than a periscopic survey of such literature, I here adopt the lens of the telescope, raising broader historical and cultural issues through a focus on a carefully selected body of literature. It supplements the range of textual forms we have considered so far, from the recruitment play *Bāngāli Palṭan* and Punjabi verses to various forms of life-writing, but this is a more self-consciously and recognisably 'literary' body of writing. Indeed, it whirls the 'cosmos' of First World War literature into fresh and uncharted territories. The writers considered here range from elite figures, both men and women, such as the Nobel Laureate Rabindranath Tagore, his elder sister Swarnakumari Devi and the poet-nationalist Sarojini Naidu to the talented Hindi scholar Chandradhar Sharma Guleri and the immensely popular Bengali poet Kazi Nazrul Islam, to the unknown 'poet and Havildar' Nand

---

[3] Quoted in DeWitt C. Ellinwood, *Between Two Worlds*, 396–397.
[4] Campbell, 'Combat Gnosticism', 203–215.
[5] Michael Longley, 'War Poetry: A Conversation', in Santanu Das (ed.), *The Cambridge Companion to the Poetry of the First World War* (Cambridge: Cambridge University Press, 2013), 260.

Singh; the writings accordingly range across lyric poetry, short story and epistolary novel, as well as the recently unearthed *Vaddā Jung Europe*, a 2,000-line-long piece of war verse. Mulk Raj Anand's war novel *Across the Black Waters* (1940) is discussed in the next chapter. While editing the *Cambridge Companion to the Poetry of the First World War* (2014), I had argued, with reference to British war poetry, that 'Neither the transparent envelope of experience nor just language whispering to itself about itself, First World War poetry represents one of those primal moments when poetic form bears most fully the weight of historical trauma.'[6] Working on South Asian literature, I realised how much such a formulation needs to be revised.

These works open up the home front in fresh ways, including its complex relationship to the war front. At an immediate level, they point to a remarkably engaged and diverse literary culture, to its multiple currents and traditions and the ways they respond to the war. At a deeper level, they provide insights into the emotional and political 'undertones' – the anxieties, aspirations, fears and fantasies – surrounding India's participation in the conflict and bear witness through the poetics of form to some of the ideological contradictions and complexities we considered in Chapter 1 and will return to in Chapter 10. By the turn of the century, many of the cities, from Calcutta and Bombay to Lahore and Amritsar, had a thriving middle class and a highly developed literary scene, with an explosion of print culture.[7] It is to this educated civilian milieu that many of the texts recovered here would have spoken, though some, like Guleri's short story, might have had points of contact with the actual sepoy-world. On the other hand, *Vaddā Jung Europe*, as we will see, is very different from the rest of the literary production considered here, with its solid roots in personal combat experience and in the rich oral culture of Punjab we examined in Chapter 2. Starting with the writings of Tagore, Devi and Naidu, either translated into or originally written in English during the war years, I examine a variety of texts written in vernacular languages, and conclude with *Vaddā Jung Europe*.

Rabindranath Tagore, Swarnakumari Devi and Sarojini Naidu

If war poems started pouring into newspaper offices in Britain the day it declared war on Germany, a number of elite Indians, including barristers,

[6] Das, 'Introduction', *The Cambridge Companion to the Poetry of the First World War*, 3.
[7] See Sanjay Joshi, *Fractured Modernity: Making of a Middle Class in Colonial North India*, 16–43; Abhijit Gupta and Swapan Chakravorty (eds), *Print Areas: Book History in India* (Delhi: Permanent Black, 2004).

civil servants and prominent citizens, similarly felt the need to match
the hour. Poems such as 'England's Cause Is Ours', 'Ode to an Indian
Army', 'India to England' and 'The War Songs for the Indians' started
appearing in the pages of a variety of journals in English. These poems
were, in many ways, the testimony to Lord Macaulay's dream-generation
of a class 'Indian in blood and colour, but English in tastes, in opinions,
in morals and in intellect'.[8] As early as 1914, a war journal entitled *Indian
Ink*, which included contributions from both British and Indian writers,
was founded in Calcutta; in 1915, the *Indian Review* published the compendious war volume *All about the War*, collecting various war-related
publications.[9]

The brightest star in the South Asian literary firmament was the Bengali
writer and Nobel Laureate Rabindranath Tagore. His earliest recorded
response to the conflict is a classic example of the orientalist-mystic lens
through which he was viewed. In the summer of 1914, he had suffered from
a 'mysterious and unbearable weight of mental oppression'.[10] On 21 May,
he wrote to his close friend, the English theologian C. F. Andrews, 'My feet
are bleeding and I am toiling with panting breath … God knows, it is the
death-pang that is tearing open my heart.'[11] A few days later, he composed
an eerily prescient poem titled 'Is It the Destroyer Who Comes?', which for
Andrew retrospectively became a sign of Tagore's 'highly sensitive nature
[that] had made him feel dimly beforehand the tragedy which was about
to happen'.[12] When Andrews asked him about 'the inner wireless', Tagore
had said, with seemingly messianic foreboding, 'It is not enough to call it
a war. This is a momentous meeting of epochs [yuga-sandhi samāgata].'[13]
A number of his 'war poems' appeared in the pro-war *Times*, the first being
'The Trumpet'. The cultural politics around its 'translation' is revealing.

---

[8] 'Macaulay's Minute on Indian Education' (2 February 1935), http://oldsite.english.ucsb.edu/faculty/
rraley/research/english/macaulay.html.
[9] *Indian Ink: Splashes from Various Pens* (Calcutta: Thacker, Spink & Co., 1914–1918); 'Poems on
the War', in Natesan (ed.), *All about the War*, 257–261. Also see Santanu Das, 'Sepoys, Sahibs and
Babus: India, the Great War and Two Colonial Journals', in *Publishing in the First World War: Essays
in Book History*, ed. Mary Hammond and Shafquat Towheed (London: Palgrave, 2007), 61–77.
[10] C. F. Andrews (ed.), *Letters to a Friend: Rabindranath Tagore's Letters to C. F. Andrews* (Delhi: Rupa,
2002), 18.
[11] Rabindranath Tagore, *The English Writings of Rabindranath Tagore*, ed. Sisir Kumar Das (Kolkata:
Sahitya Academy, 1996), Vol. 3, 234.
[12] See the original Bengali version of the poem ('Ebāar je ai elo sarvvaneśe go') in 'Balākā II', in
Rabindranath Tagore, *Rabindra Racanābalī* (Kolkata: Visva-Bharati, 1988), Vol. 16, 255; C. F.
Andrews (ed.), *Letters to a Friend*, 18–19. I am grateful to Uma Dasgupta for her kind help with the
letter.
[13] 'Balākā II, 255. My translation.

Published in 1914 and collected in 'War Poems from *The Times*', which included poems by Kipling and Thomas Hardy, it begins with its discovery of a 'trumpet' ('The trumpet lies in the dust') and gradually reaches a crescendo:

> Sleep is no more for me – my walk shall be through showers of arrows.
> Some shall run out of their houses and come to my side – some shall weep,
> Some in their beds shall toss and groan in dire dreams:
> For tonight thy trumpet shall be sounded.
>
> From thee I have asked peace only to find shame.
> Now I stand before thee – help me to don my armour!
> Let hard blows of trouble strike fire into my life
> Let my heart beat in pain, the drum of thy victory.
> My hands shall be utterly emptied to take up thy trumpet.[14]

Accompanied by an illustration of a Sikh sepoy leading a bayonet charge, it seems to neatly fit with the rhetoric of Indian 'loyalty'. As Simon Featherstone notes, 'the trumpets, drums and armour and exclamatory mode are of a kind with the verse of Henry Newbolt and William Watson'.[15] Yet, investigation of the textual history points to a different story. First, the Bengali original was written before the war on 26 May 1914.[16] In the original, Tagore does use a series of martial images ('raṇa-sajjā' – 'war decoration', 'jaya-ḍaṅkā' – 'the trumpet of victory') but they are used as *metaphors* to evoke a drama of spiritual conflict and purification ('hobo niṣkalaṅka'); moreover, they are interspersed with a parallel stream of images: 'pilgrims', 'temples', 'evening's offerings', 'garments washed white' or the 'lamp'. Interiority is what is lost in this translation: the sacred 'śaṅkha' ('conch-shell') is changed into the bellicose 'trumpet'; questions ('Who will fight today with the banners' ('Laḍbi ke āy dhwajā beye') are changed to exhortations ('Come fighters, carrying your flags'); touch ('sparśa') becomes 'strike' ('Strike my drowsy heart with the spell of youth'), while the blood-red hibiscus ('rakta-jabā'), associated with prayers, morphs into

---

[14] 'The Trumpet', in *The English Writings of Rabindranath Tagore: Poems*, Vol. I, ed. Sisir Kumar Das (New Delhi: Sahitya Akademi, 1994), 169. The poem appeared in a slightly different version in 'War Poems from *The Times*', *The Times*, 9 August 1915, 10. The poem was translated from the Bengali original by Tagore himself.

[15] Simon Featherstone, 'Colonial Poetry of the First World War', in Santanu Das (ed.), *The Cambridge Companion to the Poetry of the First World War* (Cambridge: Cambridge University Press, 2015), 180.

[16] The title of the poem is taken from the first line 'When I found thy trumpet lying in the dust' which is a faithful rendition of the Bengali original 'Tomār śaṅkha dhūlāy paḍe', to be found in Rabindranath Tagore, *Balākā* (Kolkata: Visva-Bharati, 1942), 8.

'poppies'. A spiritual herald becomes a battle-cry: a Hopkins-like dialogue with the Creator gets almost translated into a rallying-cry for Pax
Britannica. Has one of the empire's staunchest critics been co-opted into
imperial propaganda? Tagore's personal comments, in Bengali, to a friend
point in a different direction: he referred to the 'trumpet' as 'god's herald',
which has to announce the war 'with ill-will, with sin, with wrongness'
('akalyāṇer saṅge, pāper saṅge, anyāyer saṅge').[17] For him, the herald of
śaṅkha signified 'the first rays of the blood-stained dawn of a new age'
('nava-yuger rakta-varṇa aruṇoday') faintly visible in the east.[18]

His first 'war poem', composed on 22 August 1914 and published as
'Crossing' in *Indian Ink*, takes the motif of a lone boatman crossing the
'wild sea at night ... poisoned with black fear': 'The mast is aching because
of its full sails filled with the violent wind/Stung with the night's fang, the
sky falls upon the sea.'[19] In the poem, the boatman brings 'a white rose in
his hand and a song on his lips' to a mysterious woman who 'dwells in the
wayside hut' and waits alone, with her earthen lamp flickering and loose
hair flying in the wind; Tagore told Andrews that the woman in the poem
represented Belgium.[20] The horrors of the war and the plight of refugees
had not sunk in, or Bengali verse, like English lyric poetry in 1914, did not
yet have a vocabulary to absorb the horrors as the world's first industrial
war is turned into a romantic trope. Two years into the conflict, Tagore's
views would change radically, as he would be horrified by the reports of
violence, and he would emerge as one of the most powerful pacifist voices
in the world during his lectures in Japan and the United States in 1916, as
we will examine in Chapter 10. The change is reflected in 'The Oarsmen',
published in *The Times* in January 1916. There, he would return to the
imagery of the boatman in a dark night, but it is a richly metaphoric landscape: 'Do you hear the tumult of death afar,/The call midst the fire-floods
and poisonous clouds.'[21] The steersmen all wake up in fear as the Captain's
voice in the dark suddenly announces that 'the time in the harbour is over',
and the poem modulates into a process of acute soul-searching:

[17] See *Rabīndra Racanābalī*, Vol. 16, 256. In fact, in the earlier collection *Naibedya*, he had sharply
reacted to the jingoistic poetry coming out of the Anglo-Boer War.
[18] 'Balākā II', in *Rabīndra Racanābalī*, Vol. 16, 255. My translation.
[19] 'The Boatman', in *The English Writings of Rabindranath Tagore*, Vol. 1, 173. It was published in a
slightly different version and titled 'Crossing' in *Indian Ink* (1915). Both are versions of the Bengali
poem 'Matta sāgar dilo pāḍi' ('Voyaging across the Tumultuous Seas').
[20] 'The Boatman', 173; *Rabīndra Racanābalī*, Vol. 16, 256. Also see *The English Writings of Rabindranath
Tagore*, Vol. 3, Chapter II.
[21] 'The Oarsmen', *The English Writings of Rabindranath Tagore*, Vol. 1, 190.

All the black evils in the world have overflowed their banks,
Yet, oarsmen, take your places with the blessing of sorrow in your souls!
Whom do you blame, brothers? Bow your heads down!
The sin has been yours and ours.[22]

We will return to the poem in the final chapter and examine the 'sin' for which the war, for Tagore, was a symptom; his lectures on nationalism provide a rich context. It is worth noting briefly here that the war is evolved by the colonial intellectual into one of metaphysical anguish and civilisational critique; in the process, the experiential reality of actual sepoys making the journey exactly at this time across the 'kala pani' gets erased.

The Indian sepoys do not appear anywhere in Tagore's poems; interestingly, such silence is what drives the plot and emotions in 'Mutiny', a remarkable war story by none other than his elder sister Swarnakumari Devi. Devi's achievements get overshadowed by Tagore's. A gifted writer, musician and social worker, she is primarily known as the first woman novelist in Bengal.[23] Part reminiscence, part story, part critique, 'Mutiny' was written in Bengali and then translated, in all probability by Swarnakumari Devi herself, into English and published in 1919. The complex relation between imperial war service and national and racial honour that we discussed in Chapter 1 finds in this story one of its subtlest expressions. The story starts with the female narrator – an upper-class and educated Bengali woman – and her son at a dinner party thrown by an Englishwoman, Mrs A, who 'proudly declared that one French man is equal to five Germans, and one Englishman the equal of three Frenchmen'. At this, the Bengali narrator too feels a 'glow of pride', for are the 'English not most intimately related to us?' (228). The word 'pride' soon returns, but now joined to a sense of ignominy and indignation as she realises how the contribution of a million sepoys is being wholly deleted from this narrative: 'I, too, could have remarked with pride that our sepoys are in no degree inferior to the soldiers of other nations'. But she remains silent. The bruising realisation does, however, lead to reflections on the question of national 'pride', as the word now appears for the third time:

> Moreover, however proud we may feel at the bravery of our sepoys, can we call it a national pride? Alas! have we not lost the privilege of calling ourselves a nation? ... Even the simple rights which loyal citizens expect

[22] *Ibid.*
[23] Swarnakumari Devi, 'Mutiny', in *Short Stories* (Madras: The Cambridge Press, 1918), 226–239. See the brief but perceptive introduction to her in Margaret Higonnet (ed.), *Lines of Fire: Women Writers of World War I* (New York: Penguin, 1999), 383, where the story is also extracted. Also see Sisir Kumar Das, *Bāṅglā Chota-galpa* (Kolkata: Dey's, 1983), 57–60.

do not belong to us. We are not treated as equals, nor do we receive the affection that according to our own national ideas, rulers should show to their subjects. If one among so many millions of us shows a disloyal spirit, then we are all considered to be deserving of the gallows. (229)

India's war participation, meant to foster the imperial bond, has only served to highlight the racism and double standards at the heart of the empire – and more. Mrs A's casual comment leads the narrator to become aware not just of such hypocrisies but of the nexus between empire, class and race:

Never before had I been made to feel my racial inequality in my intercourse with English people. I had always been treated as one of themselves. But this deference and friendliness had been paid to me individually, as being due to my social position. To-day, these expressions of a woman belonging to a free nation, made me feel myself an utter stranger among English people. (231)

Stung and smarting, she now falls back on a burgeoning sense of reactionary cultural nationalism. As the conversation turns to the topic of 'sati',[24] Mrs B observes it to be 'a terrible custom'; instead of readily agreeing and condemning the practice, as is obviously expected from our enlightened narrator, she only rebuts with 'what terrible courage!', almost as a provocation. Such a response risks coming across almost as valorisation of the barbaric custom, though there could have been no doubt about Swarnakumari's own views. The plot changes gear as the conversation turns yet again – this time to the Sepoy Uprising of 1857. Mrs A now narrates in vivid and painstaking detail how one night, when her husband was away, she dreamt that she was caught up in a mutiny: she had heard some noise and picked up the words 'police', 'sepoy' and 'mutiny' and lay trembling in her bed, only to realise in the morning that it was her 'wild imagination' and the 'mutiny' was actually a squabble among the servants over a common love interest! The story ends abruptly with one of the dinner guests announcing that a cable had just arrived announcing that the first 'Indian soldiers have arrived in France and the French people have covered them with flowers'.

Disjointed and diffuse, the structure of the story is testimony to the ambivalence structuring the relationship between the British Raj and the liberal (Bengali) bourgeoisie. Wealthy, artistic and culturally confident,

---

[24] 'Sati' or 'suttee' refers to the custom of immolation of the widow on the husband's funeral pyre in some Hindu communities. Owing to the sustained campaigning by Christian missionaries and Brahmo religious reformers, particularly Raja Rammohum Roy, it was made illegal in the Bengal province in 1829. Swarnakumari's family, i.e. the Tagore clan, belonged to this enlightened Brahmo community; her father, Debendranath Tagore, was a prominent Brahmo preacher.

the Tagores were part of the emerging Bengali intelligentsia, that unique creation of the British Raj. It was a class that had opened its heart to Western liberalism and education, only to feel increasingly the humiliation and inequalities of colonial rule.[25] The narrator notes 'For it is the English who have made modern India, for which we are supremely grateful. But still the shoe pinches somewhere' (229). The pinch, as we have already explored, began to be keenly felt from the latter half of the nineteenth century onwards. While discussing the Bengali intellectual Bankim Chandra Chattopadhyay, Tanika Sarkar has observed how the middle classes were exposed to 'the most extreme and naked form of white racism' during the agitations around the Ilbert Bill of 1883.[26] The middle classes, she notes, were particularly troubled by two issues: first, in spite of having supported the Raj against the sepoys during the 1857 Uprising, they found themselves tarred by the same brush of disloyalty; second, they were worried about the reversal of the trends introduced by the liberal Lord Ripon, which in turn led to 'an intensification of both liberal and Hindu revivalist forms of anti-colonial critiques'.[27] The subtlety of the story lies in the way Swarnakumari Devi registers these various strands and embeds them in the minutiae of the everyday social self and intercourse. The war had paradoxically exposed the nexus between racism and class. It is debatable, though, whether Swarnakumari Devi intends to show up the dangers of cultural nationalism, or falls prey to it at a moment of angst.

Blurring the boundaries between reminiscence, report and the genre of the short story, 'Mutiny' shows how the war had forced to a moment of crisis the growing sense of alienation even among the liberal moderates and explores it through a succession of emotions: pride, sympathy, indignation, ignominy and a corrosive sense of loss of self. If one of the distinguishing features of the modernist short story is the sacrifice of plot for a 'blazing moment' of insight,[28] Swarnakumari Devi's plot-less narrative blazes with several such insights: the diagnosis of the relation between class and racist discrimination, the new-found sense of imagined community connecting the sepoy and the elite, and an acute realisation of the hierarchies and inequalities of empire. Joined onto such realisation is the satiric exposure

---

[25] Also see Tagore, 'Crisis in Civilisation', *The English Writings of Rabindranath Tagore*, Vol. 3, 723.
[26] Tanika Sarkar, 'Imagining *Hindurashtra*', in David Ludden (ed.), *Contesting the Nation: Religion, Community, and the Politics of Democracy in India* (Philadelphia: University of Pennsylvania, 1996), 168.
[27] *Ibid.*
[28] Gerri Kimber and Angela Smith (eds.), *The Poetry and Critical Writings of Katherine Mansfield* (Edinburgh: Edinburgh University Press, 2014), 550.

of imperial anxiety, bordering on panic, about the 'loyalty' of the native, going back to 1857, so that a casual altercation is mistaken by Mrs A for a mutiny. Swarnakumari Devi's title compacts the war and the 'mutiny', showing how memories of the Sepoy Uprising of 1857 haunted the British psyche and resurfaced during the war: was its eruption in the war-story generated by the journey of sepoys to the front, leaving India 'vulnerable', or was it that, post-1857, the sepoys were seen with mistrustful eyes, even though only a section of them had 'mutinied' half a century ago and thousands were, at the moment, giving up their lives for the empire? Or is there a suggestion of the war being an opportunity for the sepoys to 'redeem' themselves? No answers are given; part of the delicacy of the story lies in its exploration of the contradictions in the recesses of the psyche rather than having recourse to any overt polemic. The sepoys' service brings forth a surge of nationalist pride on the part of the narrator, set forth in the dedicatory poem 'To the Brave': 'Soldier and hero, O my Countryman!/In admiration of thee stands the world/And I, though little, become great in thee.'[29]

If the female narrator observed towards the conclusion of the story that 'It is believed after the war is over, India will receive her just demands', such aspirations were taken to their logical culmination by her fellow writer and educationalist Sarojini Naidu. A friend and admirer of the Tagores, and christened 'Bharat Kokila' ('Nightingale of India') by Mahatma Gandhi, Sarojini Naidu wrote in English and was at once a poet, politician and feminist. An alumna of King's College London and the future President of the Indian National Congress, she shot to fame with her collection *The Golden Threshold*, which was published in London in 1905.[30] During the war, she went back to India and, at the Madras Provincial conference in 1918, she made the following appeal:

> It is, in my opinion, imperative that India should give the flower of her manhood without making any condition whatsoever, since Indians were not a nation of shop-keepers and their religion was a religion of self-sacrifice … Let young Indians who are ready to die for India and to wipe from her brow the brand of slavery rush to join the standing army.[31]

---

[29] Devi, *Four Short Stories*, 1.
[30] The standard biographies are Tara Ali Baig, *Sarojini Naidu* (Delhi: Publication Division, Government of India, 1974) and Hasi Banerjee, *Sarojini Naidu: The Traditional Feminist* (Calcutta: K. P. Bagchi, 1998).
[31] Quoted in Bhargava, *India's Services in the War*, 208–209.

The smarting phrase 'nation of shopkeepers' reveals why this nationalist leader who declared that her aim was to 'hold together the divided edges of Mother India's cloak of patriotism' would support India's war service. Consider 'The Gift of India', written for the Report of the Hyderabad Ladies' War Relief Association, December 1915, and later collected in *The Broken Wing: Songs of Love, Death and Destiny 1915–1916*:

> Is there aught you need that my hands withhold,
> Rich gifts of raiment or grain or gold?
> Lo! I have flung to the East and West
> Priceless treasures torn from my breast,
> And yielded the sons of my stricken womb
> To the drum-beats of duty, the sabres of doom.
>
> Gathered like pearls in their alien graves,
> Silent they sleep by the Persian waves.
> Scattered like shells on Egyptian sands
> They lie with pale brows and brave, broken hands.
> They are strewn like blossoms mown down by chance
> On the blood-brown meadows of Flanders and France.
>
> Can ye measure the grief of the tears I weep
> Or compass the woe of the watch I keep?
> Or the pride that thrills thro' my heart's despair
> And the hope that comforts the anguish of prayer?
> And the far sad glorious vision I see
> Of the torn red banners of Victory?
>
> When the terror and tumult of hate shall cease
> And life be refashioned on anvils of peace,
> And your love shall offer memorial thanks
> To the comrades who fought in your dauntless ranks,
> And you honour the deeds of the deathless ones,
> Remember the blood of thy martyred sons![32]

A lush war lyric in a late Victorian vein becomes striking when produced by a nationalist Indian woman. What is remarkable is the way the

---

[32] Naidu, 'The Gift of India', in *The Broken Wing: Songs of Love, Death and Destiny 1915–1916* (London: William Heinemann, 1917), 5–6.

nationalist/feminist image of the abject Indian 'mother'[33] – a recurring trope in Naidu's poetry – is here exploited to legitimise and glorify India's 'gift' to the empire: a standard trope of anti-colonial resistance flows into and fuses with imperial support for the war with breathtaking fluency.

The poem remains a powerful example of how literature illuminates the contradictions of history: anglicisation and indigenousness, residual colonial loyalty and a burgeoning nationalist consciousness, martial ardour and female mourning are all fused and confused in the above poem. More than a tribute to India or the war, Naidu's poem is an ode to the complex and intimate processes of colonialism. The most articulate Indian woman-nationalist is here seen to be steeped by virtue of her class and education in the English patriotic and poetic tradition. While clichés such as 'drum-beats of duty, sabres of doom' and the 'torn red banners of Victory' are bel-licose and reminiscent of the school of poetry associated with Jessie Pope that Owen so famously ridiculed, the aestheticisation of the dead soldiers in the second stanza with its sensuous vocabulary – 'pale brows', 'broken hands', 'blossoms mown down by chance' with their murmur of labials and sibilance – links the poem with the verse of Wilfred Owen, looking back to Tennyson, Swinburne and Yeats. Yet, as Homi Bhabha notes, 'To be Anglicized is *emphatically* not to be English'.[34] Naidu at once inherits and interrogates the stock images and phrases of Victorian verse: the meadows of Flanders and France are for her blood-*brown* as she quietly throws a challenge to the very colour of war memory. The affective power of the war-bereaved mother in this poem is here rooted in the native trope of Mother India 'fettered' by the colonial yoke. Thus, while pro-war and seemingly derivative, it is at the same time slyly subversive: imperial war service becomes a route to its opposite, national autonomy. This is exactly the structure of the 'imperial–nationalist' conjunction we have been exam-ining in Chapter 1. Indeed, the final line of her poem recurs in a speech she made in 1916 to protest against the Arms Act of 1878, which made it almost impossible for Indians to carry arms to defend themselves: 'Have we not, the women of India, sent our sons and brothers to shed their blood on the battlefields of Flanders, France, Gallipoli and Mesopotamia, and when the hour comes, for thanks, shall we not say to them for whom they fought ... *remember the blood of martyred sons*, and remember the armies of

---

[33] The historian Tanika Sarkar notes that, 'For Bengalis, accustomed to the worship of a variety of female cults, emotional resonances connected with an enslaved mother figure tended to be particu-larly powerful' (*Hindu Wife, Hindu Nation*, 251).

[34] Homi K. Bhabha, 'Of Mimicry and Man: The Ambivalence of Colonial Discourse', in *The Location of Culture* (London: Routledge, 2002 [1994]), 85–92.

India and restore to India her lost manhood.'[35] In the poem, is she asking India to remember her sons martyred in the war, or is the empire called upon to remember India's 'gift': the maternal metaphor binds together empire, nation and the female poet. The English war panegyric, associated with empire and patriarchal glory, is ruptured through the inscription at its heart of a powerful nationalist consciousness as well as the plaintive notes of female mourning.

In the middle of another war, Virginia Woolf would famously observe that, 'As a woman, I have no country. As a woman I want no country. As a woman my country is the whole world.'[36] Ensconced at the imperial centre, Woolf, through brilliant ratiocination, could convert the marginalisation of women into a vision of international feminism, aligned to a pacifist stance. Swarnakumari Devi and Naidu were both staunch feminists, actively involved in the struggle for women's empowerment, but, battling with the history of colonial subjugation, they could not eschew nationalism, which to them was part of the anti-colonial struggle. As Amartya Sen has noted, nationalism has very different connotations in different political climates: if it resulted in the inter-European bloodshed, it also powered the Indian freedom struggle.[37] Yet, Tagore stood apart: he was both anti-colonial and anti-nationalist, para-doxically bringing him closer, than either Swarnakumari Devi or Naidu, to Woolf's position. While both Swarnakumari Devi and Naidu variously remembered and celebrated the sepoy, Tagore refused to write about the sepoy. This might have been part of his acute understanding of the sepoy's complicity in imperial violence; he remembered how, in Hong Kong, he had seen a Punjabi watchman kicking a Chinese labourer and pulling him by the braid of his hair, and he was filled with shame.[38]

History, Narrative and the Short Story: Guleri's 'Usne Kahā Thā'

In 1915, a thirty-two-year-old Indian scholar and linguist who had never set his foot outside India decided to write a short story about the First World War in Hindi, which catapulted him overnight to literary stardom. 'Usne Kahā Thā' (literally meaning 'She Said So', but more popularly translated

---

[35] Naidu, 'The Arms Act', in *Speeches and Writings* (Madras: G. A. Natesan, 1918), 102–103. My italics.
[36] Virginia Woolf, *Three Guineas* (Oxford: Oxford University Press, 2008 [1938]), 160.
[37] Amartya Sen, 'Is Nationalism a Boon or a Curse', in Bose and Manjapra (eds.), *Cosmopolitan Thought-Zones*, 23–37.
[38] Tan Chung, Dev, Amiya, Wang Bangwei and Wei Liming (eds.), *Tagore and China* (New Delhi: Sage, 2011), 79.

as 'The Troth' or 'At Her Bidding') is possibly the earliest and one of
the finest short stories in Hindi literature. A brilliant scholar of Hindi,
Sanskrit, Prakrit and Pali, Chadradhar Sharma Guleri taught Sanskrit
at Mayo College in Ajmer.[39] This elite institution would have been the
training ground for the Rajput princes, including Amar Singh, who were
the first to volunteer, but Guleri's imagination travels to the ordinary Sikh
sepoys. 'Usne Kahā Thā' is nothing short of a marvel, anticipating all the
classic features of European trench narratives: front-line experience, male
camaraderie, night attack, sacrifice. Francesca Orsini has noted that, in
the last years of the nineteenth century, Urdu and Hindi fiction consisted
mainly of *qissas* and *fasanas* of adventure and romance, as well as some
historical and detective novels.[40] At a time when Hindi literature was still
largely caught between the religious didacticism of poets such as Maithili
Sharan Gupt and the epic-romances of novelists such as Devaki Nandan
Khatri, with the first stirrings of social realism from writers such as Munshi
Premchand, Guleri mines into contemporary history and presents us with
a new genre in the language, pitch-perfect.[41]

The story begins with a wonderful narrative surplus, by plunging us
into the meandering, congested streets of Amritsar, with its madly rushing
tongas (two-wheeled vehicles) and colourful swearing: 'If a woman does not
get out of a [tonga] driver's way in spite of insistent warning his vocabulary takes on a different note – "Step aside, Precious One!", "Step Aside,
Lucky One!", "Step aside, don't your children love you?" '[42] Weaving their
way in and out of the traffic are a young boy and a young girl, both headed
for the local grocer's shop. They meet, they walk together, and as they
part, there comes the most memorable line of the story from the young
boy to the young girl: 'Are you engaged' (*Terī kudmāī ho gayī?*), which
would go on to become one of the most famous phrases in Hindi literature. The girl replies 'Dhut!', which, at one level, means 'No!' But, a sound

[39] See Jhabaramalla Sharma, *Guleri garima grantha: Jivana evam sahitya* (Kāśī: Nāgarīpracāriṇī Sabhā, 1984); Janaka Saha, *Hindi gadya ko Guleri ji ki dena* (Patna: Novelty, 2002).
[40] See Francesca Orsini's introduction to *The Oxford India Premchand* (New Delhi: Oxford University Press, 2004), xi–xix; also see Ram Prasad Mishr, *Outlines of Hindi Literature* (Delhi: S.S. Publishers, 1982), 105–110.
[41] The story has recently been turned into a work of dance-theatre by choreographer Gary Sheffield, under the auspices of Akademi, and was premiered in India and the UK as 'The Troth' (https://akademi.co.uk/project/the-troth-usne-kaha-tha). It has been a joy to be involved in the project as a creative consultant, and my understanding of the story has been substantially enriched by the whole group.
[42] Chandradhar Sharma Guleri, 'Usne Kahā Thā' ['At Her Bidding'], *Indian Literature*, XXVII, 102 (1984), 4, 41. Translated from the Hindi by Jai Ratan. Further references to the story are given in the text.

and a signifier forever in excess of a specific meaning, 'dhut' compacts a range of emotions: coyness, embarrassment, pique, rebuke, irritation, shy interest. The two meet again, the dialogue gets repeated, like a teasing game, until one day the girl abruptly announces 'Yes, I'm engaged' (42). Equally abruptly, the story shifts from Amritsar to the trenches in France. We also move some twenty years forward in time, and again meet the boy, now introduced to us as Jemadar Lehna Singh, serving in the war in France. We see him looking after the unwell Bodha Singh, a young sepoy and the son of the Subedar in his battalion. Meanwhile the platoon commander 'Leftun [Lieutenant] Saheb' appears suddenly and orders the Subedar to group together the sepoys for a sudden and unplanned trench-attack. As the Subedar prepares for the attack, Lehna Singh feels increasingly uncomfortable. As he strikes up a conversation with the 'Saheb' in Urdu, Lehna Singh's worst fears are confirmed: he realises that 'Leftun Saheb' is in fact a 'German Saheb' in the guise of an English officer. He overpowers the 'Saheb' but in the ensuing exchange of fire, he is wounded. Detective fiction meets combat narrative as a group of Germans attacks the trenches: the wounded Lehna Singh rallies his men, defends the trench and is hit again. But he hides his grievous injuries and insists that the sick Bodha Singh and his father, the Subedar (who is slightly wounded), are taken on the ambulance first and, to complete this classic plot of sacrifice, he dies. The story does not end here. Just before his death, the fevered mind of Lehna Singh travels to an earlier, hitherto unknown, moment in Amritsar. Before leaving for France, he had a chance encounter with the Subedar's wife (i.e. the mother of the young Bodha) – who he realised was none other than his childhood flame, the engaged girl in Amritsar with which the story began! In this meeting – conveyed through a wonderful use of flashback – the woman breaks down before her childhood sweetheart: 'You must guard the lives of both of them in the same manner. This is my entreaty' (54). Lehna Singh agrees. The plot springs open retrospectively as Guleri draws upon flashback as a narrative device to knit together a Punjabi village romance and the Great European war and align combat narrative with family drama; Lehna Singh dies to keep the promise as the title makes amply evident.

'Usne Kahā Thā' is the first short story to evoke the world of the trenches from the perspective of the Indian soldier. Consider the following mono-logue from Lehna Singh:

> Ram, Ram! Do you call it war? My bones have turned stiff by sitting in these damned trenches day and night. And it's freezing cold – ten times colder than in Ludhiana ... And one is knee-deep in slush all the time. The worst

of it, there's no enemy in sight. Only a gun booms every hour or so splitting one's eardrums and shaking the whole trench … If one's turban or elbow is visible above the trench, a bullet comes whistling through the air, ripping through one's turban. (42)

Both the vividness and the precision are astonishing; the numbness and sense of desolation in the trenches are in marked contrast to the bustle of Amritsar. As a Hindi scholar and school teacher, Guleri would have been likely to be called upon to read out some of the sepoy letters to the non-literate family members. In fact, Wazira Singh's claims in the story – 'The French woman's lawn is lush green and soft like velvet. She forces so much milk and fruits on us' – read like a line out of a sepoy letter: 'The apples have come into excellent flavours […] They are ripe. We wander in the orchards all day.'[43] Wazira Singh continues thus:

> Stop talking of death … Let it visit the Germans and the Turks, not us. Well, brothers, let's sing. Here I go –
>
> > O damsel dear,
> > So you're leaving Delhi for Peshwar,
> > Stop in the bazaar and buy cloves – the long ones.
> > And have a deal in pyajama cords.
> > We have a taste for pumpkins.
> > O fair one, what ripe pumpkins you dish out!
> > We must have more of pumpkin, so tasty it is!
>
> Who could believe that those bearded sober-looking Sikhs could sing such a bawdy song? The trench, from one end to the other, resounded with the song. (44–45)

In a situation where we have only the censored and translated extracts of the letters, the song in Hindi evokes the sepoy-world in all its raw, raucous humour. The seemingly improbable plot concerning the German spy may have its source in actual fact. On the night of 24 October 1914, high drama erupted in the Indian trenches when an unknown European was frogmarched before the Company Commander of Number 3 Company of the 47th Sikhs. In the story, Lehna Singh muses 'What had happened to his thick hair overnight. They looked so thin and close-cropped.' (47) In real-life, the 'spy' was actually a British officer of the 1/34th Sikh Pioneers, returning to the Brigade Headquarters; he had lost his way and, when pounced upon by four sepoys, he had lost his nerve.[44]

---

[43] Letter from Pathan sowar to Havildar, October 25 1915, *CIM*, IOR, L/MIL/5/828, Part 3 British Library.

[44] Corrigan, *Sepoys in the Trenches*, 66.

Guleri, however, develops the story in a different direction: instead of being just a fact-based historical pot-boiler, the story becomes an archive of some of the deepest anxieties and fantasies of the sepoy-heart. In the story, it is actually a German soldier in disguise who offers Lehna Singh a cigarette (showing his ignorance of Sikh cultural customs), speaks a 'bookish Urdu' and cries out 'Ankh, mein Got' as he is hit; Lehna Singh unmasks the German spy. The departure from the original story is crucial. As mentioned in Chapter 4, one of the most humiliating experiences for the Indian soldiers was their assumed 'inferiority'. Considered brave and courageous, they were nonetheless denied the qualities of leadership, strategy and decision-making. According to General James Willcocks, the Indian officer 'can never replace ... the natural instincts of the white man', while John Charteris, Chief of Intelligence for Lord Kitchener, noted that '[Indians] have quite rightly a high respect for the "white man" and the German is to them a "white" man ... Indian troops cannot fight without white officers whom they know'.[45] It is this racist colonial ideology which 'Usne Kahā Thā' responds to and systematically undermines. In the story, the 'English officer' is missing or killed, and Jemadar Lehna Singh is in charge – a situation in which real-life Indian non-commissioned officers often found themselves. More importantly, in spite of the initial confusion in the camp between the German spy and the British soldier (is this case of mistaken identities itself a dramatisation of British anxieties about the presumed inability of the Indian sepoys to differentiate between 'white men' belonging to different nationalities or indeed to distinguish the Allied cause from the German cause?), Lehna Singh unmasks the German spy. Like Ranjoor Singh in Mundy's *Hira Singh*, Lehna Singh is not just a 'loyal' and 'gallant' sepoy but is a *leader* who can think and plan and analyse. 'Usne Kahā Thā' thus becomes the fantasy of collective agency and strategic leadership on the part of the sepoys: what is denied in real-life is realised in fiction. And more. In this story published in June 1915, in the immediate aftermath of the Battle of Neuve Chapelle (March 1915) in which the Indian soldiers had played a major part and reports of which would no doubt have reached Guleri, he evolves a traumatic historical experience into a narrative of heroic sacrifice and religious self-fashioning around the figure of the Sikh sepoy:

> Just then seventy Germans, crying like hell, entered the trench. The Sikhs' guns stemmed the initial attack. Then came the second attack like an

---

[45] Brigadier-Gen John Charteris, *At G. H. Q.* (London: Cassel and Company, Ltd,1931), 66.

onrushing wave … Suddenly they heard a loud cry, 'Wahe Guru ka Khalsa!
Wahe Guru ki Fateh!' Then came a hail of bullets playing havoc with the
German backs. In a minute the Germans were caught in a cross-fire. While
Subedar Hazara Singh's jawans fired from behind, Lehna Singh and his men
made a bayonet charge from the front. More war cries, 'Victory to the Sikh
Guru.' It was the Sikh army in action. (50)

This is the literary counterpart of the picture of the 'gallant' Sikh in
the 'bayonet charge', and that too by an Indian writer: is Guleri, the
future Head of the Department of Oriental Learning at Benares Hindu
University, orientalising his own people or is it a comment on how Sikh
faith and imperial identity were made to feed into each other, erupting as
religious affect in the battlefields of France? Indeed, the above account can
be read alongside an extraordinary letter from a Sikh sepoy serving with
the Canadian Expeditionary Force:

> Shell and bullets were falling like rain and one's body trembled to see what
> was going on. But when the order came to advance and take the enemy's
> trench, it was wonderful how we all forgot the danger … we seized the
> trench and took the enemy prisoner. I did not think of our safety but felt
> that the Guru Maharaj was fighting in me. He is great and it is thanks to
> Him that I was able to do all I did.[46]

While here we have the eruption of individual religious zeal in the final
line, Guleri evolves it into a fantasy of collective action framed by cries
of 'Wahe Guru ka Khalsa': the similarities between the two are striking,
as both register the intensity of the faith and its galvanising role in the
battlefield. And it is nothing less than extraordinary when we remember
that Guleri was no war veteran but a scholar-writer imagining the moment
from India.

The politics of gender and sexuality in the story is equally remarkable.
If the young boy's question sets in heterosexual romance, its homosocial
counterpoint in the trenches is the relationship between Lehna and Bodha.
The sleeping Bodha, covered with Lehna Singh's blankets, suddenly breaks
into a groan:

> 'What's the matter, Bodha Bhai?'
> 'Give me some water.'
> Lehna Singh put a mug of water to his lips.

---

[46] Letter of 23 November 1916 from Private Waryam Singh, C Company, 9th Platoon, 38 Battalion,
Canadian Expedition Force, France to Wazir Singh, Kapurthala, Punjab, *CIM*, IOR, L/MIL/5/826/
9/1482, British Library.

'How are you feeling' Lena Singh asked. 'Any better?'
Putting down the mug, Bodha said, 'I've got a shiver. Tremors are
running down every fibre of my body. Oh, how my teeth chatter.'
'All right, Have my jersey.'
'And you?'
'Don't worry about me. I've got a charcoal burner. I feel like almost
breaking into a sweat.' (45)

Guleri's story opens up this rich, stirring space of same-sex intimacy but
also complicates it: is Lehna Singh working only to fulfil the 'promise'
made to his childhood sweetheart, i.e. Bodha's mother? Or is he acting
here as a surrogate mother himself, or perhaps as the potential father he
would have been if the childhood romance had come to fruition? Personal
history freights this scene of trench camaraderie. Different impulses are
fused and confused as we see failed heterosexual romance flower into
tenderness between men. The moment looks forward to a later moment
of touch and intimacy as Lehna Singh, drenched in blood, lies dying in
Wazira Singh's lap: 'Bhaiyya [brother], will you please raise me a little? And
place my head on your thigh' (54). That classic closing moment in R. C.
Sherriff's *Journey's End* (1929) – as the young Raleigh lies dying in the arms
of Stanhope – seems to have been rehearsed in the very first year of the war
in this unknown Hindi short story of an Indian university teacher who had
never been abroad.

At the same time, the story equally looks beyond the trenches. Is 'Usne
Kahā Thā' pro-war or anti-war, an imperial adventure or a nationalist allegory? The story neither affirms nor dissents. Its tremendous sophistication
and subtlety lie in the way it moves beyond these categories towards the
fulfilment of the promise: Lehna Singh's commitment is neither to the
country nor to the empire, not even to childhood romance, but to accede,
at the cost of his own life, to the desperate entreaty of a mother that he
safeguard her only son. The story does not sentimentalise or trivialise
childhood memory, but grafts it onto the figure of the anxious mother.[47]
Indeed, her centrality is extraordinary at a time when the woman figure
was marginalised even in European war literature. Lehna Singh dies not
for gallantry or honour on the battlefield but to preserve the sanctity of
the 'promise'; in the process, the very ideas of 'sacrifice' and 'honour' are
reclaimed and redefined, from the domain of war to the intimate realm of
personal relations.

---

[47] This aspect came out strongly during the rehearsals for 'The Troth' at Akademi.

'Soldier-Rebel-Poet' Kazi Nazrul Islam: War, Revolution and the Aesthetics of Violence

In the history of Indian literature, Kazi Nazrul Islam (1899–1976) enjoys the unique label of 'soldier-poet' – a title usually reserved for the British trench-poets of the First World War. In India, he was the only literary figure to undergo military training for the First World War; however, contrary to local myth, he never went to Mesopotamia or experienced actual warfare; one is not even sure whether he ever learnt to use firearms.[48] Yet, his three years in the military barracks, first in Nowshera and then in Karachi, were fundamental to his self-fashioning as the 'sainik' (soldier)-turned-'vidrohī' (rebel) poet of Bengal in the interwar years; the label 'havildar' was dearer than the epithet 'poet' to him in the post-war years. The army life was also vital to his revolutionising of the very nature of Bengali poetry, infusing it with martial imagery and rhythms as well as with Persian and Arabic words and tunes he had picked up in the cantonment. These words would brush against colloquial Bengali in his poetry, as do Hindu and Islamic myths and metaphors – appositely for a poet who tirelessly championed Hindu–Muslim unity.[49] For Nazrul, the war was not so much an imperial crisis or even a singular historical event: it was an intensely subjective and overwritten space, incandescent with 'terrible beauty'.[50] Its images, music and destructive energies would be mined to form his aesthetic of revolutionary violence. The breathtaking fluency of his transition from an imperial soldier-writer to a nationalist rebel-poet and song-writer in the post-war years takes us back to the complex relation between loyalism and nationalism examined in Chapter 1, which finds in his writing one of its strangest expressions.

Nazrul is one of the most exciting, flamboyant and lovable personalities in the history of South Asian literature.[51] Now ensconced as the national

---

[48] See Rafiqul Islam, *Nazrul-Jīvanī* (Dhaka: Dhaka University, 1972), 44–45 and Priti Kumar Mitra, *The Dissent of Nazrul Islam: Poetry and History* (Delhi: Oxford University Press, 2009), 29–33. Also see Ghulam Murshid's important article, 'Kavir Unmeṣ', *Pratham Ālo* (Dhaka), June 2017, 329–356. I am grateful to Abhishek Sarkar for this reference, as indeed I am to him for reading the section on Nazrul at very short notice, during the copyediting stage, and making a series of acute comments. See his excellent forthcoming piece 'Affective Self-Fashioning and the Bengali Imaginary: The Great War In Kazi Nazrul Islam's Life and Fiction', which I came to know about only when this book was already in production.

[49] See 'Kazi Nazrul Islam', in Kalpana Bardhan (ed.), *The Oxford India Anthology of Bengali Literature, Vol. I, 1861–1941* (Delhi: Oxford University Press, 2010), 49.

[50] 'Easter 1916', in W. B. Yeats, *Selected Poetry* (London: Macmillan, 1974), 93.

[51] Important biographies include Rafiqul Islam, *Nazrul-Jīvanī* and Arun Kumar Mitra, *Nazrul Jīvanī* (Kolkata: West Bengal Academy, 1990); and Mitra, *The Dissent of Nazrul Islam*. Several powerful

poet of Bangladesh and the rebel poet of West Bengal, he burst into the literary scene in Bengal with the force and suddenness of a 'Dhūmketu' or 'Comet', which was the name of his literary journal.[52] Tagore referred to him as 'uddām' ('irrepressible'), referring to his music as 'the sound of swords' uniting in 'jhaṅkār' ('resonance').[53] Tempestuous, dissident and startlingly original, he entranced readers in the interwar years with his vision of political revolution and lyric exuberance, set forth in appropriately named poetry collections such as *Agnivīṇā* (*The Fiery Lyre*), *Viṣer Bānśi* (*The Poison Flute*) and *Pralay Śikhā* (*Flames of Destruction*). Poems, songs, novels, short stories, essays, literary criticism, political tracts flowed from his pen. He was involved with a number of influential publications, including the anti-communal evening daily *Nabayug* (*New Age*) (1920), which he edited with his Marxist comrade Muzaffar Ahmad, the anti-colonial *Dhūmketu* (*Comet*) (1922), which became the organ for the Bengal revolutionaries, and the socialist *Lāṅgal* (*The Plough*), a mouthpiece for the peasants. He toured the country, mingled freely with people, flirted with politics, and gave fiery speeches; he composed several thousand songs, sang them at political meetings, and introduced the Persian *ghazal* to Bengal. Between 1920 and 1940, he was the enfant terrible of Bengali literati: a poem published in *Dhūmketu* led to his arrest in November 1922, which only increased his popularity.

He did not come from an elite background, unlike most Indian writers of the time. On the contrary, Nazrul – the sixth son of a poor Muslim couple – was nicknamed 'Dukhu Mian' ('Mr Miserable') and grew up amidst the creative milieu of the rural underclass. At school, through his favourite teacher Nibaran Chandra Ghatak, he came to know about the 'Yugāntar' ('New Age') group of Bengal revolutionaries and their philosophy of liberation through armed rebellion.[54] It thus might seem curious that Nazrul would decide to join the British Indian army for imperial war service rather than the ranks of the Bengali anti-colonial nationalists. However, as I have argued in Chapter 1 with reference to *Bāṅgāli Palṭon*, the lines between imperial war service and the nationalist cause were

memoirs have been written about him: in particular, see Shailajananda Mukhopadhyay, *Keu Bhole Nā Keu Bhole* (Kolkata: New Age Publishers, 1960); Muzaffar Ahmad, *Kāzi Nazrul Prasaṅge* (*Smritikathā*) (Kolkata: Twentieth-Century Publishing, 1959); and Pranatosh Chattopadhyay, *Kāzi Nazrul* (Kolkata: A. Mukherji & Co., 1977). Also see Sugata Bose's brief but perceptive discussion of Nazrul in *A Hundred Horizons*, 130–133 and, more recently, Ghulam Murshid, 'Kavir Unmeṣ'.
[52] Mitra, *The Dissent of Nazrul Islam*, 55.
[53] 'Kazi Nazrul Islam', *The Oxford India Anthology*, 49.
[54] See Pranatosh Chattopadhyay, *Kāzi Nazrul*, 27–30; Mitra, *The Dissent of Nazrul Islam*, 27.

porous; Nazrul's close associate Muzaffar Ahmad remembered the tremendous enthusiasm around the '49th Bengalis', noting how war service was viewed as a 'badge of patriotism', bringing honour and glory to the Bengalis.[55] Nazrul's decision cannot be attributed with any certainty to a political cause, whether one of 'loyalism' or some anti-colonial plot; in fact, it is highly doubtful whether the eighteen-year-old adolescent was politically all that conscious when he joined the army.[56] It was a combination of his innate restlessness, a sense of adventure, the promise of a career and a certain lure of heroic masculinity, rather than any formulated political stance, that made him enlist. Thus, in 1917, the young Nazrul joined the '49th Bengalis', expanded from the smaller 'Bengali Double Company' started in 1916.[57] This itself, as we have noted before, was a singular regiment, not merely comprising 'non-martial' Bengalis but made solely of 'citizen-soldiers'.[58] He first underwent training in Nowshera camp for three months; he was then stationed in the army barracks in Karachi for the next three years, until the 49th Bengalis was disbanded in 1920. He quickly rose through the ranks, working successively as a Lance Naik, Havildar and finally battalion Quarter-Master Havildar.[59] As his biographer Priti Kumar Mitra notes, 'during the period of his service in the army his mind transcended not only Bengal but India itself, and embraced the Muslim Middle East as well as revolutionary Russia'.[60] Here, Nazrul started reading Persian and Arabic literature with the help of a Punjabi *moulvi*, discovered the poetry of Hafez, started singing ghazals and playing various musical instruments belonging to a resident military band. The influence of the war years can be detected not only in a few explicit 'war' writings, but in a more general sense, from his greater confidence to his self-fashioning as a 'sainik' (soldier) to infusing Bengali poetry with martial images and rhythms it had not known before.

[55] Ahmad, *Kāzi Nazrul Prasaṅge*, 10.
[56] Murshid makes this point convincingly in 'Kavir Unmeṣ', 347–348. His friend Shailajananda Mukhopadhyay has attributed it to unrequited love, though again this cannot be ascertained. There is a celebrated story of Nazrul apparently carrying the hair-pin of his beloved throughout his military life, though her identity would never be disclosed.
[57] The 49th Bengali Regiment, as mentioned in Chapter 1, was a unit of 'citizen-soldiers' and the raising of the regiment generated tremendous excitement in Bengal. They were sent to Karachi for training, and some of them were sent to Mesopotamia in August 1917. They were employed at the Tamminah Royal Air Force base and did not see action. See note 131 in Chapter 1, 68.
[58] Among the other *bhadralok* soldiers were Kumar Adhikram Mazumdar, a lawyer, Khaza Habibullah, a nawab of Dhaka, and businessman Ranoda Prosad Saha. See Sujon Dutta, 'The Bhadralok Goes to War', *The Telegraph*, 1 January 2014. A memorial to the 49th Bengalis can be found in College Square, Kolkata.
[59] Rafiqul Islam, *Nazrul-Jivanī*, 44.
[60] Mitra, *The Dissent of Nazrul Islam*, 35.

Nazrul's war writings work at two levels. At a simple level, they provide insights into the tremendous excitement caused by the creation of the '49th Bengalis' in Calcutta. In his memoir, Muzaffar Ahmad remembers a big leaving party organised for the recruits in Calcutta Town Hall; Nazrul notes that they were greeted 'as if they had come from Mars'.[61] In his short story 'Rikter Vedan' ('The Pain of the Destitute') (1924), he mentions the 'enormous crowd' ('vipul janatā') and frenzied scenes of leave-taking at the Howrah Station and evokes the feelings of the sepoys as they leave for battle: 'For the good of their motherland, with what immense, limitless enthusiasm ['agādh-asīm utsāha'] do these Bengali boys race to give themselves up in the fire of some dim and distant land – oh my brothers! What smouldering fire and energy are caged in these dull khaki uniforms!'[62] In *Bāndhan-Hārā* (*The Unfettered*) (1927), an epistolary novel structured as a series of letters from Havildar 'Nurul Huda' stationed in the North West Frontier Province to family and friends, he evokes life in the barracks – the bugle calls, parades, marches and bayonet-training. As clouds mass over the hills of the North West Frontier Province, the homesick Bengali sepoys sing Tagore songs; soon, raucous folk tunes follow, and more sepoys join in, drumming tables, books and bedsteads until it evolves into a full-scale party. Nazrul writes that 'It was like the student days again. There was always a wholesome irrepressible pulse of joy dancing in the air. It was heart-rending to see such carefree laughter among men who were going to die tomorrow.'[63]

At a more complex level, the war opened up for the tempestuous youth and avant-garde artist a rich imaginative space, replete at once with desire and violence, with violence *as* desire. In *Bāndhan-Hārā*, the author's alterego Nurul Huda explains his decision to enlist in a letter:

> The orders for our mobilisation have come. Therefore there's hustle and bustle all around the camp. Very soon we will have to cross the Arabian Sea and jump into the fire of Mesopotamia, I cannot control my sense of joy. I wanted fire – only fire – fire raging across the air and the sky, within and without, and amidst it all I shall stand with the world-engulfing fire raging in my heart and see how fire meets fire. I also wanted blood. I wish I could wring the necks of all the people in the world and suck all their blood – that would

---

[61] 'Rikter Vedan', in *Nazrul racanā samagra* (Calcutta: West Bengal Bangla Academy, 2005), Vol. 1, 320. All prose translations, including those of 'Henā', 'Rikter Vedan', 'Vyathār Dān' and *Bāndhan-Hārā* are mine.

[62] *Ibid.*, 317.

[63] *Bāndhan-Hārā* ('The Unfettered') in *Nazrul racanā samagra* [*Collected Works of Nazrul*] (Calcutta: West Bengal Academy, 2001), Vol. 2, 277 (269–370).

quench my thirst. Why do I have such hostility towards my fellow beings?
Have they done me any harm? I can't answer that. They are not my enemies
and yet I have an intense desire to drink their blood. The most curious fact
is that the tiniest suffering of these men is enough to turn my heart into
a wasteland like the Sahara, wailing uncontrollably. These two contrary
impulses of the human heart [the will to destruction, and the sympathy] –
where is their source, no one knows. This restlessness, this unwarranted
burning of my heart across the ages [*anek anadhikārī āmār e jvālā*] –
Bhabhishahiba, you don't understand, you won't understand … I feel drunk
and some long-drawn wail of eternal anguish chokes my throat like poison –
I cannot write any more.[64]

One of the strangest passages in the pantheon of war writing, what we
have here is the evolution of the war into a fantasy and a celebration of
destructive violence. The excess is quintessentially Nazrulite. Underlying
the image of the desire for blood (*'raktapāne ākul ākāṅkṣā'*) and the wish
to 'suck all their blood' (*'cho cho kore tāder samasta rakta śuṣe ni'*) is the
figure of the goddess Kali, the naked warrior-goddess, who defeats the
asuras (demons), drinks their blood and goes on a spree of frenzied violence. In the early twentieth century, the cult of Kali, particularly her
Tantric image as 'Chinnamastā', was powerfully appropriated by the
Hindu revolutionary nationalists in Bengal.[65] The above passage, published
in 1924, soon after his release from prison in 1923, was part of Nazrul's
self-fashioning as the arch-poet of revolution and chimes closely with his
1922 poems such as 'Vidrohī' ('The Rebel') and 'Bhāṅgār Gān' ('Song of
Destruction'). What is extraordinary, though, is the way First World War
service is appropriated and refashioned as a paean to revolutionary violence. In fact, in his imagination, the war gets joined to other conflicts of
the time, including the October Revolution, the Third Afghan War and the
Turkish War of Independence, as well as the Indian anti-colonial struggle;
they form one continuous sheet of violence which gets rewritten as the
rebellion of the people against despotic authority.[66] Interestingly today, a

[64] *Bāndhan-Hārā*, 314.
[65] Hugh Urban, '"India's Darkest Heart": Kali in the Colonial Imagination', in Rachel Fell
McDermott and Jeffrey J. Kripal (eds.), *Encountering Kali: In the Margins, at the Centre, in the West*
(Berkeley: University of California Press, 2003), 187.
[66] In *The Dissent of Nazrul Islam*, Mitra acutely notes that Nazrul's periodical *Dhumketu* represented
no particular ideology or political party but the 'very spirit of rebellion itself'. Mitra connects
the revolutionary movements, such as Bolshevism and Turkish nationalism, and how they are
refashioned in the periodical 'in a unique attempt to derive inspiration for a revolutionary struggle
for freedom of India'. (56). The most startling and seemingly incongruous ingredient in this heady
mix, I would argue, is the First World War and Nazrul's own involvement in it, which provide
him with an overarching imaginary and vocabulary. One may also include among Nazrul's war

hundred years later, historians in works such as *Empires at War: 1911–1923* (2015) are redefining the time-frame of the war in similar terms, looking beyond 1914–1918.

In addition to *Bāndhan-Hārā* (first serialised in 1920–1921 and published as a book in 1927), Nazrul wrote a number of stories dealing with the war – 'Baouṇḍeler ātmakāhini' ('The Autobiography of a Vagabond', 1919), 'Henā' (1919), Vyathār Dān' ('The Gift of Pain') (1919), 'Ghumer Ghore' ('In a Drowsy Spell', 1919), and 'Rikter Vedan' ('The Pain of the Destitute', 1924). Most of the above works were written when he was stationed in the Karachi cantonment while his mind followed the journey of the sepoys around the world. Set variously in France, Africa, Mesopotamia and Central Asia, they are some of the most bizarre imaginings of the war, often shot through with the pain of failed romantic love, which probably had its origins in his personal circumstances. Published in a series of Bengali periodicals (to which Nazrul would post his stories from Karachi), they are, however, startlingly different from Bengali stories of the time – whether those of Prabhat Kumar Mukhopadhyay, the main practitioner of the genre during the war years, or the young Premendra Mitra.[67] Realism and romance, awareness of the cost of violence and yet a 'demonic joy' in imagining it, nationalist sacrifice and erotic thrill are yoked together in ways that threaten the coherence of the narrative. Consider the description of the trenches of Verdun in 'Henā': 'The sky and the earth [*'āsmān-jamin'*] are glowing red with the constant fire of bombardment! But redder still is the blood gushing out of the bayonet wounds of those poor boys! Redder than red! Only red, and still more red! [*'śudhu lāl ār lāl'*]. Every time a sepoy gets martyred, he turns red like a newly-wedded bridegroom' [*biyer naośā*].'[68] We seem to have an eruption of Oscar Wilde in the world of Wilfred Owen. Overwritten, messy and excessive, the very form of the stories bears testimony to ideological fractures and literary crosscurrents as the world of mythic romance mined out of *qissas* and *fasanas* is transposed onto contemporary violence. 'Henā' is divided into nine vignettes, each set in a different place, from Verdun and the Hindenburg Line to Peshawar and Kabul. The story dwells on the hallucinatory consciousness of Sohrab, an Afghan sepoy, serving in Verdun. His unrequited love for Henā in Peshawar is contrasted with his rejection of the feelings of a French girl;

---

narratives his short novella *Ghumer Ghore* (*In a Drowsy Spell*) set in an army camp in Africa, with a central romance plot. See *Ghumer Ghore* by Kazi Nazrul Islam, https://bdebooks.com/books/ghumer-ghore-by-kazi-nazrul-islam.

[67] See Sisir Kumar Das, *Bāṅglā Chota-galpa*, 150.

[68] 'Henā', *Nazrul racanā samagra*, Vol. 1, 262.

only when Sohrab returns home after the war and decides to join the Emir's army against the British in the third Anglo-Afghan war does Hena accept him: 'Even if as an Afghan I had spent my life abroad, to come back and sacrifice my life for my own country, this is what she wanted.'[69] The story ends with Sohrab and Hena joining the forces of the Emir, getting wounded and dying together: what had begun as an imperial war story reaches its operatic crescendo as a nationalist romance.

'Rikter Vedan', on the other hand, is set in Mesopotamia – Karbala, Aziziya, Kut-al-Amara. But such geographical specificity is swamped by heavy-handed orientalism: religious ecstasy is coupled with Arab romance, as the sepoy-figure is followed by a young, burkha-clad, ghazal-singing, rifle-wielding Bedouin girl named Gul belonging to the enemy side. During a direct confrontation, the girl refuses to shoot him but, after an agonising moment of dilemma, the protagonist orders his fellow sepoys to shoot her: 'A cry of pain came across – Amma! Ma! Ah!'[70] Out of the dark night, the 'Amma' – the disconsolate mother of the dead girl – suddenly appears and fills the landscape with her lament; she forgives the sepoy, kisses him on the forehead and addresses him as 'farzand' – the Arabic word for 'my dear son'.[71] The two embrace amidst a reciprocity of tears. In metaphoric terms, is the final encounter with the bereaved mother and her forgiveness an effort on the part of Nazrul, a Muslim subject, to soothe his own conscience about the Indian sepoys' role in the war in the Middle East? Is Gul then the object of love the Indian Muslim sepoys end up killing as they invade their religious birthplace and fight against their religious brethren?

His deeply conflicted feelings about the Indian occupation in Mesopotamia find powerful expression in his poem 'Śāt-il-Ārab': 'Śāt-il-Arab! Śāt-il-Arab! Throughout the ages your banks have been holy!' It was published in May 1920 in the magazine *Muslim Bhārat*, whose frontispiece carried a picture of the place. Shatt-il-Arab is the point where the Tigris and Euphrates meet and flow into the Persian Gulf; it was also the site of the landing of the 6th Poona Divisions on 6 November 1914, from where they went on to capture the city of Basra.[72] But Nazrul's poem is not a paean of victory but one of passionate lament and empathy. His sense

[69] 'Henā', 271.
[70] 'Rikter Vedan', *Nazrul racanā samagra*, Vol. I, 328 (317–377).
[71] *Ibid.*, 329.
[72] Fawaz, *A Land of Aching Hearts*, 63.

of identification is conveyed linguistically in his use of a highly Urdu-inflected Bengali as he commemorates the 'enemy' dead:

> Śahīder lohu, dilirer khun dheleche jekhāne ārab-vīr
> Yujheche ekhāne turki-senānī , yunānī, misri, ārbi, kenani
> Luteche ekhāne mukta āzād, bedouinder cāṅgā śir
> Nāṅgā śir-
> Śamśer hāte, ānsu-ānkhe hethā mūrti dekhechi vīr-nārīr[73]

> The blood of fearless martyrs streams freely from the brave Arabs,
> Here have fought the Turkish soldiers, Egyptians, Greeks, Arabs,
>   Canaanites[74]
> Rolled here the proud heads of the Bedouins, fiercely free,
> the naked heads,
> Brave women have I seen here, swords in their hands and tears in their
>   eyes.[75]

It is indeed in such lines, with Arabic and Persian words brushing against Sanskritized Bengali, that we hear what Tagore called the jhaṅkār ('resonance') of Nazrul's verse. More than many poets, Nazrul bears out the dictum that poetry is what is lost in translation: in his verse, sound *is* sense. The accretive intensity of repetition with variation – 'śahīder lohu, dilirer khun' ('the blood of martyrs, the blood of courage') or 'mukta āzād' (both words mean 'liberation', the first in Sanskrit, the second in Urdu), the use of Arabic words such as 'lohu' and 'khun' and later the Sanskritic 'rakta' for 'blood', the internal rhymes connecting the races even as they fight (senānī/yunānī/kenāni), the visceral imagery of 'luṭeche ekhane … nāṅgā śir' ('rolls … naked heads') and above all the heavily stressed consonantal rhythm all create an extraordinary music that Bengali poetry had never known before. His diction is an immensely powerful testimony to the syncretism of the Bengali language of the time, as compared with our current sanitised and depleted vocabulary. If the names of the various participants – Turks, Greeks, Arabs, Canaanites – all united in death show the macabre cosmopolitanism of the war, Nazrul's own linguistic cosmopolitanism hints at the deep history of cultural contact and intimacy between Arabs, Persians and Indians which the sepoys have violated through their invasion. If in Shakespeare's *Macbeth* the protagonist's crime had turned 'the

---

[73] 'Śāt-il-Ārab', in *Nazrul racanā samagra* [*Collected Works of Nazrul*] (Calcutta: West Bengal Academy, 2001), Vol. 1, 36 (36-37).

[74] The 'Canaanites' ('kenani') roughly correspond to the Israelites who lived in parts of Canaan.

[75] This is an approximate translation by Diya Gupta and myself of a stanza we found rather difficult to translate.

multitudinous seas incarnadine/Making the green one red', for Nazrul, the
First World War had turned the Middle East into a similar blood-bath:

> The surging waters of the roaring Tigris
> Are now filled with the blood shed at Amara;
> The disgorged blood dances in you, Tigris, in a terrible drunkenness
> The restless waters of the bloodied river, the Euphrates, roar
> 'I have punished the insolent!'
> The Tigris–Euphrates-bearing river Śāt-il
>
> Throughout the ages your banks have been holy.

The holy shrines of Shatt are now for him forever defiled, with the blood
of Muslims shed by other Muslims; indeed, the war for many Muslims
would have been nothing less than fratricide. The terrifying image of 'rakta
Gaṅgā' (literally 'blood-Ganges') leaps out of the page, blurring religious
and geographical borders. For him, the waves are fiercely alive, glistening
with blood and twisting with anger, as if it had 'drunk' the 'blue blood' of
the men. The imagery indicates the tremendous ideological and emotional
conflict felt by this Muslim poet at the imperial aggression on Islamic
lands, a sentiment which can no longer be repressed:

> The battalions of Iraq! This really is some story.
> Who would have known here one day the Bengali forces
> Would cry 'Mother mine!', burning with tears at your sorrow,
> Blood–congealed-milk! – O subjugated one,
> Inflicted with the same pain, the faithful brave shed tears,
> Land of martyrs! Farewell! Farewell!
> This wretch today bows his head to you.[76]

A poem on imperial conquest becomes an elegy for the subjugated
motherland: the Turks and Arabs are hailed as 'martyrs' ('śahīd') and
'āzād' ('liberators'), fighting for freedom, while the invading army is cast
as 'pindaries' or 'mercenaries'. The lines of identification are clear. The
empathy that men such as Kalyan Mukherji and Sisir Prasad Sarbadhikari
felt with the local people and the resulting ambivalence about the Indian
role in Mesopotamia reach in this Muslim anti-colonial revolutionary poet
its shattering climax. More than any historical testimony, it is Nazrul's
poetry that bears witness to what Sugata Bose, a historian himself, calls
'the enigma of feeling in time'.[77] The next year, in October 1921, Nazrul

---

[76] For a slightly different translation, see 'Shat-il-Arab', in Rafiqul Islam (ed.), *Kazi Nazrul Islam: A
New Anthology* (Dhaka: Bangla Academy, 1990), 26.
[77] Sugata Bose, *A Hundred Horizons*, 132. Bose, in his study, draws on Paul Ricœur, *Time and Narrative*
(Chicago: University of Chicago Press, 1990).

celebrated the Turkish victory over Greece in his famous poem 'Kāmāl Pāśā'. Often considered the 'greatest literary ballad in Bengali', he would here once more inject Bengali poetry with words, tunes and the beat of military marches he had picked up during his life in the camp: 'Oi khepeche pāglī māyer dāmāl chele kāmāl bhāi ... Ho, Ho, Kāmāl! Tu ne kāmāl kiyā bhāi! ... Quick March!/Left! Right! Left!!/Left! Right! Left!/ [There stirs the irrepressible brother Kāmāl, the reckless son of a mad mother ... Ho, Ho, Kāmāl! You have worked a miracle! ... Quick March!/Left! Right! Left!!/ Left! Right! Left!/].[78]

It was in the military camp in 1919 that Nazrul, a staunch socialist and a keen admirer of Gorky, heard about the October Revolution. His close friend Jemadar Sambhu Ray remembered how one evening, in late 1917, Nazrul invited a group of friends into his room to celebrate the success of the Red Army with music and poetry recitations; he also showed them a foreign newspaper which reported on the revolution.[79] In his novella 'Vyathār Dān', the First World War and the October Revolution merge. The story revolves around a ménage-à-trois between the betrayed lover Dara, the fallen but essentially good woman Bedoura and the repentant seducer called Saif-ul-mulk. Dara and Saif-ul-mulk, in the course of their travels, join a 'Liberation Army'; Muzaffar Ahmad, the editor of *Muslim Literature*, where this story was first published, recounted that Nazrul had initially written 'Red Army', which Ahmad changed to 'Liberation Army' to avoid charges of sedition.[80] Nazrul's narrative might have had historical roots. Both Ahmad and the revolutionary leader M. N. Roy, who was heading the Turkestan Bureau of the Communist International, recounted how some Indian sepoys posted around the oilfields of Baku in Transcaucasia had defected to the Red Army.[81] Whether or not Nazrul knew about this, the story shows him moving beyond nationalist politics to a more transnational vision of revolution:

> Brother Dara! We don't give awards like the Victoria Cross or the Military Cross, because we cannot congratulate ourselves on our own work. The fruit of our bravery and courage is the welfare of the whole world. But we hail as heroes only those few who like you have shown such selflessness and sacrifice ... You have become blind, you have become deaf, your whole

[78] 'Kāmāl Pāśā', in *Nazrul racanā samagra*, Vol. 1, 20–21.
[79] Letter of Jemadar Sambhu Roy (24 June 1957), quoted in Pranatosh Chattopadhyay, *Kāzi Nazrul*, 290–291.
[80] Ahmad, *Kāzi Nazrul Prasaṅge*, 64.
[81] Muzaffar Ahmad, *Kāzi Nazrul Prasaṅge*, 65–67; also see M. N. Roy, *Memoirs* (Bombay: Bombay Allied Publishers, 1964), 391–395.

body shows signs of ravage [*sārā aṅge jakhamer kaṭhor cinha*] – I would say
this is the best award for your bravery.[82]

Nazrul at once evokes and throws away references to imperial war
decorations as he supplants such service with the narrative of a global
anti-imperialist struggle. The sacrificial, if perverse, logic of blindness and
deafness as the 'best award' for 'bravery' chimes with the contemporary
vocabulary of 'sacrifice' – not in the cause of the empire (as in official
discourses), but rather for its overthrow, as with the Bengali revolutionary
nationalists. Dara becomes at once a timeless revolutionary and a recognisable figure from the early twentieth century, as the First World War,
the October Revolution and the Indian anti-colonial struggle leach across
their ideological frontiers.

Nazrul's war stories are necessarily fractured, for they bear witness to a
central tension between narrative and ideology: to tell the story of imperial
war service and yet infuse it with the revolutionary intensity of anti-imperialist liberation struggle. In 'Henā', this is achieved by making the Afghan
sepoy abruptly join the Emir's forces; in 'Vyathār Dān', he takes refuge
in an anonymous 'Liberation struggle'; and it reaches a breaking-point in
'Rikter Vedan' where, as the sepoys leave for imperial battle, they cry out
the nationalist slogan 'Vande Mātaram' ('Hail to the Mother').[83] Nazrul
never addressed the paradox himself, nor was it unique to him. Ahmad
notes that Bengali First World War sepoys exchanged the nationalist slogan
as a greeting; in *Bāṅgāli Palṭan*, as we saw, the cry 'Victory for George V'
modulates seamlessly to 'Victory for Bengal'; en route to the training camps
of Nowshera, the Bengali sepoys would be welcomed at the Lahore railway
station by none other than Sarala Devi, the daughter of Swarnakumari Devi
and a prominent nationalist leader, who was involved in the recruiting process and gave a series of firebrand lectures to encourage Bengali recruits.[84]
Nazrul's stories register the complexity and contradictions of the 'imperial–
nationalist' conjunction at its most extreme, tied to the affect of revolutionary violence and heroic masculinity. This fluidity is evident in his
celebrated poem 'Vidrohī' ('The Rebel'), whose apocalyptic energy and
images of boats, torpedoes and mines – 'I sport with loaded boats/And send
them down to the sea's bottom/I'm a torpedo/An explosive mine'[85] – come

[82] 'Vyathār Dān', 259.
[83] *Ibid.*, 320, 318.
[84] See Sarala Devi, 'Bengal Double Company', *Bhārati*, Baiśākh 1325; Mitra, *The Dissent of Nazrul Islam*, 29–30.
[85] 'The Rebel', *New Anthology*, 20–23.

out of the First World War. During the war years, the adventures of the German light cruiser *SMS Emden*, shelling and sinking boats in the Indian Ocean, caused widespread panic in the subcontinent.[86]

On 31 October 1922, Nazrul wrote an editorial titled 'Āmi Sainik' ('I am a Soldier') for his literary journal *Dhūmketu*.[87] The war years cemented this identity while encouraging, rather dangerously, the fetish-isation of violence and martial masculinity in the absence of his exposure to any combat experience. One almost gets the sense that it does not matter for him which side someone is fighting for, as long as he is fighting; indeed, his own identity as the anti-colonial rebel poet was forged on the anvil of imperial war service. There is a tremendous naivety and fragility to the construction as well as the celebration of a heroic, militant masculinity. If there is a remarkable imaginative expansiveness and power in his rewriting of the war, the evolution of contemporary traumatic history into a cele-bratory narrative of revolutionary energy is deeply disturbing. Indeed, as we read his idealised images of violence, we are tempted to ask the same question Virginia Woolf asked of Rupert Brooke: had he witnessed actual warfare, 'what would he have been, what would he have done'?[88]

Punjabi War Poetry: *Vaddā Jung Europe*

Nazrul remains, in many ways, the South Asian 'soldier-poet' without having ever actually gone to war, but do we have similarly ambitious and self-conscious literary works *by the combatants themselves*? In Chapter 5, in connection with the sepoy letters, we discussed a number of short poems which were often enclosed in the letters: these range from short witty lyrics to page-long poetic narratives, trying to process and describe the war. These poems enclosed within the letters – written behind the lines, in hospitals or on leave – all have the quality of notes from the battlefields. But is there no war poem – more ambitious, large-scale and reflective – from the men who served and survived, written after the heat of battle? It is at such moments that the implications of the widespread non-literacy among the troops becomes starkly visible.

An extraordinary poetic record has recently come to light: *Vaddā Jung Europe* ('The Great European War'), a Punjabi historical verse narrative

---

[86] See 'The Kaiser's Pirate Ship – The Astounding Voyage of SMS Emden', http://militaryhistorynow .com/2013/05/08/the-kaisers-pirate-ship-the-unbelievable-voyage-of-the-sms-emden.
[87] 'Āmi Sainik' ['I am a Soldier'], *Nazrul Racanābali*, Vol. 1, 686–688.
[88] Quoted in Julia Briggs, *Virginia Woolf: An Inner Life* (Orlando: Harcourt, 2005), 87.

in Gurmukhi by 'Nand Singh Havaldar', a sergeant in the Malay State Guide.[89] It was begun, we are told, when he was stationed in Taiping Penang, and was finished on 7 June 1919 while he was in Aden. Running to 2,000 lines, it is the most compendious and elaborate poetic record of the South Asian experience of the First World War. The poetic quality is admittedly uneven, but its historical value is quite unmatched. Yet nothing much is known about this poem, except what it tells us:

> I learnt writing poetry at a young age and pleased my friends through it.
> I enrolled myself in the Malay Guards Battalion as money enticed me
>   into it.
> My job was the defence of my government; I've been with a rifle since
>   childhood.
> I boarded a ship and moved to Taiping, Penang (for service) …
>
> Please forgive my mistakes and omissions, I apologise to all readers
> Man is forgetful by nature [but] I have placed the word [*vāk*] of the Guru
>   within my heart
> The art of poetry is really difficult; and I was not up to it.
> I have just written poetry for soldiers and for fun-loving people, and
>   narrated the war in Europe. (77)

Once more, we have the example of a combatant turned into a poet because of the war and the desire to narrate its fortunes; remarkable too, in the light of our discussion in Chapter 2, is the open admission of the financial attractions of the service. We are further told that the second edition was published in August 1934 by 'Kavishar' (cappella Punjabi folk performers). At first a thousand copies were printed and the 'famous shop near the clock tower in Ludhiana' was asked to stock them. Like an African *griot*, Nand Singh is a teller of tales, 'reciting' anecdotes in verse, but the pressures and anxieties of the emergent print culture are present: he warns that, if anyone publishes 'even an amended version of this ballad, I shall call him a plagiarist', and concludes 'Nand Singh tells himself to meditate upon the name of God and bow before him with clasped hands'.

Vaddā Jung Europe is most closely allied to the genre of 'Jungnamah' (literally meaning 'Book of War').[90] The 'Jungnamah' was a genre of

[89] Nand Singh Havilar, *Vaddā Jung Europe* (Ludhiana: Kavishar Gurdit Singh and Gajan Singh, 1934). I was alerted to the poem by Jeevan Deol in 2002 and, during a research trip to Chandigarh in 2005, found a copy of the poem. Dilgeer Singh kindly translated the whole text for me. The translations used here are by Arshdeep Singh Brar.
[90] The poem shares affinities with the more popular genre of *qissa* (meaning 'story' – the most famous being Waris Shah's *Heer Rānjhā*) as well as with *var*, which are battle ballads about Punjabi folk heroes.

epic-length verse narratives about historical wars, deeply intertwined with the turbulent martial history of Punjab: the most celebrated example was Shah Mohammed's *Jungnamah Hind-Punjab*, written shortly after the first Anglo-Sikh War of 1845, though the genre went back to the sixteenth century.[91] Like the *Qissas* and *Fasānah*, the 'Jungnamah' was rooted in the oral traditions of pre-colonial Punjab, and meant to be recited, or even sung to musical accompaniment.[92] Though these genres increasingly entered print culture from the middle of the nineteenth century onwards, they continued to be widely performed.[93] *Vaddā Jung Europe* follows the formal contours of these genres by opening with an invocation to Hindu deities, the Muslim Prophet and Sikh Gurus before turning to 'destiny':

'Role of Destiny'
O Nand Singh! In the hour of misfortune, man loses his wits.
It has befallen spiritual men; it has happened to powerful people.
It brings waste with it; and it has [earlier] happened to Hindustan.
It befell Mansur, when he raised the cry of 'Anā al-haq'[94]
It wrecked Hassan and Hussain, the sons of Ali,
It befell Brahma, Vishnu, Shiva, it fell upon Lord Krishna
There's a small principality in Europe, it's called Serbia ... [page torn]
There is the Austro-Hungarian empire, with an army of *lakhs* ...
   [page torn]
Some are born to destroy their families [*kulān*], placing the blame on
   the Lord ... [page torn]
28th of June 1914 was an hour of evil, the Prince was killed by a Serbian.
No one could stop destiny (7)

The war of 1914–1918 is placed in the longue durée of Indian battles culled from myth and legend; and is constructed as the latest episode in the

---

[91] See R. P. Malhotra and Kuldeep Arora (eds.), *Encyclopaedic Dictionary of Punjabi Literature* (Delhi: Global Vision Publishing House, 2003), Vol. 2, 571–586 and P. K. Nijhawan, *The First Punjab War: Shah Mohammed's Jungnamah* (Patiala: Punjabi University Press, 2000). Also see the blogpost by Raman Singh Chhina, 'Nand Singh and Jangnamah Europe'. The post appeared just as when the book was going into production – it is the only mention of the poem I have come across.

[92] Stuart H. Blackburn, Peter Claus, Joyce B. Flueckiger and Susan S. Wadley (eds.), *Introduction to Oral Epics in India* (Berkeley: University of California Press, 1989), 11. Blackburn and A. K. Ramanujan have argued that, in the Indian scenario, the oral and textual tradition do not just co-exist but are symbiotic: 'borrowing from one to the other has never ceased' (4).

[93] See Mir, *The Social Space of Language*, 12–17.

[94] The line refers to the persecution of Mansur Al-Hallaj, a Sufi mystic, 858–922 AD, Hijri. 244–309 AH.

inexorable working of destiny. The poem itself is at once a heroic narrative, a religio-philosophical meditation and an elegy for Punjabi youth. At the formal level, the refrain 'O Nant Singh' or the constant repetition at the end of the lines quoted above ('Hindustān utte' 'Jān utte' 'āyi nuksān utte' 'Krishan bhagwān utte') are mnemonic traces of an oral culture within the burgeoning economy of print, gesturing towards what Sheldon Pollock has called a 'sociotextual community'.[95]

Vaddā Jung Europe remains a testimony to how a vernacular genre is made to accommodate global warfare. It is divided into eighty-five sections with the grand narrative of the war alternating with the story of the Indian experience in France, Mesopotamia and Gallipoli. Its global reach is both capacious and precise. Starting with the killing of the Duke, it follows a rough chronology of events, from Belgium's appeal for help through brief references to key battles to the peace treaty (of Brest-Litovsk) in March 1918 between the new Bolshevik government of Soviet Russia and the Central Powers and the signing of the Armistice. Against this broad-brush framework, the story of the Indian experience unfolds in meticulous, painstaking detail, unit by unit: news of the war reaching India, the recruitment campaigns, responses of the village women, the voyage to Europe, Mesopotamia and East Africa, names of the regiments and dates of their movements, the kind of warfare, the nature of casualties, the details of what they are seeing, eating or feeling, the internal pressures, anxieties, conflicts. But *Vaddā Jung Europe* is no exercise in simple cataloguing: the grand narrative of war is regularly interrupted by dialogues, missives, 'scenes', commands, prayers, gossip as the mood oscillates between excitement, anger, elegy and protest. Eschewing but not wholly abandoning linear narrative, it is made up of a series of 'scenes' or 'voices' ranging from a 'request from the Belgian Minister' to his emperor to the 'Dialogues of women in an ordinary village' to a description of the 'Bravery of the 14th Sikh regiment' to details about Nand Singh's own regiment – their headquarters in Taipeng, Malaysia, its origins in the Perak Sikh Force or its departure on 26 September 1915 to join the Aden Field Force.[96] Such a narrative mode testifies to the democratic impulse of the genre, with its roots in oral folk culture; one can imagine regular listeners participating

---

[95] Sheldon Pollock (ed.), 'Introduction' to *Literary Cultures in History: Reconstructions from South Asia* (Berkeley: University of California Press, 2003), 7.

[96] For a brief but informative note on the Malay Sikhs, including the 'First Battalion Perak Sikhs', see Ranjit Singh Malhi, 'Early Sikhs Were Police, Convicts and Mercenary Soldiers', www.thestar.com .my/opinion/letters/2017/05/08/early-sikhs-were-police-convicts-and-mercenary-soldiers/.

and even adding to the narrative so that the poem published in 1936 might even have been much longer than the one completed in 1919.

Is *Vaddā Jung Europe* 'poetry' or 'history in verse'? The genre of 'Jungnamah' actively defies such taxonomies: its purpose was at once to educate, entertain and reflect. Towards the end of the narrative, Nand Singh notes that 'I have not written it as a ballad/My real ambition was to give you history'. In a way, *Vaddā Jung Europe* is the most sustained attempt at subaltern history of the Indian war experience, the perfect antithesis of Amar Singh's war *Diaries*. It does not have the searing testimonial quality of the letters, but its historical lens is wider: it is the voice of the community – the recruiters, the soldiers, the women, the widows, the village elders – that we hear. The chronicler in Nand Singh occasionally overpowers the versifier, as in the section 'Names of some of the war battalions' ('14th, 15th, 45, 35 and 36th battalions have Sikh soldiers/23, 32, 33, 47, 53 & 54 are also fine battalions'), but he also summons up a world we do not find in the letters: of *chowkidars* announcing the war in the villages, of the village women berating them, or of the panic created by the light cruiser *Emden*. *Vaddā Jung Europe* does not just fill in such historical gaps. Rhyme, repetition, refrain and variation in line-length and metrical scheme are some of the artistic resources brilliantly employed to give a sense of pace, progression and pulse to the narrative. If the official archives tell us about the expansion of the recruitment base in 1917 to include 'non-martial' castes, the poem vivifies such factual details with local colour and drama:

> *Sarvari, Kanauji, Garhwalis* have given up *Vedic* instructions of not
>   going beyond the sea and have chosen to pick up rifles
> O Nand Singh! Now the *Paharis, Ahirs* and *Acharyas* are up next!
> Placing *sārangis* and *dhols* aside, handsome young boys of *Ramdasis*
>   and sons of *dharamshaliyān* too have come in groups,
> O Nand Singh! Even *Chhimbas* have flocked to join the army; they say
>   they have never seen battle. (14–15)

What we have here is a sonorous roll-call of groups and castes, previously barred from the military profession, now flocking to join the army, from *Paharis* ('hill-people') to *Ramdasis* (so-called 'low-caste' groups) exchanging their musical instruments (*sārangis* and *dhols*) for the rifle, to *dharamshaliyān* (Sikh priests) and even *Chhimbas* (tailors). The long metrical beat of *kabit* in the original Punjabi, the accretive intensity of the names and the succession of exclamations convey the sense of astonishment, almost of wonder, in the

villages of all these 'non-martial' men becoming soldiers. And more: we are
not just given precise names and dates but intimate details of the leave-taking:

> It was 22nd of December and the year was 1917
> The 7th Rajputs had received an earful (for not fighting at the front)
> Each one was preparing *pūris* and packed them in their bags
> They bowed before the picture of Ram Chand and Sita
> Chanting the name of Shiva, the brave Hindu soldiers left for the
>   battle-field, never
> looking back at anyone. (60)

The scared and the profane – from bowing to the mythical elders (here
'Ram Chand and Sita' from the *Rāmāyaṇa*) to the packing of *pūris* (fluffy
pancakes) – are mixed up as the soldiers leave for the battlefront, all the
more poignant when described retrospectively. For long before we come to
this section, we have been told, some forty pages earlier, of what remains
of them in the battlefield:

> As bundles of straw [*pulliyān*] lie neglected in the fields of the farmers
> Similarly, the delicate bodies of soldiers lie in the battlefields,
> Their long hair reminded people that they were Sikhs,
> They were lying at peace in France, far away from their homeland
> The Hindu's *janeus* (sacred thread) around their body lay and could not
>   save their lives.
> The Muslims had shaved themselves and had gone to the battlefields
>   wearing thread [*ganiyān*] on their wrists.
> The whites [*goriyān*] had really fair skin. They were in the prime of their
>   youth. (22)

The simile 'bundles of straw' (*pulliyān*) occurs in the letters too, showing
a shared repository of words and images rooted in rural life. One is reminded
of the counterpart of the above lines in British trench poetry, from the tenderness of Wilfred Owen's 'full-nerved still-warm' male bodies in 'Futility'
to the grotesquery of Sassoon's 'naked sodden buttocks, mats of hair' in
the 'plastering slime' in 'Counter-Attack'.[97] Nand Singh at once concurs
and diverges. The above verses, camera-like, linger over the bodies of the
Sikhs, Hindus, Muslims and Europeans mingling in the trenches; there is
also an internal rhyme of sorts, linking *pulliyān* (to describe the Sikhs) and
ganiyān (for the Muslims) and *goriyān* (Europeans) to provide the Punjabi
sonic counterpart of the 'macabre cosmopolitanism' of the trenches. Such
intimate details are woven into the larger framework, moving beyond the

---

[97] 'Futility', in *The Poems of Wilfred Owen*, ed. Jon Stallworthy (London: Chatto and Windus, 1990),
    135; 'Counter-Attack', in Siegfried Sassoon, *Collected Poems 1908–1956* (London: Faber, 1984), 68.

war to the outbreak of Black Fever and the Wilsonian principle of self-determination. War, empire, Europe, the Middle East, the Spanish flu, Wilson: *Vaddā Jung Europe* is possibly the first Punjabi narrative poem of substantial length to register the global pulse of events of 1914–1918.

Is *Vaddā Jung Europe* aligned to the imperial centre or is it an act of subaltern anti-colonial protest? The poem refuses to be tied down to such categories. Since it was written after the devastations of war, the bellicosity that we saw in the 'The Raag of Recruitment' is absent here. The rhetoric of loyalty persists: 'But all the soldiers loved [their duty] and were ever-ready to make sacrifices' (17), but critique of the war wells up powerfully in the two most moving sections in the poem, as in the women's 'Lamentations of the Dead':

> I'd keep saying 'get your name off the list!'
> If you paid any heed to me, why would you have gone to *l'arme*
> How shall I bear the pain of this separation
> I will buy poison [*sankhiyā*] and die …
> I will mourn and beat my thighs … (22)

and the 'Bewailing by the wives':

> The women mourn the demise of their husbands,
> 'Today we have become widows [*randiyān*]
> We have discarded clothes and ornaments
> We don't need necklaces and embellishments.
> We won't be wearing these anymore,
> May you Germans perish, you are shameless and sinners' (26)

The eruption of the first person is peculiarly haunting. The final line in Punjabi ('Hove ainve janiyān tū marein Germanā … Aayi tainū papiyā ve koi sharam nā'), with its explicit address to 'Germany' and describing it as 'sinful' (*papi*) and 'shameless' (*koi sharam nā*), resonates with the Punjabi folksong 'Germanā', with its similarly resonant plea: 'Take the bachelors to war,/then victory will be yours.' In the Punjabi world of soldiering, the pain of separation (*sall*), world of widowhood (*randiyān*) or suicide through consuming 'poison' (*sankhiyā*) seem to be the choices available to women.

Like the folksongs we discussed in Chapter 2, such passages provide insights into the emotional history of the women in the villages; moreover, the poem in this way involves them in the poetic composition as protagonists, participants and listeners. Even though the poem refers to particular accounts of heroism, as of the 47th Sikhs, there is no glorification of battle. Instead, passages such as the above point to its waste and ask for peace. The omniscient narrator notes that 'every home [in India] is bewailing/The sufferings of mothers will never be subdued.' The whole poem culminates in a powerful plea:

'The Poet's Plea' [*Kavi di pukār*]
Hear, my Master [*Malikā*], please listen to my prayer, O God, stop this bloody [*khūnī*] battle.
The power is in your hands, the reins are in your hands; you started it, and now you should provide a reprieve
Stop the cannons, the guns and machinery of war. Please restore the ruined villages
You are bountiful [*bakhshind*], you are the giver. Please cease for now and provide relief to the poor …
There is no other source of support except you, without you nobody has ever won or lost,
The armies are yours and so is the battle … (66)

Like Guleri's story, the poem on the whole neither affirms nor protests but simply chronicles. Yet, in this section towards the end, in the phrase 'bloody battle' (*khūni laam*), is distilled the stinging verdict of the poet-narrator as the poem now modulates to a cry for peace; what we have is a heroic narrative acutely conscious of the *cost* of war and underpinned by a deeply elegiac sense of loss and waste. Though the poem was written after the war, the narrative voice locates us within the immediacy of the war, in the middle of anxiety and pain and suspense. When shall the war end? When will the men return? Since it was meant to be recited or sung, rather than read in silence, it might well have had a cathartic effect, taking the villagers through the emotions and motions of the war.

The literature of the First World War, as I noted before, still remains dominated by the English trench-poets. Indeed, the 'global turn' in the military and cultural history has not yet happened in the field of war literature which remains, even a hundred years after the war, steadfastly Eurocentric. Here I have tried to recover both the range and the complexity of a self-conscious body of literary works produced in India, from the elite verse of Tagore and Naidu to a folk genre such as *Vaddā Jung Europe* with its deep roots in the oral tradition. While one hopes that such recovery is a step towards a more 'global' literature of the war, what these works open up more immediately and urgently are the undertones of the war on the Indian home front – intimate, contested, diverse – through the enigma of form.

CHAPTER 9

Across the Black Waters
Emotion, Experience and 'Pigeon-English'

'One of the few officers who could talk Hindustani well and who remembered the names of the sepoys, he was yet somewhat un-understanding of the sepoy heart' (*Across the Black Waters*)[1]

'The intensely, stiflingly human quality of the novel is not to be avoided; the novel is sogged with humanity ... Human beings have their great chance in the novel.' (E. M. Forster, *Aspects of the Novel*)[2]

Of all the literary engagements with the Indian war experience, the most sustained and powerful is Mulk Raj Anand's novel *Across the Black Waters* (1940). It is the middle part of his celebrated Lalu trilogy, which starts with *The Village* (1939) and concludes with *The Sword and the Sickle* (1942). The novel opens up a whole new world in travel and combat literature in English as he shows Lal Singh and his fellow sepoys – peasant-warriors from Punjab – landing in Marseilles and encountering Europe and love and war for the first time; the history of a small village in South Asia is aligned to the defining event of twentieth-century Europe. If post-war British literary culture had become too crowded with the voices of English 'subalterns' – young middle-class army officers – the novel pulls towards the more postcolonial meaning of the term 'subaltern' as he recovers both the racial and plebeian dimensions of the conflict; effectively, he issues a challenge to the very colour of war memory. But this is no simple exercise in subaltern recovery, nor is it an exercise in 'nationalist allegory', either of brutalisation or heroism in battle or of anti-colonial awakening in the trenches.[3] A devotee at once of Gandhi and Forster, Anand focusses on common, unheroic peasant-warriors from Punjab and their daily lives on

---

[1] Mulk Raj Anand, *Across the Black Waters* (Delhi: Orient, 1949 [1940]), 256. The officer mentioned here refers to the seemingly stern Major Peacock, who is here being contrasted with the gentler 'Owen Sahib'.
[2] E. M. Forster, *Aspects of the Novel* (Harmondsworth: Penguin, 2005 [1927]), 39, 147.
[3] The phrase 'nationalist allegory' refers to Frederic Jameson's 'Third World Literature in the Era of Multinational Capitalism', *Social Text*, No. 15 (1986), 65–88.

343

the Western front; what he evokes with almost unparalleled delicacy is the
minutiae of the sepoy heart – the ebb and flow of feeling – buffeted by the
demands of war service in foreign fields but equally troubled by other histories, more local, ingrown, complex, intensely felt.

Anand's novels *Untouchable* (1935) and *Coolie* (1936) have remained in
the public eye in Britain, though accounts of Indo-British modernism and
postcolonial fiction habitually leave him out. Yet he was a vital figure in
both fields.[4] This fiery nationalist situated between India and Britain had
already served a prison sentence in India for his political activities before
arriving in London. In London, he was part of the 'Asian Bloomsbury',
that group of politically radical South Asian writers living in London
in the 1920s and 1930s.[5] He worked as the secretary to T. S. Eliot and
then later, during the Second World War, for the BBC Eastern service, running a series of important lectures to combat fascism. By that
time, he had established himself as a distinct and rather fierce presence
in the literary and socialist circles in London and was known to writers
and artists as diverse as Virginia and Leonard Woolf, Nancy Cunard and
Edgell Rickword and above all George Orwell, to whom he reported in
the BBC; E. M. Forster wrote the preface to his first novel *Untouchable*
(1935). Anand went on to become one of the most prolific Indian writers,
moving back to India in 1945, and continued to write novels, short stories,
monographs, essays, reviews and articles.[6] Having come into contact with
both Gandhi and Nehru during his visit to India in 1932, he spoke and
wrote passionately on issues such as poverty and Indian nationalism. He
started thinking about *Across the Black Waters* when he was working against
fascism, between speaking at the 1936 Anti-Fascist Writers' Conference in
London and crossing over to Spain to join the International Brigades in
the fight against Franco in the Spanish Civil War (1936–1939). The novel,
Anand tells us, was out in a rough draft in Barcelona, Madrid, during
January and April 1937, and entirely rewritten in England between July
and December 1939. In many ways, the timing was both apposite and
awkward: as Britain entered another world war and Indian troops were
summoned again, Anand – while supporting the war effort – boldly joined

---

[4] Saros Cowasjee's monograph *So Many Freedoms: Major Fiction of Mulk Raj Anand* (Oxford: Oxford
     University Press, 1977) has been a glorious exception and gives a wealth of information. Also see
     Kristin Bluemel, *George Orwell and the Radical Eccentrics* (London: Palgrave, 2004) for a powerful
     reassessment of Anand.
[5] See Anand, *Conversations in Bloomsbury* (Delhi: Oxford University Press, 1981); Susheila Nasta (ed.),
     India in Britain: South Asian Networks and Connections, 1858–1950 (London: Palgrave, 2013).
[6] Saros Cowasjee, *So Many Freedoms*, 1–35.

the critique of the past war to the critique of empire. Back in India, the people were wholly divided between the rising force of nationalism and support for the war against fascism so that the word 'freedom', as Raghu Karnad has recently noted, was pulled in different directions in 1939: did the word mean freedom for the people of Europe or freedom from the people of Europe?[7] Some of this ambivalence inevitably courses through the veins of Anand's First World War sepoys, giving the novel a retrospective political edge and emotional ambivalence absent in much of the Indian literature written in 1914–1918; the historical short-change would be literature's gain. In this respect, Anand's novel is comparable to Abdullah Hussein's majestic *Udaas Naslain* (*The Weary Generations*), written in 1963, which has a short section on the First World War.

The conflict was also personal. Anand grew up in Peshawar in Punjab in a military environment. He dedicated the novel to 'the memory of my father Subedar Lal Chand Anand, M.S.M', who had worked his way up to become Head Clerk in the Dogra Regiment – a relentlessly ambitious and obsequious colonial servant for whom his nationalist son had little respect. Anand's father did not take part in the war, but many of his friends did, and Anand would have known many of the returned soldiers and their stories. On the one hand, he wanted to give voice to these people he had known so intimately, and he would have been freshly emboldened by his socialist politics and involvement in Gandhi's grass-root nationalism, including a tour of India in 1932.[8] He had love for many of the individual people, but, for the radical Anand, it was a highly conservative, hypermasculine, prejudice-ridden, feudal–military world that he not only had left far behind but actively shunned. In a highly conflicted but revealing passage in the novel, he writes:

> A passionate people, prone to sudden exaltations and depressions, more faithful than any other if they believed, they were neutral in this war, because this was not a war for any of the religions of their inheritance, nor for any ideal which could fire their blood and make their hair stand on end. Ordered about by the Sarkar, they were as ready to thrust their bayonets into the bellies of the Germans as they had been to disembowel the frontier tribesmen, or their own countrymen, for the pound a month which the sahibs paid them. But they were like conscripts, brutalised and willing to fight like trained bulls, but without a will of their own, soulless automatons in the execution of the army code, though in the strange dark deeps of their

[7] Raghu Karnad, *Farthest Field*, 23
[8] Saros Cowasjee, *So Many Freedoms*, 32. Hereafter abbreviated as *SMF*.

nature, unschooled by the Sarkar, there lay the sensitiveness of their own
humanity, their hopes, their fears and their doubts. (133)

The convoluted syntax – the pile-up of clauses, twisting and turning
through 'because', 'but', 'though' and the accretive intensity of commas –
shows the double ambivalence at work: the sepoys' towards the Raj, and
Anand's towards the sepoys. The causes of recruitment, as we have seen,
were multiple and diverse, but, in Anand's thirties vision, they were hired,
conscripted, 'ordered'. He acknowledges their 'passionate' and 'faithful'
nature but, in trying to emphasise the coercive and involuntary nature
of the service ('they were like conscripts'), he risks robbing these men of
agency: they are depicted here as a hapless underclass, bullish and brutal,
reminiscent of his hero Karl Marx's famous description of Indian peasant
life as 'undignified, stagnant and vegetative'.[9] But peasant consciousness is
recovered in the final sub-clause in the lyrical admission of the 'strange
dark deeps of their nature' which the novel will now spectacularly proceed to plumb and dramatise. Indeed, the naivety of the assumption that
the sepoys are 'soulless automatons' ready 'to thrust their bayonets into
the bellies of the Germans' will be challenged by one of his own sepoy-
creations: 'They [the Germans] think we are all Gurkhas with kukries in our
mouths, savages who will creep up to them by surprise and kill them' (141).

Anand focusses on the fortunes of a mixed company – the 69th
Rifles – composed of Dogra, Baluchi, Sikh and Punjabi Mohammedan
companies – which can be traced to the 57th Wilde's Rifles.[10] His is a
multi-religious, multi-ethnic vision of agrarian–military India from below.
The place of action is the front line near Marseilles and Orléans; the time-
frame is set not around some distinguished operation such as in Neuve
Chapelle, March 1915, but earlier when the Indians suffered considerable setbacks. In keeping with narratives such as Aldington's *Death of a
Hero* (1929), the focus is very much on the common, the humdrum, the
unheroic. Starting with the arrival of the troops at Marseilles, their introduction to the horrors of the trenches and the gradual death of almost all
but Lalu (who is taken a prisoner of war), the novel very much follows
the arc of the post-war British combat narrative, with Lalu emerging
as the eponymous tragic anti-hero: 'Why is it that men like Kirpu, Dhanoo
and Lachman, who were so good, should have suffered and died when I a

[9] Karl Marx, 'The British Rule in India' (1853), in *Marx and Engels, Articles on Britain* (Moscow: Progress
    Publishers 1971), 166–172.
[10] For details, see the unit Diary of the 57th Rifles in the National Archives, London, WO95/3923. Also
    see *SMF*, 108.

wretch am alive?' (255). Its sequel *The Sword and Sickle* follows Lalu's return to the post-war nationalist milieu.[11] In formal terms, its social realism is sometimes perceived as somewhat naive, clothy, sentimental. Yet, given the historical weight of the subject, Anand's brand of social realism is peculiarly effective; radical experimentation, in the case of a novel such as David Jones's *In Parenthesis* (1937), would not have worked for the very *first* Indian war novel. Defying categorisation as a 'First-' or 'Third-' World text, *Across the Black Waters* blurs the boundaries between travelogue, trench narrative, indigenous and Anglophone novel in the early epoch of its flowering.

Given how singular Anand's novel is – the only novel in English about the Indian war experience – it is extraordinary how it was largely forgotten, both within war literature and in the context of Indian writing in English. However, in recent years, with the global turn in First World War studies and in modernism, the novel is beginning to be read, reprinted and commented on again. As Claire Buck has recently reminded us, the novel is 'much more than a simple corrective to a historical record in which India's contribution is erased'.[12] My focus here, in the light of the previous chapters, is different: in a context where sepoy-consciousness can only be recovered through 'fugitive fragments', Anand's novel, I would argue, provides the most powerful 'illumination' of the sepoy's inner world. Going far beyond the recovery of hidden history or the voicing of imperial dissent, the novel can be read as one of the most acute imaginings of sepoy-sensibility – an excavation of an inner realm of feeling – shaped by but not reducible to the multiple and intersecting histories of race, class, war, social relations and empire. I shall read the novel alongside archival and historical documents not merely to 'historicise' it, but to explore the singularity of fiction in being able to represent, nuance and complicate the conventionally 'historical' by getting under the skin of our consciousness; in the process, the novel provides insights into some of the central issues we have

---

[11] While *The Sword and the Sickle* is fascinating for understanding the relation of war service and post-war nationalism in India, the focus of this chapter, given the scope of the study, will be on *Across the Black Waters*.

[12] Claire Buck, *Conceiving Strangeness in British First World War Writing*, 35. In Buck's perceptive reading, the novel's representational techniques are 'a means to critique the imperial and racial foundations of European civilisation' (35). Even before the centennial years, the novel had its dedicated advocates, from Jane Marcus in *Hearts of Darkness: White Women Write Race* (New Brunswick: Rutgers University Press, 2003) to Kristin Bluemel in *George Orwell and the Radical Eccentrics* (2004). Most recently, Margaret R. Higonnet has drawn attention to its linguistic cosmopolitanism in 'Code Switching and Representations of the Great War', in Debra Rae Cohen and Douglas Higbee (eds.), *Teaching Representations of the First World War* (New York: MLA, 2017), 69–71.

been considering: cultural encounters, the sepoy-heart, processes of touch and intimacy, and loyalty and ambivalence.

Brownness As Feeling: Encounters and Self-encounters in 'Vilayet'

Colonial encounters have long been the staple of European travel narratives. The few Indian accounts which reverse the gaze have largely been by the cultural elite, sailing to the imperial centre and more rarely to France, ranging from I'tisam al-Daula's *Wonders of Vilayet* (1827) recounting his travels in France and Britain to figures such as Raja Rammohum Roy who, as an admirer of the French Revolution, apparently insisted on boarding a French ship at the Cape.[13] But the war provided Anand with a unique opportunity to democratise the experience as he shows working-class villagers from Punjab disembarking at Marseilles and encountering 'Vilayet' for the first time. If the 'soldier as tourist' is a common trope in Australian and New Zealand war literature, no war novel quite conveys with such power or humour the sense of arrival. 'Marsels! We have reached Marsels. Hip, hip, hurrah!', they shout from the deck as Marseilles comes into view, as Anand underscores both the exhilaration and the robust (mis)translation. The first one-third of the novel is a tour de force. Taking a cue from the stories he would have heard from his father's friends, he recasts war narrative as travelogue and shows the sepoys 'discovering' Vilayet: they wander around Orléans and look at and comment on its farms, statues, shops, people, houses and clothes, and make the occasional visits to the bar and the brothel.

It is unlikely Anand ever saw any sepoy letters; reading them alongside the novel is therefore all the more rewarding, for they reveal the historical depth of his imagining, especially compared with Kipling, who, as we have seen, not only had access to them but surreptitiously recycled them in *The Eyes of Asia*. He is remarkably attentive to the body as it inhabits new spaces or encounters novelty: Dhanoo slips off the commode seat as he tries to adjust to European toilet habits, while his comrades gape at a French couple kissing on the mouth (do women like being kissed on the mouth?) with the same degree of wonder as at an aeroplane ('a wooden

---

[13] Claude Markovits, 'Indian Soldiers' Experiences in France', 42. Also see Michael Fisher, *Counterflow to Colonialism: Indian Travellers and Settlers in Britain 1600–1857* (Delhi: Permanent Black, 2004).

bird') hovering overhead. These details could easily have appeared in the letters, but the differences between the two are deeply revealing. Compare the variations on the same theme, the first from a letter by a sepoy in France on 30 April 1916, and the second from the novel:

> I have not the ability to sing the praises of France, indeed ... The inhabitants are extremely kind and pleasant. All round you are cities that make you gasp with astonishment. All the skill, adornment, bravery and beauty of the world are collected in France.[14]

> So absorbed was Lalu that while Kirpu crossed the street, he continued on his way, fascinated by the chocolates, cakes and sweets arrayed in the window of an adjacent shop, and then by the tables and chairs, arrayed as in a room, and by the neckties, shirts and collars, all the richest things he had ever seen and which he would never be able to buy, but among which he felt happy to be moving at leisure. (39)

Both are overwhelmed. What Claude Markovits has called 'Occidentalism from below'[15] with reference to the letters is re-imagined by Anand, at a material and sensuous level, through encounter with the world of things. This is the Punjabi sepoy as the modern *flaneur*; there is perhaps in Lalu something of the young Anand who, as he tells us in the autobiographical *Seven Summers* (1951), emulated 'Europe through an exaggerated respect for hats, top boots, hockey sticks, cricket bats, shorts, trousers, push bikes'.[16] But such window-shopping could not be passed over without critique from a self-confessed 'intellectual in the thirties' who believed in the 'necessity of national freedom and socialism'.[17] As Lalu is blinded by the dazzle of shop-windows, Uncle Kirpu cuts him short: 'Son, that is a question of rupees ... Our cook-shop keepers have little money to spend on decorations' (37). Indeed, if 'Lalu had aspired to this Europe as to some heaven', Kirpu replies sharply, 'The sahibs travel first class ... The Indian officers second class, Tommies, havildars, naiks and sepoys in the third class – remember this and don't be led astray.' (38). One is reminded of the rickshaw puller's comment in *Coolie*: '[The English] have a caste system more rigid than ours.'[18]

---

[14] From __, France, to __, Peshwar, 25 April 1916, *CIM*, IOR, L/MIL/5/828/2, 342v, British Library.

[15] Markovits, 'Indian Soldiers' Experiences in France', 40.

[16] Anand, *Seven Summers: The Story of an Indian Childhood* (London: Hutchinson, 1951), 120.

[17] Anand, *Apology for Heroism: A Brief Autobiography of Ideas* (New Delhi: Arnold Heinemann, 1975), 141–142.

[18] Anand, *Coolie*, excerpted in Atma Ram (ed.), *Mulk Raj Anand: A Reader* (New Delhi: Sahitya Akademi, 2005), 183.

If the sepoy letters in the opening months help to recast an imperial war as a process of cultural encounters, what Anand the novelist does is to burrow, mole-like, underneath these moments to prise open their cultural and psychic frontiers. Anand's vision of Indo-European intimacy is not one of easy inter-racial camaraderie or sepoy–civilian romance but largely limited to curious glances and shy smiles; occasionally awkward phrases are exchanged, in trains, cafes, shops. Curiosity and goodwill are combined with distance and restraint; there is no overt racism. Instead, he shows, more insidiously, how the racist and colonial ideology is internalised by the sepoys as he tunnels deep and dramatises a series of encounters. 'Inferior' is a recurring word and feeling in the novel: 'The sepoys could not get over their feeling of inferiority to the sahibs, however, and they could not easily shake off their fear of the Sarkar' (238). Wartime France confronted the non-white soldiers with a rather tantalising space where racist structures and institutions continued and yet the barriers had relaxed. 'I feel afraid to enter,' Kirpu whispered as he stood in the doorway of a cafe, 'We might be reported' (199). 'This is not Hindustan but France', replies Lalu, showing how war experience had generated an understanding of the limit of colonial rule. Yet, habits persist:

> 'What does he say!' asked one of the sepoys.
>
> 'Something in Francisi, Allah knows what,' answered another.
>
> At that the Frenchman bowed very politely, smiled and went his way.
>
> 'Salaam Huzoor,' said the sepoys saluting and almost coming to attention in the face of the white man. For all white men, military or civil, were to them superior like the English sahibs in India who surrounded themselves with princely airs. (37)

This was the ultimate triumph of the British Raj: colonialism not as political or economic domination but as mental subjugation. Anand here anticipates theorists such as Frantz Fanon and Ashis Nandy who have written so incisively of colonialism as a 'state of mind'.[19] But 'brownness' as feeling is seldom purely a matter of colour or colonialism. The semi-literate sepoys from rural Punjab feel their brownness in a way wholly different from Prince Amar Singh or the middle-class Sisir Prasad Sarbadhikari – or, within the novel, Lalu's friend and competitor Jemadar Subah Singh, educated at Bishop Cotton School – who would not have *salaamed*. Amar Singh, as we have seen, takes offence at not being *salaamed* by junior white officers.

---

[19] Nandy, *The Intimate Enemy*, 1.

As internalisation of colonial and racial hierarchies, such 'brownness' gets compounded in *Across the Black Waters* with 'an arsenal of complexes', to use Fanon's term, which in this case include issues of class, education and provincialism, among others.[20] 'Compared to them [the white officers], we folk from Punjab', Kirpu notes, 'are truly like oxen' (43). The 'martial race' tag does little to relieve such shame. 'Brownness' as feeling is something the sepoys, particularly Lalu, bring to almost every encounter: 'Lalu felt embarrassed, afraid and inferior to be going to a stall where there were only white men' (25). When addressed by a French woman, he is terrified to be caught talking to a 'memsahib'; forbidden to look through the gates at the colonial bungalows in Ferozepur, he is scared even to loiter in the streets of Orléans (18); he feels 'too humble to stare at this superior life' displayed behind shop-windows (39); invited to dinner at a French house, he cannot take his seat at the table as long as 'Owen sahib' sits at the same table. His self-inhibition is only proportionate to his Europhilia, his 'utterest happiness' to be in 'Vilayet' (42). He feels thrilled to be with the Tommies (110) or to be smoking a cigarette (111) in a cafe; yet as he casts a 'furtive glance at the rich atmosphere', he feels 'ashamed and inferior and afraid lest the intrusion of his stare be interpreted as rudeness by the sahibs there' (42). Lalu becomes for us at once a nerve-centre and a micro-history of what many sepoys would have thought and felt and how they would have behaved; what Anand does with extraordinary acuity is to explore colonialism and regionalism through the history of feeling, and embed that feeling in the quotidian story of the everyday. Anand is equally interested in differences *between* brown masculinities: if the provincial Lalu falters before a bar, Subah, the son of Major Arbel Singh, drags him in with the confidence of his 'three years at the Bishop Cotton School' (25). If, in recent years, there has been a burgeoning interest in understanding imperial relations through 'zones of contact' and 'geographies of intimacy',[21] Anand shows how the most fleeting of encounters is not free from the weight of history.

At the same time, the power and subtlety of Anand's art lie in the equal knowledge that such moments are never wholly determined by histories of race and empire; our multiple identities at any one point intervene. Consider the dramatisation of two very different encounters in terms of

<hr />

[20] Frantz Fanon, *Black Skin, White Masks*, ed. Charles Lam Markmann (London: Pluto, 1986 [1952]), 30.
[21] See Tony Ballantyne and Antoinette M. Burton (eds.), *Bodies in Contact: Rethinking Colonial Encounters in World History* (Durham: Duke University Press, 2005).

gender, race and power-relationships. The first is a meeting between a
sepoy and a little girl:

> 'Come children,' Uncle Kirpu said, affectionately to the boys and girls who
> had left their game and rushed excitedly to join their playmates who already
> stood staring at the sepoys. Then he beckoned to a little girl who clung to
> an elder sister.
>
> The child held her finger dubiously in her mouth and stood shyly hesitant.
>
> 'Come, Mooni, come here,' Uncle Kirpu called her endearingly in his
> dialect.
>
> The elder sister of the child encouraged her to talk but the little girl stood
> peering at the strange phenomena of turbaned, brown men, with her
> untrusting hazel eyes.
>
> 'Come, daughter, come,' Daddy Dhanoo coaxed.
>
> But she still stood shy and enigmatic.
>
> Whereupon Uncle Kirpu lunged forward and picked her up in his arms and
> caressed her in the best fatherly tradition of India. Just then Major Peacock
> Sahib, the regimental second-in-command came that way. Kirpu did not
> know what to do. He was half-afraid to be seen holding a child, because in
> the Indian cantonment the sepoys were asked to refrain from touching the
> English children … But the Major Sahib, hard in ordinary times, smiled to
> see the pale, flustered Kirpu, changed his course and left the doting sepoys
> to amuse themselves. (95)

and the second, not so much an encounter, but rather an experience of
proximity and curiosity, as the Indian sepoys stare at 'a platoon of stalwart
black troops':

> 'Habshis' [pejorative term used to refer to people of African descent], said
> someone in an undertone half-suppressed by the clatter of marching feet,
> and there were other inquisitive whispers.
>
> 'They are sepoys like us of the Francisi Army,' said Havildar Lachman Singh.
> 'Watch your step, boys, watch your step! …'
>
> 'But they have got curly hair and are jet black and not brown as we are'
> young Kharhu protested, his belief in the superior brown skin of his inher-
> itance shocked by the comparison which Lachman had put them to. …
>
> Lalu felt guilty at having averted his eyes from them. At Marseilles he
> had seen a few African soldiers talking openly to girls in the cafes and the
> French sahibs did not mind, though he himself had been rather surprised,
> for the English did not like even the brown-skinned Indians to look at white
> women. He wondered how the English liked the French being so free and
> easy. And if the French liked the blacks, why shouldn't he like them? Why
> had he thought himself superior? He felt ashamed …

'Ohe, fool, Uncle, we didn't return the salaams of those Moorish sepoys'
Lalu said impatiently.

'They are surely savages, are they not?' ventured Dhanoo. (93–94)

At an immediate level, the exaggerated *salaam* to the French troops, the
anxiety around the Belgian girl and the racist contempt for the North
African soldiers are interlinked processes through which Anand examines
the weight of colonial and racial history in the labyrinth of the colonial
psyche. Yet the final encounter is also one which evolves into a profound
moment of self-encounter.

The two extracts above, quoted at length, show how Anand exploits
the capaciousness of fiction to explore a fundamental issue in these inter-
racial wartime encounters: the relation between racial difference and
humanistic universalism. He approaches the same issues through two very
different routes. The first passage with Kirpu and the little girl is consonant with regular reports in letters and memoirs of the colonial troops
of their encounters with children; it can be read alongside the photograph
of a sepoy offering a gift to a small boy while others look on (Figure 9.1).
Anand, however, goes much further as he shows body, emotion and etiquette jousting at the most intimate frontiers of the empire in the encounter
between Kirpu and the small French girl.[22] The delicacy of the novel lies
in the complexity of such moments: paternal impulse triumphs over racial
boundary and colonial etiquette; spontaneity and trepidation rub against
each other; processes of touch and intimacy are indulged in, tenderly,
tentatively, as racist codes of civilian society are both evoked and thrown
away in wartime France. ' "Come, Mooni, come here," Uncle Kirpu called
her endearingly in his dialect.' The moment is tender, but Anand is no
simplifier: race intrudes as visual difference. The French girl stares with her
'untrusting' hazel eyes, 'shy and enigmatic'. However the distrust is born of
unfamiliarity rather than deformed by the fear and prejudice with which
the white child accosts the black man in Fanon's famous account: 'Look, a
Negro … Mum, look at the Negro. I'm frightened.'[23] As Kirpu physically
picks her up, Anand adds 'in the best Indian tradition', though Kirpu's
anxieties perhaps have more to do with the codes of racial segregation
rather than with child sexuality. Later, when Major Peacock appears, he is

[22] Recent scholars such as Ann Laura Stoler have shown how the colonial authorities relied not just
on refashioning trade and the army in the colonies but often on a more subtle reorganisation of the
domain of the intimate. See Ann Laura Stoler, *Carnal Knowledge and Imperial Power: Race and the
Intimate in Colonial Rule* (Berkeley: University of California Press, 2002).
[23] Fanon, *Black Skin, White Masks*, 22.

Figure 9.1   A French boy with Indian soldiers. British Library, Photograph Collection of H. D. Girdwood. Courtesy of the British Library Board (Photo 24/074).

perceived as humane, non-racist and tactful, but the mutual registering of the colonial code of touch and its transgression leaves a tremor on the scene. Anand's humanism accommodates paternity and tenderness alongside the legacies of colonialism which inflect the intimate history of emotions but cannot hijack it. In the second passage, in sharp contrast, we have a grotesque internalisation and deflection of the racist hierarchies. Instead of political and racial identification with the black troops, the Indian sepoys behave like some of the local French women who initially regarded the African troops as 'cannibalistic'.[24] And worse: the village-women were afraid, the sepoy is contemptuous. But such racism is part of his insidious identity-formation in the world of colonial and racial hierarchies: accused of 'savagery' himself, the sepoy here – insecure and beleaguered – projects a 'brown over black' hierarchy, exults 'at the superior brown skin of his inheritance' and tries to assert his 'humanity'. Lalu, however, questions and resists, even if such questioning is mimetic: 'And if the French liked the blacks, why shouldn't he like them? Why had he thought himself superior?' His memory travels back to his childhood days as Anand shows how such racist hierarchies are replayed with local variations in India: Lalu remembers how, in his village school, the dark-skinned South Indian children used to be bullied by the fair-skinned Punjabi children. If Anand in writing *Across the Black Waters* issues a challenge to the colour of war memory, it is equally a challenge to the Indian obsession with skin colour, with the exact shade of brown. One of the nicest things about Anand, as we will see with Tagore, is that he is so balanced with his chastisements.

At the same time, differences within whiteness start opening up for Lalu.[25] If on arrival there was a perception of there being just one superior 'white' race, he gradually learns to differentiate – 'he wondered how the English liked the French being so free and easy' – followed by a demystification of 'whiteness' itself. If, in Henri Barbusse's *Under Fire* (1916), the sight of black bodies rotting in the heat promotes fears of racial miscegenation, the sight of a white Tommy defecating in fear takes away the last vestige of 'white superiority' for Lalu. In effect, it also humanises whiteness. As he sees French boys leaving for war and their mothers crying, these women remind him of his own mother as she 'had cried when he had left home after the

[24] See Christian Koller, 'Military Colonialism in France', in Dominiek Dendooven and Piet Chielens, *World War I: Five Continents in Flanders* (Ypres: Lannoo, 2008), 13.
[25] For 'whiteness' as construction, see Geoff Dyer, *White: Essays on Race and Culture* (London: Routledge, 1997).

holiday' (84). In a context where imperialism depended on the mystification of 'difference-cum-superiority', Lalu is the Pax Brittanica's greatest fear
come true: he realises there is no essential difference between the two races.
If the war can be reconceptualised as the process of cultural encounters,
Anand would fully exploit the capaciousness of fiction to dramatise such
moments and turn them into intimate processes of self-encounter and self-
realisation. Lalu's self-encounter with prejudice is the beginning of a new
journey: it is the first step towards 'cosmopolitan sympathies', not just with
British Tommies and French women but with fellow non-white subjects
and victims. This is the site of politicisation for Lalu and a radical moment
in a South Asian text. The exposure of the sepoys' racism and Lalu's resistance were no doubt shaped by their creator's anti-colonial cosmopolitanism
forged in London through contact with anti-imperial socialists such as
E. M. Forster, Leonard Woolf and George Orwell.[26]

Camp-Life: Ambivalence, Intimacy, One-Upmanship

In *The Sepoy and the Raj* (1994), David Omissi notes how the scholars of
the Subaltern project with their bias towards 'moments of resistance and
protest' often ignore 'the peasant-soldier groups who voted with their feet
in favour of colonial power – as if peasants ceased to be subordinate, or
conscious, or potentially dissident once they had enlisted'.[27] More recently,
the novelist Amitav Ghosh has noted that 'across those centuries of service
one thing that remained constant was the sepoy's ambivalent relationship
to his job'.[28] If questions of sepoy loyalty and dissent have fuelled some of
the most heated debates within South Asian military studies, as discussed
in Chapter 2, Anand provides one of the most nuanced portraits as he
delves into the structure of ambivalence in sepoy-consciousness.

   Through a varied cast of characters, Anand undercuts any homogeneous
notion of loyalty or dissent and shows its varying cadences through a range
of attitudes: from Dhanoo's naive loyalty to the brave Lachman Singh's
increasing disenchantment to the seasoned veteran Uncle Kirpu's clear-
sighted exposure of the systemic hypocrisies and hierarchies of the Raj.

---

[26] See the fascinating project 'Making Britain: South Asians in Bloomsbury', which has a wealth of
    detail on its website www.open.ac.uk/arts/research/asianbritain/making-britain. The phrase 'cosmo-
    politan sympathies' comes from Isaac Rosenberg's poem, 'Break of Day in the Trenches'.
[27] Omissi, *The Sepoy and the Raj*, xix; also see Kristin Bluemel, *George Orwell and the Radical
    Eccentrics*, 320.
[28] Amitav Ghosh, 'Introduction', in Vedica Kant, *'If I Die, Who Will Remember Me?': India and the
    First World War* (Delhi: Roli Books, 2014), 9.

In an earlier and symbolic moment in the text, Lalu and his comrades come across the monument of 'Jean d'Arc' in the Place du Martin. This has resonances in the archives: photographs show Indian sepoys in front of the statue, while, in October 1915, sepoy Jal-ud-Din Ahmad wrote from Rouen: 'Four hundred years ago that woman gained some notable victories in war against the English.'[29] The double significance of gender and Anglo-French conflict would not be lost on Anand. 'Then, do you mean to say that the Angrez Sahib and the Francisis were enemies at one time', a sepoy asks, rather shocked, while another replies 'A girl Jarnel who drove out the Angrezi army!' (40–41). In Lalu's consciousness, Joan of Arc blends with the figure of Rani of Jhansi, a nationalist heroine of the Sepoy Uprising of 1857, and he feels 'blood coursing in his veins' as he aims to 'follow her on the path of glory'. As we saw in the case of Nazrul Islam, imperial war and nationalist resistance get conflated in the excitement of military service. Indeed, it is repeatedly asked why are they fighting, where is the war, how many guns does the British army have? 'No one knew – nobody knew anything' is the refrain that runs through the novel (78). Anand's critique of empire and war is, however, no black-and-white affair. His attack is directed more at the colonial war machine, rather than at individual British officers, who are perceived as kind and paternalistic. As the Indian troops advance, there is no defensive covering fire and the sepoys are mowed down. 'Where are our guns', Lalu asks with desperation, to which Uncle Kirpu hisses back, with 'red hot anger', 'Where are our guns? Where are the guns? We haven't got any guns' (147). The suggestion of Indians being used as cannon-fodder is at once raised and thrown away as Kirpu blames incompetence rather than racism: 'We haven't got any big guns, otherwise they could have saved the *Goras* [whites] on the right from destruction ... But this bitch of a Sarkar hasn't got as many big guns as the Germans' (148). Anand's anti-colonialism is combined with his socialism as he follows the thesis of 'lions led by donkeys' and portrays both working-class Tommies and sepoys as victims of the war and empire.

The whole debate between claims of loyalty and dissent finds one of its earliest and most powerful portraits in the character of Kirpu. He is a seasoned veteran who had served in China and other imperial wars, one of those 'guardians of the Raj' one expects to meet in the narratives of Kipling, but, in Anand's hands, he becomes a nuanced and complex character. Razor-sharp, big-hearted and robustly anti-authoritarian, his identity is fiercely rooted in regimental service and loyalty, but he does

[29] Jal-ud-Din Ahmad, from Rouen, France, 14 October 1915, *CIM*, IOR, L/MIL/825/7, 1100.

not have any delusions about the fairness of his employers: 'The Sarkar is a like a bitch, son ... It barks its orders and does not explain' (103). He is no card-carrying loyalist, but he is no mutineer either; he may grouse against the Sarkar but it does not incite him towards dissent. Instead, he carries on with his job and takes pride in it. Neither an imperial loyalist nor a proto-nationalist, Kirpu remains a singularly powerful example of the complex sepoy-consciousness, deeply ambivalent about the Sarkar and yet wholly devoted to his regiment and comrades, defying the reductive binaries of loyalty and dissent. Funny, generous, clear-sighted, incorrigibly irreverent and immensely lovable, he also has elements of the Shakespearean fool as he exposes the pretentiousness of his fellow sepoys and undermines authority at every level; his lament at the death of Lachman Singh has all the poignancy of Dai's elegy at the death of Aneirin Lewis in Jones's *In Parenthesis* (1937). The moral centre of the Indian camp and of the narrative, Kirpu is the most powerful character in the novel. Indeed, the emotional core of the novel is the Kirpu–Lalu dyad: the homosocial intensity between Stanhope and Raleigh, as in Sherriff's *Journey's End* (1928), is replaced by an 'Uncle–Son' relationship. When Lalu fainted at the smell of blood, Uncle Kirpu 'fanned' and 'caressed' him: 'Come, my son' (79). If life in the trenches was often the extension of the public-school system for the English officers, as Robert Graves famously noted, in *Across the Black Waters* it has all the emotional shades and nuances of an extended family transposed from a Punjabi village. At the same time, Anand injects such family drama with generous doses of war camaraderie redolent of British war poetry and memoirs (and, later, Paul Fussell's *The Great War and Modern Memory*) as he shows sepoys bathing together or having a snow-fight (276) or sleeping with their bodies grouped together in the 'smallest' space (81). Such scenes are the fine-point where, in terms of world literature, the plebeian world of *Coolie* meets the rich world of touch and intimacy celebrated by Wilfred Owen and Siegfried Sassoon.

But the Indian camp is no Utopian haven: no other war novel shows a regiment so internally divided or bristling with such tension. If the empire is under attack in *Across the Black Waters*, so too is a kind of hyper-competitive, power-hungry, insecure, Indian masculinity constituted as much through colonialism as through a feudal economy obsessed with privilege and hierarchy. 'We are rotten. Never so happy as when we are up and someone else is down', says Kirpu (243). The British officers, in comparison, are represented as kind and paternalistic, whereas the Indian officers are often depicted as vicious, revelling in one-upmanship and in the assertion of what Shakespeare, in a telling phrase, calls 'a moment's brief little authority'.[30] Because these petty Indian officers have so little authority, its exercise, when the opportunity comes, is brutal. The main representative for this is Subah, the son of Major Arbel Singh. Early in the narrative, Subah tells Lalu: 'You will be my friend, even when I am an officer' (23). Once Subah has been promoted through nepotism to the rank of a Jemadar (Lieutenant), he becomes 'overbearingly masterful and all-knowing': humiliation of others becomes his way of asserting his fragile ego. Jealous of Lalu's intimacy with Marie, he orders him to parade; drunk during a trench raid, he lies and blames his fellow brethren for the failed attack. The biggest exposure of him comes during the sepoys' visit to the brothel. While the censored letters of the sepoys hint at sexual activity – 'I intend to enjoy whatever pleasures there are', wrote Jai Sigh in November 1916[31] – Anand's imagining of the scene is remarkably sordid. Subah runs out of money and yet, sexually excited, tries to grab and kiss the women, and the whole scene degenerates into 'slaps, fisticuffs, kicks' and the sepoys get thrown out. Claire Buck has noted that, in the imaginary of the scene, the sepoys 'can pay to look, but not possess';[32] one wonders whether the anxiety is equally on the part of their creator Anand, the self-consciously cosmopolitan intellectual, at the idea of his rustic brethren being able to handle paid sex with French sex-workers. Sexual encounters in the novel involve little sex and a whole world of cultural insecurity, difference and anxiety. As riposte to Dhanoo's comment that the Europeans 'drink wine and make eyes at women', Lalu notes that 'We are all "bledy fools" … Hypocrites' (73).

If Subah is a combination of a buffoon and a bully, equally sinister are the officers Suchet Singh and Lok Nath. In May 1915, General Willcocks had several men shot for malingering.[33] Anand dramatises the scene vividly as he shows the three officers – Subah, Lok Nath and Suchet Singh – exercising their authority with sadistic force as they shoot a dissenting junior colleague accused of malingering:

> 'Oh Suberdarji, forgive me, leave me here, I have got fever, forgive me!' the soft voice of the tall lemur-like Hanumant Singh could be heard. 'I can't fight! I will not fight for this dirty Sarkar.'

---

[30] Shakespeare, *Measure for Measure*, ed. J. W. Lever (London: Bloomsbury, 2008), 46.

[31] Jai Sigh, France to Sirdar Singh, Lahore, Punjab, 6 November 1917, *CIM*, IOR, L/MIL/5/827/5, 662, British Library.

[32] Buck, *Conceiving Strangeness*, 39.

[33] See 'Court-Martial Convictions in the Indian Corps', October 1914 to February 1914, The National Archives, WO, 154/14. Also see Morton-Jack, *The Indian Army*, 173.

'Stand up! Coward!'
'Up!'
'Son of a swine!'
The voices of officers multiplied.

But Hanumant simply lay down, resisting like a child, and stubbornly
rolled on the ground, refusing to get up.

'Stand up!' roared Lok Nath.
'Ohe illegally begotten!' shouted Subah.

'I shall deal with him,' said Suchet Singh, taking out his revolver. 'If you
don't get up while I count three … one, two … three …' And he shot at
Hanumant Singh so that sepoy shrieked and doubled over with a 'Hai, hai
oh my …' (178)

One of the ugliest moments in the text, the above scene is far more of a
savage attack on the native officer-collaborators who grease the wheels of
the colonial state than on the punitive war machine. If Hanumant Singh
is the only voice of active dissent in the whole novel, Anand shows how
quickly and brutally it is stamped out by his own 'comrades', guided by
their sense of 'duty' to the Sarkar. The ugliness is only rivalled by another
later when Lance-naik (Lance corporal) Lok Nath, filled with resentment
at Kirpu's promotion, tears off his recently-awarded Lance-naik's stripe
and tries to have him court-martialled for insubordination. Thrown into
prison and filled with a sense of shame, Kirpu commits suicide, marking
the bleakest point in the text. Abrupt and melodramatic, the suicide of
Kirpu underscores the rancour and in-fighting within the Indian camp.
The viciousness in the Indian camp is as much for critique in the text as
are the workings of imperial power.

Both cultural encounters and camp in-fighting constantly add an extra
layer to the otherwise standard trench narrative of mud, rats, bombardment, failed offensives and perilous trench-raids that Anand draws upon;
Lachman Singh is killed in an offensive, Daddy Dhanoo gets drowned in
the mud, Lalu is taken as a prisoner of war. *Across the Black Waters* is much
more than a combat narrative. While it is a critique of empire and war, it
will be restrictive to view the novel only within an anti-colonial nationalist parameter. Having been brought up in feudal Punjab, and fighting
the forces of fascism, Anand was particularly sensitive to the insidious
workings of power – be it British imperialists or Punjabi feudal landlords
or native military officers. In *Apology for Heroism* (1946), he remembered
rural life in Punjab as a 'subhuman' experience where 'a few privileged
persons preyed upon others like strong birds on the weaker members of

the flock'.[34] In portraying officers such as Subah or Lok Nath, he might have been drawing upon painful memories of his ruthlessly socially ambitious and politically servile father. In *Seven Summers*, he recalls his father's responses to a small gift from a British officer:

> 'The Karnel is a very good man!' he said to my mother, full of pride. 'And that basket which he has sent me is a shoe [with the meaning of being a 'slap'] in the face of all my enemies. They can go on back-biting now if they like, for I have got the Sahibs on my side ... I have served the Sarkar all these years and I shall not betray the salt I have eaten ... let us have some of the fruit now.'[35]

Rather than an uncomplicated homage to his now-dead father, *Across the Black Waters* may well have been an act of Oedipal rebellion. However, the political edge of the novel lies not in its attack upon individuals but rather in the exposure of the psychic perversities and contradictions engendered by the intersecting histories of colonialism, feudalism and the war.

Indo-englishness: Affect, Politics and Linguistic Cosmopolitanism

In his article 'Pigeon-Indian: Some Notes on Indian-English Writing' (1972), Anand predicted the enduring power of 'Indian-English writing', for 'it is based on Indian-English language of the most vital character'. He goes on to quote a celebrated passage from Raja Rao's preface to *Kanthapura* (1938):

> One has to convey in a language that is not one's own the spirit that is one's own. One has to convey the various shades and omissions of a certain thought movement that look maltreated in an alien language. I used the word 'alien'. Yet English is not really an alien language to us ... we are all instinctively bilingual, many of us writing in our own language and in English. We cannot write like the English. We should not. We cannot write only as Indians. We have grown to look at the large world as part of us.[36]

Anand similarly remembered how, in Mall Road in Delhi, certain words struck 'dithyrambically on the tympanum' of his ears: 'Hello ji', 'Thank you ji', 'By God yaar' or 'have you finished your *khana* [food]'. Such 'pidgin-English' is transformed into 'pigeon-English' by creative writers writing in

[34] Anand, *Apology for Heroism*, 21–22.
[35] Anand, *Seven Summers*, 120.
[36] Raja Rao, 'Preface' to *Kanthapura* (New Delhi: Oxford University Press, 1937), vii.

Indian English.[37] Here we have one of the earliest insights into linguistic
hybridity that has now become such a staple fiction of Indian literature in
English, particularly in the hands of writers such as Salman Rushdie and
Amitav Ghosh.

Raja Rao speaks of 'us' – educated middle-class Indians – as 'instinct-
ively bilingual', meaning proficiency in English and in one's mother tongue,
something most of the sepoys were not. What we have in *Across the Black
Waters* is a sustained act of translation: the words and thoughts of a group
of people who might have picked up a few words of English or French are
being articulated by a bilingual writer in self-consciously 'Indian English',
full of exclamations, swear-words, expletives, wordplays, songs, snatches of
conversations. Why? In 'Pigeon-Indian', he notes, echoing Raja Rao, that
'There is a psychological truth behind this kind of synthetic speech. It is
this: even when Indians know English grammar and have been used to
speaking the alien tongue for a long time, they tend to feel and think in
their mother tongues. And often, the native speech enters into the shell of
the sentence in the foreign language through certain indigenous words.'[38]
In *Across the Black Waters*, he tries to recreate certain soundscapes to not just
evoke but access the sepoy heart. If the use of English necessarily creates
distance, Anand tries to cancel some of the gap by drawing on Punjabi
words, particularly half-articulate expressions of intimacy, fear, affection,
annoyance, impatience – 'Ohe', 'Oof', 'Wah! Wah', 'Hai' – and swear-words
such as 'rape-daughter' or 'Saleh'. He once mentioned that he conceived of
dialogues in his novel in his native Punjabi, even while writing in English.
Given the subject of *Across the Black Waters*, the use of Punjabi words and
phrases would have been related, at an intimate and mnemonic level, to the
art of recreating the sepoy milieu.

Anand's use of English has attracted attention: while Kristin Bluemel
places Anand's 'weird English' in a tradition of 'imperial dissent' through
narrative disorientation, Margaret Higonnet has noted that, 'just as the
sepoys are mystified by the new world of the French ... the reader may be
mystified by Anand's incorporation of Hindi and Punjabi terms.'[39] There

[37] Anand, 'Pigeon-Indian: Some Notes on Indian-English Writing', in M. K. Naik (ed.), *Aspects of
Indian Writing in English* (New Delhi: Macmillan, 1979), 28 (24-44), republished in *Journal of
Postcolonial Writing*, 21, 2 (1982), 325–336.
[38] *Ibid.*
[39] Kristin Bluemel, 'Casualty of War, Casualty of Empire: Mulk Raj Anand in England', in Shafquat
Towheed (ed.), *New Readings in the Literature of British India 1780–1947* (Stuttgart: ibidem-Verlag,
1997), 301–326; Higonnet, 'Code Switching and Representations of the Great War', 70.

is indeed both a political and a creative dimension. The use of English is to be understood in relation not only to empire but also to different strands within Indian nationalism itself; alongside imperial dissent, there is an equally strong politics of class. In early twentieth-century India, the English language had evolved in metropolitan India as the language of bourgeois civility and elite nationalism: Nehru could speak Urdu and Hindi but wrote only in English; Jinnah worked mostly in English; the national (as opposed to regional) functions of parties such as the Indian National Congress and the Muslim League were largely carried out in English.[40] In political terms, Anand marks his distance from such conformist and upper-middle-class use of English. Influenced instead by Gandhi's grassroots nationalism and inspired by the robust Punjabi dialect with which he had grown up, the prose of *Across the Black Waters* is a sustained assault particularly on the bourgeois conventions of the English language: words are wrenched off their standard lexical and syntactical frameworks, new words and images are coined, Punjabi, English and occasionally even French words rub against each other. In fact the use of 'Indian English' cannot be interpreted as anti-colonial dissent only: it is used in a variety of registers, from the language of the colonial rule, as used by the Indian officers – ' "Get up, you gum-eyed bastards!" came Jemadar Subah Singh's orders' – to the undermining of such authority, as one form of 'Indian English' brushes against another:

> 'Get ready!' Lok Nath bawled as he walked with lifted chest towards the passage way. 'Take your "biscoots" and tea.'
> 'Wah, ohe Mishtar Lok Nath!' Lalu mumbled at the Lance-Naik's Anglicism. 'Wah!' (175)

Lok Nath's supercilious jibe ('biscoots') is undercut by Lalu's thickly (deliberately?) accented playful 'Mishtar'. At the same time, there is a strange double-bind in English being exposed as a tool of privilege and power in an Anglophone novel.

Language is not always just a mode of communication or resistance: for a novelist, it is a source of jouissance, an exercise in playfulness, a creative act. *Across the Black Waters* is possibly the *noisiest* war novel ever written. In no other novel do the soldiers talk, shout, brawl, chatter, gossip, mimic,

[40] Aijaz Ahmad makes this point convincingly in *In Theory: Classes, Nations, Literatures* (Delhi: Oxford University Press, 1992), 76. It is deeply ironic that supposedly the first time an Indian spoke in vernacular before the Viceroy was when Gandhi supported the resolution to raise 200,000 recruits in 1918.

banter, pray or curse as much as they do here as Anand tries to communicate in English the exuberant cadences of Punjabi and Hindi; they are
joined by other voices, accents, dialects. The Hindu, Sikh and Muslim
pray, and raise the war cry in their respective tongues as they charge forward; the British Tommies, encountering the sepoys, show off their
colonial under-tongue; General Willcocks speaks with a 'Sahib's broken
Hindustani' ('Hindustani bahut acche', 235), in contrast to Owen Sahib's
more fluent Hindi 'Bohat mushkil hai' ('It's a difficult situation') (163); the
French devise their own kind of pidgin English for the sepoys: 'This town!
Shell! Horribil! ... Celagare!' (201); Lalu speaks to Marie in a 'hotch-potch
of Punjabi and French' (236). If the trauma of the First World War put language on the edge, it also facilitated a sort of linguistic Babel. Few novels
in English have so inexhaustible or exuberant a fund of swear-words: rape-
daughter, rape-mother, rape-sister, son of sea-cow, jackal of an elephant of
a fool, one-eyed son of a gun, lop-eared sons of wretches, cockeyed sons
of blind bastards, gum-eyed bastards, hinneying like donkeys, festival of
mother's marriage, sucked up stone of a sour mango. While rather vicious
and misogynist, they also have a certain rhetorical excess, as when Lok
Nath says 'Come, I will rape your mother, your grandmother and her
mothers for ten generations' (248). Repositories of a range of feelings, such
swear-words and expletives are also diagnostic for Anand of the culture of
Punjab. Sexual repression leads to sexual overload at the verbal level: 'Rigid
orthodoxy and custom', he writes, had forced the sepoys to 'extremes of
asceticism, obscenity and a mawkish sentimentality which found expression in snatches of maudlin songs or abuse' (238). Indeed, one realises
afresh the acuteness of Anand's imagination as one reads the swear-words
in the novel along the grain of such historical fragments as Mir Mast's
notebook, discussed in the Introduction, with its explosion of words such
as 'testacles', 'brests', 'penis', 'harsehole' [sic].[41]

However, the use of such expletives was by no means an Indian, let alone
Punjabi, trait. John Brophy and Eric Partridge recover a similar stock in
their book *The Long Trail: What the British Soldier Sang and Said in the
Great War of 1914–1918* (1965); there are ruder lists in French, German and
Russian. 'Who's the poor bastard, Dai?', asks the guide of an injured man
in Robert Graves's *Goodbye to All That* (1929), to which the stretcher-bearer
replies 'Sergeant Gallagher' and goes on to describe how he was injured by
his own bomb: 'Silly booger aims too low, it hits the top of the parapet

---

[41] Mir Mast, 'Trench notebook', National Archives of India, Delhi, Foreign and Political War B
(Secret), February 1916, 8–9; see also Figure 0.9.

and bursts back. Deoul! Man, it breaks his silly f____ing jaw and blows a
great lump from his silly f____ face, whatever. Poor silly booger!'[42] Such
trench realism – combining various shades of affection, grief, horror and
the regional accent – had to pass, in the case of Anand, through the prism
of a foreign tongue. At the same time, swear-words also function as a
sign of almost inarticulate intimacy between old friends as both relish the
creativity and mischief of language:

> 'What are the rape-daughters saying?' asked Kirpu, playing on the last word
> affectionately to take away the sting of abuse latent in the classical curse in
> India.
>
> 'What becomes a monkey of a mirror's beauty!' said Lalu, adapting his
> phrase to the current description of the hill-men as monkeys. (15)

Non-literate they may be, but not immune to the pleasure of words, when
it is all they have in a foreign country. As the mood gradually darkens, such
playful words, differently intoned, become railings against fate.

Across the Black Waters remains the only South Asian novel in English
and one of the very few Anglophone novels to address the non-white war
experience. In this respect, its wartime cousins would be found in the
Harlem Renaissance, in novels such as Jessie Fauset's *There Is Confusion*
(1924) and Victor Daly's *Not Only War* (1932), both of which interweave
the African American war experience with the struggle for racial equality.[43]
It is not known whether Anand was familiar with either of the works
but, in its plot and structure, the resonances of *Across the Black Waters*
are with European war literature. While its social realism and concern for
the rural poor are reminiscent of vernacular traditions, as in the Hindi
novelist Munshi Premchand's celebrated *Godaan* (1936), its affinities are
more specifically with the British combat novel. The classic ingredients
of British trench literature that Paul Fussell identifies in *The Great War
and Modern Memory* (1973) – the mud and blood, comradeship, bathing
scenes, corpses, raids, trench-foot – are to be found here as Anand foists
the blood-dimmed iconography of the Western front onto Indian fiction
in English. The description of Dhanoo's death in slime – with the 'mouth
still open' – is reminiscent of the 'death by drowning' sequences so vividly
evoked in Henri Barbusse's *Under Fire* (1916), while Siegfried Sassoon's
'I'm going stark, staring mad because of the guns'[44] has its echo in Khuki

[42] Robert Graves, *Goodbye to All That* (1929; Harmondsworth: Penguin, 1988), 84.
[43] See Mark Whalan, *The Great War and the Culture of the New Negro* (Gainesville: University Press of Florida, 2008).
[44] Siegfried Sassoon, 'Repression of War Experience', in *The War Poems* (London: Faber, 1983), 84.

Ram's 'I shall go mad' (203). Above all, the generally despondent tone is very much in keeping with the war fiction of the 1920s and 1930s, such as Richard Aldington's *Death of a Hero* (1928). But, in certain fundamental ways, *Across the Black Waters* is also the classic English war novel turned upside down: in its exploration of the undertones of racial encounters, or the joining of the critique of empire and Indian feudalism to that of war, or robust use of Punjabi words, it opens up whole new worlds in war literature in English. It is not an aria for the death of European bourgeois consciousness, as with Remarque or Blunden, but tries to find a voice for the working-class non-white peasant-soldier. Given the singularity of the novel, its relative invisibility in the canon of both First World War literature and Indian writing in English is astonishing, but the tide, it seems, is finally turning – indeed, the novel appears, albeit briefly, in three essays in the recently published *Teaching Representations of the First World War* (2017), published by the Modern Languages Association, as it becomes the hook on which to hang the global dimensions of war literature. As we move beyond the centennial years, it is to be hoped that attention will also focus on its brilliant sequel *The Sword and the Sickle* (1942), which looks at the post-war period in India. The war is definitely a site of politicisation, in multiple senses of the term, for the village-boy Lalu, but Anand shrewdly and carefully avoids drawing any direct links in this novel with the anti-colonial struggle; that would be reserved for the sequel where he would align Lalu, freshly returned from Germany where he was held as a POW, to the nationalist movement.[45] But that takes us to a different context, a different place and time: the Amritsar massacre would be a crack in the table of history for the Indian subcontinent.

[45] This final part of the Lalu trilogy is compelling for its literary investigation of post-war India through the eyes of a First World War veteran, but it takes us beyond the time-frame of the current monograph.

CHAPTER 10

Post-war World and 'the Future of All Humanity'

Aurobindo, Iqbal and Tagore

In 1920, the Indian Nobel Laureate Rabindranath Tagore visited the battlefields of the Western Front for the first time. In 'Creative Unity', written in English in 1922, he reminisced:

> Lately I went to visit some battlefields of France which had been devastated by war. The awful calm of desolation, which still wore wrinkles of pain – death-struggles stiffened into ugly ridges – brought before my mind the vision of a huge demon, which had no shape, no meaning, yet had two arms that could strike and break and tear, a gaping mouth that could devour, and bulging brains that could conspire and plan. It was a purpose, which had a living body, but no complete humanity to temper it. Because it was passion – belonging to life, and yet not having the wholeness of life – it was the most terrible of life's enemies.

> Something of the same sense of oppression in a different degree, the same desolation in a different aspect, is produced in my mind when I realise the effect of the West upon Eastern life – the West which, in its relation to us, is all plan and purpose incarnate, without any superfluous humanity.

> …

> The wriggling tentacles of a cold-blooded utilitarianism, with which the West has grasped all the easily yielding succulent portions of the East, are causing pain and indignation throughout the Eastern countries. The West comes to us, not with the imagination and sympathy that create and unite, but with a shock of passion – passion for power and wealth. This passion is a mere force, which has in it the principle of separation, of conflict.[1]

Tagore's visceral description of the trenches as 'wrinkles of pain' – 'death-struggles stiffened into ugly ridges' – compares to the finest metaphors in First World War poetry. In 'The Show', the British war poet Wilfred Owen – who had read Tagore in the trenches and would recite the poem

---

[1] Rabindranath Tagore, 'Creative Unity', in *The English Writings of Rabindranath Tagore, Plays, Stories, Essays*, ed. Sisir Kumar Das (Kolkata: Sahitya Academy, 1996), Vol. 2, 531–532.

'When I go from hence' to his mother during his last leave – would describe the landscape of the Western Front as 'pitted with great pocks and scabs of plagues' across which the soldiers' agonies, insect-like, 'curl, lift and flatten'.[2] But Tagore's description soon develops into something altogether more terrifying: the vision of a demon, shapeless and formless, but with arms and jaws and brain that can plot and kill, grotesquely *alive*. *Bhaugolik apadevatā* ('geographical monster') was Tagore's term for aggressive nationalism, which, as he noted in a poem written during the Boer War (1899–1902), had made 'the world its food'.[3] In the same year that Tagore visited the battlefields, the master-psychologist Sigmund Freud was conceptualising his idea of the *Todestrieb* or death drive in *Beyond the Pleasure Principle*; in *Civilisation and Its Discontents* (1929), his response to the war, Freud would further develop his thesis about 'the blindest fury of destructiveness' as something inherent in the human psyche.[4] The poet and the psychologist would meet in Vienna in 1926.

War-as-demon becomes a common trope in European literature and art in the post-war years, but the colonial intellectual pushes it in a different direction: the demon becomes the 'West' *itself* in the way the imagery of hands resurfaces in the metaphor of the tentacles. Indeed, the image of the 'West' red in tooth and claw with the blood of imperial expansion resonates with anti-western and Pan-Asian discourses of the time, where Europe is often described as fighting like 'wolves and jackals' over the 'scraps of meat in the Orient'.[5] 'Passion' is a key word in the above passage, transferred from the demon of war to the predatory 'West', the word itself – from the Latin *'passio'* meaning 'suffering' and suggestive of the 'Passions of Christ' – a telling reminder of how very far Europe had moved from its Christian credo of 'suffering'. Tagore was one of the first intellectuals to emphasise the cost of imperialism not just for Asians and Africans but for Europe itself, as the humanist lamented the corruption of the 'large-hearted liberalism' of the British: '[I] wonder how imperialist greed could bring about so ugly a transformation in the character of so great a race.'[6] The extended

---

[2] Wilfred Owen, 'The Show', *The War Poems*, 42. For the story of Owen reading Tagore in the trenches, see Krishna Dutta and Andrew Robinson, *Rabindranath Tagore: The Myriad-Minded Man* (London: Bloomsbury, 1995), 2–3.

[3] See Ashis Nandy, *The Illegitimacy of Nationalism: Rabindranath Tagore and the Politics of Self* (Delhi: Oxford University Press, 1994), 7.

[4] Freud, *Civilisation and Its Discontents, The Standard Edition of the Complete Psychological Works*, ed. and trans. James Strachey *et al.* (London: Hogarth, 1953–74), Vol. XXI, 121.

[5] See Sven Saaler and Christopher W.A. Szpilman (eds.), *Pan Asianism: A Documentary History, 1850–1920* (London: Rowman and Littlefield, 2011), Vol. 1, 136.

[6] Tagore, 'Crisis in Civilisation', in *The English Writings of Rabindranath Tagore, A Miscellany*, ed. Sisir Kumar Das (Kolkata: Sahitya Academy, 1996), Vol. 3, 722, 725.

imagery of the 'demon' provides shrewd political insights into empire and the war: the violence on the Western Front was nothing wholly new but an extension into Europe of the barbarity that imperial Europe had inflicted on other parts of the world. The 'desolation' of the trenches recalled for Tagore the similar desolation caused by the 'West upon Eastern life'. It was an insight that would be echoed by intellectuals as diverse as Hannah Arendt, Jean-Paul Sartre and Simone Weil with reference to the brutalities unleashed in Europe during the thirties.[7]

In recent years, scholars have powerfully drawn attention to a range of anti-colonial and anti-Western imaginaries, from that of Jamal al-Din al-Afghani, the father of the Pan-Islamic movement, to Okakura Kakuzō (who wrote under the pseudonym Okakura Tenshin), the pioneer of Japanese Pan-Asianism and a friend of Tagore.[8] In *The Politics of Anti-Westernism in Asia* (2007), Ceymil Aydin notes the rise in the nineteenth century of 'strategic essentialism against the European discourses of race, Orient, and empire and a legacy of the universalism inherited from the non-Western humanistic traditions of Islam, Confucianism or Buddhism'.[9] Ideas of Pan-Asianism and Pan-Islamism reached India and intersected with a variety of nationalisms which varied from 'official nationalisms' adopted from Europe to the powerful imagination of an 'inner spiritual space', as in the iconography of 'Bharat Maata' or Bankim Chandra Chattopadhyay's *Anandamath* (1882).[10] The destructiveness of the First World War gave such ideas an unprecedented boost. More than ever, the war seemed to provide confirmation of the moral crisis of the Eurocentric world-order, and strengthened the appeal of Pan-Asian and Pan-Islamic ideas on the global stage.[11] The unprecedented violence of the war made colonial intellectuals (who were often critical admirers of Europe) wonder 'whether the torch of European civilisation was not meant for showing light but to set

---

[7] Pankaj Mishra, *From the Ruins of Empire: The Revolt Against the West and the Remaking of Asia* (London: Penguin, 2013), 254. Mishra's book contains one of the most illuminating discussions of the postwar moment in a global context.

[8] See Pankaj Mishra, *From the Ruins of Empire*; Cemil Aydin, *The Politics of Anti-Westernism in Asia*; Kris Manjapra, *Age of Entanglement*; Rustom Bharucha, *Another Asia: Rabindranath Tagore and Okakura Tenshin* (Delhi: Oxford University Press, 2006).

[9] Aydin, *The Politics of Anti-Westernism in Asia*, 201.

[10] Partha Chatterjee, *Nationalist Thought and the Colonial World: A Derivative Discourse* (London: United Nations University, 1986); Tanika Sarkar, *Hindu Wife, Hindu Nation*; Kris Manjapra, *Age of Entanglement*, 42.

[11] See Prasenjit Duara, 'The Discourse of Civilisation and Pan-Asianism', *Journal of World History*, 12, 1 (2001), 103–104; also see Harald Fischer-Tiné, 'Indian Nationalism and the "World Forces": Transnational and Diasporic Dimensions of the Indian Freedom Movement on the Eve of the First World War', *Journal of Global History*, 2, 3 (2007), 325–344.

fire'.[12] While a shell-shocked Europe saw itself as an Eliotian 'waste land' and Western liberalism could speak only through the 'ou-boum' of the Marabar Caves, as in Forster's *A Passage to India* (1924), colonial intellectuals, in contrast, were filled with a sense of hope for a more equitable post-war world.

If the fictional imagination of the war in India has clustered around the figure of the semi-literate sepoy, this final chapter examines the First World War in relationship to Indian intellectual history with reference to three outstanding poet-thinkers of modern India: Aurobindo Ghosh, Muhammed Iqbal and Rabindranath Tagore.[13] In the process, it explores the complexity and contradictions of that history. There are three impulses that underlie the argument. First, while these men, particularly Aurobindo and Iqbal, are often regarded as 'nationalist' heroes, this chapter shows the internationalist nature of their imaginings during the war years: all three were intimately familiar with both European and Asian intellectual cultures, and their anti-colonialism emerged out of rich 'cosmopolitan thought-zones'.[14] Second, the horrors of the war made them evolve their anti-colonial stances into civilisational critiques whose conceptual foundations went far beyond an 'Indian' or nationalist imagining. Combining an ethical critique of empire and an idealist critique of industrial modernity, they were fired by a vision which, in Tagore's words, embraced 'the future of all humanity'.[15] Such aspiration was immensely powerful and poignant, but also fractured, I would contend, by the weight of that history and the misprision of language, as each put forward his particular vision of a redemptive Asia in answer to a blood-stained West. Of course, neither the 'West' nor 'Asia' was a stable category in their thoughts, which, as we shall see, differed among these three writers; moreover, their responses were partly shaped by the audiences they were addressing or the particular 'thought-zones' in which they wished to intervene. Third, while these essays are studied as 'political'

---

[12] Quoted in Tan Chung, Amiya Dev, Wang Bangwei and Wei Liming (eds.), *Tagore and China* (Delhi: Sage, 2011), 79.

[13] Intellectual history is a burgeoning field in the context of South Asia: see Shruti Kapila (ed.), *An Intellectual History for India* (Cambridge: Cambridge University Press, 2012) for an excellent collection of essays. Here, I refer to each of the three figures by the name under which they are best recognised: Aurobindo Ghosh as Aurobindo, Rabindranath Tagore as Tagore (his family name) and Muhammed Iqbal, also known as Allama Iqbal, as Iqbal.

[14] See Manjapra, 'Introduction' to Bose and Manjapra (eds.), *Cosmopolitan Thought Zones*, 1–19, where Manjapra convincingly argues for a sort of 'anticolonial cosmopolitanism'. The idea resonates with Cemil Aydin's thesis of 'anti-Westernism' in *The Politics of Anti-Westernism in Asia*, and the 'ethical style of anti-colonial dissent' in Leela Gandhi's *The Common Cause: Postcolonial Ethics and the Practice of Democracy* (Chicago: Chicago University Press, 2014).

[15] Tagore, *Nationalism*, ed. Ramchandra Guha (London: Penguin, 2009 [1917]), 41.

or 'social' treatises, they can productively be read as *literary* texts – metaphoric, allusive, fractured – each bearing witness to the turbulence and hope of an immediately post-war world.

Aurobindo Ghosh: Politics, *Dharma* and Language

Poet, essayist, translator, literary and art critic, political theorist and philosopher: the sheer variety of 'lives' of Aurobindo Ghosh (or Sri Aurobindo to his followers) as well as his sudden departure from the heat of revolutionary nationalist politics in 1910 to become a mystic visionary or *yogi* are responsible for the strange neglect of this brilliant and original thinker and writer.[16] Alone of all the Indian nationalists, Aurobindo grew up in Europe. Christened Aurobindo 'Ackroyd' Ghosh by his Anglophile father, he was sent to St Paul's in London and then to Cambridge. There he distinguished himself as a brilliant classicist, and was also introduced to Indian spirituality and nationalism.[17]

Aurobindo returned to India in February 1893. Opposed to both the colonial state and the 'middle-class machine' that was the Indian National Congress, he formed a secret revolutionary group in 1900 and founded the English-language newspaper *Bande Mataram*, a veritable 'international compendium of political insurgency'.[18] At a time when the Indian National Congress was arguing for dominion status, he issued a call for full independence – 'Our ideal is that of *Swaraj* or absolute autonomy free from foreign control.'[19] During a period of solitary confinement for his involvement in the Alipore bomb case of 1908, he had a series of mystical experiences, whereupon he famously retired from politics and departed from Calcutta to Pondicherry in February 1910. There, he would live as a religious recluse, absorbed in meditation and immersing himself in German philosophy, the *Bhagavad Gita* and the Vedanta and the practice of *yoga*. Combining elements from the German philosopher-historian Karl Gotthard Lamprecht, the *Upanishads* and the *Bhagavad Gita*, he formed a complex theory of individual and social evolution towards a 'greater Reality', which he set forth over several years in *The Human Cycle* and

---

[16] Peter Heehs, *The Lives of Sri Aurobindo* (New York: Columbia University Press, 2008); Peter Heehs, *Sri Aurobindo, A Brief Biography* (Delhi: Oxford University Press, 1989). A good selection of his writings can be found in *The Essential Writings of Sri Aurobindo*, ed. Peter Heehs (Delhi: Oxford University Press, 1998).

[17] Peter Heehs, *Sri Aurobindo, A Brief Biography*, 9, 10–19.

[18] Manjapra, *Age of Entanglement*, 46.

[19] 'An Open Letter to My Countrymen', in *The Essential Writings of Sri Aurobindo*, 5.

The Life Divine.[20] In August 1914, he co-founded, with the French writer Paul Richard and his wife Mirra Richard, the landmark journal *Arya*. When Richard was called back to France in February 1916, Aurobindo assumed its editorship and published on literature, poetry, philosophy, the *Bhagavad Gita*, and social and political thought. 'All told', notes his biographer Peter Heehs, 'between 1914 and 1921, he published the equivalent of a dozen books.'[21] While the conflict shaped his major works such as *The Ideal of Human Unity* (serialised during the years 1915–1918) and *The Human Cycle* (serialised from August 1916 to July 1918), his most sustained engagement would be in a selection of interlinked essays collected in *War and Self-Determination* (1920). They include 'The Passing of War', 'The Unseen Power', 'Self-Determination' and '1919', published in *Arya* between 1916 and 1920, and a foreword to the whole volume and 'The League of Nations' were added in 1920.[22] What characterises the essays is a combination of astute political analysis and religious mysticism which blurs generic definitions and undermines any particular critical approach.

What occupies Aurobindo are the very causes of war in an age of liberalism when its 'passing' or prevention is the cherished aim (576). Thus, in 'The Passing of War', the eruption of this world war leads him to an examination of nineteenth-century liberalism itself; he argues that the so-called guarantors of world peace such as international trade links, the establishment of democracy and the international 'Courts of Arbitration' (584) are actually 'illusions' which have merely changed rather than actually prevented warfare.[23] For him, the cherished ideal of peace on the part of nineteenth-century Europe is itself a form of imperial greed:

> For the statesman and the governing classes the idea is to have peace and security for the maintenance of past acquisitions and an untroubled

---

[20] Peter Heehs, 'Introduction', in *Situating Sri Aurobindo*, xiii; B. S. Chimni, 'Retrieving "Other" Visions: Sri Aurobindo and the Ideal of Human Unity', in Peter Heehs (ed.), *Situating Sri Aurobindo: A Reader* (New Delhi: Oxford University Press, 2013), 135–138.

[21] Heehs, *The Lives of Sri Aurobindo*, 258; and *The Essential Writings of Sri Aurobindo*, xv. A Francophile in spite of his anti-colonialism, Aurobindo keenly followed the German advance from his semi-seclusion in Pondicherry. On 15 September 1914, he wrote down in his diary that 'the great German defeat satisfies at once *trikaldristi* and *aishwarya*'; when General von Kluck changed direction just before Paris, he thought that the spiritual intervention by him and Mirra Richard (who came to be known as the Mother) had saved the day for the Allies. See Heehs, *Lives*, 257.

[22] 'Foreword' to 'War and Self-Determination' (1920), in *Social and Political Thought* (hence abbreviated as *SPT*), *Sri Aurobindo Birth Centenary Library* (Pondicherry: Sri Aurobindo Ashram Trust, 1971), Vol. 15, 575. The essays comprising 'War and Self-Determination' are 'Foreword', 'The Passing of War', 'The Unseen Power', 'Self-Determination', '1919' and 'The League of Nations'. All references to any of these essays are to this edition, unless otherwise stated.

[23] 'The Passing of War', *SPT*, 576, 584.

domination by the great highly organised imperial and industrial nations without the perturbing appearance of new unsatisfied hungers and the peril of violent unrests, revolts, revolutions ... (577)

His analysis of an inequitable world-order resonates not just with that of Iqbal and Tagore, as we will see, but with one of the most hallowed thinkers on war and peace: Immanuel Kant. In *Zum ewigen Frieden: Ein philosophischer Entwurf* (*Perpetual Peace: A Philosophical Essay*) (1795), while discussing 'cosmopolitan right' as the basis of a new world-order, Kant notes that the main deterrent to true peace is the 'inhospitable behaviour of the civilised nations, especially the commercial states of our continent' which 'fills us with horror'. He continues thus: 'Oppression of the natives followed [as well as] famine, insurrection, perfidy and all the rest of the litany of evils which can afflict mankind.'[24] Both for Kant and for Aurobindo, an unequal world-order is incompatible with 'perpetual peace'; for the latter, early-twentieth-century imperialism was necessarily caught up in a vicious cycle of injustice and violent reprisal, of which the Russian Revolution was the most recent and powerful example.

However, Aurobindo soon leaves the realm of the political to plumb the depths of the psychological. War, he would go on to argue, was a 'psychological necessity', for 'what is within us, must manifest itself outside.'[25] At about the same time, Freud was writing about the preponderance of violence in our psychic lives: 'If we are to be judged by our unconscious wishful impulses, we ourselves are, like primaeval man, a gang of murderers ... [War] strips us of the later accretions of civilisation and lays bare the primal man in each of us.'[26] Yet, the differences between the psychologist and the *yogi* were substantial: if the war made Freud move beyond the pleasure principle into the detection of the death-drive, it made Aurobindo move from the psychological to the spiritual and insist on an 'inner change': 'War and violent revolution can be eliminated ... on the condition that we get rid of the inner causes of war and the constantly accumulating *Karma* of successful injustice of which violent revolutions are the natural reactions. Otherwise, there can be only at best a fallacious period of artificial peace.'[27] Its biggest example for him was the formation

---

[24] Immanuel Kant, *Perpetual Peace: A Philosophical Essay*, trans. M. Campbell Smith with a preface by Robert Latta (New York and London: Garland Publishing, 1972), 139.
[25] 'The Passing of War', *SPT*, 587.
[26] Freud, 'Thoughts for the Times on War and Death', in *The Standard Edition of the Complete Psychological Works*, Vol. XIV, 297, 299.
[27] 'Foreword', *SPT*, 577.

of the League of Nations – this 'ill-jointed, stumbling and hesitating machine' (599).

In 'After the War' (1920), he emphasises two fallouts from the war as most 'momentous for the future': the struggle between 'Capital and Labour', and that of a 'resurgent Asia'.[28] Aurobindo's essay, published just a week after the Second World Congress of the Comintern in Moscow in the summer of 1920 – when M. N. Roy, on Lenin's invitation, spoke memorably and Bolshevik support for anti-imperialism was adopted as a policy – is a poignant testimony to the brief period of hope and alliance in the relationship between Bolshevism and the anti-colonial struggle.[29] Lenin's exposure of the secret agreement among France, Britain and Tsarist Russia to carve up and appropriate the Middle East attracted admiration from the colonial intellectuals, including from the Bengali economist Benoy Kumar Sarkar, who called it 'an extraordinary and incredibly supermanic promulgation of a new international morality'.[30] Similarly, Aurobindo hailed the union as a 'moral alliance' between the 'intellectual idealism of Europe and the soul of Asia',[31] while his friend Paul Richard proclaimed that 'We are working for Asia – for a free and united Asia – to prepare in her and through her the world for the great Dawn, the Dawn of Man.'[32] Aurobindo pushed such ideas further as he spoke of an 'Asiatic unrest … from Egypt to China' and reiterated the demand for political independence: 'self-government, Home Rule, democracy, national independence'.[33] But, in the essay, such acute socio-historical insights give way to his theory of social and spiritual 'evolution'.[34] The conjunction of Bolshevism and Asian resurgence was only 'an acute stage of crisis', the 'first of an ascending series of changes to the creation of a greater humanity'.[35] What was needed, beyond economic reorganisation and political change, was an 'inner change' as he now reconceptualises the Wilsonian doctrine of 'self-determination' from

---

[28] 'After the War', *SPT*, 640.
[29] See John Patrick Haithcox, *Communism and Nationalism in India: M. N. Roy and Comintern Policy, 1920–1939* (Princeton: Princeton University Press, 1971); also see Aydin, *Politics of Anti-Westernism*, 145–149, who notes how, between 1919 and 1923, the relationship 'moved from a stage of friendly cooperation to hostile competition' as the Bolsheviks, despite their anti-colonial agenda, 'could not accept the idea of an alternative Eastern civilisation' (149).
[30] Benoy Kumar Sarkar, 'The International Fetters of Young China', *The Journal of International Relations*, 11, 3 (1921), 355.
[31] 'After the War', *SPT*, 646, 648.
[32] Paul Richard, 'Some Answers', *Asian Review*, 1, 1 (1920), 42.
[33] 'After the War', *SPT*, 644–645.
[34] Sachidananda Mohanty (ed.), *Sri Aurobindo: A Contemporary Reader* (London: Routledge, 2008), 96.
[35] 'After the War', *SPT*, 640; 'The Unseen Power', *SPT*, 589.

the realm of political sovereignty to that of 'an inner and larger self other than the mere ego': 'True freedom is only possible if we live in the infinite, live, as the Vedanta bids us, in and from our self-existent being.'[36] Yet, there is little attention in the essays to the material bases of such transformation, such as social movements or the political economy.

What makes these essays at once exhilarating and frustrating is the combination of analytical acuity and the subordination of these political, psychological and sociological analyses to his theory of spiritual evolutionism. We seem to be borne at a hundred miles an hour through the worlds of political philosophy, human psychology and contemporary history, only to be finally asked to fixate our vision on 'life divine': the cares of the world seem to be stripped away before the vale of soul-making. Even an historian as humanistic and nuanced as Sumit Sarkar notes ironically, 'So the nationalist leader becomes the yogi of Pondicherry.'[37] There is a tension between the political and the mystical, the material and the metaphysical throughout the essays which is never resolved, and yet to try to shear one off from the other is to miss their singularity. Consider the following extract:

> And now we see militarism and commercialism united in a loving clasp, coalescing into a sacred biune duality of national life and patriotic aspiration and causing and driving by their force the most irrational, the most monstrous and nearly cataclysmic, the hugest war of modern and indeed of all historic times ...

> As this great materialistic civilisation of Europe to which the high glowing dawn of the Renaissance gave its brilliant birth and the dry brazen afternoon of nineteenth-century rationalism its hard maturity, is passing away and the bosom and the soul of man heave a sigh of relief at its going, so whatever new civilisation we construct after this evening of the cycle, *yugasandha*, on which we are entering ...

> But a *dharmarajya* of the half-penitent *Vaishya* is not to be the final consummation of a time like ours pregnant with new revelations of thought and spirit and new creations in life, nor is a golden or rather a copper-gilt age of the sign of the Balance to be glorious reward of this anguish and travail of humanity. It is surely the kingdom of another and higher *Dharma* that is in preparation.[38]

Politics, poetry and prophecy are combined; irony and hope, Lamprecht and the *Vedanta*, critique and hope are held in balance as metaphor and

---

[36] 'Self-determination', *SPT*, 604, 599.
[37] Sarkar, *The Swadeshi Movement in Bengal 1903–1908*, 316.
[38] 'The Passing of War', *SPT*, 583; 'The Unseen Power', *SPT*, 589; 593.

imagery become the mode of ratiocination – a method that Tagore will perfect in his essays on 'Nationalism'. Central to the passage quoted above is the imagining of a double birth or invagination, from *adharma* to that of *svadharma*. The ironic imagery of consummation and progeny ('clasp', 'birth', 'pregnant', 'revelation', 'creation') begins with the satanic embrace of 'militarism' and 'commerce', legitimated by the ideology of Western patriotism and imperialism and giving violent birth to the war. 'Irrational', 'monstrous', 'cataclysmic': the denunciation is precise and unequivocal at a time when Gandhi and Naidu were preaching the rewards of 'sacrifice' for the war. Aurobindo's critique of the West proceeds through sound and imagery. Sound becomes sense through the alliterative embrace of 'clasp', 'coalesce', 'cause' and gives way to 'biune', 'birth' and 'brazen', while nineteenth-century Europe is reduced to one 'dry brazen afternoon'; the vision also accords with the successive stages of his evolutionary philosophy, as set out in *The Human Cycle*. Yet, there is a certain poignancy in the image of the rebirth in 'bosom and soul' of man: the shift is both temporal and spatial as we move from the light of the day to '*yuga-sandhya*' ('epochal evening'), the vocabulary itself registering the shift from Europe to Asia. Steeped as he was in the *Bhagavad Gita* and the *Upanishads*, is this also a classic instance of the Europe-educated colonial intellectual who must speak in his native tongue and create an alternative *language* of discourse?

Language, like Eliot's view of history, has 'cunning passages, contrived corridors/And issues, deceives with whispering ambitions'.[39] In this extract from Aurobindo, framing a vision so cosmic and universal, is a robustly Hindu vocabulary embedded in caste hierarchies, as when he distinguishes the 'higher *dharma*' from the 'dharmarajya of the half-penitent *Vaishya*'. The term 'Vaishya' refers to the third of the four Hindu castes, comprising farmers and merchants: if the phrase is meant ironically to refer to greedy nations dividing up the spoils of war, the critique of imperialism here gets caught up in the no less reprehensible politics of caste. Indeed, the tension between spiritual cosmopolitanism and a religio-linguistically determined vocabulary runs throughout his writing, as in his repeated use of the word '*dharma*'. The term, meaning 'duty' or 'religion', is an ancient Sanskrit word going back to the Vedas; a complex and polysemic concept, it was resurrected powerfully in nineteenth-century Bengal by the writer Bankim Chandra Chattopadhyay, who used it to define a predominantly Hindu spiritual realm against the onslaught of an outer,

---

[39] T.S. Eliot, 'Gerontion', *The Complete Poems and Plays 1909–1950* (New York: Harcourt, Brace & Company, 1952), 22.

Western domain of *vijñān* (Science).[40] The term *dharma* came to embody a powerful Hindu revivalist poetics and ethics which became the ground of nationalist resistance. Aurobindo inherited the word from Bankim, but he further expanded its scope.[41] In his famous Uttarpara speech, he noted that 'We shall devote ourselves not to politics alone, nor to social questions alone, nor to theology or philosophy or literature or science by themselves, but we include all these in one entity which we believe to be all-important, the *dharma*, the national religion which we also believe to be universal.'[42] In a spirited defence of Aurobindo, Sugata Bose has argued that Aurobindo's *sanātan dharma* 'was no narrow or bigoted creed, but as large as "life itself"' and that the inversion of its 'humanistic aspiration … is the signal achievement of our secularist historians, not of Aurobindo'.[43] The moot question is whether a religious and culturally specific vocabulary can fully accommodate a universalist vision.

Hindu imagery came to Aurobindo as leaves to the trees. The war reminded him of Arjun's responses to *Kurukshetra* of the *Mahābhārata*: 'As a swarm of moths with ever-increasing speed fall to their destruction into a fire that someone has kindled, so now the nations with ever-increasing speed are entering into Thy jaws of doom.' The outcome of this destruction, Krishna tells Arjun, will be 'the *dharmarajya*, the kingdom of the *Dharma*' (592), which mirrors his vision of the post-war 'spiritual reconstruction'.[44] While such religious imagery was a source of affective power and was often enmeshed in the very fabric of language, especially in its vernacular forms, it also limited the appeal of the vision to particular groups. The Muslim intellectual Muzaffar Ahmad – Aurobindo's contemporary, and Nazrul's friend – noted how the dominance of Hindu imagery in early-twentieth-century nationalism made it difficult for men like him to align themselves to the movement; citing a line from the song *Vande Mātaram*, translated by Aurobindo ('For, thou hast ten-armed Durga's power'), he noted 'How could a monotheist Muslim youth utter this invocation?'[45] This is not to

---

[40] There has been an important body of work on the reconceptualisation of 'dharma' in nineteenth-century Bengal, particularly with reference to Bankim: see Sudipta Kaviraj, *The Unhappy Consciousness: Bankimchandra Chattopadhyay and the Formation of Nationalist Discourse in India* (New York: Oxford University Press, 1998); Manjapra, *Age of Entanglement*, 44–45; Tanika Sarkar, 'Imagining Hindurashtra', 162–184.
[41] See Andrew Sartori, 'The Transfiguration of Duty', in Peter Heehs (ed.), *Situating Sri Aurobindo: A Reader* (Delhi: Oxford Unversity Press, 2013), 98–99.
[42] 'Uttarpara Speech', Ghosh, *The Essential Writings of Sri Aurobindo*, 41.
[43] Sugata Bose, 'The Spirit and Form of an Ethical Polity', in Peter Heehs (ed.), *Situating Sri Aurobindo*, 119.
[44] 'The Unseen Power', *SPT*, 591–592.
[45] See Suchetana Chattopadhyay, 'War, Migration and Alienation in Colonial Calcutta', 221.

question the universal humanism of Aurobindo's vision but to enquire into the politics of representation and the fabric of lived-in language; we will return to this problem at the end of the chapter. The explicit Hindu register is, however, absent from his final imagining of a post-war world: 'In India the notion of an Asiatic, a spiritualised democracy has begun to be voiced, though it is as yet vague and formless.'[46] 'Spiritualised democracy' was far closer than any religious creed to Aurobindo's understanding of *dharma*. However, at the end of the essay, both the idea of Asia and *dharma* are left behind and history and politics fade before the poetics of 'a greater unknown ... concealed and in preparation, not yet formulated, in the experimental laboratory of Time'.[47]

Muhammed Iqbal: Islam, Post-war Reconstruction and 'Inner Revolution'

In the grandeur of his vision and its universalist aspiration, Muhammed Iqbal provides the Islamic counterpart to Aurobindo. There is, however, a fundamental difference: if Aurobindo's vision is ultimately spiritualist, unbounded by religious affiliation even though drawing on Hindu imagery, Iqbal's was self-consciously Islamic. In the aftermath of the war, Iqbal, like Aurobindo, envisaged a new world order – an alternative humanistic socio-economic ethic and polity represented by Islam as the antidote to the war-ravaged West. Iqbal is usually ensconced within South Asian studies as the ideological father of Pakistan, but the scope and richness of his imagination far exceed the bounds of either nation or conventional Islam. Referring to the First World War, Iqbal noted that 'The storm of the West has made the Muslim into a real Muslim.'[48] Yet, defining who is a 'real' Muslim, or what Islam is, for him, becomes a process of philosophical enquiry rather than a doctrine. Nor does Iqbal's conception of Islam exist in simple opposition to a monolithic 'West'.[49]

---

[46] 'After the War', *SPT*, 645.

[47] '1919', *SPT*, 650.

[48] 'Tulu-i-Islam', in Iqbal, *Call of the Marching Bell [Bāṅg-i-dāra]*, trans. M. A. K. Khalil (Newfoundland: Khalil, 1997), 360.

[49] See Javed Majeed, *Muhammed Iqbal: Islam, Aesthetics and Postcolonialism* (London: Routledge, 2009) and the introduction to Javed Majeed, *The Reconstruction of Religious Thought in Islam* (Stanford: Stanford University Press, 2013), xi–xxx, for a thoughtful investigation of his poetic and religious selves. Also see Iqbal Singh Sevea, *The Political Philosophy of Muhammed Iqbal: Islam and Nationalism in Late Colonial India* (Cambridge: Cambridge University Press, 2002). There are short but perceptive discussions of Iqbal in Stephen N. Hay, *Asian Ideas of East and West: Tagore and His Critics in Japan, China and India* (Cambridge: Harvard University Press, 1970), 295–303 and Mishra, *From the Ruins of Empire*, 257–261.

Iqbal is a classic example both of the cosmopolitanism and of the contradictions engendered by the multi-religious fabric of Indian society as well as by British colonial rule. He was born in 1877 in Punjab into an orthodox Kashmiri family, and read Arabic, English and philosophy in Lahore. He travelled to Europe in 1908 to read philosophy at Trinity College Cambridge and law at Lincoln's Inn, London; he then went to Heidelberg to study Goethe and Heine and on to Munich to write his PhD on metaphysics in Persia.[50] As various scholars have noted, his years in Europe were transformational. On one hand, he became increasingly disillusioned about the materialism and racial inequities of the West, and predicted, like Aurobindo, its demise: 'Your civilisation will commit suicide/With its own sword.'[51] On the other hand, he became 'hyperconscious' of his Muslim identity while simultaneously falling under the spell of Nietzsche, particularly his idea of the Superman.[52] Thus, here was an anti-imperialist whose intellectual formation partly lay in the West and who took pride at being knighted; an otherwise cosmopolitan intellectual who became obsessively convinced about the superiority of Islam to other religions or political systems; an anti-nationalist and ardent believer in Pan-Islamism who nonetheless advocated in 1930 the formation of a 'consolidated North-West Indian Muslim State'.[53] Like Aurobindo, Iqbal too turned his gaze to a 'resurgent Asia', but the land he saw was very different from that of the *karmayogi*. The springs of his anti-colonial dissent were nourished not by Hindu nationalists such as Bankim Chandra Chattopadhyay but by trans-national thinkers such as Jamal al-Din al-Afghani, the founder of Pan-Islamism, who had lamented in the nineteenth century that 'The Islamic states today are unfortunately pillaged and their property stolen; their territory is occupied by foreigners ... What a great catastrophe has fallen [on us]!'[54] On his trip back from Europe, Iqbal gazed at the coast of Sicily – now the 'tomb of Muslim culture' but once the site of its greatest empire – and similarly lamented 'Whose annals lie lost in your ruins?/... I who weep here will make others weep there.'[55] In 1911, at the brutal seizure of

---

[50] For biographical details, see Iqbal Singh, *The Ardent Pilgrim: An Introduction to the Life and Work of Iqbal* (Delhi: Oxford University Press, 1997).

[51] Quoted in Singh, *Ardent Pilgrim*, 49.

[52] See Zafar Anjum, *Iqbal: The Life of a Poet, Philosopher and Politician* (New Delhi: Random House India, 2014), especially Part II (1905–1908, Europe).

[53] 'Presidential Address Delivered at the Annual Session of the All-India Muslim League, 29 December 1930', *Speeches and Statements of Iqbal* (Lahore: Shamloo, 1948), 34.

[54] Quoted in Sayid Jamāl al-Dīn al-Afghānī and Abdul-Hādī Hā'irī, 'Afghānī on the Decline of Islam', *Die Welt des Islams*, New Series, 13, 1/2 (1971), 124–125.

[55] 'Sicily', *Poems from Iqbal* trans. V.G.Kiernan (John Murray: London, 1955), 13–14.

Libya by Italy, a bewildered Iqbal accosted God directly in 'Shikwā': 'But you bestow grace on their habitations,/And your thunderbolts strike only our dwellings?'[56]

For Iqbal, educated in England and Germany, the First World War must have been a painful conflict between mentors, though he supported the Allied cause and initially even wrote in favour of George V. But, like it did for Tagore, the war confirmed his disillusionment with Western civilisation and opened up a space for both reflection and critique. But, unlike Tagore's humanistic message, Iqbal's response could be sharp and satirical:

> The West develops wonderful new skills
> In this as in so many other fields
> Fine are the ways it kills,
> And great are its skill's yields.
>
> …
>
> Its submarines are crocodiles
> With all their predatory wiles.
> Its bombers rain destruction from the skies.
> Its gases so obscure the sky
> They blind the sun's world-seeing eye.
> Its guns deal death so fast
> The Angel of Death stands aghast,
> Quite out of breath
> In coping with this rate of death.
> Despatch this old fool to the West
> To learn the art of killing fast – and best.[57]

Here he combines the satirical wit of the nineteenth-century Urdu poet Akbar Allahabadi with the conceit of the English metaphysical poet John Donne. If Allahabadi had sarcastically exhorted his colonised Muslim readers to 'give up your literature, say I; forget your history', Iqbal uses such rapier-sharp wit to satirise the role of Western science in the present carnage; the 'busy old fool, unruly sun' of John Donne's 'The Sun Rising' is at once invoked and banished from the lovers' bedroom to the killing fields of France and Flanders.

During the war years, Iqbal would embark on a remarkable poetic project of exploring the *khudi* or the creative self – a vital concept in his poetry – as evident in the very titles: *Asrār-e-Khudi* (*Secrets of the Self*) and *Ramuz-e-Bekhudi* (*Mysteries of Selflessness*).[58] As the world descended into

---

[56] Iqbal, 'Shikwā', as quoted in Singh, *Ardent Pilgrim*, 67.
[57] Iqbal, 'The Wisdom of the West', *Payām-i-Mashriq* [*A Message from the East*], trans. M. Hadi Husain (Lahore: Iqbal Academy Pakistan, 1977), 91.
[58] See Majeed, *Muhammad Iqbal* for discussion of these works and the concept of *khudi* (18–57).

nationalist strife, Iqbal would set forth his vision of Islam: 'Our essence is not bound to any place/The vigour of our wine is not contained in any bowl; .../Neither is our heart of India, or Syria or Rum/Nor any fatherland do we profess except Islam.'[59] It was against the backdrop of world events – from the horrors of the Western front to wartime Pan-Islamism, from the mutilation of the Ottoman empire to the rise of the *Khilafat* – that Iqbal wrote some of his most important works: *Payām-i-Mashriq* (*Message of the East*, 1923) in Persian, the poetry collection *Bāṅg-i-dāra* (*Call of the Marching Bell*, 1924) in Urdu, as well as *The Reconstruction of Religious Thought in Islam* (1932). Yet the term 'Islam' is multiform and fractured in his thought, and it is not always in simple opposition to a monolithic 'West'; Nietzsche, Bergson, Hegel, Marx and Wordsworth all play a part in his reconstruction of Islam. As Javed Majeed notes, 'His work ranges from an oppositional, postcolonial Islam in relation to a globally dominant West, to subtler and more constructive engagement with the latter's philosophy and science, in which he also reworks Islamic Hellenism in distinctive ways.'[60] At the same time, such reworking of Islam was also responsive to a number of points outside the East–West axis, depending on the 'thought-zone' in which he wished to intervene: it ranged from the need to accommodate a creative *khudi*, so vital to his own work, to countering the Hindu-dominated nationalism within India to the dominance of Persian influences within Islamic thought.[61]

Iqbal once wrote to Edward Thompson that it was his interest in Islam as 'moral polity' that drove him to politics, and he feared that nationalism – whether European or Indian – would lead to 'irreligiousness', which he partly blamed for the war.[62] If the war made intellectuals around the world look eastwards, Iqbal turned specifically to the Muslim East. Consider the preface to *Payām-i-Mashriq* (*Message of the East*, 1922), a work modelled on Goethe's *West–östlicher Diwan* (*West–Eastern Divan*):

> Europe's Great War was a catastrophe which destroyed the old world order in almost every respect, and now out of the ashes of civilisation and culture Nature is building up in the depths of life a new Adam and a new world for him to live in … The East, and especially the Muslim East, has opened its eyes after a centuries-long slumber. But the nations of the East should

[59] Quoted in Sevea, *The Political Philosophy of Muhammed Iqbal*, 126.
[60] Majeed, *Muhammed Iqbal*, xxvi.
[61] See Majeed, *Muhammed Iqbal*, 64–66. Majeed notes that 'It was a pristine spirit of Arabian Islam that Iqbal sought to recapture, as he tried to shear off the Hellenic, Persian and Indian elements later added to it' (65).
[62] Sevea, *The Political Philosophy of Muhammed Iqbal*, 140–141.

realise that life can bring no revolution in its surroundings until a revolution takes place in its inner depths.[63]

If Aurobindo's vision was one of spiritual *evolution*, Iqbal's would be one of an 'inner' *revolution*. In 1915, when Shaukat Ali – a Pan-Islamist and the future leader of the *Khilafat* movement – had asked for his support, Iqbal had declined; similarly, as the *Khilafat* movement gathered momentum, Iqbal showed little interest in it and instead formulated his own complex vision of a post-war world.[64] It is his collection of Urdu verse *Bāng-i-Darā* (*Call of the Marching Bell*), published in 1924, and in particular the celebrated poems 'Khizr-e-Rāh' ('The Traveller's Guide') and 'Tulu'-i-Islām' ('The Renaissance of Islam') that show the most powerful engagement with the post-war moment.

'Khizr-e-Rāh' was first read at a session of the Anjuman Himayat-e-Islam in 1921. It is an extended allegory on the state of the post-war world and the place of Islam in it. Iqbal casts the poem in the form of an extended dialogue as, one still night, the contemplative poet chances upon the 'globe-trotting Khizr' by the 'river-bank'. Khizr is one of the most mysterious figures in the Qur'an. 'Khizr' literally means 'green'; his knowledge is green and original, drawn from Allah's own presence. In the poem, he sees, Tiresias-like, 'those storms/Whose tumults are still sleeping quietly in the river'. The poet-narrator asks him 'What is the secret of life? What is imperialism?/And what is this struggle between labour and capital?' However, Iqbal joins to such contemporary references to empire and the October revolution the post-war partitioning of the Middle East:

> The ancient patched garment of Asia is being torn
> The youth of parvenu nations are adorned with ornaments![65]

The original line describing Asia reads as follows:

> *Ho Rahā Hai Asiā kā Kharqā-e-Dairinā Chāk*
> *Naujawān Aqwām-e-Nau Daulat ke Hain Perāyā Posh.*

Kharqā is a traditional Sufi costume; *Dairinā* means organic: the image of Asia in her ancient organic costume is built up in the first hemistich, only to be followed by a second hemistich ending with the forceful

---

[63] Iqbal, *A Message from the East*, xvii–xviii.
[64] See Gail Minault, *The Khilafat Movement: Religious Symbolism and Political Mobilization in India* (New York: Columbia University Press, 1982), 11.
[65] Muhammed Iqbal, 'Khizr-e-Rāh', which in this edition is transliterated as 'Khidar-I-Rah', *Bāng-i-dāra* [*Call of the Marching Bell*], English translation and commentary by M. A. K. Khalil (Newfoundland : M. A. K. Khalil, 1997), 349.

monosyllabic *chāk*, meaning ripped apart, knifed, savaged. Asia emerges mutilated and bruised; it is a powerful reference to the partitioning of the Ottoman Empire through a series of pacts, including the Treaty of Sèvres (1920) following the victory of the Entente Powers, by which a French mandate was acknowledged for Syria and Lebanon, and a British mandate for Mesopotamia (later Iraq) and Palestine, among others.[66] Iqbal draws on similar sartorial imagery in his equally bitter poem 'The League of Nations': 'All I know about it is/That a few thieves of grave-clothes have set up/A body for dividing the world's graves', a reference to British and French appropriation of territories in Asia and North Africa in the post-war period.[67] If Aurobindo had referred to the League of Nations as 'a mockery and a bye-word', with Asia and Africa re-partitioned as 'the personal property of two or three great European powers',[68] Iqbal's bitterness would erupt through the sarcastic image of the 'monster of despotism' parading as the chimera-like 'blue-mantled fairy' (*Neelam Pari*):

> The monster of despotism is dressed up in democracy's robes,
> And you consider it to be the blue-mantled fairy?

> The legislative assembly, the reforms, the rights and concessions
> In Western medicine the tastes are sweet, the effect is soporific!

> May God protect us from the fever of speeches of members of assemblies
> This is also the capitalists' sham quarrelling to deceive the poor.[69]

For both Aurobindo and Iqbal, what the post-war 'peace' exposed was the 'chimera' of Western liberalism, as imperial plunder was dressed up in a vocabulary of reforms, rights and concessions.

The post-war moment saw Iqbal trying to recast Islam as a universalising religion whose key message was 'de-racialisation'. It was meant as a spiritual and moral bulwark against the dominant ideology of racial hierarchies, both in Europe and in the wider Islamic world.[70] He instead wanted the Muslims to be endowed with the 'Turkoman's dignity, Indian's intellect, Arab's eloquence'.[71] Thus, trying to overcome the secular, territorially

---

[66] See Paul C. Helmreich, *From Paris to Sèvres: The Partition of the Ottoman Empire at the Peace Conference of 1919–1920* (Columbus: Ohio State University Press, 1974).
[67] Iqbal, 'The League of Nations', *A Message from the East*, 160.
[68] Aurobindo, 'After the War', *SPT*, 638.
[69] Iqbal, 'Khizr-e-Rah'. Here I follow Khalil's translation from *Call of the Marching Bell*, 351, except for the first two lines quoted above.
[70] Majeed, *Muhammed Iqbal*, 67.
[71] 'Tulu'-i-Islam', in *Bāṅg-i-dāra* [*Call of the Marching Bell*], trans. M. A. K. Khalil (Newfoundland: M. A. K. Khalil, 1997), 360. Also see Muhammad Iqbal, *Poems from Iqbal: Renderings in English Verse with Comparative Urdu Text*, trans. V. G. Kiernan (Karachi: Oxford University Press, 2004 [1955]).

based system of nationhood or *qawmiyyat* which he believed had led to the European war as well as trying to knit together Muslims from different *mazhabs* and sects within the wider 'Islamic fold', he envisioned for the post-war world an alternative transnational and transcultural socio-political order based on *millat* or a religious community.[72] Iqbal took exception to any suggestion that his conviction in the superiority of Islam stemmed from his faith and argued instead that he was guided by 'practical and not patriotic concerns': 'It was Islam and Islam alone which, for the first time, gave the message to mankind that religion was neither national and racial, nor individual and private, but purely human and that its purpose was to unite and organize mankind despite its natural distinctions'.[73] For Iqbal, such a vision of Islam had universalist aspirations, but his exhortation was aimed specifically at Muslims: 'The dream of universal freedom which was seen by Islam/Oh Muslims, you should watch the interpretation of that dream today!'[74]

'Tulu'-i-Islam' is, in many ways, an expansive answer to the questions posed in 'Khizr-e-Rāh'. 'This is not a rosy dawn of a new age on the horizon of the West', Iqbal famously said of the First World War, 'but a torrent of blood.'[75] In 'Tulu', such an image is reworked, as if the blood-letting in the West had infused the East with new blood: 'The sun has risen over the horizon; the time of deep slumber has passed./The blood of life runs in the veins of the dead East.' Yet, neither the imagery nor the East–West divide is stable as the metaphor resurfaces with reference to the Ottoman empire: 'If a mountain of grief collapsed upon the Ottomans, then why lament?/For the dawn arises from the blood of a hundred thousand stars.' Such ideas of a renaissance through the apocalypse of war could be found in the West as well, as in the poetry of D. H. Lawrence, such as 'Resurgence': 'I lift my tender flame/Of pure and lambent hostage from the dead.'[76] Iqbal's, in contrast, is one of Islamic resurgence:

> This principle rises from the story of the Radiant Community
> You are the guardian of the nations of the land of Asia.[77]

---

[72] The terms themselves are often fluid and ambiguous, defined not only in relationship to the Western secular-state but different traditions and terminologies within Islam itself. See Sevea, *The Political Philosophy of Muhammed Iqbal*, 147–163 for an extensive discussion of *Millat*.

[73] Iqbal, *Speeches and Statements*, 206–207.

[74] 'Khidar-I-Rah', 354.

[75] Quoted in Ali Hashmi, 'Three Poems by Allama Iqbal', https://blogforwords.wordpress.com/2011/08/09/three-poems-by-allama-iqbal.

[76] 'Resurrection', in *The Complete Poems of D. H. Lawrence*, ed. Vivian de Sola and F. Warren Roberts (Harmondsworth: Penguin, 1964), 745.

[77] The translation of these two lines differs from that of Khalil in *Call of the Marching Bell* for stated reasons; otherwise I follow his translation of 'Tulu'-i-Islam'. Also see http://iqbalurdu.blogspot.co.uk/search?q=Sargazhat-E-Millat.

[*Ye Nuktāh Sarguzasht-e-Millat-e-Baizā Se Hai Paidā
Ke Aqwām-e-Zamīn-e-Asiā Kā Pāsbān Tū Hai*]

'Sarguzasht-e-Millat' means '[story of] Radiant community' rather than 'the history of the Muslim nation', as Khalil gives us in his translation, but it clearly refers to the Muslim community; and soon, the guardianship of the Asian states expands into 'responsibility for the whole world'. At the same time, Islam also undergoes a powerful interpretation and expansion as he asks for the 'idols of colour and blood' to be lost in the '*millat*'.[78] The richness for many of us today lies not so much in the message or even in the quality of the faith but in the beauty and poignancy thrown into that call. What gets developed is not so much a particular credo but a state of consciousness erupting through images and metaphors:

> O God, light the candle of Longing in the tulip's heart
> Make every speck of garden's dust a martyr searching for the Truth …

> The Muslim's destination is beyond the azure-coloured sky
> You are the caravan the dust of whose trail are stars! …

> Come, so that we may sprinkle flowers and pour wine in cup
> Rend asunder the sky's roof and establish a new foundation.[79]

The focus, however, remains on the 'Muslim's destination', which leads the way towards the world's 'new foundation'. The tension, once again, is between universalism and particularity. While it would be a travesty to see this radiant vision through the blood-dimmed lenses of the future Partition or, even more crudely, through Islamic extremism – each of which would have horrified Iqbal – his is nonetheless a vision of Islam and Islam alone as the saviour of humanity, however profound, expansive or universal. Equally interesting is how the war in turn puts pressure on the very concept of Islam, paving the way for Iqbal's magisterial work *The Reconstruction of Religious Thought in Islam* (1932).

Rabindranath Tagore: Resistance, Retribution and Redemption

On 11 November 1918, as the guns fell quiet on the Western front, Prime Minister Clemenceau asked the Comtesse de Noailles to read him poems from Tagore's *Gitanjali*.[80] Indeed, during and after the war years, Tagore

---

[78] 'Tulu'-i-Islam', 360–361.
[79] 'Tulu'-i-Islam', 360–363.
[80] Rathindranath Tagore, *On the Edges of Time* (Calcutta: Orient Longman, 1958), 127.

emerged as the *guru* from the East as he lectured to packed and enthralled audiences from Kobe to Boston to Frankfurt. As the first non-European to win the Nobel Prize, Tagore during the war years had the status of a contemporary rock star: in Japan, Buddhist monks welcomed him by burning incense; in Germany, people queued to touch the hem of his robe, and a little child even mistook him for Jesus Christ![81]

In his final prose work 'Sabhyatār Saṅkaṭ' ('Crisis in Civilisation', 1941), written amidst the Second World War, Tagore famously noted 'As I look around I see the crumbling ruins of a proud civilisation [Europe] strewn like a vast heap of futility. And yet I shall not commit the grievous sin of losing faith in man.'[82] This statement, written on his eightieth birthday, holds the key to the intricately nuanced, robustly cosmopolitan and profoundly humanistic world of Tagore. Born in 1861 into a wealthy, talented and creative family in Calcutta, Tagore was part of the emerging Bengali intelligentsia – a class that had opened its heart to Western liberalism and education, only to feel increasingly the ignominious pinch of British colonial rule. Tagore remembered how his childhood days and nights were 'eloquent' with the 'stately declamations of Edmund Burke, Macaulay's long-rolling sentences and discussions of Shakespeare's drama', but 'I began increasingly to discover how easily those who accepted the highest truths of civilisation disowned them with impunity whenever questions of national self-interest were involved.'[83] Such realisations, like Aurobindo's and Iqbal's, shaped his anti-colonial cosmopolitanism: he was a fierce critic of British imperialism but openly admitted his 'deep love and great respect for the British race as human beings', citing individuals such as David Hare and C. F. Andrews.[84] His relation to the Indian nationalist movement was equally ambivalent. He maintained a warm relationship with Gandhi but he distanced himself from his Non-cooperation Movement: 'We of the Orient should learn from the Occident ... to say that it is wrong to co-operate with the West is to encourage the worst form of provincialism.'[85] When queried, he famously retorted that 'Patriotism cannot be our final spiritual shelter; my refuge is humanity. I will not buy glass for the price of diamonds and I will never allow patriotism to triumph over humanity as long as I live.'[86]

[81] Stephen Hay, *Asian Ideas of East and West*, 131.
[82] 'Crisis in Civilisation', 726.
[83] 'Crisis in Civilisation', 723.
[84] 'Nationalism', 42.
[85] Quoted in Krishna Kripalini, *Rabindranath Tagore: A Biography* (New Delhi: National Book Trust, 1962), 294.
[86] Letter of 19 November 1908, in *Selected Letters of Rabindranath Tagore*, ed. Krishna Dutta and Andrew Robinson (Cambridge: Cambridge University Press, 1997), 72.

While Aurobindo and Iqbal remained in India during the war years, Tagore roamed the world.[87] Unable to sail to Europe, he accepted a high-profile lecturing tour, from May 1916 to February 1917, in Japan and the United States; these celebrated lectures would form the basis of his book *Nationalism*. As the world was rent apart by violence, Tagore's oceanic voyage – going from Calcutta through Rangoon, Penang, and Hong Kong to Kobe en route to the United States – was opening up for him an alternate world of contact and exchange. It was followed up by further voyages in the immediate post-war years: a fifteen-month tour of Europe and the United States in May 1920, visits to China and Japan in 1924, and again across Europe in 1926. During these trips, he met some of the leading intellectuals in each of the countries he visited, from Liang Qichao in China and Noguchi in Japan to Bergson, Rolland, Mann and Freud in Europe. During and immediately after the war years, Tagore thus opened up a rare dual traffic, with the Far East on the one hand and Europe and the United States on the other. Some of the ideas we most associate with Tagore – his humanism, his ceaseless championing of the relation between the East and the West and his critique of nationalism – have pre-war origins but find during the war years some of their most powerful and compelling shapes as well as a global audience. Indeed, the internecine European conflict made him think, as he told his American audience in 1916, about 'the future of all humanity' and facilitated the shift, in Stephen Hay's words, from 'poetry to prophecy'.[88]

In a speech to the Anglo-American Association in Peking in 1924, Tagore recounted the following experience:

> Following the end of the War I went to Europe where I was received with a warmth of welcome which overwhelmed me. I could not believe that it was because of my books or my work. Then I decided that it must be that the nations of the West were looking for some new ideal from the East which would reconstruct their civilisation on a better basis.

[87] See Prasanta Kumar Pal, *Ravijīvanī (1914–1920)* (Kolkata: Ananda Publishers, 1997), Vol. 7 and Ramachandra Guha, 'Introduction: Travelling with Tagore', in Ramachandra Guha (ed.), *Nationalism* (Delhi: Penguin, 2009), vii–ix. References to the essays 'Nationalism in Japan' and 'Nationalism in the West' are to this edition, and Guha's introduction has pointed me to several valuable sources. Two other remarkable works have been important to my thinking in this chapter: they are Stephen N. Hay, *Asian Ideas of East and West* and Rustom Bharucha, *Another Asia*. Also see Krishna Kripalani, *Rabindranath Tagore: A Biography*, and Krishna Dutta and Andrew Robinson, *Rabindranath Tagore: The Myriad-Minded Man* and the online Tagore Variorum, http://bichitra .jdvu.ac.in. Also see K. L. Tuteja and Kaustav Chakraborty (eds.), *Tagore and Nationalism* (New Delhi: Springer, 2017), particularly Sukanta Chaudhuri's excellent essay on 'Tagore, Nationalism and Imperialism', 67–75.
[88] 'Nationalism in the West', 41; Stephen Hay, *Asian Ideas of East and West*, 26.

This looking to the East touched me deeply. I realised the great responsibility and felt that I must in my own humble way help to bring together the two hemispheres which were drifting apart every day.

With this aim I founded Visva-Bharati in which I endeavoured to give expression to the ideal of the present age. The peoples of the world have come close to one another through science but they must also come together in spirit.[89]

Indeed, such 'wild praise' from the West, as Amartya Sen has noted, 'genuinely influenced' him; his conversations with civilisational critics such as Romain Rolland and W. B. Yeats partly shaped his thinking and the way he would present his 'message' from the East (which sometimes differed from his Bengali writings).[90] His carefully groomed image with long white beard, flowing robes and intense gaze, and messages with their combination of spiritual admonition and cultural harmony embodied what a war-ravaged West wanted to see in the East – wise, peaceful, sacrosanct – as orientalism occasionally flowed into self-orientalism. While the essays on 'Nationalism', delivered as lectures in Japan and the United States, have accrued a long and distinguished list of commentators, I will here examine them in the specific context of the First World War. I will also consider the influence of war on his socio-political vision more generally, along with some of his Bengali essays.

When Tagore published his lectures in 1917, he prefaced the book with a poem opening with the following lines:

> The last sun of the century sets amidst the blood-red clouds of the
>   West and the whirlwind of hatred.
> The naked passion of self-love of Nations, in its drunken delirium
>   of greed, is dancing to the clash of steel and howling verses of
>   vengeance.
> The hungry self of the Nation shall burst in a violence of fury from
>   its own shameless feeding.
> For it has made the world its food.
> And licking it, crunching it and swallowing it in big morsels,
> It swells and swells.
>
>   'The Sunset of the Century'[91]

---

[89] Tagore, *Visit to China* (Shantiniketan: Visva-Bharati, 1924), 20.

[90] Amartya Sen, 'Tagore and China', in Tan Chung, Amiya Dev, Wang Bangwei and Wei Liming (eds.), *Tagore and China*, 8

[91] 'Śatābdīr Sūrya' ['The Sunset of the Century'] in 'Naivedya' (poems 64 and 65), *Rabīndra Racanābalī* (Kolkata: Visva-Bharati, Ashwin 1346 – 25 Baishākh 1372 [September 1939 – May 1965]), Vol. 8, Bhadra 1348, [August 1941]), 51–52. All further references are to this edition of twenty-six volumes. Written in Bengali but translated and published in 1918 as part of his book on *Nationalism*. See 'The Sunset of the Century', in *The English Writings of Rabindranath Tagore*, Vol. 2, 466.

This eerily First World War-like poem was written in Bengali on the last evening of the nineteenth century. It was his response to the Boer War (1899–1902). A full fourteen years before the First World War's outbreak, he had grasped the intimate relationship between nationalism, imperial ambition and global violence. Here we have an early characterisation of the nation as a monstrous force which erupts, as we saw, in his vision of the 'demon' in the trenches and which he would soon make the subject of his lectures.[92] As early as 1901, he had observed with strange clairvoyance that 'This conflict is increasingly becoming a thorn [*kaṇṭakita*] at the edges of European civilisation. There is an early indication that there will be a tussle and scramble [*ṭhelāṭheli kāḍākāḍi*] over the possession of the world.'[93] Thirteen years later, the First World War provided a resounding, if perverse, validation of not just a prediction but a whole thesis. The war, for Tagore, was neither a sudden eruption of violence nor a case of Europe sleep-walking into war: it was inscribed in the very 'logic' of 'Nationalism', manufactured in the West and spelt with a capital 'N', which had not just spurred but, more insidiously, made morally acceptable the hunger for power and imperial aggression. The horrors of the war that Tagore would have been reading about perhaps explain the 'hysterical excess' that creeps into the language of his lectures, almost matching in its histrionic force Kipling's 'The Hun is at the gate.'[94] Tagore's understanding was obviously very different – almost diametrically opposite – to Kipling's. Picking up the metaphor of the 'thorn' from his old letter, Tagore trenchantly noted in 'Laḍāier Mūl' ('The Cause of Conflict') in 1914 that 'Today, it is a thorn in its own side. Even though Germany has become drunk [*mātāl*] in this wrong [*anyāy*] war, this is not bred in Germany alone but written in the current history of European civilisation.'[95] The 'this' in the essay is not wholly identified as nationalism, but rather the desire for mastery (*prabhutva*).

In the wartime lectures, we have a rapid intensification and coming together of certain issues he had been developing in a number of essays over a few years about nation, patriotism and conflict. In 'Nation Kī?' ('What Is the Nation?', 1901), an explication of the French historian Ernest

---

[92] He was briefly attracted to the Swadeshi movement (1903–1908) in Bengal and wrote several poems and songs, but he soon distanced himself from it as he realised its potential for violence. Sumit Sarkar's *The Swadeshi Movement in Bengal 1903–1908* remains the authoritative account of the movement.

[93] 'Prācya O Pāścātya Sabhyatā' ['Eastern and Western Civilisation'] (1901) in *Rabīndra Racanābalī*, Vol. 4 (Shraban 1347 [July 1940]), 420.

[94] Rudyard Kipling, 'For All We Have and Are', in *The Years Between* (London: Methuen, 1919), 21.

[95] 'Laḍāier Mūl ['The Cause of Conflict'] (1914), in 'Kalāntar', *Rabīndra Racanābalī*, Vol. 24, (*Poush 1354* [December 1947]), 272.

Renan's famous lecture 'Qu'est-ce qu'une nation?' (1882), Tagore notes
that there is no equivalent word in Bengali. He carefully distinguishes the
word 'nation' from 'jāti' (which can indicate caste or 'varṇa') as well as
race, but it is not yet an altogether bad thing. He defines it as 'a living
entity, a substance of the mind' ('sajīv sattā, ekṭi mānas padārtha) and
locates its appeal in two principles – an ancient fund of shared memory
and the desire to live together which goes beyond the claims of ethnicity,
language, religion, commerce or territory; he even concludes by pondering
over the application of Renan's ideas to India.[96] A few months later, in
'Prācya O Pāścātya Sabhyatā' (1901), he refers to the European state as
inherently 'selfish' and observes that, overriding the call of '*dharma*', it feels
little hesitation or embarrassment in claiming that 'might is right'.[97] The
word 'nation' appears again the following year in his perceptive essay titled
'Virodhmūlak Ādarśa' ('The Ideology Rooted in Conflict') (1901), in which
he warns about the steady militarisation and denigration of other nations
being carried on in Britain. 'Blindness, injustice and cruelty' are associated
with the nation. 'In fact this blindness', he carries on, is 'the main illness
of nationalism ['*nation-tantrā*']' as he coins a new Bengali word, adding
the Sanskrit suffix 'tantra', equivalent to the Greek 'kratia', to the noun
'nation'.[98] 'Whether it be through falsehood or error, one has to prove one's
superiority to oneself and in the process, denigrate other nations – this is
the main '*dharma*' of the nation, the refuge of patriotism ... for the very
backbone of the nation is self-interest [*svārtha*].'[99] For him, in sharp contrast to the concept of 'nation', the essence of a civilisation like India, which
different marauding tribes have made their home, lies in its slightly clichéd
'unity amidst diversity', in its commingling of different races and religions,
and foregoing of particularity in the interest of a common humanity.[100] In
1914, at the outbreak of the war, Tagore would return to his analysis of the

---

[96] 'Nation Kī?' ['What is the Nation'] (1901), in '*Ātmaśakti*,', *Rabīndra Racanābalī*, Vol. 3 (Baishākh 1347 [April 1940]), 518.

[97] 'Prācya O Pāścātya Sabhyatā', 420.

[98] I am grateful to Abhishek Sarkar for this insight.

[99] 'Virodhmūlak Ādarśa' ['The Ideology Rooted in Conflict'], *Rabīndra Racanābalī*, Vol. 10, 594.

[100] See Tagore, 'Hindutva'; later published as 'Bhāratbarṣer Samāj' where he contrasts '*samāj*' with 'Nation'. 'Bhāratbarṣer Samāj' ['The Civilisation of India'] (1901), *Rabīndra Racanābalī*, Vol. 3 (Baishākh 1347 [April 1940]), 520. In 'Prācya O Pāścātya Sabhyatā', he observes that the 'evolving History of India' is testimony to how each internal group can override its particularity (*viśeṣ ākār*) in the service of a fuller history of the 'whole of mankind' ('*samasta mānaver sāmagrī*) and create a 'Greater India' (*brihat bhāratvarṣa*). Yet, the principle of difference is at work in different essays. Indeed, in 'Nation Kī', he translates Renan's argument that 'at the present time the existence of nations is a good thing' as 'for the present these differences [*bhinnatā*] of nations are good'. See Amartya Mukhopadhyay's astute essay ' "Bhinnata of Nations": Tagore's Search in Nationalism,

causes of the conflict. In the appropriately titled 'Laḍāier Mūl' ('The Cause of Conflict'), he notes that

> The desire for domination [*prabhutva*] is a real obstacle, it comes in the way of the free interaction of human beings. It is this struggle for domination [*prabhutva-ceṣṭā*] which is at the root of all major conflicts ...
>
> At one time, this drive towards mastery was limited only to the Brahmins and the Kshatriyas. It is for this reason that the conflict over arms and scripture was limited to them. The professional did not have a care in the world for such fights, he would just carry on with his daily round of activities.
>
> In recent times, the world has declined to an age of the Vaishya-rule [*vaiśya-rājak*]. Commerce is no longer mere commerce, there has now been a marriage [*gāndharva vivāha*] between commerce and empire ...
>
> At one time, the Vaishyas have been owners only of commodities, now even human beings have become his property [*sampatti*].
>
> Instead of the age-old business dealings between nations, we now see the transactions of the empire being conducted day and night. As a result, there is something wholly new that is happening in the history of the world – the rule of one country over another, even when the two countries are on either side of the seas.
>
> Never before in the world has there been the urge to dominate on such an immense [*vipul*] scale.
>
> The areas for domination [*prabhutvar kṣetra*] for Europe are Asia and Africa.
>
> Now, Germany is in trouble. He has woken up far too late from his sleep. He has arrived at the feast only at the end, huffing and puffing. He is hungry, he can even smell the fish, but nothing is left for him except the bones. His body is now shaking with rage. He says that if a place has not been laid at the table for me, I do not care for an invitation. I shall grab a place at the table by might.[101]

The essay works at two levels. He starts by drawing a parallel between the European war and the caste wars in India between the Brahmins and Kshatriyas as he delves into the psychological roots of human conflict. Interestingly, the caste-laden vocabulary with the denigration of the 'Vaishyas' or business-class ('*vaiśya-rājak*' – rule of the Vaishyas or '*vaiśyer sampatti*' – 'the property of the Vaishyas') would be largely excised from his lectures in English for his Western audience. He then goes on to develop this thesis by turning to Europe. Tagore had written elsewhere how, when

"Bharatavarsiya Samaj and Beyond"', in Sanjukta Dasgupta and Chinmoy Guha (eds.), *Tagore: At Home in the World* (New Delhi: Sage, 2013), 125–151.
[101] 'Laḍāier Mūl', 271–272.

the members of the East India Company first landed on India's shores, they were welcomed with the ancient custom of hospitality extended to guests; but now, commerce has been supplanted by empire, redrawing the very map of the world. For Tagore, as for Aurobindo and Lenin, the present war was one for imperial domination but, unlike them, he cuts across any socio-economic analysis to detect a more fundamental impulse in 'prabutya', a word repeated throughout the passage, meaning desire for domination and control. While his canny analysis of Germany's late imperialism is evolved into the witty and elaborate metaphor of the hungry latecomer at the feast, what was far more dangerous for him was the legitimisation of imperial 'might' ('gāyer jor') through the doctrine of 'Nationalism'.

In many ways, the lectures on 'Nationalism' (written in English) that Tagore would deliver in Japan and then in the United States were the cul-mination of his decade-long thinking around empire, modernity and their discontents that we see in the above Bengali essays. But there are several striking differences, or rather developments. Ideas crystallise here around the concept of 'nationalism' in a way they had not in the Bengali essays; the First World War gives the idea a contemporary relevance and *raison d'être* on a global scale, helping Tagore to evolve his critique of empire into a larger civilisational and ethical critique whose centre remains nationalism and the lust for power. Moreover, there is a certain excess and intensifica-tion in his language that we do not find in the Bengali version. Consider the following passage from 'Nationalism in Japan':

> The political civilisation which has sprung up from the soil of Europe [and] is overrunning the whole world, like some prolific weed, is based on exclu-siveness. It is always watchful to keep at bay the aliens or to exterminate them. It is carnivorous and cannibalistic in its tendencies, it feeds upon the resources of other peoples and tried to swallow their whole future. It is always afraid of other races achieving eminence, naming it as a peril, and tries to thwart all symptoms of greatness outside its own boundaries, forcing down races of men who are weaker, to be eternally fixed in their weakness.[102]

The 'feeding' imagery of 'Śatābdīr Sūrya' is here combined with the argu-ment about the pernicious logic of nationalism that Tagore was formu-lating in 'Birodhmūlak Ādarśa', but there is a new-found flamboyance and excess to his lectures in English: nationalism here is at once a 'prolific weed', an exterminator, a carnivore and a cannibal as metaphors are pushed out of

---

[102] 'Nationalism in Japan', 8.

joint. Later, he could compare it to a giraffe, a machine which presses bales of humanity, a hydraulic dam: the metaphors show a visceral abhorrence which goes far beyond the 'illegitimacy of nationalism'.[103] According to Tagore, the nation is the 'organised self-interest of a whole people, where it is least human and least spiritual' and an 'organisation of politics and commerce'; it symbolised the 'survival of that part of man which is the least living'.[104] In an essay titled 'To the Nation', written in 1917, he noted that the 'physiognomy' of its dominance is 'everywhere the same from San Francisco to London, from London to Tokyo'. What galled him particularly, he added, was not just 'its career of aggressive selfishness', whether in appropriating foreign land or in its commercial dealings, but the way it *legitimated* the 'cult of selfishness' as a 'moral duty'.[105]

Ironically, Tagore's first stop would be at Japan, one of the most aggressively nationalist Asian states, where he spoke at Osaka on 1 June, 1916. Japan's sensational victory over Russia in 1905 had sent shockwaves around the non-Western world, from Egypt and Turkey to Vietnam and China. In 1895, it had defeated China, and in 1910, it annexed Korea; at the outbreak of the First World War, Japan offered to help Great Britain on the condition that it could take Germany's Pacific territories.[106] After invading Shandong on 2 September 1914, and capturing Tsingtao in November 1914, Japan would present China with its Twenty-One Demands in January 1915. Thus, even before Tagore had reached the war-ravaged West, this self-confessed Japanophile saw in this Asian state the immediate proof of how nationalist intoxication fuelled imperial greed and legitimated racial arrogance: how is he going to fit this new Japan into his thesis of a 'spiritual Orient'? Tagore's essay 'Nationalism in Japan' is a fractured and dissonant text whose richness comes not so much from its message as from its gaps, strenuous argument and mixed metaphors. Starting indeed with high praise for Japan's ancient culture and values, and its contemporary emergence as the 'natural leader'

---

[103] Bharucha makes the point convincingly, noting that 'it is easy to fall into the trap of what has been theorised as the "illegitimacy of nationalism"', referring to Nandy's influential reading of Tagore's Nationalism. At the same time, as Bharucha goes on to observe, 'the rejection of nationalism does not mean that Tagore's affiliation to the imaginary of the nation, at civic and creative levels, should be summarily dismissed, or collapsed into his critique of nationalism at the level of the state and government' (*Another Asia*, 69–70).

[104] 'Nationalism in the West', 41, 39; 'Creative Unit', 548.

[105] 'To the Nation', in Sisir Kumar Das (ed.), *The English Writings of Rabindranath Tagore, Volume 3, A Miscellany* (Calcutta: Sahitya Akademi, 1996), 859, 861 (859–862). The phrase 'career of aggressive selfishness' is not in the volume edited by Sisir Das but occurs in other versions of the essay.

[106] Robert O'Neill, 'Churchill, Japan, and British Security in the Pacific 1904–1942', in Robert B. Blake and William Roger Louis, *Churchill: A Major New Assessment of His Life in Peace and War* (Oxford: Clarendon Press, 1993), 276.

who had 'infused hope in the heart of all Asia', he changes gear abruptly as warm praise modulates into scarcely-veiled criticism:

> What is dangerous for Japan is not the imitation of the outer features of the West, but the acceptance of the motive force of western nationalism as her own. Her social ideals are already showing signs of defeat at the hand of politics. I can see her motto, taken from science, 'Survival of the fittest', writ large at the entrance of her present-day history … We can take anything from science but not this elixir of moral death. Never think for a moment that the hurts you inflict upon other races will not infect you, or that the enmities you sow around your homes will be a wall of protection to you for all time to come.[107]

The references to Japan's treatment of China and Korea are clear; after such knowledge, one may ask, what vision of a spiritual Orient could remain? Phrases such as 'the hurts you inflict upon other races will not infect you' are astonishingly perceptive and resonant today, given the whole contemporary field of study of the damage wrought by imperialism and racism on the emotional history of Europe as well. But the above extract, and the whole essay more generally, raise two broader questions. First, was Tagore absolute in his argument for the repudiation of military power; and second, did Tagore seriously believe 'nationalism' to be a solely Western malady? Reading 'Nationalism in Japan' alongside his private correspondence reveals a far more ambivalent attitude. In Letter no. 15 in 'Jāpānyātrī' (1916), he wrote

> In the whole of Asia only Japan realised one day that Europe could be countered only through that force through which she had become triumphant in the whole world. Otherwise, she must have to fall under her wheels, and once she has fallen, there would be no way of rising ever again.[108]

This is not an endorsement of militarism by any means, but it comes far short of the denunciation that he espouses in 'Nationalism in Japan': such a rueful outburst does not undermine Tagore's stance against war but does show its embattled nature in a colonial context, of how tempting and easy it was for an anti-colonial intellectual to subscribe to a militaristic Pan-Asianism which is able to combat imperialism. But such militarism, while countering Western hegemony, could equally become a menace to Japan's Eastern neighbours. In a letter written the previous year – June 1915, i.e. just a year before his lecture on nationalism in Japan – he had observed 'I am

---

[107] 'Nationalism in Japan', 3, 21–22.
[108] 'Jāpānyātrī' ['The Traveller to Japan'], *Rabīndra Racanābalī*, Vol. 19 (Baishākh 1352 [April 1945]), 291.

sure that Japan has her eyes on India'. 'She is hungry', he continued, 'she is munching Korea, she has fastened her teeth upon China and it will be an evil day for India when Japan will have her opportunity.'[109] In spite of this realisation, Tagore seemed to have clung on to his thesis. In 'Nationalism in the West', he writes 'The West in the voice of her thundering cannon had said at the door of Japan – Let there be a Nation – and there was a Nation.'[110] As late as 1932, when militant nationalism had taken over Japan, Tagore lamented in a private diary entry that 'In Japan's blood has entered the poison of imperialism from the West … We see Europe's best pupil in Asia, Japan, copying in Korea and in China its master's arrogance of might.'[111] Was it an exercise in strategic essentialism or, as would have been more likely the case, was it that because the reach of European imperialism at the time was so much vaster, more global and well-organised that it led Tagore to this categorisation of imperialism as an intrinsically Western disease somewhat infecting Japan? This assumption of a spiritual 'East' and a power-hungry 'West' would have been further strengthened by the orgiastic violence of the First World War. This essentialist vision would soon be powerfully challenged. Neither the Japanese officials nor the Pan-Asianists could endorse Tagore's view of a 'spiritual East' untainted by the West or his denunciation of the national spirit. Referring to him as 'the beautiful flower of a ruined country', they lamented his 'resignation-ism', which they thought was apposite for an intellectual from a country *horobiru*: ruined, lost, 'deceased'.[112] Yet, such 'resignation-ism', as I shall argue, was fundamental to Tagore's poetics and politics of an alternative non-militant and anti-nationalist Pan-Asian unity as a counterpoint both to Western nationalism and to the aggressive Pan-Asianism coming out of Japan.[113]

From Japan, Tagore set sail towards the United States, where he would develop his thesis with an almost hysterical force. There he lectured in some twenty cities, including Chicago, New Haven, Iowa, Washington, San Francisco, Buffalo and Ann Arbor. In Boston, he spoke for eighty

---

[109] Dutta and Robinson, *Rabindranath Tagore*, 200. As early as 1917, Taraknath Das, a former fellow in political science and economics at Washington, had written *Is Japan a Menace to Asia?* (Shanghai: Taraknath Das, 1917).

[110] 'Nationalism in the West', 54.

[111] Tagore, *Journey to Persia and Iraq: 1932*, transl. from Bengali by Surendranath Tagore and Sukhendu Ray and ed. Supriya Roy (Shantiniketan: Visva-Bharati, 2003), 29.

[112] Hay, *Asian Ideas of East and West*, 87, 117.

[113] One of the main architects of a militant nationalist Pan-Asianism was Ōkawa Shūmei, who would selectively quote from Tagore's lecture and distort his vision to argue that it was Japan's 'mission to unite and lead Asia'. See Mishra, *From the Ruins*, 232; Aydin, *The Politics of Anti-Westernism*, 89–91, 236 and Xu Guoqi, *Asia and the Great War: A Shared History* (Oxford: Oxford University Press, 2017).

minutes to a 3,000-strong audience. For Tagore, even more than for Iqbal, Europe or even Britain was no homogeneous or stable entity. All his life, Tagore maintained a careful distinction between the 'Englishman', as represented by the petty 'Burrasahib' ('chief officer') – 'merchant, or a military man or a bureaucrat' – and 'the high-souled Englishman like David Hare'; in Japan, he had spoken about 'that Europe which is great and good' and 'the Europe which is mean and grasping'.[114] This ambivalence gets split into the 'Spirit of the West' and 'the Nation of the West'. If the 'Spirit' signified English literature, science and its 'large-hearted liberalism', nationalism now emerges as a demoniacal and soul-destroying machine with 'the conscience of a ghost and the callous perfection of an automaton' (39) and constituted of 'forge and hammer and turn-screw' (55).[115] Fuelled by the 'mutual jealousy of the powers', it had inexorably led the whole world to war. Consider the grand finale to his lecture on 'Nationalism in the West' delivered across the United States as his imagination reaches its feverish pitch:

> This European war of Nations is the war of retribution … The time has come when, for the sake of the whole outraged world, Europe should fully know in her own person the terrible absurdity of the thing called the Nation.
>
> The Nation has thriven long upon mutilated humanity. Men, the fairest creations of God, came out of the National manufactory in huge numbers as war-making and money-making puppets, ludicrously vain of their pitiful perfection of mechanism. Human society grew more and more into a marionette show of politicians, soldiers, manufacturers and bureaucrats, pulled by wire arrangements of wonderful efficiency …
>
> And this Nation may grow on to an unimaginable corpulence, not of a living body, but of steel and steam and office buildings, till its deformity can contain no longer its ugly voluminousness, – till it begins to crack and gape, breathe gas and fire in gasps, and its death-rattles sound in cannon roars. In this war the death-throes of the Nation have commenced. Suddenly, all its mechanism going mad, it has begun the dance of the Furies, shattering its own limbs, scattering them into the dust. It is the fifth act of the tragedy of the unreal.

The war had opened up for an Asian intellectual the vantage point from which to judge and chastise Europe. Poetry, polemic and affect are blended with a fine excess, and social diagnosis evolves into moral denunciation without a break or mediating pause: 'In this frightful war the West has

---

[114] 'East and West', 456; 'Nationalism in Japan', 28.
[115] 'Nationalism in the West', 39, 55.

stood face to face with her own creation, to which she had offered her soul. She must know what it truly is.'[116]

The essay is well known, yet its extraordinary language is seldom examined. Tagore's imaginative and linguistic exuberance is key to his argument: conceptual connections are forged through the texture of language, images beget fresh images and metaphor becomes the mode of ratiocination. The transition from the idea of the 'Nation' as demoniac and corpulent to men as 'money-making and war-making puppets' to the description of the state bureaucracy as a 'marionette show' is both breathless and seamless, lurching between visions of bodily decay and soulless mechanisation. Yet, it is in the final paragraph that Tagore bares his full arsenal. At a time when industrial weaponry was tearing apart the human body ('her humanity shattered into bits on her battlefields'),[117] Tagore's metaphoric imagination brings together his two old enemies – the nation and the machine – as the 'Nation' becomes a corpulent body of 'steel and steam and office-buildings' before morphing into the 'ugly voluminousness' of the trench-landscape with its gas and fire and cannon-roar. Nationalism, industrial capitalism and mechanisation are all implicated with each other as his moral vision seizes on the war as the logical, shattering climax of their unholy nexus.

Tagore was, however, no Moses crying in the wilderness. 'I have not come here', he asserted with grand authority, 'to discuss the question as it affects my own country, but as it affects the future of all humanity.'[118] He was part of an international conversation. His understanding of the war, like that of Aurobindo and Iqbal, has points of contact with Lenin's thesis of it being the product of 'half a century of development of world capitalism and of its billions of threads and connections' (though there were significant differences between Lenin and Tagore in their overall responses to the war).[119] Moreover, the Austrian pacifist Bertha von Suttner, who had invited Tagore to the Peace Congress in Vienna in January 1914, had written specifically about the links between exaggerated nationalism and armaments in her book *Das Maschinenzeitalter* (*The Machine Age*) in 1899. In fact, Tagore's views had resonances across a broad spectrum of social and political theories of the time, from Max Weber's discontent with the 'total domination of the bureaucratic way of life' through the British political theorist Leonard

---

[116] *Ibid.*, 61, 62.
[117] *Ibid.*, 54.
[118] *Ibid.*, 41.
[119] V. I. Lenin, *The Tasks of the Proletariat in Our Revolution* (Moscow: Progress Publishers, 1980 [1917]).

Hobhouse's critique of soulless nature of the state to Hannah Arendt's diagnosis of 'cog mentality' in the origins of totalitarianism.[120] But there were two important differences. First, for Tagore, all causes of modern 'evil' – from industrial capitalism to late imperialism to the war – coalesced round the idea of the 'Nation'. Second, he often forges the connections at the level of metaphor and imagery: the fabric of his prose becomes his critique. In the context of the war, 'mutilation' accretes intensities of meaning, moving from a metaphor for the individual (crippled by the nation-state) to the nation-state itself 'shattering its own limbs' to the 'shattering' of flesh and limbs on the Western Front. The nation-state here emerges as nothing more than a war machine: inexorable, relentless, demoniacal. Behind the various *m*-sounds that animate the passage (mutilation, manufactory, marionette, manufacturers, mechanism) lurks the barely repressed word 'murder'. However, his critique was no anti-Western diatribe; in fact, it was an index of his love for the 'spirit of the West'. As he poignantly wrote to his friend C. F. Andrews in 1916, 'Will Europe never understand the genesis of the present war, and realize that the true cause lies in her own growing scepticism towards her own ideals – those ideals that have helped her to be great?'[121]

Abroad, he became the most visible symbol of the 'East'. The idea of a 'spiritual East' as the antidote to a materialist Europe was originally a Western invention, which appeared in the writings of European travellers, missionaries and writers as early as the eighteenth century. It was then revived powerfully in the humanistic scholarship of the nineteenth-century European and American Orientalists and enthusiastically adopted and modified by the Indian spiritual revivalists, partly in conjunction and partly in competition with the Christian missionaries. Tagore would have been familiar with the work of a number of charismatic nineteenth-century religious reformers such as the Brahmo preacher Keshab Chandra Sen and the Hindu religious reformer Swami Vivekananda, who had blazed the trail for him by lecturing in Europe and the United States on 'Greater Asia' as the complement to European technology and science: 'India dies not. China dies not. Japan dies not. Therefore we

---

[120]   Quoted in David Beetham, *Max Weber and the Theory of Modern Politics* (Cambridge: Polity Press, 1985), 81; Leonard Hobhouse, *The Metaphysical Theory of the State: A Criticism* (Los Angeles: Hard Press Publishing, 2013); Hannah Arendt, *The Origins of Totalitarianism* (New York: Harcourt, 1951), 41. Also see Mukhopadhyay, '"Bhinnata of Nations"', 125–151.

[121]   'Letters to a Friend', Tagore's letter to C. F. Andrews, 11 July 1915, in *The English Writings of Rabindranath Tagore*, Vol. 3, 246.

must always remember that our backbone is spirituality.'[122] His vision of a Pan-Asian universalism resonated with and was possibly indebted to his friend, the Boston-based Japanese art critic Okakura Tenshin, who had introduced him to 'such a thing as an Asiatic mind'.[123] Tagore follows in this grand tradition, but introduces several key differences. First, his social and political contexts are very different from those of his nineteenth-century predecessors. In Tagore's version, the First World War becomes a war of *retribution* and the nineteenth-century vision of the 'spiritual East' is consequently turned into an urgently-needed *redemptive* potential as he embarks on what Rustom Barucha has succinctly called 're-orienting the Orient'.[124]

But how far was Tagore himself convinced by his own redemptive project? As early as in Japan in 1916, mentioned earlier, his audience refused to be convinced by Tagore's idea of a 'spiritual Orient' untainted by the West. His lecturing juggernaut came famously to a halt in China in 1926 when young communists boycotted his lecture; the intellectual and anarchist Wu Chih-hui was voicing a powerful strand within the popular response when he called Tagore's 'interpretation of Eastern and Western civilization as shallow and ridiculous as a blind man's babblings'.[125] No one was perhaps as acutely aware of this as Tagore himself. While his distinction between the 'Spirit' and 'Nation' of the West undercuts any homogeneous notion of Europe, his private wartime correspondence complicates the picture further. On 11 July 1915, he wrote to C. F. Andrews that

> In India, when the upper classes ruled over the lower, they forged their own chains. *Europe is closely following Brahmin India*, when she looks upon Asia and Africa as her legitimate fields for exploitation … She seems to have exhausted the oil that once lighted her lamp. Now she is feeling a distrust against the oil itself, as if it were not at all necessary for the light.[126]

---

[122] Quoted in Hay, *Asian Ideas of East and West*, 40. See *Asian Ideas of East and West*, 82–124; Carolien Stolte and Harald Fischer-Tiné, 'Imagining Asia in India: Nationalism and Internationalism', *Comparative Studies in Society and History*, 54, 1 (2012), 76.

[123] Tagore, 'City and Village', in *Talks in Japan*, 185. Also quoted in Hay, *Asian Ideas of East and West*, 38–39.

[124] See Bharucha, *Another Asia*, 70–76. Bharucha also makes the important point that Tagore's 'sense of being in the world' should be evoked more in terms of 'universality' rather than 'cosmopolitanism', given its philosophical and spiritual ambition (*Another Asia*, 136).

[125] Hay, *Asian Ideas of East and West*, 218. He pointed out that the famous champion of Eastern spirituality had stayed in the best modern hotel, ridden the latest of the Western automobiles and used the best foreign clubs for meetings.

[126] 'Letters to a Friend', Tagore's letter to C. F. Andrews, 11 July 1915, in *The English Writings of Rabindranath Tagore*, Vol. 3, 246. Emphasis added.

Lurking underneath the binary of the East and West, we have here an alternative map: Brahmin India and 'Nation of the West' are here aligned on a common axis in their lust for power, which is pitted against a tradition of liberalism and spirituality which binds together the 'spirit' of the West and the mythical Orient. This was no new insight: in a number of his essays in Bengali, such as 'Ācārer Atyācār', Tagore powerfully drew attention to the insidiousness of the caste system. Part of the compelling power of Tagore's essay on 'Nationalism' lies in its repressed or half-acknowledged realisation of conjunctions and alliances crosscutting the categories he had set up, of the looming presence of the 'Nation of the East' threatening to choke the 'Spirit of the East', even as the categories of 'nation' and 'spirit' prove unstable. His dream of a Pan-Asian unity came to a cruel end, first with the Japanese conquest of Manchuria in 1931–1932 and then with Japan's invasion of China in 1937. In 1938, when the Japanese poet Yone Noguchi wrote to Tagore for his support, arguing that the war was one of 'Asia for Asia', the latter struck back in print. Noting that Noguchi's conception of Asia was 'raised on a tower of skulls', he ended by 'wishing the Japanese people, whom I love, not success, but remorse'.[127]

Tagore's concept of a unified and spiritual Orient, his distinction between the 'nation' and the 'spirit' of the West, and his diatribe against the 'Nation' as the cause of everything that disagreed with him seem naive today. At the same time, his intuitive grasp of the connections between imperialism, nationalism and industrial modernity, fanning out through similes and metaphors, remains amazingly acute. As does his insight into the relation between victory pageants and the psychology of war. What distressed him most in Japan, he noted, was not the 'policies of kings and generals' (22) but the exhibition of war-trophies in schools. In a lecture in China in 1924, he revisited his memories from Japan in 1916:

> I passed through Japan and while there I realised for the first time, or really not the first time, but more strongly than ever, the terrible suffering with which the whole world was afflicted. I saw in Japan the war trophies from China publicly exhibited. I failed to understand this gloating attitude, this joy in the humiliation of another nation which had suffered defeat.[128]

Here, we have an early but acute diagnosis of the relation between military regalia and fascist psychology that Virginia Woolf would develop

---

[127] *Poet to Poet* (Calcutta: Visva-Bharati, 1939), 21.
[128] When he had asked, he was told that they would help to 'train the minds of people … for future warfare', *Rabindranath Tagore's Visit to China* (Calcutta, 1924), 17.

so spectacularly in *Three Guineas* (1938). In fact, while the author of *Nationalism* is often compared with political and social theorists and periodically pulled up for his deficiencies, his affinities – in style and sensibility – are perhaps more akin to Woolf. Like Woolf's, his is a powerful defence of the aesthetic and the personal against the compromises of the political. Like Woolf, he writes not with the political acumen of a seasoned statesman but with the metaphoric richness and allusiveness of the poet. Second, he flies in the face of social Darwinism and nationalism to make an impassioned plea for individual freedom and universalism whose roots go back to romantic aesthetics. His conclusion 'We the No-Nations ...' has all the subtle understandings of power and its repudiation found in Virginia Woolf's 'As a woman I have no country; as a woman, I want no country; as a woman, my country is the whole world.'[129] Living under colonial subjugation, Tagore obviously could not, like Woolf, say that 'I want no country', but there was a combination of extraordinary courage, political acuity and deep loneliness in his swimming against the nationalist current, both at home and in the world, and carefully distinguishing between his own anti-colonial patriotism for his country and jingoistic nationalism. A hundred years later, in the context of the world at large – whether Brexit-ridden Britain, Trump's America or India in the grip of burgeoning nationalism – his insights into the xenophobic, intolerant and divisive aspects of nationalism remain not just relevant but radioactively so.

The Fragility of Hope: A Conversation?

A number of scholars, from Ceymil Aydin to Pankaj Mishra, have noted how the massacre on the Western Front made a mockery of the narrative of progress woven around Western technological modernity. How could Europe continue with its claim of 'civilising mission' when it could not contain its own barbaric violence? Even people who had been qualified admirers of the West now recoiled in horror. If at the close of the previous century Tagore had envisioned 'blood-red clouds', the sun itself appeared like 'blood' in a post-war fog-bound London to Liang

---

[129] 'Nationalism in the West', 63; Virginia Woolf, *Three Guineas* (Oxford: Oxford University Press, 2008 [1938]), 197.

Qichao, the future architect of China, as he sipped tea in a garden party at Buckingham Palace; 'the great European War', he noted, 'nearly wiped out human civilisation'.[130] Meanwhile the British philosopher Bertrand Russell noted that 'the Great War showed that something went wrong with our civilisation', while the French poet Paul Richard, a friend of both Aurobindo and Tagore, noted that 'peace will come from Asia'.[131]

Aurobindo, Iqbal and Tagore all participate in this tumultuous moment. A reading of the three together brings out some of the internal dissonances in their thoughts as well as their differences from each other, while revealing points of contact. For all three, the 'European war' was in essence an imperial war fought for the possession of Asia and Africa; for each, its terrible violence and destruction were symptomatic of a deeper spiritual malaise, and the violence and destruction almost a divine act of retribution for the excesses of European imperialism. The war also strengthened the deep ambivalence that Aurobindo, Iqbal and Tagore shared about the nation-state. If, in his war writings, Aurobindo called the nation 'a convenience, and a rather clumsy convenience' which will ultimately wither away, in *The Human Cycle*, he defined its '*dharma*' as 'self-protection and self-expansion by devouring others'. Tagore too used the word to the same sarcastic effect when he noted that 'the main *dharma* of the nation' is to 'denigrate other nations' and fuel racial arrogance. Iqbal, however, objected on different grounds: for him, the beauty of Islam was in its transnational scope, and he believed that nationalism would lead to 'irreligiousness', which he considered to be one of the causes of the war.[132] Yet, none of these positions was stable: Aurobindo was a former nationalist revolutionary, while Iqbal would, in later life, advocate a separate nation-state on the grounds of religion. Indeed, Iqbal's writings during and immediately after the war testify to his embrace of a more syncretic culture, which he later would sadly abandon. With Tagore, of course, we have a very particular interpretation of 'nationalism'. It is debatable whether the reservations of either Aurobindo or Iqbal about nationalism extended to anti-colonial nationalism, as with Tagore. In fact, it was during the war years that Tagore would write his novel *Ghare Baire* (*The Home and the World*) (1915), a sustained critique of

---

[130] Joseph R. Levenson, *Liang Ch'i-Ch'ao and the Mind of Modern China* ([S.I]: Thames and Hudson, 1959), 203.

[131] Bertrand Russell, *The Problem of China* (London: G. Allen & Unwin, 1922), 14; Paul Richard, 'Introduction' to William Winstanley Pearson, *For India* (Tokyo: Asiatic Association of Japan, 1917), iv.

[132] Sevea, *The Political Philosophy of Muhammed Iqbal*, 140–141.

the Swadeshi movement in Bengal – even though his patriotism erupted at the level of emotion and affect through songs and lyric verse.

What all three share is a certain global imagining and an ethical–spiritual impulse. All three think about the 'future of all humanity' in a postwar world; what each of them advocates, with eerie resonance, is not a vision of Indian political independence or even of 'anti-colonial cosmopolitanism'[133] but something much deeper and more fundamental: the necessity of a 'spiritual revolution' for any meaningful social and political change to happen which, in turn, would usher in a more just world. For each, the problem lay in the increasing gap between what Tagore termed the 'spirit' and the 'nation', and each, in his own way, sought to ethicise the political and spiritualise public life. But it was no straightforward process, as they all fell back on a spiritual–religious discourse with all its power and perils. For Aurobindo, as we have seen, it was the realisation of 'life divine' through an expanded spiritual consciousness which he calls 'dharmarājya'; while the vision itself was secular, the framing vocabulary and images came from Hindu scriptures. With Iqbal, the vision itself was one of reconstructed Islam. While it was no narrow religious creed for either of these men but founded on humanistic principles and infused with universalist aspiration, Aurobindo's Hindu-inflected 'evolutionary consciousness' and Iqbal's 'reconstructed Islam' might have the same alienating effect on other groups.

There are two questions involved: first, whether a universal humanistic vision could be articulated through the framework of any particular religion; second, whether language itself, particularly in vernacular forms, is implicated, consciously or unconsciously, in religious registers. Tagore, it seems, was acutely alert to both problems. While his Bengali writings employ, or get enmeshed in, Hindu vocabulary, he tried to expunge his political writings in English, meant for a broader audience, of words and images with specific Hindu or even Brahmo connotations. Vernacular linguistic forms are often tied up in the world of religious affect and imagery which in fact gives them their poetic and emotional intimacy; to sanitise such language into secular modes of expression is also to flatten it. This was a problem that all three would have known with particular acuity, for each was a poet and had a spiritual vision: language, poetics and spirituality for all of them were finely blended. Iqbal was writing in Persian and Urdu for a largely Persian- and Urdu-speaking readership. While Tagore's poems in Bengali were similarly meant for a local audience, his essays on

---

[133] Manjapra, 'Introduction', to *Cosmopolitan Thought-Zones*, 2 (1–19).

'Nationalism', by dint of being in English for a largely Western audience, could more easily be 'secularised'. Aurobindo, in that sense, was a more curious example: the pervasive nature of Hindu imagery in his writings – though they are all in English – only goes to show the affective power of such ideas and images, and the intensity of his faith.

Of the three, the most cosmopolitan – in terms of both vision and vocabulary – was Tagore; his Brahmo background may have played a part. Consider, for example, his war-poem 'The Oarsmen', where the war is interpreted as an act of divine retribution. There is a corresponding need to essay forth into a post-war new world through a 'daring venture of faith', but its religious shade is left undefined:

> All the black evils in the world have overflowed their banks,
> Yet, oarsmen, take your places with the blessing of sorrow in your souls!
> Whom do you blame, brothers? Bow your heads down!
> The sin has been yours and ours.
> The heat growing in the heart of God for ages –
> The cowardice of the weak, the arrogance of the strong, the greed
> of fat prosperity, the rancour of the wronged, pride of race, and
> insult to man –
> Has burst God's peace, raging in storm.[134]

The poem is marked by the same combination of ethical critique and humanistic idealism that we have noted in the essay 'Nationalism in the West', though here the responsibility is shared – 'the sin has been yours and ours' – rather than the sole handiwork of the West. The tone of the poem too resonates with the finale of the essay: 'When the morning comes for cleansing the blood-stained steps of the Nation along the high-road of humanity, we shall be called upon to bring our own vessel of sacred water – the water of worship – to sweeten the history of man into purity.'[135] What would have possibly been *gaṅgā jal* ('holy water of the Ganges'), had the essay been in Bengali, is shorn of any explicit Hindu reference and folded into an image of 'sacred water'. But, lurking behind the poem, as in much of his post-war writing, and going far beyond the vagaries of religion and language, was a different bias.

On meeting Tagore for the first time in 1921, Romain Rolland wrote rhapsodically about the poet's beauty – 'too handsome almost' – and spiritual calm, but also added rather ruefully that, 'Despite his charming

---

[134] Tagore, 'The Oarsmen', in *English Writings*, Vol. 1, 190.
[135] 'Nationalism in the West', 63.

politeness, one sees that he is perfectly convinced of the moral and intellectual superiority of Asia – above all, of India – over Europe.'[136] While Tagore's remarkable poise and confidence may have ruffled Rolland's European *hauteur*, he was perhaps not wholly wrong: there was indeed in all three thinkers we have considered here a conviction about the moral superiority of Asia, and particularly of India. It may have been a case of inherited belief or an exercise in strategic anti-colonial essentialism or a necessary buffer – emotional, intellectual and moral – against Western imperialism and a Eurocentric world-order, or a combination of all three. Whatever it was, such a view was strengthened through the horrors of the two world wars. A few days before his death, in the middle of the Second World War, he observed 'Perhaps that dawn will come from this horizon, from the East where the sun rises.'[137] In the tentative 'perhaps' lies both the fragility of hope and the humility of the assumption. It was fitting indeed from a poet whose name 'Rabi' (*'ravi'* in Sanskrit) meant the 'sun', and Aurobindo and Iqbal could not have agreed more. Yet, the sun would have appeared with a different tinge to each of the three.

[136] Entry for 19 April 1921, in Rolland, *Inde: Journal 1915–1943*, as quoted in Hay, *Asian Ideas of East and West*, 132.
[137] Tagore, 'Crisis in Civilisation', *SE*, 268.

Afterword
The Colour and Contours of War Memory

At the time of writing *The Indian Corps in France* (1918), Lieutenant-Colonel J. W. B. Merewether and Sir Frederick Smith felt that the 'present struggle' had been waged on so immense a scale that many units had failed to receive 'contemporary justice', but 'perhaps none more conspicuously than those of the Indian Army Corps'.[1] For Amar Singh, the Rajput aristocrat and diarist, the answer lay in the realm of art: as mentioned earlier, he stressed the need of bringing *Charans* (hereditary poet-historians) from Jodhpur State to the Western Front to document sepoy experiences for posterity.[2] Here, I would like to briefly reflect on the afterlives of the sepoys, with a focus on the centennial commemoration. In recent years, there has been an overall broadening, as well a simultaneous process of sanitisation, of the memory of the First World War with regard to the colonial experience. The colour of First World War memory in Britain today is no longer white; the Indian sepoys have in recent years been more visible than ever before.[3] Indeed, an inspection of the sepoy-story may help us to ask some of the deeper questions about commemoration itself: what do we mean by the term, whose memory are we talking about, and why and in what form do we seek to remember?

Before we embark, it is important to briefly pause on the relationship of the sepoy contribution to the history of undivided India until 1947, which, in turn, has shaped the nature of remembrance in Bangladesh, Myanmyar (Burma), Pakistan and India. Indeed, what do we know about the post-war lives of the sepoy-veterans, especially those who were injured

---

[1] Lt Col. Merewether and Sir Frederick Smith, *The Indian Corps in France*, xvi–xvii.

[2] DeWitt Ellinwood, *Between Two Worlds*, 396–397.

[3] Santanu Das, 'The First World War and the Colour of Memory', *The Guardian*, 22 July 2014, www .theguardian.com/commentisfree/2014/jul/22/first-world-war-whitewashed-eurocentric. A YouGov poll, done in the UK between October 2012 and August 2014, showed a 24% increase in public awareness of the Indian soldiers who fought for Britain in 1914, rising to 68% in 2014 from 44% in 2012. See 'New Study Finds Strong Appetite for Learning WW1 History', www.britishfuture.org/ articles/news/new-study-strong-appetite-learning-wwi.

406

or shellshocked? What is the relationship between war service and the post-war nationalist movement? Did the war hasten the process of modernity and decolonisation? Each is a vast and compelling topic which warrants further investigation and is beyond the scope of this present study; it is likely that, in the post-2018 period, the focus will move from the soldiers' wartime experiences to their post-war lives, and the significance of the war – socially, culturally, politically – for the interwar history of these former colonies. For Malcolm Darling, the financial commissioner of Punjab, the wartime experiences of the sepoys had opened the eyes of Punjab peasantry to the wider world and catapulted them to modernity. From agricultural innovations and the building of schools to greater regard for women and dignity of labour, the returned peasant-warrior apparently implemented on his native soil what he had only marvelled at in France: the war, for Darling, had induced in the sepoy a 'new humanity'.[4] A veil of silence is here drawn over the thousands who would have returned home mutilated or shellshocked. On the other hand, for the nationalist historians and novelists, the trenches of the Western Front become the site for political radicalisation: our Lalu heads from the trenches via the POW camps in Germany to nationalist rallies in India as we move from Anand's *Across the Black Waters* to its sequel *The Sword and the Sickle* (1942).

The reality, as always, was messier. While it is indisputable that some returned soldiers *did* implement agricultural and educational changes, further research is needed to find out how widespread or sustained these were and whether they were indeed the direct consequences of their experiences in France. On the other hand, the nationalist interpretation needs to be equally scrutinised. It is undeniable that the experiences abroad made the soldiers more confident, robust and aware of their rights: when interviewed in 1972, a veteran noted that 'when we saw various peoples and got their views, we started protesting against the inequalities and disparities which the British had created between the white and the black'.[5] Such politicisation must surely have helped in the bid for equality and freedom. But it would indeed be premature – if rather seductive – to draw a straight line from war service via the protests against the Rowlatt Act in Punjab to the nationalist movement and subsequent independence. The minutiae of

---

[4] Malcolm Darling, *Wisdom and Waste in the Punjab Village*, 332.
[5] Interview with Lance-Naik Khela Singh conducted by Ellinwood and Pradhan, quoted in Pradhan, 'The Sikh Soldier', in Pradhan and Ellinwood (eds.), *India and World War I*, 224. Also see Upendra Narayan Chakravorty, *Indian Nationalism and the First World War 1914–1918* (Kolkata: Progressive Publishers, 1997) for one of the few book-length studies on the topic.

social history and the structures of feeling do not fit into such comfortable grids. At a local level, one can draw a strong link between the brutal (over) recruitment in 1918 and the fury that blazed across the streets of Amritsar in 1919, further fuelled by new taxes, inflation and the flu.[6] At the same time, we cannot forget the painful fact that the soldiers who obeyed the orders of General Dyer and gunned down the unarmed mob in Jallianwala Bagh on 13 April 1919 were not British officers but Gurkha, Sikh and Pathan bothers-in-arms of our First World War soldiers (there remains the tantalising possibility of a few First World War veterans among those killed). Such incidents defy any neat teleological narrative relating the war-returned sepoys and the nationalist movement; the connections between the two are more oblique but, for that matter, no less deep. The disillusionment with the Montagu–Chelmsford reforms of 1919, the Khilafat movement and Indian nationalism in the 1920s under the leadership of Gandhi were very much in the shadow of the war and the legitimate expectations that the country's 'loyalty' and its contribution of nearly 1.5 million men had aroused.[7] The war did not directly lead to decolonisation; but it was the beginning of the end in that, in conjunction with the Amritsar massacre, it dispelled any illusions Indians might have had about British rule in their country. Rabindranath Tagore famously renounced his knighthood in protest against the Amritsar massacre. 'The time', he noted, 'has come when badges of honour make our shame glaring in their incongruous context of humiliation, and I for my part wish to stand, shorn of all special distinctions, by the side of those of my countrymen, who, for their so-called insignificance, are liable to suffer a degradation not fit for human beings.'[8] Yet, in one more instance of the complex and contradictory history of India, in the same year, on 19 July (1919), the Indian troops took part in the Victory Parade and Peace Pageant to the Cenotaph in London.

In 1921, the Duke of Connaught laid the foundation stone in Delhi for the All India War Memorial (now known as the India Gate) designed by Edwin Lutyens, and it was inaugurated formally on 12 February 1931. It is dedicated to the Indian dead of the First World War as well as to those killed in the Third Anglo-Afghan War – with the names of both groups etched on the walls – showing how the two conflicts bled into each other. Today, the India Gate has been so seamlessly assimilated into

[6] See Kim Wagner, ' "Calculated to Strike Terror": The Amritsar Massacre and the Spectacle of Colonial Violence', *Past and Present*, 233, 1 (2016), 185–225. I am grateful to Kim Wagner for discussing with me the relationship between the war and the protests against the Rowlatt Bill.
[7] Bose and Jalal, *Modern South Asia*, 102–119.
[8] Krishna Dutta and Andrew Robinson (eds.), *Selected Letters of Rabindranath Tagore* (Cambridge: Cambridge University Press, 1997), 223.

the post-independence history of the country that few even know about its First World War origins. Indeed, was Lutyens' monument an ode to empire or to the Indians who died, or to both? Is it today an imperial relic or a nationalist icon? 'One way to adapt the notion of *lieux de mémoire* in postcolonial scholarship', notes Jay Winter, 'is to insist upon the hybrid character of colonial and postcolonial sites of memory. Each and every one is a palimpsest, an overwritten text.'[9] Such hybridity is inscribed into the very architecture of the other substantial site of sepoy remembrance: the Neuve Chapelle War Memorial to the Missing, with its circular enclosure, domed chattris, carved stone tigers and inscriptions in Roman, Arabic, Gurmukhi and Devnagari scripts. It was designed by Herbert Baker and unveiled on 7 October 1927. At its centre stands a fifteen-foot-high column, with a lotus capital, the Star of India and the imperial crown; on its walls are panels with the names of 4,700 Indian soldiers and labourers who died on the Western Front and have no known graves.[10]

Speaking with a double tongue, these two monuments were, however, unusual in their democratic impulse to record the names of *all* the Indian dead or missing they wished to commemorate, irrespective of rank. The more common practice, particularly for colonial memorials outside Europe, was to record the names of only the officers. For example, the memorial to the Missing of Mesopotamia, unveiled at Basra in 1929, records the 665 Indian officers by name, but not the 33,222 other ranks who are mentioned numerically (even though many of their names were known, in contrast to British privates who are all commemorated by name), a merciless testimony to the double cross of race and rank that these men bore through the war.[11] Kipling's phrase for the inscription on the graves of the missing – 'Known Unto God' – accretes fresh intensities of meaning in this context.

Across the world, from sepoy names emblazoned on the Menin Gate at Ypres to commemorative plaques at the Haydarpasha English Cemetery in Istanbul or the Taveta 'Indian' Cemetery in Kenya to memorials scattered across South Asia, one finds recognition, in varying scale, of the Indian contribution.[12] But a general amnesia soon set in: as Europe started recovering from its wreckage, its thoughts naturally turned to its own dead, mutilated

[9] Jay Winter, 'In Conclusion: Palimpsests', in Indra Sengupta (ed.), *Memory, History and Colonialism: Engaging with Pierre Nora in Colonial and Postcolonial Contexts* (London: German Historical Institute, 2009), 167.
[10] See Stanley Rice, *Neuve Chapelle: India's Memorial in France, 1914–1918* (London: Hodder & Stoughton, 1928); also see 'Neuve-Chapelle Memorial', www.cwgc.org/find/find-cemeteries-and-memorials/144000/neuve-chapelle-memorial.
[11] See Michèle Barrett, 'Death and the Afterlife: Britain's Colonies and Dominions', in Santanu Das (ed.), *Race, Empire and First World War Writing* (Cambridge: Cambridge University Press, 2011), 310. Currently, efforts to rectify this are being made by the Commonwealth War Graves Commission.
[12] See Chhina, *The Last Post: Indian War Memorials around the World* (Delhi: USI, 2010)

and bereaved. Meanwhile, in post-war India, the nationalist movement gathered momentum under the leadership of Gandhi, and, in this heated atmosphere, there was little scope for remembrance. In a joint article, Rana and Adil Chhina have astutely observed that financial compensation took the place of commemoration in post-war India: no narrative space was created, at the national or public level, around the country's war casualties or veterans.[13] The Amritsar massacre of 1919 pushed these men deeper and darker into the shadow: Mahatma Gandhi, who had helped to recruit the men in 1918, now condemned the sepoys as 'hired assassins of the Raj'.[14] The war service was viewed as little more than an 'occupational hazard', with the loss of a limb or an eye as the price.[15] Yet, memories persisted, privately, stubbornly. A few years ago, in Kolkata, I interviewed the Punjabi novelist Mohan Kahlon, who had lost his two uncles in Mesopotamia. He told me how his grandmother had gone mad with grief at the loss of her sons and their house in the village of Lyallpur in Punjab came to be known as 'pagalkhana' ('asylum'). Around the same time, I also interviewed, in Delhi, the family of Lieutenant Colonel Raj Singh Gursey.[16] His grandfather Pat Ram was also killed in the war, but the memories were very different. Pat Ram had helped in the local recruitment campaign and received silver coins and cash for his efforts; at the time of his death, his wife was just twenty-two and she continued to draw a war pension for another fifty-four years. She had the silver coins made into a necklace, which she used to wear proudly, and the family used the cash to buy land during the Partition. Like the experience of the sepoys, there is no homogeneous memory of the war in South Asia: any commemoration has to include both these narratives.

Therefore, it is not surprising that only after a hundred years is South Asia finally coming to terms with its participation in the two world wars; the centenary has finally made a space for these subterranean memories to emerge. In each of these nation-states - Bangladesh, Nepal and Pakistan – there is a burgeoning interest from the common people and there have been several official programmes to mark the centennial anniversary, though such activities have been more visible and organised in the case of India. After some initial debates in the Indian national press about whether Indian sepoys should be honoured at all, the common consensus has been to commemorate them – irrespective of the cause or

---

[13] See Rana Chhina and Adil Chhina, 'Commemoration: Cult of the Fallen (India)', https://encyclopedia.1914-1918-online.net/article/commemoration_cult_of_the_fallen_india.
[14] Quoted in Sugata Bose, *His Majesty's Opponent*, 51.
[15] Shashi Tharoor, 'Why the Indian Soldiers of WW1 are forgotten', www.bbc.co.uk/news/magazine-33317368.
[16] Interview with Mohan Kahlon in Kolkata, 18 December 2014; interview with Colonel Raj Singh Gursey, New Delhi, 22 January 2015.

motive – with a steady trickle of articles in the press and some commemorative events and volumes.[17] The Indian Prime Minister Narendra Modi made a high-profile visit to the Neuve Chapelle War Memorial in April 1915 while Prince William and his wife Kate Middleton, during their visit to India in April 2016, laid a marigold wreath at the India Gate. Rana T. S. Chhina, a retired Squadron Leader and the secretary of the United Service Institution of India, has played a vital role in India in highlighting the contribution of the First World War sepoys, from organising commemorative activities and trying to build up a digital resource to collaborating on a range of projects, both in India and abroad.[18] While Chhina is passionately interested in the First World War – both his grandfathers served in that war – his work has a wider aim: to create a space, as it were, for war remembrance in India in the absence of institutions such as the Imperial War Museum or the Australian War Memorial, especially as we move towards the anniversary of the Second World War.

By way of conclusion, I would briefly like to turn to the centennial commemoration of the Indian soldiers in a part of the world where war remembrance has been a central part of socio-cultural life since the First World War: Great Britain. Britain has seen an extraordinary outburst of energy and activities around the centenary of the war, one to which I have been a witness and an occasional participant. There has been a significant interest in various 'marginalised' or 'hidden' histories. What has been particularly heart-warming is the work of hundreds of 'citizen-historians', often spurred on by radio and television programmes (the BBC has played a prominent part in this commemorative fever), or community projects supported by organisations such as the Heritage Lottery Fund. The experience of the South Asian soldiers has enjoyed reasonable visibility, from programmes such as the acclaimed *The World's War: Forgotten Soldiers of Empire* on BBC 2 presented by David Olusoga to a host of radio programmes, YouTube videos and various community projects ('Whose Remembrance?', 'Salt of the Sarkar', 'We Were There Too', 'Empire, Faith and War') to exhibitions, light and sound shows, concerts, dance-theatre and creative re-enactments.[19] This phenomenal work has been accompanied by the recovery of fresh primary material – possibly the most lasting legacy

---

[17] See, for example, the special First World War issue of *Outlook (100 Years of War)*, 31 March 2014.
[18] See Rana T. S. Chhina, *The Last Post: Indian War Memorials around the World* (Delhi: United Service Institution, 2010). Chhina's reflections on India's role in the war and some of the aims of the USI-MEA centenary project can be found at 'USI–MEA World War I Centenary Tribute Project to Shed New Light on India's Role', http://blogs.icrc.org/new-delhi/2014/04/11/usi-mea-world-war-i-centenary-tribute-project-to-shed-new-light-on-indias-role.
[19] There have been too many interesting projects in recent years to give a full list. In addition to the range of community projects, there have been a radio play ('Subterranean Sepoys'), a dance-theatre

of this centenary – and an almost instantaneous process of dissemination through online sources, such as project websites, YouTube videos, twitter, blog posts and Facebook accounts. If *The Battle of the Somme* (1916) was the most watched film during the war years, online media have played a similarly vital role in the centennial upheaval.

Such media frenzy has been supplemented by several powerful cases of on-site commemoration. In the same year as the foundation stone of the India Gate was laid in Delhi, the Prince of Wales unveiled a dome-like *Chattri* (meaning 'umbrella' or 'pavilion') Memorial at Patcham on the South Downs in Sussex – the place of cremation of the fifty-three Sikh and Hindu sepoys who died in the hospitals in Brighton.[20] The memorial gradually fell into neglect and disrepair, and even served as a target for rifle-practice by troops during the Second World War until, in the 1990s, it came to the attention of a local Sikh teacher, Davinder Dhillon, who revived the annual commemoration ceremony.[21] On 26 September 2010, a memorial tablet bearing the names of all fifty-three of the sepoys cremated there was unveiled by the Commonwealth War Graves Commission. A very similar story is to be discovered in relation to the Muslim burial ground at Horsell Common, at Woking, Surrey. Commissioned by the War Office, it was completed in 1917, with ornate brick walls and a domed archway and minaret, in tandem with the architecture of the neighbouring Shah Jahan Mosque; during the war, it received some seventeen bodies, with another ten being received during the Second World War. Post-First World War neglect, in this case, was compounded by post-Second World War racist vandalism, and in 1968 the bodies had to be exhumed and transferred to the Brookwood cemetery. As with the Chattri group, the local people rallied together, a grant from the Heritage Lottery Fund was organised in 2012 for restoration, and the grounds were finally re-opened in 2015, with a beautiful Islamic-style 'peace-garden'.[22] At the heart of both these inspirational stories of community enterprise has been a common sentiment: a

('The Troth') based on Guleri's story 'Us Ne Kahā Thā' by Akademi, a musical programme 'Sacred Sounds: Sikh Musical Traditions and the First World War' by Alchemy, the film 'Farewell My Indian Soldier' by Vijay Singh, the play 'Wipers' by Ishy Din and the exhibitions 'Empire, Faith and War' by UK Punjab Heritage in 2014 and 'Legacy of Valour' in 2015. Also see my BBC Radio 4 programme 'Soldiers of the Empire', and short youtube documentary, *From Bombay to the Western Front* (www.youtube.com/watch?v=6stybO5v7SY).

[20] There were special crematoria at Patcham (Sussex), Netley and Brockenhurst (Hampshire) for Hindu and Sikh soldiers.

[21] The annual gathering of the Chattri has now vastly expanded in scope, with several hundred people coming together on the Chattri Memorial day. See the website Chattri, www.chattri.org, for a full account of the activities of the group.

[22] For a potted history of the place, see 'The Peace Garden', www.horsellcommon.org.uk/sites/the-peace-garden. A short BBC documentary, *Britain's Muslim Soldier*, was also made at the time. Also

genuine impulse to recognise and recover the South Asian war experience (looking through our post-independence and post-partition lenses today) and the mobilisation of such memory to give the Indian, Pakistani and Bangladeshi communities a sense of their ethnic 'British' identities, shored up through the 'shared past' of their ancestors fighting for Pax Britannica, and pave the way for greater racial integration.

Indeed, over the centennial years, colonial war memory is increasingly being reinvented in the UK as the grand stage on which to play the anthem of multiculturalism. There has been a central tension here between this much-needed expansion of war memory and a simultaneous process of sanitisation of the painful dimensions of colonial war service from that narrative. 'Ultimate sacrifice for a cause he didn't even understand', noted Zafar Iqbal, a policy officer at Woking Borough Council and a galvanising force for the restoration of the burial ground, with reference to one of the Muslim soldiers originally buried at Horsell. These men, we are told, were examples of the 'shared history' that bound Britain and South Asia, and go to show that 'there's no conflict between being Muslim and being British'.[23] In 2012, Baroness Sayeeda Warsi, the first Muslim woman to sit in cabinet as part of the government, had set the tone as she led the 'Commonwealth' war commemoration:

> And 'our boys' on the front line weren't just Tommies; they were Tariqs and Tajinders as well – one million Indian soldiers fighting and dying for our country.
>
> There were also black British Soldiers, like the iconic footballer Walter Tull, who died in 1918 as he helped his men retreat in heavy gunfire.
>
> These are the people we must remember – people who everyone in today's Britain can relate to.
>
> I'm sure the far right will try and get their grubby hands on this moment, just as they try to own our Union flag.
>
> ...
>
> As the daughter of Pakistani immigrants, I proudly bang the drum for Britain's heritage, because it's mine too.
>
> After all, both my grandfathers fought with the Allies.
>
> I am also proud to serve in a government which respects our troops and resources them properly, honouring our Military Covenant.
>
> So two years from now, 100 years since the Great War began, let us all come together under one flag to remember what our heroes did for every single one of us.

see Santanu Das, 'Are Faith-Specific War Memorials the Best Way to Remember the Fallen?', www.independent.co.uk/news/world/world-history/are-faith-specific-war-memorials-the-best-way-to-remember-the-fallen-a6727821.html.
[23] Quoted from the BBC documentary *Britain's Muslim Soldier* (2015).

Afterword

I will make it my mission to ensure that the centenary is a chance for everyone
to learn about the contribution of the Commonwealth soldiers. After all, our
shared future is based on our shared past.[24]

What Warsi does here is in many ways crucially important: she issues a
direct challenge to the colour of war memory in the lead-up to the centenary.
Equally importantly, hers is a view faithful to the multi-religious composition of the British Indian army, inclusive of the Muslim Tariq and the Sikh
or Hindu Tajinder. And yet, on closer scrutiny, the vocabulary seems rather
dissimulating: '"Our boys" ... [including] one million Indian soldiers fighting
and dying for our country'. Which country? Did the soldiers actually know
or knowingly 'sacrifice', when most joined, as we have seen, to keep hunger at
bay? The complex and sometimes contradictory motives of the Indian soldiers
are here instead flattened into a paean of British conservative loyalism eerily
reminiscent of George V's call to the empire in 1914; indeed, in the references
to a government respecting 'our troops' and resourcing them, do we have a
parallel agenda here of targeting ethnic minorities for current recruitment in
the British armed forces? Moreover, the language of imperial bonding veils
much that was painful and unattractive. If there are heart-warming tales of
Indo-European friendship, the colonial and racial hierarchies were firmly in
place: fences around the Brighton Pavilion Hospital, as we have seen, kept the
Tariqs and Tajinders apart from the Tommies.

Colonial war commemoration often slips into 'celebration', as if the
only way to reclaim these men is by turning them into 'war heroes' or
'martyrs'. What is often forgotten amidst such valorisation is that these
are histories of violence and trauma; they were at once victims and killers.
Consider the riposte from Sofia Ahmed (a journalist and blogger, and, like
Warsi, a British Muslim woman):

I'm a prime target for these initiatives, coming from a 'Martial Race' as I do.
My great, great grandfather was awarded an 'order of merit' and given title
of 'Subedar Major' for his 'bravery' during the First World War. However,
the fact that he was probably fighting on the Mesopotamian campaign
against the Muslim Ottoman empire, doesn't exactly fill me with ecstatic
pride. It actually makes me a bit nauseous to think about what 'brave' act
he must have carried out to be given the highest military award in the land.[25]

---

[24] Baroness Warsi, "Our Boys Weren't Just Tommies – They Were Tariqs and Tajinders Too", http://
sayeedawarsi.com/2012/10/16/the-sun-our-boys-werent-just-tommies-they-were-tariqs-and-
tajinders-too. Warsi has reiterated the message in various forms; the final paragraph in the above
extract is quoted from her speech, as reported in Jane Merrick and Kashmira Gander, 'Tommies and
Tariqs Fought Side by Side', *The Independent*, 22 June 2013, www.independent.co.uk/news/uk/home-
news/special-report-the-centenary-of-wwi-tommies-and-tariqs-fought-side-by-side-8669758.html.

[25] Initially written as a blog response to the phenomenon of the 'poppy hijab' for Muslim women,
Ahmed's piece was published in *The Independent* on 4 November 2015. See Sofia Ahmed, 'No,

War memory to Ahmed is a poisoned chalice as she undercuts the celebratory sacrificial rhetoric of Warsi: the two may be said to mark the opposite ends of the spectrum. Moreover, it is often overlooked that, while there were extraordinary soldiers such as Khudadad Khan with their heart-stirring tales, most sepoys, like the English Tommies, would have trembled like leaves and shat in their trousers as the shells burst. If asked about imperial sacrifice or shared history, they would have pointed, like Wilfred Owen, to 'the old lie' – they were only human in inhuman circumstances. Vulnerability, rather than tales of heroism, may be a more fruitful way of understanding the war, i.e. the *cost* of war, the first step towards preventing it.

What we note is a tension between what can be called the instrumental and ethical uses of the Indian war experience. The instrumental use of colonial war memory, which has largely characterised the community projects and commemorative programmes, aims for greater recognition of the role of colonial troops, partly with a view to use it for a more multi-cultural agenda and to combat everyday racism and xenophobic nation-alism. Interestingly, as this book goes into print, the Windrush scandal is engulfing the country, and the black British MP David Lammy mem-orably invoked the contribution of the West Indian soldiers in the two world wars to demand better treatment for the Windrush generation. Understandably, ethnic community groups insist on telling 'positive' stories, even if it involves conscious sanitisation; on occasions, the 'posi-tive' element can get out of hand and border on ethnic nationalism and unreconstructed heroism.[26] On the other hand, an ethical use of memory would involve greater attention to the minutiae of history, in all its asym-metries and messiness, as well as to the moral and cultural complexities.[27] Does commemoration of the contribution of a particular group inevitably involve renewed othering and denigration of the 'enemy'? How do we, for example, remember a hypothetical underage sepoy, forcibly recruited, who ends up killing a Turkish soldier? Is there a way of remembering both at the same time, without any note of triumphalism? Moreover, why is it

---

I Won't Wear the "Poppy Hijab" to Prove I'm Not a Muslim Extremist', www.independent.co.uk/voices/no-i-wont-wear-the-poppy-hijab-to-prove-im-not-an-extremist-a6720901.html.

[26] It becomes particularly difficult to critically examine these stories when they are narrated by descendants of colonial soldiers. I have in mind two such gatherings in the House of Commons in 2014, convened respectively by Sayeeda Warsi and Diane Abbott, when the descendants arrived with various pieces of war memorabilia and started airing their views. Even though I did not always agree, I could not help being deeply moved by and admiring the intensity of their investment in these often celebratory stories.

[27] See Cécile Fabre, *Cosmopolitan Peace* (Oxford: Oxford University Press, 2016). Also listen to her illuminating podcast 'Remembering War', https://podcasts.ox.ac.uk/remembering-war.

that, in the field of non-white colonial contribution, the tension between 'commemoration' and 'celebration' is at its most intense?

My own engagement with these questions has been long and vexed. If I had always issued caveats against strictly instrumental uses of the past, there have been a couple of occasions where I have had bouts of intense soul-searching and questioned my own assumptions – particularly after the terrorist attacks in London and Paris in 2016 and 2017. Indeed, if an expedient version of colonial war experience can actively help, as we are told, in racial integration in these perilous times – both against Islamic extremism and the rising tide of Islamophobia often following the attacks – what right do a few of us have to demur? If such stories can help in restoring confidence, why not? In April 2016, a few of us working on the field convened a seminar 'Beyond Commemoration: South Asia and the First World War' at King's College London, where we got together people from diverse fields interested in the topic – academics, people from the army and the navy, political activists and community leaders, museum archivists and curators, poets and artists and policy makers.[28] What emerged from the compelling discussion was the need to look at these painful histories squarely in the eye, and that instrumental and ethical uses of the past are not mutually incompatible. Now that the initial aim of gaining recognition of these soldiers has been achieved, we need to get beyond simple commemoration and create a space for critique and discussion. Any uses of war memory, if they are to be effective and resonant, must be historically and ethically responsible; if greater racial integration and harmony is the common aim for all of us, we cannot have a robust multicultural society without a robust engagement with the past, however painful or messy it may be.

A related question that arises is one of genre: is a plinth or plaque or monument with a cryptic one-line message the most apt way to commemorate such complex stories? Hidden histories are often the most contested. A more expansive form of commemoration – such as a literary work or an exhibition with the scope for multiple narratives – may be a more appropriate even if less visible testament. The exhibition 'Five Continents in Flanders' (2008) in the In Flanders Museum, Ypres, Kamila Shamsie's war novel *A God in Every Stone* (2014) and the poetry of Amarjit Chandan are important steps in that direction.

---

[28] A blog of the event by Iqbal Hussein is to be found at 'Beyond Commemoration: South Asia and the First World War', http://blog.nationalarchives.gov.uk/blog/beyond-commemoration-south-asia-first-world-war, with a link to an audio-recording and a short YouTube video.

India, Empire, and First World War Culture similarly seeks to open up a multi-dimensional space, at once critical and affective, by taking us back to the war years and embedding us in the richness and variety of the cultural sources and discourses. In what is now an iconic moment in the literary history of First World War, Wilfred Owen quoted the following lines from Tagore to his mother as he left home for France for the final time:

> When I go from hence, let this be my parting word
> That what I have seen is unsurpassable.[29]

Tagore's fellow-countrymen and colonial brethren – combatants and non-combatants, officers and labourers – could not have agreed more as they travelled to various parts of the world not just to see but take part in the 'unsurpassable' – occasionally wonder, but more often horror. As we have seen, literary and cultural artefacts have the power to transmit that sense of the 'unsurpassable'; equally, they point beyond the sepoy-story to its reach in the minutiae of everyday life within the Indian homefront, affecting both men and women. The war was a crack in the table of history not just in Europe. Aural, visual and literary artefacts, in their combination of historical testimony and formal sensuousness, are peculiarly alert to and often enmeshed in the contradictions and complexities of the time; we need to pay attention to the various intensities of meaning that pulse underneath their surfaces. Now that the first, essential step of 'recovery' of the colonial non-white contribution to the war efforts is well underway, these artefacts, it is hoped, will facilitate a more complex interrogation of the colonial dimensions of war service – the worlds of experience and feeling they spawned and their difficult post-war legacies. A hundred years on, these objects, images and tunes, often accompanied by words – or re-configured in the realm of poetry and fiction – have themselves the 'unsurpassable' power of conjuring up the past, taking us beyond a sanitised version of history sealed in medals and memorials into something altogether more palpable, intractable, and incorrigibly plural.

---

[29] Tagore, 'When I go from hence', in *The English Writings of Rabindranath Tagore*: Poems, Vol. 1, 76.

Select Bibliography

ARCHIVES

Australia
Australian War Memorial, Canberra
Mitchell Library, State Library of New South Wales

Belgium
In Flanders Fields Museum, Ypres

France
Bibliothèque de documentation internationale contemporaine, Nanterre
Musée d'Histoire Contemporaine, Paris
Service historique de la défense, Paris

Germany
Brandenburgische Akademie der Wissenschaften, Berlin
Lautarchiv der Humboldt-Universität zu Berlin
Museum Europäischer Kulturen, Staatliche Museen zu Berlin – Preußischer Kulturbesitz
Staatsbibliothek Berlin
Politisches Archiv des Auswärtigen Amtes, Berlin

India
Dupleix Museum, Chandernagore, West Bengal
General Amar Singh Kanota Museum and Library, Jaipur
Haryana Academy, Gurgaon, New Delhi
National Archives of India, New Delhi
National Library, Kolkata
Nehru Memorial Library, New Delhi
Punjab Government State Archives, Chandigarh

United Services Institution of India, New Delhi
West Bengal State Archives, Kolkata
Visva-Bharati Archives, Shantiniketan

New Zealand

Alexander Turnbull Library, Wellington
Auckland War Museum, Auckland

United Kingdom

India Office Record and Library (IOR), Asia, Africa and Pacific Collections,
    British Library
Brighton History Centre, Brighton
Cambridge University Library
Imperial War Museum, London
Liddell Hart Centre for Military Archives, London
National Army Museum, London
The National Archives, Kew, London
The Keep, Brighton

Private Collections

Avtar Singh Bahra, London
Sunanda Das, Kolkata
Indrani Haldar, Kolkata
Romola Sarbadhikari, Kolkata
Domique Faivre, Neuve Chapelle
Paul Richards, Oosterdam
Eric Deroo, Paris
Raj Singh, New Delhi
Rajinder Bath, London

Newspapers and Periodicals

The following are in addition to passages from various newspapers, as extracted in
    Reports of Native Newspapers, 1914–1921
Amrita Bazar Patrika
Asian Review
Bengalee
Bhāratvarṣa
Bhāratī
Daily Mirror
Hindostan
Jat Gazette
Kölnische Zeitung
L'Illustration

Mānasī O Marmavāṇī
Modern Review
The Bystander
The Illustrated London News
The Pioneer
The Statesman
The Times
The Tribune
The War Illustrated

PUBLISHED PRIMARY SOURCES

47th Sikhs: War Records of the Great War, 1914–1918 (Chippenham, 1992 [1921])
Ghadar dī Gūnj (San Francisco: Hindustani Ghadar Press, 1916)
India's Contribution to the Great War (Calcutta: Superintendent Government Printing, 1923)
Indian Ink: Splashes from Various Pens (Calcutta: Messrs Thacker, Spink and Co., 1915)
Punjab Government Gazetteer of the Lahore District, 1883–4 (Lahore: Sang-e-Meel Publications, 1989)
Patiala and the Great War: A Brief History of the Services of the Premier Punjab State (London: The Medici Society Ltd, 1923)
Speeches of Indian Princes on the World War (no details, 1919)
Statistics of the Military Effort of the British Empire during the Great War, 1914–1920 (London: HM Stationery Office, 1920)
Abbasi, Anis Ahmad, *Bahār-i-Jung* [*The Spring of War*] (Aminabad, Lucknow: Mahadev Prasad Varma, 1917)
al-Afghānī, Sayid Jamāl al-Dīn and Hā'irī, Abdul-Hādī, 'Afghānī on the Decline of Islam', *Die Welt des Islams*, New Series, 13, 1/2 (1971), 121–125
Alexander, Herbert, *On Two Fronts, Being the Adventures of an Indian Mule Corps in France and Gallipoli* (New York: Dutton, 1917)
Anand, Mulk Raj, *The Village* (London: Jonathan Cape, 1939)
  Across the Black Waters (Delhi: Orient Longman, 1940)
  The Sword and the Sickle (London: Jonathan Cape, 1942)
  Seven Summers: The Story of an Indian Childhood (London: Hutchinson, 1951)
  Apology for Heroism: A Brief Autobiography of Ideas (New Delhi: Arnold Heinemann, 1975)
  Conversations in Bloomsbury (Delhi: Oxford University Press, 1981)
  Untouchable (London: Penguin, 2014 [1935])
Anderson, Maj. M. H., *With the 33rd 'Q.V.O.' Light Cavalry in Mesopotamia: The Diaries of Major M. H. Anderson, November 1914 to April 1915*, ed. Capt. E. S. J. Anderson (Uckfield: Naval and Military Press, 2014)
Andrews, C. F. (ed.), *Letters to a Friend: Rabindranath Tagore's Letters to C. F. Andrews* (Delhi: Rupa, 2002)
Ashok, Shamsher Singh (ed.), *Prāchin Varan te Jangnāme* (Amritsar: Shiromani Gurdwara Parbandhak Committee, 1950)
Austin, Frederic Britten, 'The Magic of Muhammed Din', *The Strand Magazine*, August 1917

Azad, Bishan Sahai and Dattatreya, Piyare Mohan, *Fasānah-i-Jung-i-Yūrap* [*The Saga of the War in Europe*] (Lahore: C. L. Alam and Company, 1914)

Barber, Charles, *Besieged in Kut and After* (London, 1917)

Barbusse, Henri, *Under Fire* (London: Dent, 1965 [1916])

Bardhan, Kalpana, *The Oxford Anthology of Bengali Literature, Volume 1, 1861–1941* (Delhi: Oxford University Press, 2010)

Barrier, N. G., *Banned: Controversial Literature and Political Control in British India, 1907–1947* (Delhi/Columbia: Manohar/University of Missouri Press, 1974)

Barstow, A. E., *Handbook on Sikhs* (New Delhi: Uppal Publishing House, 1989 [1928])

Basu, Bhupendranath, *Why India Is Heart and Soul with Britain in This War* (London: Macmillan, 1914)

Bhargava, M. B. L., *India's Services in the War* (Allahabad: M. B. L. Bhargava, 1919)

Bhattacharya, Sabyasachi (ed.), *The Mahatma and the Poet: Letters and Debates between Gandhi and Tagore, 1915–1941* (New Delhi: The National Book Trust, 1997)

Bibikoff, Massia, *Our Indians in Marseilles*, trans. L. Huxley (London: Smith, Elder, & Co., 1915)

Bismal, Sukh Dev Prashad Sinha, *Bahār-i-English* [*The English Spring*] (Allahabad: Asrar-i-Karimi Press, 1916)

Bonarjee, P. D., *A Handbook of the Fighting Races of India* (Calcutta: Thacker, Spink & Co., 1899)

Borden, Mary, *The Forbidden Zone* (London: William Heinemann, Ltd, 1929)

Candler, Edmund, *The Long Road to Baghdad* (London: Routledge, 2016 [1919])

The Sepoy (London: John Murray, 1919)

Charteris, Brigadier-Gen. John, *At G. H. Q.* (London: Cassel and Company, Ltd, 1931)

Chattopadhay, Satish Chandra, *Bāṅgāli Palṭan* (Calcutta: Madhuri Workshop, 1916)

Cunningham, Col. A. H., *A Short History of the Corps of King George's Own Bengal Sappers and Miners during the War, 1914–1918* (publication details unknown, 1930; available at the British Library)

Darling, Malcolm Lyall, *The Punjab Peasant in Prosperity and Debt* (Oxford: Oxford University Press, 1925)

Wisdom and Waste in the Punjab Village (London: Oxford University Press, 1934)

Das, Taraknath, *Is Japan a Menace to Asia?* (Shanghai: Taraknath Das, 1917)

Datta, V. N. (ed.), *New Light on the Punjab Disturbances in 1919* (Simla: Indian Institute of Advanced Study, 1975)

Devi, Mokkhada, *Kalyāṇ-Pradīp: The Life of Captain Kalyan Kumar Mukhopadhyay I.M.S.* (Calcutta: Satish Chandra Mukhopadhyay and Rashik Law Press, 1928)

Devi, Sarala, 'Bengal Double Company', *Bhāratī*, April 1918

Devi, Swarnakumari, *Short Stories* (Madras: The Cambridge Press, 1918)

Dobson, Austin (ed.), *The Complete Poetical Works of Oliver Goldsmith* (unknown location: Andesite Press, 2017)

Fazil, Muhammad Khan, Raja, *Maujūdah Jung-i-Yūrap ke asbāb aur Jarman tahzib* [*The Causes of the War in Europe and German Culture*] (Lahore: Islamiyah Steam Press, 1915)

Forster, E. M., *Aspects of the Novel* (Harmondsworth: Penguin, 2005 [1927])

Freud, Sigmund, *The Standard Edition of the Complete Psychological Works*, trans. James Strachey (London: Hogarth Press, 1953–1974)

Frobenius, Leo, *Der Völkerzirkus unsere Feinde* (Berlin: Eckart-Verlag, 1916)

Gandhi, M. K., *The Collected Works of Mahatma Gandhi* (Ahmedabad: Government of India, 1965)

An Autobiography or The Story of My Experiments with Truth (London: Penguin, 1982)

Hind Swaraj and Other Writings, ed. Anthony J. Parel (Cambridge: Cambridge University Press, 1997)

Ghose, Babu Aurobindo (ed.), *Bal Gangadhar Tilak: His Writings and Speeches* (Madras: Ganesh & Co., 1919)

Ghosh, Amitav, *The Imam and the Indian: Prose Pieces* (New Delhi: Ravi Dayal Publisher, 2006)

Flood of Fire (London: John Murray, 2015)

Ghosh, Aurobindo, *Collected Works by Sri Aurobindo, Birth Centenary Library* (Pondicherry: Sri Aurobindo Ashram Trust, 1971), 30 volumes

The Essential Writings of Sri Aurobindo, ed. Peter Heehs (Delhi: Oxford University Press, 1998)

Sri Aurobindo: A Contemporary Reader, ed. Sachidananda Mohanty (London: Routledge, 2008)

Graves, Robert, *Goodbye to All That* (Harmondsworth: Penguin, 1988 [1929])

The Collected Poems of Robert Graves (London: Penguin Classics, 2003)

Grimshaw, Capt. Roly, *Indian Cavalry Officer, 1914–15*, ed. Col. J. Wakefield and Lt Col. J. M. Weippart (Tunbridge Wells: Costello, 1986)

Gu XinQing, *Ou Zhan Gong Zuo Hui Yi Lu* [*Memories of My Work in the European War*] (Hong Kong: Commercial Press, 1937)

Guleri, Chandradhar Sharma, 'Usne Kaha Thah' ['At Her Bidding'], *Indian Literature*, XXVII, 102 (1984), 4, 41

Hamid Merathi, Muhammad 'Abd al-Hamid, *Mussadas-I Jung-I Karimā, ma'rufbih … Nazm-I hāl-I Tarabulus* (Aligarh: Urdu Press, 1913)

Higonnet, Margaret R. (ed.), *Lines of Fire: Women Writers of World War I* (New York: Penguin, 1999)

Hobhouse, Leonard, *The Metaphysical Theory of the State: A Criticism* (Los Angeles: Hard Press Publishing, 2013 [1918])

Hogarth, D. G., 'The Eastern Mind', *Monthly Review*, 15, 43 (1904)

Husain, Khadim, *Jungnāmah-I Rusva Jāpān, al-ma'rufbihMikadu-namah-I manzum* [*The Chronicles of War in Russia and Japan*] (Ambala: Allah Baksh and Hafiz 'Ali Hasan, 1907)

Hussain, Fazl-I (ed.), *Bahār-i-Jarman* [*The Spring of the Germans*] (Moradabad: Afzal-al-Matabi, 1915)

Hussein, Abdullah, *The Weary Generations* [translation of *Udas Naslain*, 1963] (London: Peter Owen, 1999)

Hypher, P. P., *Deeds of Valour Performed by Indian Officers and Soldiers, during the Period from 1860 to 1925* (Simla: Liddell's Press, 1927)

Iqbal, Muhammed, *Speeches and Statements of Iqbal* (Lahore: Shamloo, 1948)

Poems from Iqbal: Renderings in English Verse with Comparative Urdu Text, trans. V. G. Kiernan (Karachi: Oxford University Press, 2004 [1955])

A Message from the East [Payām-i-Mashriq], trans. M. Hadi Husain (Lahore: Iqbal Academy Pakistan, 1977)

Call of the Marching Bell [Bāṅg-i-dāra], trans. M. A. K. Khalil (Newfoundland: M. A. K. Khalil, 1997)

The Reconstruction of Religious Thought in Islam, ed. M. Saeed Sheikh and intro. Javed Majeed (Stanford: Stanford University Press, 2013)

Islam, Kazi Nazrul, *Kazi Nazrul Islam: A New Anthology*, ed. Rafiqul Islam (Dhaka: Bangla Academy, 1990)

Nazrul Racanāvalī [Collected Works of Nazrul], ed. Abdul Qadir (Dhaka: Bangla Academy, 1993)

Nazrul Racanā Samagra [Collected Works of Nazrul] (Calcutta: West Bengal Academy, 2001 and 2005), 2 volumes

Jaffrelot, Christophe (ed.), *Hindu Nationalism: A Reader* (Princeton: Princeton University Press, 2007)

Jarboe, Andrew Tait (ed.), *War News in India: The Punjabi Press during World War I* (London: I. B. Tauris, 2016)

Jünger, Ernst, *Storm of Steel*, trans. Michael Hofmann (London: Allen Lane, 2003 [1920])

Kahlon, Mohan, *Veh Gaye Pani* (New Delhi: Chetna Parakasha: 2010)

Kashi Nath, P., *Indian Labourers in France* (Bombay: Oxford University Press, 1919)

Kanda, K. C., *Urdu Ghazals: An Anthology: From 16th to 20th Century* (New Delhi: Sterling, 1995)

Kanrei Shaiza, *Apuk Apaga Rairei Khare. France Khava, 1917– 1918 [The First Great War Worldwide. To France, 1917–1918]* (Imphal: publisher not known, 1974)

Kant, Immanuel, *Perpetual Peace: A Philosophical Essay*, trans. M. Campbell Smith with a preface by Robert Latta (New York and London: Garland Publishing, 1972)

Karkaria, Nariman, *Rangbhumini Rakhad [Roaming a Performance Stage or Travels of Interesting Places]* (Bombay: Manek Printing Press, 1922)

Kendall, Tim (ed.), *Poetry of the First World War* (Oxford: Oxford University Press, 2013)

Kimber, Gerri and Smith, Angela (eds.), *The Poetry and Critical Writings of Katherine Mansfield* (Edinburgh: Edinburgh University Press, 2014)

Kipling, Rudyard, *The Eyes of Asia* (New York: Doubleday, Page & Company, 1918)

The Years Between (London: Methuen, 1919)

Kim, ed. Edward Said (London: Penguin, 1987)

The Collected Poems of Rudyard Kipling, ed. R. T. Jones (Ware: Wordsworth, 2001)

Kreyer, Maj. J. A. C. and Uloth, Maj. G., *The 28th Light Cavalry in Persian and Russian Turkistan 1915–1920* (Oxford: Slatter & Rose Ltd, 1926)

La Mazière, Pierre, *L'H.C.F.: L'hôpital chirurgical flottant* (Paris: Albin Michel, 1919)

Lall, Joel Waiz, *Haqīqat-i-Jung* [*The Truth of the War*] (Delhi: J. & Sons Barqi Press, 1915)

Lawrence, D. H., *The Complete Poems of D. H. Lawrence*, ed. Vivian de Sola and F. Warren Roberts (Harmondsworth: Penguin, 1964)

Leigh, M. S., *The Punjab and the War* (Lahore: Sang-e-Meel Publications and Superintendent Government Printing, 1997 [1922])

Lenin, V. I., *The Tasks of the Proletariat in Our Revolution* (Moscow: Progress Publishers, 1980 [1917])

Lind, Col. A. G., *A Record of the 58th Rifles F.F. in the Great War 1914–1919* (Waziristan: Commercial Steam Press, 1933)

Long, P. W., *Other Ranks of Kut* (Uckfield: The Naval and Military Press, n.d.)

Lucas, Charles, *The Empire At War*, Vol. V (London: Oxford University Press, 1926)

Lüders, Heinrich, 'Die Gurkhas', in Wilhelm Doegen (ed.), *Unter fremden Völkern: Eine neue Völkerkunde* (Berlin: Stollberg, 1925), 126–139

Luschan, Felix von, *Kriegsgefangene* (Berlin: Dietrich Reimer, 1917)

MacGill, Patrick, *The Great Push* (London: Herbert Jenkins, 1917)

MacMunn, G. F., *The Armies of India* (London: Adam & Charles Black, 1911)
India and the War (London: Hodder and Stoughton, 1915)
The Martial Races of India (London: Sampson Low, 1933)

Marx, Karl, 'The British Rule in India' (1853), in *Marx and Engels, Articles on Britain* (Moscow: Progress Publishers, 1971)

Masters, John, *The Ravi Lancers* (London: Michael Joseph, 1972)

Merewether, Lt Col. J. W. B. and Smith, Sir Frederick, *The Indian Corps in France* (London: John Murray, 1918)

Mundy, Talbot, *King of the Khyber Rifles* (London: Constable & Co., 1917)
Hira Singh: When India Came to Fight in Flanders (London: Cassell & Co., 1918)

Naidu, Sarojini, *The Broken Wing: Songs of Love, Death and Destiny 1915–1916* (London: William Heinemann, 1917)
Speeches and Writings (Madras: G. A. Natesan, 1918)

Natesan, G. A. (ed.), *All about the War: The India Review War Book* (Madras: G. A. Natesan, 1915)

Neilson, J. Fraser, *Muhārabah-I ʿālam*, trans. from the English into Urdu by Sayyid Muʿin al-Din (Budaun: Nizami Press, 1916)

Niedermayer, Oskar von, *Meine Rückkehr aus Afghanistan* [*My Return from Afghanistan*] (Munich: Wolf, 1918) (under the pseudonym Hadschi Mirza Hussein)
Unter der Glutsonne Irans: Kriegserlebnisse der deutschen Expedition nach Persien und Afganistan [*Under the Scorching Sun of Iran: War Experiences of the German Expedition to Persia and Afghanistan*] (Dachau: Einhornverlag, 1925)

Nizami, Khvajah Hasan, *Jarman-nāmah* [*The Book of the Germans*], compiled by Qudsi Muhammadi al-Nizami Bhopali (Delhi: Halqah-I Mashaʾikh; Meerut, 1915)

O'Dwyer, Michael, *India As I Knew It, 1885–1925* (London: Constable, 1925)

Omissi, David (ed.), *Indian Voices of the Great War: Soldiers' Letters, 1914–1918* (London: Macmillan, 1999)

Owen, Harold and Bell, John, *Wilfred Owen: Collected Letters* (Oxford: Oxford University Press, 1967)

Owen, Wilfred, *The Poems of Wilfred Owen*, ed. Jon Stallworthy (London: Chatto & Windus, 1990)

   The War Poems, ed. Jon Stallworthy (London: Chatto & Windus, 1994)

Palit, D. K., *Saga of an Indian I.M.S. Officer – The Life and Times of Lt Col. A. N. Palit, OBE 1883–1972* (New Delhi: United Service Institution of India, 2006)

Pearson, William Winstanley, *For India* (Tokyo: Asiatic Association of Japan, 1917)

Prashad, Shiv, *Jarmani ke aslī hālāt* [*The Actual Circumstances in Germany*] (Faizabad: Ta'aluqdar Press, 1915)

Pratap, Rajah Mahendra, *My Life Story 1886–1979*, ed. Vir Singh (Delhi: Originals, 2004)

Premchand, *The Oxford India Premchand*, intr. Francesca Orsini (New Delhi: Oxford University Press, 2004)

Pritam, Amrita, *Alone in the Multitude*, ed. and trans. Suresh Kohli (New Delhi: Indian Literary Review, 1979)

Rafiullah, Mohammed, *Gwalior's Part in the War* (London: Hazell, Watson & Viney, 1920)

Ram, Atma (ed.), *Mulk Raj Anand: A Reader* (New Delhi: Sahitya Akademi, 2005)

Rao, Raja, *Kanthapura* (New Delhi: Oxford University Press, 1937)

Ray, Krishna Behari, 'Captive of the Turks in the Battle of Kut, as narrated by Sitanath Bhatta', *Mānasī O Marmavāṇī*, September 1919, 121–125

Rice, Stanley, *Neuve Chapelle: India's Memorial in France, 1914–1918* (London, Hodder & Stoughton, 1927)

Richard, Paul, 'Some Answers', *Asian Review*, 1, 1 (1920)

Roberts, Frederic Sleigh, *Forty-One Years in India: From Subaltern to Commander-in-Chief* (London: Macmillan, 1897)

Rowcroft, C. H., *With Hodson's Horse in Palestine* (Bombay: Thacker & Co. Ltd, 1919)

Roy, Ashutosh, 'Yuddhavandīr Ātmakathā' ['Autobiography of a Prisoner of War'], *Bhāratvarṣa*, January 1920 (Part 2, Vol. 2), 194–197

Roy, M. N., *Memoirs* (Bombay: Bombay Allied Publishers, 1964)

Rudolph, Susanne and Rudolph, Lloyd (eds.), *Reversing the Gaze: Amar Singh's Diary: A Colonial Subject's Narrative of Imperial India* (Delhi: Oxford University Press, 2000)

Rudra, Maj. Gen. A. A., *His Service in Three Armies and Two World Wars*, ed. Maj. Gen. D. K. Palit (New Delhi: Reliance Publishing House, 2000)

Russell, Bertrand, *The Problem of China* (London: G. Allen & Unwin, 1922)

Sandes, Major E. W. C., *In Kut and Captivity: With the Sixth Indian Division* (London: John Murray, 1919)

Sarbadhikari, Sisir Prasad, *Abhi Le Baghdad* (Kolkata: privately printed, 1957)

Sarrut, Paul, *British and Indian Troops in Northern France – 70 Sketches 1914–1915* (Arras: H. Delepine, 1915)

Sassoon, Siegfried, *Memoirs of an Infantry Officer* (London: Faber & Faber, 1965 [1930])

The War Poems (London: Faber, 1983)

Collected Poems 1908–1956 (London: Faber, 1984)

Sen, Kunal C., *Through War, Rebellion & Riot 1914–1921: Being a Narrative of My Career in Egypt, the Dardanelles, the Balkans, Mesopotamia and in Iraq, under 'Shot and Shell', and Its Finale under the 'lathi' of Bombay Rioters* (Calcutta: Art Press, n.d., according to Worldcat, between 1921 and 1939)

Sen, Prafulla Chandra, 'Bengal Ambulance Corps-er Katha' ['The Story of Bengal Ambulance Corps'], *Mānasī O Marmavāṇī*, December 1922 (Year 13, Part 2, Vol. 5), 459–466, January 1924 (Year 15, Part 2, Vol. 6), 536–542 and June 1925 (Year 17, Part 1, Vol. 5), 495–500

Sever, Adrian, *Documents and Speeches on the Indian Princely States* (Delhi: B. R. Publishing Corporation, 1985)

Shakespeare, William, *Measure for Measure*, ed. J. W. Lever (London: Bloomsbury, 2008)

The Tempest (Arden Shakespeare), ed. Alden T. Vaughan and Virginia Mason Vaughan (London: Bloomsbury, 2011)

Shamsie, Kamila, *A God in Every Stone* (London: Bloomsbury, 2014)

Singh, Nand, *Vaddā Jung Europe* [*The Great European War*] (Ludhiana: Kavishar Gurdit Singh and Gajan Singh, 1934)

Singh, Sant, *Na'ra-i-Jung* [*The Call of War*] (Lahore, 1918)

Singh, Tara, *Bharti* [*On Recruiting*] (Lahore, 1915)

Sinha, Kumar Manindra Chandra, *Writings and Speeches by Kumar Manindra Chandra Sinha* (Calcutta: unknown publisher, n.d.)

Stiehl, Otto, *Unsere Feinde: 96 Charakterköpfe aus deutschen Kriegsgefangenenlagern* [*Our Enemies: 96 Faces with Striking Features from German POW Camps*] (Stuttgart: Verlag Julius Hoffmann, 1917)

Tagore, Rabindranath, *Visit to China* (Shantiniketan: Visva-Bharati, 1924)

Poet to Poet (Calcutta: Visva-Bharati, 1939)

Rabīndra Racanābalī [*Collected Works of Rabindra(nath Tagore)*] (Kolkata: Visva-Bharati, 1940–1950), 27 volumes

The English Writings of Rabindranath Tagore, ed. Sisir Kumar Das (Delhi: Sahitya Akademi, 1994–1996)

Selected Letters of Rabindranath Tagore, ed. Krishna Dutta and Andrew Robinson (Cambridge: Cambridge University Press, 1997)

Journey to Persia and Iraq: 1932, transl. from Bengali by Surendranath Tagore and Sukhendu Ray and ed. Supriya Roy (Shantiniketan: Visva-Bharati, 2003)

Selected Essays (Delhi: Rupa, 2004)

Selected Poems (Oxford Tagore Translations), ed. Sukanta Chaudhuri and intro. by Sankha Ghosh (New Delhi: Oxford University Press, 2004)

Nationalism, ed. Ramchandra Guha (London: Penguin, 2009 [1917])

Tennant, Lt Col. E, *The Royal Deccan Horse in the Great War* (Aldershot: Gale & Polden Ltd, 1939)

Tilak, Bal Gangadhar, *Writings and Speeches*, ed. Aurobindo Ghose (Madras: Ganesh & Co., 1919)

Townshend, Charles, *My Campaign in Mesopotamia* (London: Thornton Butterworth Ltd, 1920)

Walter, George (ed.), *The Penguin Book of First World War Poetry* (London: Penguin, 2004)

Watson, Sir Harry, *A Short History of the Services Rendered by the Imperial Service Troops during the Great War, 1914–18* (Calcutta: Government of India Central Publications Branch, 1930)

Willcocks, Gen. Sir James, *With the Indians in France* (London: Constable and Company, 1920)

Wilson-Johnston, Lt Col. W. E., *An Account of the Operations of the 18th (Indian) Division in Mesopotamia, December 1917 to December 1918* (London: Finden Brown & Co. Ltd, 1920)

Woolf, Virginia, *Three Guineas* (Oxford: Oxford University Press, 2008 [1938])

Yeats, W. B., *Selected Poetry* (London: Macmillan, 1974)

SECONDARY SOURCES
Books

Abraham, Itty, *How India Became Territorial: Foreign Policy, Diaspora, Geopolitics* (Stanford: Stanford University Press, 2014)

Ahmad, Aijaz, *In Theory: Classes, Nations, Literatures* (Delhi: Oxford University Press, 1992)

Ahmad, Muzaffar, *Kāzi Nazrul Prasaṅge* (*Smritikathā*) (Kolkata: Twentieth-Century Publishing, 1959)

Akçapar, Burak, *People's Mission to the Ottoman Empire: M. A. Ansari and the Indian Medical Mission, 1912–1913* (Delhi: Oxford University Press, 2014)

Ali, Imran, *The Punjab under Imperialism, 1885–1947* (Princeton: Princeton University Press, 1988)

Anderson, Benedict, *Imagined Communities: Reflections on the Origin and Spread of Nationalism* (London: Verso, 2006 [1983])

Anjum, Zafar, *Iqbal: The Life of a Poet, Philosopher and Politician* (New Delhi: Random House India, 2014)

Arendt, Hannah, *The Origins of Totalitarianism* (New York: Harcourt, 1951)

Argov, Daniel, *Moderates and Extremists in the Indian Nationalist Movement 1883–1920, with Special Reference to Surendranath Banerjea and Lajpat Raj* (London: Asia Publishing House, 1968)

Aydin, Cemil, *The Politics of Anti-Westernism in Asia: Visions of World Order in Pan-Islamic and Pan-Asian Thought* (New York: Columbia, 2007)

Baig, Tara Ali, *Sarojini Naidu* (Delhi: Publication Division, Government of India, 1974)

Balesi, Charles John, *From Adversaries to Comrades-in-Arms: West Africans and the French Military 1885–1918* (Massachusetts: African Studies Association, 1979)

Ballantyne, Tony and Burton, Antoinette M. (eds.), *Bodies in Contact: Rethinking Colonial Encounters in World History* (Durham: Duke University Press, 2005)

Bandyopadhyay, Sekhar, *From Plassey to Partition: A History of Modern India* (Hyderabad: Orient Blackswan, 2009)

(ed.), *Nationalist Movement in India: A Reader* (Delhi: Oxford University Press, 2009)

Banerjee, Hasi, *Sarojini Naidu: The Traditional Feminist* (Calcutta: K. P. Bagchi, 1998)

Barbeau, Arthur E. and Henri, Florette, *The Unknown Soldiers: African-American Troops in World War I* (New York: Da Capo Press, 1996 [1974])

Barkawi, Tarak, *Soldiers of Empire: Indian and British Armies in World War II* (Cambridge: Cambridge University Press, 2017)

Barker, A. J., *The Neglected War: Mesopotamia 1914–1918* (London: Faber, 1967)

Townshend of Kut: A Biography of Major-General Sir Charles Townshend, K.C.B., D.S.O. (London: Cassell, 1967)

Barooah, Nirode K., *Chatto: The Life and Times of an Indian Anti-Imperialist in Europe* (New Delhi: Oxford University Press, 2004)

Barrier, N. G. and Wallace, Paul, *The Punjabi Press, 1880–1905* (East Lansing: Michigan State University Press, 1970)

Barthes, Roland, *Camera Lucida: Reflections on Photography* (New York: Hill and Wang/Farrar, Straus and Giroud, 1981)

Basu, Shrabani, *For King and Another Country: Indian Soldiers on the Western Front, 1914–1918* (London: Bloomsbury, 2014)

Bates, Crispin and Rand, Gavin (eds.), *Military Aspects of the Indian Uprising* (London and New Delhi: Sage, 2013)

Bayly, C. A. (ed.), *The Raj: India and the British 1600–1947* (London: National Portrait Gallery Publications, 1990)

The Birth of the Modern World: Global Connections and Comparisons, 1780–1914 (Oxford: Blackwell, 2004)

Beer, Gillian, *Open Fields: Science in Cultural Encounter* (Oxford: Oxford University Press, 1999)

Beetham, David, *Max Weber and the Theory of Modern Politics* (Cambridge: Polity Press, 1985)

Bhabha, Homi, *The Location of Culture* (London: Routledge, 1994)

Bharucha, Rustom, *Another Asia: Rabindranath Tagore and Okakura Tenshin* (Delhi: Oxford University Press, 2006)

Bhatnagar, R., *Sarojini Naidu: The Poet of a Nation* (Allahabad, n.d.)

Blackburn, Stuart H. and Ramanujan, A. K., *Another Harmony: New Essays on the Folklore of India* (Berkeley: University of California Press, 1986)

Blackburn, Stuart H., Claus, Peter, J., Flueckiger, Joyce B. and Wadley, Susan S. (eds.), *Oral Epics in India* (Berkeley: University of California Press, 1989)

Blake, Robert B. and Louis, William Roger (eds.), *Churchill: A Major New Assessment of His Life in Peace and War* (Oxford: Clarendon Press, 1993)

Bley, Helmut and Kremers, Anorthe (eds.), *The World during the First World War* (Essen: Klartext, 2014)

Bloxham, Donald, *The Great Game of Genocide: Imperialism, Nationalism and the Destruction of the Ottoman Armenians* (Oxford: Oxford University Press, 2005)

Bluemel, Kristin, *George Orwell and the Radical Eccentrics* (London: Palgrave, 2004)

Boehmer, Elleke, *Indian Arrivals 1870–1915: Networks of British Empire* (Oxford: Oxford University Press, 2015)

Bondurant, Joan V., *Conquest of Violence: The Gandhian Philosophy of Conflict* (Berkeley: University of California Press, 1965)

Bose, Arun Coomer, *Indian Revolutionaries Abroad, 1905–1922: In the Background of International Developments* (Patna: Bharati Bhawan, 1971)

Bose, Sugata, *A Hundred Horizons: The Indian Ocean in the Age of Global Empire* (Harvard: Harvard University Press, 2006)

His Majesty's Opponent: Subhas Chandra Bose and India's Struggle against Empire (Cambridge: Harvard University Press, 2011)

Bose, Sugata and Jalal, Ayesha, *Modern South Asia: History, Culture, Political Economy* (London: Routledge, 2011)

Bose, Sugata and Manjapra, Kris (eds.), *Cosmopolitan Thought-Zones: South Asia and the Global Circulation of Ideas* (London: Palgrave, 2010)

Braybon, Gail (ed.), *Evidence, History and the Great War: Historians and the Impact of 1914–18* (New York and Oxford: Berghahn Books, 2003)

Briggs, Julia, *Virginia Woolf: An Inner Life* (Orlando: Harcourt, 2005)

Brown, Judith, *Gandhi: Prisoner of Hope* (New Haven: Yale University Press, 1989)

Brown, Judith and Pare, Anthony, *The Cambridge Companion to Gandhi* (Cambridge: Cambridge University Press, 2011)

Buck, Claire, *Conceiving Strangeness in British First World War Writing* (London: Palgrave, 2014)

Burton, Antoinette, *At the Heart of the Empire: Indians and the Colonial Encounter in Late-Victorian Britain* (Berkeley: University of California Press, 1998)

Butler, Judith, *Precarious Lives: The Power of Mourning and Violence* (London: Verso, 2006)

Cannadine, David, *Ornamentalism: How the British Saw Their Empire* (Oxford: Oxford University Press, 2002)

Caplan, Lionel, *Warrior Gentlemen: Gurkhas in the Western Imagination* (New York and Oxford: Berghahn Books, 1995)

Carmichael, Jane, *First World War Photographers* (London and New York: Routledge, 1989)

Cashman, Richard, *The Myth of Lokmanya: Tilak and Mass Politics in Maharashtra* (Berkeley: University of California Press, 1975)

Cecil, Hugh and Liddle, Peter H. (eds.), *Facing Armageddon: The First World War Experienced* (Barnsley: Leo Cooper, 1996)

Chakrabarty, Dipesh, *Provincializing Europe: Postcolonial Thought and Historical Difference* (Princeton: Princeton University Press, 2000)

Chakravorty, Upendra, *Indian Nationalism and the First World War, 1914–1918* (Calcutta: Progressive Publishers, 1997)

Chandra, Bipan, *The Rise and Growth of Economic Nationalism in India* (New Delhi: People's Publishing House, 1966)

Chatterjee, Partha, *Nationalist Thought and the Colonial World: A Derivative Discourse* (London: United Nations University, 1986)

The Nation and Its Fragments: Colonial and Postcolonial Histories (Princeton: Princeton University Press, 1994)

Chattopadhyay, Pranatosh, *Kāzi Nazrul* (Kolkata: A. Mukherji & Co., 1977)

Chaudhary, Zahid R., *Afterimage of Empire: Photography in Nineteenth-Century India* (Minneapolis: University of Minnesota Press, 2012)

Chhina, Rana T. S., *The Indian Distinguished Service Medal* (New Delhi: InvictaIndia, 2001)

The Last Post: Indian War Memorials around the World (Delhi: United Service Institution, 2010)

Les Hindous, The Indian Army on the Western Front, 1914–1918 (Delhi: USI, 2016)

Clarke, Joseph and Horne, John (eds.), *Peripheral Visions: European Military Expeditions As Cultural Encounters in the Long 19th Century* (London: Palgrave, 2018)

Clifford, James and Marcus, George E. (eds.), *Writing Culture: The Poetics and Politics of Ethnography* (Berkeley: University of California Press, 1986)

Cohen, Debra Rae and Higbee, Douglas (eds.), *Teaching Representations of the First World War* (New York: MLA, 2017)

Collins, Joyce, *Dr. Brighton's Indian Patients, December 1914–January 1916* (Brighton: Brighton Books, 1997)

Collins, Michael, *Empire, Nationalism and the Postcolonial World: Rabindranath Tagore's Writings on History, Politics and Society* (London: Routledge, 2012)

Condos, Mark, *The Insecurity State: Punjab and the Making of Colonial Power in British India* (Cambridge: Cambridge University Press, 2017)

Cooter, Roger, Harrison, Mark and Sturdy, Steve (eds.), *Medicine in Modern Warfare* (Amsterdam: Rodopi Press, 1999)

Corrigan, Gordon, *Sepoys in the Trenches: The Indian Corps on the Western Front 1914–1918* (Staplehurst: Spellmount, 1999)

Cowasjee, Saros, *So Many Freedoms: Major Fiction of Mulk Raj Anand* (Delhi: Oxford University Press, 1978)

Crowley, Patrick, *Kut 1916: Courage and Failure in Iraq* (Stroud: The History Press, 2009)

Das, Santanu, *Touch and Intimacy in First World War Literature* (Cambridge: Cambridge University Press, 2006)

(ed.), *Race, Empire and First World War Writing* (Cambridge: Cambridge University Press, 2011)

(ed.), *The Cambridge Companion to the Poetry of the First World War* (Cambridge: Cambridge University Press, 2013)

L'Inde dans la Grande Guerre: Les cipayes sur le front de l'Ouest [*India in the Great War: The Sepoys on the Western Front*], trans. Didier Debord and Annie Perez (Paris: Gallimard, 2014)

1914–1918: Indian Troops in Europe (Ahmedabad: Mapin Publishing, 2015) [English translation of *L'Inde dans la Grande Guerre*, published in India]

Das, Santanu and Kate McLoughlin, *First World War: Literature, Culture, Modernity* (Oxford: Oxford University Press, for the British Academy, 2018)

Das, Sisir Kumar, *Bāṅglā Chota-galpa* (Kolkata: Dey's Publishing, 1986)

Davis, Paul K., *Ends and Means: The British Mesopotamian Campaign and Commission* (Madison: Associated University Presses, 1994)

Dempsey, L. James, *Warriors of the King: Prairie Indians in World War I* (Regina: Canadian Plains Research Centre, 1999)

Dendooven, Dominiek and Chielens, Piet, *World War I: Five Continents in Flanders* (Ypres: Lannoo, 2008)

Desai, Ashwin and Vahed, Goolam, *The South African Gandhi: Stretcher-Bearer of Empire* (Stanford: Stanford University Press, 2015)

Devji, Faisal, *The Impossible Indian: Gandhi and the Temptation of Violence* (Harvard: Harvard University Press, 2012)

Dirks, Nicholas, *Castes of Mind: Colonialism and the Making of Modern India* (Princeton: Princeton University Press, 2001)

Doherty, Simon and Donovan, Tom, *The Indian Corps on the Western Front: A Handbook and Battlefield Guide* (Brighton: Tom Donovan Editions, 2014)

Dowling, Timothy C. (ed.), *Personal Perspectives: World War I* (California: ABC-CLIO, 2006)

Duckers, Peter, *The British-Indian Army 1860–1914* (Buckinghamshire: Shire Publications, 2003)

Dutta, Krishna and Robinson, Andrew, *Rabindranath Tagore: The Myriad-Minded Man* (London: Bloomsbury, 1995)

Dyer, Geoff, *White: Essays on Race and Culture* (London: Routledge, 1997)

Echenberg, Myron, *Colonial Conscripts: The Tirailleurs Sénégalais in French West Africa, 1857–1960* (London: James Curry, 1991)

Edwards, Elizabeth, *Raw Histories: Photographs, Anthropology and Museums* (Oxford: Berg, 2001)

The Camera as Historian: Amateur Photographers and Historical Imagination, 1885–1918 (Durham: Duke University Press, 2012).

Ellinwood, DeWitt C., *Between Two Worlds: A Rajput Officer in the Indian Army, 1905–1921* (Lanham: Hamilton, 2005)

Ellinwood, DeWitt C. and Pradhan, S. D. (eds.), *India and World War I* (Delhi: Manohar, 1978)

Erikson, Erik, *Gandhi's Truth: On the Origins of Militant Nonviolence* (New York: W. W. Norton, 1969)

Evans, Andrew, *Anthropology at War: World War I and the Science of Race in Germany* (Chicago: University of Chicago Press, 2010)

Fabre, Cécile, *Cosmopolitan Peace* (Oxford: Oxford University Press, 2016)

Fanon, Frantz, *Black Skin, White Masks*, ed. Charles Lam Markmann (London: Pluto, 1986 [1952])

The Wretched of the Earth (London: Penguin, 1991 [1961])

Fawaz, Leila, *A Land of Aching Hearts: The Middle East in the Great War* (Cambridge: Harvard University Press, 2014)

Fell, Alison S. and Sharp, Ingrid (eds.), *Women's Movements: International Perspectives, 1914–1919* (London: Palgrave, 2007)

Fisher, Michael H., *Counterflow to Colonialism: Indian Travellers and Settlers in Britain 1600–1857* (Delhi: Permanent Black, 2004)

Fogarty, Richard, *Race and Empire in France: Colonial Subjects in the French Army, 1914–1918* (Baltimore: Johns Hopkins University Press, 2008)

Fogarty, Richard and Jarboe, Andrew Tait (eds.), *Empires in World War I: Shifting Frontiers and Imperial Dynamics in a Global Conflict* (London: I. B. Tauris, 2014)

Fox, Richard G., *Lions of the Punjab: Culture in the Making* (Berkeley: University of California Press, 1985)

Fussell, Paul, *The Great War and Modern Memory* (Oxford: Oxford University Press, 1975)

Gandhi, Leela, *Affective Communities: Anticolonial Thought, Fin-de-Siècle Radicalism, and the Politics of Friendship* (Durham: Duke University Press, 2006)

The Common Cause: Postcolonial Ethics and the Practice of Democracy (Chicago: Chicago University Press, 2014)

Gardner, Nikolas, *Trial by Fire: Command in the British Expeditionary Force in 1914* (Westport: Praeger, 2003)

The Siege of Kut-al-Amara: At War in Mesopotamia, 1915–1916 (Bloomington: Indiana University Press, 2014)

Gerwarth, Robert and Manela, Erez (eds.), *Empires at War: 1911–1923* (Oxford: Oxford University Press, 2014)

Giara, Marzban Jamshedji, *The Contribution of the Parsi Community during the First World War (1914–1918)* (Navsari: Sorabji Burjorji Garda College Trust, 2016)

Gilroy, Paul, *The Black Atlantic: Modernity and Double Consciousness* (London: Verso, 1993)

Postcolonial Melancholia (New York: Columbia University Press, 2005)

Gould, Tony, *Imperial Warriors: Britain and the Gurkhas* (London: Granta Books, 1999)

Green, Martin, *Dreams of Adventure, Deeds of Empire* (Routledge: London, 1979)

Greenblatt, Stephen, *Learning to Curse: Essays in Early Modern Culture* (New York: Routledge, 1990)

Gregory, Adrian and Paseta, Senia (eds.), *Ireland and the Great War* (Manchester: Manchester University Press, 2002)

Gressieux, Douglas, *Les Troupes Indiennes en France, 1914–1918* (Saint-Cyr-sur-Loire: Allan Sutton, 2007)

Guha Thakurta, Tapati, *Monuments, Objects, Histories* (New York: Columbia University Press, 2004)

Gupta, Partha Sarathi and Deshpande, Anirudh (eds.), *British Raj and Its Indian Armed Forces, 1857–1939* (Delhi: Oxford University Press, 2002)

Haithcox, John Patrick, *Communism and Nationalism in India: M. N. Roy and Comintern Policy, 1920–1939* (Princeton: Princeton University Press, 1971)

Hammond, Mary and Towheed, Shafquat (eds.), *Publishing in the First World War: Essays in Book History* (London: Palgrave, 2007)

Harder, Hans (ed.), *Bankimchandra Chattopadhyay's Srimadbhagabadgita: Translation and Analysis* (New Delhi: Manohar, 2001)

Hardiman, David, *Gandhi in His Time and Ours* (London: Hurst, 2003)

Harrison, Mark, *The Medical War: British Military Medicine in the First World War* (Oxford: Oxford University Press, 2014)

Hay, Stephen N., *Asian Ideas of East and West: Tagore and His Critics in Japan, China and India* (Cambridge: Harvard University Press, 1970)

Heehs, Peter, *Sri Aurobindo: A Brief Biography* (Delhi: Oxford University Press, 1989)

  The Lives of Sri Aurobindo (New York: Columbia University Press, 2008)

  (ed.), *Situating Sri Aurobindo: A Reader* (New Delhi: Oxford University Press, 2013)

Helmreich, Paul C., *From Paris to Sèvres: The Partition of the Ottoman Empire at the Peace Conference of 1919–1920* (Columbus: Ohio State University Press, 1974)

Hight, Eleanor M. and Sampson, Gary D. (eds.), *Colonialist Photography: Imag(in) ing Race and Place* (London: Routledge, 2002)

Hirschkind, Charles, *The Ethical Soundscape: Cassette Sermons and Islamic Counterpublics* (New York: Columbia University Press, 2006)

Hodges, Geoffrey, *The Carrier Corps: Military Labour in the East African Campaign of 1914 to 1918* (Massachusetts: Westwood, 1986)

Höpp, Gerhard, *Muslime in der Mark: Als Kriegsgefangene und Internierte in Wünsdorf und Zossen, 1914–1924* (Berlin: Verlag das Arabische Buch, 1997)

Horne, John (ed.), *State, Society and Mobilization in Europe during the First World War* (Cambridge: Cambridge University Press, 1997)

  (ed.), *A Companion to World War I* (Hoboken: Wiley-Blackwell, 2010)

Howe, Glenford, *Race, War and Nationalism: A Social History of West Indians in the First World War* (Kingston: James Currey, 2002)

Hunt, James D., *Gandhi in London* (Delhi: Promilla, 1978)

Huttenback, Robert A., *Racism and Empire: White Settlers and Coloured Immigrants in the British Self-governing Colonies, 1830–1910* (Ithaca: Cornell University Press, 1976)

Isemonger, F. C. and Slattery, J., *Account of the Ghadr Conspiracy (1913–1915)* (Delhi: South Asia Books, 1998)

Islam, Rafiqul, *Nazrul-Jivani* (Dhaka: Dhaka University, 1972)

Jalal, Ayesha, *Self and Sovereignty: Individual and Community in South Asian Islam since 1850* (New York: Routledge, 2000)

Jeffery, Keith, *Ireland and the Great War* (Cambridge: Cambridge University Press, 2000)

Johler, Reinhard, Marchetti, Christian and Scheer, Monique (eds.), *Doing Anthropology in Wartime and War Zones: World War I and the Cultural Sciences in Europe* (Bielefeld: transcript Verlag, 2010)

Johnston, Hugh J. M., *The Voyage of the Komagata Maru: The Sikh Challenge to Canada's Colour Bar* (Delhi: Oxford University Press, 1979)

Josh, Bhagwan, *Communist Movement in Punjab 1921–1947* (Delhi: Anupama, 1979)

Joshi, Sanjay, *Fractured Modernity: Making of a Middle Class in Colonial North India* (Delhi: Oxford University Press, 2001)

Kant, Vedica, *'If I Die, Who Will Remember Me?': India and the First World War* (Delhi: Roli Books, 2014)

Kapila, Shruti (ed.), *An Intellectual History for India* (Cambridge: Cambridge University Press, 2010)

Karnad, Raghu, *Farthest Field: An Indian Story of the Second World War* (London: William Collins, 2015)

Katyal, Anjum, *Habib Tanvir: Towards an Inclusive Theatre* (New Delhi: Sage, 2012)

Kaviraj, Sudipta, *The Unhappy Consciousness: Bankimchandra Chattopadhyay and the Formation of Nationalist Discourse in India* (New York: Oxford University Press, 1995)

Kayleyss, Margot, *Muslime in Brandenburg – Kriegsgefangene im 1. Weltkrieg: Ansichten und Absichten* (Berlin: Staatliche Museen zu Berlin, 2000)

Keene, Jennifer and Nieberg, Michael (eds.), *Finding Common Ground: New Directions in First World War Studies* (Leiden: Brill, 2011)

Kerr, Andrew, *I Can Never Say Enough about the Men: A History of the Jammu and Kashmir Rifles throughout Their World War One East African Campaign* (Gloucestershire: PMC Management Consultants, 2010)

Kerr, Douglas, *Eastern Figures: Orient and Empire in British Writing* (Hong Kong: Hong Kong University Press, 2008)

Khan, Yasmin, *The Raj at War: A People's History of India's Second World War* (London: The Bodley Head, 2015)

Killingray, David and Omissi, David (eds.), *Guardians of Empire: the Armed Forces of the Colonial Powers c. 1700–1964* (Manchester: Manchester University Press, 1999)

Kitchen, James, *The British Imperial Army in the Middle East: Morale and Military Identity in Sinai and Palestine Campaign* (London: Bloomsbury, 2015)

Kohli, Suresh (ed.), *Alone in the Multitude* (New Delhi: Indian Literary Review, 1979)

Koller, Christian, *'Von Wilden aller Rassen niedergemetzelt': Die Diskussion um die Verwendung von Kolonialtruppen in Europa zwischen Rassismus, Kolonial- und Militärpolitik (1914–1930)* (Stuttgart: Franz Steiner, 2001)

Krauss, Rosalind, *The Optical Unconscious* (Cambridge: MIT Press, 1994)

Kripalini, Krishna, *Rabindranath Tagore: A Biography* (Oxford: Oxford University Press, 1962)

Kritzman, Lawrence D. (ed.), *Realms of Memory: Rethinking the French Past*, trans. Arthur Goldhammer, 3 vols. (New York: Columbia University Press, 1996–1998)

Kurzman, Charles (ed.), *Modernist Islam 1840–1940: A Sourcebook* (New York: Oxford University Press, 2002)

Lange, Britta, *Die Wiener Forschungen an Kriegsgefangenen 1915–1918: Anthropologische und ethnografische Verfahren im Lager* [*The Viennese Researches on Prisoners of War 1915–1918. Anthropological and Ethnographic Methods in the Camp*] (Vienna: Verlag der Österreichischen Akademie der Wissenschaften, 2011)

Lebow, Richard Ned, *White Britain and Black Ireland: The Influence of Stereotype on Colonial Policy* (Philadelphia: Institute for the Study of Human issues, 1976)

Lee, Hermione, *Body Parts: Essays on Life-Writing* (London: Pimlico, 2010)

Liebau, Heike, Bromber, Katrin, Hamza, Dyala, Lange, Katharina and Ahuja, Ravi (eds.), *The World in World Wars: Experiences, Perceptions and Perspectives from Africa and Asia* (Leiden: Brill, 2010)

Long, Roger D. and Talbot, Ian (eds.), *India and World War I: A Centennial Assessment* (London: Routledge, 2018)

Longworth, Philip, *The Unending Vigil: A History of the Commonwealth War Graves Commission* (London, Pen and Sword Military, 1988)

Lowe, D. A. (ed.), *Soundings in Modern South Asian History* (Berkeley: University of California, 1968)

Ludden, David (ed.), *Contesting the Nation: Religion, Community and the Politics of Democracy in India* (Philadelphia: University of Pennsylvania Press, 1996)

Lunn, Joe, *Memoirs of a Maelstrom: A Senegalese Oral History of the First World War* (Portsmouth: Heinemann, 1999)

Lyons, Martyn, *The Writing Culture of Ordinary People in Europe, c. 1860–1920* (Cambridge: Cambridge University Press, 2012)

MacKenzie, John M. (ed.), *Imperialism and Popular Culture* (Manchester: Manchester University Press, 1989)

Mago, Pran Nath, *Contemporary Art in India* (Delhi: National Book Trust, 1985)

Majeed, Javed, *Autobiography, Travel and Postnational Identities* (London: Palgrave, 2007)

    Muhammed Iqbal: Islam, Aesthetics and Postcolonialism (London: Routledge, 2009)

    The Reconstruction of Religious Thought in Islam (Stanford: Stanford University Press, 2013)

Malhotra, Anshu and Mir, Farina (eds.), *Punjab Reconsidered: History, Culture and Practice* (Delhi: Oxford University Press, 2012)

Malhotra, R. P. and Arora, Kuldeep (eds.), *Encyclopaedic Dictionary of Punjabi Literature* (Delhi: Global Vision Publishing House, 2003)

Malik, Kenan, *The Meaning of Race* (London: Palgrave, 1996)

Manela, Erez, *The Wilsonian Moment and the International Origins of Anticolonial Nationalism* (Oxford: Oxford University Press, 2009)

Manjapra, Kris, *Age of Entanglement* (Cambridge: Harvard University Press, 2014)

Marcus, Jane, *Hearts of Darkness: White Women Write Race* (New Brunswick: Rutgers University Press, 2003)

Marcus, Laura, *Auto/biographical Discourses: Theory, Criticism, Practice* (Manchester: Manchester University Press, 1994)

Marrin, Albert, *The Church of England in the First World War* (Durham: Duke University Press, 1974)

Marston, Daniel and Chander Sundaram (eds.), *A Military History of India and South Asia: From the East India Company to the Nuclear Era* (Bloomington: Indiana University Press, 2007)

Mason, Philip, *A Matter of Honour: An Account of the Indian Army, Its Officers & Men* (London: Jonathan Cape, 1974)

Mazumder, Rajit, *The Indian Army and the Making of Punjab* (Ranikhet: Permanent Black, 2003)

McClenaghan, Tony and Richard Head, *Maharajas' Paltans: History of the Indian State Forces, 1888–1948* (Delhi: Manohar, 2013)

McLoughlin, Kate, *Authoring War: The Literary Representations of War from the Iliad to Iraq* (Cambridge: Cambridge University Press, 2011)

McPherson, Kenneth, *Muslim Microcosm: Calcutta, 1918–1935* (Ann Arbor: University of Michigan Press, 1974)

Menezes, S. L., *Fidelity and Honour: The Indian Army from the Seventeenth to the Twenty-First Century* (Oxford: Oxford University Press, 1999)

Metcalf, Thomas R., *Ideologies of the Raj* (Cambridge: Cambridge University Press, 1998)

Michel, Marc, *L'Appel à l'Afrique, contributions et réactions à l'effort de guerre en A.O.F. (1914–1919)* (Paris: Publications de la Sorbonne, 1982)

Minault, Gail, *The Khilafat Movement: Religious Symbolism and Political Mobilization in India* (New York: Columbia University Press, 1982)

Mir, Farina, *The Social Space of Language: Vernacular Culture in British Colonial Punjab* (Berkeley: University of California Press, 2010)

Mishr, Ram Prasad, *Outlines of Hindi Literature* (Delhi: S.S. Publishers, 1982)

Mishra, Pankaj, *From the Ruins of Empire: The Revolt against the West and the Remaking of Asia* (London: Penguin, 2013)

Mitra, Arun Kumar, *Nazrul Jibani [The Life of Nazrul]* (Kolkata: West Bengal Academy, 1990)

Mitra, Priti Kumar, *The Dissent of Nazrul Islam: Poetry and History* (Delhi: Oxford University Press, 2009)

Moore-Gilbert, Bart, *Postcolonial Life-Writing: Culture, Politics and Self-Representation* (London: Routledge, 2009)

Morris, Rosalind C. (ed.), *Can the Subaltern Speak? Reflections on the History of an Idea* (New York: Columbia University Press, 2010)

Morton-Jack, George, *The Indian Army on the Western Front: India's Expeditionary Force to France and Belgium in the First World War* (Cambridge: Cambridge University Press, 2014)

Mosse, George, *The Jews and the German War Experience 1914–1918* (London: Leo Baeck Institute, 1977)

Moyd, Michelle R., *Violent Intermediaries: African Soldiers, Conquest, and Everyday Colonialism in German East Africa* (Athens: Ohio University Press, 2014)

Mukherjee, Mridula, *Colonizing Agriculture: The Myth of Punjab Exceptionalism* (Delhi: Sage, 2001)

Mukhopadhyay, Durga Das, *Folk Arts and Social Communications* (Delhi: Ministry of Information and Broadcasting, 1994)

Mukhopadhyay, Shailajananda, *Keu Bhole Nā Keu Bhole* (Kolkata: New Age Publishers, 1960)

Murphy, Mahon, *Colonial Captivity during the First World War: Internment and the Fall of the German Empire, 1914–1919* (Cambridge: Cambridge University Press, 2017)

Mustafa, Aksakal, *The Ottoman Road to War in 1914: The Ottoman Empire and the First World War* (Cambridge: Cambridge University Press, 2008)

Nair, Janaki, *Mysore Modern: Rethinking the Region under Princely Rule* (Minneapolis: University of Minnesota Press, 2011)

Nancy, Jean-Luc, *Listening* (New York: Fordham University Press, 2007)

Nanda, Bal Ram, *Three Statesmen: Gokhale, Gandhi and Nehru* (Delhi: Oxford University Press, 2004)

Nandy, Ashis, *The Intimate Enemy: Loss and Recovery of the Self under Colonialism* (Delhi: Oxford University Press, 1983)

The Illegitimacy of Nationalism: Rabindranath Tagore and the Politics of Self (Delhi: Oxford University Press, 1994)

Bonfire of Creeds: The Essential Ashis Nandy (New Delhi: Oxford University Press, 2004)

Nasta, Susheila (ed.), *India in Britain: South Asian Networks and Connections, 1858–1950* (London: Palgrave, 2013)

Nelson, Cary and Grossberg, Lawrence (eds.), *Marxism and the Interpretation of Culture* (London: Macmillan, 1988)

Nijhawan, P. K., *The First Punjab War: Shah Mohammed's Jungnamah* (Patiala: Punjabi University Press, 2000)

O'Brien, Tim, *The Things They Carried* (New York: Mariner Books, 2009)

Olusoga, David, *The World's War* (London: Head of Zeus, 2014)

Omissi, David, *The Sepoy and the Raj: The Indian Army, 1860–1940* (London: Macmillan, 1994)

Page, Melvin (ed.), *Africa and the First World War* (Basingstoke: Macmillan, 1987)

The Chiwaya War: Malawians and the First World War (Boulder: Westview Press, 2000)

Pal, Prasanta Kumar, *Ravijīvanī (1914–1920)* (Kolkata: Ananda Publishers, 1997)

Parker, Peter, *The Last Veteran: Harry Patch and the Legacy of War* (London: Fourth Estate, 2009)

Parrat, Saroj Nalini Arambam, *The Court Chronicles of the Kings of Manipur* (London: Routledge, 2005)

Pasha, Mustapha Kamal, *Colonial Political Economy: Recruitment and Underdevelopment in the Punjab* (Karachi: Oxford University Press, 1998)

Pati, Budheshwar, *India and the First World War* (Delhi: Atlantic Publishers, 1996)

Pick, Daniel, *Faces of Degeneration: A European Disorder 1848–1918* (Cambridge: Cambridge University Press, 1993)

Penny, H. Glenn and Bunzl, Matti (eds.), *Worldly Provincialism: German Anthropology in the Age of Empire* (Ann Arbor: University of Michigan Press, 2003)

Pinney, Christopher, *The Coming of Photography to India* (London: The British Library, 2008)

Photography and Anthropology (London: Reaktion, 2012)

Poliakov, Leon, *The History of Antisemitism: Suicidal Europe 1870–1933*, Vol. IV, trans. George Klin (Oxford: Oxford University Press, 1985)

Pollock, Sheldon (ed.), *Literary Cultures in History: Reconstructions from South Asia* (Berkeley: University of California Press, 2003)

Porter, Patrick, *Military Orientalism: Eastern War through Western Eyes* (London: Hurst and Company, 2009)

Power, Paul F., *Gandhi on World Affairs* (London: George Allen and Unwin, 1960)

Pradhan, S. D., *Indian Army in East Africa* (New Delhi: National Book Organisation, 1990)

Prasad, Yuvaraj Deva, *The Indian Muslims and World War I* (New Delhi: Janaki Prakashan, 1985)

Pratt, Mary Louise, *Imperial Eyes: Travel Writing and Transculturation* (New York: Routledge, 1992)

Pugsley, Chris, *Te Hokowhitu a Tu: The Maori Pioneer Battalion in the First World War* (Reed: Auckland, 1995)

Puri, Harish K., *Ghadar Movement: Ideology, Organisation, and Strategy* (Amritsar: Guru Nanak Dev University Press, 1993)

Raghavan, Srinath, *India's War: World War II and the Making of Modern South Asia, 1939–1945* (London: Penguin, 2016)

Ramnath, Maia, *Haj to Utopia: How the Ghadar Movement Charted Global Radicalism and Attempted to Overthrow the British Empire* (Berkeley: University of California University Press, 2011)

Ramusack, Barbara N., *The Indian Princes and Their States* (Cambridge: Cambridge University Press, 2004)

Ray, Rajat Kanta, *The Felt Community: Commonality and Mentality before the Emergence of Indian Nationalism* (New Delhi: Oxford University Press, 2003)

Raychaudhuri, Tapan, *Europe Reconsidered: Perceptions of the West in Nineteenth-Century Bengal* (Oxford: Oxford University Press, 2005)

Ricœur, Paul, *Time and Narrative* (Chicago: University of Chicago Press, 1990)

Robb, George, *British Culture and the First World War* (London: Palgrave, 2002)

Robb, Peter (ed.), *The Concept of Race in South Asia* (Delhi: Oxford University Press, 1997)

Rogan, Eugene, *The Fall of the Ottomans: The Great War in the Middle East, 1914–1920* (London: Allen Lane, 2015)

Roper, Michael, *The Secret Battle: Emotional Survival in the Great War* (Manchester: Manchester University Press, 2010)

Rosenwein, Barbara H., *Emotional Communities in the Early Middle Ages* (Ithaca: Cornell University Press, 2007)

Roy, Kaushik (ed.), *War and Society in Colonial India, 1807–1945* (Delhi: Oxford University Press, 2006)

Brown Warriors of the Raj: Recruitment and the Mechanics of Command in the Sepoy Army, 1859–1913 (New Delhi: Manohar, 2008)

The Army in British India: From Colonial Warfare to Total War 1857–1947 (London: Bloomsbury, 2012)

Sepoys against the Rising Sun: The Indian Army in Far East and South East Asia, 1941–45 (Leiden: Brill, 2015)

Roy, Kaushik, *The Indian Army in the Two World Wars* (Leiden: Brill, 2012)

Roy, Kaushik and Gavin Rand (eds.), *Culture, Conflict and the Military in Colonial South Asia* (Routledge: Abingdon, 2017)

Roy, Franziska, Liebau, Heike and Ahuja, Ravi (eds.), '*When the War Began, We Heard of Several Kings': South Asian Prisoners in World War I Germany* (Delhi: Social Science Press, 2011)

Ruck, Calvin, *The Black Battalion 1916–1920: Canada's Best Kept Military Secret* (Halifax: Nimbus Publishing Limited, 1987)

Rutherford, Jessica, *The Royal Pavilion: The Palace of George IV* (Brighton: Brighton Borough Council, 1994)

Ryan, James, *Picturing Empire: Photography and the Visualization of the British Empire* (Chicago: Chicago University Press, 1997)

Saaler, Sven and Szpilman, Christopher W. A. (eds.), *Pan Asianism: A Documentary History, 1850–1920* (London: Rowman and Littlefield, 2011)

Saha, Janaka, *Hindi gadya ko Guleri jī kī dena* (Patna: Novelty, 2002)

Said, Edward W., *Culture and Imperialism* (London: Random House, 1994)

Samson, Anne, *World War I in Africa: The Forgotten Conflict among the European Powers* (London: I. B. Tauris, 2012)

Sarkar, Sumit, *The Swadeshi Movement in Bengal 1903–1908* (Ranikhet: Permanent Black, 2011 [1973])

Modern India 1885–1947 (Delhi: Macmillan India, 2002 [1983])

Sarkar, Tanika, *Hindu Wife, Hindu Nation: Community, Religion and Cultural Nationalism* (Bloomington: Indiana University Press, 2001)

Sathia, Priya, *Spies in Arabia: The Great War and the Cultural Foundations of Britain's Covert Empire in the Middle East* (Oxford: Oxford University Press, 2008)

Saunders, Nicholas, *Trench Art: A Brief History and Guide 1914–1939* (Barnsley: Pen & Sword, 2011)

Saunders, Nicholas and Cornish, Paul (eds.), *Modern Conflict and the Senses* (London: Routledge, 2016)

Saxena, Shyam Narain, *Role of Indian Army in the First World War* (New Delhi: Bhavana Prakashan, 1987)

Scarry, Elaine, *The Body in Pain: The Making and Unmaking of the World* (Oxford: Oxford University Press, 1985)

Schorske, Carl E., *Fin-de-siècle Vienna: Politics and Culture* (New York: Knopf Doubleday Publishing Group, 1981)

Scott, James C., *Domination and the Arts of Resistance: Hidden Transcripts* (New Haven: Yale University Press, 1992)

Sehrawat, Samiksha, *Colonial Medical Care in North India: Gender, State and Society, c. 1840–1920* (Delhi: Oxford University Press, 2013)

Sengupta, Indra (ed.), *Memory, History and Colonialism* (London: German Historical Institute, 2009)

Sevea, Iqbal Singh, *The Political Philosophy of Muhammed Iqbal: Islam and Nationalism in Late Colonial India* (Cambridge: Cambridge University Press, 2002)

Sharma, Jhabaramalla, *Guleri garimā grantha: Jīvana evam sāhitya* (Kāśī: Nāgarīpracāriṇī Sabhā, 1984)

Shaw, Graham and Lloyd, Mary (eds.), *Publications Proscribed by the Government of India* (London: The British Library, 1985)

Sherry, Vincent, *The Great War and the Language of Modernism* (New York: Oxford University Press, 2004)

Showalter, Elaine, *The Female Malady: Women, Madness and English Culture* (New York: Virago, 1987)

Singh, Amarinder, *Honour and Fidelity: India in World War I* (Delhi: Roli Books, 2015)

Singh, Gajendra, *The Testimonies of Indian Soldiers and the Two World Wars: Between Self and Sepoy* (London: Bloomsbury, 2014)

Singh, Iqbal, *The Ardent Pilgrim: An Introduction to the Life and Work of Iqbal* (Delhi: Oxford University Press, 1997)

Sinha, Mrinalini, *Colonial Masculinity: The 'Manly Englishman' and the 'Effeminate Bengali'* (Manchester: Manchester University Press, 1995)

    Spectres of Mother India (Durham and London: Duke University Press, 2006)

Skaria, Ajay, *Unconditional Equality: Gandhi's Religion of Resistance* (Minneapolis: University of Minnesota Press, 2016)

Smith, Leonard V., *The Embattled Self: French Soldiers' Testimony of the Great War* (Ithaca: Cornell University Press, 2007)

Smith, Richard, *Jamaican Volunteers in the First World War: Race, Masculinity and the Development of National Consciousness* (Manchester: Manchester University Press, 2004)

Sohi, Seema, *Echoes of Mutiny: Race, Surveillance, and Indian Anticolonialism in North America* (New York: Oxford University Press, 2014)

Spivak, Gayatri Chakravorty, *A Critique of Postcolonial Reason: Towards a History of the Vanishing Present* (Cambridge: Harvard University Press, 1999)

Stanley, Peter, *Die in Battle, Do Not Despair: The Indians on Gallipoli, 1915* (London: Helion, 2015)

Stewart, Pamela and Strathern, Andrew, *Witchcraft, Sorcery, Rumours and Gossip* (Cambridge: Cambridge University Press, 2004)

Stewart, Susan, *Poetry and the Fate of the Senses* (Chicago: Chicago University Press, 2002)

Stoler, Ann Laura, *Carnal Knowledge and Imperial Power: Race and the Intimate in Colonial Rule* (Berkeley: University of California Press, 2002)

    Along the Archival Grain: Epistemic Anxieties and Colonial Common Sense (Princeton: Princeton University Press, 2009)

Stovall, Tyler and Van Den Abbeele, Georges (eds.), *French Civilisation and Its Discontents* (Lanham: Lexington, 2002)

Strachan, Hew, *The First World War* (New York: Viking, 2005)

The First World War: To Arms (Oxford: Oxford University Press, 2011)

Streets, Heather, *Martial Races: The Military, Race and Masculinity in British Imperial Culture, 1857–1914* (Manchester: Manchester University Press, 2004)

Talbot, Ian, *Punjab and the Raj, 1849–1947* (Delhi: Manohar, 1988)

Tan Chung, Dev, Amiya, Wang Bangwei and Wei Liming (eds.), *Tagore and China* (New Delhi: Sage, 2011)

Taves, Brian, *Talbot Mundy, Philosopher of Adventure: A Critical Biography* (London: McFarland Books, 2006)

Tharoor, Shashi, *Inglorious Empire: What the British Did to India* (London: Hurst, 2017)

Tinker, Hugh, *Separate and Unequal: India and the Indians in the British Commonwealth 1920–1950* (London: Hurst, 1976)

Todman, Dan, *The Great War: Myth and Memory* (London: Bloomsbury, 2005)

Towheed, Shafquat (ed.), *New Readings in the Literature of British India 1780–1947* (Stuttgart: ibidem-Verlag, 1997)

Townshend, Charles, *When God Made Hell: The British Invasion of Mesopotamia and the Creation of Iraq 1914–1921* (London: Faber, 2010)

Tuteja, K. L. and Chakraborty, Kaustav (eds.), *Tagore and Nationalism* (New Delhi: Springer, 2017)

Vanita, Ruth and Kidwai, Saleem (ed.), *Same-Sex Love in India: Readings from Literature and History* (London: Palgrave, 2000)

Visram, Rozina, *Asians in Britain* (London: Pluto Press, 2002)

Wagner, Kim, *Of Rumours and Rebels: A New History of the Indian Uprising of 1857* (London: Peter Lang, 2016)

Wakefield, Alan and Moody, Simon, *Under the Devil's Eye: Britain's Forgotten Army at Salonika 1915–1918* (Stroud: Sutton Publishing, 2004)

Wakefield, Col. J. and Weippart, Lt Col. J. M. (eds.), *Indian Cavalry Officer: Captain Roly Grimshaw* (Tunbridge Wells: Costello, 1986)

Walsh, Michael and Andrekos Varnava ed. *The Great War and British Empire* (London: Routledge, 2017)

Whalan, Mark, *The Great War and the Culture of the New Negro* (Gainesville: University Press of Florida, 2008)

Wilcox, Ron, *Battles on the Tigris: The Mesopotamian Campaign of the First World War* (Barnsley: Pen & Sword, 2006)

Williams, Raymond, *Marxism and Literature* (Oxford: Oxford University Press, 1977)

Wilson, Jon, *India Conquered: British Raj and the Chaos of Empire* (London: Simon & Schuster, 2016)

Winter, Jay, *Sites of Memory, Sites of Mourning: The Great War in European Cultural History* (Cambridge: Cambridge University Press, 1996)

(ed.), *America and the Armenian Genocide of 1915* (Cambridge: Cambridge University Press, 2008)

War beyond Words: Languages of Remembrance from the Great War to the Present (Cambridge: Cambridge University Press, 2017)

Winter, Jay and Sivan, Emmanuel (eds.), *War and Remembrance in the Twentieth Century* (Cambridge: Cambridge University Press, 1999)

Xu Guoqi, *Strangers on the Western Front: Chinese Workers in the Great War* (Cambridge: Harvard University Press, 2011)

Asia and the Great War: A Shared History (Oxford: Oxford University Press, 2017)

Yong, Tan Tai, *The Garrison State: The Military, Government and Society in Colonial Punjab, 1849–1947* (New Delhi: Sage, 2005)

Chapters in Edited Books

Ahuja, Ravi, 'The Corrosiveness of Comparison', in Heike Liebau, Katrin Bromber, Dyala Hamza, Katharina Lange and Ravi Ahuja (eds.), *The World in World Wars: Experiences, Perceptions and Perspectives from Africa and Asia* (Leiden: Brill, 2010), 131–166

Anand, Mulk Raj, 'Pigeon-Indian: Some Notes on Indian-English Writing', in M. K. Naik (ed.), *Aspects of Indian Writing in English* (New Delhi: Macmillan, 1979), 24–44

Anderson, Ross, 'Logistics of the IEF D in Mesopotamia, 1914–1918', in Kaushik Roy (ed.), *The Indian Army in the Two World Wars* (Leiden: Brill, 2011), 105–144

Barrett, Michèle, 'Subalterns at War: First World War Colonial Forces and the Politics of the Imperial War Graves Commission', in R. C. Morris (ed.), *Can the Subaltern Speak?: Reflections on the History of an Idea* (New York: Columbia University Press, 2010), 156–176

'Death and the Afterlife: Britain's Colonies and Dominions', in Santanu Das (ed.), *Race, Empire and First World War Writing* (Cambridge: Cambridge University Press, 2011), 301–320

Benjamin, Walter, 'A Little History of Photography', in *Selected Writings, Volume 1 Part 2, 1931–1934*, trans. Rodney Livingstone and others, ed. Michael W. Jennings (Cambridge: Belknap Press, 1999)

Black, Jonathan, 'Our Brown Brethren': Identity and Difference in images of non-white soldiers' in Michael Walsh and Andrekos Varnava ed. The Great War and British Empire (London: Routledge, 2017), 129–150

Bluemel, Kristin, 'Casualty of War, Casualty of Empire: Mulk Raj Anand in England', in Shafquat Towheed (ed.), *New Readings in the Literature of British India 1780–1947* (Stuttgart: ibidem-Verlag, 1997), 301–326

Bose, Sugata, 'The Spirit and Form of an Ethical Polity', in Peter Heehs (ed.), *Situating Sri Aurobindo: A Reader* (New Delhi: Oxford University Press, 2013), 111–129

Chaudhuri, Sukanta, 'Tagore, Nationalism and Imperialism', in K. L. Tuteja and Kaustav Chakraborty (eds.), *Tagore and Nationalism* (New Delhi: Springer, 2017), 67–75

Chhina, Rana, 'Their Mercenary Calling: The Indian Army on Gallipoli, 1915', in Ashley Ekins (ed.), *Gallipoli: A Ridge Too Far* (Wollombi: Exisle Publishing, 2013), 232–253

Chimni, B. S., 'Retrieving "Other" Visions: Sri Aurobindo and the Ideal of Human Unity', in Peter Heehs (ed.), *Situating Sri Aurobindo: A Reader* (New Delhi: Oxford University Press, 2013), 130–153

Das, Santanu 'India, Women and the First World War', in Alison Fell and Ingrid Sharp (eds.), *Women's Movements: International Perspectives, 1914–1919* (London: Palgrave, 2007), 18–37

'Sepoys, Sahibs and Babus: India, the Great War and Two Colonial Journals', in *Publishing in the First World War: Essays in Book History*, ed. Mary Hammond and Shafquat Towheed (London: Palgrave, 2007), 61–77

'Imperialism, Nationalism and the First World War', in Jennifer Keene and Michael Nieberg (eds.), *Finding Common Ground: New Directions in First World War Studies* (Leiden: Brill, 2010), 67–85

'Indians at Home, Mesopotamia and France', in Santanu Das (ed.), *Race, Empire and First World War Writing* (Cambridge: Cambridge University Press, 2011), 70–89

'Writing Empire, Fighting War', in Susheila Nasta (ed.), *India in Britain: South Asian Networks and Connections, 1858–1950* (London: Palgrave, 2013), 28–45

'Entangled Emotions: Race, Encounters and Anti-colonial Cosmopolitanism', in Santanu Das and Kate McLoughlin (eds.), *First World War: Literature, Culture, Modernity* (London: British Academy and Oxford University Press, 2018), 241–261.

Das, Veena, 'The Signature of the State: The Paradox of Illegibility', in Veena Das and Deborah Poole (eds.), *Anthropology in the Margins of the State* (Santa Fe: SAR Press, 2004), 225–252

Devji, Faisal, 'Gandhi's Great War', in Roger D. Long and Ian Talbot (eds.), *India and World War I: A Centennial Assessment* (London: Routledge, 2018), 191–206

Evans, Andrew, 'Capturing Race: Anthropology and Photography in German and Austrian Prisoner-of-War Camps during World War I', in Eleanor M. Hight and Gary D. Sampson (eds.), *Colonialist Photography: Imag(in)ing Race and Place* (London: Routledge, 2002), 226–256

Featherstone, Simon, 'Colonial Poetry of the First World War', in Santanu Das (ed.), *The Cambridge Companion to the Poetry of the First World War* (Cambridge: Cambridge University Press, 2015), 173–184

Freud, Sigmund, 'Beyond the Pleasure Principle', in *Standard Edition of the Works of Sigmund Freud*, trans. James Strachey (London: Hogarth Press, 1920–1922), Vol. XVIII, 7–65

'Thoughts for the Times on War and Death' (1915), in *The Standard Edition of the Complete Psychological Works*, trans. James Strachey (London: Hogarth Press, 1953–1974), Vol. XIV, 273–302

Ghosh, Amitav, 'Foreword' to Kant, *'If I Die, Who Will Remember me?': India and First World War*, 9–10

Guha, Ramachandra, 'Introduction: Travelling with Tagore', in Ramachandra Guha (ed.), *Nationalism* (Delhi: Penguin, 2009), vii–lx

Higonnet, Margaret, 'Code Switching and Representations of the Great War', in Debra Rae Cohen and Douglas Higbee (eds.), *Teaching Representations of the First World War* (New York: MLA, 2017), 69–71

Jones, Heather, 'Imperial Captivities: Colonial Prisoners of War in Germany and the Ottoman Empire, 1914–18', in Santanu Das (ed.), *Race, Empire and First World War Writing* (Cambridge: Cambridge University Press, 2011), 175–193

Kayleyss, Margot, 'Indian POWs in World War I Photographs as Source Material', in Franziska Roy, Heike Liebau and Ravi Ahuja (eds.), *'When the War Began, We Heard of Several Kings': South Asian Prisoners in World War I Germany* (Delhi: Social Science Press, 2011), 207–230

Koller, Christian, 'Military Colonialism in France', in Dominiek Dendooven and Piet Chielens, *World War I: Five Continents in Flanders* (Ypres: Lannoo, 2008), 11–22

'Representing Otherness: African, Indian and European Soldiers' Letters and Memoirs', in Santanu Das (ed.), *Race, Empire and First World War Writing* (Cambridge: Cambridge University Press, 2011), 127–142

'German Perception of Enemy Colonial Troops', in Franziska Roy, Heike Liebau and Ravi Ahuja (eds.), *'When the War Began, We Heard of Several Kings': South Asian Prisoners in World War I Germany* (Delhi: Social Science Press, 2011), 130–148

Lange, Britta, 'South Asian Soldiers and German Academics', in Franziska Roy, Heike Liebau and Ravi Ahuja (eds.), *'When the War Began, We Heard of Several Kings': South Asian Prisoners in World War I Germany* (Delhi: Social Science Press, 2011), 149–184

Liebau, Heike, 'Kaiser Ki Jay: Perceptions of World War I and the Socio-religious Movement among the Oraons in Chota Nagpur, 1914–1916', in Heike Liebau, Katrin Bromber, Dyala Hamza, Katharina Lange and Ravi Ahuja (eds.), *The World in World Wars: Experiences, Perceptions and Perspectives from Africa and Asia* (Leiden: Brill, 2010), 251–276

Markovits, Claude, 'Indian Soldiers' Experiences in France during World War I', in Heike Liebau, Katrin Bromber, Dyala Hamza, Katharina Lange and Ravi Ahuja (eds.), *The World in World Wars: Experiences, Perceptions and Perspectives from Africa and Asia* (Leiden: Brill, 2010), 29–54

Moyd, Michelle, ' "We Don't Want to Die for Nothing": Askari at War in German East Africa, 1914–1918', in Santanu Das (ed.), *Race, Empire and First World War Writing* (Cambridge: Cambridge University Press, 2011), 90–107

Mukhopadhyay, Amartya, ' "Bhinnata of Nations": Tagore's Search in Nationalism, "Bharatavarsiya Samaj and Beyond" ', in Sanjukta Dasgupta and Chinmoy Guha (eds.), *Tagore: At Home in the World* (New Delhi: Sage, 2013), 125–151

O'Neill, Robert, 'Churchill, Japan, and British Security in the Pacific 1904–1942', in Robert B. Blake and William Roger Louis (eds.), *Churchill* (Oxford: Clarendon Press, 1993), 275–290

Owen, H. F., 'Towards Nation-wide Agitation and Organisation: The Home Rule Leagues, 1915–1918', in D. A. Lowe (ed.), *Soundings in Modern South Asian History* (Berkeley: University of California, 1968), 159–195

Pradhan, S. D., 'The Sikh Soldier in the First World War', in DeWitt Ellinwood and S. D. Pradhan (eds.), *India and World War I* (Delhi: Manohar, 1978), 213–225

Rabinow, Paul, 'Representations Are Social Facts', in James Clifford and George E. Marcus (eds.), *Writing Culture: The Poetics and Politics of Ethnography* (Berkeley: University of California Press, 1986), 234–261

Roy, Kaushik, 'Logistics and the Construction of Loyalty: The Welfare Mechanism in the Indian Army 1859–1913', in Partha Sarathi Gupta and Anirudh Deshpande (eds.), *British Raj and Its Indian Armed Forces, 1857–1939* (Delhi: Oxford University Press, 2002), 98–124

'The Army in India in Mesopotamia from 1916–1918: Tactics, Technology and Logistics', in Ian Beckett (ed.), *1917: Beyond the Western Front* (Leiden: Brill, 2009), 131–158

Sarkar, Tanika, 'Imagining Hindurashtra', in David Ludden (ed.), *Contesting the Nation: Religion, Community, and the Politics of Democracy in India* (Philadelphia: University of Pennsylvania, 1996), 162–184

'Gandhi and Social Relations', in Judith M. Brown and Anthony Parel (eds.), *The Cambridge Companion to Gandhi* (Cambridge: Cambridge University Press, 2011), 173–195

Sartori, Andrew, 'The Transfiguration of Duty', in Peter Heehs (ed.), *Situating Sri Aurobindo: A Reader* (Delhi: Oxford University Press, 2013), 93–109

Sen, Amartya, 'Is Nationalism a Boon or a Curse', in Sugata Bose and Kris Manjapra (eds.), *Cosmopolitan Thought-Zones: South Asia and the Global Circulation of Ideas* (London: Palgrave, 2010), 23–37

Seth, Sanjay, 'Rewriting Histories of Nationalism: The Politics of "Moderate Nationalism" in India, 1870–1905', in Sekhar Bandyopadhyay (ed.), *Nationalist Movement in India: A Reader* (Delhi: Oxford University Press, 2009), 30–48

Sibley, David, 'Over the Dirty Waters: The Experience of British Indians in World War I', in Timothy Dowling (ed.), *Personal Perspectives: World War I* (Santa Barbara, California: ABC-Clio, 2006), 29–50

Singha, Radhika, 'Front Lines and Status Lines: Sepoy and 'Menial' in the Great War 1916-1920', in Heike Liebau et al. (eds.), *The World in the World Wars* (Leiden: Brill, 2010), 55–106

'The Recruiter's Eye on "the Primitive": To France – and Back – in the Indian Labour Corps, 1917–18', in James E. Kitchen, Alisa Miller and Laura Rowe (eds.), *Other Combatants, Other Fronts: Competing Histories of the First World War* (Cambridge: Cambridge Scholars Press, 2011), 199–224

'India's Silver Bullets: War Loans and War Propaganda, 1917–18', in Maartje Abbenhuis, Neill Atkinson, Kingsley Baird and Gail Romano (eds.), *The Myriad Legacies of 1917: A Year of War and Revolution* (London: Palgrave, 2018), 77–102

Spivak, Gayatri, 'Can the Subaltern Speak?', in Cary Nelson and Lawrence Grossberg (eds.), *Marxism and the Interpretation of Culture* (London: Macmillan, 1988), 271–316

'Three Women's Texts and Circumfession', in Alfred Hornung and Ernstpeter Ruhe (ed.), *Postcolonialism & Autobiography: Michelle Cliff, David Dabydeen, Opel Palmer Adisa* (Amsterdam: Rodopi, 1998), 7–22

Stadtler, Florian, 'Britain's forgotten volunteers: South Asian contributions to the Two World Wars', in Ruvani Ranasinha et al. (eds.), *South Asians and the shaping of Britain, 1870–1950* (Manchester: Manchester University Press, 2012), 80-100

Stovall, Tyler, 'Love, Labour and Race: Colonial Men and White Women in France during the Great War' in Tyler Stovall and Georges Van Den Abbeele (eds.), *French Civilisation and Its Discontents* (Lanham: Lexington, 2003), 297–319

Sunder Rajan, Rajeswari, 'Death and the Subaltern', in Rosalind C. Morris (ed.), *Can the Subaltern Speak? Reflections on the History of an Idea* (New York: Columbia University Press, 2010), 117–138

Urban, Hugh, ' "India's Darkest Heart": Kali in the Colonial Imagination', in Rachel Fell McDermott and Jeffrey J. Kripal (eds.), *Encountering Kali: In the Margins, at the Centre, in the West* (Berkeley: University of California Press, 2003), 169–195

Wadley, Susan S., 'Why Does Ram Swarup Sing? Song and Speech in the North Indian Epic Ḍholā', in Arjun Appadurai, Frank J. Korom and Margaret A. Mills (eds.), *Gender, Genre, and Power in South Asian Expressive Tradition* (Philadelphia: University of Pennsylvania Press, 1991), 201–223.

Winter, Jay, 'In Conclusion: Palimpsests', in Indra Sengupta (ed.), *Memory, History and Colonialism: Engaging with Pierre Nora in Colonial and Postcolonial Contexts* (London: German Historical Institute, 2009), 167–173

Journal Articles

Adam, Leonhard, 'A Marriage Ceremony of the Pun-Clan (Magar) at Rigah (Nepal)', *Man: A Monthly Record of Anthropological Science*, 34, 23 (1934), 17–21

Anand, Mulk Raj, 'Pigeon-Indian: Some Notes on Indian-English Writing', *Journal of Postcolonial Writing*, 21, 2 (1982), 325–336

Atia, Nadia, ' "A Relic of Its Own Past": Mesopotamia in the British Imagination, 1900–14', *Memory Studies*, 3, 3 (2010), 232–241

Baer, Ulrich, 'Photography and Hysteria: Towards a Poetics of the Flash', *The Yale Journal of Criticism*, 7, 1 (1994), 41–77

Bardgett, Suzanne, 'Indians in Britain during the First World War', *History Today*, 65, 3 (2015), unpaginated

Barrett, Michèle, 'Subalterns at War: First World War Colonial Forces and the Politics of the Imperial War Graves Commission', *Interventions: International Journal of Postcolonial Studies*, 9, 3 (2007), 451–474

Bayly, Chris, 'India, the Bhagavad Gita and the World', *Modern Intellectual History*, 7, 2 (2010), 275–295

Beckett, Ian F. W., 'The Singapore Mutiny of February 1915', *Journal of the Society for Army Historical Research*, LXII (1984), 132–153

Brock, Peter, 'Gandhi's Non-violence and His War Service', *Gandhi Marg* (New Delhi), 23 February 1981, 601–616

Campbell, James, 'Combat Gnosticism: The Ideology of First World War Poetry Criticism', *New Literary History*, 30 (1999), 203–215

Chatterjee, Partha, 'Tagore, China and the Critique of Nationalism', *Inter-Asia Cultural Studies*, 12, 2 (2011), 271–283

Chattopadhyay, Suchetana, 'War, Migration and Alienation in Colonial Calcutta', *History Workshop Journal*, 64, 1 (2007), 212–239

Danzig, R., 'The Multilayered Cake: A Case Study in the Reform of the Indian Empire', *Modern Asian Studies*, 3, 1 (1969), 57–74

Das, Santanu, 'The Singing Subaltern', *Parallax*, 17, 60 (2011), 4–18
   'Indian War Experience: Archive, Language and Feeling', *Twentieth Century British History*, 25, 3 (2014), 391–417
   'Reframing Life/War "Writing": Objects, Letters and Songs of Indian Soldiers, 1914–1918', *Textual Practice*, 29, 7 (2015), 1265–1287

Duara, Prasenjit, 'The Discourse of Civilisation and Pan-Asianism', *Journal of World History*, 12, 1 (2001), 99–130

Fischer-Tiné, Harald, 'Indian Nationalism and the "World Forces": Transnational and Diasporic Dimensions of the Indian Freedom Movement on the Eve of the First World War', *Journal of Global History*, 2, 3 (2007), 325–344
   '"Unparalleled Opportunities": The Indian YMCA's Army Work Schemes for Imperial Troops during the Great War (1914–1920)', *Journal of Imperial and Commonwealth History* (forthcoming, 2018)

Ganachari, Aravind, 'First World War: Purchasing Indian Loyalties', *Economic and Political Weekly*, 19 February 2005, 779–788

Gardner, Nikolas, 'Sepoys and the Siege of Kut-al-Amara, December 1915–April 1916', *War In History*, 11, 3, (2004), 307–326
   'Morale and Discipline in a Multiethnic Army: The Indian Army in Mesopotamia (1914–1917)', *The Journal of the Middle East and Africa*, 4, 1 (2013), 1–20

Greenblatt, Stephen, 'Touch of the Real', *Representations*, No. 59 (1997), 14–29

Greenhut, Jeffery, 'Race, Sex and War: The Impact of Race and Sex on Morale and Health Services for the Indian Corps on the Western Front, 1914', *Military Affairs*, 45, 2 (1981), 71–74
   'The Imperial Reserve: the Indian Corps on the Western Front, 1914–1915', *Journal of Imperial and Commonwealth History*, 12 (1983), 54–73

Hiley, Nicholas, 'Hilton DeWitt Girdwood and the Origins of British Official Filming', *Historical Journal of Film, Radio and Television*, 13, 2 (1993), 129–148

Horne, John, 'Immigrant Workers in France during World War I', *French Historical Studies*, 14, 1 (1985), 57–88

Hunter, Kathryn, '"Sleep on Dear Ernie, Your Battles are O'er": A Glimpse of a Mourning Community, Invercargill, New Zealand, 1914–1925', *War in History*, 14, 1 (2007), 36–62

Jameson, Frederic, 'Third World Literature in the Era of Multinational Capitalism', *Social Text*, No. 15 (1986), 65–88

Jarboe, Andrew Tait, '"Healing the Empire": Indian Hospitals in Britain and France during the First World War', *Twentieth Century British History*, 26, 3 (2015), 347–369

Jeffery, Keith, 'An English Barrack in the Oriental Seas? India in the Aftermath of the First World War', *Modern Asian Studies*, 15, 3 (1981), 369–386

Kamtekar, Indivar, 'The Shiver of 1942', *Studies in History*, 18, 1 (2002), 81–102

Kelly, Saul, 'Crazy in the Extreme? The Silk Letters Conspiracy', *Middle Eastern Studies*, 49, 2 (2013), 162–178

Killingray, David and Matthews, James, 'Beasts of Burden: British West African Carriers in the First World War', *Canadian Journal of African Studies*, 13, 1/2 (1979), 7–23

Kundu, Kalyan, 'Rabindranath Tagore and World Peace', *Asiatic*, 4, 1 (2010), 77–86

Levine, Philippa, 'Battle Colors: Race, Sex and Colonial Soldiery in World War I', *Journal of Women's History*, 9, 4 (1998), 104–130

Lieven, Michael, 'Contested Empire: Bertram Mitford and the Imperial Adventure Story', *Paradigm*, No. 25 (1998), unpaginated, available at http://faculty.education.illinois.edu/westbury/paradigm/lieven2.html

Lunn, Joe, '"Les races guerrières": Racial Preconceptions in the French Military about West African Soldiers during the First World War', *Journal of Contemporary History*, 34, 4 (1999), 517–536

'Remembering the Tirailleurs sénégalais and the Great War: Oral History as Methodology of Inclusion in French Colonial Studies', *French Colonial History*, 10 (2009), 125–149

Mahmood, Tahir, 'Collaboration and British Military Recruitment: Fresh Perspective from Colonial Punjab, 1914–1918', *Modern Asian Studies*, 50, 5 (2016), 1474–1500

Manjapra, Kris K., 'The Illusions of Encounter: Muslim "Minds" and Revolutionaries in First World War Germany and After', *Journal of Global History*, 1, 3 (2006), 363–382

Martin, Gregory, 'The Influence of Racial Attitudes on British Policy Towards India in the First World War', *Journal of Imperial and Commonwealth History*, 14 (1986), 91–113

'German and French Perceptions of the French North and West African contingents, 1910–1918', *Militärgeschichtliche Mitteilungen*, 56 (1997), 31–68

McKenzie, R., 'The Laboratory of Mankind: John McCosh and the Beginnings of Photography in British India', *History of Photography*, XI (1987), 109–118

Meyers, Jeffrey, 'The Politics of "A Passage to India"', *Journal of Modern Literature*, 1, 3 (1971), 329–338

Morton-Jack, George, 'The Indian Army on the Western Front, 1914–1915: A Portrait of Collaboration', *War in History*, 13 (2006), 329–362

Mukhopadhyay, Priyasha, 'Of Greasy Notebooks and Dirty Newspapers: Reading the Illegible in *The Village in the Jungle*', *The Journal of Commonwealth Literature*, 50, 1 (2015), 59–73

'On Not Reading the Soldier's Pocket-Book for Field Service', *Journal of Victorian Culture*, 22, 1 (2017), 40–56

Murshid, Ghulam, 'Kavir Unmeş', *Pratham Ālo* (Dhaka), June 2017, 329–356

Omissi, David, 'Europe through Indian Eyes', *English Historical Review*, 122 (2007), 371–396

Pandey, Gyan, 'The Long Life of Rumour', *Alternatives*, 27(2002), 165–191

Pinney, Christopher, 'Classification and Fantasy in the Photographic Construction of Caste and Tribe', *Visual Anthropology*, 3 (1990), 259–288

Robinson, Catherine, 'Neither East nor West: Some Aspects of Religion and Ritual in the Indian Army of the Raj', *Religion*, 26, 1 (1996), 37–47

Sarkar, Benoy Kumar, 'The International Fetters of Young China', *The Journal of International Relations*, 11, 3 (1921), 347–368

Sathia, Priya, 'Developing Iraq: Britain, India and the Redemption of Empire and Technology', *Past and Present*, No. 197 (2007), 211–248

Sen, Satadru, 'Chameleon Games: Ranjitsinhji's Politics of Gender and Race', *Journal of Colonialism and Colonial History*, 2, 3 (2001), electronic journal

Singh, Gajendra, 'India and the Great War: Colonial Fantasies, Anxieties and Discontent', *Studies in Ethnicity and Nationalism*, 14, 2 (2014), 343–361

'Throwing Snowballs in France: Muslim Sipahis of the Indian Army and Sheikh Ahmad's Dream, 1915–1918', *Modern Asian Studies*, 48, 4 (2014), 1024–1067

Singh, Nazar, 'Newspapers, Politics, and Literature in Nineteenth Century Delhi and Punjab', *Panjab Past and Present*, 24, 2 (1990), 392–407

Singha, Radhika, 'Finding Labor from India for the War in Iraq: The Jail Porter and Labor Corps, 1916–1920', *Comparative Studies in Society and History*, 49, 2 (2007), 412–445

'The Short Career of the Indian Labour Corps in France, 1917–1919', *International Labour and Working-Class History*, No. 87 (2015), 27–62

Sinha, Mrinalini, 'Premonitions of the Past', *The Journal of Asian Studies*, 74, 4 (2015), 821–841

Stanley, Peter, ' "An Entente ... Most Remarkable": Indians at Anzac', *Sabretache*, XXII, 2 (1981), 17–21

Stirr, Anna, 'Sounding and Writing a Nepali Public Sphere: The Music and Language of Jhyaure', *Asian Music*, 46, 1 (2015), 3–38

Stolte, Carolien and Fischer-Tiné, Harald, 'Imagining Asia in India: Nationalism and Internationalism', *Comparative Studies in Society and History*, 54, 1 (2012), 65–92

Stovall, Tyler, 'The Color Line behind the Lines: Racial Violence in France during the Great War', *The American Historical Review*, 103, 3 (1998) 737–769

Subrahmanyam, Sanjay, 'Taking Stock of the Franks: South Asian Views of Europeans and Europe, 1500–1800', *The Indian Economic and Social History Review*, 42 (2005), 69–100

Tinker, Hugh, 'India in the First World War and After', *Journal of Contemporary History*, 3, 4 (1968), 89–107

VanKoski, Susan, 'Letters Home 1915–16: Punjabi Soldiers Reflect on War and Life in Europe and Their Meanings for Home and Self', *International Journal of Punjab Studies*, 2, 1 (1995), 43–63

Visram, Rozina, 'The First World War and Indian Soldiers', *Indo-British Review*, XVI (1989), 17–26

Wagner, Kim, ' "Calculated to Strike Terror": The Amritsar Massacre and the Spectacle of Colonial Violence', *Past & Present*, 233, 1 (2016), 185–225

Winter, Jay, 'Shell-Shock and the Cultural History of the Great War', *Journal of Contemporary History*, 35, 1 (2000), 7–11

Woods, Philip, 'Film Propaganda in India, 1914–1923', *Historical Journal of Film, Radio and Television*, 15, 4 (1995), 543–553

Unpublished Texts

Bromber, Katrin, Lange, Katharina and Liebau, Heike, 'First World War Historiographies: Commemoration, New Research and Debates during the Centennial in/on Africa, the Middle East and South Asia'

Fischer-Tiné, Harald, 'Keep Them Pure, Fit, and Brotherly! The Indian Y.M.C.A.'s Army Work Schemes during the Great War (1914–1920)'

Ghosh, Amitav, 'Shared Sorrows: Indians and Armenians in the prison camps of Ras el-'Ain'

Jarboe, Andrew Tait, 'Soldiers of empire: Indian sepoys in and beyond the imperial metropole during the First World War, 1914–1919', PhD Dissertation (Northeastern University, 2013)

Liebau, Heike, 'Encounters of a Gurkha in Europe (1914–1918): Gangaram Gurung'

Nath, Ashok, 'A Bengali Infantry Regiment in the Great War'

Ng, Katie, 'Identity in Perspectives of Chinese Labourers in WWI'

Sarkar, Abishek, 'Affective Self-Fashioning and the Bengali Imaginary: The Great War in Kazi Nazrul Islam's Life and Fiction'

Yadav, K. C., 'Donning the Khaki: Recruitment in Punjab during World War I'

Online Sources

'1914–1918-online. *International Encyclopaedia of the First World War*', www.1914–1918-online.net/ [particularly the section on India, with essays by various scholars]

Ahmed, Sofia, 'No, I Won't Wear the "Poppy Hijab" to Prove I'm Not a Muslim Extremist', www.independent.co.uk/voices/no-i-wont-wear-the-poppy-hijab-to-prove-im-not-an-extremist-a6720901.html

'Ariel L. Varges', http://bufvc.ac.uk/newsonscreen/search/index.php/person/952

Awan, Mahmood, 'Not Their War', http://tns.thenews.com.pk/world-war-i-not-punjabis-war/#.V6cPTOgrKUl

'The Feminine Metaphor', http://tns.thenews.com.pk/poetry-the-feminine-metaphor/#.V6cNoegrKUl

Baroness Warsi, 'The Sun myView: "Our Boys Weren't Just Tommies – They Were Tariqs and Tajinders Too" ', http://sayeedawarsi.com/2012/10/16/the-sun-our-boys-werent-just-tommies-they-were-tariqs-and-tajinders-too

Bichitra: Online Tagore Variorum, http://bichitra.jdvu.ac.in

'Brighton Warrior: Manta Singh', www.sikhmuseum.com/brighton/warriors/manta/index.html

Chandan, Amarjit, 'How They Suffered: World War One & Its Effect on Punjabis', http://apnaorg.com/articles/amarjit/wwi

'Punjabi Poetry on War', www.sikhfoundation.org/sikh-punjabi-language-studies/punjabi-poetry-on-war-amarjit-chandan

Chattri, www.chattri.org

Chhina, Raman Singh, 'Nand Singh and Jungnamah Europe: Subaltern Insights on the Wars of Empire', http://blogs.lse.ac.uk/southasia/2017/04/05/nand-singh-and-jangnamah-europe-subaltern-insights-on-the-wars-of-empire

Chhina, Rana and Chhina, Adil, 'Commemoration, Cult of the Fallen (India)', https://encyclopedia.1914-1918-online.net/article/commemoration_cult_of_the_fallen_india

Chhina, Rana T. S., 'USI–MEA World War I Centenary Tribute Project to Shed New Light on India's Role', http://blogs.icrc.org/new-delhi/2014/04/11/usi-mea-world-war-i-centenary-tribute-project-to-shed-new-light-on-indias-role

'Cultural Exchange in a Time of Global Conflict: Colonials, Neutrals and Belligerents during the First World War', http://sourcebook.cegcproject.eu/

Das, Santanu, 'Are Faith-Specific War Memorials the Best Way to Remember the Fallen?', *The Independent*, 9 November 2015, www.independent.co.uk/news/world/world-history/are-faith-specific-war-memorials-the-best-way-to-remember-the-fallen-a6727821.html

From Bombay to Flanders: Indian Sepoys in Europe in First World War, youtube documentary for Arts and Humanities Research Council, UK, March 2015, www.youtube.com/watch?v=6stybO5v7SY

'Indian Sepoy in the First World War', podcast for Oxford University, September, 2012, https://podcasts.ox.ac.uk/indian-sepoy-first-world-war

'Soldiers of the Empire, BBC Radio 4, September 2014, www.bbc.co.uk/programmes/b04lozq5

'The First World War and the Colour of Memory', *The Guardian*, 22 July 2014, www.theguardian.com/commentisfree/2014/jul/22/first-world-war-white washed- eurocentric

'The Indian Sepoy in the First World War', British Library, www.bl.uk/world-war-one/articles/the-indian-sepoy-in-the-first-world-war

'Dr. Ram Mohan Dattatreya', www.ikashmir.net/tributes/rmdatatreya.html

Dutta, Sujon, 'The Bhadralok Goes to War', *The Telegraph*, 1 January 2014, www.telegraphindia.com/1140101/jsp/nation/story_17740177.jsp

'Eugène Burnand', www.eugene-burnand.com

Fabre, Cécile, 'Remembering War', https://podcasts.ox.ac.uk/remembering-war

'First World War Recruitment Posters', www.iwm.org.uk/learning/resources/first-world-war-recruitment-posters

Ghosh, Amitav, 'The Home and the World in Iraq, 1915–17' and 'Istanbul and Indian Soldiers', archived at amitavghosh.com/blog

Hussein, Iqbal, 'Beyond Commemoration: South Asia and the First World War', http://blog.nationalarchives.gov.uk/blog/beyond-commemoration-south-asia-first-world-war

Jain, Anurag, 'Introduction to *Eyes of Asia*', www.kiplingsociety.co.uk/rg_asia_intro.htm

J. N. Sen, www.bbc.co.uk/news/uk-england-leeds-31761904

Khalid, Haroon, 'A World without Written Words: The Remnants of Pakistan's Oral Tradition', www.dawn.com/news/1316665

'Komagata Maru: Continuing the Journey', http://komagatamarujourney.ca

Lange, Britta, 'Archive, Collection, Museum: On the History of the Archiving of Voices at the Sound Archive of the Humboldt University', *Journal of Sonic Studies Issue 13 Online*, http://sonicstudies.org/post/156170371867/journal-of-sonic-studies-issue-13-online

Liebau, Heike, 'Prisoners of War (India)', in the *1914–18 Online Encyclopedia*, https://encyclopedia.1914-1918-online.net/article/prisoners_of_war_india

Maguire, Anna Mary, *Cultural Encounters during the First World War: The Experience of Troops from New Zealand, South Africa and the West Indies*, PhD Thesis, King's College London (2017), https://kclpure.kcl.ac.uk/portal/files/66980846/2017_Maguire_Anna_1239996_ethesis.pdf

Mahmood, Tahir, 'Punjab and the First World War: Expectations and the Enticement of the "Oriental Mind"', http://pu.edu.pk/images/journal/history/PDF-FILES/2%20TM_v51No2_2014.pdf

'Making Britain: South Asians in Bloomsbury', www.open.ac.uk/arts/research/asianbritain/making-britain

Merrick, Jane and Gander, Kashmira, 'Tommies and Tariqs fought side by side', *The Independent*, 22 June 2013, www.independent.co.uk/news/uk/home-news/special-report-the-centenary-of-wwi-tommies-and-tariqs-fought-side-by-side-8669758.html

Mundy, Talbot, *Hira Singh: When India Came to Fight in Flanders* (1918), www.gutenberg.org/files/4400/4400-h/4400-h.htm

'Neuve-Chapelle Memorial', www.cwgc.org/find/find-cemeteries-and-memorials/144000/neuve-chapelle-memorial

Pennell, Catriona, 'Remember the World as well as the War', www.britishcouncil.org/sites/default/files/remember-the-world-as-well-as-the-war-report.pdf

Punjab Government Gazetteer of the Lahore District, 1883–1884 (Lahore: Sang-e-Meel Publications, 1989), www.asafas.kyoto-u.ac.jp/kias/pdf/kb6/14sunaga .pdf

'Punjabi Folksongs', www.mptmagazine.com/poem/punjabi-folksongs-703

Quayum, Mohammed A., 'Imagining "One World": Rabindranath Tagore's Critique of Nationalism', https://mukto-mona.com/Articles/mohammad_quayum/Tagore_Nationalism.pdf

'Report of the Commissioners', https://archive.org/stream/reportofthecommi032063mbp/reportofthecommi032063mbp_djvu.txt

Sharma, Manimugdha, 'Delhi brings alive World War 1 Memory', *The Times of India*, 14 March, 2015, https://timesofindia.indiatimes.com/india/Delhi-brings-alive-WWI-memory/articleshow/46560017.cms

Sharma, Sarika, '100 years On, Voices from World War I', *The Tribune*, 20 May, 2018, www.tribuneindia.com/news/spectrum/society/100-years-later-voices-from-wwi/591837.html

'Sikhs and World War I', http://www.empirefaithwar.com [compiled and hosted by UKPHA)

Singh, Gajendra, 'Revolutionary Networks', in 1914–1918 Online Encyclopedia, https://encyclopedia.1914-1918-online.net/article/revolutionary_networks_india

Singh, Yumnam Rajeshwor, '87 Brave Manipuries of the First World War', http://kanglaonline.com/2015/11/87-brave-manipuries-of-the-first-world-war

Singha, Radhika, 'Labour (India)', https://encyclopedia.1914-1918-online.net/article/labour_india

'Terrible Beauty: Music & Writing of FWW CEGC' (concert recording), www.youtube.com/watch?v=yVyyrm-Feno

Tharoor, Shashi, 'Why the Indian Soldiers of WW1 are Forgotten', www.bbc.co.uk/news/magazine-33317368

'The Baloch Regiment in Camp', https://en.wikipedia.org/wiki/British_Expedition_to_Abyssinia#/media/File:The_Abyssinian_Expedition,_1868_Q69868.jpg

'The German Mission to Afghanistan 1915–16 (The Niedermayer–Hentig Expedition)', http://s400910952.websitehome.co.uk/germancolonial uniforms/afghan%20mission.htm

'The Kaiser's Pirate Ship – The Astounding Voyage of SMS Emden', http://militaryhistorynow.com/2013/05/08/the-kaisers-pirate-ship-the-unbelievable-voyage-of-the-sms-emden

'The Peace Garden', www.horsellcommon.org.uk/sites/the-peace-garden

'The Troth – Usne Kaha Tha', https://akademi.co.uk/project/the-troth-usne-kaha-tha

'The Unlikeliest of Pals', www.leeds.ac.uk/news/article/3670/the_unlikeliest_of_pals_an_indian_soldier_alone_among_yorkshiremen

'WW1 and the Royal Pavilion', https://brightonmuseums.org.uk/royalpavilion/history/wwi-and-the-royal-pavilion

Index

Page numbers in *italics* denote illustrations. *n* = footnote; *t* = table/diagram.